Officers who died in the Service of the Royal Navy, Royal Naval Reserve, Royal Naval Volunteer Reserve, Royal Marines, Royal Naval Air Service and Royal Air Force 1914-1919.

S.D. & D.B. Jarvis

Clean, Simple, Valiant, Well Beloved,
Flawless in Faith and Fame.

Kipling.

ISBN 1873058 31 4

INTRODUCTION

Volume 1 of The Cross of Sacrifice series has quite correctly been acknowledged as possibly the most significant book for researchers, military historians, libraries and regimental museums in the last 50 years. The compilers have received tributes from all over the world for their diligence and accuracy.

In this Volume Mr S.D. Jarvis, and his father, Mr D. B. Jarvis, break totally new ground by compiling the names of the officers of the Royal Navy and associated services. No one has attempted such a task before. For good measure and to ensure all officers names are eventually recorded they have added a section to cover the officers of the Royal Air Force formed on the 1st April, 1918.

It must be appreciated that the conflict was so great, the number of deaths so enormous, that no reference book on the subject of the Great War can be perfect. The information given at the time was subject to mis-spelling and of course mis-recording. Taking as their source documents the registers of the War Graves Commission they have accurately recorded what they have seen and read. For those who wish to research further many opportunities exist.

A fresh approach has long been needed to the compiling of information on the Great War Messrs. S. D. and J. B. Jarvis have thrown enormous energy and time into ensuring those who died will be remembered. The appearance of this Volume will be gratefully acknowledged by the great majority of collectors, historians and researchers.

Trevor J Davies November 1993.

HOW TO INTERPRET THE INFORMATION GIVEN

ACLAND-HOOD, Charles Alexander John Midmn, RN HMS Invincible kia 31.5.16 MR3

SURNAME:	ACLAND-HOOD
FIRST NAMES:	Charles Alexander John
RANK:	Midshipman
DECORATIONS:	None identified
CAUSE OF DEATH:	Killed in Action
DATE:	31.5.16
SERVICE:	The Royal Navy HMS Invincible
OTHER REFERENCE:	
REGISTER:	MR3 (see Appendix 1)
INFORMATION FROM	
ALTERNATIVE SOURCES:	None

AINSWORTH G.G., ResN Sister RN QARNNS RN Hosp Peebles 29.10.18. CR Scot 671

SURNAME:	AINSWORTH
FIRST NAMES:	G.G.,
RANK:	Reserve Nursing Sister
DECORATIONS:	None
CAUSE OF DEATH:	Not known
DATE:	29.10.1918
UNIT:	Queen Alexander's Royal Naval Nursing Service
OTHER REFERENCE:	
REGISTER:	CR Scotland 671 (see Appendix 1)
INFORMATION TAKEN	
FROM ALTERNATIVE	
SOURCES:	None

ALLEN, Victor William, M.C., M.M. 2Lt, RAF + 4SA1, 103 Sqdn, 9.6.18 CR France 360

SURNAME:	ALLEN
FIRST NAMES:	Victor William
RANK:	2nd Lieutenant
DECORATIONS:	Military Cross, Military Medal
CAUSE OF DEATH:	Not recorded
DATE:	9.6.1918
UNIT:	Royal Air Force and 4th South African Infantry
OTHER REFERENCE:	
REGISTER:	CR France 360.

A small number of Royal Navy names have very brief details listed. These names have been seen recorded in various documents but have not been found in the War Registers.

SECTION I

OFFICERS WHO DIED IN THE SERVICE OF THE ROYAL NAVY, ROYAL NAVAL RESERVE, ROYAL NAVAL VOLUNTEER RESERVE, ROYAL MARINES AND THE ROYAL NAVAL AIR SERVICE

A

ABBOTT,Frank Maclean   Lt   RN   HMS Surprise kld 23.12.17 MR1
ABELSON,Edward Gordon   T2Lt   RMLI   1.12.16   CR France85
ABERCROMBIE,Cecil Halliday   Lt   RN   HMS Defence kia   31.5.16MR2
ABIGAIT,Edward A   T2Lt   RMA   A/A Bde   17.3.16   CR Belgium171
ABINGER,Shelley Leopold Lawrence THonComdr   RNVR   23.5.17 CR Surrey160
ABRAHAM,Felix   FtPaymr   RN   HMS President   4.11.17CR Hamps57
ABRAMS,John   TSkipper   RNR   HMTrawler Arfon   kld   30.4.17MR1
ACLAND-HOOD,Charles Alexander John   Midmn RN   HMS Invincible   kia   31.5.16MR3
ACTON,Fitzmaurice.CMG.   Cmdr   RN   HM Coastguard   7.8.20 CR Eire292
ADAM,Herbert Algernon.OBE,   Capt   RN   HMS Pembroke   27.9.20 CR Kent46
ADAMS,Charles Edgar.RD.   LtComdr   RNR   HMS Egmont(lost in SS Pundit)   kia   9.6.18 MR3
ADAMS,Cyril Henwood   Clerk   RN   HMS Defence kia   31.5.16MR2
ADAMS,George William Henry   Asst Clerk   RN   HMS Formidable   kia   1.1.15 MR1
ADAMS,P.   Gnr   RN   HMS Cordelia   1.3.20   CR Europe150A
ADAMS,S.   Gnr   RN   HMS Vivid   1.11.15CR Devon1
ADAMS,Samuel Alan TEng Lt   RN   HMS Indefatigable   kia   31.5.16MR2
ADDIS,George AWt Mech   RN   HMS GoodHope   kia   1.11.14MR3
ADLAM,Leslie Edwin TFlt Sub-Lt   RNAS Dunkirk   9.9.17   MR20
AGASSIZ,Thomas Roland   Comdr RNR   HMYacht Conqueror   kia   26.9.16MR3
AGNEW,Thomas Randal   Skipper   RNR   HMTug Raven 3   drd   20.1.17   CR Numb96
AINSWORTH,G.G.   ResNSister   RN   QARNNS RN Hosp Peebles   29.10.18 CR Scot671
AIREY,George Ryder.MC.   TLt   RNVR Howe Bn RNDiv   dow   24.11.16 CR France40
AIREY,Harold Ferguson   TFlt Sub-Lt   RNAS   23.11.17 CR Lancs95
AITKEN,William James Lightbody   Sub Lt RNVR HMS Colleen   16.4.17 CR Eire434 &Eire14
AKERS,Frederick William   TFlt Sub-Lt   RNAS   20.7.17 CR Belgium175 FltLt
ALBURY,L.F. Lt   RM   1RM Bn RNDiv   27.9.18 CR France530
ALDCROFT,William Henry   Eng Lt RNR   HMS ebble   17.5.18   CR Greece10
ALDERSON,Dixwell L.   Midmn RN   HMS Conqueror   15.12.17 CR Yorks569
ALDRIDGE,Douglas John   TLt   RMLI   1RM Bn RNDiv   kia   26.10.17 CR Belgium126
ALEXANDER,Frederick.DSO.   Eng Cmdr   RN   HMS Cleopatra   2.7.20 CR Hamps5
ALEXANDER,James Morrow FltSubLt   RN/RNAS   acckld 12.9.15   CR Kent67
ALEXANDER,John W.   Lt   RNR   HMTug Dalkeith   29.4.18 CR Italy24
ALEXANDER,Philip George BA   Chapn RN   HMS Hampshire   kld   5.6.16 MR3
ALLAN,Alexander   TLt   RNR   see ALLEN,A
ALLAN,Eric Hugh   Sub-Lt RNR   HMS Bombala kia   25.4.18MR3
ALLAN,Hugh TFlt Sub-Lt   RNAS   3Sqn   kia   6.7.17 CR Belgium24
ALLAN,William   TSkipper   RNR   HMTrawler Borneo   kld   18.6.17MR3
ALLARDYCE,William Swirles   TSurg Prob   RNVR HMS Negro   drd   21.12.16 MR1
ALLAWAY,William   TFlt Sub-Lt   RNAS   drd   31.7.17   MR1
ALLDRIDGE,Douglas Robert George Paul TSub-Lt   RNVR Nelson Bn RN Div   13.11.16 MR21
ALLEN,Alexander   TLt   RNR   HMTrawler Morococala   kld   19.11.17 MR2 ALLAN
ALLEN,Frank Reginald   Midmn RNR   HMS Ebro   dedacc 19.10.15 CR Staffs35
ALLEN,J.R.   Carp LtRN   HMS Vivid   19.1.16   CR Cornwall136
ALLEN,John Alexander Cameron   TEng Sub-Lt   RNR   HMS Beramot kia   13.8.17MR2
ALLEN,Matthew   ChBosn   RN   HMS Vivid   18.7.17 CR Devon1
ALLEN,RobertLt   RNVR HMS Actaeon ded   29.11.18 CR Numb1
ALLENDER,FrederickTEng Sub-Lt   RN   HMS Vanguard   kld   9.7.17 MR1
ALLERTON,Frank Hilton   Lt   RNR   HM S/M G7   kld   1.11.18MR3
ALLFREE,Geoffrey Stephen   Lt   RNVR HMML 247   drd   29.9.18   MR3
ALLIN,L.J.W. Sub Lt RN   HMS President   6.3.19   CR Cambs16
ALLISON,Joseph Leyland   Flt Sub Lt   RNAS   18.3.18 CR France525
ALLIX,John Philip.MID   TLt   RNR   HMDrifter Jean   kld   17.10.17 MR3
ALLSOP,Anthony Victor George   Midmn RN   HMS Aboukir kia   22.9.14MR1
ALLSOP,W.B. Sub Lt RNR   HMS Pembroke   6.3.19   CR Ches26
ALLTREE,E.W.   Lt   RNR   HMS India   29.10.18 CR Europe136
ALTON,Wingfield Wooley   Ft Paymr   RN   HMS Defence kia   31.5.16MR2

1

AMOS,Henry CharltonLt   RM   RMDivEngs RNDiv   22.7.15 CR Gallipoli14
AMY,John H Wt Wardmaster RN   HMS Hyacinth   3.7.17 CR SAfrica158
ANDERSON,Alexander Bannatyne   Lt   RNR   HMS Diana   28.9.18 MR65
ANDERSON,Bernard Lt   RNR   HMS Bombala kia   25.4.18 MR2
ANDERSON,Charles Coventry   Lt   RNVR Anson Bn RNDiv   8.5.15   MR4
ANDERSON,Francis M.   Flt Off RNAS   1.1.18 CR Yorks172
ANDERSON,George Skipper   RNR   HMDrifter Campania II   drd   5.3.17 CR Scot843
ANDERSON,James   Ch Art Eng   RN   HMS Viking kld   29-1-16   MR3
ANDERSON,Kenneth Angus Naval Cadet   RN   HMS Bulwark   kld   26.11.14 MR3 Midmn
ANDERSON,L.D.   Midmn RN   HMS Agamemnon   9.5.18 CR Greece10
ANDERSON,Samuel Mate   RN   HM S/M C16   16.4.17 CR Kent67
ANDREW,James   Sub-Lt RNR   RFA Sokoto   9.11.18CR Norfolk85
ANDREWS,B.G.   Capt   RMLI 1Bn   22.8.18 CR France214
ANDREWS,Christopher B   Capt   RM   Plymouth Bn RNDiv   11.5.15 MR4
ANDREWS,Eric Osterfield Arliss   TFlt Sub-Lt   RNAS   drd   8.11.17MR1
ANDREWS,Ernest Lancelot Capt   RM   1RM Bn RNDiv   25.8.18 CR France744
ANDREWS,H.G.   Lt Cmdr   RNVR 2Res Bn RNDiv   22.11.18 CR Hamps1
ANGUS,Matthew   Eng Lt RN   HMS Ocean   ded   16.6.17   CR Devon172
ANGUS,Robert   Lt   RNR   HMCMB 33A kia   12.4.18CR Belgium24
ANNAND,Wallace Moir   TLt Comdr   RNVR Collingwood Bn RNDiv   4.6.15 MR4
ANNESLEY,Earl Francis   TSub-Lt   RNVR RNAS   5.11.14MR1
ANSELL,Charles   Lt   RN   HMS President   26.12.17 CR Numb4
ANSON,John Henry Algernon Sir   Lt   RN   HM S/M H5   drd   2.3.18 MR1
ANTRAM,Herbert Wilkins   TLt   RNR   HM S/M K17 drd   31.1.18   MR1
APTHORP,Reginald John   TSub-Lt   RNVR Hood Bn RN Div   14.11.16 MR21
ARBERRY,Henry   Wt Tel RN   HMS Defence kia   31.5.16MR2
ARBUTHNOT,Robert Keith Sir KCB.MVO.Rear-Admiral RN   HMS Defence kia   31.5.16MR2
ARMES,W.E. Insp of Engine Fitters RFA Reliance   16.5.18 CR Greece10
ARMITAGE,George Geoffrey Allen   PTFlt Sub-Lt RNAS   11.12.15 CR Glouc124
ARMSTRONG,Frederick Carr DSC Flt Cmdr   RNAS   25.3.18 MR20
ARMSTRONG,Harold Gage Bewes   Maj   RMLI Portsmouth Bn RNDiv kia   5.5.15 CR Gallipoli31
ARMSTRONG,Lionel Eric   TMidmn   RNR   HMS Marmiondrd   21.10.17 MR2
ARMSTRONG,Percy Towns   Lt   RNVR RNAS kldacc 26.5.17   CR Numb7
ARMSTRONG,Philip Furlong Sub-Lt RN   HM S/M G8   kld   3.1.18 MR3
ARNOLD,Charles V Flt Lt RNAS   16.8.17 CR Essex40
ARNOLD,H.J.DSO. Flt Lt RNAS Eastchurch   20.3.18 CR Kent68
ARNOT,George Henry.RD.   Cmdr   RNR   28.10.17 CR Ches6
ARON,Eustace M.   Sub Lt RNVR 189Bde MG Coy RNDiv   13.11.16 CR France339
ASBURY,Charles Percy   TLt   RNVR Hood Bn RN Div   23.4.17 MR20
ASH,Basil Drummond Lt   RN   RNAS   30.9.14 MR1 FltLt
ASHFORD,W.J.S.   Bosn   RN   HMS Repulse   16.4.19 CR Hamps9
ASHLEY,Alexis William   Midmn RN   HMS Verulam kld   3.9.19 MR1
ASHLEY,Thomas   Skipper   RNR   HMTrawler Margate kia   24.4.17MR1
ASLIN,Robert Lt   RNR   HMS Hyacinth   6.12.15CR EAfrica124
ASTON,Ernest Reginald   Lt   RNVR Howe Bn RNDiv   kia   13.11.16 CR France339
ATKIN-BERRY,Harold Harding   Lt   RN   HM S/M E26 kld   6.7.16 MR3
ATLAY,H.T. Lt Cmdr   RN   HMS Revenge   11.11.14 CR Kent2
ATTFIELD,Cecil   Sub Lt RNVR Drake Bn RNDiv   kia   29.9.18CR France241
ATTWOOD,D.R.DSC.Lt   RNR   HM S/M G5   24.11.18 CR Durham88
AULD,John Hamilton Midmn RNR   HMS Clan McNaughton   drd   3.2.15 MR1
AULD,Robert McDonald   TMidmn   RNR   HMS Calgarian   14.6.16 CR Canada745A
AUSTEN,Mark   Midmn RN   HMS Queen Mary   kia   31.5.16MR3
AUSTEN,Thomas   Surg Cmdr   RN   HMS Pembroke   22.10.18 CR Kent46
AUSTIN,Alan Murray APaymr   RN   HMS Hawke kia   15.10.14 MR1
AVERY,George Gladstone   TFlt Sub-Lt   RNAS   drd   14.5.17   MR1
AYRES,Ernest Alfred TEng Sub-Lt RNR   HMS Stonecrop   kia   18.9.17MR3

B

BABBAGE,Sidney John   Lt   RN   HMS President   acckld 15.5.19 CR Devon2
BABBINGTON,Hugh DSC,MID   Lt   RN   HMS Fox   27.11.19 CR Surrey21
BACK,Eric Percy Coventry   Capt   RN   HMS Natal   kld   30.12.15 MR1
BACK,Hatfield Arthur William   Chapn RN   HMSVanguard kld   9.7.17 MR1
BACKWOOD,Thomas A   TEng Sub-Lt   RNR   3.16
BACON,Francis Hugh TAsst Paymr   RNR   HMYacht Aries   31.10.15 CR Europe67
BACON,Henry L.   Lt   RN   HMS Raglan   20.1.18 CR Gallipoli1
BADHAM,Francis Molyneaux TLt   RNVR Collingwood Bn RNDiv   4.6.15 MR4
BAGGS,A.G. ChGnr RN   HMS Excellent   5.6.19 CR Scot816
BAGOT,Maurice John Hervey Lt   RN   HMS Monmouth   kia   1.11.14 MR2
BAGSHAWE,Adair Grey   TSub-Lt   RNVR Collingwood Bn RNDiv   4.6.15 MR4
BAILEY,Bernard Michael Hon.   Midmn RN   HMS Defence kia   31.5.16 MR2
BAILEY,Donald Frank TSub-Lt   RNVR Hood Bn RNDiv   23.4.17 MR20
BAILEY,Frederick Maurice   TWt Tel   RNR   HMS Champayne   kia   9.10.17 MR2
BAILEY,Leslie Frank TMidmn   RNR   HMS Bayano kia   11.3.15 MR3
BAILEY,Royal Hubert Silas   T2Lt   RMLI   1 RM Bn RNDiv   5.1.18 MR21
BAKER,Bertie Napier Sub-Lt RNVR HMS President   21.12.18 CR France146
BAKER,Cecil Robert Morshead   StaffSurg   RN   HMS Ganges ded   26.5.18   CR Suffolk128
BAKER,Frank TSub-Lt   RNVR   6.15
BAKER,George William   EngLt RN   HM S/M K5   drd   20.1.21   MR1
BAKER,Montague Samuel   Sub Lt RNVR Howe Bn RNDiv   kia   29.7.17 CR France452
BAKER,William   Sig Bosn   RN   HMS Queen Mary   kia   31.5.16 MR3
BAKER,William Alfred   Wt Mech   RN   HMS Warspite acckld 3.3.18 CR Essex105
BAKEWELL,Alfred   Lt   RN   HMS Onslaught   31.5.16 CR Scot722
BALCOMBE,Francis Cedric   TLt   RMLI   1 RM Bn RNDiv   26.10.17 MR30
BALCOMBE,James   Ch Gnr RN   HMS Glatton dow   18.9.18   CR Hamps8
BALDRY,George William   Skipper   RNR   HMTrawler Kaphrida kld   8.6.16 MR1
BALDWIN,Anthony Edward   Midmn RN   HMS Queen Mary   kia   31.5.16 MR3
BALDWIN,Hubert R   TLt   RNVR   7.15
BALE,C.J.   Sub-Lt RNR   HMS India   7.12.15 CR Europe135
BALL,Alwyn Lancaster   TSub-Lt   RNVR Nelson Bn RNDiv   13.11.16 MR21
BALLANTYNE,Ernest Orford Cmdr   RN   HMS Viknor   13.1.15 CR Scot262
BALLANTYNE,Kenneth   AGnr   RN   HMS Viknor   13.1.15 CR Hamps9
BALLARD,Charles Frederick Comdr RN   HMS Formidable   kia   1.1.15 MR1
BANFIELD,George   ChArtEng   RN   HMS Bittern   drd   4.4.18 MR2
BANKES-PRICE,John Thearsby   TFlt Lt RNAS   17.9.16 MR34
BANNING,Arthur H   TSub-Lt   RNVR   4.17
BARBER,Charles Ashton   Lt   RMLI   1RM Bn RNDiv   kia   21.8.18 CR France518
BARBER,Cyril Frederick   Maj   RMLI   HMS Goliath kia   13.5.15 MR1
BARBER,Cyril Roaf   Flt Sub Lt   RNAS   1Wing 2Sqn   7.1.18 CR France1359
BARBER,Frederick Norman   Ch Carp   RN   HMS Queen Mary   kia   31.5.16 MR3
BARBER,James   Eng Capt   RN   HMS President   9.3.17 CR Surrey2
BARBER,John TMidmn   RNR   HMS Ebro   kld   6.3.17 MR1
BARBER,John Byron Lt   RN   HMS Bulldog kld   16.4.16 MR1
BARBOUR,W.Sub Lt RNVR Drake Bn RNDiv   21.8.18 CR France518
BARCHARD,Geoffrey Bruce   Midmn RN   HMS Aboukir kia   22.9.14 MR1
BARCLAY,Ivan Curror Christie   TSurg Prob   RNVR HMS MaryRose   kia   17.10.17 MR1
BAREHAM,Archibald G MC Lt   RMLI   1 RN Bn RNDiv   8.10.18 MR16
BARIN,Anthony J   Lt   RN   10.17
BARKER,Charles Rowley   Sub Lt RNVR Anson Bn RNDiv   24.12.17 CR France379
BARKER,Godfrey   Maj   RM   Drake Bn RNDiv   29.4.15 CR Gallipoli6 29.5.15
BARLING,George Reuben.MID   Lt   RNR   HMDrifter Floandi   kia   15.5.17 CR Italy6
BARLOW,Arthur Horace Charles   Sub-Lt RN   HMS BlackPrince   kia   31.5.16 MR3
BARLOW,George   TEng Lt   RN   HMS Natal   kld   30.12.15 MR1
BARNARD,Charles Henry   TLt   RNVR HM Mersey Examination Vessel No1   kld   28-12-17 MR2

3

BARNES,Alfred   Gnr   RN   HMS Torrent kld   23.12.17 MR3

BARNES,Douglas M Flt Lt   RNAS   6.15

BARNES,Jack Clixby ALt   RM   Plymouth Bn RNDiv   11.5.15 MR4

BARNETT,Harry Percival   Paymr Lt Cmdr RN   HMS Pekin   6.2.19 CR Lincs123

BARON,Maurice Nelson   TFlt Sub-Lt   RNAS   kia   15.8.17 CR Belgium173

BARRAS,William George   Staff Surg   RNVR HMS Vanguard   kld   9.7.17 MR1

BARRATT,George   Gnr   RN   5.16

BARRETT,James   Surg   RN   HMS Imperieuse   acckld   18.12.14 MR3

BARRETT,William John   Bosn   RN   HMS Monmouth   kia   1.11.14 MR2

BARRON,John   Skipper   RNR   HMTrawler Evadne   kld   27.2.17 MR3

BARRON,Thomas George   TWt Tel   RNR   HMS Leviathian(lost in SS AlnwickCastle) drd   19.3.17 MR1

BARROW,John Gerald   ASub-Lt   RN   HM S/M E3   kia   18.10.14 MR3

BARROW,Joseph   Ch Gnr RN   HMS Valiant   29.12.15 CR Lancs146

BARROW,Thomas P Ch Art Eng   RN   HMS Geranium   28.4.16 CR Europe6

BARRY,James Bosn   RN   HMS Bulwark kld   26.11.14 MR3

BARRY,James R.   Midmn RNR/RNAS   1.8.17 CR Iraq8

BARRY,Joseph   AGnr RN   8.15

BARTHOLOMEW,James John   TSkipper   RNR   HMDrifter Excel   5.7.17 CR France85

BARTLETT,Charles Sydney Ellis   Midmn RN   HMS Goliath kia   13.5.15 MR1

BARTLETT,Geoffrey Edward Rose   PMidmn   RNR   HMS Bulwark kld   26.11.14 MR3

BARTTELOT,Nigel Kenneth Walter LtCmdr   RN   HMS Libert   28.8.14 CR Sussex52

BASKERVILLE,Gilbert Thomas   Clerk   RN   HMS Cressy kia   22.9.14 MR1

BASSETT,Thomas Arthur   Cmdr   RNR   HMS Presidentdedacc   29.9.18   CR Hamps57

BASTIN,Edward   Capt   RMLI   190MG Coy RNDiv   kia   13.11.16 CR France1490

BASTOW,William Henry   2Lt   RFA att RNAS   26.11.15 CR Gallipoli1

BATCHELOR,Harold James   Flt Sub-Lt   RNAS   drd   11.5.15   MR1

BATES,Edwin Raymond   Midmn RN   HMS Indefatigable   kia   31.5.16 MR2

BATES,George 121407   Ch Off   HM Coastguard Stn Par Cornwall   4.5.19 CR Devon3

BATES,John Richard Lt   RMLI   1RM Bn RNDiv   5.9.18 CR France646

BATES,J T G Sub-Lt RNVR HMS Norsholt   17.11.18 CR Surrey91

BATSON,William S Sub-Lt RN   HMS Marmiondrd   21.10.17 MR2

BATTING,William John   Art Eng   RN   HMS Hogue kia   22.9.4 MR1

BATTLE,Thomas James   Art Eng   RN   HM TB D6   ded   3.10.18 CR Hamps5

BATTSON,Reginald Alan   Lt   RNVR HMS Waterfly   12.10.17 CR Iraq8

BAUDRY,Royce Gustave Andre   Flt Lt   RNAS   2.8.16 MR20

BAVIN,Anthony James   Lt   RN   HMS Mary Rose   kia   17.10.17 MR1

BAYFIELD,Geoffrey Harry Verrall   Lt   RN   HMS BlackPrince   kia   31.5.16 MR3

BEAL,Arthur Reginald George   Fleet Paymr   RN   HMS Goliath kia   13.5.15 MR1

BEAL,Basil Arthur   Lt   RN   HM S/M E49   kld   12.3.17 MR3

BEALE,Ernest E   ATFlt Lt   RNAS   13.12.17 CR Lincs78

BEALE,William   TSub-Lt   RNVR HMS Fauvette kld   9.3.16 MR1

BEALES,Arthur   Wt Elect   RN   HMS Indefatigable   kia   31.5.16 MR2

BEARBLOCK,Walter James Fleet Surg   RN   HMS Invincible   kia   31.5.16 MR3

BEARD,Eva Gladys   NSister RN   QARNNS   14.3.20 CR Staffs94

BEARD,George Harry.DSC.   AFlt Commr   RNAS   kia   7.9.16 MR1

BEATON,Henry Alexander Fullerton Lindsay Carnegie TEng RNR HMS Trent   ded   15.5.15   CR Asia60

BEATTIE,Charles Percival   ATLt   RNR   HMS Ramsey kia with 'Meteor'   8.8.15   MR3

BEATTIE,William J Flt Sub-Lt   RNAS   30.9.17 CR France193

BEATTY,David   Sub-Lt RNVR Drake Bn RNDiv   25.3.18 MR20

BEAUMONT,Freund TAsst Paymr   RNR   HMS Laurentic   kld   25.1.17 MR2

BECKETT,Frederick Richard TSkipper   RNR   HMTrawler Merse   kld   22.5.17 MR2

BECKWITH,Alfred Edward   Surg(Prob)   RNVR HMS Oriole   ded   1.8.18 CR Hamps5

BEDELL-SIVRIGHT,David Revell   TSurg   RN   Medical Unit RNDiv   ded   5.9.15 MR3

BEDFORD,Arthur   TSkipper   RNR   HMTrawler Remarko kld   3.12.16 MR1

BEE,George   Ch Skipper   RNR   HMTrawler Gambri   kld   18.1.18 MR1

BEER,Francis John   Bosn (Retd) RN   HMS Aboukir kia   22.9.14 MR1

BEEVOR,Charles Francis   Flt Lt RNAS   5.11.14 MR1

BEGG,Rivers G.   Flt Sub Lt   RNAS Brit Adriatic Sqn 6Wing   17.7.17 CR Italy37

BELFIELD,James Stewart   Eng Sub Lt   RIM   attIWT   24.4.19 MR65

BELL,Albert Henderson   Asst Paymr   RNR   HMS Goliath kia   13.5.15 MR1

BELL,David Courtenay   Lt   RN   HM S/M C25 kia   6.7.18 CR Suffolk130
BELL,Fred   Eng   RNR   HMS Viknor   drd   13.1.15   MR3
BELL,John Henry   Wt Vict   RN   HMS Queen Elizabeth   18.1.21 CR Hamps7
BELL,Laurence Wellington   TSub-Lt   RNR   HMS Laurentic   kld   25.1.18MR2
BELL,Norman Leven Russell Lt Comdr   RN   HMS Vanguard   kld   9.7.17 MR1
BELL,William Atherton   ATLt RNR   HM WaterTank'Provider'   ded   11.9.16 MR3
BELTON,Henry   Skipper   RNR   HMTug Ben Braec   12.4.17 CR Yorks2
BENCKE,J.A. Eng Sub Lt   RNR   Cable Ship John Pender   14.2.19 CR Hamps9
BENDYSHE,Richard Nelson LtCol RMLI   Cmdg Deal Bn RNDiv   1.5.15 CR Gallipoli7
BENJAMIN,John Duxfield   TLt   RNR   HMTrawler Asia   kld   12.9.17MR1
BENJAMIN,Nathan Henry   TSub-Lt   RNVR   Drake Bn RNDiv   dow   25.4.17 CR France95 Lt
BENNETT,Austin Douglas   ALt   RNR   HMS Ebro   kia   14.1.16MR1
BENNETT,C.P.MBE. Gnr   RN   HMS Furious   26.12.19 CR Hamps8
BENNETT,Frank Norman   Eng Lt RN   HMS Natal   kld   30.12.15 MR1
BENNETT,Hugh Donald   Lt   RNR   HMS Cressy   kia   22.9.14MR1
BENNETT,James   Gnr   RN   11.14
BENNETT,Samuel Lowe   TFlt Sub-Lt   RNAS   29.4.17 MR20
BENNETTS,Eric A.   Flt Sub Lt   RNAS   17.8.17 CR France924
BENNIE,Harold Edwin   TLt   RMLI   2Bn   dow   6.2.17 CR France52
BENOY,William Vevers   Eng Lt-Commr RN   HMS Nomad kia   31.5.16MR3
BENSON,William Francis   Sub Lt RNVR Drake Bn B'Coy RNDiv   kia   8.10.18CR France403
BENYON,Godfrey Berkeley John   Lt Comdr   RN   HMS Good Hope   kia   1.11.14MR3
BEODYSHE,Richard N   Maj/BtLtCol(Retd) RM   5.15
BERKS,R.   Flt Sub Lt   RNAS Westgate   13.3.17 CR Kent27
BERNAYS,Leopold Arthur.CMG.DSO.   AComdr   RN   HMS Vala   kia   21.8.17MR3
BERRIDGE,Raymond Winchester   Flt Sub Lt   RNAS 6Sqn attRFC 14Wing kld   3.5.17 CR France164
BESANT,Thomas Fleming   Lt Comdr   RN   HMA S/M AE1 lent to RAN   drd   14.9.14   MR2
BESSON,Frank   Flt Sub-Lt   RNAS   kia   20.12.15 MR1
BETHELL,Edwin   TCh Eng   RNR   HMS India   kia   8.8.15 MR1
BETHELL,Maurice John   Lt   RN   HMS Nestor   kia   31.5.16MR3
BETTINGTON,Aylmer F.   SqnCmdr   RNAS   12.9.17 CR Kent65
BETTS,John Henry   Lt   RN   HMS President   29.3.18 CR Numb4
BEVAN,George Parker.CMG.DSO.AM.   Capt   RN   HMS Triad   ded   14.1.20   CR Asia60
BIBBY,Harold Mowbray   TLt   RNR   HMYacht Verona   kld   24.2.17MR2
BIBBY,John Richard TFlt Sub-Lt   RNAS   11.6.17 CR Europe6
BIBBY,Walter Jackson   TLt   RNR   HMTrawler Corientes kld   23.6.17MR2
BICKMORE,Brian Somerset Lt   RN   HMS Comet   kld   4.8.18 MR2
BIDWELL,Leonard John   Midmn RN   HMS President   17.7.16 CR London9
BIGGS,Geoffrey Nepean   Lt Comdr   RN   HM S/M E30   kld   22.11.16 MR3
BIGGS,Herbert Benjamin   Lt   RNVR Hawke Bn RNDiv   3.9.18 MR16
BILES,Harry   AssPaymstr   RNVR 2Bde HQ RNDiv   13.7.15 CR Gallipoli14
BILLING,Charles G.   Capt   RMLI   Deal Bn RNDiv   (/.6.15)8.1.16 CR Gallipoli2
BILSON,Harold   Eng Sub-Lt   RNR   HMS Sarnia   kia   12.9.18MR3
BINKS,Arthur J.   Flt Sub Lt   RNAS   9.2.18 CR Derby34
BIRCH,Douglas Alexander Colvin   Midmn RN   HMS Invincible   kia   31.5.16MR3
BIRCH,Russell Ernest Lt   RN   HM S/M E24   kld   27.3.16MR3
BIRD,James Harkness.MID   Skipper   RNR   HMTrawler Helgian   kld   6.9.17   MR3 John
BIRD,Albert Edgar   AArt Eng   RN   HMS Good Hope   kia   1.11.14MR3
BIRKS,Rowland   TFlt Sub-Lt   RNAS   3.17
BISHOP,Arthur Anderson   Flt Sub Lt   RNAS   kld   14.9.17CR Kent7
BISHOP,Arthur Godfrey   Gnr   RN   HM S/M C33   kld   5.8.15 MR2
BISHOP,Hubert Drew Eng Lt-Commr RN   HMS Goliath kia   13.5.15MR1
BISSON,PhilipTLt   RNR   HMS Waterwitch attHMS Louvain   kia   20.1.18 MR2
BLACK,Cecil John Trower   2Lt   RMLI   Potsmouth Bn RNDiv   9.5.15 MR4
BLACK,Hatfield A W ATChapn   RN   7.17
BLACK,James Douglas (Dudley)   TSub-Lt   RNVR 189 Bde MG Coy RNDiv   13.11.16 MR21
BLACK,Leslie Gordon TSub-Lt   RNVR Hawke Bn RNDiv   dow   13.12.16 CR Essex37
BLACK,Norman   TFlt Sub-Lt   RNAS 9Sqn   12.10.17 CR Belgium132
BLACK,Ronald George   ALt   RN   HMS Tyrant   accdrd 4.11.17MR3
BLACK,Sidney Arthur Flt Sub Lt   RN/RNAS 3Wing   8.1.16 CR Gallipoli1

BLACK,William	TEng Lt	RN	HMS Natal	kld	30.12.15 MR1

BLACK,William   TEng Lt   RN   HMS Natal   kld   30.12.15 MR1
BLACK-BARNES,Charles Talbot.MID   Lt   RN   HMS Royal Oak   ded   21.2.19   CR Hamps219
BLACKBURN,Lewis Frederick   Capt   RN   HMS President   5.1.16 CR London24
BLACKFORD,William James Eng Cmdr   RNR   HMS Engadine   1.1.20 CR Kent5
BLACKWOOD,Thomas Anderson   Eng Sub-Lt   RNR   HMS Fauvette kld   9.3.16 MR1
BLAGROVE,Cecil Richard   TFlt Lt   RNAS   kia   7.2.17 CR Belgium353
BLAIR,George Wilson Skipper   RNR   HMS Firefly   6.10.18CR Europe6
BLAIR,James Penney Eng Lt RN   HMS Arno   drd   23.3.18   MR3
BLAKE,Francis George   Eng Lt RN   HMS Cormorant   6.5.16 CR Europe23
BLAKE,Ian Hamilton Flt Cadet   RNAS   kldacc   26.11.17 CR France1844
BLAKE,Laurence Wortland Acton   Sub-Lt RN   HMS Ariel   kld   2.8.18 MR3
BLAKE,William H.   Prob Schmstr RN   HMS Impregnable   18.4.21 CR Devon3
BLAKER,Arthur Wilfrid.MID Lt   RN   HMSInflexible dow   19.3.15   MR1
BLAKEY,Andrew Hunter   Lt   RNR   HMS Mastiff   19.2.19 CR Durham19
BLAMPEY,John Charles Richard   Art Eng   RN   HMS Genista kia   23.10.16 MR2
BLANE,Charles Rodney Sir   Comdr RN   HMS Queen Mary   kia   31.5.16MR3
BLANSHARD,Thomas R.   Lt   RNR   HMS Thetis   10.9.17 CR NIreland52
BLIGH,Edward Henry Swinburne   Lt   RNVR Draker Bn RNDiv   dow   10.9.15   CR Gallipoli1
BLISSETT,Jack Patrick Murray   ALt   RN   HM S/M E14 kia   28.1.18MR3
BLISSETT,Samuel   TSkipper   RNR   HMTrawler Courtier kld   6.1.16 MR1
BLOMEFIELD,Thomas Charles Alfred   Comdr RN   HMS Juno   dow   14.8.15   MR1
BLOW,Harold Lt   RNR   HMS Black Prince   kia   31.5.16MR2
BLUETT,Bertie William   Lt Comdr   RN   HMS Monmouth   kia   1.11.14MR2
BLUMFIELD,Louis   Lt   RN   HMS Inflexible   ded   23.7.18   CR Scot722
BLYTH,R.A.   Flt Sub-Lt   RNAS   23.1.18 CR Belgium115
BLYTH,Reginald Edward   Lt   RN   HMS Barham dow   31.5.16   MR40
BOARDMAN,Harry.DCM.   2Lt   RMLI   RNDiv(Res)   kldacc   16.7.17   CR Yorks529
BOASE,Harold   Lt   RN   HM S/M C16   16.4.17 CR Suffolk130
BODDY,Andrew John TFlt Sub-Lt   RNAS HMS Killingholme   kia   27.4.16MR1
BOISSIER,William A M   TLt   RMA   27.7.17 CR Belgium24
BOLAM,John William TSub-Lt   RNR   SS Heathersidekia   24.8.17MR1
BOLAS,James Sydney TFlt Sub-Lt   RNAS   12.1.16 MR4
BOLES,Noel Henry   Lt   2DorsetR att RNAS   kia   11.1.16CR Gallipoli1
BOLINGBROKE,Russell   Sub-Lt RN   HMS Paragon kia   17.3.17MR3
BOLTON,Edward   TSub-Lt   RNVR Hood Bn RNDiv   kia   3.11.17CR Belgium125
BOLTON,Stuart Bladen Nelson   Midmn RN   HMS Indefatigable   kia   31.5.16MR2
BOLTON,Wilfred   TSub-Lt   RNVR Collingwood Bn RNDiv   4.6.15 MR4
BOND,James William Midmn RN   HMS Russell kld   27.4.16MR1
BOND,V.J.   Ch Wt Eng   RNR   HMS Minotaur   24.2.20 CR Scot280
BONE,John Turner   Flt Sub Lt   RNAS   18.10.15 CR France1361
BONHAM,Thomas Parry   Capt   RN   HMS Black Prince   kia   31.5.16MR3
BONNETT,Ernest C   T2Lt   RMLI   1RM Bn RNDiv   27.10.17 CR Belgium63
BONNEYWELL,Percy AGnr   RN   HMS P26   kld   10.4.17MR1
BONTOR,Lawrence Sidney   Lt   RN   HM S/M L10 kia   4.10.18MR3
BOOKLESS,James H TSub-Lt   RNVR Nelson Bn RNDiv   4.5.15 MR4
BOOTH,C.   Lt   RNR HMS Hazel   13.12.18 CR Greece10
BOOTH,F.   Flt Sub Lt   RNAS   3.1.18 CR France924
BOOTHBY,James Robert   LtCmdr   RNVR attArmoured Car Div RNAS   kia   1.5.15 CR Gallipoli30
BOR,Thomas Humphrey   ALt   RNR   HM S/M E5   kld   11.3.16MR3
BORRETT,John Cyril FitzRobert   Lt Comdr   RN   HMS Invincible   kia   31.5.16MR3
BORROWES,Kildare Henry   Midmn RN   HMS Queen Mary   kia   31.5.16MR3
BORROWES,Walter Lt   RN   HM S/M C31 kld   7.1.15 MR3
BORTHWICK,George Gnr   RN   HMS Turbulent   kia   31.5.16MR3
BOSWELL,Walter Osler   Lt   RNVR HMML240   3.3.19 CR Surrey1
BOULTON,James Forster   Midmn RN   HMS Monmouth   kia   1.11.14MR2
BOULTON,R.   Lt(Retd)   RN   3.4.19 CR Devon1
BOWDEN,John Noah TSub-Lt   RNVR Anson Bn RNDiv   13.11.16 MR21
BOWDEN-SMITH,Victor James   LtCmdr   RN   HMML No403 kld   22.8.18MR3
BOWER,Harold A   Flt Lt RNAS   2.9.16 CR London23
BOWLE-EVANS,Stephen   Cmdr RN   HMS Hyacinth   29.11.16 CR SAfrica158

6

BOWLES,Edward John   Eng Lt RN   HM S/M K5   drd   20.1.21   MR3
BOWLES,Geoffrey C TSub-Lt   RNVR   4.17
BOWLES,William George   Skipper   RNR   HMTrawler Strathrannock   kld   6.4.17 MR1
BOWLY,Edmond Mansel   Lt   RN   HMS Narbrough   drd   12.1.18   MR3
BOWMAN,Geoffrey Glendinning   TFlt Sub-Lt   RNAS 1 Sqdn   19.5.17 MR20
BOWYER,Richard Grenville Lt   RN   HMS Paragon   kia   17.3.17 MR3
BOYCE,Harold C Woollcombe   see WOOLLCOMBE-BOYCE,H C
BOYLE,Fred. Lt   RNR   HMDrifter Campania II   5.3.17   CR Yorks2
BRACE,William Percy Sub-Lt(Paymr) RNVR HMS Pembroke   25.10.18 CR Mon67
BRADBURN,Thomas S. ·   Surg   RN   HMS President   8.3.18 CR Warwick152
BRADDOCK,Arthur Leslie   Asst Paymr   RNR   HMS Cressy kia   22.9.14 MR1
BRADE,Frank Tomkinson.DSC.   LtCmdr   RNR   HMCMB No67A   kia   18.8.19 MR2
BRADFORD,Bertram Hamilton Malcolm Lt (Retd)   RN   HMS Aboukir   kia   22.9.14   MR1 LtCmdr
BRADFORD,George Nicholson.VC. LtCmdr   RN   HMS Iris II   kia   23.4.18 CR Belgium371
BRADING,William Ernest   ArtEng RN   HMS Exe   kld   27.3.18 MR3
BRADLEY,Charles W.Raymond   Sub Lt RNVR Drake Bn RNDiv   13.11.16 CR France339
BRADLEY,John   Eng   RNR   HMS Viknor drd   13.1.15   MR3
BRADSHAW,George W   Gnr   RN   5.16
BRAIN,Arthur Thomas   TLt   RNR   MFA Eleanor kia   12.2.18 MR3
BRAINE,Carl Svend Lt   RNR   HMS Anchusa kia   16.7.18 MR2
BRANDER,Robert William   Surg   RN   HMS Crescent kldacc 1.5.18 CR Scot764
BRANDON,Arthur F. Flt Lt RNAS   26.10.17 CR Kent25
BRANDT,Frank   Capt   RN   HMS Monmouth   kia   1.11.14 MR2
BRANNON,Bertram Robert Urry   Eng Lt RN   HMS Plover   8.11.18 CR Scot252
BRATTAN,Arthur Crosfield ALt   RNR   HMS Ayano kia   11.3.15 MR3
BRAY,Charles Willoughby   Lt   RNR   HMS Aquarius   15.11.17 CR Greece10
BRAY,Frank TFlt Sub-Lt   RNAS   15.7.17 MR20
BRAY,Raymond Earl Prob Flt Off RNAS   14.8.17 CR Bucks54
BRAYBROOKE,C.W. Maj   RM   24.3.20 CR Kent63
BREAKSPEAR,Arthur John   ChGnr RN   HMS Bulwark   26.11.14 CR Kent46
BREARLEY,Harold B.   Flt Sub Lt   RNAS   30.1.18 CR Scot252
BREBNER,William Frederick Mate (E)   RN   HMS Queen Mary   kia   31.5.16 MR2
BRETT,Leslie Henry Flt Sub Lt   RNAS   22.7.17 CR Greece10
BREUELL,S. Lt   RNR   SS Transylvania   5.5.17 CR Italy13
BREWER,Charles Edward William   Lt   RN   HMS Ariel   kld   2.8.18 MR3
BRIDGE,Bryant Henry TFlt Sub-Lt   RNAS   drd   9.8.17 MR1
BRIDGEMAN,Richard Orlando Beaconsfield.DSO.Hon Cmdr RN   HMS Hyacinth drdacc 9.1.17 CR Tanzania1
BRIDGLAND,Charles TSub-Lt   RNVR Drake Bn RNDiv   dow   11.12.15 MR3
BRIERLEY,James Roger Ingham   SubLt RN   HM S/M J6   drd   15.10.18 MR1
BRIGGS,Ernest Frederick   Paymr Sub-Lt RNR   HMS Teutonic   20.12.18
BRIGGS,George Leonard Clayton   Sub-Lt RN   HMS Genista kia   23.10.16 MR3
BRIGHT,C.T. Art Eng   RN   HM S/M J6   15.10.18 CR Numb36
BRIGHT,Eli Francis Gnr   RN   HMS Pathfinder   kia   5.9.14 MR3
BRIMER,Charles Torryburn   TFlt Sub-Lt   RNAS   drd   4.12.16 MR1
BRINJES,Stanley Lionel   Lt   RNR   HM S/M L10 kia   4-10-18   MR3
BRINSMEAD,Cecil Horace   Flt Sub Lt   RN/RNAS 3Wing   kia   11.1.16 CR Gallipoli1
BRITTAIN-SMITH,Sydney Francis   Lt   RNVR attRNAS   ded   7.9.17 CR Greece9
BROAD,Dennis Gurney   TFlt Sub-Lt(Ass Paymr) RNAS(RNR)HMS Kilingholme   kia   27.4.16 MR1
BROAD,Frank.MID   Skipper   RNR   HMDrifter Ocean Fisher   kld   16.6.18 MR1
BROCKMAN,W.   Lt   RN   HMS Talbot   11.9.14 CR Devon1
BRODIE,Donald Francis O'Callaghan Lt   RN   HM S/M D5   kld   3.11.14 MR3
BRODIE,Theodore Stuart   Lt Comdr   RN   HM S/M E15 kia   17.4.15 CR Asia52
BRODIE,Thomas Patterson   TEng Sub-Lt   RNR   HMS Dundee kia   2.9.17 MR3
BROGAN,Thomas William   T2Lt   RMLI   2 RM Bn RNDiv   26.10.17 MR30
BROOKE,E.DSO.   Lt Cmdr   RN   HMS Strongbow   10.2.19 CR Yorks642
BROOKE,Patrick Harry   Sub Lt RN   HMS Courageous   24.5.17 CR Scot287
BROOKE,Rupert   TSub-Lt   RNVR   4.15
BROOKING,Charles W   AGnr   RN   9.14
BROOKS,Frances Edward(Tommy)MM&Bar.Sub Lt RNVR Anson Bn RNDiv   kia   10.11.18 CR France1142
BROOKS,Thomas Brownhill TAsst Paymr   RNR   HMS Tipperary   kia   1.6.16 MR3

7

BROTCHIE,Robert Traill   Surg   RNVR   HMS Bulwark kld   26.11.14   MR3
BROTHERS,James Harold   TSub-Lt   RNVR 189 Bde MG Coy RNDiv   13.11.16 MR21
BROTHERTON,A.S. Capt   Merchant Marine attAdmiralty Salvage Draft   6.11.18CR France1848
BROUGHTON,Alfred William Delves   Capt   RMLI   see DELVES-BROUGHTON,A.W   5.16
BROWN,David   TEng Lt   RNR   MFA Eleanor   kia   12.2.18MR1
BROWN,David   TLt   RNR   HMYacht Sandra   kia   25.9.15   MR1
BROWN,Douglas Burn Buchan   Lt   RN   HMS Indefatigable   kia   31.5.16MR2
BROWN,Ernest Arthur   ATLt   RNR   HMS Bayano   kia   11.3.15MR3
BROWN,Geoffrey Edelman   PMidmn   RNR   HMS Clan McNaughton   drd   3.2.15   MR1
BROWN,George   TSurg Prob   RNVR   HMS Marmion   21.10.17 CR Europe146 Surg
BROWN,George Kendall   Art Eng   RN   HMS Defence kia   31.5.16MR1
BROWN,Harry Cliff 2Lt   RMLI   1RM Bn RNDiv   17.2.17   CR France514
BROWN,James Robert   TEng Sub-Lt   RNR   HMS Laurentic   kld   25.1.17MR2
BROWN,John TEng Lt   RNR   HMS Stephen Furness kia   13.12.17 MR3
BROWN,John TEng Lt   RNR   MFA Whitehead   kia   15.10.17 MR3
BROWN,Leonard   Skipper   RNR   HMTrawler Silver Queen   15.2.18 CR Kent7
BROWN,Lewis   Prob Flt Off RNAS   kld   21.3.18CR Lancs43
BROWN,Peter Eng Lt RNR   HMS Otranto   6.10.18CR Scot31
BROWN,Robert   Lt   RNR   HMS Sarnia   kia   12.9.18MR3
BROWN,Robert   Skipper   RNR   HMTrawler James Secker   drd   25.9.17   MR3
BROWN,Stephen   Eng Lt-Comdr RN   HMS Strongbow   kia   17.10.17 MR1
BROWN,William   PMidmn   RNR   HMS Clan McNaughton   drd   3.2.15   MR1
BROWN,William Fraser   TLt   RNVR   Anson Bn RNDiv   4.6.15   MR4
BROWN,William George   Lt   RNR   HMS Duchess of Rothesay   8.3.19   CR London3
BROWNE,Ernest Robert DSC   Skipper   RNR   HMDrifter Cromorna   7.4.19   CR Norfolk21
BROWNE,George Edmund Rangecroft   Lt   RNR   HMS Laurentic   kld   25.1.17MR2
BROWNE,Harold Rollo Gore Asst Paymr   RN   HMS Invincible   kia   31.5.16MR3
BROWNE,Murdoch Campbell DSC   TCapt RMLI   1 RM Bn RNDiv   13.11.16 MR21
BROWNE,William D TSub-Lt   RNVR Hood Bn RNDiv   7.6.15   MR4
BROWNING,Guy Arrott   Chapn & Instr RN   HMS Indefatigable   kia   31.5.16MR2
BRUCE,David Eng   RNR   HMS Viknor   drd   13.1.15   MR3
BRUCE,Gervase Ronald   Midmn RN   HMS Monmouth   kia   1.11.14MR2
BRUCE,John TSkipper   RNR   HMDrifter Charity   drd   24.10.15 MR3
BRUCE,William.DSC.TSkipper   RNR   HMTrawler Bradford drd   26.10.16 MR3
BRYAN,Richard Albert   Midmn RN   HMS Russell kld   27.4.16MR1
BRYANS,Fraser M   TFlt Sub-Lt   RNAS ded UK buried Canada 11.10.17   ded   17.7.17   CR Canada1688
BUCHAN,Alexander TSkipper   RNR   HMTrawler Violet May   kia   15.2.18MR3
BUCHAN,Peter   TSkipper   RNR   HMDrifter Morning Star   kld   8.1.16   MR3
BUCHANAN,Colin James   ASub-Lt   RNR   HM S/M C33 kld   5.8.15   MR3
BUCHANAN,W.M.   Lt   RNR   HMS President   19.2.19   CR Hamps5
BUCKLE,Harry James Eng Lt RN   HMS Excellent   17.8.19   CR Hamps9
BUCKLEY,Eric James Kershaw   TFlt Sub-Lt   RNAS   drd   28.9.17   CR Europe90
BUCKNILL,James Riddell   Lt   RN   HMS Negro   drd   21.12.16 MR1
BUDD,Victor John   Flt Sub-Lt   RNAS   drd   20.2.18   MR1
BULEY,John Webber TSkipper   RN(RNR) HMT Calumsia   15.11.17 CR Egypt1
BULLOCK,Edward Noah   TSkipper   RNR   HMTrawler Jay   kia   11.8.17MR1
BULTEEL,Edward W. Lt   RN   HM TB12   10.5.15   CR Suffolk130
BUNBURY,Evan Campbell   Cmdr   RN   HMCMB No71A   drd   15.10.18 MR3
BUNCE,John Frederick.MC.   Sub Lt RNVR Howe Bn RNDiv   dow   19.2.17   CR France177
BUNGARD,George   Gnr   RN   1.15
BURCHELL,William Thomas Hays   AGnr   RN   HMS Good Hope   kia   1.11.14MR3
BURDEN,Charles E   TFlt Lt RNAS   1.18
BURGE,Norman Ormsby.MIDBvtLtCol   RMLI   Nelson Bn RNDiv   kia   13.11.16 CR France701
BURGESS,H. Mate   RN   HMS Furious   27.1.19   CR Hamps138
BURGESS,Nathaniel Gordon   Lt   RNR   HM S/M H5   drd   2.3.18   MR1
BURGON,Peter   TSkipper   RNR   HMTrawler Resono   kld   26.12.15 MR1
BURKILL,George Arthur   Midmn RNR   HMS Himalaya   23.11.16 CR Tanzania1
BURLINSON,Arthur Sub-Lt RNR   HMS Clan McNaughton   drd   3.2.15   MR1
BURN,John.RD.   Cmdr   RNR   HMS Victory ded   18.5.20   CR Hamps7
BURNELL,Harry   AWt Tel   RN   HMS Barham   kia   31.5.16MR3

8

BURNELL,James Jago Mate   RN   HMS Vivid   5.5.15 CR Devon3
BURNETT,J.   Lt   RNVR HMS President   21.7.18 CR Sussex151
BURNETT,Lionel C Lt (Retd)   RN   Killed serving in the army   8.17
BURNETT,William Josiah   TFlt Sub-Lt   RNAS 1 Sqdn   26.9.17 MR20
BURNETT,William Leslie DCM   TSub-Lt   RNVR Drake Bn RNDiv   30.12.17 MR21
BURNS,John.DSC.   TEng Lt   RNR   HMS Vala   kia   21.8.17 MR1 James
BURNS,Erasmus Joseph   Gnr   RN   HMS Archer   accdrd 22.2.19   MR2
BURNS,Frederick George   Lt   RNVR HMS Presidentded   23.11.18 CR Greece23
BURR,Henry Adam John   TSub-Lt   RNVR Hawke Bn RNDiv   23.4.17 MR20
BURR,Ronald Eric   Flt Sub Lt   RN/RNAS   dow   18.2.18   CR France297
BURRELL,William   Lt   RNVR MotorBoatRes accdrd 18.11.14 MR3
BURT,John Cooper   Carp   RN   HMS Bulwark kld   26.11.14 MR3
BURT,Walter Saxon Midmn RN   HMS Queen Mary   kia   31.5.16 MR3
BURTON,Cecil R.   2Lt   RMLI 1RM Bn RNDiv   17.2.17 CR France514
BURTON,Joseph Henry.DSC. Gnr   RN   HMS Tower   accdrd 1.12.17 MR2
BURTON,R.DSC.   Capt   RMLI 6Bn   8.9.19 MR70
BURTON,Reginald Edward George   Capt   RMLI HMS Irresistible   dow   1.4.15 CR Europe6
BURTON-FANNING,Newel Edward Eden   TCapt RMLI 2 RM Bn RNDiv   28.4.17 MR20
BURWOOD,Frederick Henry TSkipper   RNR   HMDrifter Dewey   drd   12.8.17   MR1
BURWOOD,Samuel Robert   TSkipper   RNR   HMDrifter Kent County   kld   8.12.16 MR1
BURY,George Wyman Lt   RNVR HMS Egmont   23.9.20 CR Egypt10
BUSBY,Eric William TFlt Sub-Lt   RNAS 4Sqn   kia   10.7.17 CR Belgium171
BUSH,Richard Eldon Flt Lt RNAS   24.4.17 CR Somerset103
BUSHELL,John William   Bosn   RN   HMS Good Hope   kia   1.11.14 MR1
BUSK,Hans Acworth Flt Commr   RNAS   6.1.16 MR4
BUTCHER,James Frederick AGnr   RN   HMS Vanguard   kld   9.7.17 MR1
BUTCHER,Samuel Edmund   Gnr   RN   HMS Natal   kld   30.12.15 MR2
BUTLER,Basil George Midmn RNR   HMS Clan McNaughton   drd   3.2.15 MR1
BUTLER,Edmund Artis   Skipper   RNR   HMTrawler Lock Naver   kld   13.5.18 MR3
BUTLER,James   Skipper   RNR   HMTrawler Cotsmuir kld   2.2.17 MR3
BUTLER,Ralph T   Clerk RN   HMS Hampshire   drd   5.6.16 CR Scot900
BUTT,Leonard Stephen   Paymr Sub-Lt RNR   31.12.15 CR NIreland52
BUXTON,James   Art Eng   RN   HMS Cowslip kia   25.4.18 MR3
BYRNE,Erl Stanley Frederic   TMidmn   RNR   HMS Torrent kld   23.12.17 MR3
BYRNE,Felix.MID   Lt   RNR   HMS Begonia kia   6.10.17 MR3
BYRNES,James William   Skipper   RNR   Trader Tourazo   24.12.14 CR Kent46
BYRON,Charles G.   Lt   RNR   HMS Earl of Peterborough   ded   10.12.18 CR Italy83

C

CABLE,Alfred Charles   Skipper   RNR   HMS Vesper   4.4.18 CR NIreland52
CADLE,Ernest Geoffrey   Midmn   RN   HMS Formidable   kia   1.1.15 MR1
CADMAN,Maurice Danks   Surg Prob   RNVR HMS Rival   kld   4.6.18 MR3
CADMAN,William   Comdr RN   HMS Vanguard   kld   9.7.17 MR1
CAIN,P.E.   LtCmdr   RN   23.3.21 CR Sussex183
CAINE,Ernest Wilfred Eng Lt RN   HMS Black Prince   kia   31.5.16 MR3
CAKEBREAD,A.   Lt   RNVR HMS Juno   7.7.19 CR Asia9
CALBOURNE,Robert Henry   Midmn RN   see COLBOURNE,R H
CALDER,Harry.RD. LtCmdr   RNR   HMYacht Aries   31.10.15 CR Scot247
CALLAN,W.D.   ChGnr RN   HMS Ark Royal   8.3.20 CR Europe6
CALLENDER,George Marshall   SubLt RNVR Howe Bn RNDiv   4.6.15 CR Gallipoli2
CALLENDER,William G M   TSub-Lt   RNVR prob same as CALLENDER,G M   6.15
CALTHROP,Edward Spencer Surg   RN   30.7.17 CR Surrey55
CALVERT,Francis J Gnr   RN   HMS Partridge   12.12.17 CR Europe146
CAMERON,Alistair Gordon.DSC.MID   TSub-Lt   RNR   HM S/M E16 kld   22.8.16 MR3
CAMERON,Mark William   Gnr   RN   HMS Invincible   kld   31.5.16 MR3
CAMPBELL,A.V.MC. LtCmdr   RNVR   Howe Bn RNDiv   30.12.17 CR France662 A.U.
CAMPBELL,Adair Melfort Gerald   Midmn RN   HMS Defence kia   31.5.16 MR2

9

CAMPBELL,Charles Allen   TSkipper   RNR   HMTrawler Silanier   accdrd 25.9.16   MR21
CAMPBELL,Donald   TAsst Eng   RNR   HMS Princes Irene   kld   27.5.15MR3
CAMPBELL,Donald Rhodes   Lt   RN   HMCMB 71A kia   15.10.18 CR Belgium24
CAMPBELL,George   Ch Offr   CG   HMCG Craster Stn   3.3.20 CR Yorks172
CAMPBELL,George Richard Colin   LtCmdr   RN   CompassDept(Slough)HMSPresident drd in RMS Leinster 10.10.18 CR Eire14
CAMPBELL,Gunning Morehead.CB.   MajGen   RM   AdjtGen   29.11.20 CR Hamps7
CAMPBELL,Guy   Paymr RN   HMS Venerable   ded   25.11.18 CR Devon3
CAMPBELL,John   TCapt RMLI   2 RM Bn RNDiv   28.4.17 MR20
CAMPBELL,Keith Morehead Gunning   Sub-Lt RN   HM S/M C31 kld   7.1.15 MR3
CAMPBELL,Malcolm Drury Lt   RNVR Howe Bn RNDiv   2.5.15 CR Gallipoli14
CAMPBELL,O.M.OBE.   Constructor   RN   CIR   kld   28.8.21CR Yorks2 (24.8.21)
CAMPBELL,Philip S. LtCmdr   RNVR Drake Bn RNDiv   13.11.16 CR France339
CAMPBELL,Patrick Duncan Melver   StaffSurg   RN   HMS Sentinel   21.3.15 CR Kent46
CAMPBELL,Thomas Lt   RN   HMS President   29.8.18 CR Lancs2
CAMPBELL-COOKE,Alan Gordon   Sub-Lt RN   HMS Invincible   kia   31.5.16MR3
CAMPION,Elbert   Skipper   RNR   HMT AchillesII   26.6.18 CR Devon46
CANDEY,Henry William   WtTel RNR   kldacc 14.9.17   CR Newfndland59
CANDY,Philip Sadler Midmn RN   HMS Monmouth   kia   1.11.14MR2
CANNIN,Herbert Bernard   TSub-Lt   RNVR Nelson Bn RNDiv   10.1.18 MR21
CANT,Andrew EngLt RNR   HMS Ashtree   15.12.17 CR Wales17
CAPPLEMAN,Thomas Warcup WSA1559   Skipper   RNR   HMDrifter Witham   ded   24.6.18   CR Yorks42
CAPPLEMAN,Wilkinson   Skipper   RNR   HMT Recepto drd   16.2.17   CR Numb96
CAPPS,Frederick Albert   Ft Surg RN   HMS Defence kia   31.5.16MR2
CARD,L H   Sub-Lt RNVR Hood Bn RNDiv   2.10.18CR France1184
CARD,Thomas Philip Lester   Gnr   RN   in HM FltMessenger Ermine HMS Abercrombie kia 2.8.17 MR1
CARDEW,Basil St Merryn   Clerk RN   HMS Monmouth   kia   1.11.14MR2
CARDEW,John St Erme   Lt   RN   HMS Canada   9.2.17 CR Glouc30
CARLES,Alan James Lt   RN   HM S/M E22 kia   25.4.16MR3
CARLISLE,James   EngLt RNR   HMS Laurentic   25.1.17 CR Eire295
CARLISLE,Reginald Henry   Lt   RNVR HMS Sarnia kia   12.9.18MR3
CARLYLE,Thomas   Surg Sub-Lt   RNVR HMS Relentless   21.10.18 CR London8
CARMICHAEL,Alexander D Gibson   see GIBSON-CARMICHAEL,Alexander D
CARMICHAEL,Ian Neil   FltSubLt   RN   RNAS   20.7.16 CR Scot54
CARMICHAEL,James TAsst Eng   RNR   HMS Princess Irene   kld   27.5.15MR3
CARMICHAEL,John Duncan Lt   RNAS/RNVR Depot HMS President   19.3.18 CR France102
CARMICHAEL,John.DSO.   EngCmdr   RNR   HMS Princess Margaret   2.4.18 CR Lancs7
CARMICHAEL,William Albert   Lt   RNR   HMT St Ives   21.12.16 CR Yorks2
CARPENTER,Edward Berry   TCapt RMLI   Plymouth Bn RNDiv dow   18.8.15   MR2
CARPENTER,George TSkipper   RNR   HMTrawler Drumtochty   kld   29.1.18MR2
CARR,Henry Cecil   Comdr RN   HMS Bayano kia   11.3.15MR3
CARR,Josephine   Clerk WRNS G4985 SS Leinster   kia   10.10.18 MR2
CARRE,Edward Cambridge   Lt   RN   HM S/M E47 kld   20.8.17MR3
CARROLL,Alexander TSkipper   RNR   HMTrawler Glenprosen   kld   3.11.16 MR1
CARROLL,John George   Flt Sub-Lt   RNAS   28.3.18 MR20
CARTE,Edward A L   TSub-Lt   RNR   11.16
CARTER,Eccles James   Lt   RN   HMS Pathfinder   kia   5.9.14 MR1
CARTER,Edwin   Eng Comdr   RN   HMS Goliath kia   13.5.15MR1
CARTER,Francis   AArt Eng   RN   HMS Bulwark kld   26.11.14 MR3
CARTER,George Leslie Lewis NavalInstr   RN   HMS Pomone ded   29.7.18   CR Devon67
CARTER,Gerald Ernest Berkeley   Lt   RN   HM S/M C33 kld   5.8.15 MR3
CARTER,Richard Hector   Paymr RN   HMS Defence kia   31.5.16MR2
CARTWRIGHT,Francis J W.DSO.   Maj/TLt Col   RMLI   1Bn   dow   30.4.17   CR France113
CARY,Byron Plantagenet.DSO.Hon   Lt Comdr   RN   HM S/M G9 drd   16.9.17   MR3
CASE,E.J.   LtCmdr   RN   HMS Victory   18.4.18 CR Hamps9
CASEY,Francis Dominick.DSC.   ATFlt Comdr   RNAS 3Sqn   kia   10.8.17CR Belgium172
CASEY,Thomas Daniel   Gnr   RN   HMS Alcantara   kia   29.2.16MR3
CASHMORE,Ernest W.   SubLt RNVR Nelson Bn RNDiv   13.11.16 CR France339
CASSAP,James   Lt   RNR   HMS Victory   3.11.17CR Sussex144
CASSIDY,John   Ch Gnr RN   HMS Russell   27.4.16 CR Europe6

CATER,Edward Howell   Cmdr   RN   HMS Lord Nelson   7.8.15 CR Gallipoli30
CATHIE,Richard Archibald   Cmdr   RN   20.3.18 CR Eire5
CATLEY,Charles   Gnr   RMA   HMS Queen Mary   kia   31.5.16 MR3
CATLIN,Edward James   AGnr   RN   HMS Cressy   kia   22.9.14 MR1
CATON,Jack   SubLt RNVR Anson Bn RNDiv   27.3.18 CR France233
CATON,Peter EngSubLt   RNR   HMS Laurentic   25.1.17 CR Eire295
CAWSEY,William Arthur   Carp   RN   HMS Inflexible   kia   18.3.15 MR2
CAY,Arthur Lindesay Capt   RN   HMS Invincible   kia   31.5.16 MR3
CENTER,William R   Ft Surg RN   HMS Russell   28.4.16 CR Europe6
CHADWICK,Arnold J.DSO?(DSC)   ATFlt Comdr   RNAS 4Sqn   28.7.17 CR Belgium172
CHALLINOR,Charles Gnr   RN   HM TB No96   drd   1.11.15 MR3
CHAMBERLAIN,Arthur Beaumont Goddard Twyford Lt   RN   HMS Neptune kia   23.4.18 CR Kent7
CHAMBERLAIN,Edgar Warner   Eng Comdr   RN   HMS Bulwark kld   26.11.14 MR3
CHAMBERLAIN,Henry Neville   Lt   RNR   HMS Anchusa kia   16.7.18 MR2
CHAMBERLAIN,Louisa Charlotte   ResNSister   QARNNS   HMHS China kld   10.8.18 MR1
CHAMPNESS,Eric Treeve   TEng Sub-Lt   RN   HMS Queen Mary   kia   31.5.16 MR3
CHANCE,Arthur Ernest Newton   TSub-Lt   RNVR Howe Bn RNDiv   13.11.16 MR21
CHANDLER,John Alfred   AssPaymstr   RNR   HMS Arabis   kia   11.2.16 MR2
CHANDLER,Joseph   ChOff CG   HM Coastguards   5.2.16 CR Eire309
CHAPELLE,Reginald Charles Sub Lt RNVR HMS St.Steiriol   kld   25.4.18 MR1
CHAPLIN,B.DSC.   Lt   RNR   HM Yacht Seadawn   6.7.18 CR Hamps58
CHAPLIN,Charles Geoffrey   Lt   RN   HMS Natal   kld   30.12.15 MR1
CHAPLIN,Harold G.   Surg   RN   HMS Hampshire   drd   5.6.16 CR Scot900
CHAPMAN,Alfred Henry   Lt   RMLI 190Bde MGCoy RNDiv   13.11.16 MR21
CHAPMAN,Charles Hamilton Murray FltLt   RNAS   23.2.18 CR Kent65
CHAPMAN,Charles Manners Sutton.DSC&Bar Lt   RN   HM S/M L55   kia   9.6.19 CR Hamps5
CHAPMAN,Donald Frank   TEng Sub-Lt   RNR   HMS Mechanician   kia   20.1.18 MR3
CHAPMAN,John Downie   TCh Eng   RNR   HMS Clan McNaughton   drd   3.2.15 MR1
CHAPMAN,Richard Keppel George Sutton Midmn   RN   HMS Bulwark kld   26.11.14 MR3
CHAPMAN,W.   SubLt RNVR Hawke Bn RNDiv   4.9.18 CR France646
CHARLTON,Adolph Coles   TLt   RNR   HMS Hampshire   kld   5.6.16 MR3
CHARTERS,William Lt   RNR   HMS Patrol   accdrd 3.2.18 CR Glouc5
CHATER,C.W.   Sub Lt RNR   HMS Lady Cory Wright   kia   26.3.18 MR3
CHEETHAM,Charles Joseph Lt Col RMA retd 63 Regtl Dist Recruiting Office   ded   9.12.16 CR Lancs416
CHERRY,Alfred   Gnr   RN   HMS Defence kia   31.5.16 MR2
CHERRY,Lancelot A   TSub-Lt   RNVR Drake Bn RNDiv   11.5.15 MR4
CHESSEX,Robert Ernest Aini TLt   RNVR HMS Vanguard   kld   9.7.17 MR1
CHETWOOD,George Albert   ChGnr RN   HMS Patia   4.3.18 CR Hamps9
CHICHESTER,Robert Charles Lt   RN   HMS Black Prince   kia   31.5.16 MR3
CHICK,Reginald Samuel John Sub Lt RNVR HMS Sarnia   kia   12.9.18 MR3
CHILD,Bernard   Eng Lt RN   HMS Monmouth   kia   1.11.14 MR2
CHILD,Herbert Alexander.CMG.   Lt   RN   HMS Cumberland   drd   21.10.14 MR2
CHILD,Thomas F Dampier   see DAMPIER-CHILD,Thomas F
CHISHOLM,James.RD.   EngCmdr   HMS Armadale Castle   27.4.19 CR Scot761
CHISHOLM,Robert Fellowes Lt Comdr   RN   HM S/M E37 kld   3.12.16 MR3
CHITTOCK,William Hubbard TEng Sub-Lt   RNR   HMS Newmarket   kld   17.7.17 MR3
CHOLMLEY,George Francis Lt Comdr   RN   HM S/M E3   kia   18.10.14 MR3
CHORLEY,Dudley Cecil   AAsst Paymr   RNR   HMS Bayano   kia   11.3.15 MR3
CHRISTIAN,Harold   Capt   RN   HMS President   15.11.17 CR Glouc30
CHRISTIAN,William   Skipper   RNR   HMTrawler Euston   kld   12.2.17 MR2
CHRISTIE,Dennis Peter   Sub-Lt RN   HMS Surprise kld   23.12.17 MR1
CHRISTIE,Peter   Skipper   RNR   HMTrawler Briton   21.7.15 CR Suffolk130
CHRISTMAS,William Thomas   Gnr   RN   HMS Vanguard   kld   9.7.17 MR3
CHURCH,James Brodrick Tilney   Lt   RN   Collingwood Bn RNDiv   4.6.15 MR4
CHUTER,John William(Jack) FltSubLt   RN   attRNAS(E Medn)   9.6.17 CR Greece9
CLAPTON,Thomas   Lt   RNR   HMS President   14.1.19 CR Canada1028
CLARK,Frederick John   Art Eng   RN   HMS Queen Mary   kia   31.5.16 MR3
CLARK,George   ATLt   RNR   HMYacht Kethailes   drd   11.10.17 MR1
CLARK,James TLt   RNVR HMPMS Nepaulin   kld   20.4.17 MR3
CLARK,Robert Brown TLt   RNR   HMS Louvain kia   20.1.18 MR2

11

CLARK,Sydney Broford   ALt   RNR   HMS India   kia   8.8.15 MR1
CLARK,Thomas Henry   Mate   RN   HMS Black Prince   kia   31.5.16MR1
CLARK,Wilfrid Thomas De Lacy   Maj   RMLI   24.2.19 CR Guernsey144
CLARK,William   Lt   RNR   10.16
CLARKE,Benjamin Jacob   Lt   RN   HM S/M K5   drd   20.1.21   MR3
CLARKE,Frank   Lt   RN   HMS Bulwark kld   26.11.14 MR3
CLARKE,James S   Lt   RN   HMS Vernon   31.3.17 CR Hamps9
CLARKE,James Benjamin   Carp   RN   HMS Cressy   kia   22.9.14MR1
CLARKE,William A.St.A.   SubLt   RNVR RNDiv 190 MG Coy   30.12.17 CR France1483
CLARKE,William Reginald 1472   Skipper   HMT AnnFord Melville   3.3.19 CR Scot288
CLARKSON,Frederic WilliamLt Comdr   RN   HMS Hawke   kia   15.10.14 MR1
CLARKSON,George TWt Tel   RNR   HMTrawler Columbia kia   1.5.15 MR3
CLARKSON,James Wallace   Eng Sub Lt   RNR   HMS Otranto   drd   6.10.18MR1
CLARKSON,William Herbert MC   TSub-Lt   RNVR Drake Bn RNDiv   30.12.17 MR21
CLAYTON,Gerald Edward Cririe   2Lt   RM   RNDiv ded   2.9.15 CR Wales546
CLAYTON,Henry   AArt Eng   RN   HMS Formidable   kia   1.1.15 MR3
CLAYTON,Ralph Lyall   Lt Comdr   RN   HMS Queen Mary   kia   31.5.16MR3
CLEARE,Henry Thornton   Mate (E)   RN   HMS Black Prince   kia   31.5.16MR1
CLEGG,Hubert JosephEng Comdr   RN   HMS Indefatigable   kia   31.5.16MR2
CLEGHORN,William Howie Eng Lt-Comdr RN   HMS MaryRose   kia   17.10.17 MR1
CLEMENS,Frederick William Theodor TSurg   RN   HMS Defence kia   31.5.16MR2
CLERK,Cecil A.   SubLt   RNVR Nelson Bn RNDiv   dow   31.12.17 CR France398
CLEVES,Reginald Vaughan   SubLt   RNVR Hood Bn RNDiv   kia   23.4.17CR France924
CLIFFORD,Ernest A   TSub-Lt   RNVR Howe Bn RNDiv   4.6.15 MR4
CLIFTON-MOGG,H.R.   LtCmdr   RN   HMS Milne   2.11.15CR Suffolk130
CLIVE,Reginald D.   FltSubLt   RNAS   10.11.17 CR Warwick63
CLORAN,Gerald J.   SubLt RNR   HNYacht Ombra   7.11.17CR Kent2
COATES,William Herbert.DSO.RD.   Comdr RNR   HMS Redbreast   kia   15.7.17MR1
COBB,Thomas Humphrey   ASub-Lt   RN   HMS Invincible   kia   31.5.16MR3
COBBE,Mervyn Hugh Capt   RN   HMS Princess Irene   kld   27.5.15MR3
COCHRANE,B R   Lt   RN   HMS President   14.3.19 CR Surrey158
CODE,Lawrence   TPFlt Offr   RNAS   20.8.17 CR Lincs78
CODRINGTON,J.R.A.LtCmdr   RN   HMS Ambrose   1.11.18CR Devon1
COEY,John Smiley   Midmn RN   HMS Formidable   kia   1.1.15 MR1
COKE,Arthur George Hon   TLt   RNVR Armoured Car Divn   kia   21.5.15MR4
COLBOURNE,Robert Henry   Midmn RN   HMS Vanguard   kld   9.7.17 MR1
COLBY,John James   TSkipper   RNR   HMDrifter Clover Bank   kia   15.2.18MR1
COLCHESTER,Edward Cromwell   Lt   RN   HMS Irresistible   kia   18.3.15MR3
COLE,Harold Arthur Eng Lt RNR HMS Bombala   kia   25.4.18MR1
COLE,John Francis Herbert   Comdr RN   HMS Lynx   kld   9.8.15 MR3
COLE,Richard James ASig Bosn   RN   HMS Cressy   kia   22.9.14MR3
COLE,Sidney L.F.   AssPaymr   RNR   HMS Princess Irene   27.5.15 CR Kent67
COLE,Thomas Art Eng   RN   HMS Black Prince   kia   31.5.16MR3
COLEMAN,Harry E   Gnr   RN   8.15
COLEMAN,Humphrey Parry   Sub Lt RNR   RFA Industry kia   18.10.18 MR3
COLEMAN,Robert   Lt   RNR   HMTrawler Marton   31.1.16 CR Devon258
COLES,Vyvian Harcourt   Paymr RNR   HMS Vala   kia   21.8.17MR1
COLLET,Charles Herbert.DSO.MIDx2   FltCmdr   RNAS 3Wing (& Capt RMA) doi   19.8.15CR Gallipoli1
COLLETT,Arthur Benjamin   Lt   RNVR HMPMS Plumpton   kld   19.10.18 CR France1359
COLLETT,Norman C. F/O   RNAS   29.1.18 CR Kent91
COLLIER,Edward des Forges ALt   RNR   HM S/M E22 kia   25.4.16MR3
COLLIER,Edward Wilme MC   2Lt   RMLI 2 RM Bn RNDiv   22.3.18 MR20
COLLIER,Martin Huntly   Lt   RN   HM S/M H10 kld   19.1.18MR1
COLLIER,Ronald Inglis   Lt   RN   HMS Tipperary   kia   1.6.16 MR3
COLLIN,William   TSkipper   RNR   HMDrifter Christia Craig   kia   15.2.18MR1
COLLINGS,Albert E. EngCapt   RN   HMS Vivid   4.9.16 CR Devon1
COLLINGWOOD,George Frederick Ch Gnr RN   HMS Black Prince   kia   31.5.16MR3
COLLINS,Bernard John   Lt   RNVR HMS Vernon   29.10.18 CR Hamps5
COLLINS,George   Ch Gnr RN   HMS Goliath kia   13.5.15MR3
COLLINS,Gerald Thurston Cole   Lt   RN   HMS Tipperary   kia   1.6.16 MR3

12

COLLINS,Henry   TSkipper   RNR   HMDrifter Spotless Prince   kia   26.10.16 MR1
COLLINS,Hugh Duppa   Lt Comdr   RN   HMS Monmouth   kia   1.11.14 MR2
COLLINS,Major Martyn   TSub-Lt   RNVR   Hawke Bn RNDiv   4.2.17 MR21
COLLINS,Reginald Charles.MID   EngLt   RNR   HMS Quadrille   26.11.18 CR Essex287
COLLINS,Ronald Felix   TFlt Sub-Lt   RNAS   10Sqn   28.4.17 CR Belgium171
COLLINS,Thomas Shorrock   SubLt   RNVR   Hood Bn RNDiv   23.11.17 CR France13
COLQUHOUN,Robert Crosthwaite   Maj   RMLI   HMS Invincible   kia   31.5.16 MR3
COLQUHOUN,William George   Eng Comdr   RN   HMS Tipperary   kia   1.6.16 MR3
COLSON,Douglas Nowell.DSC.   Sub-Lt RNR   HM S/M E18   kld   11.6.16 MR3
COLSTON,Charles Sydney.DSC.   Capt   RN   &RAF   25.11.18 CR Essex145
COLTON,Alfred John AGnr   RN   HMS Invincible   kia   31.5.16 MR2
COMLEY,George William   Gnr   RMA   HMS Lion   10.8.15 CR Scot722
COMYNS,Charles William   TLt   RMA   HB RM   kia   9.11.17 CR Belgium176
CONBY,Henry Brodie.DSC MID   TLt   RNR   HMDrifter GeorgeV   kld   3.6.17 MR1
CONNAH,Edward George 1029   Skipper   RNR   HMT 770   ded   11.11.15 CR Yorks2
CONNOP,Harold Arno   FltSubLt   RNAS   31.3.18 CR France1359
COO,Harold Thomas F/O   RNAS   22.1.18 CR France1844
COOK,Albert Edward TSkipper   RNR   HMDrifter GeorgeV   kld   3.6.17 MR1
COOK,Austin Pugh   Lt   RMLI   2RM Bn RNDiv   kia   26.7.17 CR France1192
COOK,Cecil B.   FltSubLt   RNAS   20.8.17 CR Kent95
COOK,Charles Gustar Asst Clerk   RN   HMS Good Hope   kia   1.11.14 MR2
COOK,Duncan Gibson Paymstr   RNR   HMS Begonia   kia   6.10.17 MR3
COOK,Frank TWt Tel   RNR   HMS Stonecrop   kia   18.9.17 MR1
COOK,Frederick   Mate   RN   HMS Hampshire   drd   5.6.16 CR Scot900
COOK,James A.   SubLt   RNVR   Hawke Bn RNDiv   13.11.16 CR France1490
COOK,Percy Sidney   Skipper   RNR   HMTrawler Offa II   ded   19.4.19   CR Norfolk131
COOK,Robert Duff   Eng Sub Lt   RNR   HMTrawler Lochiel   kia   24.7.18 MR1
COOK,Thomas   ATLt   RNR   HMPMS Queen of the North   kld   20.7.17 MR1
COOK,Thomas Arthur TSkipper   RNR   HMTrawler King Emperor   drd   4.2.16 MR1
COOKE,Alan G Campbell   see CAMPBELL-COOKE,Alan G
COOKE,Arthur Stanley   TSub-Lt   RNVR   Hood Bn RNDiv   23.4.17 MR20
COOKE,Christopher Arthur Gresham Midmn RN   HMS Vanguard   kld   9.7.17 MR1
COOKE,Guy Proudfoot   TSub-Lt   RNVR   Nelson Bn RNDiv   3.5.15 MR4
COOKE,Harold Maynard   Sub Lt RNVR HMTrawler Thomas Cornwall drd   29.10.18 MR3
COOKE-HURLE,W.A.   Capt   RN   ded   1.5.20 CR Canada146
COOKES,John Weatherstone Sub-Lt RNVR Drake Bn RNDiv   30.12.17 MR21
COOKSON,Alfred Owen   Lt   RNVR Hawke Bn RNDiv   8.10.18 MR16
COOKSON,Edgar Charles.VC.DSO. Lt Comdr   RN   HMS Verulam   kld   3.9.19   MR1 Sub Lt
COOKSON,Edgar Christopher.VC.DSO. LtCmdr   RN   HMS Clio   kia   28.9.15 CR Iraq5
COOMBE,Allen Sandby   TPFlt Offr   RN/RNAS   4.9.17 CR Essex40
COOMBES,Harold Victor   TAsst Paymr   RNR   HMS Indefatigable   kia   31.5.16 MR2
COOMBS,Arthur Erskine Gurney   Lt   RN   HMS Hawke   kia   15.10.14 MR1
COOPER,Alfred Hay Lt   RNR   HMTrawler Princess Mary   13.3.18 CR Europe6
COOPER,Douglas B.   Lt   RN   HMS Melbourne   28.5.15 CR Bermuda1
COOPER,Frederick Augustus Midmn RN   HMS Monmouth   kia   1.11.14 MR2
COOPER,Hanway   Sub-Lt RN   HMS Monmouth   kia   1.11.14 MR2
COOPER,John McD.   SubLt   RNR   HMS Viknot   13.1.15 CR Dorset48
COOPER,John Ft Paymr   RN   HMS Monmouth   kia   1.11.14 MR2
COOPER,John George Lt   RNR   HMS Cowslip kia   25.4.18 MR3
COOPER,Percy B A   Lt Comdr(Retd)RN   Killed serving in Army   8.16
COOPER,William Francis Reginald Ashley Midmn   RN   HMS Indefatigable   kia   31.5.16 MR2
COPELAND,Eric Neville van der Ben Lt   RNVR 63MG Bn RNDiv   kia   26.3.18 CR France233
COPLAND,Joseph Uriah   Gnr   RN   HMS Formidable   kia   1.1.15 MR1
COPLESTONE,Frederick Lewis   Lt Comdr   RN   HM S/M D2   kld   1.12.14 MR3
COPLESTONE-BOUGHEY,Alfred Fletcher Comdr   RN   HMS Defence kia   31.5.16 MR2
CORBETT,Arthur C Flt Sub-Lt   RNAS   12.16
CORBYN,Vernon Hector   Midmn RN   HMS Cressy   kia   22.9.14 MR1
CORDNER,A.A.   Maj   RMLI   (Zeebrugge raid)   23.4.18 CR Devon236
CORNER,John ChArtEng   RN   HMS Ghurka   8.2.17 CR Kent46
CORNISH,Edwin   Capt   RN   23.9.17 CR Italy12

13

CORRIE,L   Paymr Sub-Lt RNR   HMS Hermoine   23.10.18 CR Surrey160
CORY,William Tucker   Mate   RN   HMS Invincible   kia   31.5.16 MR2
COSSEY,Arthur E.   EngCmdr   RN   HMS Hampshire   drd   5.6.16 CR Scot900
COTTER,Francis John Anson ASub-Lt   RN   HMS Good Hope   kia   1.11.14 MR3
COTTER,Leonard Edmund   Lt   RNR   HMYacht Iolaire   drd   1.1.19   MR3
COTTER,Reginald Alexander Midmn RNR   HMS Pheasant drd   1.3.17 CR Scot900
COTTON,Henry Perceval Coode   Midmn RN   HMS Malaya kia   31.5.16 CR Scot900
COTTRELL,Clement Fraser   Sub-Lt RN   HM S/M G9   drd   16.9.17   MR3
COTTRELL-DORMER,Humphrey Randle Upton LtCmdr   RN   HMS Princess Irene   kld   27.5.15 MR3
COUCH,Herbert William   Eng Lt-Comdr RN   HMS Good Hope   kia   1.11.14 MR3
COULL,John TSkipper   RNR   HMDrifter Laurel Crown   kld   22.6.16 MR3
COULSON,Harry.G.C.   Lt   RMLI   1RM Bn RNDiv   17.2.17 CR France514
COURTIS,Ernest George   Ch Gnr RN   HMS Clan McNaughton   drd   3.2.15 MR2
COVERDALE,Frederick William   Lt   RNR   HMS Newmarket   kld   17.7.17 MR3
COWAN,Donald   Lt   RNR   MFA Princess Alberta   21.2.17 CR Greece10
COWAN,Ian Colquhoun   Lt   RN   HMS Defence kia   31.5.16 MR2
COWIE,James Alexander   TLt   RNR   HMTrawler Fulmar   kld   17.1.16 MR1
COWIE,Joseph TSkipper   RNR   HMDrifter Freuchny   kld   8.1.16   MR3
COWLEY,Charles Henry.VC. LtCmdr   RNVR SS Julnar   24.4.16   MR38
COWLING,J.W.   Midmn RNR   HMS Teutonic   22.12.18 CR Cornwall163
COWLING,William Robert   ·Wt EngRNR   HMS Hawke kia   15.10.14 MR1
COWPER,Carlton Valentine De Mornay Capt RN   HMS President in SS Queen kia   28.6.18 MR1
COWPER,William Pearson   Surg   RN   HMS Valiant   1.2.19 CR London12
COX,Arthur   AGnr RN   HMS Invincible   kia   31.5.16 MR3
COX,Edmund Ft Surg RN   HMS Vanguard   kld   9.7.17 MR1
COX,Herbert A Snead   see SNEAD-COX,Herbert A
COX,Howard J Hamilton   see HAMILTON COX,Howard J
COX,James Ellis   ABosn RN   HMS Cressy kia   22.9.14 MR1
COX,William TSub-Lt   RNR   HMWaterTank Progress   drd   21.12.16 MR1
COXE,Hugh Clifford Holled   Lt   RN   HMS Formidable   kia   1.1.15   MR1
CRABB,Joseph   Bosn   RN   HMS Indefatigable   kia   31.5.16 MR2
CRABTREE,Samuel R.   Cmdr   RN   HMYacht Zaida   30.9.16 CR Iraq8
CRACKNELL,George Noel   LtPaymr   RN   HMS Iron Duke   12.8.21 CR Kent46
CRADOCK,Christopher George Francis Maurice KCVO.CB RAdml RN   HMS Good Hope   kia   1.11.14 MR3
CRAGG,Noel Henry.MID   Lt   RN   HMS Victory kia   20.9.15 CR France1360
CRAGG,W.A. Lt   RNVR HMS Victory   21.10.18 CR Ches59
CRAIG,A.   SubLt RNR   HMTug Epic   4.11.18 CR Cornwall96
CRATTER,Richard Andrew.DSC.   TLt   RNR   HMDrifter Clover Bank   kia   15.2.18   MR3 CRAFTER
CRAVEN,Harry Lees Dacre   Lt Comdr   RN   HMS Glory lost in SS Irena kia   4.11.17 MR3
CRAWFORD,Alexander Hendry   ATLt   RNR   HMS Marguerite   accdrd 26.7.17   MR1
CRAWFORD-WOOD,James P.   PF/O   RNAS   23.10.17 CR Oxford3
CREED,Algernon H.E.   RevChpn   RN   HMS Orvieto   ded   21.5.17 CR Hamps151 A.H.G.
CRESSMAN,Fred Christie . TFlt Sub-Lt   RNAS   drd   24.12.17 MR1
CRESSWELL,J.B.   Lt   RN   HMS Excellent   16.10.20 CR Numb78
CRESWELL,Colin Fraser   Lt   RN   HM S/M E47 kld   20.8.17 MR3
CRICHTON,George Edward Allan   Eng Comdr   RN   HMS Black Prince   kia   31.5.16 MR3
CRIPPS,John Walter Davies   Flt Sub Lt   RNAS   drd   12.9.17   MR1
CRISP,Thomas.VC.DSC.   TSkipper   RNR   HMsmack Nelson   kia   15.8.17 MR1
CROCKER,William R Flt Comdr(Lt) RNAS(RN) RN AirStn(PortSaid)   6.3.16 CR Egypt7
CROFT,Richard Bernard   Midmn RN   HMS Indefatigable   kia   31.5.16 MR2
CROFTON,Harold Mowatt Maxwell PaymrSubLt   RN   HMS Curacon   29.11.18 CR Suffolk130
CROMIE,Francis Newton Allen.CB.DSO.Capt   RN   Naval Attaché Petrograd   31.8.18   CR Europe180 &MR70
CROOK,James Sig Bosn   RN   HMS Indefatigable kia   31.5.16 MR3
CROSBY,Albert Walter Gordon   TPFlt Offr   RNAS   kld   10.3.18 CR Lincs78
CROSS,Thomas Kingston   TSub-Lt   RNVR Hood Bn RNDiv   dow   24.4.17   CR France95
CROSS,Wilfrid Norman   FltSubLt   RNAS   6.3.18 CR Kent25
CROSSLEY,Charles V DSC TLt   RNR   HMS Duchess   13.2.18 CR Lincs123
CROUCHER,George Beaver   Lt   RNVR HMS President   16.4.18 CR Lincs156
CROUCHER,William FltSubLt   RNAS   dedacc 18.9.15   CR Sussex5
CROWE,H.Laurence Flt Sub Lt   RNAS   kld   22.6.17 CR Canada1688

CROWE,Thomas Mervyn   TSub-Lt   RNVR Anson Bn RNDiv   4.6.15 MR4
CROWTHER,Johnny SubLt RNVR Anson Bn RNDiv   2.11.18 CR France232
CROWTHER,Oswald Hubert TLt   RNVR/RNAS kia   20.8.16 MR1
CRUDDAS,Seymour Capt   RMA   HMS Bellerophon   6.3.17 CR Scot900
CRUMMACK,Alfred Geoffrey   TLt   RNR   HM S/M H10 kld   19.1.18 MR1
CRUSE,Percy Staff Paymr   RN   HMS Hampshire   kld   5.6.16 MR3
CUBBIN,E.Le M.   SubLt RNR   HMS Arlanya   27.9.18 CR Ches182
CUBBIN,William   Paymr RN   HMS Actaeon   6.1.18 CR Devon3
CUDDEFORD,Frederick William Francis Lt RN   HM S/M K5   drd   20.1.21   MR3
CUDDY,Ernest James Lt Comdr   RN   4Bn RNDiv   5.12.17 CR Europe99
CULLIMORE,Bertie Harold   PMidmn   RNR   HMS Viknor   drd   13.1.15   MR3
CULLING,Thomas Grey DSC TFlt Lt RNAS   8.6.17 MR20
CUMMING,George Edward   Lt Comdr   RN   HMS Good Hope   kia   1.11.14 MR3
CUNDY,Louis   1284   Skipper   RNR   HMTrawler Balfour   dedacc 8.10.17 CR Devon2
CUNNINGHAM,Andrew Coutts   Midmn RNR   HMCMB No33A   kia   12.4.18 MR3
CUNNINGHAME,David Duncan   Eng Lt-Comdr RN   HMS Surprise drd   23.12.17 CR Europe100
CUNSTANCE,Gustavus William Musgrove Surg   RN   HMS Hawke   kia   15.10.14 MR1
CURREY,Edward Hamilton.MID   Cmdr RN   HMS Eagle   ded   10.12.16 CR Ches3
CURRIE,W.D.K.   ChEng   AdmiraltyTransport Breslau   25.3.17 CR France8
CURTIN,Morris   Lt   RM   Chatham Bn RNDiv   4.5.15 MR4
CUST,Arthur John Purey.MID Sub-Lt RN   HMS Strongbow   kia   17.10.17 MR1
CUSTANCE,Aldwyn Douglas Lt   RN   HMS Exmouth   22.7.15 MR2
CUTHBERT,Benjamin   TSub-Lt   RNR   HMYacht Zarefah   kld   8.5.17 MR1
CUTHBERT,Henry Kenmore Duff   PMidmn   RNR HMS Good Hope   kia   1.11.14 MR3
CUTHBERTSON,S.J. Gnr(Retd)   RN   HMS Vivid   9.8.18 CR Devon1
CUZNER,Albert Edward   Flt Sub-Lt   RNAS   30.4.17 MR20

D

DACEY,Henry Edward   Mate (E)   RN   HMS Defence kia   31.5.16 MR2
DAGLISH,George Richard Gordon   FltLt   RNAS   kld   1.3.17 CR Numb97
DAILLIE,Mathew   TLt   RNR   SS Heathersidekia   24.8.17 MR3
DALBY,Edwin Ballard   Lt   RNR   SS Joshua Nicholson   kia   18.3.17 MR3
DALE,Wellington Treveluan ASub-Lt   RNR   Submarine Sect RNDiv   ded   11.5.15   CR Egypt6
DALE-RICHARDS,Hedley Norman   Surg   RN   HMS Cowslip kia   25.4.18 MR3
DALES,Thomas   TSkipper   RNR   HMTrawler Amy   4kld   11.4.17 MR1
DALLAS,William Edward Barnett   Lt   RN   HMS Arlanza   ded   6.10.18 CR Staffs65
DALRYMPLE-CLARK,Ian H W S   Sqd Comdr   RNAS   8.9.16 CR Lincs78
DALY,Denis HeywoodFltSubLt   RNAS   17.7.17 CR France1359
DALZIEL,W. Sub Lt RNR   HMS Sunhill   2.5.19 CR Europe6
DAMPIER-CHILD,Thomas Henry Fielder Eng Lt Comdr RNHMS Opal   drd   12.1.18   MR3
DANIEL,Charles Tregenna   Lt   RNR   HMS Presidentded   19.2.19   CR France377
DANIEL,Horace Stroud   Lt   RNR   HMS Dido   11.3.19 CR Devon1
DANIELS,J K Comn Gnr   RN   HMS Wallington for HMD P52   4.11.19 CR Essex62
DANIELS,Sidney Charles   Bosn   RN   HMS Bombala kia   25.4.18 MR3
DANN,Philip Whitley SubLt RNVR Hood Bn RNDiv   24.5.18 CR France252
DANVERS,H. Surg   RN   18.3.20 CR France1775
DARLEY,Arthur Tudor   Comdr RN   HMS Good Hope   kia   1.11.14 MR3
DARRELL,C.H.   SubLt RNVR Hawke Bn RNDiv   25.8.18 CR France1504
DARROCH,Archibald Lt ·   RNR   HMYacht Rhouma   18.10.18 CR Scot677
DASENT,Manuel   Cmdr RN   HMS Hampshire   drd   5.6.16 CR Scot900
DATHAN,Joseph Duncan   Chpn   RN   HMS Pembroke   7.1.18 CR Kent46
DAUNT,Thomas   Bosn   RN   HMS Natal   kld   30.12.15 MR1
DAVEY,Reginald Argyle   TLt   RNVR HMS Campania   drd   8.9.16 MR1
DAVID,Thomas Morgan   Eng Lt Comdr RN   HMS Hawke   kia   15.10.14 MR1
DAVIDSON,Alexander Clyne TSub-Lt   RNR   HMS Bayano   kia   11.3.15 MR3
DAVIDSON,Arthur Leslie   TEng Sub-Lt   RNR   HMS Atlanta   6.6.16 CR Middx25
DAVIDSON,Ernest George William   Capt   RN   HMS Otranto   6.10.18 CR Scot31

15

DAVIDSON,George Thorold TSub-Lt   RNVR Hood Bn RNDiv   26.10.16 MR21
DAVIDSON,J. ChArtEng   RN   HMS Gunner   23.1.19 CR Kent46
DAVIDSON,John Duncan   EngLt RNR   HMS Lady Moira   15.5.19 CR Wilts62
DAVIDSON,William TSkipper   RNR   HMDrifter Great Heart   kld   24.9.15MR3
DAVIE,Herbert G F T2Lt RM   see FERGUSON-DAVIE
DAVIES,Herbert Edward   Lt   RNR   RFA Hughli   drd   26.4.19   MR2
DAVIES,John Eric   TSub-Lt   RNVR Collingwood Bn RNDiv   4.6.15 MR4
DAVIES,Thomas R. Lt   RNR   HMYacht Conqueror II   27.9.16 CR Shrops93
DAVIES,William Read   Asst Clerk   RN   HMS Irresistible   kia   18.3.15MR3
DAVIS,Albert Robert Wilberforce   Paymstr   RNR   HMS Stonecrop   kia   18.9.17MR3
DAVIS,Cyril Frederick Lan...?Flt Lt   RN/RNAS HMS Ark Royal   missing 14.10.15 MR1
DAVIS,Eric James   TMidmn   RNR   HMS Indefatigable   kia   31.5.16MR2
DAVIS,F.J.   LtCmdr   RNR   HMS President   13.5.19 CR Lancs34
DAVISON,William James   LtCmdrPayMstr RN   HMS Warspite   27.2.20 CR Europe34
DAVY,Bernard WalterMidmn RNR   HMS Ark Royal attRNAS   kld   10.7.16CR Gallipoli1
DAW,Arthur William Perryman   Art Eng   RN   HMS Bulwark kld   26.11.14 MR3
DAW,Harold William Bennett SubLt   RNVR HMS Perthshire   ded   28.3.17   CR Scot900
DAWES,E.J.DSC. Lt   RNR   HMS Epsom   27.10.18 CR Lancs256
DAWSON,John M. FltOff RNAS   7.9.17 CR Yorks172
DAWSON,John Robert   TSkipper   RNR   HMTrawler Lord Airedale   drd   19.3.15   MR1 & CR Norfolk131
DAY,Elystan Tidmarsh   Midmn RNR   HMS Caronia   6.9.15 MR3
DAY,Harold.DSC.   FltSubLt   RNAS   kia   5.2.18 CR France1723
DAY,Miles Jeffrey Game.DSC.   ATFlt Comdr RNAS   kia   27.2.18MR1
DAY,Thomas Morris Lt   RNR   HMS President   7.8.21 CR Yorks2
DAY,William Art Eng   RN   HMS Monmouth   kia   1.11.14MR2
DAYMOND,George Henry   EngLt RNR   HMS Laurentic   25.1.17 CR Eire295
DAYRELL-REED,Archibald.DSO&Bar.   Lt   RN   18.8.19 MR70
de BLAQUIERE,Allan Boyle Hon   Sub-Lt RN   HMS Antrim on HMS Laurentic   kld   25.1.17MR1
de BLESS,Gervase Anthony David Herewyt Midmn RN   HMS Revenge   23.3.16 CR NHants82
DE BURGH,Francis Vavasour Cmdr   RIM   attAden FF   7.12.18MR65
de BURGH,John Maurice Truscott   ASub-Lt   RN   HMS Colossus accdrd 14.9.15   MR2
De la MOTHE.Claude Douglas Fenelon Lt   RNVR Howe Bn RNDiv   13.11.16 CR France339
DE LA WARR,Gilbert George Reginald 8thEarl Lt   RNVR HMML California   16.12.15 CR Italy42
de SEGUNDO,Arthur WilliamMidmn RN   HMS Vanguard   kld   9.7.17 MR1
de St LEGIER,Archibald Samuel   Eng Lt RN   HMS Negro   drd   21.12.16 MR1
de VERTEUIL,Fernand Louis Joseph Marie Surg   RN   HMS Good Hope   kia   1.11.14MR3
de WET,Eric Oloff.DSC.MID Sub-Lt RN   HMS Narbrough   drd   12.1.18   MR3
De WILDE,Joseph Sylvan   TFlt Sub-Lt RNAS   3 Sqdn   27.9.17 MR20 John
DEAKIN,Harold Barnett   TSub-Lt   RNR   HMDrifter Lily Reaichkld   25.2.16MR1
DEANE,Herbert Albert   Lt   RNR   HMS Aboukir kia   22.9.14MR1
DEANE,Thomas Alexander David   Lt   RMLI   Portsmouth Bn RNDiv kia   3.5.15 MR4
DEANE-MORGAN,C F Hon TAsst Eng   RNR   see FITZMAURICE-DEAN-MORGAN,C Hon
DEANS,J.E. Lt   RNR   HMS Cumberland   5.10.18CR Lancs7
DEARDEN,Robert   TEng Sub-Lt   RNR   HMPMS Queen of the North   kld   20.7.17MR1
DEARMER,Christopher   TLt   RNVR/RNAS dow 6.10.15MR1
DEED,John Cyril Capt   (RMRes)RMLI HMS Formidable   kia   1.1.15 MR1
DEESON,L.A. Schmstr   RN   HMS Africa   28.9.18 CR WAfrica30
DEIGHTON,Thomas EngSubLt   RNR   HMS Pembroke II   27.9.18 CR London23
DELMEGE,Claude Phillipe   Midmn RN   HMS Cressy   kia   22.9.14MR1
DELVES-BROUGHTON,Alfred William   Capt   RMLI   HMS Black Prince   kia   31.5.16MR1
DENHAM,Herbert E Art Eng   RN   HMS Monarch   19.11.16 CR Hamps9
DENHOLM,Robert Miller   ProbFltOff   RNAS   28.7.17 CR Scot677
DENMAN-DEAN,George Walpole Winthrop TLt   RM   2RM Bn RNDiv   dow   7.11.17CR France145
DENNIER,William Harrison Stott   Wt EngRNR   HMS Aboukir kia   22.9.14MR1
DENNING,Charles Gordon   SubLt RN   HMS Morris   24.5.18 CR Hamps198
DENNIS,James Ch Gnr RN   HMS Vanguard   kld   9.7.17 MR1
DEVEREUX,Edmund Bourchier   Lt(Flt Lt)   RN(RNAS) HM Airship P2   drd   26.11.17 MR1
DEVINE,Charles L TLt   RNR   1.18
DEWAR,Lancelot John Austen(Jack) 2Lt   RMLI   2RM Bn RNDiv   kia   13.11.16 CR France339
DEWDNEY,Harold James   Lt   RNVR Anson Bn RNDiv   kia   21.8.18CR France214

DICK,James Douglas   Capt   RN   HMS Vanguard   kld   9.7.17 MR1
DICKEN,A   Sub-Lt RNVR Hawke Bn RNDiv   12.9.15 CR Middx48
DICKINSON,Arthur   Lt   RNR   HMS Victory   1.7.19 CR Lincs160
DICKINSON,Cecil William   Flt Lt   RNAS   HM Airship C8   drd   9.6.16 MR1
DICKSON,Andrew Ferguson TSub-Lt   RNR   HMS India   kia   8.8.15 MR1
DICKSON,Archibald William Midmn RN   HMS Queen Mary   kia   31.5.16MR3
DICKSON,David Angus   Midmn RN   HMS Hawke   kia   15.10.14 MR1
DICKSON,James Johnston   AArt Eng   RN   HMS Good Hope   kia   1.11.14MR3
DICKSON,Joseph Muir Findlay   TSub-Lt   RNVR Nelson Bn RNDiv   13.7.15 MR45
DICKSON,Thomas Seaborn Dudfield TLt   RNR   HMTrawler Cantatrice kld   5.11.16MR1
DIEHL,William Henry Lt   RNR   HMS Presidentded   5.10.18CR Scot674
DIGBY,Ronald R.   Skipper   RNR   HMT Pitstruan   13.4.17 CR Scot280
DIMSDALE,Reginald Thomas Lt   RN   HM S/M E22   kia   25.4.16MR3
DINGLE,Hugh John   SurgProb   RNVR HMS Petard   31.5.16 CR Scot722
DISNEY,Edward Ogle Lt Comdr   RN   HMS Arethusa accdrd 4.1.16 MR1
DISSETTE,Arthur Clarke   TFlt Sub-Lt   RNAS   2.6.17 CR Belgium18
DIVINE,Charles Lawford   Lt   RNR   HMS M28   20.1.18 CR Gallipoli1
DIXIE,Albert Edward LtCmdr   RN   HMS Crescent   16.5.20 CR Scot245
DIXON,Albert James FltSubLt   RNAS 8Sqn   4.1.18 CR France1290
DIXON,John Francis.DSC.   Flt Lt   RNAS HMAirship C27   kia   11.12.17 MR1
DIXON-WRIGHT,Henry Dixon.MVO.   Chpn   RN   HMS Barham   dow   1.6.16   CR Scot900 /.5.16
DOBELL,John Willett Lt   RN   HMS President   1.3.19 CR Devon102
DOBINSON,George William Ch Carp   RN   HMS Aboukir kia   22.9.14MR1
DOBSON,Reginald   TPFlt Offr   RNAS   8.3.18 CR Lancs34
DODD,Reginald   Wt Offr 2   RNAS HMS Pegasus accdrd 17.9.17   MR1
DOLLERY,W.H.   Lt   RMLI   23.4.18 CR Hamps4
DOLPHIN,William Henry   Art Eng   RN   HMS Natal   kld   30.12.15 MR1
DOMVILLE,James Henry Sir Lt   RN   Cmdg HM Destroyer P19   13.9.19 CR London8
DONALDSON,Richard.MC.   Lt   RNVR Anson Bn RNDiv   kia   5.9.18 CR France689
DONALDSON,Thomas   Skipper   RNR   HMDirfter Fizzer   6.6.16 CR Scot640
DONNELL,Ernest Tudor   Lt   RN   HMS Shark   kia   31.5.16MR3
DONOVAN,Denis   Comm Mech   RN   HMS Contest kia   18.9.17 MR2
DONOVAN,Edgar C TSub-Lt   RNVR RN SiegeGuns   26.4.17 CR Belgium24
DONOVAN,Patrick John   TLt   RNR   HMTrawler Lotus   23.6.16 CR Hamps5
DONOVAN,William Thomas ABosn RN   HMS Invincible   kia   31.5.16MR2
DORMAN,Thomas Stephen Leurs.DSO.   Lt Comdr   RN   HMS Lavenderkia   5.5.17 MR2
DOUBLEDAY,Charles H.   AssPaymr   RN   HMS Leviathan   11.6.17 CR WIndies29
DOUBLEDAY,George Hambrook Dean.DSC MID ALt   RNR   HMS Cullist   kia   11.2.18MR3
DOUGAL.J.   Skipper   MMR HMDrifter Isabel Colven   11.11.15 CR Scot558
DOUGHERTY,Eric Barnard Compton Lt   RM   Portsmouth Bn RNDiv   14.7.15 MR4
DOUGLAS,A.R.   SubLt RN   HMS President   17.2.19 CR Cambs16
DOUGLAS,David William Shafto   Lt Comdr   RN   HMS Black Prince   kia   31.5.16MR3
DOUGLAS,F.T.   SubLt RNR   HMS Teakol   14.3.19 CR Scot795
DOUGLAS,James Sholto   LtCmdr   RNVR/RNAS ded   18.12.16 CR Ches28
DOUGLAS,William   TSub-Lt   RNVR Howe Bn RNDiv   26.10.17 MR30
DOUGLASS,Percy.C.D.   FltCmdr   RN   attRNAS   10.12.17 CR Greece9
DOWDING,Geoffrey Marischal   PMidmn   RNR   HMS Good Hope   kia   1.11.14MR3
DOWNIE,David   Lt   RNR   HMS President   1.2.19 CR Numb96
DOWNING,Dawson Calybut FltLt   RNAS   25.2.15 CR Wilts116
DOWNS,John Peter   Lt   RNR   HMTug Gosforth   29.3.19 CR Asia51
DOYLE,Harry ThomasSubLt RNR   HMYacht Verona   kld   24.2.17CR Essex112
DRAKE,John Harold   Lt   RNR   HMS Pegasus kia   20.9.14CR Tanzania1
DRAKE-BROCKMAN,Lewis Arthur Maj   RMLI   10.5.19 MR70
DREW,George Montford.MID ATLt   RNR   HM S/M E14   kia   28.1.18MR3
DREW,Reginald James Blakeney   LtCmdr   RN   HMS Glatton   kld   16.9.18CR Kent46
DREWRY,George Leslie.VC. Lt   RNR   HMTrawler William Jackson   2.8.18 CR Essex1
DRIVER,Charles   Wt EngRNR   HMS Monmouth   kia   1.11.14MR1
DRIVER,Ernest   Art Eng   RN   HMS Hawke   kia   15.10.14 MR3
DRUMMOND,G.A.DSC.   Lt   RNR   HMPMS Plupton   kld   19.10.18 CR France1359
DRUMMOND-HAY,E.de Vis Lt   RN   HMS Emperor of India   12.5.20 CR Europe6

DRURY,W.B. Cmdr RN   21.6.17 CR Egypt9
DUCKWORTH,Cyril Gordon Flt Sub Lt   RNAS   accdrd 21.2.18   MR1
DUCKWORTH,Joseph   Art Eng   RN   HMS Good Hope   kia   1.11.14 MR3
DUFF-DUNBAR,Kenneth James.DSO.   Lt Comdr   RN   HM S/M E16   kld   22.8.16 MR3
DUFFIN,R.   EngLt RN   HMS Laconia   5.3.15 CR SAfrica158
DUGGAN,Edward   Gnr   RN   HMS Opal   drd   12.1.18   MR2
DUKE,Alan C.H.   LtCmdr   RN   HMS Vanguard   11.7.17 CR Scot900
DUKE,Gordon Ezra   FltSubLt   RNAS   kld   10.1.16 CR Sussex144
DUNBAR-DUNBAR-RIVERS,Evelyn Lt   RN   HMS Vanguard   kld   9.7.17 MR1
DUNCAN,David Alan TFlt Sub-Lt   RNAS   kld   2.6.17 CR London8
DUNCAN,James Chrystal   SubLt RNVR Tug George Robinson   25.11.18 CR Yorks154
DUNCAN,Robert   TLt   RNVR Anson Bn RNDiv   8.5.15 MR4
DUNDAS,Kenneth R.Hon   Lt   RNVR Anson Bn RNDiv   7.8.15 CR Gallipoli26
DUNDEE-HOOPER,Stewart Briscoe Lt   RN   HM S/M E4   15.8.16 CR Suffolk130
DUNN,A.   SubLt RNR HMS Kilcock   8.3.19 CR Suffolk130
DUNN,Edward Paschal   Gnr   RN   HMS Queen Elizabeth drd   1.12.20 CR Hamps8
DUNN,Samuel William   Lt   RN   HMS Topaze   10.7.18 CR Italy6
DUNNING,Edward Lancelot Sub-Lt RNVR Anson Bn RNDiv   9.4.18 MR27
DUNNING,Edwin H.DSC.   SqnCmdr   RNAS   7.8.17 CR Essex270
DUNPHY,Bernard   Lt   RNR HMS Bayano kia   11.3.15 MR3
DUPEN,A.P.L.Eng Capt   RN   HMS Egmont   25.12.18 CR Europe6
DUPREY,Seymour Gordon   TAsst Paymr   RNR   HMS Ramsey(in Meteor?)   kia   8.8.15 MR1
DURHAM,Arthur Edwin   Lt   RN   HMS Laforey kld   23.3.17 MR1
DURLACHER,Richard Frederic   Midmn RN   HMS Indefatigable   kia   31.5.16 MR2
DURRANT.Humphrey M.L.   Midmn RN   HMS Queen Mary   6.6.16 CR Scot722
DUTHIE,Robert   TSkipper   RNR HMDrifter Beneficent kia   1.6.16 MR3
DUTHIE,Walter Nicol TSub-Lt   RNVR HMPMS Queen of the North   kld   20.7.17 MR1
DUTTON,Ernest   Lt   RNR HMS Suva   kldacc 7.11.18 CR Egypt15
DYER,Ernest Humphrey McArthur   Ft Paymr   RN   HMS Indefatigable   kia   31.5.16 MR2
DYETT,E.L.A.Lt   RNVR Nelson Bn RNDiv   shot at dawn 5.1.17 CR France1553
DYMOCKE,Maurice Dymoke Asst Paymr   RN   HMS Indefatigable   kia   31.5.16 MR2
DYMOTT,Edwin   Wt Tel RN   HMS Tipperary   kia   1.6.16   MR3
DYOTT,Kenelm Mitchill   TSurg RN   HMS Stephen Furness kia   13.12.17 MR3
DYSON,Eric H   TPFlt Offr   RNAS   3.12.17 CR Lincs78
DYSON,H.R.MM.   SubLt RNVR RNDiv attRAF   25.11.18 CR Yorks547

E

EADIE,John   Lt   RN   HMS Defence kia   31.5.16 MR2
EAGLES,Charles Edward Campbell.DSO.MID Maj   RMLI Chatham Coy RM Bn kia   23.4.18 CR Warwick30
EASBY,Harold Richard   Obs Sub-Lt   RNAS   7.1.18 CR France1359
EASTON,Montague George   AComdr   RNR HMS Louvain kia   20.1.18 MR2
EASTON,Thomas Henderson Lt   RNVR Clyde Examination Service   21.8.16 CR Scot674
EATON-SHORE,John J   TLt   RM   Div Engrs RNDiv   dow   13.11.16 CR France41
ECKETT,U.T.M.   Lt   RNVR HMS Research   21.2.19 CR Lancs155
EDDIS,C.J.F. LtCmdr   RN   HMS Scimitar   19.10.18 CR Scot900
EDE,Ernest Grant   Eng Lt Comdr RN   HMS Pellew kia   12.12.17 MR3
EDEN,William Nicholas   Midmn RN   HMS Indefatigable   kia   31.5.16 MR2
EDGAR,Alfred   Lt   RN   HMS Monmouth   kia   1.11.14 MR2
EDGAR,Harold John Martin TLt   RNVR Drake Bn RNDiv   11.5.15 MR45
EDGECOMBE,Arthur Wilfrid Midmn RN   HMS Verulam kld   3.9.19 MR1
EDMONDSON,Cyril Arthur.MID   Lt   RNVR Hood Bn RNDiv   kia   13.11.16 CR France339
EDMUNDS,William Henry   Surg RN   HMS Pembroke   4.10.16 CR Heref&Worc107
EDWARDS,Caroline Maud   ResNSister   QARNNS   HMHS Drina on HMS Natal kld   30.12.15 MR1
EDWARDS,Frederick William   Art Eng   RN   HMS Flirt   drd   1.6.16 CR Kent67
EDWARDS,George K Eng Capt   RN   HMS Sokoto   18.12.16 CR Devon258
EDWARDS,Harrington Douty.DSO. Lt Comdr   RN   HM S/M E5   kld   11.3.16 MR3
EDWARDS,Herbert L Capt   RN   HMS Calypso   17.11.17 CR Scot722

EDWARDS,Hugh.DSO.   Capt   RN   HMS President   5.12.16 CR Hamps206
EDWARDS,John Warden   Sub-Lt RNVR Nelson Bn RNDiv   5.6.15 CR Gallipoli14
EDWARDS,Robert Charles George   TSub-Lt   RNVR Hawke Bn RNDiv   13.11.16 MR21
EDWARDS,Trevor   TCapt RMLI 3 RM Bn RNDiv   26.10.17 MR30
EDWARDS,Victor Lawrence TLt   RNVR HMS President II   21.8.17 CR Asia81
EDWARDS,William Henry   TSub-Lt   RNVR Nelson Bn RNDiv   13.7.15 MR4
EGAN,Charles Edward Francis   Lt   RN   HMS Ardent   kia   1.6.16 MR3
EGREMONT,John   Asst Paymr   RN   HMS Good Hope   kia   1.11.14 MR3
ELDER,Kenneth Edward   Lt   RNR HM S/M E47   kld   20.8.17 MR3
ELGOOD,Reginald Lloyd   ALt   RN   HMS Vanguard   kld   9.7.17 MR1
ELIOT,Francis Geoffrey.MC. Capt RM   1 RM Bn RNDiv   kia   27.9.18 CR France530
ELKES,Frederick J G M   Lt Comdr   RNR HMS Ocean   _1.15_   CR Iraq6 7.12.14
ELLICE,William   Midmn RN   HMS Bulwark kld   26.11.14 MR3
ELLINGTON,Robert Smith   Skipper   RNR HMTrawler Drumoak kld   5.10.14 MR3
ELLIOTT,Bertram Nowell.DSO.   LtCol RMLI   23.4.18 CR Kent42
ELLIOTT,George Littleton   TEng Sub-Lt   RNR HMS Laurentic   kld   25.1.17 MR2
ELLIOTT,George Walter   ALt   RNR HM S/M E50 kld   31.1.18 MR3
ELLIOTT,Henry   Ft Paymr   RN   HMS Eagle   ded   23.2.17   CR Lancs391
ELLIOTT,Joseph   Ch Gnr RN   HMS Himalaya   20.2.17 CR SAfrica158
ELLIOTT,R.   SubLt RNR HMS Lagos   15.9.15 CR WAfrica61
ELLIOTT,William   Skipper   RNR   1.3.18 CR Lincs156
ELLIOTT,William C A   2Lt   RM   RMLI 1 RM Bn RNDiv   17.7.16 CR France559
ELLIS,A.   Lt   RNR HMS Ravenswood   1.11.18 CR Durham26
ELLIS,Anwyl Lt   RNVR MB Res   drd   18.11.14 CR Scot956
ELLIS,Bernard Henry.DSO.DSM.   Cmdr RNVR Hawke Bn RNDiv   dow   21.4.18   CR France64
ELLIS,Edward _V_ezian.MC. Lt&Adjt   RNVR Howe Bn RNDiv   kia   7.2.17   CR France383 W.
ELLIS,Edward White Lt   RNVR Hawke Bn RNDiv   3.2.17 MR21
ELLIS,Frank Gnr   RN   HMS Derwent   2.5.17 CR France85
ELLIS,George Lt   RN   HMS Wildfire   13.10.17 CR Hamps9
ELLIS,George Skipper   RNR HMTrawler Evangel   21.8.15 CR Lincs123
ELLIS,J.W.   2Lt   RN   10RWFus B'Coy attRNDiv   24.5.18 CR France215
ELLIS,Oliver Barnard TFlt Sub-Lt   RNAS   19.5.17 MR20
ELLIS,Sidney E   TFlt Sub-Lt   RNAS   dedacc 12.7.17   CR Belgium171
ELLIS,Stanley Venn Capt RN   HMS Defence kia   31.5.16 MR2
ELLISON,Frederick Thomas TSkipper   RNR HMTrawler Towhee   kld   15.6.17 MR1
ELLISON,Herbert William.DSM.   Gnr   RN   HMS Laverock ded   3.12.17 CR Devon1
ELVEN,Arthur Robert James Lt   RNR HMS Ghurka kld   8.2.17 MR3
ELVENS,Eliza Millicent   ResNSister   QARNNS   HMS Natal   kld   30.12.15 MR1
ELWELL,Charles B Lt Comdr   RN   9.14
ELY,Hedley Thomas   Lt   RNVR Hood Bn RNDiv   21.8.18 MR16
EMERSON,John H   Sub-Lt RNVR Nelson Bn RNDiv   13.11.16 CR France339
EMMETT,Cyril William   Flt Sub-Lt   RNAS   15.3.18 CR France1359
EMPSON,Richard W H M   Lt   RM   Portsmouth Bn RNDiv   1.5.15 CR Gallipoli31
EMSON,Francis Reginald   Asst Paymr   RNR HMS Clan McNaughton   drd   3.2.15 MR1
EPPSTEIN,Maurice William Wallis   FltSubLt   RNAS   kld   12.5.17 CR France1359
ERRINGTON,Albert George TLt   RNR HMS Candytuft   kia   18.11.17 CR WAfrica12
ERSKINE,Fentoun A.MID   T2Lt RMLI   5.5.15 MR4
ERSKINE,Henry David   Midmn RN   HMS Minotaur kldacc 31.3.15   CR Surrey160
ESMONDE,John Henry Grattan   Midmn RN   HMS Invincible   kia   31.5.16 MR3
ESPLIN,David Sub-Lt RNR HMS Pembroke   6.3.16 CR Scot764
ESSON,William   Maj   RMLI HMS Russell kld   27.4.16 MR3
EUSTIS,Thomas John Bosn RN   HMS Indefatigable   kia   31.5.16 MR2
EVANS,Benjamin George   Art Eng   RN   HMS Queen Mary   kia   31.5.16 MR3
EVANS,Bertram Sutton.MVO.   Capt RN   HMS Europa ded   2.3.19 CR France457
EVANS,Charles Lt   RNVR HMS Eileen   13.6.18 CR Canada1694
EVANS,Frederick Richardson Lt   RNR   4.10.15 CR Devon1
EVANS,Herbert Clyde.MID   Lt Comdr   RNVR Nelson Bn RNDiv   kia   5.6.15 CR Gallipoli14
EVANS,John Archibald   TLt   RNR HMYacht Conqueror II kia   26.9.16 MR3
EVANS,Tim Evelyn   Sub-Lt RN   HM S/M C29 kld   29.8.15 MR2
EVELEGH,Edmund George.MIDx2   Lt Col RM   Cmdg Nelson Bn RNDiv   14.7.15 CR Gallipoli14

EVERITT,Alfred Everitt   Eng Comdr   RN   HMS Aboukir kia   22.9.14 MR1
EWART,Victor Alexander   Lt   RN   HMS Queen Mary   kia   31.5.16 MR3
EYRE,Cyril A Flt Lt RNAS   7.7.17 CR France705
EYRE,Edward Geoffrey A   TFlt Sub-Lt   RNAS   21.10.17 MR20

F

FAED,James Ronald Herdman Midmn RN   HMS Goliath kia   13.5.15 MR1
FAIRNIE,Simon   Skipper   RNR   HMTrawler Renarro   kld   10.11.18 MR3
FALCONER,Percy Albert Gordon   ALt   RNR   HM S/M E10   kld   21.1.15 MR3
FALGATE,Samuel Charles   TSkipper   RNR   HMDrifter Hilary II   kld   25.3.16 MR1
FANE,Robert Gerald Cmdr RN   HMS Dartmouth   kia   15.5.17 CR Italy17
FANNING,Newel E E Burton   see BURTON-FANNING,Newel E E
FAREBROTHER,George Henry   Art Eng   RN   HMS Monmouth   kia   1.11.14 MR2
FARMERY,J C   Wt Tel RNR   HMS Leviathan   18.10.15 CR SAmerica6
FARQUARSON,C.G.MC.   LtCol   RMLI   2RM Bn RNDiv   24.3.18 CR France177
FARQUHAR,Alistair C.N.   Lt   RN   HMS Eden   17.6.16 CR Scot329
FARRAR,Joseph   Ch Art Eng   RN   HMS Paragon kia   17.3.17 MR2
FARRELL,William Edward   Lt   RN   HMS Ruby   ded   11.10.18 CR Italy17
FARROW,Edwin Percy   SubLt   RNVR   Hawke Bn RNDiv   25.8.15 CR Gallipoli6
FARWELL,John Ralph Bax   Lt   RN   HM S/M E30   kld   22.11.16 MR3
FAULKNER,Robert Irvine   Lt   RN   HMS Black Prince   kia   31.5.16 MR3
FAVELL,Ernest Torre Lt Comdr   RN   HMS Pathfinder   kia   5.9.14 MR1
FAWCETT,H. Maj   RMLI   29.12.18 MR70
FAWCUS,Victor Clarence Barick   Midmn RN   HMS New Zealand   5.4.19 MR65
FEDARB,Frederick   SurgCmdr   RN   HMS Vernon   25.5.19 CR Hamps7
FEETHAM,James   TLt   RNR   HMTrawler Worsley   kld   14.8.15 MR1
FEILDING,Hugh Cecil Robert Hon   Lt Comdr   RN   HMS Defence kia   31.5.16 MR2
FELLOWES,Edmund Ethelberht   PMidmn   RNR   HMS Hampshire   kld   5.6.16 MR3
FELLOWES,Ivan Gordon   Midmn RN   HMS Irresistible   kia   18.3.15 MR3
FENN,C.H.   Lt   RNR   HMS Thistle   9.4.19 CR SAfrica158
FENNER,Athelstan Alfred Lennox   Lt Comdr   RN   HM S/M K4   drd   31.1.18   MR3
FENNER,Eric Athelstan   SubLt   RNVR   Anson Bn RNDiv   dow   12.10.18 CR France512
FERGUSON,Alex Burns   SubLt   HMS Veronica   12.7.20 CR NZ134
FERGUSON,Dugald Lt   RNR   HMS Begonia kia   6.10.17 MR3
FERGUSON,James   EngLt   RNR   FleetMessenger Race Fisher   ded   12.10.15 MR40 &MR4 ?
FERGUSON,John White   Lt   RNVR   Hood Bn RNDiv   4.6.15 MR4
FERGUSON-DAVIE,Herbert George 2Lt   RM   Portsmouth Bn RNDiv   9.5.15 MR4
FERGUSSON,Nigel Robert   Lt   RN   HMS Bulwark kld   26.11.14 MR3
FERNIE,David Gnr   RN   HMS Pelican   ded   25.3.17   CR Hamps8
FERRIER,Robert England   Sub-Lt RN   HMS Partridge kia   12.12.17 MR3
FERRIER,William Francis   TPFlt Offr   RNAS   kld   26.8.17 CR France1844
FERRIS,David Henry TSurg Prob   RNVR   HMS Broke   kia   31.5.16 MR3
FETHERSTON,John McDonald   SubLt   RNVR   HM ML218   6.12.18 CR Greece10
FFIELD,B O   Flt Sub-Lt   RNAS   24.12.14 CR Middx29
FIELD,Clifford Capt   RMLI   HMS Aboukir kia   22.9.14 MR3
FIELD,George Henry RMGnr   RMLI   HMS Indefatigable   kia   31.5.16 MR1
FIELD,Thomas Mostyn   Midmn RN   HMS Queen Mary   kia   31.5.16 MR3
FIELDEN,Herbert   T2Lt   RMLI   2 RM Bn RNDiv   9.3.18 MR20
FIELDING,Allen   Cmdr   RNR   HMS Orama   11.7.17 CR SAfrica158
FIELDING,James MID   T2Lt   RMLI   1 RM Bn RNDiv   28.4.17 MR20
FILKIN,Robert Thomas Norman   Lt   RNR   HM S/M D6   kia   24.6.18 MR1
FINCH,Edward Terence Doyne   Lt   RN   HMS Bulwark kld   26.11.14 MR3
FINCH,Sydney William   Paymr RN   HMS Pathfinder   5.9.14 CR Devon1
FINCH-DAWSON,Humphrey Cmdr RN   HMS Daedalus   13.8.16 CR Kent46
FINCKEN,Cuthbert Abraham Taylor   Art Eng   RN   HMS Hampshire   kld   5.6.16 MR2
FINDLAY,George   TSkipper   RNR   HMDrifter Protect   kld   16.3.17 MR3
FINLAISON,Hilton Evans Bear   Surg   RNAS (may be RNASBR)   ded   2.8.18 CR London8

FINLAY,James   AArt Eng   RN   HMS Invincible   kia   31.5.16 MR3
FINNIS,Frank.CVO.   Adml   RN   17.11.18 CR Sussex204
FIRMAN,Humphrey Osbaldston Brooke.VC.Lt   RN   SS Julnar   24.4.16 MR38
FIRTH,Edward Skipper   RNR   HMTrpt Northumbria   5.10.20 CR Lincs156
FISH,Sidney Howard MC   Lt Cmdr   RNVR Hood Bn RNDiv   25.8.18 CR France578
FISHENDEN,J.W.   Gnr   RN   HMS Pekin   20.9.19 CR Hamps5
FISHER,Charles Dennis   TLt   RNVR HMS Invincible   kia   31.5.16 MR3
FISHER,D'Arcy George   SubLt RNVR HMS Presidentded   30.11.18 CR Cornwall49
FISHER,Edward Garlick   SurgLt RN   HMS Vigorous   12.5.19 CR NIreland47
FISHER,Ernest Edward   Gnr   RN   HMS Turbulent   6.2.21 CR Hamps5
FISHER,John Maurice Haig   Lt   RN   HMS Good Hope   kia   1.11.14 MR3
FISHER,Sydney   Art Eng   RN   10.16
FISHER-ROWE,Seymour   Cmdr   RN   HMS Falmouth   27.2.16 CR Norfolk101
FISKEN,Peter WtEng RNR   HMS Hampshie   5.6.16 CR Scot900
FITZHERBERT-BROCKHOLES,Roger Hubert Lt   RN   HMS Glory   kld   2.7.19 MR3
FITZMAURICE-DEANE-MORGAN,Cormac Hon Asst Engr RNR   HMS Princess Irene   kld   27.5.15 MR3
FITZPATRICK,Michael Joseph DSM Gnr   RN   HMS Raglan   kia   20.1.18 CR Gallipoli1
FITZROY,Edward Henry   Lt   RN   HMS Simoom kia   23.1.17 MR1
FLANNERY,Arthur H.   Surg   RN   31.12.16 CR Eire12
FLANNERY,Patrick   Skipper   RNR   HMTrawler Strathalva ded   12.12.19 CR Lincs156
FLEET,Herbert Percy Skipper   RNR   17.12.17 CR Lincs156
FLEMING,Bruce   EngSubLt   RNR   HMS Teutonic   30.11.16 CR Scot1030
FLEMING,Ernest Kingston   EngLt RN   HMS Glorious   20.3.19 CR Lancs14
FLEMING,George Rivers Sanderson FltLt   RNAS   17.4.17 CR France1632
FLEMMING,Thomas Thomas Stewart Lt   RN   HMS Invincible   kia   31.5.16 MR3
FLETCHER,Christopher George Ost SubLt RNVR Howe Bn RNDiv   kia   13.11.16 CR France339
FLETCHER,William John Wall   Lt   RN   HMS Black Prince   kia   31.5.16 MR3
FLOCKHART,John   Lt   RNVR HMS Tarlair   29.9.18 CR Scot137
FLOOD,Cecil Ernest Cloar   TSub-Lt   RNVR Anson Bn RNDiv   10.6.15 MR4
FLOYD,William Eric PF/O   RN   RNAS kld   21.1.18 CR Ches8
FLYNN,Harold John PF/O   RNAS   5.7.17 CR Kent28
FOLLETT,Edwin.DSC.   Lt   RNR   HMS Proserpine   ded   2.10.18 CR Iraq8
FOORD,H.R. SubLt RNVR 2(Res)Bn RNDiv   4.4.19 CR Hamps1
FOOTE,Richard Christopher Georges Lt   RMLI   9RM Bn RNDiv   dow   15.10.14 CR Belgium353
FORBES,Arthur Walter.DSO. Lt   RN   HM S/M H5   drd   2.3.18 MR1
FORBES,James Arthur Charles   Midmn RN   HMS Tiger   dow   1.6.16 MR2
FORBES,Spencer Dundas   Comdr RN   HMS Monmouth   kia   1.11.14 MR2
FORD,George ChBosn   RN   HMS Drake   dedacc 7.3.17 CR Devon1
FORD,Philip Henry Sig Bosn   RN   HMS Pathfinder   kia   5.9.14 MR4
FORD,Victor Bosn RN   HMS Blake   25.3.20 CR Kent46
FORD,William J.   ChCarp   RN   HMS President   15.2.17 CR Cornwall136
FORD,W.L.   Chpn   RN   HMS Suffolk   9.5.18 CR Europe195 &MR70
FOREMAN,Victor Oswald   Eng Lt RN   HMS Kent   ded   21.7.15   CR Canada154
FORMAN,Leonard Eales   TPFlt Offr   RN/RNAS HMS President   kld   16.8.17 CR Essex40
FORREST,James   EngLt RNR   HMS Acasta   31.5.16 CR Kent46
FORRESTER,Adrien Andrew Ft Surg RN   HMS Implacable   kia   25.4.15 MR1
FORRESTER,Frank C MC   Lt   RNVR Hawke Bn RNDiv   25.3.18 MR20
FORRESTER,James David   Capt   RAMC attRNDiv   kia   14.11.16 CR France701
FORTIER,R.L.DSO.RD.   ACmdr RNR   ded   7.3.21 CR Canada609
FOSTER,Harold Arthur   TSub-Lt   RNVR Drake Bn RNDiv   13.11.16 MR21
FOSTER,William John   Lt Comdr   RN   HM S/M E6   kld   26.12.15 MR3
FOULIS,Archibald P Liston   see LISTON-FOULIS,Archibald P
FOUQUET,David   Skipper   RNR   HMT Craigewan   19.9.16 CR Scot288
FOWLER,Horace Vernon   Lt   RIM   SS Nearsuch   15.7.17 MR65
FOX,Alfred Frank   Bosn   RN   HMS Tiger   12.2.21 CR Devon3
FOX,Charles   ChOff CG   HM Coastguards Stn Padstow   27.7.17 CR Devon1
FOX,Cedric Earle   TFlt Sub-Lt   RNAS   drd   7.1.18 MR1
FOX,Charles Leonard Lt Comdr   RN   HMS Mary Rose   kia   17.10.17 MR1
FOX,Ernest I W   TLt   RNR   Naval ViceConsul Cadiz   5.3.18 CR Europe34
FOX,John James de la Tour   Sub Lt (TFlt Sub-Lt)   RN(RNAS)   drd   9.3.17 MR1

21

FOX,Reginald William   PaymrSubLt   RNVR HMS Wallington   ded   7.1.19 CR Devon3
FOX,Robert Edwin Alston   TLt   RNR   HMTrawler Merse   kld   22.5.17MR1
FRAMES,Neville Wall   TFlt Sub-Lt   RNAS 1Sqn   28.1.16 CR Belgium171
FRANCE-HAYHURST,Cecil Halsted Cmdr RN   HMS Patuca   24.2.15 CR Ches119
FRANCIS,David   TSub-Lt   RNVR Nelson Bn RNDiv   13.11.16 MR21
FRANCIS,Leslie Curil Kendall   Lt   RN   HM S/M L9   accdrd 12.7.18   MR3
FRANCKLIN,Philip MVO   Capt   RN   HMS Good Hope   kia   1.11.14MR3
FRANKLIN,Charles.OBE.   Maj&QM   RMLI   5.9.19 CR Hamps7
FRANKLIN,C C   PFlt Offr   RNAS   20.3.18 CR Lincs78
FRANKUM,A V   ChEng RN   HMS Quarta   1.6.17 CR Egypt15
FRASER,Norman   TLt   RNR   HMDrifter Jennie Murray   kia   15.2.18MR3
FRASER,Percival Victor   WO 2 RNAS   kld   10.1.16CR Sussex144
FRASER,William   TSub-Lt   RNVR att Anson Bn RNDiv dow   27.10.17 CR Belgium3
FRASER,William St John   Lt Comdr   RN   HM S/M E10 kld   21.1.15MR3
FREELAND,James Henry   Gnr   RN   HMS Tornado kld   23.12.17 MR3
FREEMAN,Edmund APFltSubLt   RNAS   14.7.16 CR Berks82
FREEMAN,Gerald Stewart   TSurg Prob   RNVR HMS Lassoo   kld   13.8.16MR2
FRENCH,Edward John   Lt   RNR   HMS Good Hope   kia   1.11.14MR3
FREYBERG,Lancelot Percy   Lt Comdr   RN   HMS Russell kld   27.4.16MR1
FREYBERG,Oscar   TSub-Lt   RNVR Collingwood Bn RNDiv   4.6.15 MR4
FROST,John Stuart   TAsst Paymr   RNR   HMS Russell kld   27.4.16MR1
FROST,Robert Skipper   RNR   HMT Orcades   14.4.16 CR Yorks2
FROUDE,John AubreyMidmn RN   HMS Cressy   kia   22.9.14MR1
FRY,Ernest William   Sub-Lt RNVR Drake Bn RNDiv   4.9.18 MR16
FRY,Frederick Charles   Art Eng   RN   HMS Invincible   kia   31.5.16MR3
FRY,Howard   TSub-Lt   RNVR Howe Bn RNDiv   dow   16.11.16 CR France102
FRY,William Mervyn TSub-Lt   RNVR HMPMS Ludlow   kld   29.12.16 MR1
FRYER,Ernest George ASub-Lt   RNR   HMS Vengeance   dow   15.6.15   MR3
FULCHER,Clarence Alban   LtCmdr   RN   HMS Presidentded   2.10.16CR Kent46
FULLARTON,Kenneth   Lt   RNVR HM ML43   ded   17.11.18 CR Suffolk85
FULLER,John Joseph TEng Sub-Lt   RNR   HMWaterTank Progres   drd   21.12.16 MR1
FULLER,William George   Art Eng   RN   HMS Queen Mary   kia   31.5.16MR3
FULTON,Joseph Henry Coldbook   T2Lt   RM   Portsmouth Bn RNDiv   3.5.15 MR4
FURLONG,Allan Hyde   Lt   RNR   HMS Carol   14.3.20 CR Sussex95

G

GABBETT,Edmond Poole   Lt Comdr   RN   HMS Cressy   kia   22.9.14 MR1
GAIMES,John Austin.DSO.   Lt Cmdr   RN   HM S/M K5   drd   20.1.21   MR3
GALBRAITH,W   Lt   RN   HMS Thesus   16.10.18 CR Italy6
GALE,William I   ChGnr RN   HMS Attentive   16.12.17 CR Kent7
GALE,William Thomas   Gnr   RN   HMS Shark   kia   31.5.16MR2
GALLETLY,William TEng   RNR   HMS Princess Irene   kld   27.5.15MR3
GANDY,Herbert Howard   Gnr   RN   HM TB7   kld   5.6.17 CR Sussex183
GANE,Herbert T   TSub-Lt   RNR   2.17
GANNAWAY,Philip Corliss   Lt   RNVR HMS Vanessa ded   6.11.18CR Wales463
GARDEN,James   TSkipper   RNR   HMDrifter Ferndale   drd   27.12.15 MR3
GARDINER,William Norman Lt   RN   HMS Defence kia   31.5.16MR2
GARDNER,Frederick L   Lt   RN   Staff of DNTO(Dieppe) Late RIM   28.5.17 CR France377
GARDNER,George Frederick Sig Bosn   RN   HMS Hogue   kia   22.9.14MR1
GARDNER,Jack Thornton   Lt   RMA   RM Eastney   7.11.18CR Hamps5
GARDNER,Leonard S SubLt   RNVR Nelson Bn RNDiv   13.11.16 CR France339
GARNHAM,Percy Claude   TLt   RNVR Nelson Bn RNDiv   3.5.15 MR4
GARNHAM,Robert William   ChGnr RN   HMTrawler Valpa   19.3.16 CR Germany2
GARNISH,Charles Arthur   Skipper   RNR   HMTrawler Kirkland kld   20.8.17MR2
GARNSWORTHY,Charles Stanley   ALt   RNR   HMS Clan McNaughton   drd   3.2.15 MR1
GARROD,Edward   Skipper   RNR   HMTrawler Clifton   18.2.17 CR Suffolk85
GARTSIDE-TIPPING,Henry Thomas Lt Comdr   RN   HMYacht Sanda   25.9.15 MR31

GARTSIDE-TIPPING,Stuart Mrs Wife of LtCmdr above Womens Emergency Canteens   6.3.17 CR France864
GASKELL,Gerald Bruce   Lt Comdr   RN   HMS Good Hope   kia   1.11.14MR3
GASKELL,Holbrook Lance   FltSubLt   RNAS   kia   2.5.17 CR Greece1
GATES,Arthur J   TSkipper   RNR   HMDrifter Unity   1.9.17 CR France1359
GATES,R T   Flt Lt RNAS   14.9.14 CR Middx30
GATT,Laurence   Wt Elect   RN   HMS Queen Mary   kia   31.5.16MR3
GEALER,Harry   SubLt RNVR Hood Bn RNDiv   13.11.16 CR France339
GEAR,John D SurgSubLt   RNVR HMS Melampus   ded   10.11.18 CR Surrey1
GEATON,William Christopher   Ch Carp   RN   HMS Defence kia   31.5.16MR2
GEDDES,Alexander   TSkipper   RNR   HMTrawler Fraser   kld   17.6.17MR3
GEDDES,George   Skipper   RNR   HMDrifter Speedwell V   28.10.16 CR Eire522
GEDDES,George M   TSkipper   RNR   HMDrifter Clavis   kia   9.7.16 MR3
GEDDES,John Skipper   RNR   HMTrawler Charles Astie   kld   26.6.17MR3
GEDGE,Joseph Theodore   Staff Paymr   RN   HMS Amphionkld   6.8.14 MR2
GEE,Ronald James   TSub-Lt   RNVR Anson Bn RNDiv   13.11.16 MR21
GELDARD,J Capt   RM   Plymouth Divn RNDiv   20.8.18 CR Camb2
GEMMELL,John   EngSubLt   RNR   HMS Ophir   19.9.18 CR USA246
GEOGHEGAN,Herbert Lyne Ft Surg RN   HMS Black Prince   kia   31.5.16MR3
GEORGE,H A Skipper   RNR   HMDrifter Troophead   21.10.18 CR Suffolk85
GEORGE,Robert Edward   TSkipper   RNR   HMTrawler Senator   kld   21.5.17MR1
GERRARD,Ernest Dundas   ATLt   RNR   HMTrawler Robert Smith   kld   20.7.17MR1
GIBBINS,George   Capt   RMLI   2 RM Bn RNDiv   23.3.18 MR20
GIBBINS,James W   TEng Lt   RNR   see GIBBONS,J W
GIBBON,Charles James.DSC. Lt   RNR   HMS DreelCastle   ded   29.10.18 CR Yorks294
GIBBONS,B.C.   Midmn RNR   HMS Otranto   6.10.18CR Scot31
GIBBONS,James William   EngLt RNR   HMS Laurentic   25.1.17 CR Eire295
GIBBS,Valentine Francis   Cmdr RN   Cmdg HMS Iris Ex HMS Tiger   dow   23.4.18   CR Devon274
GIBSON,Edmund Herbert   TLt   RNVR Hood Bn RNDiv   dow   25.10.15 MR3
GIBSON,George   Skipper   RNR   Naval Base Kingston   2.11.16CR Lincs156
GIBSON,George Henderson   TAsst Eng   RNR   HMS Viknor drd   13.1.15   MR3
GIBSON,Mungo Campbell   TLt Comdr   RNVR Nelson Bn RNDiv   3.5.15 MR4
GIBSON-CARMICHAEL,Alexander David Sub-Lt RN   HM S/M E16 kld   22.8.16MR3
GIDNEY,Edwin   Eng Sub Lt   RNR   HMS Empress of Russia   ded   10.6.15   MR3
GIFFARD-BRINE,Robin George Bruce   Midmn RN   HMS Invincible   kia   31.5.16MR3
GIFFORD,John Ernest Ch Art Eng   RN   HMS Indefatigable   kia   31.5.16MR2
GILBERT,Alfred Stephen   Lt   RNR   HMYacht Zarefah   8.5.17 CR Scot258
GILBERT,J.   Gnr   RN   HMS Nimrod   18.10.18 CR Hamps9
GILBERT,Thaddeus   38146   Skipper   RNR   HMT Garmo   20.12.14 CR Yorks185
GILBERT,Wilfred V. SubLt RNVR Nelson Bn RNDiv   3.6.15 CR Gallipoli14
GILES,Alfred Edward Boscawen.DSO. ALt RN   HMS Manley accdrd 25.10.17 MR1
GILL,Thomas Attwood Eng Lt RNR   HM SalvageTug Hughli   26.4.19 CR Belgium24
GILLAM,Henry James Lt   RNR   HMS Egmont   7.4.18 CR Italy35
GILLESPIE,Leslie Herbert Gray   FltSubLt   RNAS HMS Ark Royal   kld   2.12.17CR Greece10
GILLESPIE,Robert   Eng Lt RN   ded   4.1.21 CR Canada1687
GILLIES,Daniel   Lt   RNVR HM MB71   30.4.15 CR Scot86
GIPPS,George Comdr RN   HMS Grafton kia   3.1.16 MR3
GLASGOW,Theodore Linscott TFlt Sub-Lt   RNAS 105Sqnkia   19.8.17CR Belgium18
GLEDHILL,Alfred   TLt   RNR   HM S/M E6   kld   26.12.15 MR3
GLENDINNING,J   Div Ch Offr   CG   Bridge of Don CG Stn   28.6.18 CR Scot288
GLOVER,Maurice John   WtSchmr   RN   HMSGlatton kld   22.9.18CR Ches133
GLOVER,S J Mate RN   HMS Mersey   6.1.19 CR Europe30
GOAD,Edwin George Wt Elect   RN   HMS Lion   kia   31.5.16MR3
GODBEHERE,HerbertGnr   RN   HMS Lassoo kld   13.8.16MR2
GODDARD,Denis Gerald Ambrose   Midmn RN   HMS Queen Mary   kia   31.5.16MR3
GODFREY,James Douglas.DSC.   Lt   RN   HMS Attentive Ex HMS Arethusa   31.10.17 CR Kent231
GODSAL,Alfred Edmund.DSO.   Cmdr RN   Cmdg HMS Vindictivekia   10.5.18CR Belgium175
GOLD,Harry SubLt RNVR Hawke Bn RNDiv   14.11.16 CR France293
GOLDFINCH,J R   ChOff RN   HMCoastguard   21.1.19 CR Hamps5
GOLDSMITH,Cecil de la Mere.RD. Cmdr RNR   21.1.17 CR WAfrica24
GOLDSMITH,John   Capt   RMLI   1RM Bn RNDiv   dow   11.5.17   CR France40

GOOCH,L D EMidmn RN　　　HMS Implacable　　　　　4.10.15CR Essex141
GOOCH,Thomas Shirley　　　Cmdr　RN　　　　　11.12.18 CR Surrey160
GOODESS,James F　Gnr　　RN　　HMS President　　26.11.17　CR Hamps9
GOODHART,Francis Herbert Heveningham.DSO Cmdr　　RN　　HM S/M K13 drd　　29.1.17　　　CR Scot81
GOODWIN,Godfrey J W　　FltSubLt　　　RNAS　　　kld　　12.3.18CR France1359
GOODWIN,Matthew Dean　　Sub Lt RNR　HMS Arabis　kia　　11.2.16MR2
GOODWIN,Squire　2Lt　RMLI　1RM Bn RNDiv　　kia　　10.11.18 CR Belgium246
GORDON,Archibald　TObs Sub-Lt　RNAS　　　drd　　7.1.18　MR1
GORDON,James R.　　AssPaymr　RNR　HMS Patrol　　　20.2.18 CR Scot54
GORDON,Ralph Lacy　SubLt　RNVR HMS Tarlair　　19.6.18 CR Scot93
GORDON,Thomas　　Sub Lt RNR　RFA Hughli　drd　26.4.19　　　MR3
GORE BROWN,Harold R　　Asst Paymr　RN　　see BROWNE,H R G
GORE-BROWNE,Geoffrey George　　Midmn RN　　HMS Aboukir kia　　22.9.14MR1
GORMAN,Joseph　　FltLt　RNAS NthnSqn 6Wing　　dedacc　17.12.17 CR Italy48
GOSNEY,William Charles　　Bosn　RN　　HMS Formidable　kia　1.1.15　MR1
GOSS,John Henry　　RMGnr　　RMLI HMS Lion　kia　31.5.16MR2
GOTT,Francis Stuart　Sub LTRN　　HMS Badminton　　accdrd 2.10.20MR1
GOUGH,Harold Brentnall　　TMidmn　　RNR　HMS Bayano　kia　11.3.15MR3
GOULD,William Henry Felix TSub-Lt　　RNR　HMS Stephen Furness kia　13.12.17　MR3
GOW,Charles Humphrey　　TSurg Lt　RN　att Anson Bn RNDiv　13.11.16 MR21
GOW,Roderick Charles Alister　　Lt　RN　HMS Defence kia　31.5.16MR2
GRACE,Edmund Victor Joseph　　Flt Sub-Lt　RNAS 10 Sqdn　　19.9.17 MR20
GRAHAM,A.E.　　ChEng1Cl　　HMOiler Tiflis　20.1.19 CR Asia51
GRAHAM,Charles Walter DSO　　Flt Lt RNAS 1 Wing kld　8.9.16 CR Surrey3
GRAHAM,Henry Davenport　FltLt　RNAS　　21.3.17 CR Greece7
GRAHAM,Malise Stewart　Sub-Lt RN　HM S/M G8　accdrd　22.6.17　　MR3
GRAHAM,Robert　Midmn RNR　HMS Vivid　ded　2.10.18CR Devon1
GRANT,Duncan Stuart Ogilvie　FtPaymr　RN　HMS Duncan　18.1.15 CR Devon1
GRANT,Ferris Nelson Lt Comdr(Retd)RN　DoW Recieved in Army Capt 5RSuss R　kia　9.5.15 MR22
GRANT,James Douglas　FltSubLt　RNAS drd　3.10.17CR Scot280
GRANT,John TSkipper　RNR　NMDrifter Tuberose　kld　31.8.16MR3
GRANT,John Francis Haughton　Sub-Lt RNVR　10.12.19 CR London30
GRANT,Robert　TSkipper　RNR　HMDrifter Lily Reaichkld　25.2.16MR3
GRANT-DALTON,Harold.MC.　Lt　RNVR Hood Bn RNDiv　dow　28.4.18　　CR Germany3
GRAVES-BURTON,Richard H.RD.　Cmdr RNR　HMS Excellent　29.9.17 CR Hamps5
GRAY,Alan Theodore Flt Sub-Lt　RNAS　16.8.17 MR20
GRAY,George C.　SubLt RNR　HMS Sachem　15.12.17 CR Lancs14
GRAY,George Smith Booth.RD.　Cmdr RNR　HMS Cumberland　accdrd 21.10.14 MR3
GRAY,Gordon Evelyn Elliott Lt　RN　HMS Good Hope　kia　1.11.14MR3
GRAY,John　Bosn　RN　HMS Indefatigable　kia　31.5.16 MR1
GRAY,Samuel ATLt　RNR　HMS Vala　kia　21.8.17MR3
GRAZEBROOK,Robert HenryEng Comdr　RN　HMS Cressy　kia　22.9.14MR1
GREEN,Charles Arthur　Skipper　RNR　HMDrifter City of Liverpool kld　31.7.18MR1
GREEN,G　Paymr Sub-Lt RNR　HMS President V　25.4.19 CR Surrey160
GREEN,James William　Lt　RNR　HMTrawler Dirk　kia　28.5.18MR1
GREEN,John Alexander　Capt　RN　8SStaffR attAnson Bn RNDiv dow　18.8.18　　CR France69
GREEN,S.W.B.DSO.　Cmdr RN　HMS Glowworm　26.8.19　MR70 & CR Europe179
GREEN,Thomas Fleming　TAsst Paymr　RNR　HNS Paxton　kia　20.5.17MR1
GREEN,Wilfred Steuart Miall Lt Cmdr　RNVR Benbow Bn RNDiv　20.9.15 MR3
GREENE,David W　TSub-Lt　RNVR　　1.18
GREENHILL,Benjamin P K　ALt　RNVR HMS Hampshire　drd　5.6.16 CR Scot900
GREENSHIELDS,Thomas Edwards　Lt Comdr　RN　HMS Venerable　kia　9.8.15 MR3
GREENWAY,William Stephen　Skipper　RNR　HMTrawler Mary　kld　5.11.14MR2
GREENWELL,Arthur Robert PTFlt Sub-Lt RNAS　kld　20.10.16 CR Lincs78
GREENWELL,Evelyn Eyre　Lt　RNVR HMS Research　23.2.19 CR Surrey27
GREENWOOD,Charles Thomas　FltSubLt　RNAS　15.3.18 CR Lancs237
GREER,James Alfred TAsst Eng　RNR　HMS Viknor　drd　13.1.15　　MR3
GREEVES,Thomas Malcolmson　FltSubLt　RNAS 12Sqn 5Wing kld　23.12.17 CR France1359
GREGORY,A.W.　Lt　RM　1RM Bn RNDiv　27.9.18 CR France530
GREGORY,H.W.　LtCmdr　RN　HMS Hoverfly　10.9.17 CR Iraq6

24

GREIFFENHAGEN,Rider Maurice Waterhouse Lt   RN   HM S/M E24   kld   27.3.16MR3
GREIG,Donald.OBE. Cmdr RN   27.7.21 CR Iraq6
GREIG,George Anthony   AChapn   RN   HMS Russell ded   28.4.16   CR Europe6
GREY,Arthur Thomas Skipper   RNR HMT R.R.S.   16.11.18 CR Norfolk131
GREY,Eric Verner   Lt   RN   HMS Hampshire   kld   5.6.16   MR3
GREY-SMITH,John E Lt Comdr   RN   see SMITH,J E G
GRIER,William James Bosn RN   HMS Black Prince   kia   31.5.16MR3
GRIERSON,Frank J. TAsst Eng   RNR HMS Princess Irene   kld   27.5.15MR3
GRIERSON,James C. SubLt RNVR HMS Zaria   3.7.15 CR Scot1014
GRIERSON,John   TEng Sub-Lt   RNR HMS Mechanician   kia   20.1.18MR3
GRIFFIN,E.A.DSC.   ChBosn   RN   HMS Stephen Furness   25.6.18 CR Hamps8
GRIFFIN,George   Lt   RN   HMS Victory   11.6.15 CR Hamps8
GRIFFIN,John Joseph Gnr   RN   15.1.21 CR Hamps5
GRIFFITH,Hubert William Douglas   Lt   RN   HMS Pheasant kld   1.3.17 MR2
GRIFFITH,William Llewelyn   Midmn RN   HMS Indefatigable   kia   31.5.16MR2
GRIFFITHS,Edwin   TSub-Lt   RNR HMYacht Zaida   kia   17.8.16MR1
GRIFFITHS,John Stanley   PMidmn   RNR HMS Triumph dow   6.3.15 MR2
GRIGSON,Mabel Edith   Sister QARNNS   RNHospital Malta   3.10.18CR Europe6
GRINLAW,Thomas   TSkipper   RNR HMTrawler Orsino   kia   28.9.16MR2
GRINLING,Charles Stuart   ALt   RM   Chatham Bn RNDiv   3.5.15   MR45
GROGAN,W.J.   RrAdml   RN   HMYacht Sapphire II   14.3.15 CR Glouc27
GROVER,JohnMaj   RM   Plymouth Bn RNDiv   24.6.15 CR Gallipoli2
GROW,Roderick Charles Alister   Lt   RN   see GOW,R C A
GRUBB,Walter Bousfield Watkins   Lt Comdr   RN   HMS Cressy   kia   22.9.14MR1
GRUNDY,Howard Eckhardt   TPFlt Offr   RNAS   kld   1.5.17 CR Lincs78
GUDGEON,Athole Edwin   Lt   RNR HMS Ettrick   dow   27.8.17   CR Hamps201
GUEST,Harold Victor TMidmn   RNR HMS Indefatigable   kia   31.5.16MR2
GUILD,Robert William   TSkipper   RNR HMDrifter Diadem II   28.3.16 CR Lincs156
GULLETT,Albert E.   PFltOffRNAS   18.2.18 CR Essex1
GULLIVER,Montague Edwin Allen   Skipper   RNR HMTrawler Epsworth drd   22.5.17   MR2
GULLY,Lewis Vincent   Eng Sub Lt   RNR HMS Cullist   kia   11.2.18MR3
GUNN,Alexander John   ATLt RNR HM S/M E26   kld   6.7.16 MR3
GUNNER,Edward Geoffrye   Sub-Lt RN   HMS Bulwark kld   26.11.14 MR3
GUNNING,James Meluish   TSub-Lt   RNVR HMS Opal   drd   12.1.18   MR3
GYE,Alexander Hugh.MID   Lt Comdr   RN   HMS Negro   drd   21.12.16 MR1

H

HACKETT,J. Lt   RN   HMS Nimrod   10.10.18 CR Dorset27
HADDICAN,Edward TSkipper   RNR HMTrawler Apley   kld   6.12.17MR1
HADWEN,J. SurgLtCmdr RN   HMS Lancaster   23.10.18 CR USA11
HAIG,James Douglas TFlt Sub-Lt   RNAS Royal Ark 2 Wing   20.5.17 MR40
HAINES,Cyril L   TObs Sub-Lt RNAS   26.5.17 CR Belgium390 HAINS Lt
HAINES,William R   TSub-Lt   RNVR Howe Bn RNDiv   17.2.17 CR France514
HAKIN,William Charles MC TSub-Lt   RNVR Howe Bn RNDiv   13.11.16 MR21
HALAHAN,Henry Crosby.DSO.   Capt   RN   HMS Presidentkia   23.4.18MR1
HALAHAN,Robert Crosby   Lt Comdr   RN   HM S/M E18   kld   11.5.16MR3
HALE-WHITE,Leonard   Lt   RN   HMS Natal   kld   30.12.15 MR1
HALFYARD,Sidney John Barnes   Gnr   RN   HMS M28   kia   20.1.18MR2
HALL,A.   WtEng RNR HMS Carnarvon   21.10.18 CR Hamps5
HALL,Alexander   TSkipper   RNR HMTrawler Princess Beatrice kld   5.10.14MR3
HALL,Alfred AtkinsonLt   RNR HM S/M D3   drd   15.3.18   MR3
HALL,C.L.   Maj   RMLI Portsmouth Div   29.7.18 CR Somerset126
HALL,Dudley Walter Rowland   Lt   RMLI 1Bn   dow   27.3.18   CR France145
HALL,Ernest Turrell TSub-Lt   RNR HMS Marsa   drd   17.11.17 MR1
HALL,Fitzroy Henry AComdr   RN   HMS Newmarket   kld   17.7.17MR3
HALL,Frederick Spencer   EngSubLt   RNR HMS Mantua   6.11.16CR Essex13
HALL,George Lt   RNR HMMS Blackmorevalekld   1.5.18 MR2

HALL,George Rome ALt RNR HMS Invincible kia 31.5.16MR3
HALL,Herbert Flt Lt RNAS HM Airship C27 kia 11.12.17 MR1
HALL,Joseph.DSC. EngLt RNR HMPMS Kempton kia 24.6.17 CR France1359
HALL,Oswald Probyn Lt RNR HMS Otranto drd 6.10.18 MR1
HALL,William Chpn&Instr RN HMS Venerable 4.11.16CR Devon1
HALL,W.J.H. Gnr RN HMS Diadem 5.2.15 CR Hamps5
HALL,William BrasierEngCmdr RN HMS Venerable ded 23.9.17 CR Glouc164
HALLETT,Percival Henry Gnr RN HMS Formidable kia 1.1.15 MR1
HALLETT,William Amos Shpt RN HMS Commonwealth 17.2.17 CR Kent46
HALLIDAY,Charles FrederickLt RNR HMS Black Prince kia 31.5.16MR3
HALLIDAY,Stephen Lionel Sub-Lt RN HMS Lark accdrd 3.2.16 MR1
HALLWRIGHT,William W.DSO. LtCmdr RN HMS Q16 21.4.17 CR Warwick9
HAM,Harry Bosn RN 11.17
HAM.Henry R.W. LtCmdr RN HMS President 18.3.16 CR Devon1
HAM,John Burtlett ChGnr RN HMS Excellent 31.3.21 CR Devon6
HAMBLY,John Richard ChGnr RN HMS Excellent ded 5.3.19 CR Hamps9
HAMILTON COX,Howard Jack Capt RMA att RN Siege Guns 22.10.17 CR Belgium24
HAMILTON,Alexander C. SubLt RNVR 188Bde MG Coy RNDiv 13.11.16 CR France339
HAMILTON,Alexander Douglas Peel ALt RMLI HMS Defence kia 31.5.16MR1
HAMILTON,Frederick Tower.GCVO.KCB.Sir Adml RN CinC Rosyth 4.10.17CR Scot139
HAMILTON,Gordon Midmn RNR HMS M25 kia 28.8.18 CR Europe179
HAMILTON,James.DSC. Ch Gnr RN HMTB No90 drd 25.4.18 MR2
HAMILTON,John Allan PMidmn RNR HMS Viknor drd 13.1.15 MR3
HAMMOND,Hilgrove Eng Comdr RN HMS Triumph kia 25.5.15MR2
HAMMOND,John William Gnr RN HM S/M K4 drd 31.1.18 MR3
HAMMOND,Stanley John Lt RNR HMS Rhododendron kia 5.5.18 MR1
HANCOCK,Isaac.MIDGnr RN HMS Mary Rose kia 17.10.17 MR2
HANCOCK,Reginald Lionel.DSO. Cmdr RN HMS Endeavour lost in HMS Comet kld 4.8.18 MR1
HANCOCK,Stanley George TMidmn RNR HMS Viknor drd 13.1.15 MR3
HANCOCK,Stanley Pearce.MID SubLt RNVR Hawke Bn RNDiv dedacc 2.6.16 CR France1545
HANCOCK,William Thomas Dignam Bosn RN HMS Liverpool 24.3.17 CR Italy17
HANLY,John Malby Bergin Lt RN HMS Queen Mary kia 31.5.16MR3
HANSON,Francis J. Lt RMLI 2RM Bn RNDiv 13.11.16 CR France339
HANSON,Oswald H Lt Comdr RNVR Benbow Bn RNDiv 11.10.14 CR Belgium365
HANWELL,Meynell Osborne Midmn RN HMS Defence kia 31.5.16MR2
HARDIMAN,Arthur Montague Midmn RN HMS Cornwallis kia 25.4.15MR1
HARDING,Albert Ewart PaymstrLt RNR HMS Colleen 10.12.18 CR Eire76
HARDING,Wilfrid John MC Chapn 4cl att Drake Bn RNDiv 31.10.17 MR30
HARDSTAFF,Leslie Hewitt Flt Lt RNAS Felixstowe AirStn attAdmlty Aero Test Staff kld 28.10.16 CR Kent65
HARDY,Guy B WO2 RNAS 4.16
HARDY,Philip Ernest Redford T2Lt RMLI 2 RM Bn RNDiv 28.4.17 MR20
HARDY,William Frank Sub-Lt RNVR Anson Bn RNDiv 25.8.18 MR16
HARDY,W.H. Lt RN HMS Badger 24.12.18 CR Europe6
HARLAND,Eustace William PFltOffRNAS kldacc 18.3.18 CR Yorks228
HARLOCK,Philip Lt RN HM S/M E37 kld 3.12.16MR3
HARMSWORTH,Vere Sidney Tudor Hon Lt RNVR Hawke Bn RNDiv 13.11.16 CR France339
HAROLD,Geoffrey Charles Midmn RN HMS Hogue kia 22.9.14MR1
HARPER,Colin Grahame Lt RN HMS Princess Irene kld 27.5.15MR3
HARPER,Maurice Harry de Jersey TSurg RN HMS Queen Mary kia 31.5.16MR3
HARRIS,George Alexander ATLt RNR HM S/M E24 kld 27.3.16MR3
HARRIS,Henry James TEng Sub-Lt RNR HMS Mechanician kia 29.1.18MR3
HARRIS,Joseph Orlando.DSO. SubLt RNVR Hawke Bn RNDiv dow 10.10.18 CR France380
HARRIS,Malcolm Alfred Milner Midmn RN HMS Defence kia 31.5.16MR2
HARRIS,Norman Midmn RN HMS Bulwark kld 26.11.14 MR3
HARRISON,Arthur Leyland.VC. Lt Cmdr RN HMS Lion kia 23.4.18 CR Belgium391
HARRISON,Douglas William TFlt Sub-Lt RNAS HMS Torrent kld 23.12.17 MR1
HARRISON,George Basil Lt Comdr RN HMS Natal kld 30.12.15 MR1
HARRISON,Gerard Younghusband Sub-Lt RN HMS Vanguard kld 9.7.17 MR1
HARRISON,Harold TSkipper RNR HMTrawler Drumtochtly kld 29.1.18MR1
HARRISON,Richard Gnr RN HMS Bayano kia 11.3.15MR3

HARRISON,Thomas Edmund Lt Comdr   RN   HMS Aboukir kia   22.9.14 MR1
HARRISON,Walter   Skipper(WO) RNR HMS Vasco de Gama ded   19.2.19   CR Yorks6
HARRISON,William Crawford   Lt Comdr   RN   HMS Formidable   kia   1.1.15 MR1
HARRY,F C   Sub-Lt RNVR Hawke Bn RNDiv   8.10.18 MR16
HART,Arthur Reginald   SubLt RNVR Hood Bn RNDiv   kia   13.11.16 CR France339
HATTON,Edward Allen Smeathman Capt   RMLI Chatham Bn RNDiv   29.4.15 CR Gallipoli30
HART,Bertram Welby FltSubLt   RNAS HMS Pembroke   acckld   24.1.15   CR Devon1
HART,John Churchward   Asst Paymr   RN   HMS Queen Mary   kia   31.5.16 MR3
HART,John William   Sub Lt RNVR Collingwood Bn RNDiv   4.6.15 MR4
HART,Maurice William   Asst Paymr   RN   HMS Hermes kia   31.10.14 MR1
HARTIGAN,T J   Surg   RN   HMS Espiegle   30.5.18 CR Egypt7
HARTLAND,Frederick George   Ch Carp   RN   HMS Monmouth   kia   1.11.14 MR2
HARTLEY,William Ernest   TNaval Instr RN   HMS Vanguard   kld   9.7.17 MR1
HARVEY,Arthur F   PTFltSubLt   RNAS   24.3.17 CR Ches182
HARVEY,Bernard Matheson Lt Comdr   RN   HMS Cressy kia   22.9.14 MR1
HARVEY,Charles Russell   Ft Paymr   RN   HMS Queen Nary   kia   31.5.16 MR3
HARVEY,Francis John William.VC. Maj   RMLI HMS Lion   kia   31.5.16 MR1
HARVEY,John Stephen   ATLt RNR HM S/M E49 kld   12.3.17 MR3
HARVEY,W. ChOff CG   HM Coastguard Wireless Tel Stn Rame Head   15.3.20 CR Cornwall138
HARVIE,Edward Alexander Gordon TSub-Lt   RNVR Anson Bn RNDiv   13.11.16 MR21
HASTIE,Alexander   Skipper   RNR HMTrawler drd   21.2.18   MR1
HATCH,George Cliffe Lt   RN   HMS Vehement   2.8.18 CR Lincs160
HATCH,H.R. Lt   RNR   17.5.17 CR EAfrica24
HATHORN,George Hugh Vans   Lt   RMLI HMS Formidable   kia   1.1.15 MR1
HATTERSLEY-SMITH,G.A. Lt   RN   HMS Lark   1.11.15 CR Devon1
HATTON,Edward Allen Smeathman Capt   RMLI Chatham Bn RNDiv   29.4.15 CR Gallipoli30
HAWKER,Frederick G.   ChGnr RN   HMS Vivid   9.10.17 CR Devon1
HAWKINS,Astley Ralph   Lt   RNR HMS Attentive ded   16.2.19   CR Kent7
HAWKINS,Claude Ernest Vincent   Lt   RN   HMS Erin   kia   23.4.18 CR Belgium391
HAWTHORN,Walter Lt Cmdr   RNR HMTrawler Columbia kia   1.5.15 MR1
HAY,Alan John   Clerk RN   HMS Defence kia   31.5.16 MR2
HAY,Douglas A   TFlt Sub-Lt   RNAS   9.15
HAYCOCK,Harry   Gnr   RN   HMS Gloucester   1.1.18 CR Italy17
HAYDON,Francis Chatterley Eng Lt Comdr RN   HMS Cressy kia   22.9.14 MR1
HAYES,Walter F   TLt RNVR Collingwood Bn RNDiv   4.6.15 MR4
HAYHOE,Frederick George   Skipper   RNR HMDrifter Frigate Bird   drd   11.3.18   MR1
HAYLES,Bernard Surman   WtEng RNR HMS Victory   16.5.15 CR Hamps5
HAYLES,Trevor George Lawless   Midmn RN   HMS Defence kia   31.5.16 MR2
HAYWARD,Arthur Frederick Lt   RMLI   10.5.15 CR Egypt6
HAYWARD,F Ch Offr   CG   31.7.19 CR Suffolk85
HAZARD,George C.J. Gnr   RN   HMS Jason   16.4.15 CR Scot902 G.C.T.
HAZEON,Cyril S.   Capt   RM   HMS Hampshire   drd   5.6.16 CR Scot900
HEAD,Charles Harold Evelyn LtCmdr   RN   HMS Vesuvius kldacc 22.5.15   CR Scot764
HEAD,Clement Gordon Wakefield   Lt Comdr   RN   HM S/M D2 kld   1.12.14 MR3
HEADLEY,Alfred Norman   TLt   RNR HM S/M E37 kld   3.12.16 MR3
HEALD,Ivan Lt   RNVR Hood Bn RNDiv   4.12.16 CR France924
HEALY,Richard May Art Eng   RN   HMS Good Hope   kia   1.11.14 MR3
HEAP,Thomas Reginald   Lt Comdr   RNR HMTrawler Burnley   kld   25.11.16 MR1
HEARN,Henry John.MID   Lt Comdr   RN   HM S/M K17 drd   31.1.18   MR1
HEARN,Henry Walter Edward   ALt   RN   HMS Pheasant kld   1.3.17 MR2
HEARN,John Henry Creamer EngLtCmdr   RN   HMS Saumarez   5.2.16 CR Devon1
HEASLEY,John W   Wt EngRNR   HMS Russell   28.4.16 CR Europe6
HEATH,Fred Charles SubLt RNR HMS Carol   ded   18.1.17   CR Scot252
HEATON-ELLIS,Michael   Sub-Lt RN   HMS Taurus   24.1.19 CR Middx29
HEBWORTH,Sidney Lt   RNVR Anson Bn RNDiv   dow   10.4.18   CR France62
HELBERT,A B   Flt Sub-Lt   RNAS HMS President II   29.8.17 CR Surrey160
HELLYER,Albert John   Carp RN   HMS Good Hope   kia   1.11.14 MR3
HENDERSON,Frank Hannam.CMG.DSO.   VAdml   HMS President ded   26.6.18   CR Hamps5
HENDERSON,P.D.   LtCmdr   RNR &Nigerian Marine   28.3.15 CR Cornwall23
HENDERSON,Richard   ASub-Lt   RN   HMS Invincible   kia   31.5.16 MR3

27

HENRY,Willoughby John   ASub-Lt&Adjt RNVR Anson Bn RNDiv   4.6.15 MR4
HENTON,Aubrey Warner   SubLt RNVR HMS Ark Royal attRNAS   kld   9.6.17 CR Greece9
HEPWORTH,Campbell Melville Willis CB Capt   RNR   25.2.19 CR Middx48
HERBERTSON,James Dougall   Lt   RNVR HMML No378 drd   30.11.19 MR3
HEREWYT DE ELEAS,Gervase A D Midmn RN   3.16
HERFORD,Bernard Henry   TLt   RM   Chatham Bn RNDiv   dow   2.5.15 MR1
HERFORD,Geoffrey Maurice Ivan   Capt   RMLI   HMS Monmouth   kia   1.11.14MR3
HERLIBY,Sidney Holloway   Gnr   RN   HMS Pheasant   kld   1.3.17 MR2 HERLIHY
HERON,Andrew   TLt   RNR   HMS Brilliant   18.9.16 CR Essex40
HERRING,Edwin Trueman   2Eng   HM Tug Grappler HM Dockyard Portsmouth kld   22.10.15 CR Hamps5
HERRIOTT,George Hodges   FltSubLt   RNAS   dedacc 6.11.17CR Kent25 HERRIOT
HERRON,William Robinson   AArt Eng   RN   HMS Good Hope   kia   1.11.14MR3
HERVEY,William B TLt   RNVR Airship C11   21.7.17 CR Surrey2
HESKETH,William Pemberton   TMidmn   RNR   HMS Nessus   kia   31.5.16MR2
HEWETSON,George Hayton Chapn RN   HMS Bulwark kld   26.11.14 MR3
HEWETSON,J.C.C.   SubLt   RN   HMS Royal Sovereign   23.8.19 CR Sussex178
HEWITT,Holt Charles TSub-Lt   RNVR Nelson Bn RNDiv   23.4.17 MR20
HEWITT,Joseph Hall Lt   RNVR HMS Arrogant ded   26.2.19   CR Surrey1
HEWLETT,Donald Graham   FtPaymr   RN   HMS St George   18.7.17 CR Greece7
HIBBERD,William Drummond   TLt   RNR   HMTug Chichester   accdrd 1.1.16 MR1
HIBBERT,Septimus   Surg   RNVR HMS Formidable   kia   1.1.15 MR1
HICKLEY,S.A.   Capt   RN   27.11.14 CR Kent268
HICKMAN,Henry Percy Valentine   Capt   RN   HMS Undaunted   ded   9.11.18CR Yorks619
HICKS,Edwin James Mate   RN   HMS Itchen   kia   6.7.17 MR2
HIGGINS,Kenneth Aislabie Longuet   ALt   RMLI   see LONGUET-HIGGINS,A.L.
HIGGS,Eric S. Lt   RNVR HMS Newbury   15.2.18 CR Kent83
HIGH,John   TSkipper   RNR   HMTrawler John High kld   7.8.16 MR3
HILL,Cuthbert Alexander   Midmn RN   HMS Invincible   kia   31.5.16MR3
HILL,E.   ArtEng RN   HMS Ceres   13.4.18 CR Yorks2
HILL,Edmund Arnott Lt   RN   HMS Formidable   kia   1.1.15 MR1
HILL,F.C.MC. Lt   RNVR HMS Excellent   2.8.19 CR Devon276
HILL,Frederick   SubLt   RNVR Hawke Bn RNDiv   25.12.17 CR France379
HILL,Henry   Eng Lt RNR   HMS Sarnia   kia   12.9.18MR3
HILL,Samuel G.   Lt   RNVR HM ML534   13.4.17 CR Italy6
HILLABY,Eric Crowther   TFlt Sub-Lt   RNAS 1Sqn kia   6.7.17 CR Belgium140
HILLAM,George   Skipper   RNR   HMTrawler Numitor kld   20.4.18MR1
HILLIARD,Gerald W Flt Sub-Lt   RN/RNAS   8.9.15 CR Norfolk85
HILLIER,P.C.A.   EngrCmdr   RN   HMS Colombo   30.10.18 CR Wilts87
HILLS,Henry Skipper   RNR   HMS Roche Castle   8.5.15 CR Wales168
HINDE,George Herbert   TSub-Lt   RNVR Howe Bn RNDiv   26.10.17 MR30
HINDLEY,Robert Muir   Paymstr   RNR   HMS Cullist kia   11.2.18 MR3
HINDMARSH,Michael Johnson   Eng Lt RNR   HMS Lady Cory Wright   kia   26.3.18MR3
HINE,John McLennan TEng Lt   RN   HMS Invincible   kia   31.5.16MR3
HINES,Reginald George   Eng Lt Comdr RN   HMS Turbulent   kia   1.6.16 MR3
HIRTZEL,George Henry   Eng Lt Comdr RN   HMS Hampshire   kld   5.6.16 MR3
HISLOP,John TSurg Prob   RNVR HMS Nessus   kia   31.5.16MR2
HITTER,George EdgarTSkipper   RNR   HMDrifter Pelagia   kld   28.11.16 MR16
HOADLEY,William Cecil   Midmn RNR   HMS Bittern   drd   4.4.18 MR2
HOARE,Harry MID   TCapt RM   1 RM Bn RNDiv   13.11.16 MR21
HOBBS,Owen Jardine SubLt RNVR Anson Bn RNDiv   13.11.16 CR France339
HOBBS,William R P Ch Schmstr   RN   HMS Victory   15.10.17 CR Hamps5
HOBSON,Matthew Brooks   Art Eng   RN   HMS Hampshire   kld   5.6.16 MR3
HOCKING,William   PTFlt Sub-Lt RNAS/RN   kld   21.4.16MR1
HODDINOTT,J.R.   EngCmdr   RN   HMS Toreador   9.10.18CR Hamps5
HODGE,Roy Norman Clare   TSub-Lt   RNR   HMS Viknor   drd   13.1.15   MR3
HODGES,Charles Raymond Walker   TFlt Sub-Lt   RNAS   18.8.17 MR20
HODGES,Leonard W. FltSubLt   RNAS   31.5.16 CR Iraq6
HODGMAN,William Henry Skipper   RNR   HMTrawler Lord Ridley   kld   10.5.17MR1
HODGSON,Edward Thomas Midmn RN   HMS Invincible   kia   31.5.16MR3
HODKINSON,Enoch Dennis Wt Tel RNR   HMS Tarlair   ded   14.11.18 CR Lancs24

28

HOGG,James TEng Sub-Lt RNR HMS Mavis kia 3.6.17 MR1
HOLBECK,Gilbert Stuart TSub-Lt RNR HMS Syria 25.8.16 CR Hamps5
HOLDEN,Charles TSkipper RNR HMTrawler Ben Earn 14.2.17 CR Lincs123
HOLDSWORTH,Wesley CopeSurg Prob RNVR HMS Begonia kia 6.10.17MR3
HOLLAMBY,George Reginald Billinghurst Lt RM 1RM Bn RNDiv 27.9.18 CR France530
HOLMES,Edmond C. Lt RN HMS Astraea 11.10.18 CR SAfrica158
HOLMES,Henry Clarence T2Lt RMLI 1 RM Bn RNDiv 28.4.17 MR20
HOLMES,J. Eng RM HMS Titania 21.7.20 CR Asia33
HOLROYD,Harold Sykes PFlOff RN RNAS kld 21.8.17CR Yorks715
HOLT,Cecil William Midmn RN HMS Hogue kia 22.9.14MR1
HOLTON,Alfred Edward.MC. Lt RMA HB 22.2.19 CR France34
HOOD,Horace Lambert Alexander.KCB.DSO.MVO.RAdml RN HMS Invincblekia 31.5.16MR3
HOOD,Martin Arthur Frankland Lt Cmdr RN 14.5.19 CR Lincs239
HOOD,Maurice Henry Nelson Hon TLt RNVR Hood Bn RNDiv 7.6.15 MR4
HOOD,Thomas Samuel Stanley TFlt Sub-Lt RNAS drd 26.4.17 MR1
HOOK,Robert Medway Sig Bosn RN HMS Black Prince 15.5.16 CR Scot900
HOOPER,Alfred Oswald Staff Surg RN HMS Natal kld 30.12.15 MR1
HOPCROFT,George Midmn RN HMS Queen Mary kia 31.5.16 MR3 HOPCRAFT
HOPE,William Hayhurst FltSubLt RNAS 1Wing dow 24.11.16 CR France598
HOPKINS,Cyril Burnett Mate (E) RN HMS Indefatigable kia 31.5.16MR3
HOPKINS,Istrian Victor Sub Lt RNR HMCMB No33A kia 12.4.18MR2
HOPPS,Hugh James Surg RN HMS Aboukir kia 22.9.14MR1
HORBURY,Arthur ChGnr RN HMS Bellerophon drd 3.12.14CR Scot899
HORDERN,Cedric TSurgProb RNVR HMS Kale ded 21.6.15 CR Scot253
HORNBY,Hugh Stanton Lt RN HM S/M C26 1.5.16 CR Kent5
HORNE,George TSkipper RNR HMTrawler Lena Melling kld 23.4.16MR1
HORNER,William Frith.DSC. Flt Comdr(ALt)RNAS(RN) HM Airship P4 drd 21.12.17 MR1
HORROCKS,Frank TAsst Paymr RNR HMS Redbreast kia 15.7.17MR2
HORSEY,Arthur Mather Surg Prob RNVR HMS Recruit kld 9.8.17 MR2
HORSFIELD,John Nixon Lt RNVR Hawke Bn RNDiv 19.6.15 CR Gallipoli1 V.
HORSWELL,Bazil Whittle TFlt Sub-Lt RNAS kld 11.10.17 CR Middx39
HORWOOD,Frederick John ADiv Offr CG Wireless Tel Stn HMCG Sheerness 8.2.18 CR Kent67
HOSKYNS-ABRAHALL,Christopher Henry Maj RMLI Portsmouth Bn RNDiv dow 4.5.15 MR3
HOUGH,John Elswood Chaffey Flt Sub-Lt RNAS 24.10.17 MR20
HOUGHTON,Reginald Robert Rees EngLt RNR HMS Camito ded 27.2.19 CR Lancs18
HOULDSWORTH,H.J. SubLt RN HMS President 23.2.19 CR Warwick112
HOUSE,Joseph.DSC. EngLt RN HMS Verulam 3.9.19 MR70
HOUSTON-STEWART,William TFlt Sub-Lt RNAS 26.5.17 CR Belgium390
HOWARD,Andrew Capt RAF ex RNVR (2Lt)Ass Paymr HMS Carribean 28.10.19 CR Lancs8
HOWARD,George William TSkipper RNR HMTrawler Remindo kld 2.2.18 MR1
HOWARD,Henry V. SubLt RNVR Howe Bn 13.11.16 CR France1490
HOWELL,John Henry SubLt RNR HMS Astraea 3.7.16 CR Wales219
HOWELLS,John Francis SurgLt RN attRAMC 19FA ded 6.11.18CR France332
HOWLETT,James Frederick TSkipper RNR HMDrifter Datum kia 26.10.16 MR1
HUDDLESTON,Leslie G TPFlt Offr RNAS 22.1.18 CR London28 HUDDLESTONE
HUDDY,John ALt RNR HMS Bayano kia 11.3.15MR3
HUDSON,W.C. SubLt RNVR HMYacht Jason II 7.11.18CR Essex185
HUDSON,William Henry Fisher Eng Lt Comdr RN HMS Defence kia 31.5.16MR2
HUGHES,Basil Frederick Murray TFlt Sub-Lt RNAS accdrd 1.12.15CR Europe23
HUGHES,George Henry William TSub-Lt RNVR Anson Bn RNDiv 28.4.17 MR20
HUGHES,Hugh Robert ALt RNR HMS Bulwark kld 26.11.14 MR3
HUGHES,J. SurgProb RNVR HMS Arabis RNDiv 11.2.16 CR Germany2
HUGHES,John TLt RNR 4.16
HUGHES,Robert TAsst Paymr RNR HMS Folkestone on HMS Louvain kia 20.1.18MR2
HULBERT,E.W.L.R. SubLt RNVR Hood Bn RNDiv 25.5.18 CR France233
HULME,Thomas Ernest TLt RMA Naval Siege Bty kia 28.9.17CR Belgium24
HUMBLE,Edward William George TEng RNR HMS Bayano kia 11.3.155 MR3
HUME,John Douglas DSC TFlt Lt RNAS HMS Presidentkld 10.12.16 CR Kent67
HUMPHREY,Edmund William Alfred ALt RNR HMS Formidable kia 1.1.15 MR1
HUMPHREY,Ernest F. Lt RNR HMS Spey 7.3.17 CR Kent46

29

HUMPHREYS,Arthur Idwal   Lt   RNVR Howe Bn RNDiv   kia   5.2.17 CR France383
HUMPHREYS,Ernest Evan   Lt   RNVR HMS Tarlair   14.1.19 CR Devon3
HUMPHRYS,Frederick James Surg   RN   11Sqn Armoured Cars RNAS dow   5.9.15 CR Gallipoli27
HUNNINGS,Robert Percy   Bosn   RN   HMS Duncan accdrd 4.3.17 MR1
HUNT,Ernest John   Gnr   RN   HM S/M H10   kld   19.1.18 MR1
HUNT,George Percy Edward.DSO.   Capt   RN   HMS Vivid   22.8.17 CR Heref&Worc90
HUNT,H.L.   2Lt   RMA Siege Guns   kia   29.5.18 CR Belgium24
HUNT,John Thomas   WtEng RN   HMS Rugby   22.9.20 CR Kent46
HUNT,William Clarke Ch Gnr RN   HMS Invincible   kia   31.5.16 MR3
HUNTER,George M.   WtEng RNR   HMS Hampshire   drd   5.6.16 CR Scot900
HUNTER,George   SubLt RNVR Drake Bn RNDiv   kia   21.8.18 CR France1485
HUNTER,William   Lt   RNR   HM S/M E4   15.8.16 CR Suffolk130
HUNTER,William   SubLt RNVR Anson Bn RNDiv   4.1.18 CR France668
HURREN,Robert George.DSC.   TSkipper   RNR   HMDrifter Gleaner of the Sea kia   26.10.16 MR1
HURST,Allan James   Art Eng   RN   HMS Shark   drd   31.5.16 CR Europe178A Allen
HURST,Charles Edwin   TEng Comdr   RNR   HMS Laurentic   kld   25.1.17 MR2
HURST,N.   EngSubLt   RNR   RFA Reliance   9.10.18 CR Greece10
HUTCHIESON,G.P.   SubLt RNVR HMS Pactolus   14.12.20 CR Glouc9
HUTCHINGS,John   Comdr RN   HMS Natal   kld   30.12.15 MR1
HUTCHINGS,John Percy   Gnr   RN   HMS Fortune kia   1.6.16 MR3
HUTCHINSON,Ernest Henry Lt   RNR   10.1.20 CR Somerset197
HUTCHINSON,Thomas   Bosn (Retd)   RN   8.15
HUTCHINSON,William Scrope   ASub-Lt   RN   HMS Invincible   kia   31.5.16 MR3
HUTCHISON,Thomas McLaren   Sub-Lt RNVR HMS Black Prince   kia   31.5.16 MR3
HUTTON,Illtyd Arthur Stewart   Cmdr   RN   HMS Tamar   ded   2.4.21 CR Asia20
HUTTON,James   Wt EngRNR HMS Tara   kia   5.11.15 MR2
HUTTON,Ronald Winder   Capt   RMA   att Egyptian Army   3.4.17 CR EAfrica116
HUTTY,Alfred Irving SubLt RNAS   21.8.17 CR France1359
HYDE,John Brasons MID   Eng Lt Cmdr   RN   HMS Sable   25.10.18 CR London12
HYLAND,John Edward   2Lt   RMLI Portsmouth Bn RNDiv   10.5.15 MR45
HYSLOP,John William   TSub-Lt   RNR   HMS Champagne   kia   9.10.17 MR2

I

ILIFF,Alan Chadwick   Sub-Lt RNVR Nelson Bn RNDiv   20.6.15 CR Gallip[oli14
INCH,John Lumsden   TSkipper   RNR   HMS Prize   kia   14.8.17 MR2
INGHAM,Joshua M   TFlt Sub-Lt   RNAS   3.17
INGLE,Jack Alexander   AsstPaymstr   RNR   HMS Anchusa kia   16.7.18 MR2
INGLES-CHAMBERLAYNE,Rupert Henry   Midmn RN   HMS Hawke kia   15.10.14 MR1
INGMIRE,Gilbert Maynard   AssPaymr   RNR   HMS Dalhousie   7.8.16 CR Iraq6
INMAN,Edward Tyrrell   Comdr RN   HMS Simoom kia   23.1.17 MR1
INNES,William   Skipper   RNR   HMDrifter Norfolk County   25.3.18 CR Europe6
INSKIP,Sydney Hope Elsdale Lt   RMLI kia   23.4.18 CR Essex1
INWOOD,Arthur William   Wt EngRNR HMS Aboukir kia   22.9.14 MR1
IRELAND,de Courcy Wyndor Plankett SqnCmdr   RNAS   21.2.16 CR Kent46
IRELAND,Ralph   Lt Comdr   RN   HMS Southampton   drd   19.1.17   MR3
IRELAND,Thomas Berry   ABosn RN   HMS Monmouth   kia   1.11.14 MR2
IRVINE,James Lt   RNR   HMTrawler Corona   23.3.16 CR Kent28
ISAAC,Frederick William   ChGnr RN   HMS Charguinola   drd   30.1.19   CR Hamps9
ISAACS,Walter Albert FltSubLt   RNAS   3.11.17 CR Essex7
ISITT,Robert   Ch Carp   RN   HMS New Zealand   10.12.16 CR Middx15
IVES,Derrick Sub-Lt RN   HM S/M H10   kld   19.1.18 MR1
IXER,Sydney Henry Howard   Lt   RNVR HMS Constance   dow   20.8.18   CR Hamps51

J

JACKETT,William Robert   Gnr   RN   HMS Queen Mary   kia   31.5.16   MR3

JACKMAN,John   Gnr   RN   HMS Paragon kia   18.3.17 MR1

JACKSON,Charles George   TLt   RNVR/RNAS   ded   6.2.17 CR Middx26

JACKSON,Edward George Oliphant   TFlt Sub-Lt   RNAS   HM Airship C17   kia   21.4.17 MR1

JACKSON,Francis L H   TLt   RNVR Howe Bn RNDiv   26.10.17 CR Belgium125

JACKSON,John Metcalfe   Cmdr   RN   SurveyingTrawler Daisy   7.3.18 CR Kent7

JACKSON,Joseph   Lt   RMLI   HMS Iris   23.4.18 CR Lancs34

JACOBS,Trevor   SubLt   RNVR Hood Bn RNDiv   4.2.17 CR France514

JAGGER,Oliver Robin Octavius   Midmn RN   HMS Bulwark kld   26.11.14 MR3

JAMES,David Thomas Emyr   Lt   RNR   HMS Laurentic   kld   25.1.17 MR2

JAMES,Henry Skipper   RNR   HMTrawler Elise   kia   22.9.18 MR1

JAMES,Samuel George   TSub-Lt   RNVR Hood Bn RNDiv   9.10.17 CR Belgium92

JAMESON,Arthur George   Lt Comdr   RN   HN S/M D2   23.11.14 MR3

JAMESON,Harold Walter   TSkipper   RNR   HMTrawler Ruby   kia   17.10.17 MR1

JAMIESON,Andrew   Lt&QM   RMLI   Chatham Div   13.8.19 CR Kent46

JAMIESON,Thomas   TEng Lt   RNR   HMS Laurentic   kld   25.1.17 MR2

JAQUES,William   2Lt   RMLI   1Bn   dow   30.12.17 CR France398

JARVIS,Hugh Townley   TEng Sub-Lt   RNR   HMS Calgarian   kia   1.3.18 MR3

JAUNCEY,Henry Cyril Adlum   Sub-Lt RN   HMS Defence kia   31.5.16 MR2

JEFFERS,Percival Thomson Edward   ATLt   RNR   HMTB No11   kld   7.3.16 MR2

JEFFERSON,Ingleby Stuart   Lt   RN   HM S/M C34 kia   21.7.17 MR3

JEFFERY,Richard Gilbert   Eng Lt RN   HMS Carnarvon   ded   6.10.14 MR2

JEFFREYS,Robert   Comdr RN   HMS Clan Mcnaughton   drd   3.2.15 MR1

JEHRING,William Ernest   TSub-Lt   RNVR Nelson Bn RNDiv   28.10.17 MR30

JENKIN,Conrad   Lt   RN   HMS Warspite ded   24.12.16 CR Scot899

JENKINS,James Reed Gnr   RN   HMS Exe   kld   27.3.18 MR3

JENKINSON,George Eric   Lt   RN   HM S/M H3   kld   15.7.16 MR3

JENNINGS,Herbert.J. Gnr   RN   HMS Hampshire   drd   5.6.16 CR Scot900

JENNINGS,Harry Clarence   Lt   RN   HM S/M L55   kia   9.6.19 CR Hamps5

JEPHSON,George Douglas   Cmdr   RN   HMS Dartmouth   ded   7.2.16 CR France1776

JERMAIN,Philip Lloyd Lawless   T2Lt   RM   Portsmouth Bn RNDiv   24.6.15 MR4

JERRAM,Harry Escombe Ravenhill   Midmn RN   HMS Hawke   kia   15.10.14 MR1

JEWELL,Cyril FltSubLt   RNAS   (Stonehenge)   8.2.18 CR Kent143

JOEL,Edgar Cecil   Lt   RNR   HMS Clan McNaughton   drd   3.2.15 MR1

JOHNS,Alfred Thomas   Art Eng   RN   HMS Monmouth   kia   1.11.14 MR2

JOHNS,William   Carp   RN   HMS Cochrane   accdrd   10.4.17   MR3

JOHNSON,Alan Archibald   TLt   RNVR Drake Bn RNDiv   30.12.17 MR21

JOHNSON,Colin   Flt Lt   RNAS   acckld 17.3.16   CR Kent47

JOHNSON,George Moore   TSurg RN   HMS Defence kia   31.5.16 MR2

JOHNSON,Henry.DSC.   TLt   RNR   HMS Vala   kia   21.8.17 MR3

JOHNSON,J. Skipper   RNR   HMTrawler John Cowarden   28.11.18 CR Lancs48

JOHNSON,Oswald Maughan   Sub-Lt RN   HMS Pheasant kld   1.3.17 MR2

JOHNSON,Robert Warren   Capt   RN   HMS Cressy   kia   22.9.14 MR1

JOHNSON,William Charles Michael   TLt   RNR   HMS Viknor   drd   13.1.15   MR3

JOHNSTON,Alexander Keith   TAsst Paymr   RNR   HMS Defence kia   31.5.16 MR2

JOHNSTON,David Keith   Flt Lt   RNAS see KEITH-JOHNSTON,David

JOHNSTON,James   TSurg Prob   RNVR HMS Alcantara   kia   29.2.16 MR3

JOHNSTON,James Barlow   SubLt   RNVR Hawke Bn RNDiv   8.10.18 CR France403

JOHNSTON,Macfie Keith   see KEITH-JOHNSTON,Macfie

JOHNSTON,Philip Andrew   ATFlt Comdr RNAS   17.8.17 MR20

JOHNSTON,Randal William McDonnell Midmn   RN   HMS Vanguard   kld   9.7.17 MR1

JOHNSTON,William TFlt Sub-Lt   RNAS RNR   kld   20.1.18 MR1

JOHNSTON,William   Sub Lt RNVR Anson Bn RNDiv   17.11.18 CR Europe149

JOHNSTONE,Arthur Townsend   Comdr RN   HMS Defence kia   31.5.16 MR2

JOHNSTONE,Herbert Kenneth   TSub-Lt   RNVR Hawke Bn RNDiv attRFC 22Sqn   kia   3.12.17 CR France31

JOHNSTONE,Leopold Edward   ASub-Lt   RN   HMS Invincible   kia   31.5.16MR3
JONES,August C.   FltSubLt   RNAS   27.6.17 CR France1359
JONES,Charles   TSen Eng   RNR   HMS Bayano   kia   11.3.15MR3
JONES,Charles John   Gnr   RN   HMS Queen Mary   kia   31.5.16MR3
JONES,C H   Lt   RNVR   27.10.18 CR Yorks114
JONES,Cyril Oscar Howe   TSurg   RN   HMS Invincible   kia   31.5.16   MR3
JONES,Edward Lewis   Lt   RNR   HMS Queen Victoria   1.12.18CR Warwick3
JONES,Eynon Llewellyn   Sub-Lt   RNR   HMS Indefatigable   kia   31.5.16MR2
JONES,Francis   TSkipper   RNR   HMTrawler Speeton   kld   31.12.15 MR1
JONES,Frederic Percival   Eng Lt   RN   HMS Begonia   kia   6.10.17MR3
JONES,Henry Platen Lewis   Midmn   RN   see LEWIS-JONES,H.P.
JONES,Henry.DSC.   Lt   RNR   HMTrawler Sapper   kld   29.12.17 MR3
JONES,Herbert Owen   TAsst Paymr   RNR   HMS India   8.8.15 CR Europe131
JONES,John Cecil   Asst Paymr   RNR   HMS Hawke   kia   15.10.14 MR1
JONES,Loftus William.VC.   Comdr   RN   HNS Shark   kia   31.5.16CR Europe178A
JONES,Myrddin Emrys   SurgLt   RN   HMS Indomitable   4.12.18CR Wales462
JONES,Richard Hugh   TEng   RNR   HMS Clan Mcnaughton   drd   3.2.15 MR1
JONES,Stuart Gale   VD   Lt Cmdr   RNVR Hawke Bn RNDiv   kia   25.8.18 CR France578
JONES,Thomas Elwyn   TNaval Instr   RN   HMS Defence   kia   31.5.16MR2
JONES,Valentine Howard Sutton   Capt   RMLI   1 RM Bn   8.5.17 CR Hamps6
JONES,William Basil Loxdale.MID   TFlt Obs   RNAS   drd   7.1.18 MR1
JONES,William George   Ch Gnr   RN   HMS Indefatigable   kia   31.5.16MR2
JONES,William Hamley   Lt   RN   HM MFR Ungeni   ded   2.1.16 CR Scot900
JONES-PARRY,Jeffreys Ivor   Sub-Lt   RNR   HMS Wolverine   kia   28.4.15MR3
JUKES,Ronald Worthington   TSub-Lt   RNVR Collingwood Bn RNDiv   4.6.15 MR4
JUTSAM,J N   Skipper   RNR   HMS St George   20.6.16 CR Middx39

K

KANAAR,John Adrian Gerard   PMidmn   RNR   HMS Hampshire   kld   5.6.16 MR3
KANE,James F.   SubLt   RNR   HMYacht Zarefah   8.5.17 CR Scot900
KAY,Thomas Henry   TSkipper   RNR   HMTrawler Vivanti   drd   7.3.17 MR2
KAYLL,Hugh Oswald   Lt   RNVR HMS Colleen   11.12.18 CR Eire301
KEABLE,H.B.   Lt   RNVR HMS Manxman   11.9.15 CR Italy61
KEAN,Cuthbert Benedict   ATLt   RNR   HMS Jessamine in SS Cooray   kia   29.8.17MR1
KEARNEY,Charles Henry   T2Lt   RMLI   2 RM Bn RNDiv   28.4.17 MR20
KEARNEY,William Arthur   Wt Mech   RN   HMS Warspite   30.8.16 CR NIreland37
KEARNS,Michael   Sig Bosn   RN   HMS Defence   kia   31.5.16MR2
KEEN,William E   Wt Eng   RNR   HMS Cressy   kia   22.9.14 MR1
KEIGHLEY,Harold Sugden   SubLt   RN   HMS Julius   ded   8.1.21 CR Sussex144
KEIGHTLEY,Gordon   TSub-Lt   RNVR/RNAS   20.5.17 MR40
KEITH,Clive Arthur   Midmn   RN   HMS Hawke   kia   15.10.14 MR1
KEITH-JOHNSTON,David   Flt Lt   RNAS   kia   10.8.15CR Belgium173
KEITH-JOHNSTON,Macfie   TFlt Sub-Lt   RNAS   12.9.15 CR Kent67
KELL,Philip Arthur Graham   Lt   RNR   HMS Cressy   kia   22.9.14MR1
KELLAND,R.S.   SubLt   RNVR Hawke Bn RNDiv   20.5.18 CR France1013
KELLETT,Richard Pinder   Lt   RN   HMS Flirt   kia   26.10.16 MR3
KELLY,Frederick S.DSC.   LtCmdr   RNVR Hood Bn RNDiv   13.11.16 CR France232
KEMP,A.J.   Lt   RNR   HMYacht Alchymist   22.10.18 CR Devon3
KEMP,Ernest   Wt Tel   RN   HMS Invincible   kia   31.5.16MR3
KEMP,Frederick Robert   Skipper   RNR   HMT Ameer   kld   18.3.16CR Yorks2
KEMP,Horace   Skipper   RNR   HMDrifter Launch Out   29.10.16 CR Suffolk86
KEMP,John Archibald   Lt   RN   HMS Tipperary   kia   1.6.16 MR3
KEMPSON,John Reginald   Midmn   RN   HMS Hawke   kia   15.10.14 MR1
KENDALL,Edward Hext   TFlt Sub-Lt   RNAS   kld   12.7.17CR Belgium132
KENNEDY,Alec Norman   ALt   RN   HMS Torrent   kld   23.2.17MR3
KENNEDY,Cecil Gordon   TMidmn   RNVR HMS Narbrough   drd   12.1.18   MR3
KENNEDY,Fergus   EngSubLt   RN   HMS Rowan   28.8.18 CR Scot752

KENNEDY,Patrick S TFlt Sub-Lt   RNAS   26.9.16 CR Lincs78
KENNY,Bernard William   TSub-Lt   RNVR Nelson Bn RNDiv   19.12.15 MR415
KENNY,Henry Alexander Harold Symonds Sub-Lt   RNVR Anson Bn RNDiv   26.3.18 MR20
KENT,B.R.G.DSO.   Lt   RNR   HMSOtranto   6.10.18CR Scot32
KEOGH,John Ambrose   Surg Cmdr   RN   HMS Pembroke   5.2.19 CR Middx26
KEOHANE,Denis   ChBosn   RN   HMS Victory   9.1.18 CR Hamp5
KER,David R TFlt Sub-Lt   RNAS see KERR,D R
KER,William TLt   RNVR Hawke Bn RNDiv   13.11.16 MR21
KERR,David,Ross   FltSubLt   RNAS   11.11.17 CR Kent25
KERR,John.DSO.   Lt   RNR   HMS Mitchell   27.2.18 CR Devon1
KETT,Ernest Charles Eng Lt RNR HMS Otranto   drd   6.10.18MR1
KEWNEY,George Stanley   Chapn & Instr RN   HMS Queen Mary   kia   31.5.16MR3
KIDD,Sydney James Rewa   EngLt RNR   HMS Polly Bridge   14.10.18 CR Essex1
KILLHAM,G.F.   ChGnr   RN   HMS Vesuvius   28.5.18 CR Hamps9
KILNER,Bertram Denison   Flt Cmdr   RNAS   drd   6.10.18MR1
KILNER,Harold   TSub-Lt   RNVR Anson Bn RNDiv   13.11.16 MR21
KINCAID,Frank   TEng   RNR   HMS Clan McNaughton   drd   3.2.15 MR1
KING,Christopher   Lt   RNR   HMS Albyn   2.9.17   CR France1359
KING,George.W.   Gnr   RN   HMTrawler Tenby Castle   7.2.18 CR Scot1014
KING,George Alfred   Gnr   RN   HMS Crusader accdrd   21.1.17   MR3
KING,Henry Stuart   ASub-Lt   RN   HMS Indefatigable   kia   31.5.16MR2
KING,Joseph R   ATLt Comdr   RNR   HMTrawler Marion   kld   23.2.18MR3
KING,Patrick John   Eng Lt Comdr RN   HMS Indefatigable   kia   31.5.16MR2
KING,Percival EngLtCmdr   RN   HNMS Winchester   ded   23.10.19 CR Devon68
KING,Thomas Gerrard Wt Mech   RN   HMS Aboukir kia   22.9.14MR3
KING,Vernon Lt   RM   attRAF kia   11.4.18CR France95
KING,William Edward   Gnr   RN   HMS Bulwark kld   26.11.14 MR3
KINGCOME,William John Hore   PaymstrLt   RN   Devonport Barracks   11.8.18 CR Devon3
KINGDOM,William Wilfred AGnr RN   HMS Good Hope   kia   1.11.14MR2
KINNEAR,George Robertson Gnr RN   HMS Queen Mary   kia   31.5.16MR3
KIPPIN,Alfred George TSkipper   RNR   HMTrawler Picton Castle   kld   19.2.17MR2
KIRKLAND,John Stuart   Sub-Lt RN   HMS Turbulent   kia   1.6.16 MR3
KITCHIN,Geoffrey Gordon   ASub-Lt   RN   HMS Queen Mary   kia   31.5.16MR3
KLEMP,Charles Thomas   ATLt RNR   HM S/M E4   drd   15.8.16MR3
KNEEL,Jack Arthur Charles   Asst Clerk   RN   HMS Defence kia   31.5.16MR2
KNIGHT,Alfred Robert   TSub-Lt   RNVR Hawke Bn RNDiv   13.11.16 MR21
KNIGHT,N.T.CIE.   EngCapt   RIM   18.10.18 MR66
KNIGHT,Ronald V.   FltSubLt   RNAS   12.3.17CR Somerset186
KNIGHT,Stanley Charles   Lt   RMA   A/A Bde   12.7.15CR Belgium171
KRIKORIAN,Charles Fielding Lt   RNVR 2Drake Bn RNDiv   ded   22.5.16CR Dorsetp
KYNASTON,A.E.F.   Surg   RN   HMS Devonshire   13.10.14 CR Scot926

L

LAIDLAW,Robert Stewart   Lt   RN   lent to RAN HMS Melbourne ded   23.4.19 MR2
LAING,Henry George Stobart Lt   RN   HMS Indefatigable   kia   31.5.16MR2
LAIRD,Arthur H   Asst Paymr   RNR/RNAS   28.3.16 CR London30
LAIRD,John Knox.CB.   Capt   RN   SNO Aberdeen   21.12.20 CR Scot281
LAKE,Frederick   TSkipper   RNR   HMS Prize   kia   14.8.17MR2
LAKE,J.H.   ChOff CG   HM CoastguardStn Sunderland   12.9.19 CR Durham27
LAKE,William Addison   T2Lt   RMLI 2 RM Bn RNDiv   28.4.17 MR20
LAMB,R.M.   Lt   RNVR Hood Bn RNDiv   16.7.19 CR Scot253
LAMBE,Michael Joseph   AArt Eng(WO) RN   HMS Indefatigable   kia   31.5.16MR2
LAMBERT,Harry Ernest   WtWardMstr   RN   RN Hospital   17.12.19 CR Wales402
LAMONT,A.DSC.   Lt   RNR   HMS Asteria   21.9.19 CR Asia51
LANDALE,Walter Luke   Lt   RN   HM S/M E18 kld   11.6.16MR3
LANE,Arthur E.   EngLt RN   HM S/M K13   drd   29.1.17   CR Scot81
LANE,Arthur Geoffrey Napier LtCmdr   RN   HMS Assistance   8.11.18CR Warwick19

33

LANE,Edward Reginald MacDonald Lt   RN   HM S/M H3   kld   15.7.16MR3
LANE,Jeremiah   Bosn RN   HMS Marlborough   12.2.19 CR Kent46
LANE,Julius Albert   Cmdr RN   HMS Columbine   19.10.15 CR Hamps5
LANE,Thomas Edward   Mate RN   HMS Ocean   kia   13.3.15MR2
LANE-POOLE,Francis Gainsborough Capt   RMA   23.12.15 CR Middx26
LANG,Hugh   TEng Sub-Lt   RNR   HMYacht Eriska   accdrd 2.1.17 MR2
LANGFORD,John Alfred   SubLt RNVR Drake Bn RNDiv   13.11.16 CR France701
LANGFORD,M.H.DSO.   SurgLtCmdr   RN   HMS Challenger   15.12.18 CR EAfrica36
LANGSTONE,Harold C.   F/O   RNAS   22.1.18 CR France1844
LANGSTRETH,Edmund   SubLt RNVR Nelson Bn RNDiv   13.11.16 CR France339
LANYON,James   Lt   RN   HMS Vivid   drd   28.12.17 MR2
LARKING,Alfred George   TMidmn   RNR   HMS Hampshire   kld   5.6.16 MR3
LARMOUR,Edward Archibald Rice   TEng Lt   RNR   HMS Laurentic   kld   25.1.17MR2
LARTER,Norman IvanTFlt Sub-Lt   RNAS   drd   9.12.17MR1
LATHAM,Leslie Stephen   Gnr   RN   HMS Bittern   drd   4.4.18 MR2
LATTEY,Alexander Davidson Midmn RN   HMS Hawke   kia   15.10.14 MR1
LAUGHTON,Bertram Douglas   TSub-Lt   RNVR Hawke Bn RNDiv attRFC   dow   1.10.17CR Belgium18
LAVIGNE,Joseph Louis   PFltOffRNAS   acckld 15.4.17   CR Essex9
LAW,Cecil Robert de Vaux   Sub-Lt RN   HMS Indefatigable   kia   31.5.16MR2
LAW,Harry D. Cmdr   RN   HMS Victory   20.10.17 CR Hamps234
LAW,Herbert Lt   RNR   HMTrawler Achilles IIkld   26.6.18MR1
LAWLER,E.A. Gnr   RN   HMS Strenuous   30.3.20 CR Hamps4
LAWRENCE,Henry William   Ch Gnr RN   HMS Dido   8.2.17 CR Hamps5
LAWRENCE,Robert Reginald.MID Lt   RNVR HMS Queen Cmdg HM ML506   ded   31.1.19   CR Italy6
LAWRENCE,Samuel Louis   WtOrdnanceOff RN   HMS Vivid   ded   2.4.20 CR Devon3
LAWRIE,George Hume   TSub-Lt   RNVR Hood Bn RNDiv   30.12.17 MR21
LAWS,G.V.   Lt   RNVR   3.12.19CR Hamps220
LAWS,Henry Alexander   EngSubLt   RNR   HMS Egmont   19.10.18 CR Essex287
LAWSON,Frederick Herman ATLt RNR   HMS Dundee kia   16.3.17MR3
Le MESURIER,Charles E.CB. Capt   RN   HMS Calliope   10.11.17 CR Hamps195 Comdore2Cl
LE PAGE,Edward James   TEng Sub-Lt RNR   HMS Alcantara   kia   29.2.16MR3
LE PATOUREL,Wallace Mackenzie Chapn RN   HMS Defence kia   31.5.16MR2
LE SEELLEUR,Gordon J.   SubLt RNVR Drake Bn RNDiv   11.8.17 CR France1191
LE SEELLEUR,John Thomas Lt   RMLI   HMS Invincible   kia   31.5.16MR2
LEAF,Alfred Walter   WtShptRN   HMS Fox   26.3.19 CR Kent46
LEATHER,Gerald   Lt   RN   HMS Pathfinder   kia   5.9.14 MR1
LEATHWOOD,John Pearson AGnr   RN   HMS Aboukir kia   22.9.14MR1
LEE,Bernard Richards TFlt Sub-Lt RNAS   drd   15.2.16   MR1
LEE,Cedric   SubLt RNVR Anson Bn RNDiv   13.11.16 CR France339
LEE,Charles Alexander.RD. Cmdr RIM   Ex RNR   ded   6.2.18 CR Italy6
LEE,Douglas Baillie   Asst Paymr RN   HMS Monmouth   kia   1.11.14MR2
LEE,George.MIDx2   ATLt RNR   HMTrawler Remarko kld   3.12.16MR1
LEE,Reginald Arthur   EngLtCmdr   RN   HMS Violent   25.10.18 CR Devon6
LEE,Robert Thomas Hawton Valentine Ch Gnr   RN   HMS Monmouth   kia   1.11.14MR2
LEE,William James   Gnr   RN   HMS Motagua kld   19.3.18MR1
LEES,Charles Cunningham Dumville Lt   RN   HMS Verulam kld   3.9.19 MR1
LEES,John Arnold   Lt Comdr   RN   HMS Monmouth   kia   1.11.14 MR2
LEES,Robert H.   SubLt RNR   HMS Arabis   16.12.15 CR NIreland181
LEGARD,William Remmington DSO TMaj (LtComdr)RMA(RN)   23.7.17 CR Middx16
LEGGE,Walter H   TSub-Lt(Lt)   RNVR att RFC   11.2.17 CR Essex40
LEIGH-CARTE,Edward Alexander   SubLt RNR   HMS Overton   17.11.16 CR Greece7
LEIGHTON,A.A.DSM.   SubLt RNVR Hawke Bn RNDiv   3.9.18 CR France1252
LEMARCHARD,Francis Wharton   SurgSubLt   RNVR HMS Phoebe   12.2.19 CR Devon17
LEMON,Hubert Charles MID TFlt Lt RNAS   kld   28.2.18CR London27
LEMON,Randolph Charles   Midmn RNR   HMS Exe   kld   27.3.18CR Kent46
LEONARD,William Henry   Art Eng   RN   HMS Russell   28.4.16 CR Europe6
LESLEY,Henry Norman   Lt   RN   HM S/M G9   drd   16.9.17   MR3
LESMOND,Gerald Lawrence TSub-Lt   RNVR HMPMS Duchess of Montrosekld   18.3.17MR3
LETLEY,Leonard William   Midmn RNR   HMS Excellent   drd   27.4.19   MR3
LEVER,F.K.   Midmn RNR   PC 69   8.10.18CR Lancs170

LEWES,Price Vaughan.CB.DSO.   Capt   RN   HMS Superb   9.11.14CR Devon3
LEWIN,Joseph TLt   RNR   HMTrawler Robert Smith   kld   20.7.17MR1
LEWIS,Albert Edward Gnr   RN   HMS Challenger   8.3.15 CR WAfrica61
LEWIS,Charles Anthony   Lt   RNVR HMS Egmont   17.12.18 CR Greece17
LEWIS,Charles Williams   TSurg RN   HMS Queen Mary   kia   31.5.16MR3
LEWIS,David Llewellyn   Surg Lt RN   HMS Pembroke   2.3.19 CR Essex40
LEWIS,Frank LtCmdr   RN   HMS Vivid   28.3.16 CR Devon1
LEWIS,Frank Concanen   FltSubLt   RNAS   kia   21.8.17CR France285
LEWIS,Frederick George   ALt   RNR   HMS Clan Mcnaughton   drd   3.2.15 MR1
LEWIS,H.   EngSubLt   RNR   HMS Kildonan Castle   4.12.18CR Essex13
LEWIS,Ivor Morgan   Chapn RN   HMS Goliath kia   13.5.15MR1
LEWIS,James Christopher Francis   Lt   RN   HMS Castor   accdrd 26.4.18   MR3
LEWIS-JONES,Henry Platen Midmn RN   HMS Hawke   kia   15.10.14 MR1
LEWIS-LLOYD,Robert Evan ALt   RN   HMS Opal   drd   12.1.18   MR3
LEWITT,Benjamin   Surg   RN   HMS Otranto drd   6.10.18MR1
LEYBORNE-POPHAM,Arthur   Lt Cmdr   RN   HMS Clan McNaughton   drd   3.2.15 MR1
LIDDELL,B.M.   Lt   RNR   29.10.19 CR Shrop70
LIDDLE,Morton Robert Bridges   ALt   RN   HMS Tornado kld   23.12.17 MR2
LIDDLE,Thomas Dickson MB   Staff Surg   RN   HMS Thames   2.4.15 CR Kent67
LIDDLE,Thomas Robson   PTFlt Sub-Lt RNAS   kld   30.4.16 CR Canada1522 Lt
LIGERTWOOD,Peter ACapt RMLI   2RM Bn RNDiv   26.10.17 CR Belgium126
LILLEY,Arthur L   Bosn   RN   HMS Hampshire   drd   5.6.16 CR Scot900
LILLIE,Alexander William Hewson   TLt   RNR   HMS Pretoria   10.10.17 CR EAfrica67
LILLIE,William Philip.DSC.   Lt   RN   HMS S/M E34   20.7.18 CR Germany2
LILLY,A.   Skipper   RNR   HMTrawler Sulby   21.11.15 CR Lancs48
LIMBRICK,Frederick W.   Skipper   RNR   HMS Unity   4.10.16CR Wales389
LIMOND,Percy   TAsst Eng   RNR   HMS Pricess Irene   kld   27.5.15MR3
LIMRICK,W.S.   AssPaymr   RNR   HMS Arlanya   23.3.18 CR Lancs149
LINCOLD,George William   TSkipper   RNR   HMDrifter Michaelmas Daisy kld   26.11.16 MR1
LINDNER,Leonard Hubert   Lt Comdr   RN   HMS Indefatigable   kia   31.5.16MR2
LINDSAY,William James   Lt   RNR   HMTrawler Alberia   21.8.17 CR Cornwall40
LING,Percy John   Ft Paymr   RN   HMS Formidable   kia   1.1.15 MR1
LINTOTT,William   TSub-Lt   RNVR Nelson Bn RNDiv   12.7.15 MR4
LINWOOD,Francis G   TWt Tel   RNR   HMS Newsbury   15.2.18 CR Middx77
LION,Neville Isidore TLt   RMLI   1 RM Bn RNDiv   28.4.17 MR20
LISTER,Charles Alfred Hon.MID   Lt   RM   Hood Bn RNDiv   28.8.15 CR Greece10
LISTER,Francis Henry EngRrAdml   RN   HMS Colleen   20.8.18 CR Eire76
LISTON-FOULIS,Archibald Primrose.MID LtCol   RMA   attRGAkia   30.11.17 CR France415
LITTLE,Howard W   TSub-Lt   RNVR Hawke Bn RNDiv   19.6.15 MR4
LITTLE,J S OBE   Staff Paymr   RNR   HMS President   19.5.18 CR Surrey152
LITTLEBOY,Vernon H   TFlt Sub-Lt   RNAS   22.12.17 CR Surrey160
LIVERMORE,Albert George Nathaniel Gnr RN   HMS Ardent kia   31.5.16CR Europe178A
LIVERSIDGE,Raymond Allan TAsst Paymr   RNR   HMS Invincible   kia   31.5.16MR3
LIVESEY,James Trevor   Gnr   RN   HMS Fandango   kld   3.7.19 MR2
LIVINGSTONE,David TLt   RNR   HMDrifter Cosmos   kia   15.2.18MR3
LIVINGSTONE,John Alexander   Lt   RNR   HMTrawler Hero   ded   23.2.19   CR Wales9
LLEWELYN,Robert Harman Comdr RN   HMS Queen Mary   kia   31.5.16 MR3
LLOYD,Maurice Charles Humphrey.DSO&Bar.MIDx2 SubLt RN   HMS Hindustan   dow   24.4.18   CR Kent7
LLOYD,Pennant Athelwold Iremonger Capt RN   HMS President   15.9.16 CR Wales658
LLOYD,Seisyllt Hugh TFlt Sub-Lt   RNAS 10 Sqdn   kld   14.8.17MR20
LLOYD,Thomas Frederick   EngLt RNR   RFA Waterwitch   ded   29.10.15 CR Greece10
LLOYD-ROBERTS,Henry George   Clerk RN   HMS Hogue kia   22.9.14MR1
LOARD,Frank W   Lt Col RM   7.15
LOBB,Francis Frederick   Ft Surg RN   HMS Queen Mary   kia   31.5.16MR3
LOCHTIE,David   Lt   RNR HMS Seagull drd   30.9.18   MR2
LOCK,Henry John   Lt   RMLI HMS Bulwark kld   26.11.14 MR1
LOCKIE,Keith F/O   RNAS   24.9.17 CR France1844
LOCKIE,Thomas Corbett   EngLt RN   HMS Glatton   7.10.18CR Scot671
LOCKWOOD,Arthur William Carden   SubLt   HMS Eden   drd   17.6.16 CR France377 orA.C.W.
LONGLEY,Charles Raynsford Midmn RN   HMS Indefatigable   kia   31.5.16MR2

LONGTON,E.R.D.   SubLt RNVR   18.11.14 CR Scot756
LONGUET-HIGGINS,Kenneth Aislabie   Lt   RMLI Deal Bn RNDiv   dow   2.5.15 MR1
LORD,Reginald   FltSubLt   RNAS   kld   10.8.15 CR Kent27
LORD-FLOOD,James Aloysius   Surg Prob   RNVR HMS Anchusa kia   16.7.18 MR2
LOUTIT,Arthur Justice   Sub-Lt RNVR Hood Bn RNDiv   8.10.18 MR16
LOVE,Arthur Richard Gordon SubLt RNVR Drake Bn RNDiv   21.8.18 CR France518
LOVE,Harold Ewart   Flt Sub Lt   RNAS RN Seaplane Base(PortSaid) dedacc 28.3.18   CR Egypt7
LOVE,R.   ChGnr RN   HMS President   5.1.19 CR Hamps9
LOVE,Thomas E   TSub-Lt   RNVR Hood Bn RNDiv   14.6.15 MR4
LOVEGOOD,Thomas E.   Lt   RN   CG DistOff HM CstGds   3.4.16 CR Scot442
LOVETT,Frederick John   TWt Tel   RNR HMS India   8.8.15 CR Europe131
LOVETT,Hugh McVey   ALt   RNR   HMTrawler Sarah Alice   kia   26.9.16 MR2
LOWCOCK,A.W.B.   Lt   RNVR HM ML367   ded   12.11.18 CR Greece10
LOWE,Frank Augustus   TLt   RNVR Collingwood Bn RNDiv   7.6.15 MR4
LOWES,Joseph Edward   Art Eng   RN   HMS Russell kld   27.4.16 MR1
LOWN,James TSkipper   RNR   HMTrawler Kingsway   7.8.17 CR Lincs156
LOWNDES,Alexander C.B.   Capt   RN   HMS Impregnable   20.3.21 CR Devon3
LOWTHER,Cecil   TFlt Sub-Lt   RNAS   8.17
LOXLEY,Arthur Noel Capt   RN   HMS Formidable   kia   1.1.15 MR1
LOXLEY,Vere Duncombe   Capt   RM   1RM Bn RNDiv   13.11.16 CR France220
LUARD,Frank William   Col   RM   Portsmouth Bn RNDiv   13.7.15 CR Gallipoli14
LUARD,Herbert Du Cane   Cmdr RN   Coastguard Plymouth   21.2.19 CR Essex285
LUBBOCK,Alexander Nevile Lt Cmdr   RN   HMS Donegal in SS Orensa   kia   28.4.18 MR2
LUCAS,Claude de Neufville   Lt   RN   HMS Indefatigable   kia   31.5.16 MR2
LUCAS,George Henry TSkipper   RNR   HMTrawler George Milburn kld   12.7.17 MR1
LUCE,Philip Stanley   Lt   RNVR Anson Bn RNDiv   25.8.18 CR France578
LUCKING,Christopher H   ALt   RNR   HMS Viknor drd   13.1.15   MR3
LUKE,Thomas Ralph Carpt RN   HMS Ariadne ded   2.9.17 CR Devon3
LUKER,Frederick   Ch Bosn   RN   HMS Invincible   kia   31.5.16 MR3
LUMSDEN,Frederick William.VC.CB.DSO.BrigGen RMA   Cmdg 14Bde   4.6.18 CR France502
LUND,John   Gnr   RN   HMS Natal   kld   30.12.15 MR3
LUSCOMBE,Geoffrey Alfred Lt Cmdr   RN   HMMS Blackmorevalekld   1.5.18 MR2
LUSHINGTON,Guye Wellesley   Capt   RMA HMS Bellerophon   ded   8.5.16 CR Sussex95
LYALL,William   TSkipper   RNR   HMDrifter Gavenwood   kld   20.2.16 MR3
LYDALL,Cecil Wykeham   Chapn RN   HMS Lion   kia   31.5.16 MR2
LYON,Harold Vernon Lt   RN   HM S/M E2 drd   8.9.15 MR3
LYON,Herbert Inglis Nigel.MID   Lt Comdr   RN   HMS Marmiondrd   21.10.17 MR2
LYON,Herbert.CB.   Adml(Retd)   RN   ded   15.3.19   CR Europe3

M

MABERY,W H   Skipper   RNR HMS Firefly   14.8.18 CR France1571
MABROOK,J. ?   ?   HMS Soudan   2.6.18 CR Scot722
MacALISTER,D.   Lt   RNR HMT Mikasa ded   16.2.19   CR Scot25
MacALONEY,Ralph Gordon TFlt Sub-Lt   RNAS HMS Hawke kia   15.10.14 MR1
MacALPINE,C.B.   Lt   RNR HMS Glory   4.11.18 MR70
MacCORMAC,John Sides Davies   TSurg RN   HMS Black Prince   kia   31.5.16 MR3
MACDONALD,Colin Gordon Flt Sub Lt   RNAS   kia   11.3.18 CR Belgium24
MacDONALD,Donald Gnr   RN   HMS Recruit kld   9.8.17 MR3
MACDONALD,Donald   Lt   RNR HMS President   17.3.18 CR Canada745A
MACDONALD,Donald Roy   Lt   RN   HMS Hawke kia   15.10.14 MR1
MacDONALD,John Robert   TSkipper   RNR HMDrifter Laurella   accdrd 29.11.17 MR3
MACDONALD,RobertTAsst Eng   RNR HMS Princess Irene   kld   27.5.15 MR3
MacDONALD,William Norman   Eng Comdr   RN   HMS Vanguard   kld   9.7.17 MR1
MacELWEE,Archibald M.   TEng Lt   RNR HMPMS Duchess of Montrosekld   18.3.17 MR3
MACFARLANE,Robert Craig Midmn RN   HMS Hawke kia   15.10.14 MR1
MACFARLANE,T.L. Lt   RNVR HMS Glowworm   25.8.19 CR Europe179 &MR70
MacFARLANE,Thomas Morton   Eng Lt RNR HMS Knight Templar kia   7.4.18 MR3

MacGLIP,William Graham   TAsst Paymr   RNR   HMS Queen Mary   kia   31.5.16MR3
MacGREGOR,Donald Piriaulx   Lt Comdr   RN   HMS M28   kia   20.1.18 MR2
MacGREGOR,J.   Lt   RNR   HMS Mallina   24.4.18 CR Scot283
MACHAN,John Sydney   Eng Lt Comdr   RN   HMS Endymion   drd   26.10.17 MR2
MACINTYRE,John Ebenezer TSurg Prob   RNVR HMS Ardent   31.5.16 CR Europe148
MACK,Ralph Michael Lt Comdr   RN   HMS Tornado kld   23.12.17 MR2
MACKAIL,David Rankin Fleming   Eng Sub Ly   RNR   HMS Sarnia   kia   12.9.18MR3
MACKAY,Frederick B.   LtCmdr   RNR   HMS Ceto   17.4.16 CR Scot674
MACKAY,John   Gnr   RN   HMS Espiegle ded PoW 29.10.16 MR38
MacKAY,William Gordon   Eng Sub Lt   RNR   RFA Industry kia   18.10.18 MR3
MacKENZIE,A A   Capt   IWT,RE   ex Sub-Lt RNR   ded   3.11.19CR Wales568
MACKENZIE,Colin Roy.DSO.   FltCmdr   RNAS   24.1.17 CR France517
MACKESON,Donald Fairfax ALt   RN   HMS Tower   accdrd 1.12.17MR1
MACKIE,Alexander   TAsst Eng   RNR   HMS Princess Irene   kld   27.5.15MR3
MacKINNON,Neil Shaw.DSC.   Eng Lt RNR   HMS Cullist   kia   11.2.18MR3
MACKINTOSH,Evelyn Mary AssPrincipal WRNS   18.12.18 CR Scot424
MACKIRDY,Peter Mackay   TLt Comdr   RNVR   Anson Bn RNDiv   dow   25.5.15   MR3
MacKNIGHT,Dundas Simpson   Surg Lt RN   HMS Britannia   9.11.18CR Europe23
MACKPHERSON,R.M.   SurgProb   RNVR HMS Narwhale   26.12.17 CR Scot900
MACLACHLAN,Angus Hope Lt   RN   HMS Vindictive   kia   10.5.18CR Belgium175
MacLARTY,John   PTFlt Sub-Lt RNAS   drd   24.8.15   MR1
MACLEAN,Archibald TSub-Lt   RNR   HMS Redbreast   kia   15.7.17MR3
MACLEAN,Hector Forbes   Sub Lt RN   HMCMB No62BD   kia   18.8.19MR3
MacLENNAN,George Gordon TFlt Lt RNAS   kia   21.7.17 CR Belgium175 Flt Cmdr
MACLEOD,Torquil Harry Lionel   Midmn RN   HMS Goliath kia   13.5.15MR1
MacMULLEN,Alfred Robinson.DSC&Bar Surg   RN   Hood Bn RNDiv   dow   7.9.18 CR France52
MACPHEE,Michael   EngSubLt   RNR   HMPMS Albyn   9.11.18CR France1359
MACPHERSON,John Midmn RN   HMS Bulwark kld   26.11.14 MR3
MACPHERSON,Roderick M TSurg Prob   RNVR   12.17
MACRATH,Stewart Chichester   Lt Cmdr   RNR   HMS Pekin   4.6.18 CR Lincs156
MADDISON,Brian Armitage SubLt RNR   HMS Simoon   23.1.17 CR Kent7
MAGGS,Ivor Alphonso   Eng Lt RN   HMS Kale   kld   27.3.18MR1
MAHON,Patrick Singleton   AAsst Paymr   RNR   HMS Aboukir kia   22.9.14MR1
MAILE,Charles Grenville   Paymstr   RNR   HMS Perth   kia   1.10.18MR1
MAIN,C.   EngCmdr   RN   HMS Shakespeare   31.5.18 CR Hamps160
MAIN,Reuben Eng Comdr   RN   HMS Invincible   kia   31.5.16MR3
MAINPRICE,Bernard Paul   Clerk   RN   HMS Bulwark kld   26.11.14 MR3
MAINPRICE,Ernest William Loxley   Ft Paymr   RN   HMS Invincible   kia   31.5.16MR3
MAIR,James   TSkipper   RNR   HMTrawler Waltham kia   10.10.17 MR3
MAITLAND,Henry   EngLt RNR   HMS Nepaulin   20.4.17 CR France1359
MAITLAND,Henry Jervois Rualt   Sub Lt RNVR HMS President   17.3.18 CR Canada745A
MALAN,Charles Caesar Merindol   Lt Comdr   RN   HMS Opal   drd   12.1.18   MR3
MALET DE CARTERET,Philip Reginald Midmn   RN   HMS Queen Mary   kia   31.5.16MR3
MALET,Francis Arthur Rivers FltSubLt   RNAS   acckld 12.11.16 CR Kent46
MALLARD,N. FltSubLt ·   RN   RNAS   30.3.18 CR Yorks438
MALLER,Henry   Lt   RNVR HM ML375   2.9.17 CR Scot241
MALLET,Clement Stanley Bertram   TMidmn   RNR   HMS Hampshire   kld   5.6.16 MR3
MALLETT,Cecil Horace   SubLt RNVR Anson Bn RNDiv   12.4.18 CR France64
MALONE,John Joseph DSO TFlt Sub-Lt   RNAS   30.4.17 MR20
MALONEY,Adrian E. SubLt RNVR Hawke Bn RNDiv   8.3.18 CR France711
MANKEY,John   EngLt RN   HMS Spindrift   8.8.21 CR Devon1
MANN,Alfred Thomas Osborne   FltSubLt   RNAS 3Wing   29.11.16 CR France1826
MANN,John   SubLt RNVR HMS San Foin   17.2.19 CR Hamps5
MANNING,Charles William   TSkipper   RNR   HMSmack Ethel & Millie   kia   16.8.17MR1
MANNING,E.S.MID   AssEngRNR   HMS Clementina   20.9.15 CR NIreland14
MANNING,Job H   Mate   RN   HMS Berwick   10.1.17 CR Bermuda1
MANSBRIDGE,Frederick Henry   Ch Bosn   RN   HMS Black Prince   kia   31.5.16CR Europe178A
MANSEL,Charles Pleydell   Lt Cmdr   RN   HMS Celtic   ded   26.3.15   MR3
MANSFIELD,Cyril James.MVO.   DepSurgGen RN   ded   7.5.16 CR Hamps5
MANTON,Charles   Art Eng   RN   HMS Cressy   kia   22.9.14MR1

37

MANTON,Joseph Maurice 268174   ArtEng RN   HMS Bulwark   23.9.14 CR Dorset57
MARCHANT,Macnamara   Midmn RN   HMS Vanguard   kld   9.7.17 MR1
MARESCAUX,Gerald Charles Adolphe.CB.CMG.MIDx4 V/Adml RN   ded   3.9.20 CR Kent46
MARKEY,Charles Aloysius   TSubLt RNVR Hood Bn RNDiv   23.1.20 CR Eire12
MARKHAM,Herbert Edward TLt   RMLI 2 RM Bn RNDiv   26.4.17 MR20
MARKS,W.   ComnShpt   RN   HMS Talbot   15.11.16 CR Devon1
MARSH,Frank Sydney T2Lt   RMLI 1 RM Bn RNDiv   28.4.17 MR20
MARSH,Thomas E L Lt   RM   HMS Russell   27.4.16 CR Europe6
MARSHALL,C.D.   StaffSurg   RNVR HMS Dalhousie   14.9.18 MR65
MARSHALL,Francis T A J   T2Lt   RM   Depot Eastney   12.5.15 CR Hamps5
MARSHALL,Herbert Myers   DentalSurg   RNVR HMHS China kld   10.8.18 MR1
MARSHALL.John   Comdr RN   HMS Victory   3.2.17 CR Hamps5
MARTIN,C.W.   Lt   RMLI 1RM Bn RNDiv   13.11.16 CR France339
MARTIN,Cecil Taylor Asst Clerk   RN   HMS Monmouth   kia   1.11.14 MR2
MARTIN,Charles James   TSub-Lt   RNVR Hood Bn RNDiv   4.6.15 MR4
MARTIN,Charles Walter   T2Lt   RMLI 1 RM Bn   13.11.16 CR France339
MARTIN,John Anthony   Lt   RNR   HMS Lobster accdrd 6.10.19 MR1
MARTIN,Lionel Arthur   Surg   RN   HMHS China kld   10.8.18 MR1
MARTIN,Richard   Surg Lt RN   HMS Grenville   accdrd 25.12.19 MR2
MARTIN,William Henry   TLt   RNR   HMYacht Aries   kld   31.10.15 MR3
MARTYN,J.L. Lt   RNR   HMS Vivid   25.10.18 CR Cornwall4
MARWOOD,Thomas Art Eng   RN   HMS Goliath kia   13.5.15 MR1
MASKELL,Albert George Glover   TEng Sub-Lt   RNR   HMS Duke of Albany kia   24.8.16 MR2
MASON,David R.MIDTLt Comdr   RNR   HMS Osmanieh   kia   31.12.17 CR Egypt1
MASON,N.G.M.MC. Maj   RFA   RN DAC   13.9.18 CR France560
MASON,Philip   TSkipper   RNR   HMTrawler Tugela   kld   26.6.16 MR1
MASON,Richard Gordon William.RD.   Cmdr RNR   HMYacht Iolaire   drd   1.1.19 MR3
MASSEY,Hugh A.   SubLt RNVR Howe Bn RNDiv   26.8.15 CR Greece10
MASSON,Donald Howe   FltSubLt   RNAS   20.4.17 CR France1359
MASTER,Harold Onslow   Lt   RNR   HMS Indefatigable   kia   31.5.16 MR2
MASTERS,Trevor Munro Hoare   Midmn RN   HMS Formidable   kia   1.1.15 MR1
MATHEWS,George Joseph   Eng Lt Comdr RN   HMS Tornado kld   23.12.17 MR2
MATHEWS,Sidney Herbert   TEng   RNR   HMSSV No14 kia   30.5.15 MR2
MATHIAS,John.RD. Cmdr RNR   HMS Laurentic   4.12.16 CR Ches182
MATON,Eustace Newton Gerald   Lt   RN   HMS Tipperary   kia   31.5.16 MR3
MATTHEWS,Frank George   Midmn RN   HMS Cressy   kia   22.9.14 MR1
MATTHEWS,G.E.   LtCmdr   RN   HMS Sable   18.10.18 CR Scot722
MATTHEWS,Godfrey Estcourt.CB.CMG. TBrigGen RMLI Cmdg 198 Inf Bde   dow   13.4.17   CR France80
MATTHEWS,Humphrey   Lt   RN   HMS Hampshire   drd   5.6.16 CR Scot900
MATTHEWS,Vernon Lickfold   Surg   RN   HMS Viknor   drd   13.1.15   MR3
MATTHEWS,W.C.B. 2Lt   RMLI 1RM Bn RNDiv   25.8.18 CR France84
MAULEVERER,Claude du Pre Stansfeld Gowan Midmn   RN   HMS Vanguard   kld   9.7.17 MR1
MAURICE,Thomas Hector Molesworth   Comdr RN   HMS Princess Irene   kld   27.5.15 MR3
MAXWELL,Aylmer Edward TLt Col   RM   Cmdg Collingwood Bn RNDiv   dow   9.10.14 CR Belgium342
MAXWELL,John Earle   SubLt RNVR attA Sqn 2Wing RNAS   kia   30.3.17 CR Greece19
MAXWELL,William Leigh   LtCol RM   HQ Staff 2Bde RNDiv   9.5.15 CR Gallipoli14
MAXWELL-LEFROY,Patrick Egerton   Lt   RN   HMS Mosquito   kia   25.4.15 MR1
MAY,John Frederick Lt   RM   Plymouth Bn RNDiv   25.4.15 MR4
MAY,Theodore Charles   TFlt Sub-Lt   RNAS   kld   24.7.17 MR20
MAY,William Henry.MBE.   LtCmdr   RN   HMS Pembroke   23.3.19 CR Kent46
MAYNARD,Alfred Frederick TLt   RNVR Howe Bn RNDiv   13.11.16 MR21
McADAM,A.C.   Lt   RMLI   4.9.18 CR France103
McALISTER,John William   Art Eng   RN   HMS Vanguard   kld   9.7.17 MR3
McALLISTER,G.H.   Lt   RNR HMS Pontypool   23.5.19 CR Gallipoli1
McALLISTER,John Norquay 2Lt   RNAS   attRFC 10Wing   23.6.17 CR France268 FltSubLt
McALPINE,C.B.   Lt   RNR HMS Glory   4.11.18 CR Europe179
McBARNET,Edward James.RD.   Lt Comdr   RNR   HMS Albion dow   16.8.15   CR Egypt3
McBRIDE,Robert Anderson.AM.   Lt   RNVR HMS President V   6.7.18 CR Scot752
McCARTHY,Charles Gnr   RN   HMS Goliath kia   13.5.15 MR3
McCARTHY,Charles Gnr   RN   HMS Onslaught   kia   1.6.16 CR Scot722

McCARTHY,Thomas Edward James Ch Carp   RN   HMS Pembroke   30.10.16 CR Kent67
McCLELLAND,H.W. Gnr   RN   HMS Natal   28.8.15 CR Hamps9
McCLORRY,James Richard Lt   RNR   HMTrawler H.E.Stoud   26.10.16 CR C'land&W'land50
McCORMICK,Ian Campbell SubLt RNVR Hood Bn RNDiv   24.1.17 CR France701
McCORMICK,John Arthur Rice   Lt   RNVR Nelson Bn RNDiv   5.6.15 CR Gallipoli14
McCORQUODALE,J. Lt   RNR   HMS Columbine   24.10.15 CR Scot764
McCOY,Charles   Ch Gnr RN   HMS Enchantress   12.11.17 CR Hamps9
McCULLOCK,James TSub-Lt   RNR   HMYacht Kethailes drd   11.10.17 MR3
McCURRACH,William   TSub-Lt   RNVR 190 MG Coy RNDiv dow   27.5.17   CR France95
McDONALD.William Begg.DSC.   Eng Lt RNR   HMS Stonecrop   kia   18.9.17MR3
McFARLAND,Malcolm   Paymstr   RNR   HMS Cowslip kia   25.4.18 MR3
McGHIE,John Allen   Lt   RIM   18.10.16 MR65
McGINTY,John   Gnr   RN   HMS Cyclops   3.12.16CR Ches182
McGLADDERY,William   SubLt RNVR MFA Hughli   26.4.19 CR France1359
McGRATH,Percival Wainman Lt   RNVR Drake Bn RNDiv   kia   24.6.15CR Gallipoli1
McGREGOR,Alexander Thomson   TEng Lt   RNR   HMS Stephen Furness kia   13.12.17 MR3
McGREGOR,David John   Eng Lt Comdr RN   HMS Hawke kia   15.10.14 MR1
McGREGOR-ROBERTSON,Thomas Bollen Seath Lt   RN   HM S/M E36   kld   19.1.17MR3
McHARDY,Robert P. Cmdr   RN   HMS Antrim   15.7.17 CR Devon1
McINDOE,Edward Phillips   PFltOffRNAS   kld   27.2.18CR Durham26
McINNES,J.   EngLt RNR   18.8.18 MR65
McINTOSH,Alexander Fraser Surg   RN   HMS Pekin   drd   4.3.18 CR Lincs1
McINTOSH,Henry B TLt   RNVR Howe Bn RNDiv   4.6.15 MR4
McINTOSH,James   Skipper   MMR HMTrawler Cinceria ded   10.12.18 CR Scot886
McINTOSH,James Alexander TSub-Lt   RNR   HMT Falmouth III   kld   19.11.15 CR Europe96
McKAY,Alexander   Skipper   RNR   HMDrifter Friendly Girls   ded   10.9.18   CR Scot288
McKAY,James Art Eng   RN   HMS Pathfinder   kia   5.9.14 MR1
McKECHNIE,William Skipper   RNR   HMS Osiris   ded   19.4.16   MR2
McKEAG,John Joseph EngLt RNR   RFA Carol   4.4.18 CR Scot900
McKELVEY,Charles James   TEng Sub-Lt RNR   HMS Clacton kia   3.8.16 MR3
McKENNA,W.Skipper   RNR   HMT Hatano   21.10.18 CR France85
McKENZIE,Murdoch   ArtEng   RN   HMS Pembroke   7.12.14 CR Kent46 Murdock
McKINNON.H.   Lt   RNR   FleetMessenger The Viceroy   30.9.15 CR Scot761
McKIRDY,Peter Mackay   see MacKIRDY,P.M.
McLACHLAN,Duncan Campbell   TSkipper   RNR   HMTrawler Othello II kld   31.10.15 MR2
McLAREN,D.L.   SubLt RNR   HMS Ashtree   21.7.18 CR Wales17
McLAUGHLIN,C.E.DSO.   Lt   RN   HMS Humber   11.8.19 CR Europe179 &MR70
McLEOD,Alexander TSub-Lt   RNVR Collingwood Bn RNDiv   4.6.15 MR4
McLEOD,Arthur   TEng Sub-Lt RNR   HMS Champagne   kia   9.10.17MR2
McLEOD,George   Lt   RNR   HMS Cowslip kia   25.4.18MR3
McLEOD,J.K.DSO. LtCmdr   RN   HMS Victory   26.9.20 CR Hamps5
McMAHON,Maurice.DSO.AM.   LtCmdr   RNR   HMS President   25.10.19 CR Lancs156
McMILLAN,John Archibald TSub-Lt   RNVR Anson Bn RNDiv   13.11.16 MR21
McMULLEN,Alexander Percival   Lt   RN   HMS Invincible   kia   31.5.16 MR3
McNAIR,George McFarline Lt   RNR   HMS Europa ded   6.1.19 MR3
McNALLY,Hugh Francis   TSurg RN   HMS Hampshire   kld   5.6.16 MR3
McNAMEE,George   Head Schlmr RN   HMS Queen Mary   kia   31.5.16MR3
McNEIL,Allan 2Lt   RMLI   ded   24.2.19   CR Scot774
McNEIL,Percy Gordon TFlt Sub-Lt RNAS   3.6.17 MR20
McNEIL-SMITH,Henry Churchill   Clerk RN   HMS Russell kld   27.4.16MR1
McNEILL,William Alexander Lt   RNR   HMS Laurentic   25.1.17 CR Scot435 &MR2
McNICOL,John   Lt   RNR   FleetMessenger Silverfield   29.9.15 CR Greece11
McQUEEN,Andrew   Paymstr   RNR   RFA Hughli drd   26.4.19   CR Belgium175
McREDDIE,George Sydenham   Sub Lt RNR   HMS Anchusa kia   16.7.18MR2
McVICAR,John   TEng Sub-Lt RNR   HMS Laurentic   kld   25.1.17MR2
McWATTIE,J.J.H.   Lt   RNR   HMTrawler Aspasia   2.1.19 MR70
McWILLIAM,Donald McLeod EngLtCmdr   RNR   HMS Orama   1.3.16 CR Scot360
MEAD,Claud,Frederick   Capt   RM   Deal Bn RNDiv   kia   13.12.15 CR Gallipoli2
MEAKIN,William   Gnr   RN   HMS Peregrine   9.12.18CR hamps8
MEAL,Percy Sig Bosn   RN   HMS Champion   7.7.16 MR2

MEALE,George Samuel   Skipper   RNR   HMDrifter Frons Olivae   12.10.15 CR Suffolk91
MEARNS,William   Surg   RN   HMS Formidable   kia   1.1.15 MR1
MEATS,Harold Stephen   ATLt RNR   HM S/M E30 kld   22.11.16 MR3
MEDLICOTT,Stephen Flt Lt (Lt)   RN att RNAS Seaplane 928   kld   26.4.15CR Hamps5
MEE,Cecil Henry   Lt   RNR   HMS Bombala kia   25.4.18MR1
MEEHAN,Michael A. SurgLt RN   HMS Earl of Peterborough   13.12.18 CR Italy83
MEESON,Edward Hickman Tucker.DSO. Eng Comdr   RN   HMS Defence kia   31.5.16MR2
MELLAND,Brian Trevor Roper   TSub-Lt   RNVR Anson Bn RNDiv   6.5.15 MR4
MELLAND,Frederick BernardTLt   RNVR Hawke Bn RNDiv   24.4.17 MR20
MELLERSHIP,George.DSC. Skipper   RNR   HMT Irawadi   24.5.16 CR Yorks1
MELSOME,Robert Percy   ALt   RNR   HMTug Char drd   16.1.15   MR3
MELVIN,John AssEngRNR   HMS Partridge dedacc 29.9.15   CR Greece10
MENZIES,John   Sub-Lt RNVR Hood Bn RNDiv   21.4.18 MR16
MERCER,David.KCB.MIDx2 Sir   MajGen   RM   AdjtGen RM   1.7.20 CR Kent2
MESSENGER,William Geoffrey DSC   Lt   RNR   HMTrawler Kunishi   30.12.18 CR Surrey142
METCALFE,William Burton ALt   RN   HM S/M E50 kld   31.1.18MR3
METHUEN,Paul Thomond Gape   LtCmdr   RN   HMS Hercules ded   26.5.18   CR Dorset33
MICKLEBOROUGH,William Lawrence   Skipper   RNR   HMTrawler Quintia   26.11.18 CR Norfolk88
MIDDLEMIST,Robert James Menteith   Lt   RN   HM S/M K5   drd   20.1.19   MR3
MIDDLETON,Albert AArt Eng   RN   HMS Black Prince   kia   31.5.16MR1
MIDDLETON,Hugh J Lt Comdr(Retd)RN   8.14
MIDDLETON,NormanTSub-Lt   RNR   HMYacht Sanda   kia   25.9.15MR3
MIDGLEY,Ernest Edward   TEng Sub-Lt RNR   HMS Laurentic   kld   25.1.17MR2
MIEVILLE,Geoffrey Francois Clerk RN   HMS Queen Mary   kia   31.5.16MR3
MILES,Gerard Skipper   ·RNR   HMS Osiris   25.12.16 MR1
MILES,Harry William Maj   RMLI HMS Vanguard   kld   9.7.17 MR3
MILES,Irving Brock   Comdr RN   HMS Vivid   29.1.17 CR London8
MILES,Osmond Edward   TSub-Lt   RNR   HMS Hilary   drd   2.1.15 MR2
MILL,George Robertson   StaffSurg   RNVR Surg & Agent Birkenhead Mersey Div ded   11.2.18   CR Ches8
MILLER,Alexander   TLt   RNR   HMDrifter Michaelmas Daisy kld   26.11.16 MR3
MILLER,Herbert   Paymr RNR   HMS Halcyon   6.12.18CR Numb3
MILLER,Norman Heath   TLt   RNVR Howe Bn RNDiv   4.6.15 MR4
MILLER,William   Surg   RN   HMS Bulwark kld   26.11.14 MR3
MILLETT,Edward George   ArtEng RN   HMS Titania   ded   16.1.19   CR Essex7
MILLIGAN,John Desmond   SurLt RN   HMS Blake   7.1.20 CR Scot674
MILLWARD,Kenneth H.   FltSubLt   RNAS   7.7.17 CR France705
MILNE,A.E. WtEng RNR   HMS Colleen   3.3.15 CR Eire76
MILNE,Robert Conway   ATLt RNR   HMS Q27   kia   13.3.17MR2
MILNER,Dermod Ross   Chpn RN   HMHS Garth Castle   17.9.19 CR Europe179 &MR70
MILNER-BARRY,Edward Leopold   LtCmdr   RNVR HMS Wallington   7.5.17 CR Cambs25
MILROY,Douglas   TSub-Lt   RNVR Collingwood Bn RNDiv   4.6.15 MR4
MILSOM,Edward Winfrid   ALt   RN   HMS Defence kia   31.5.16MR2
MILTON,John Penn   Midmn RN   HMS Vanguard   kld   9.7.17 MR1
MILVAIN,Charles Edward Francis   Lt   RNVR Hawke Bn RNDiv   25.6.15 CR Egypt3
MINERS,Percy Edward   Eng Sub Lt   RNR   RFA Vitol   kia   7.3.18 MR1
MINERS,William Henry   Skipper 101SA RNR   HMTrawler Norman II   18.4.18 CR Devon1
MINISTER,Clement TSkipper   RNR   HMDrifter Ocean's Gift II   kld   30.8.17MR1
MITCHELL R.R.   EngLt RNR   HMS Laurentic   25.1.17 CR NIreland138
MITCHELL,Forest H. Lt   RNVR BritArmouredCarDiv   6.2.17 CR Iraq8
MITCHELL,Granville James   SubLt RNVR Hood Bn RNDiv   kia   26.2.18CR France662
MOORE,Henry   ChOff RN   HM Coastguard   7.9.19 CR Cornwall55
MITCHELL,James   Ch Bosn   RN   HMS Tiger   kia   31.5.16MR2
MITCHELL,James   TSkipper   RNR   HMDrifter Forward III kld   31.3.17MR3
MITCHELL,James   TSkipper   RNR   HMDrifter Ocean Star kld   26.9.17MR3
MITCHELL,Robert R TEng Lt   RNR   1.17
MOGG,Francis Lindsay   Eng Lt RN   HMS Invincible   kia   31.5.16MR3
MOIR,Archibald Douglas.MID   Midmn RN   HMS Mary Rose   kia   17.10.17 MR1
MOIR,Charles Jarvis TFlt Lt RNAS   10.5.17 CR Belgium175
MOLYNEUX,Cecil Richard Hon   Midmn RN   HMS Lion   kia   31.5.1616 MR2
MONKS,Frederick   ArtEng RN   HMS Cressy   22.9.14 CR Suffolk130

MONKS,Frederick Shaw   TSub-Lt   RNR   HMS Viknor drd   13.1.15   MR3
MONTAGU,Alexander Cyril Lt   RN   HMS Bulwark kld   26.11.14 MR3
MONTGOMERY,Lancelot Alexander Lt   RN   HMS Good Hope   kia   1.11.14MR3
MONTGOMERY,Richard Tichborne TLt   RNR   HMS Redbreast   kia   15.7.17MR3
MOODY,Douglas Whimster Keiller TSurg RN   HMS Natal   kld   30.12.15 MR1
MOODY,Frederick William TLt   RNR   HMTrawler Apley   kld   6.12.17MR3
MOON,George Bassett   TSurg RN   HMS Lion   kia   31.5.16MR2
MOORE,Charles Lewis   Lt   RN   lent to RAN HMA S/M AE1   drd   14.9.14   MR2
MOORE,Geoffrey   FltLt   RNAS   26.2.18 CR Greece10
MOORE,J.   FtSurg RN   HMS Pembroke   13.5.15 CR Heref&Worc24
MOORE,Thomas Stone   Sub-Lt RN   HM S/M C34 kia   21.7.17MR3
MOORE-ANDERSON,Walter Graham   Staff Surg   RN   HMS Clan McNaughton   drd   3.2.15 MR1
MOORHOUSE,Stephen John EngSubLt   RNR   HMS Chelmsford   5.2.17 CR France1359
MORAN,James   Wt Tel RN   HMS Triumph kia   7.5.15 MR1
MORAN,Joseph L   TFlt Sub-Lt   RNAS/RN   12.12.17 CR Canada1246
MORANG,George Heaven   PFlt Offr   RNAS   27.10.17 MR20
MORETON,John Alfred CMG,DSO Capt   RN   HMS Erebus   19.3.20 CR Surrey150
MORGAN,C F Dean Hon   see FITZMAURICE-DEAN-MORGAN,C. Hon
MORGAN,Edward   Lt   RNR   HMS Anchusa kia   16.7.18MR2
MORGAN,George William Faulconer Chpn   RN   HMS Invincible   kia   31.5.16MR3
MORGAN,John Emil FltLt   RNAS   30.3.17 CR Iraq8
MORGAN,Lewis   FltLt   RNAS   kld   11.5.17CR Somerset183
MORGAN,Richard   Lt   RNR   HMS Laurentic   25.1.17 CR Eire270
MORGAN,T.H.   EngLt RN   HMS Sardonyx   6.11.18CR Devon3
MORGAN,William Watkins TLt   RNVR Hawke Bn RNDiv   19.6.15 MR4
MORISON,Archibald Alexander   TSurg RN   HMS Indefatigable   kia   31.5.16MR2
MORLEY,Jack Clifford   SubLt RNVR Hood Bn RNDiv   10.10.18 CR France380
MORRIS,J.F.   Lt   RN   HMS Julius   2.2.21 CR Greece9
MORRELL,William Anthony Gnr   RN   HMS Black Prince   kia   31.5.16MR3
MORRELL,William Joseph Ch Art Eng   RN   HMS Arabis   kia   11.2.16MR2
MORRICE,John Walter   Midmn RN   HMS Formidable   kia   1.1.15 MR1
MORRIS,Charles Sebastian Lt Comdr   RN   HMS Black Prince   kia   31.5.16MR3
MORRIS,Edward   Flt Sub Lt   RNAS   accdrd   27.1.18   MR1
MORRIS,John Philip Claude Asst Paymr   RN   HMS Russell kld   27.4.16MR1
MORRISON,Henry Ernest   Gnr   RN   HMS Pathfinder   kia   5.9.14 MR1
MORRISON,James William   TLt   RNVR Hood Bn RNDiv   23.4.17 MR20
MORRISON,Louis D. FltCmdr   RNAS   21.7.17 CR Yorks2
MORRISON,Ronald B.   FltSubLt   RNAS   12.7.17 CR Kent88
MORTIEAU,Arthur James   Sig Bosn   RN   HMS Hampshire   kld   5.6.16 MR3
MORTIMER,Ernest Henry   Carp   RN   HMS Black Prince   kia   31.5.16MR3
MORTIMORE,Francis Edwin TEng Lt   RNR   HMS Clacton kia   3.8.16 MR1
MORTON,Arthur Charles   ATPaymr   RNR   MFA Eleanor kia   12.2.18MR1
MORTON,Cecil Edward Howard   Capt   RM   Portsmouth Bn RNDiv   ded   18.5.15 CR Essex149
MORTON,Herbert C Capt   RM   HMS Bulwark   26.11.14 CR Kent64
MORTON,W.M.   EngrLt RN   HMS Ark Royal   28.12.18 CR Greece14
MOSS,Charles John Gnr   RN   HMS Contest kia   18.9.17MR3
MOSS,J.G.   EngLtCmdr   RN   HMS President   12.11.18 CR Yorks338
MOTT,Alan Birkbeck Lt   RN   HMS Conqueror   13.2.19 CR Surrey42
MOUAT,Arthur Henry Cheyne   Lt   RNR   HMS Natal   kld   30.12.15 MR1
MOULTRIE,Lionel Geoffrey Fergusson Midmn   RN   HMS Valient   23.4.19 CR Surrey160
MOWAT,Alexander Skipper   RNR   HMDrifter Ruby Gem   16.2.17 CR Scot827
MOWLL,H H S   Lt   RNVR HMS Vernon   18.10.18 CR Surrey118
MOXHAM,James F. Lt   RMLI   1.5.15 CR Gallipoli7
MOYLE,William Arthur   Flt Sub-Lt   RNAS   22.3.18 MR20
MUIR,David TSub-Lt   RNR   HM FleetMessenger Ermine kia   2.8.17 MR1
MUIR,George Watson Midmn RN   HMS Monmouth   kia   1.11.14MR2
MUIR,T.   Lt   RNVR HMS Hermoine   25.4.18 CR Scot674
MUIR,Thomas Frederick   Lt   RNR   HMTrawler Longset kld   6.2.17 CR Scot909
MULES,Arthur Benjamin Stephen   Carp   RN   HMS Goliath kia   13.5.15MR1
MULLENS,Cyril John Ashley TSub-Lt   RNVR/RNAS drd   5.5.16 MR1

MULLER,Arthur Gardiner   AComdr   RN   HMS Racoon   ded   31.8.15   MR1
MULLER,George Fison   Maj   RMLI   1.5.15 CR Gallipoli7
MUNDY,Frederick C.MC.   TLt   RNVR Anson Bn RNDiv   26.10.17 CR Belgium20
MUNNELLY,Stephen Gnr   RN   HMS Indefatigable   kia   31.5.16MR2
MUNRO,Keith Ross   TFlt Sub-Lt   RNAS   9.8.17 MR20
MUNTZ,Claude Leonard Eyre Capt   RMLI 1Bn   dow   17.11.16 CR France74
MURPHY,Daniel Stephen   Bosn   RN   HMS Vanguard   kld   9.7.17 MR2
MURPHY,James K.MC.   StaffSurg   RNVR HMS Vivid   13.9.16 CR Devon1
MURPHY,John M J   Eng Comdr   RN   HMS Assistance   8.6.17 CR Hamps5
MURPHY,William David Rudolph   Lt   RNR   HMS Lobelia   1.1.19 CR Europe23
MURRAY,Alexander Gordon Lt   RN   HMS Invincible   kia   31.5.16MR3
MURRAY,Cecil   FltCmdr   RNAS   22.1.18 CR France1844
MURRAY,James A   TLt Comdr   RNVR   HMS Niobe   dedacc   6.12.17 CR Canada323A RNR
MURRAY,John   Eng Lt RN   HMTB No11   kld   7.3.16 MR1
MURRAY,John Berkeley   Lt Comdr   RN   HMS Natal   kld   30.12.15 MR1
MURRAY,John Matthew   Eng Lt Comdr RN   HMS Queen Mary   kia   31.5.16MR3
MURRAY,Petchell Burtt   FltSubLt   RNAS   4.11.14CR Lancs436
MURRAY,Philip George Wolfe   Lt   RNVR HMS Alsatian   12.10.16 CR Scot967
MURRAY,William   Skipper   RNR   HMDrifter Frigate Bird   9.7.16 CR Italy17
MURRAY,William John   Gnr   RN   HMS Racoon   drd   9.1.18 MR3
MURRAY-BROWN,Granville Lt Comdr   RN   HMS Indefatigable   kia   31.5.16 MR2 BROWNE
MUSGRAVE,Christopher   Midmn RN   HMS Monmouth   kia   1.11.14MR2
MUTCH,J.   Skipper   RNR   HMT Florence Dombey   11.2.16 CR Scot497
MUTTEN,J.   Skipper   RNR   HMS Thalia   12.7.18 CR Scot926

N

NAPER,George Wyatt Edgell   Lt Comdr   RN   HM S/M E24   kld   27.3.16 MR3
NAPIER,George Levack Mackay   Lt   RN   HMS Racoon   drd   9.1.18 MR1
NAPIER,Trevylyan Dacres Willes.KCB.MVO.Sir Adml RN CinC NAmerica St   30.7.20 CR Bermuda1
NEALE,Colin F   TSub-Lt   RNVR   4.17
NEALE,Edwin Henry ChGnr RN   HMS Vivid   ded   28.11.16 CR Cornwall132
NEEDHAM,Louis.DSC.   · LtPaymstr   RNR   HMS Godetia ded   20.12.18 CR Derby57
NEEDLEY,George   Ch Gnr RN   HMS Defence   kia   31.5.16MR2
NEILD,J H   Lt Cmdr   RN   HMS President IV   6.7.19 CR Norfolk151
NELSON,F.A. Maj   RN   HMS Hibernia   13.2.15 CR SCot722
NELSON,Robert   Lt   RNR   HMS India   kia   8.8.15 MR1
NESBIT,John George   Lt   RNR   HMT Brock   30.5.18 CR Numb2
NESBITT,Norman   SubLt RNVR Anson Bn D'Coy RNDiv   21.8.18 CR France214
NEVILE,Sandford Grant Radcliffe   Cmdr RN   HMS President   15.1.18 CR Yorks264
NEVILL,John Beamish   Lt   RNR   HMS Genista kia   23.10.16 MR3
NEWALL,Jack H.M.   SubLt RNVR Drake Bn RNDiv   kia   13.11.16 CR France339
NEWBERRY,John D   Flt Comdr   RN/RNAS   28.9.17 CR Essex40
NEWBERRY,Julius William ShptLt RN   HMS Presidentded   1.10.18CR Hamps8
NEWBERRY-BOSCHETTI,L.W.   Lt   RNR   HMS P32   26.10.18 CR Berks31
NEWBERY,Bernard Charles Croucher   TAsst Paymr   RNR   HMS Laurentic   kld   25.1.17MR2
NEWBIGGING,Robert A Mate RN   HMS Princess Irene   kld   27.5.15MR1
NEWELL,Frederick John   TSub-Lt ，   RNVR Hood Bn RNDiv   20.10.17 CR Belgium92
NEWLANDS,George Jarron   EngSubLt   RNR   HMS Thrush   11.4.17 CR Scot235
NEWSHAM,Richard Harold   EngLt RNR   Alvage Tug Hughli   ded   28.9.18   CR Durham181
NEWTON,Edward Francis   TLt   RNR   HMS Genista kia   23.10.16 MR3
NEWTON,George   Wt EngRNR   HMS Formidable   kia   1.1.15 MR1
NEWTON,John W   Bandmstr   RM   RM Barracks Plymouth   26.6.16 CR Devon1
NEWTON,Peter Joseph   Bosn   RN   HMS Africa   8.5.18 CR Warwick9
NICHOLAS,John Gould.DSC, Lt   RN   HMS Narbrough   drd   12.1.18   MR3
NICHOLLS,Harry   Art Eng   RN   HMS Bulwark kld   26.11.14 MR3
NICHOLS,William Robert   Skipper   RNR   HMTrawler Bombardier   drd   27.3.19   MR1
NICHOLSON,Victor FltLt RN   RNAS 2Wing   10.7.16 CR Gallipoli1

NICHOLSON,Victor Hills   Sub-Lt RN   HMS Recruit   kld   9.8.17   MR2
NICHOLSON,Whitworth Brady   Lt   RN   HMS Swift   6.5.18   CR Kent7
NIVEN,James Douglas Eng Lt Comdr RN   HMS Black Prince   kia   31.5.16 MR3
NIX,Percival Kent   FtSurg RN   HMS Bulwark   26.11.14 CR Hunts111
NIXON,Albert Edward RMGnr   RMA   HMS Invincible   kia   31.5.16 MR3
NIXON,Edwin Lt   RNR   HMS Doncaster   8.11.16 CR Scot235
NIXON,George Russell   Comdr RN   HMS Albermarle   accdrd 7.11.15 MR3
NOAKE,Basil Stratford   Lt Cmdr   RN   HMS Begonia kia   6.10.17 MR3
NOBLE,John Brecknock   BvtLtCol   RM   RM Barracks(Chatham)   ded   9.3.17   CR Kent42
NOBLE,Thomas Herbert   TAsst Paymr   RNR   HM Yacht Verona   kld   24.2.17 MR1
NOEL,George TSkipper   RNR   7.16
NOKES,Cecil Ivan   Clerk   RN   HMS Russell   kld   27.4.16 MR1
NOLAN,James Joseph TSurg Prob   RNVR HMS Candytuft   kia   18.11.17 MR2
NORMAN,Aubrey Lancelot William   Lt   RNR   HMS Newmarket   kld   17.7.17 MR3
NORMAN,John   TSub-Lt   RNVR Howe Bn RNDiv   4.6.15   MR4
NORMAN,H C D   Lt Cmdr   RNR   18.6.19   CR Norfolk85
NORMAN,William   Lt   RNR   RFA Industry kia   18.10.18   MR3
NORRIS,A.P.   Eng Lt RN   HMS Wear   14.9.15   CR Europe6
NORRIS,Hugh Leigh   Ft Surg RN   HMS Indefatigable   kia   31.5.16 MR2
NORRIS,W.C. ChBosn   RN   HMS Fisgard   21.9.20   CR Hamps9
NORTHCOTT,Henry H MacF TLt   RNVR/RNAS   17.1.16   CR Kent67
NORTHROP,John Eric   TFlt Sub-Lt   RN/RNAS   2.3.17   CR Norfolk85
NORVELL,George Robert   TSkipper   RNR   HMTrawler Speeton   kld   31.12.15 MR1
NOTT,Ryan Pierce   EngSubLt   RNR   HMS Isis   6.3.16   CR Devon1 Evan
NUGENT,Mark Lavallin O'Reilly   TAsst Paymr   RNR   HMS Hampshire   kld   5.6.16   MR3

O

O'BRIEN,Desmond   Hon   Flt Lt   RNAS   kld   16.2.15   MR1
O'BRIEN,Thomas   Gnr   RN   HMS Eden   drd   17.6.16   MR2
O'DRISCOLL,M.D.DSM.   Lt   RNR   HMS Western Queen   6.12.18 CR Eire12
O'DWYER,Arthur   Lt   RM   13.3.20   CR Kent2
O'FEE,Stewart NavlSchmr   RN   HMS Vivid   13.3.20   CR NIreland188
O'HALLORAN,Michael   Gnr   RN   HMS Flirt   1.6.16   CR Kent7
O'HARA,Bernard Patrick   Paymstr   RNR   HMS Espiegle   11.10.19   CR Europe6
O'REILLY,Frank Power   Lt   RN   HMS Invincible   kia   31.5.16 MR3
OAKDEN,Arthur Marshall.MID   Lt   RM   RNDiv Engrs 1FC   dow   21.5.15   CR Gallipoli1
OAKELEY,Francis Eckley   Lt   RN   HM S/M D2   kld   1.12.14 MR3
OAKES,G.   ArtEng RN   HM TB36   28.11.19   CR Hamps5
OAKESHOTT,Leonard England   FltSubLt   RNAS   31.3.18   CR France200
OAKLEY,A.E. EngSubLt   RNR   HMS Sunhill   2.6.19   CR Scot722
OAKLEY,Francis Albert George   Gnr   RN   HMS Good Hope   kia   1.11.14 MR3
OATES,Joseph Gnr   RN   HMS Tipperary   kia   1.6.16   MR2
OATES,Joshua Lawrence   TSub-Lt   RNVR 188 TMB RNDiv   13.11.16   MR21
ODAM,Edwin Keates   Asst Paymr   RN   HMS Defence kia   31.5.16 MR2
ODAM,John Bassett   Asst Paymr   RN   HMS Russell   kld   27.4.16 MR1
ODLE,Harold   SubLt(Obs)   RNAS HMS Ark Royal   kld   2.12.17 CR Greece10
OGILVIE,Alexander Stuart   Midmn RN   HMS Vanguard   kld   9.7.17   MR1
OGSTON,Alexander Lockhart Capt   RM   8.2.19   CR Wales171
OKELL,Alan Amery   2Lt   RMLI   1RM Bn RNDiv   kia   17.2.17 CR France514
OLDHAM,Cecil Henry   ASub-Lt   RN   HMS Vanguard   kld   9.7.17   MR1
OLIVER,Egbert C.   Lt   RNVR Hood Bn RNDiv   5.2.17   CR France514
OLIVER,Frederick William   Instr(Cookery)RN   HMS Curlew   27.9.18   CR Devon3
OLIVER,Richard   Lt   RNVR Mersey Exam Service ded   19.9.17   CR Lancs149
OLIVER,William Smith   FltSubLt   RNAS   Dunkirk   acckld   24.3.17   CR Kent7
ONSLOW,Arthur G.DSC.   LtCmdtRN   HMS Onslaught   1.6.16   CR Scot722 DSO
ORCHARD,Wallace Ernest   FltSubLt   RNAS   2.6.17   CR France512
ORDE,Herbert Walter Julian.DSC.   Lt   RN   HMS Goliath kia   13.5.15 MR1

ORFEUR,Charles Bernard   ObsSubLt   RNAS 2Sqn 1Wing   dow   1.7.17 CR France1359
ORGAN,Ambrose Francis   Gnr   RN   HM TB Nell   kld   7.3.16 MR3
ORGAN,George Frederick   Ch Gnr RN   HMS Good Hope   kia   1.11.14 MR3
ORMEROD,John R   TAsst Paymr   RNR   SS Hungerford   6.4.16 CR Egypt15
ORMEROD,Leonard William.DSC.   FltCmdr   RNAS   16.3.18 CR France1266
ORMEROD,Reginald H.   Midmn RN   HMS St Vincent   9.2.18 CR Yorks583
ORR-EWING,John Angus   Lt   RN   HMS Turbulent   kia   1.6.16 MR3
OSBISTON,Frank Gardiner   Lt   RNR   HMS Victory   3.8.18 CR Devon1
OSBORN,Arthur Ernest   Carp   RN   HMS Russell   kld   27.4.16 MR1
OSBORNE,George Robertson Eng Lt RN   HMS Whitley   drd   14.2.21   CR Europe42
OST,James George   Cmdr   RN   HMS Vernon   27.7.18 CR Sussex135
OSWALD,Donald James Strachan   LtCmdr   RN   HMS Gloucester   6.1.19 CR Italy17
OWEN,Griffith Charles Llewellyn   Midmn RN   HMS Defence kia   31.5.16 MR2
OWEN,Harold William Starr PaymrLt   RNR   HMS Julius   ded   15.2.20   CR Hamps5
OWEN,Harry Kenneth Mostyn Sub-Lt RN   HMS Sorceress   accdrd 16.2.18   MR1
OWEN,John Aubrey   Lt   RNR   HMTrawler John Pollard   27.10.17 CR Wales17
OWENS,George Bolster   Paymr RN   HMS Good Hope   kia   1.11.14 MR3
OWENS,Owen Llewellyn   TSkipper   RNR   HMS Soldier Prince   18.9.16 CR Norfolk131
OXFORD,Charles   Ch Art Eng   RN   HMS Bullfinch accdrd 16.2.15   MR2
OXLADE,Charles Herbert.RD.   Comdr RNR   HMS Arbutus kia   15.12.17 MR2
OXLEY,Kenneth L C TPObs Offr   RNAS   23.10.17 CR Kent65

P

PACE,Henry Joseph   Capt   RMA   7.8.15 CR London9
PATTERSON,Alex   TAsst Eng   RNR   HMS Princess Irene   kld   27.5.15 MR3 PATERSON
PENROSA,John Samuel Sandford   Lt Comdr   RN   HMS Bulwark   kld   26.11.14 MR3 PENROSE
PACEY,James Thomas   Skipper   MMR SS Cawdor Castle   30.3.19 CR Scot280
PAGE,Herbert Joseph TFlt Sub-Lt   RNAS   drd   15.2.16   MR1
PAGE,John Albert   FltLt   RNAS att10Sqn   kia   22.7.17 CR France705
PAGE,Robert Edward TSkipper   RNR   HMTrawler Burnley   kld   25.11.16 MR3
PAGE,Robert James   AGnr RN   HMS Good Hope   kia   1.11.14 MR3
PAILTHORPE,Harold Anderson.MID FltLt   RNAS   kia   23.5.17 CR France924
PAINE,Charles William Stanley   Capt   RMLI Benbow Bn xfered to Hood Bn RNDiv kia   17.7.15 CR Gallipoli2
PAISLEY,William   Lt   RNR   HMS Africa   ded   18.9.18   CR WAfrica30
PALK,Arthur Charles Asst Clerk   RN   HMS Indefatigable   kia   31.5.16 MR2
PALLISTER,John Edward   Lt Comdr   RNR   HMTug Sir Hugh Bell accdrd 1.7.15 MR3
PALMER,Arthur John Lt   RNVR Drake Bn RNDiv   11.8.17 CR France1192
PALMER,Cecil O.   Lt(Obs)   RNAS   26.2.18 CR Greece10
PALMER,Edmund John   TSub-Lt   RNVR Nelson Bn RNDiv   dow   27.4.17   CR France95
PALMER,Harry Hibbitt   TAsst Paymr   RNR   HMS Black Prince   kia   31.5.16 MR3
PARK,William.DSC. LtCmdr   RNVR HMS Ark Royal RNAS   ded   27.1.17   CR Kent46
PARKER,E.C. ChOff RN   HM Coastguards   6.12.19 CR Eire216
PARKER,J H Maj/BvtLtCol RMLI   29.6.18 CR Surrey37
PARKER,Leslie Hunter   TFlt Sub-Lt   RNAS   14.6.17 MR20
PARKER,Reginald Hastings Midmn RN   HMS Marlborough   kia   25.6.20 CR Asia51
PARKER,T.   SubLt RNR   HMS Sir John Moore   26.11.18 CR Lancs43
PARKER,William Pearn   Lt   RNR   HMS Manzanita   ded   10.7.16   CR Italy17
PARKINSON,Oliver Laurence TAsst Paymr   RNR   HMS Louvain kia   20.1.18 MR2
PARKINSON,Reay   Lt   RN   HM S/M E49 kld   12.3.17 MR3
PARMETER,Alfred Phillips.RD.   LtCmdr   RNR   HMS Satellite   5.5.18 CR Yorks98
PARNIS,Charles   EngLt RN   HMS Theseus   4.6.19 CR Numb2
PARRY,George Llewelyn   ALt Col   RMLI 2Bn   dow   2.2.18 CR France145
PARRY,William George   FltOt RNAS HMS President kld acc 12.6.17   CR Staffs52
PARSLOW,F.D.VC. Master/Lt   MM/RNR   HorseTransport AngloCalifornia(London)   4.7.15 MR39
PARSONS,Guy Fowell   Lt Cmdr   RN   HMS Nigella ded acc 6.3.19 MR3
PARSONS,Raymond SLt Comdr   RN   Hood Bn RNDiv   4.6.15 MR4
PARSONS,Reginald Lacey   Paymstr   RNR   HMS Lady Cory Wright   kia   26.3.18 MR3

PARTRIDGE,Charles Burnett Capt RMLI HMS Good Hope kia 1.11.14 MR2
PASCOE,John Mydhope Midmn RN HMS Monmouth kia 1.11.14 MR2
PATERSON,Andrew Lt RNR HM TB No80 accdrd 24.10.16 MR3
PATERSON,George Lt RNVR Anson Bn RNDiv 25.8.18 MR16
PATERSON,James TEng Lt Comdr RNR HMS Morea 9.7.17 CR Essex87
PATERSON,James Knox Eng Lt RNR HMPMS Ascot kia 10.11.18 MR3
PATERSON,O.D. Eng HMTrawler Lochgarry 13.9.16 CR Scot820
PATERSON,Richard E Lt RN HMS Fortune 31.5.16 CR Europe148
PATON,Graham Morton ASub-Lt RNVR Nelson Bn RNDiv dow 4.5.15 MR3
PATON,Norman Giles Sub Lt RNVR HMML No403 kld 22.8.18 MR1
PATON,William F. AssPaymr RNVR 22.5.15 CR Scot674
PATTERSON,F.W.J. ArtEng RN HMS Indomitable 27.12.19 CR Wales402
PATTISON,William Laurence.DSC. SubLt(Obs) RNAS 5Sqn attRFC 22Wing dow 17.3.18 CR France716
PAUL,Hugh Beresford ASub-Lt RN HMS Fortune kia 1.6.16 MR3
PAWSON,Robert Henry Sub-Lt RNVR Drake Bn RNDiv 25.3.18 MR20
PAYNE,Arthur E TSub-Lt RNVR HMML 429 drd 30.11.16 CR Hamps5
PAYNE,Thomas Algernon Wt Tel RNR HMS Macedonia ded 28.2.19 CR Yorks561
PAYNTER,Charles Theodore Lt RN HMS North Star kia 23.4.18 MR1
PEACH,Reginald Henry Paymr Lt RNR HMS Kingfisher 26.11.18 CR Norfolk131
PEARCE GOULD,Alfred Leslie SurgLt RN att 1RM Bn RNDiv kia 19.5.18 CR France2
PEARCE,Bertram James 2Eng MMRes HMS Albyn 2.9.17 CR France1359
PEARCE,Harry William TSkipper RNR HMTrawler Hirose kld 29.6.16 MR2
PEARCE,Isaac TSkipper RNR HMTrawler Dagon kld 8.12.16 MR1
PEARCE,Joseph John TAsst Paymr RNR HMYacht Marynthea 7.5.17 CR Europe23 RNVR
PEARN,T.Edward Warwick Gnr RN HMS Princess Irene kld 27.5.15 MR2
PEARNE,William James Carp RN HMS Indefatigable kia 31.5.16 MR2
PEARSON,Donald Eng Lt RN HMS Marmion 21.10.17 CR Europe146
PEARSON,Eugene Arthur SurgSubLt RNVR HMS Lysander ded 6.11.18 CR Kent83
PEBERDY,Warner Hutchins TFlt Lt RNAS accdrd 14.1.17 MR1
PEDRICK,Arthur Gordon Lt RN HM S/M K9 7.1.18 CR Hamps7
PEEL,Cyril Capt RN HMS Amphitrite 8.11.18 CR Scot217
PEET,Frank Conway Lt RN HMS Rocket 31.10.18 CR Scot722
PICKUP,William Howard SurgLt RN HMS Prince Rupert ded 27.11.18 CR Warwick55
PEGLER,Charles Richard TFlt Sub-Lt RNAS 12.7.17 MR20
PEIRSON,Edward Leslie TAsst Paymr RNR HMS Vanguard kld 9.7.17 MR1
PEIRSON-SMITH,Ernest Cecil Midmn RN HMS Queen Mary kia 31.5.16 MR3
PELLATT,Thomas Henry Art Eng RN HMS Exmouth ded 5.1.16 MR2
PENDER,Frederick William TAsst Eng RNR HMYacht Aries kld 31.10.15 MR3
PENDLETON,Frank Reginald Eng Comdr RN HMS Conquest kia 25.4.16 MR1
PENNELL,Harry Lewin Lee Comdr RN HMS Queen Mary kia 31.5.16 MR3
PENNEY,Douglas Eric TFlt Sub-Lt RNAS kld 9.5.17 CR London23
PENNY,Edward Bosn RN HMS Thetis 26.4.17 CR Sussex144 PENNEY
PENNY,William Ch Sig Bosn RN HMS Good Hope kia 1.11.14 MR3
PERCY,Algernon William Hon TSub-Lt RNR HMS Queen Mary 31.5.16 CR Europe146
PERKINS,Guy Struthers ALt RMLI Deal Bn RNDiv 23.11.15 CR London3
PERRY,Archibald Benjamin EngLt RNR HMS Vienna 6.10.16 CR Essex185
PERRY,Frederick William Abbott Lt RMLI 1RM Bn RNDiv kia 17.2.17 CR France514
PERSEE,Dudley Francis.DSO. Lt RN HMS Tartar 7.11.18 CR Numb4
PETRE,John Joseph.DSC. SqnCmdr RNAS kldacc 13.4.17 CR France699
PHELAN,S J RC Chapn RN 5.16
PHELPS,Thomas Sackville AssPaymstrI/C RNR HMS Gaillardia kld 22.3.18 MR1
PHILIP,John Forbes TLt RNR HMS Candytuft kia 18.11.17 MR2
PHILLIPPS-WOLLEY,Clive Lt Comdr RN HMS Hogue kia 22.9.14 MR1
PHILLIPS,Albert Markham Hood Comdr RN HMS Bulwark kld 26.11.14 MR3
PHILLIPS,Arthur William Sig Bosn RN HMS Tipperary kia 1.6.16 MR3
PHILLIPS,George Hugh TFlt Sub-Lt RNAS drd 7.1.18 MR1
PHILLIPS,George Thomas Art Eng RN HMS Goliath kia 13.5.15 MR3
PHILLIPS,Harold Lt Comdr RNR HMS Almanzola accdrd 25.1.16 MR3
PHILLIPS,James Charles Skipper RNR HMTrawler Lydian kld 18.9.15 MR2
PHILLIPS,John Lt RNR HMS Racoon 9.1.18 CR Scot422

45

PHILLIPS,Richard Lewis   TEng Sub-Lt   RNR   HMS Tara   kia   5.11.15 MR3
PHILLOTT,Charles George Rodney   Lt   RN   HM S/M E6   kld   26.12.15 MR3
PHILP,Frederick John.MC.   Sub Lt RNVR   Drake Bn RNDiv   dow   22.8.18   CR France84
PHIPPS,Francis Thomas   Midmn RN   HMS Defence kia   31.5.16 MR2
PHIPPS,Thomas George   TSkipper   RNR   HMTrawler Whooper kld   30.6.16 MR2
PICKLES,Philip Dobson   Surg   RNVR HMS Russell   28.4.16 CR Europe6
PIKE,William George Henry   Art Eng   RN   HMS Black Prince   kia   31.5.16 MR3
PILCHER,Stephen   Ch Offr   CG   6.3.18 CR Hamps5
PILKINGTON,George Lt   RN   HM S/M C31 kld   7.1.15 MR3
PINHORN,Leonard Waller   AAsst Paymr   RNR   HMS Hogue   kia   22.9.14 MR1
PIPE,David Archibald ATCapt   RMLI   1 RM Bn RNDiv   27.10.17 MR30
PIPON,J.R.   Lt   RNR   HMS Victory   4.2.19 CR Canada1694
PITCHER,Oscar John TSkipper   RNR   HMTrawler Jessie Nutten   kld   4.9.16 MR1
PITCHERS,C. Skipper   MM   SS Queen Bee   4.7.16 CR Suffolk98
PITT,Arthur Henry John   Chapn RN   HMS Good Hope   kia   1.11.14 MR3
PITT,Arthur James   Gnr   RN   HMS Raglan kia   20.1.18 CR Gallipoli1
PITT,Weston W   TPFlt Offr   RNAS   7.6.17 CR Lincs78
PITTENDRIGH,John Lt   RNR   HMS Hussar   ded   28.10.18 CR Italy12
PIZEY,Collyns Price   FltLt   RNAS   11.6.15 CR Greece21
PLACE,John Spencer   Ft Paymr   RN   HMS Barham kia   31.5.16 MR3
PLANTEROSE,Ernest A.   SubLt   RNAS   BritAdriaticSqn 6Wing   17.7.17 CR Italy37
PLATT,Maurice   SubLt   RNVR   RNDiv   26.11.18 CR Lancs427
PLATTS,Edgar Lovell Filmer TLt   RMLI   1 RM Bn RNDiv   28.4.17 MR20
PLUMMER,H.W.   Skipper   RNR   HMTrawler Freesia   2.11.18 CR Eire76
PLUNKETT,Gerald   TSub-Lt   RNVR Collingwood Bn RNDiv   4.6.15 MR4
POINTER,George Horace   EngSubLt   RNR   HMS Hermoine   ded   22.2.19   CR Hamps5
POLAND,R.A. Maj   RMLI   1RM Bn RNDiv   21.8.18 CR France518
POLLARD,Henry   Ch Eng RNR   HMS Viknor   drd   13.1.15   MR3
POLLASTRINI,Michael Lorenzo.MID TMidmn   RNR   HMS Strongbow   kia   17.10.17 MR1
POLWARTH,William AArt Eng   RN   HMS Mary Rose   kia   17.10.17 MR1
PONSONBY,Bertie Hastings Midmn RN   HMS Bulwark kld   26.11.14 MR3
POOK,Charles Harry TEng Sub-Lt   RNR   HMS Alcantara   kia   29.2.16 MR3
POOLE,John Jeffery Graham   Midmn RNR   HMS Almanzora   24.10.18 CR Kent36
POOLE,Sidney Gower SubLt   RNVR Hawke Bn RNDiv   kia   13.11.16 CR France516
POOLE,Walter Croker TLt   RNVR HM Mersey Examination Vessel No1 kld   28.12.17 MR3
POORE,John Verity   Asst Clerk   RN   HMS Cressy   kia   22.9.14 MR1
POPHAM,Arthur Leyborne   Lt Comdr   RN   see LEYBORNE-POPHAM,Arthur
PORTAL,Raymond Spencer   Asub-Lt   RN   HMS Invincible   kia   31.5.16 MR3
PORTCH,Henry Herbert   TLt   RNVR HMS Prize   kia   14.8.17 MR2
PORTER,Angus   SubLt   RN   HMS Centurion   14.3.16 CR Glouc5
PORTER,George H.   SubLt   RNVR/RNAS   4.1.17 CR Herts30
POTTER,Albert Victor   Skipper   RNR   HMT Ruthin Castle   23.4.17 CR Numb97
POTTER,Herbert Alfred   TSurg Prob   RNVR HMS Contest kia   18.9.17 MR2
POTTER,John Lewis   81/WSA   Skipper   RNR   HMT Pitstruan   10.1.15 CR Scot280
POTTER,Percival Barber   TMidmn   RNR   HMS India   kia   8.8.15 MR1
POTTIE,George Maxwell   TAsst Eng   RNR   HMS Ramsey kia   8.8.15 MR2
POTVIN,James Edward.MID   TFlt Sub-Lt   RNAS   drd   19.6.17   MR1
POUND,John Matthew   TCapt RMLI   1 RM Bn RNDiv   13.11.16 MR21
POWELL,Arthur Falkenburg   LtCmdr   RN   HMS Argus   19.6.19 CR Scot722
POWELL,John Mullinger   Clerk RN   HMS Invincible   kia   31.5.16 MR3
POWELL,Leslie Arthur   TFlt Sub-Lt   RNAS 3Sqn   kia   7.3.17 CR France41
POWELL,Owen Philip SubLt RN   HMS Verulam kld   3.9.19 MR70
POWELL,Richard Walter   Skipper   RNR   HMT Eros   kld   8.6.18 CR Yorks2
POWELL,Samuel Huntley   Sub-Lt RNVR Drake Bn RNDiv   25.3.18 MR20
POWNALL,George Harley   Lt Comdr   RN   HMS Egmont kia   25.4.15 MR3
PRATT,Herbert   Bosn   RN   HM S/M K13 drd   29.1.17   CR Scot81
PRATT,Josiah TSkipper   RNR   HMTrawler Lobelia II kld   19.4.17 MR2
PRATT,Percy Alfred Ernest   Carp   RN   HMS Princess Irene   kld   27.5.15 MR3
PRATT,Raymond Forster   SurgProb   RNVR HMS Tartar   17.6.17 CR Numb74
PRATT,William Richard   Gnr   RN   HMS Vernon   21.7.16 CR Mon52

PRATT-BARLOW,Bernhard Alexander   Comdr RN   HMS Hawke   kia   15.10.14 MR1 Bernard
PRATTENT,Francis Melville ALt   RNR   HMS Defence kia   31.5.16 MR2
PREECE,W.L. Lt   RNVR HMS President   10.11.18 CR Wales497
PRENTIS,Osmond James   Comdr RN   HMS Wolverine   kia   28.4.15 MR3
PRESCOTT,George Augustus Ludwig MID TEng Lt RNR HMS Paxton kia   20.5.17 MR2
PREST,Leslie Barton Lt   RN   HMS Clan McNaughton   drd   3.2.15 MR1
PRESTON,George Hindle   TSkipper   RNR   HMTrawler Tervani   kld   5.12.16 MR1
PRETTY,G H A   Gnr   RN   HMS King George V   10.2.19 CR NHants146
PREVOST,Annette Maud   ResNSister   QARNNS   RNHosp(Chatham)   19.11.18 CR Kent46
PRICE,Edgar Sidney TAsst Paymr   RNR   HMS Black Prince   kia   31.5.16 MR3
PRICE,Edward John   Lt   RN   HM S/M E15   16.10.18 CR Iraq8
PRICE,Guy William DSC & bar   Flt Cmdr   RNAS   18.2.18 MR20
PRICE,Vivian Franklin Lionel Rose   LtCmdr   RN   HMS Europa ded   5.11.15 CR Egypt3
PRICE,Wilfred Bartholomew Sub-Lt RN   HMS Defence kia   31.5.16 MR2
PRICE,W H   Lt   RNVR HMML 562   2.7.18 CR Middx15
PRIMROSE,Hugh Rosebery   TAsst Paymr   RNR   HMS Natal   kld   30.12.15 MR1
PRIMROSE,Walter Wingate   Lt   RM   RNDiv attRFC   27.2.17 CR Scot752
PRINCE,H.   Lt   RNR   HMS Presidentkldacc 21.2.19   CR France146
PRINSEP,Caradoc Stuart McLeod   Lt   RN   HM S/M G7   kld   1.11.18 MR3
PRITCHARD,Charles Lt   RNR   HMS Skelwith   14.3.16 CR Asia61
PRITCHARD,Henry 2Lt   16RWFus att Hood Bn RNDiv   7.4.18 MR27
PROSSER,Douglas Henry   Lt   RN   HMS Russell kld   27.4.16 MR1
PROWSE,Cecil Irby   Capt   RN   HMS Queen Mary   kia   31.5.16 MR3
PRYCE-BROWNE,William Herbert   Maj   RMLI   kia   6.10.14 CR Belgium342
PULFORD,George Bensley   TSkipper   RNR   HMDrifter Girl Eva   kld   2.10.16 MR1
PULFORD,Samuel   Lt   RNR   HMTug Stoic   26.6.17 CR Wales651
PULLEN,John Richardson Le Geyt   Midmn RN   HMS Monmouth   kia   1.11.14 MR2
PULLEYNE,Richard Ivor.DSO.DSC.MID   Lt   RN   HM S/M E34 kia   20.7.18 CR Europe96
PULLING,Edward Laston DSO   TFlt Lt RN/RNAS   2.3.17 CR Norfolk85
PUNCH,Sidney E.   Surg   RN   HMS Indefatigable   kia   31.5.16 MR2
PURDY,Claude Chester   Flt Lt RNAS   kia   15.2.18 MR1
PURSER,Frank Duleken   Lt   RNVR Nelson Bn RNDiv   27.12.17 CR France667
PURSER,Hubert Roberts MIDx2   TCapt RMA   18.3.17 CR EAfrica39
PURVIS,John Eiston   Lt   RNVR HMML No561 kld   21.10.18 MR1
PUTTOCK,Denys Ernest   SubLt RN   HMS Valorous   20.3.19 CR Devon153
PYNE,William E   TSkipper   RNR   2.18

Q

QUERIPEL,Cecil Mervyn   LtCmdr   RN   HMS Bulwark   26.11.14 CR Kent46
QUICK,Richard Henry Gnr   RN   HMS Defiance for'M31'   8.3.21 CR Cornwall175
QUILL,Maurice Desmond   Capt   RMA   dedacc 17.6.18   CR Glouc31
QUILTER,John Arnold Cuthbert   TLt Col   Gren Gds Cmdg Howe Bn RNDiv   kia   6.5.15 CR Gallipoli14
QUIRK,Frederick Whitby   Surg   RN   HMS Princess Irene   kld   27.5.15 MR3

R

RABY,Harry Lt   RNR   HMS Ramsey kia   8.8.15 MR2
RADCLIFFE,Samuel Gnr   RN   HMS Laurel kia   28.8.14 MR2
RADMORE,Archibald M.   Skipper   RNR   HMTrawler Bracklyn   11.5.17 CR Suffolk85
RADMORE,Lewis   FltSubLt   RNAS   6.9.16 CR Warwick69
RAE,David   EngSubLt   RNR   HMS Kildonan Castle   8.11.18 CR Kent46
RAILTON,John Cedric FltLt   RNAS   9.5.17 CR Cornwall96 /.3.17
RAINER,Horace   TEng Sub-Lt   RNR   HMS Fauvette kld   9.3.16 MR1
RALPH,Bertram Gray Lt   RNR   HMS Goliath kia   13.5.15 MR1
RALPH,Roderick.DSC.   Skipper   RNR   HMTrawler Neptunian drd   27.10.18 MR3

RAMAGE,George Norris.RD. Comdr RNR   HMS Duke of Albany kia   24.8.16 MR2
RAMSAY,Allan McDonald TSkipper   RNR   HMTrawler Dhoon   kld   24.11.16 MR3
RAMSAY.Donald W. FltSubLt   RNAS   7.7.17 CR France1039
RAMSEY,Frank Blashfield TLt   RNVR Hood Bn RNDiv   20.7.15 MR4
RAMSEY,Robert   Lt   RNR   HMS Manco   21.4.15 MR40
RANKIN,Charles   EngSubLt   RNR   HMYacht Iolaire   1.1.19 CR Cornwall96 &MR2
RANKIN,Edward Harold   Lt   RNVR HMMinelayer 407   6.2.19 CR Devon47
RANSFORD,Lionel Bolton   FltSubLt   RNAS   kia   18.3.18 CR France1266
RANSOME,Reginald Hugh   Lt Comdr   RN   HMS Partridge kia   12.12.17 MR3
RANSON,G A Lt   RNR   HMS Leda   11.1.19 CR Middx7
RAPER,William Ferry Sig Bosn   RN   HMS Invincible   kia   31.5.16 MR3
RATTRAY,Norman McLeod EngSubLt   RNR   HMS Research dedacc 21.7.18   CR Dorset57
RAY,Eric Swire   Lt   RN   HMS Queen Mary   kia   31.5.16 MR3
RAYNER,Edward   TSurg RN   HMS Vanguard   kld   9.7.17 MR1
RAYNER,John Andrew   TSkipper   RNR   HMTrawler Edinburgh Castle   ded   4.12.16 CR Lincs123 RAYNOR
READ,Arthur William EngSubLt   RNR   HMS Alsatian   27.10.18 CR Hamps9
READ,Ernest John.CGM.   Gnr   RN   HMS Invincible   kia   31.5.16 MR3
READ,Harry Croad   EngCmdr   RN   HMS Vivid   26.12.20 CR Cornwall140
RECKITT,Charles E TSurg RN   HMS Victory   20.1.17 CR Surrey2
REDDICK,George Adam   SubLt RNVR Nelson Bn RNDiv   13.11.16 CR France339
REDGATE,George Williams ArtEng RN   HMS Racoon   9.1.18 CR Kent14
REDMOND,Raymond O'Connell   TSurg Prob   RNVR HMS Clan McNaughton   drd   3.2.15 MR1
REECE,Frank William TWt Eng   RNR   HMS Triumph kia   25.5.15 MR2
REED,Stanley John   TSen Eng   RNR   HMS Princess Irene   kld   27.5.15 MR3
REES,Charles Edgar Art Eng   RN   HMS Tipperary   kia   31.5.16 CR Europe64
REED,Thomas 2Eng MM   HMTransport Twilight   28.6.17 CR France1359
REES,Francis Leonard TSub-Lt   RNVR att 190 MGCoy RNDiv   23.4.17 MR20
REES,Frederick Harold   Surg RN   Drake Bn RNDiv   dow   21.6.15   CR Gallipoli1
REES,George William TAsst Eng   RNR   HMS Princess Irene   kld   27.5.15 MR3
REEVE,Percy SubLt RNVR Hawke Bn RNDiv   29.9.18 CR France602
REEVES,Fabian Pember   TFlt Lt RNAS 6Sqdn   6.6.17 MR20
REGAN,Daniel   ChGnr RN   HMS Dreadnought   6.7.19 CR Eire90
REGAN,David ChGnr RN   HMS Dreadnought   6.7.19 CR Eire14
REID,Ellis Vair DSC TFlt Sub-Lt   RNAS   28.7.17 MR20
REID,Harold McK   TFlt Sub-Lt   RNAS   23.2.18 CR Canada1300
REID,J.M.   Lt   RNR   HMS M18   21.10.18 CR Scot387
REID,John Stewart Gilchrist.DSC.   Lt   RNR   HM S/M L55 kia   9.6.19 CR Hamps5
REILLY,Trevor Burke Lt   RNR   HMS Topaze ded   28.11.18 CR Asia60
REISS-SMITH.Robert Edward ChGnr RN   HMS Donegal   17.4.16 CR Devon1
REMFRY,C J Gnr   RN   HMS Pegasus   11.5.21 CR Asia51
RENNICK,Henry Edward de Parny   Lt Comdr   RN   HMS Hogue kia   22.9.14 MR1
RENNIE,Ernest   SubLt RNVR Drake Bn RNDiv   kia   15.5.18 CR France2
RENNIE,Mark Norman   TLt   RNR   HMS Vala   kia   21.8.17 MR1
RENNIE,T.C. Lt   RNR   HMS Passing   13.2.19 CR Scot252
RENNIE,William Watson   TEng RNR   HMS Princess Irene   kld   27.5.15 MR3
RENSHAW,George Robinson Lt   RNR   HMS Defence kia   31.5.16 MR2
REPETTO,Effizzio   Art Eng   RN   HMS Vanguard   kld   9.7.17 MR2
REYNOLDS,Arthur John   Wt Tel RNR   HMS Almanzora   28.10.18 MR1
REYNOLDS,J.J.   Ch Gnr RN   HMSupply Ship Carrigan Head   5.12.16 CR Europe6
REYNOLDS,Roland.MID   Lt   RN   HMDrifter Catspaw   31.12.19 CR Europe178A
REYNOLDS,William WtOff RN   HMS Spey   7.3.17 CR Kent46
RIBGY,W.J.   TAssEng   RNR   HMSpecial service vessel No3   31.5.15 CR Ches61
RIBTON,Reginald H. EngSubLt   RNR   HMS Almanzora   14.2.16 CR Scot1030
RICE,Eric Vyvyan   TSub-Lt   RNVR Nelson Bn RNDiv   13.7.15 MR4
RICHARDS,Benjamin John   Carp Lt RN   HMS Terrible   2.5.17 CR Hamps5
RICHARDS,Charles A.MC.   SubLt RNVR Anson Bn RNDiv   10.11.18 CR France1142
RICHARDS,Edwin Henry   EngLt RN   HMS President   16.9.16 CR Devon3
RICHARDS,James Marks   Ch Carp   RN   HMS Warrior kia   31.5.16 MR2
RICHARDS,John William   Lt   RMLI 1RM Bn RNDiv   kia   13.11.16 CR France339
RICHARDS,Walter H P   Capt   RM   Chatham Bn RNDiv   3.5.15 MR4

48

RICHARDSON,Alexander John Souter   ASub-Lt   RN   HMS Invincible   kia   31.5.16 MR3
RICHARDSON,Daniel Lt   RNR   HMS Lady Cory Wright   kia   26.3.18 MR3
RICHARDSON,Douglas Higham   Lt   RNR   HM TB 9   ded   1.11.18 CR Essex102
RICHARDSON,Frederick   TLt   RNR   HM S/M G9   drd   16.9.17   MR3
RICHARDSON,Henry T Eng Sub-Lt   RNR   2.18
RICHARDSON,Quinton Hume   SurgLtCmdr   RN   HMS Dragon   23.6.19 CR Cornwall140
RICHARDSON,Raymond de Dibon.DSC.   Lt   RN   HMS President   21.3.19 CR Yorks208
RICHARDSON,Samuel Spaulding   Flt Sub Lt   RNAS   drd   19.12.17 MR1
RICHARDSON,William H.   FltLt   RN   RNAS   1.8.17 CR Iraq8
RICHARDSON,William Joseph Martin   Eng Lt RNR   HMAS Kurambra   15.2.19 CR London11
RICHER,Stanley Thompson   TEng   RNR   HMSSV No14 kia   30.5.15 MR1
RICHES,A.G. SubLt RNR   HMYacht Lorna   5.12.15 CR Essex112
RICHMOND,John A H   Sub-Lt RNVR   4.6.15 MR4
RIDER,Arthur Art Eng   RN   HMS Natal   kld   30.12.15 MR1
RIDER,Clifford Heath ASub-Lt   RN   HMS Queen Mary   kia   31.5.16 MR3
RIDGE,Edwyn Manners   Sub-Lt RNVR Benbow Bn RNDiv   8.10.14 MR31
RIDING,John Henry   Sub-Lt RNR   HMYacht Sanda   kia   25.9.15 MR3
RIDLER,George John Lt   RNVR Anson Bn RNDiv   26.3.18 MR20
RIDSDILL,John Henry Skipper   RNR   HMT Strymon   27.10.17 CR Yorks6
RIGBY,Charles Newton Beaumont.MIDx2 Lt RMA   HMS Barham kld   23.4.18 CR Herts57
RIGBY,James Henry Smith   TSub-Lt   RNR   HMTrawler Xylopia   4.2.16 CR Lancs14
RIGBY,Walter J   TAsst Eng   RNR   5.15
RIGGALL,Edward Gordon   Flt Lt RNAS   kld   16.2.15 MR1
RIGGS,Henry Gnr   RN   HMS Negro   drd   21.12.16 MR2
RILEY,Herbert Lawson   Midmn RN   HMS Aboukir kia   22.9.14 MR1
RIMINGTON,Percy William.OBE.   Cmdr RN   HMS Cormorant   12.6.19 CR Europe23
RISING,John Paston   Asst Paymr   RN   HMS Black Prince   kia   31.5.16 MR3
RITCHIE,C.H. Cdt   RN   Keyham RN College   14.12.18 CR Devon3
RIVETT,Charles Henry   TSkipper   RNR   HMDrifter Jeannie Murray   kia   15.2.18 MR1 & CR Norfolk131
ROACH,Edmund Daniel   FltSubLt   RNAS   kld   1.5.17 CR France924
ROACH,Gerald   TFlt Sub-Lt   RNAS   27.7.17 MR20
ROBB,Hamilton J   ALt   RM   11.14
ROBERT,F.W.Cmdr RN   HMS Nesmar II   20.10.18 CR Scot54
ROBERT,Ivon d'Esterre.MID Maj   RFA   Cmdg AnsonBn RNDiv   4.6.15 MR4
ROBERTON,Alexander Patterson   Midmn RN   HMS Zealandia   2.2.17 CR Lancs40
ROBERTS,Edward Elwood   TLt   RNR   HMTrawler Dagon   kld   8.12.16 MR3
ROBERTS,Frank Clive   Eng Sub Lt   RN   HMS Lady Cory Wright   kia   26.3.18 MR3
ROBERTS,Griffith Hugh   TEng Sub-Lt   RNR   HMS Tara   kia   5.11.15 MR3
ROBERTS,Harry   Skipper   RNR   22.7.18 CR Suffolk23
ROBERTS,Norman   Eng Lt Comdr RN   HMS Nestor   kia   31.5.16 MR3
ROBERTS,Norman MC,DCM   TSub-Lt   RNVR Hood Bn RNDiv   31.12.17 MR21
ROBERTS,Thomas Henry   TWt Eng   RNR   HMS Defence kia   31.5.16 MR2
ROBERTS,William Richard Gnr   RN   HMS Invincible   kia   31.5.16 MR3
ROBERTSON,Alan Diarmid Campbell   Midmn RN   HMS Aboukir kia   22.9.14 MR1
ROBERTSON,Albert John   TSub-Lt   RNVR Nelson Bn RNDiv   4.1.18 MR21
ROBERTSON,J.N. FtSurg RN   HMS Blake   22.12.14 CR Devon1
ROBERTSON,James Coutts TWt Eng   RNR   HMS Natal   kld   30.12.15 MR1
ROBERTSON,Thomas Arthur Way Sub-Lt RN   HMS Queen Mary   kia   31.5.16 MR3
ROBERTSON-GLASGOW,Martin   Lt Comdr(Retd)RN   Killed serving in the Army   7.16
ROBINS,Mary Jennette   ResNSister   QARNNS   4.11.18 CR Lancs198
ROBINSON,A.W.   SubLt   RNVR Drake Bn RNDiv   5.2.17 CR France252
ROBINSON,Charles Edward Flt Comdr(Capt)   RNAS(RMLI)   8.12.15 MR4
ROBINSON,Ernest   Lt   RNR   HMS Hawke kia   15.10.14 MR1
ROBINSON,Frederick Gnr   RN   HMS Tyrian   ded   10.4.21   CR Hamps5
ROBINSON,George Brooke   Chapn RN   HMS Formidable   kia   1.1.15 MR1
ROBINSON,George William TSkipper   RNR   HNTrawler Robert Smith   kld   20.7.17 MR3
ROBINSON,James Thomas   TEng Sub-Lt   RNR   MFA Whitehead   kia   15.10.17 MR3
ROBINSON,John Stanley   NavalInstrLt   RN   HMS Royal Oak   13.11.18 CR Scot722
ROBINSON,Lancelot Alec   Asst Paymr   RNR   HMS Bulwark kld   26.11.14 MR3
ROBINSON,Lawrence William   Lt   RMLI 1RM Bn RNDiv   17.2.17 CR France514

ROBINSON,Marshall H.   NavalInstr   RN   HMSVivid   15.6.17 CR Cornwall140
ROBINSON,Oswald   Lt   RNVR HMML No424 kia   23.4.18 MR2
ROBINSON,Percival TEng Lt   RNR   HMS Newmarket   kld   17.7.17 MR3
ROBINSON,Richard A W   TSub-Lt   RNVR   2.17
ROBINSON,Richard Bertram Lt   RNVR HM ML62   10.1.18 CR Scot579
ROBINSON,Samuel   TSub-Lt   RNR   HMS Paxton   kia   20.5.17 MR3
ROBINSON,T.I.C.   SubLt RNVR 2Res Bn RNDiv   28.2.19 CR Hamps1
ROBLEY,John P.   SubLt RNVR Nelson Bn RNDiv   5.6.15 CR Gallipoli14
ROBSON,Edward Gleadall Uphill   AChapn   RN   HMS Aboukir kia   22.9.14 MR1
ROCH,Arthur TwiningTEng Lt   RN   HMS Proserine in SS Persia   drd   30.12.15 MR1
ROCK,Frank Ernest   Surg   RN   HMS Laurentic   kld   25.1.17 MR2
RODWELL,John Martin   TSkipper   RNR   HMDrifter Persistive kld   9.2.16 MR1
ROE,Cyril Charles   Lt   RMLI 1 RM Bn RNDiv   28.4.17 MR20
ROE,Frank Edward Mervyn   Lt Comdr(Retd)RN   DoW recieved in Army Capt 5att12 Rif Brig   7.6.16 CR Belgium11
ROE,Jacob Care   TSub-Lt   RNR   HMS Princess Irene   kld   27.5.15 MR3
ROGERS,Edward Eccles   Skipper   RNR   HMTrawler Ranmanika   accdrd 7.1.19 MR3
ROGERS,Harold Sidney   TLt   RNVR HMTrawler Remindo kld   2.2.18 MR1
ROGERS,Harry PowysLt   RN   HMS Monmouth   kia   1.11.14 MR2
ROGERS,Thomas   TPObs Offr   RNAS   drd   19.6.17   MR1
ROGERS,Thomas Evan   Lt   RNR   HMDrifter Frons Olivae   kld   12.10.15 MR1
ROOKE,Henry Skipper   RNR   HMTrawler Dragon II   8.10.18 CR Eire5
ROOME,Philip William   Ft Paymr   RN   HMS Aboukir kia   22.9.14 MR1
ROONEY,Gerald Christopher Maj   RMLI HMS Queen Mary   kia   31.5.16 MR2
RORKE,Alfred John   TSub-Lt   RNVR Hawke Bn RNDiv   12.2.17 CR France41
ROSE,Benjamin Tuck Skipper   RNR   HMTrawler Euripides accdrd 11.7.18   MR3
ROSE,George Albert Skipper   RNR   HMTrawler Saxon Prince   drd   28.3.16   MR1
ROSE,John H. FltSubLt   RN   RNAS 3Wing   26.11.15 CR Gallipoli1
ROSHER,Harold   FltLt   RNAS   27.2.16 CR Kent5
ROSS,Andrew DCM   Sub-Lt RNVR Drake Bn RNDiv   8.10.18 MR16
ROSS,Arthur Ellerker Lt   RNVR Anson Bn RNDiv Ex 5YorkR   8.10.18 CR France915
ROSS,George TSkipper   RNR   HMDrifter Transit   kia   15.5.17 MR3
ROSS,George Charles Cumberland   Staff Surg   RN   HMS Hawke   kia   15.10.14 MR1
ROSS,George W   TSub-Lt   RNVR Howe Bn RNDiv   4.6.15 MR4
ROSS,Gordon Fraser Lt   RNVR HM MB No254   10.5.18 CR Kent7
ROTHERA,Frank Alan   Lt   RN   HMS Ariel   kld   2.8.18 MR2
ROTHERHAM,Donald Kenneth   Lt   RN   HMS Cadmus   24.3.16 CR Asia33
ROUQUETTE,Arthur Prestwich Henry   LtCmdr   RN   HMS Grafton   15.11.18 CR Egypt8
ROUS,N.   EngLt RNR   HMPMS Belle   22.9.18 CR Lancs102
ROWE,George Moore Allender   Cmdr   RN   HMS Conqueror   acckld 30.4.20   CR Dorset57
ROWE,Henry Herbert Sig Bosn   RN   HMS Black Prince   kia   31.5.16 MR3
ROWE,Seymour F   Comdr RN   see FISHER-ROWE,S
ROWLAND,Harold Clarke   Sub Lt RNVR HMS Motagua kld   19.3.18 MR3
ROWLAND,Samuel   Skipper   RNR   HMT T.R.Ferens   10.11.17 CR Yorks6
ROWLETT,Olive Kathleen   NSisterQARNNS   HMHS Drinn on HMS Natal kld   30.12.15 MR1
ROWLEY,Bertram G TObs Sub-Lt RNAS   3.3.18 CR Leics63
ROWLEY,Frederick Douglas   TEng Lt   RNR   SS Heathersidekia   24.8.17 MR1
ROXBURGH,John Hewitt.MC.   Maj   RN   MG Bn RNDiv   2.10.18 CR France530
ROXBURGH,Robert   Midmn RN   HMS Indefatigable kia   31.5.16 MR2
ROXBY,Leycester Curzon Maude   Lt Cmdr   RN   12.8.18 CR Europe51
ROY,P.A.   EngSubLt   RNR   HMS Sobo   23.2.19 CR Scot674
ROYDS,Jasper F   Sub-Lt RN   HMS Arrogant   9.11.17 CR Lincs57
RUCK-KEENE,Ernest Laurence   Lt   RN   HMS Egmont accdrd 24.12.18 MR3
RUDD,Arthur Ernest Lillington   Lt   RNR   HMTrawler Bracklyn kld   11.5.17 MR1
RUFFLES,James Rayward   TLt   RNR   HMS Highflyer   kld   6.12.17 MR2
RUSE,Richard John   Lt   RN   HMS Mars   28.6.18 CR Devon1
RUSH,John   TEng Sub-Lt   RNR   HMPMS Fair Maid   kld   9.11.16 MR1
RUSSELL,Archibald McKerrow   TSurg RN   HMS Macedonia on HMHS Highland Corrie kia   16.5.17 MR1
RUSSELL,Charles Arthur Campbell   Lt   RN   HM S/M G7   kld   1.11.18 MR3
RUSSELL,Harry Bright   Lt   RNR   HMS Canning ded   24.9.15   MR2
RUSSELL,John George MC   TSub-Lt   RNVR Anson Bn RNDiv   26.10.17 MR30

RUSSUM,Sidney Willetts   EngSubLt   RNR   HMS Viscol   ded   11.2.19   CR Scot764
RUTHERFORD,Angus Bowie Gnr   RN   HMS Princess Irene   kld   27.5.15 MR3
RUTHERFORD,John Douglas Surg   RN   HMS Theseus   13.9.17   CR Greece10
RUTLEDGE,George Robert   TEng Lt Comdr   RNR   HMS Laurentic   kld   25.1.17 MR2
RYAN,Edward William Blackwood   Lt   RN   HM S/M E26   kld   6.7.16 MR3
RYDER,Dudley William   Lt   RN   HM S/M E36   kld   19.1.17 MR3

S

SAINSBURY,Charles William Carp   RN   HMS Hawke   kia   15.10.14 MR1
SALISBURY,J.   Gnr   RN   HMS Vivid   11.3.20 CR Devon3
SALTER,Cyril Jefferies   TLt   RNR   HMTrawler Remindo   kld   2.2.18 MR1
SAMLER,John Harman   Lt   RN   HMS Queen Mary   kia   31.5.16 MR3
SANCTUARY,James Tompson   Paymstr   RNR   HMS Bombala kia   25.4.18 MR1
SANDBACH,Joseph   SubLt RNVR Howe Bn RNDiv   20.7.15 CR Gallipoli2
SANDELL,Arthur   SubLt RNVR Howe Bn RNDiv   30.3.17 CR Iraq8
SANDERCOCK,Courtenay Lyne   Sub Lt RNVR HMTrawler Lochiel   kia   24.7.18 MR1
SANDERS,Frederick J DSO   Maj/TLt Col   RM   see SAUNDERS,F J
SANDERS,W.T.   Gnr   RN   HMS Mischief   27.10.18 CR Devon207
SANDERS,William Edward.VC DSO.TLt Comdr   RNR   HMS Prize   kia   14.8.17 MR2
SANDERS,William H Lt   RM   Portsmouth Bn RNDiv   3.5.15 MR4
SANDFORD,Joseph Herbert   TSkipper   RNR   HMTrawler Carlton   kld   21.2.16 MR1
SANDFORD,Richard Douglas VC   Lt   RN   HM S/M G11   23.11.18 CR Yorks119
SANDISON,Alexander Mundell   T2Lt   RMLI 1RM Bn RNdiv   dow   28.2.17   CR France145
SANDS,Lloyd Allison Flt Lt   RNAS   22.3.18 MR20
SANDY,Thomas   Bosn   RN   HMS Renown ded   11.7.17   CR Hamps9
SARGENT,Charles Henry   TSub-Lt   RNVR HMS Newbury   15.2.18 CR London22
SARGENT,Edwin John Gostwyck   Surg   RN   HMS Topaze   25.6.18 MR65
SAUNDERS,Frederick John.DSO.   LtCol RMLI Cmdg Anson Bn RNDiv   kia   12.11.16 CR France701
SAUNDERS,Percy Michael   TSkipper   RNR   HMTrawler Nadine   kld   1.9.15 MR1
SAUNDERS,Richard TSkipper   RNR   HMTrawler Angelus   28.2.16 CR Lincs156
SAUNDERS,Robert Girling   TFlt Sub-Lt   RNAS   24.6.17 MR20
SAVAGE,Frank   Lt   RMLI 1RM Bn RNDiv   17.2.17 CR France514
SAVILE,H.   Capt   RN   HMYacht Portia   1.11.14 CR Hamps5
SAVILL,Herbert John Capt   RN   HMS Hampshire   kld   5.6.16 MR3
SAVILL,Leslie Spencer   TSub-Lt   RNVR Howe Bn RNDiv   24.4.17 MR20
SAW,Arthur C TFlt Sub-Lt   RNAS   21.4.16 CR Hamps5
SAXBY-THOMAS,Douglas Roscoe   Lt Comdr   RN   HMS Laurentic   kld   25.1.17 MR2
SAYER,Frederick Charles.DSM.   Skipper   RNR   HMTrawler Gabir   kld   24.5.18 MR1
SAYERS,Albert Edward.DSC.TSkipper   RNR   HMTrawler Gambri   kld   18.1.18 MR1
SCARLETT,Leopold Florence Hon   Lt   RN   lent to RAN HMA S/M AE1   drd   14.9.14   MR2
SCARLL,Thomas   Skipper   RNR   HMDrifter Eyrie   kld   2.9.14 MR1
SCHAFER,John Sharpey   Cmdr RN   HMS Gaillardia   kld   22.3.18 MR1
SCHOFIELD,Edward Bandmster WO RMBand   HMS Bulwark kld   26.11.14 MR3
SCHOFIELD,William Richard Lt   RN   HM S/M C29   kld   29.8.15 MR2
SCHOLTZ,Johannes Marais   Lt   RNR   HMS Queen Mary   kia   31.5.16 MR3
SCHREIBER,Vivian George Edward Schreiber Midmn   RN   HMS Monmouth   kia   1.11.14 MR2
SCHURR,Cecil Albert Lt   RNVR CentralSupplyDepot(WormwoodScrubs)   27.6.16 CR Kent27
SCLATER,Guy Lutley Capt   RN   HMS Bulwark kld   26.11.14 CR Hamps157
SCOREY,P.L.   WtShpt RN   HMS Curacao   1.12.18 CR Wales404
SCOTCHER,C.G.   SubLt RNR HMS Welland   16.3.19 CR Hamps5
SCOTT,Albert James Gnr   RN   HMS Bulldog kia   16.4.16 CR Gallipoli1
SCOTT,Frederick S   Ch Gnr RN   HMS Astraea   4.7.16 CR SAfrica158
SCOTT,Gordon Beattie George   Flt Sub-Lt   RNAS 1 Sqdn   3.9.17 MR20
SCOTT,Harold Fawcett   Art Eng   RN   HMS P26   kld   10.4.17 MR1
SCOTT,James D.   FltSubLt   RNAS 3Wing   20.9.16 CR France1826
SCOTT,James G   TLt RNAS   25.1.18 CR Canada1531
SCOTT,John D'Urban Midmn RN   HMS Defence kia   31.5.16 MR2

SCOTT,John Stuart Binney   Lt   RN   HM S/M E3   kia   18.10.14 MR3
SCOTT,Samuel   WtEng RN   HMS Ark Royal   ded   5.6.20 CR Asia51
SCOTT,Walter Comdr RN   HMS Good Hope   kia   1.11.14 MR3
SCOTT,Walter Larmond.DSC&Bar   TLt   RNR   HMS Q20   drd   29.3.17   MR3
SCOTT,William John   Sub-Lt   RNVR HMS Hermione for HMML 364   ded   23.4.19   CR London4
SCRIMGEOUR,Alexander   ASub-Lt   RN   HMS Invincible   kia   31.5.16 MR3
SEABROOK,William Turner TEng Sub-Lt   RNR   HMPMS Queen of the North kld   20.7.17 MR1
SEAMAN,E.   ArtEng RN   HMS Britannia   15.12.18 CR Hamps9
SEARANCKE,Cyril   Lt   RN   HMS Russell   kld   27.4.16 MR1
SEARLE,Francis Charles   Surg   RN   HMS Good Hope   kia   1.11.14 MR3
SEAVERS,Thomas H AWt Tel   RN   HMS Spencer   8.3.18 CR Suffolk130
SEED,Randolph H   TPFlt Offr   RN/RNAS   11.5.17 CR Essex40
SELF,Samuel Robert Victor   Mate (E)   RN   HMS Invincible   kia   31.5.16 MR3
SENNITT,Claude Cushing   TSub-Lt   RNVR Hood Bn RNDiv   23.4.17 CR France95
SETON,Sidney James TAsst Paymr   RNR   HMS Formidable   kia   1.1.15 MR1
SEVERN,Cecil A   Comdr RN   HMS Amphitite   13.3.16 CR Hamps5
SEWELL,Herbert   TEng Lt   RNR   HMS Laurentic   kld   25.1.17 MR2 Hubert
SEYMOUR,Hobart William Theodore Rudolph Lt   RN   HMS Russell kld   27.4.16 MR1
SEYMOUR,Neville   ASub-Lt   RN   HMS Queen Mary   kia   31.5.16 MR3
SEYMOUR,Vere   Lt   RNR   HMS Coquette kld   7.3.16 MR1
SHAKESPEAR,Hastings F   Capt   RN   HMS Wildfire   16.5.17 CR Kent67
SHANE-STEWART,Patrick H Lt Comdr   RNVR   12.17
SHARLAND,William W.   EngLt RNR   HMS Pebble   2.2.17 CR Greece10
SHARMAN,John Edward.DSC&Bar   FltCmdr   RNAS 3Wing 10Sqn attRFC 22Wing kia   22.7.17 CR France705
SHARP,Maurice James Rogers.DSO   Eng Lt Cmdr   RN   HMS Recruit   kld   9.8.17 MR3
SHARPLES,Thomas H.W.   SubLt   RN   HMS Hampshire   drd   5.6.16 CR Scot900
SHATTOCK,Thomas Eng Comdr   RN   HMS Queen Mary   kia   31.5.16 MR3
SHAW,Ernest Edward Sub Lt   RNR   HMS Lady Cory Wright   kia   26.3.18 MR3
SHAW,Henry Staveley Pilkington   Sub-Lt RN   HMS Opal   drd   12.1.18   MR3
SHAW,Herman   TLt   RM   4.17
SHAW,John   EngSubLt   RNR   HMS Nepaulin kia   20.4.17 CR France8
SHAW,P.DSC.LtCmdr   RNR   HMS Sylvia   21.4.18 CR Scot252
SHAW,Samuel Skipper   RNR   HMS Octoroon   24.10.18 CR Yorks1
SHAW,Stewart Patrick Houston   LtCmdr   RNVR Hood Bn RNDiv   kia   30.12.17 CR France662
SHAW,William Joseph   Sub-Lt RNVR Howe Bn RNDiv   26.10.17 MR30
SHEA,Hubert John   TSub-Lt   RNVR Howe Bn RNDiv   17.2.17 MR21
SHEARER,Thomas Ralph   TFlt Sub-Lt   RNAS 9Sqn   13.6.17 CR Belgium171
SHEATH,Ernest Frederick   AMate RN   HMS Queen Mary   kia   31.5.16 MR3
SHEATH,Frederick Charles   AGnr   RN   HMS Bulwark kld   26.11.14 MR3
SHEE,Henry John   TSen Eng   RNR   HMS Princess Irene   kld   27.5.15 MR3
SHELFORD,Thomas Lawrie   Capt   RN   HMS Goliath kia   13.5.15 MR1
SHEPARD,Hardinge Lilford   Lt Comdr   RN   HMS Viknor   drd   13.1.15   MR3
SHEPHERD,Arthur Gelston   PFltSubLt   RNAS   10.3.15 CR Berks15
SHEPHERD,Peter George   Flt Sub Lt   RNAS   accdrd   27.10.17 MR1
SHEPPARD,James Frederick EngLt RNR   HMPMS Helper   11.11.18 CR Lancs146
SHINKFIELD,Percy Robert   2Lt   RNVR RNDiv   8.10.18 CR France338
SHINNIE,Herbert Forsyth Craig   ASub-Lt   RNR   HMS Formidable   kia   1.1.15 MR1
SHORE,Lionel Henry Comdr RN   HMS Invincible   kia   31.5.16 MR3
SHORLAND,George   TSurg RN   HMS Invincible   kia   31.5.16 MR3
SHORLAND,John Maitland   Midmn RN   HMS Invincible   kia   31.5.16 MR3
SHORT,James Hassard   Lt   RNR   HMS Bittern drd   4.4.18 MR2
SHOTTON,Harold   Lt   RNR   HMTrawler Walpole   17.12.16 CR Wales17
SHOULER,Edward James Battams   Lt   RN   HMS Viking kld   29.1.16 MR3
SHREEVE,Percy Silvester   TSkipper   RNR   HMDrifter Moss   kia   25.4.16 MR1
SHRUBSALL,William James Gnr   RN   HMS Aboukir kia   22.9.14 MR1
SIDDLE,Herbert Alfred   TSub-Lt   RNVR Nelson Bn RNDiv   23.4.17 MR20
SIKES,Richard Herbert   TSub-Lt   RNVR Howe Bn RNDiv ex RFus   24.4.17 MR20
SILLITOE,W.E.   Lt   RM   23.4.18 CR Kent2
SILVERTOP,Arthur Edward   Comdr RN   HMS Defence kia   31.5.16 MR2
SILVESTER,S.   ChArtEng   RN   HMS Victory   18.3.20 CR Hamps8

SILVESTER,William Henry TWt Tel   RNR   HMTrawler Columbia kia   1.5.15 MR1
SIMES,Henry Charles Nathaniel   Eng Lt Comdr   RN   HMS Pheasant kld   1.3.17 MR2
SIMMONS,Charles Douglas.DSO.   Lt Cmdr   RNR   HMS Otranto drd   6.10.18MR1
SIMMS,Herbert RutterFltSubLt   RNAS   kia   5.5.16 CR Oxford25
SIMMS,Wilford Suthern   TEng Sub-Lt   RNR   HMPMS Kempton   kld   24.6.17MR3
SIMONDS,Tom   EngLt RN   HMS Pactolus   13.10.15 CR Scot503
SIMPSON,Donald   Gnr   RN   HMS Black Prince   kia   31.5.16MR3
SIMPSON,Hubert Zeph   Asst Paymr   RNR   HMS Hawke   kia   15.10.14 MR1
SIMPSON,Joseph Henry   Clerk RN   HMS Natal   kld   30.12.15 MR1
SIMPSON,Walter Alfred   Sub-Lt RNVR Hood Bn RNDiv   24.3.18 MR20
SIMS,Charles Edmonds   ASub-Lt   RNR   HMS Bayano kia   11.3.15 MR3
SIMS,Edmund Ch Gnr RN   HMS President   28.5.16 CR London2
SIMS,James Theodore TFlt Sub-Lt   RNAS   26.5.17 CR Lincs6
SIMS,John   Midmn RN   HMS Bulwark kld   26.11.14 MR3
SIMS,Leonard Anderson   ALt   RNR   HMS Diana   ded   20.11.17 CR Canada323A
SINCLAIR,Peter Campbell 1472SA   TSkipper   RNR   HMTrawler Cleon   kld   1.2.18 MR3
SINCLAIR,Robert John   Gnr   RN   HMS Conqueror   18.2.19 CR Kent67
SINCLAIR,W. EngCmdr   RNR   HMS Otranto   6.10.18CR Scot31
SINCLAIR,William Baikie   AMate RN   HMS Princess Irene   kld   27.5.15MR1
SINGLE,Frank A.   SubLt RN   HMS Warspite   31.5.16 CR Scot722
SKANDIAN,C.   Intprtr   attDivHQ RNDiv   9.9.15 CR Greece10
SKETCHLEY,Ernest F.Powys.DSO.   Maj   RMLI GenStaff 63 RNDiv   kia   12.10.16 CR France2
SKINNER,Philip John Lancelot   Sub-Lt RN   HMS Formidable   kia   1.1.15 MR1
SKYNNER,William Walker   Lt   RN   HMS Hampshire   kld   5.6.16 MR3
SLACK,Ernest Ch Art Eng   RN   HMS Ardent   kia   1.6.16 MR1
SLAPP,Charles   TSkipper   RNR   HMTrawler Ina Williams   kld   30.5.17MR2
SLATER,A.   Schmr RN   25.6.18 CR Yorks396
SLATER,John Skipper   RNR   HMTrawler Thomas Cornwall drd   29.10.18 MR3
SLEDGE,William G S Gnr   RN   HMS Queen   3.5.15 CR Europe6
SLINGSBY,John   Midmn RN   HMS Formidable   kia   1.1.15 MR1
SLINGSBY,Stephen Henry   Lt   RN   HMS Defence kia   31.5.16MR2
SMILEY,Samuel Thomas   Sub Lt RNR   HMS Arabis   kia   11.2.16MR2
SMITH,A   Skipper   RNR   HMS John Cope   27.1.19 CR Scot820
SMITH,Albert ArtEng RN   HM TB9   dedacc 27.7.16   CR Yorks448
SMITH,Alexander   TSkipper   RNR   HMDrifter Active III   kld   15.10.17 MR3
SMITH,Arthur Guy   Lt   RN   HMS Good Hope   kia   1.11.14MR3
SMITH,Charles EdwinLt   RN   HMS Crescent   28.7.20 CR Scot722
SMITH,Cyril A DSO TLt   RNVR   Presumed killed6.16
SMITH,Ernest Graham   Eng Lt Comdr RN   HMS Vanguard   kld   9.7.17 MR1
SMITH,Francis Beacroft.MC Lt   RNVR RNDiv attRAF   28.5.18 CR Essex1
SMITH,Geoffrey SelbyTFlt Sub-Lt   RNAS 8Sqn   23.11.17 CR France120
SMITH,Harold L.   FltSubLt   RNAS   24.5.17 CR France1278
SMITH,Harold Dent   TFlt Sub-Lt   RNAS   drd   24.5.17   MR1
SMITH,Harold Lindsay.DSC. Art Eng   RN   HM S/M L10 kia   4.10.18MR3
SMITH,John Eric Seldon   Midmn RN   HMS Royal Oak   26.7.19 CR Surrey55
SMITH,John Essex Grey   Lt Cmdr   RN   HMS Cambrian   accdrd 17.3.17   MR2
SMITH,Joseph Arthur 2Lt   RMLI 2Bn   dow   27.3.18   CR France225
SMITH,Lewis E.   FltSubLt   RNAS   25.2.17 CR France1675 2Lt
SMITH,Langley Frank Willard.DSC. TFlt Sub-Lt RNAS   4Sqn 4Wing   kia   12.6.17 CR Belgium376 FltLt
SMITH,S.E.   Bandmr2Cl   RMB 1131 RM HMS Conqueror   21.11.18 CR Devon3
SMITH,S.G.   Lt   RNR   Gibralta   26.7.18 CR London25
SMITH,Samuel C A   Gnr   RN   2.15
SMITH,Sydney F B   TLt   RNVR   9.17
SMITH,Thomas   Midmn RNR   HMS Shark   31.5.16 CR Europe110
SMITH,Victor Adolphus   Skipper   RNR   HMDrifter Nexus   9.5.18 CR Lancs43
SMITH,William   TEng Sub-Lt   RNR   HMS Bacchante   accdrd 21.2.17   MR1
SMITH,William JamesTWt Eng   RNR   HMS Bulwark kld   26.11.14 MR3
SMYTH,Basil Wilson TSub-Lt   RNVR Nelson Bn RNDiv   13.7.15 MR4
SMYTH-OSBOURNE,Edward   Lt Comdr   RN   HMS Invincible   kia   31.5.16MR3
SNAGG,B.C.K.   Capt   RM   HQ   27.2.19 CR Sussex197

53

SNEAD-COX,Herbert Arthur Midmn RN   HMS Indefatigable   kia   31.5.16MR2
SNOOK,Ralph Edgar Lt   RN   HM S/M E50 kld   31.1.18MR3
SNOW,Edward RupertMidmn RN   HMS Ark Royal att RNAS   3.3.17 CR Gallipoli1
SNOW,Vincent Graham   Lt   RN   HMS Hampshire   kld   5.6.16 MR3
SOADY,J.C. LtCmdr   RN   HMS Egmont   28.4.16 CR Devon1
SOAMES,Eric ASub-Lt   RN   HMS Racoon drd   9.1.18 MR1
SOANES,John Skipper   RNR   HMDrifter The Throne   11.10.18 CR France123
SOLLY,Alfred TEng Sub-Lt RNR   HMPMS Queen of the South kld   20.7.17MR1
SOMERVILLE,Frank Bowfield   PMidmn   RNR HMS Formidable   kia   1.1.15 MR1
SOMERVILLE,John White   2Lt   RMLI 2RM Bn RNDiv   22.6.16 CR France558
SOMERVILLE,Kenneth Archibald May   Midmn RN   HMS Monmouth   kia   1.11.14MR2
SOREL-CAMERON,Herbert Augustus   ATLt RNR HMS Stephen Furness kia   13.12.17 MR3
SOUHAMY,John Charles   ChGnr RN   HMS Defiance   3.6.18 CR Devon3
SOUTER,Elias Suding TSub-Lt   RNR   MFA Eleanor kia   12.2.18MR3
SOUTHERN,F.   SubLt RNVR Anson Bn RNDiv   27.9.18 CR France530
SOUTHGATE,Henry Albert 2Lt   RN   3RWKentR attAnson Bn RNDiv   8.4.18 CR France252
SOUTHON,Harry   Art Eng   RN   HMS Defence kia   31.5.16MR3
SOUTHWELL,Henry Kenneth Martin Lt   RN   HM S/M L55 kia   9.6.19 CR Hamps5
SUTTON,Wilfrid JohnPaymr RN   HMS Queen Elizabeth   9.12.18CR Hamps7
SOWDEN,William Richard   PMidmn   RNR HMS Hampshire   kld   5.6.16 MR3
SOWERBY,Charles Fitzgerald   Capt RN   HMS Indefatigable   kia   31.5.16MR2
SPARKS,H E A   Lt   RNVR   28.9.18 CR Surrey6
SPARKS,John Barnes CBE Capt RN   29.3.20 CR London4
SPARKS,John James Eng Lt RNR   HMS Portwood   kia   8.8.18 MR1
SPARLING,Sydney J. TMaj   RM   Howe Bn RNDiv   4.6.15 MR4
SPEAKMAN,Solomon Ernest Lt   RNR   HMS Ganges   8.5.18 CR Lancs34
SPEARMAN,Alexander Young Crawshay Mainwaring Cmdr RN   Collingwood Bn RNDiv   4.6.15 MR4
SPEED,Walter Henry Bosn   RN   HMS Kent   ded   31.3.18   MR3
SPENCER,George DSC   Lt   RNR HMS Iris   dow   23.4.18   CR London12
SPENCER,Thomas Flt Sub-Lt   RNAS   kld   16.2.15MR1
SPENCER WARWICK,John Charles TLt   RNVR Anson Bn RNDiv   4.6.15 MR4
SPENSER,H. SubLt RNVR   13.9.14 CR Kent2
SPERLING,Charles Auriol   Lt   RN   HMS Petard   31.5.16 CR Scot722
SPILMAN,Frederick William Ch Offr   RN   HM Coast Guard   8.11.18CR Scot965
SPRANG,E.A.MC.   Lt Cmdr   RNVR Anson Bn RNDiv   26.8.18 CR France84
SPROTT,HughTEng Sub-Lt   RNR HMS Calgarion   kia   1.3.18 MR3
SPRY,William Ft Surg RN   HMS Alsatian   28.11.14 MR2
SQUIRES,Eric W.   SubLt RNVR Nelson Bn RNDiv   13.11.16 CR France339
STRICKLAND,Percy Lt   RN   HMS Dublin kia   31.5.16CR Scot879
St.JAMES,Joseph A.   FltSubLt   RNAS   3.11.17CR Kent25
ST.VINCENT-RYAN,EdmondLt   RM   ded   2.2.17 CR Scot241
STACEY,Aylmer Geoffrey   Capt RMLI HMS Minerva ded   4.10.15CR Egypt15
STACEY,Frank Wendell   TSub-Lt   RNVR Hood Bn RNDiv   4.6.15 MR4
STAHL,Henry C   Lt Comdr   RN   HMTrawler King Emperor   4.2.16 CR Surrey106
STAINER,William Gordon   Paymr RN   HMS Bulwark kld   26.11.14 MR3
STALLARD,Albert Donald   AAsst Paymr RN   HMS Princess Irene kld   27.5.15MR3
STALLARD,George T Carp   RN   HMS Hampshire   drd   5.6.16 CR Scot900
STANFORD,E.   SubLt RNVR RN Depot CrystalPalace   15.2.15 CR Kent83
STANLEY,Leonard   SubLt RNR HMS Alcantara   2.3.16 CR Scot900
STANNARD,Charles Edward TWt Tel   RNR HMS Champagne   kia   9.10.17MR2
STANTON,Robert Greenhow Openshaw   Lt   RMLI 4 Bn dow   28.4.18   CR Lincs38
STAPLETON,Thomas Lt   RN   HMS Monmouth   kia   1.11.14MR2
STARK,Adolphus Edward   Art Eng   RN   HMS Drake kia   2.10.17MR3
STARK,J.   2Eng RNR HMS Duchess of Hamilton   29.11.15 CR Suffolk130
START,Alfred AWt Mech   RN   HMS Monmouth   kia   1.11.14MR2
STARTIN,Francis Henry James.MID SubLt RNVR Nelson Bn RNDiv   dow   19.7.15   CR Gallipoli1
STAUGHTON,Albert W   TCapt RMLI 2Bn   26.12.16 CR France40
STEEDMAN,Robert Skipper   RNR   HMTrawler Ethelwulf kld   1.12.18MR1
STEEL,John Lt   RNVR HMS Peel Castle   7.2.16 CR Kent28
STEEL,John Haythorne   Lt   RN   HMS Munster accdrd 18.4.18   MR3

54

STEELE,Frank Charles   Wt Shpt   RN   HMS Cleopatra   drd   3.11.20 MR3
STEELE,Robert George   Lt   RNR   HMS Polandia drd   10.3.17   MR2
STEELE,Thomas   Lt   RNR   HMS Laurentic   drd   25.1.17   CR NIreland102
STEGGALL,John William Abbott   TNaval Instr RN   HMS Invincible   kia   31.5.16 MR3
STEGGLES,Thomas William   Mate   RN   HMS Indefatigable   kia   31.5.16 MR3
STEINTHAL,Geoffrey Rowlandson   ALt   RMLI   HMS Black Prince   kia   31.5.16 MR1
STEPHEN,Alexander Piggot   TLt   RN   HMYacht Zarefan   kld   8.5.17   MR3
STEPHENS,Arthur Kingdon   Ass Constr2Cl RCNC   HMS Queen Mary   kia   31.5.16 MR2
STEPHENS,Franklyn Frith   Bosn   RN   HMS Good Hope   kia   1.11.14 MR3
STEPHENS,Richard   SubLt   RNR   HMS Terrible   ded   7.2.19   CR Cornwall161
STEPHENSON,Reginald Leonard   Sub-Lt   RNVR   Hood Bn RNDiv   25.5.18   MR27
STERNDALE BENNETT,Waller.DSO&Bar   Cmdr   RN   Drake Bn RNDiv   7.11.17   CR Belgium16
STEVENS,Josiah Henry   TAsst Paymr   RNR   HMS President in SS Normandy   kia   25.1.18 MR1
STEVENS,Philip Bennett   Ft Paymr   RN   HMS Vanguard   kld   9.7.17   MR1
STEVENS,Walter James   FltOff   RNAS   acckld   11.3.18   CR Kent205
STEVENSON,Frederick Fotheringham Anderson Sub Lt RNR   HMS Perth   kia   1.10.18 MR1
STEVENSON,James Willasey Eng Sub Lt   RNR   HMTrawler Dirk   kia   28.5.18 MR1
STEVENSON,John   TLt   RNR   HMS Bergamot   kia   13.8.17 MR2
STEWART,Charles   ATLt   RNR   HMS Arbutus kia   15.12.17   MR2
STEWART,Claud Lapsley.MID   Eng Cmdr   RNR   HMS Patia   kia   13.6.18 MR3
STEWART,Francis Gordon   LtCmdr   RN   HMS Hampshire   drd   5.6.16   CR Scot900
STEWART,James Stenhouse   TAsst Eng   RNR   HMS Viknor   drd   13.1.15   MR3
STEWART,John   Skipper   RNR   HMDrifter John Robert   kld   1.2.19   MR3
STEWART,John William Alfred   Ch Gnr RN   HMS Cormorant   28.4.15   CR Europe23
STEWART,Peter   TEng   RNR   HMS Princess Irene   kld   27.5.15 MR3
STEWART,Thomas Louis Grenet   Surg   RN   attRNDiv   4.6.15   CR Greece10
STEWART,William S.FltSubLt   RNAS   kld   8.11.16 CR Scot11
STIRLING,Wilfred Dixon   Lt (N)   RN   HMS Monmouth   kia   1.11.14 MR2
STOCKER,Walter G   AGnr   RN   HMS Cameleon   9.6.17   CR Europe6
STOCKS,David De Beauvoir.DSO.   Comdr RN   HM S/M K4   drd   31.1.18   MR3
STOEHR,Oscar Humphrey   Lt   RN   HMS Vanguard   kld   9.7.17   MR1
STOKES,Louis Mauden   T2Lt   RMLI   2Bn   kia   13.11.16   CR France131
STOKES,Walter   Eng Comdr   RN   HMS Hogue   kia   20.10.14   CR Europe90
STONE,Arthur Edward   Wt Mech   RN   HMS Queen Mary   kia   31.5.16 MR3
STONE,Arthur Walter TLt   RNVR HMS Manxman   accdrd   24.10.17   MR1
STONE,Frederick William   TEng Sub-Lt   RNR   HMYacht Zaida   kia   17.8.16 MR1
STONE,Horace Gordon   Lt   RNVR   ded   15.12.18   CR France457
STOPFORD-SACKVILLE,Geoffrey William Lt   RN   HMS Ribble   ded   20.5.15   CR Egypt3
STOREY,T.B.   Lt   RNR   HMS Otranto   11.9.15   CR SAmerica12
STORRS,Francis Edmund   Lt   RNVR HMS President   10.11.18   CR London8
STORY,Louis Percival St.John   TSurg Prob   RNVR HMS Opal   drd   12.1.18   MR3
STOTT,Fred   EngSubLt   RNR   HMS Styx   ded   10.12.18   CR EAfrica36
STOUT,T.   Lt   see YORSTON true name
STRACHAN,Alexander Ledingham   TSurg Prob   RNVR HMS Genista kia   23.10.16   MR3
STRANG,George Nicholas   TSub-Lt   RNVR   Howe Bn RNDiv   13.11.16   MR21
STRANGE,Charles Stuart   Asst Paymr   RN   HMS President   22.4.16   CR France85
STRATHERN,Robert Stewart TEng Sub-Lt   RNR   MFA Eleanor kia   12.2.18 MR1
STRATHY,Ford Stuart   TFlt Sub-Lt   RNAS   6Sqn   kia   17.8.17 CR Belgium173
STREET,Edward Walter Lloyd   PaymrCapt   RN   HMS Pembroke   4.6.19   CR Kent46
STREET,George Campbell   Lt Comdr   RN   HMS Queen Mary   kia   31.5.16 MR3
STREET,Henry Layard   Lt Comdr   RN   HMS Formidable   kia   1.1.15   MR1
STREVENS,Charles Edward   Bosn   RN   HMS Superb   8.12.18 CR Asia81
STRICK,J.K.   Maj   RM   Unatt List   13.1.19   CR France458
STRICKLAND,Charles Walter Campbell Cmdr   RN   HMS Wildfire   14.9.18   CR London28
STRICKLAND,Herbert Slade   Sub-Lt   RNVR   Hawke Bn RNDiv   3.9.18   MR16
STRICKLAND,Percy   Lt   RN   5.16
STRINGER,Frederick Thurston   Lt   RN   HMS Redpole   26.3.19   CR Glouc178
STROWGER,Alonzo   TSkipper   RNR   HMDrifter Clover Bank   kia   24.4.16 MR1
STRUGNELL,H.F.H.   Maj   RM   dedacc   21.3.19   CR Hamps242
STUART,Dudley   Lt Comdr   RN   HMS Turbulent   kia   1.6.16   MR3

STUART,Kenneth   ProbF/O   RNAS   kld   13.6.17 CR Kent83
STUART,Marlin   Eng Lt Comdr   RN/RNAS   21.6.16 CR London8
STUBBS,John Duncan Midmn RN   HMS Aboukir kia   22.9.14 MR1
STUCKEY,Frank Stuart   Art Eng   RN   HMS Bulwark kld   26.11.14 MR3
STURROCK,Peter Alexander Crawford.DSC.Lt   RN   HMS Penarth kld   4.2.19 MR1
STURT,Albert Edward Ch Gnr RN   HMS Queen Mary   kia   31.5.16 MR3
SULIVAN,Gerald Henry   TCapt RMLI 1 RM Bn RNDiv   13.11.16 MR21
SULLIVAN,Christopher   Ch Bosn   RN   HMS Victory   27.9.17 CR Hamps5
SUMMERS,Cyril Henry Gerald   Midmn RN   HMS Indefatigable   kia   31.5.16 MR2
SUMNER,John David Ch Gnr RN   HM TB No96 drd   1.11.15 MR2
SUTCLIFFE,James Frederick Lt   RMLI Portsmouth Bn RNDiv   14.7.15 MR4
SUTHERLAND,William   Skipper   RNR HM Drifter Deliverer kia   3.11.17 MR3
SUTTON,Arthur Lawrence   Gnr   RN   HMS Hampshire   kld   5.6.16 MR3
SUTTON,Ernest Arthur   TWt Tel   RNR HM Trawler City of Dundee drd   14.9.15   MR3
SWAINSON,Andrew N.   Lt   RN   HMS Flirt   1.6.16 CR Sussex109
SWALE,John V.   T2Lt RMLI 2Bn   17.2.17 CR France41
SWALES,Robert   Skipper   RNR HMS Victory   18.10.18 CR Lancs48
SWALLOW,Richard   Flt Sub-Lt   RNAS   20.12.17 CR Sussex144
SWANSON,William John   Bosn   RN   HMS Goliath kia   13.5.15 MR2
SWEET,Algernon Sidney Osborne   Chapn RN   HMS Natal   kld   30.12.15 MR1
SWIFT,Lionel Walthew   Eng Cmdr   RN   HM Yacht Nairn   ded   24.8.19   MR2
SWINBURNE,Thomas Reid   TFlt Sub-Lt   RNAS 1 Sqdn   8.6.17 MR20
SYKES,G.J.   LtCmdr   RNR HMS Ooma   3.6.18 CR WAfrica30
SYKES,J.   Skipper   RNR HMT Swallow   26.11.16 CR Scot280
SYLK-ROWLANDS,Christopher Macaulay Sub-Lt   RNR   HMS Tartar   17.6.17 CR France102
SZULEZEWSKI,Oswald DSO.   Lt   RNVR HMS Proserpine   26.10.17 CR Iraq5

T

TABUTEAU,Augustus Elliott Ft Paymr   RN   HMS Natal   kia   30.12.15 MR1
TAIT,Joseph Cook   Eng Lt RNR RFA Industry kia   18.10.18 MR3
TALBOT,Geoffrey Richard Henry   FltLt RNAS   29.6.16 CR Herts14 /.6.16
TAMPLIN,Gerald Hornby   Lt   RNVR Hood Bn RNDiv   23.4.17 CR France452
TANNER,Charles Philip   Eng Sub Lt   RN   HMS Indefatigable kia   31.5.16 MR2
TATHAM,Trevor Hodgson Stanley   Lt   RN   HMS Formidable kia   1.1.15 MR1
TATHAM,William Inglis   Sub-Lt RN   HM S/M H3   kld   15.7.16 MR3
TATTERSALL,Donald Stewart   PMidmn   RNR HMS Formidable   kia   1.1.15 MR1
TAYLOR,A.   EngSubLt   RNR HMS Ophir   9.2.19 CR Lancs4
TAYLOR,A.   Skipper   RNR HM Drifter Enterprise   18.3.18 CR Scot280
TAYLOR,A.G.E.   Capt   RN   7RFus att RNDiv   27.5.17 CR France95
TAYLOR,Charles G.MVO.   EngCapt   RN   HMS Tiger   24.1.15 CR Devon237
TAYLOR,Frank Arnold   Sub-Lt RNVR Hood Bn RNDiv   24.3.18 MR20
TAYLOR,Godfrey   Ft Surg RN   HMS Formidable kia   1.1.15 MR1
TAYLOR,Henry Noel Aldersey   Midmn RN   HMS Queen Mary   kia   31.5.16 MR3
TAYLOR,L T Lt   RNVR HM Trawler Israel Aldcroft   8.11.18 CR London14
TAYLOR,Norman Willis   Midmn RN   HMS Bulwark   26.11.14 CR Kent46
TAYLOR,Ralph   SubLt RNVR Nelson Bn RNDiv   22.12.17 CR France662
TAYLOR,T.V. Skipper   RNR HM Trawler Stelma   3.2.19 CR Dorset57
TAYLOR,William George   Gnr   RN   HMS Defence kia   31.5.16 MR3
TEAGUE,John Cockburn Jessop   Capt   RM   Portsmouth Bn RNDiv   1.5.15 MR4
TEDBURY,Spencer George   Art Eng   RN   HMS Goliath kia   13.5.15 MR3
TENCH,Richard James   EngRrAdml   RN   1.11.18 CR Hamps10
TENISON,Julian T.   LtCmdr   RN   HM S/M E41   15.8.16 CR Suffolk130
TENNYSON,Harold C.Hon   SubLt RN   HM TBD Viking   29.1.16 CR Hamps234
TERRENEAU,Cecil Roy   TFlt Sub-Lt   RNAS   29.4.16 MR50
TERRY,Frank Goodrich   Lt Comdr   RN   HMS Fortune kia   1.6.16 MR3
TETLEY,Arthur S.MIDx2   TLt Col   RM   Drake Bn RNDiv   dow   15.11.16 CR France41 RNVR
THACKARA,Roy Arthur   Asst Eng   RNR HMS India kia   8.8.15 MR1

56

THACKER,George Daniel   TSkipper   RNR   HMDrifter Cosmos   kia   15.2.18 MR1
THACKER,William Norman Lt   RNVR   HMML 520   17.2.18 CR Eire76
THIRLWELL,Robert TSub-Lt   RNR   HMYacht Zaida   kia   17.8.16 MR1
THOMAS,Alfred   TSkipper   RNR   HMTrawler Benton Castle   kld   10.11.16 CR Hamps9
THOMAS,Aubrey   LtCmdr   RN   HMS Thalia   6.6.16 CR Scot926
THOMAS,Francis Hastings.DSC.MID Capt   RMLI   HMS Talbot   kia   15.8.16 MR2
THOMAS,John E.   FltSubLt   RNAS   3.9.17 CR Wales603
THOMAS,Leslie Morgan   SubLt RNVR   Anson Bn RNDiv   15.2.17 CR France8
THOMAS,Robert   Lt   RNR   HMS Kelvin   kia   7.7.17 CR Wales550
THOMAS,William James   StnOff HM CG   20.10.24 CR Kent28
THOMPSON,Herbert Edward TSkipper   RNR   HMTrawler Repro   kld   26.4.17 MR1
THOMPSON,Lionel G.C.   SubLt RN   21.3.16 CR Sussex164
THOMPSON,Richard James TWt Tel   RNR   HMS Laurentic   kld   25.1.17 MR2
THOMSON,Andrew TSen Eng   RNR   HMS Clan McNaughton   drd   3.2.15 MR1
THOMSON,C.W.   Lt   RNR   HMS Egmont   4.10.18 CR Europe6
THOMSON,Charles   Skipper   RNR   HMTrawler Sapper   kld   29.12.17 MR3
THOMSON,Lindsay McClure Slade   Sub-Lt RN   HMS Torrent   kld   23.2.17 MR3
THOMSON,M Wt Schmr   RN   HMS Hecla   12.2.19 CR Scot669
THOMSON,P. EngSubLt   RNR   HMS Duke of Cornwall   20.2.19 CR Lancs146
THORNBURY,Brian Lt   RN   HMS Lynx   kld   9.8.15 MR3
THORNE,Alfred L.   FltSubLt   RNAS   9.4.17 CR France583
THORNELY,John Stephen Samworth ALt   RM   Chatham Bn RNDiv ded   24.7.15   MR40
THORNHAM,Albert William TSkipper   RNR   HMTrawler Thuringia kia   11.11.17 MR1
THORNHILL,Humphrey O'Brien   Sub-Lt RN   HMS Lassoo   kld   13.8.16 MR2
THORNTON,Frank Ernest   TSkipper   RNR   HMTrawler Corona   kld   23.3.16 MR1
THORPE,William   Skipper   RNR   SS James & Walter   ded   7.3.19 CR Suffolk92
THURNALL,William Eustace Valentine 2Lt RM   HMS Commonwealth ded   1.2.21 CR Scot963
THURSFIELD,R.M.R. Surg Lt RN   HMS Glowworm   25.8.19 CR Europe179 &MR70
TILLER,George Edwin   Mate RN   HM S/M C34 kia   21.7.17 MR2
TILLING,Walter Randall   Lt   RNR   HMS Excellent Ex HMS Kent   20.10.18 CR Hamps57
TINDALL,N.S.   Cmdr RN   HMS Clematis   2.10.20 CR Europe6
TINNE,Ernest Percy James   Lt   RNR   HMS Hogue   kia   22.9.14 MR1
TIPPEN,Lewis Roland Asst Paymr   RN   HMS Invincible   kia   31.5.16 MR3
TISDALL,Arthur Walderne St Clair.VC.MID TSub-Lt RNVR   Anson Bn RNDiv   6.5.15 MR4
TITCOMB,Francis Holt Yates TPFlt Offr   RNAS   15.4.17 CR London4
TITHERIDGE,Benjamin MVO   Lt Comdr   RN   HMS Pomone   23.1.18 CR Hamps4
TITLEY,Guy Lt   RN   HMS Natal   kld   30.12.15 MR1
TIZARD,John Ellery Asst Paymr   RN   HMS Good Hope   kia   1.11.14 MR3
TODD,Allan Switzer TFlt Lt RNAS attd RFC 20 Wing   4.1.17 MR20
TODD,Hugh SenEng RNR 3SpServSqn   3.7.15 CR NIreland37
TODD,J.G.   SubLt RNVR Hawke Bn RNDiv   2.10.18 CR France530
TOLLAST,Robert Owen   Lt   RMLI   RNDiv Engrs 2FC   19.5.15 CR Gallipoli1
TOMS,Francis Hamilton   PTFlt Sub-Lt RNAS   20.2.16 CR London6
TONKINSON,Albert Joseph Surg RN   HMS Monmouth   kia   1.11.14 MR2
TOOTELL,E. Maj RM   11.1.20 CR Kent2
TOTHILL,Geoffrey Ivan Francis   Midmn RNVR   killed serving in Army 2Lt 4RFus kia   27.3.16 MR29
TOTTENHAM,Charles Loftus DSO Lt   RNR   HMS Lorna   ded   27.11.18 CR London4
TOTTENHAM,Desmond Frank Charles Loftus ASub Lt   RN   HMS Invincible   kia   31.5.16 MR3
TOTTIE,Oscar William   Lt   RN   HMS Aboukir kia   22.9.14 MR1
TOUGH,Neil Skipper   RNR   HMDrifter Mackays   1.5.18 CR Scot249
TOUGHILL,Francis Robert James   PMidmn   RNR   HMS Negro   drd   21.12.16 MR1
TOULMIN,Stewart Newnham TSurg RN   MFA Ermine   kia   2.8.17 MR2
TOWERS,Grantham TFlt Sub-Lt   RNAS   7.11.17 CR Hamps5
TOWNSEND,J.W.E. LtCmdr   RN   HMS Imperieuse   19.11.15 CR Dorset51
TOWNSEND,J T   Gnr RN   HMS Revenge   9.11.18 CR Hamps9
TOWNSEND,Richard Herbert Denney.MID Comdr RN   HMS Invincible   kia   31.5.16 MR3
TRAHERNE,Llewellyn Edmund   Cmdr RN   HMS Excellent   ded   14.10.14 CR Wales31
TRAPP,George Leonard   TFlt Sub-Lt   RNAS 10Sqn   13.11.17 CR Belgium16
TRAPP,Stanley Valentine   FltSubLt   RNAS 8Sqn att RFC 22Wing   10.12.16 CR France167
TRAVERS,William J. Lt   RNVR Drake Bn RNDiv   kia   4.2.17 CR France339

TRAYNOR,Walter E. FltLt　RNAS　RN Wing 3Sqn　　2.2.17　CR France518
TREASURE,Douglas George　Lt　　RNVR　HM PMS Kylemore　　10.3.19　CR Suffolk130
TREASURE,I.N.　　Midmn RNVR　HMS Tancred　　11.11.18　CR Scot722
TREEBY,Reginald Butcher　PMidmn　　RNR　HMS Bulwark kld　　26.11.14　MR3
TREMAYNE,John A.E.　TSub-Lt　　RNVR　Hawke Bn RNDiv　　19.6.15　MR4
TREMBETH,George　Lt　RNR　HMS Begonia kia　6.10.17MR3
TRENHOLM,F.E.　SubLt RNVR　Anson Bn RNDiv　　10.11.18　CR France1142
TREVELYAN,Percy　SubLt　RN　HMS Sable　ded　10.3.19　　CR Oxford74
TREVES,Harold Thomsett　TLt　RNVR　Nelson Bn RNDiv　dow　25.5.15　　MR3
TREW,Arthur J　TEng Lt　RNR　HMS Osmanich　drd　7.1.18 CR Egypt1
TREWEEKS,Richard Edward Lewis　Lt　RN　HMS Natal　kld　30.12.15　MR1
TREWIN,William George Knight　Bosn　RN　HMS Defence kia　31.5.16MR2
TRIGGS,Tom Kenneth.AM.(gold)　AComdr　RN　HMS Highflyer　kld　6.12.17MR2
TROLLOPE,Douglas KennedyLt　RN　HMS Tobago　ded　11.12.18　CR Scot722
TROTTER,Alfred　Art Eng　RN　HMS Penarth　kld　4.2.19　MR1
TROTTER,Warren Francis　Maj & Hon Col RMA　Cmdg Depot How.Bde(FortCumberland)&Sch/Music(Eastney)19.6.16　CR C'land&W'land100
TROUGHTON,Harold Willis　SubLt　RNVR　190Bde MG Coy RNDiv Ex HMS Temeraire kia　13.11.16　CR France339
TROUNSON,Graham Francis James　PMidmn　　RNR　HMS Good Hope　kia　1.11.14MR3
TROUNSON,Samuel Percival TAsst Eng　　RNR　HMS India　　8.8.15　CR Europe131 EngSubLt
TRUE,Albert　TSkipper　RNR　HMTrawler Tettenhall kld　23.5.17MR1
TRUMBLE,Frederick Hugh Geoffrey　Lt　RN　HMS Warwick　10.5.18　CR Kent7
TRUSCOTT,Arthur　Cmdr　RN　HMS Gunner　　4.6.18　CR Surrey160
TRUSCOTT,Cyril Alfred　TLt　RNVR　Nelson Bn RNDiv　dow　23.4.17　　CR France96
TRYON,John Francis　Lt　RN　HM S/M G8　kld　3.1.18　MR3
TUCK,John Joseph　Sen Eng　RNR　HMS Viknor　drd　13.1.15　　MR3
TUCKER,Charles Alfred Edward　TMidmn　　RNR　HMS Hampshire　kld　5.6.16 MR3
TUCKER,Louis Egbert　TSub-Lt　　RNVR　Collingwood Bn RNDiv　　4.6.15　MR4
TUCKETT,Ernest Edward　Lt　RNR　HMS Cyclops　11.10.18　CR Yorks194
TUCKEY,Charles Phelps　Capt　RMLI　Plymouth Bn　23.4.18　CR Belgium390
TUDBALL,Denzil Charles　Midmn RN　HMS Indefatigable　kia　31.5.16MR2
TUDOR,Douglas Courtenay　Lt　RN　HMS Good Hope　kia　1.11.14MR3
TULLEY,T R (or John R)　FltSubLt　　RNAS　　29.6.17　CR France1359
TUNGATE,John　Skipper　RNR　HMDrifter Piscatorial II　kld　28.12.17　MR1
TURNBULL,Alfred Edward　Surg　RNVR　HMS Cressy　kia　22.9.14MR1
TURNBULL,Frederick Carr Cedrick　SubLt　RNVR　Hawke Bn RNDiv　　13.11.16　CR France339
TURNBULL,George King　TLt　RNVR　Nelson Bn RNDiv　　23.4.17　MR20
TURNER,E.S.　Lt　RNVR　HM ML360　　6.3.19　CR Lancs154
TURNER,George William.MID　ATPaymr　　RNR　HMS Bergamot　kia　13.8.17MR2
TURNER,Gerald de La Motte　Midmn RN　HMS Bulwark kld　26.11.14　MR3
TURNER,Richard Chase　LtCmdr　RN　HMS Pegasus dow　20.9.14　　CR Tanzania1
TURNER,Warwick Hackwood　TPFlt Offr　　RNAS　ded　10.3.18　　CR Middx80
TURNEY,Kenneth V　TFlt Sub-Lt　RNAS/RN?　　28.9.17 CR Belgium378
TURTON,L.M.　Capt　RN　HMS Venus　13.10.18　CR Asia60
TUSON,Henry John　Midmn RN　HMS Indefatigable　kia　31.5.16MR2
TUTT,Frederick Leonard　Sub Lt RNVR　HMS Ariel　kld　2.8.18　MR2
TWISS,Guy K.　Lt　RN　HMS Tartar　17.6.17　CR Sussex138
TWITCHIN,Dennis Jack　Mismn RNR　HMS Vivid　ded　4.10.18CR Devon3
TWYNAM,Hugh　ALt　RNR　HM S/M E36　kld　16.1.17MR3
TYLEE,Errol Tom　EngSubLt　RNR　HMS Nairana ded　26.1.19　　CR Scot241
TYRELL,Hugo William Louis　Lt　RN　HM S/M K17　drd　31.1.18　　MR1
TYSSIL-DAVIES,JohnLt　RNR　HMS Hindustan　ded　21.1.18　　CR Kent46

U

UFFEN,Joseph S.M.   Gnr   RN   HMS M18   dedacc 14.4.17   CR Greece9
UNDERWOOD,Powell C   Capt   RN   HMS North Star II   4.6.17   CR Egypt1
UNSWORTH,W Hubert   TEng Sub-Lt   RN   HMS Invincible   kia   31.5.16 MR3
UNWIN,Edward George Cummings   SubLt   RNVR   Hood Bn RNDiv   kia   3.9.18   CR France646
UPCHER,Sidney Wodehouse   Lt   RN   HMS Vanguard   kld   9.7.17   MR1
UPHAM,Henry Edward Reginald   2Lt   RM   1RM Bn RNDiv   13.11.16   CR France339
UPSON,Charles Edwin.MC.   SubLt   RNVR   Drake Bn RNDiv   28.9.18   CR France256
USBORNE,Claude H   Sub-Lt   RNVR   HM ML534   2.5.17   CR Italy6
USBORNE,Neville Florian   WingCmdr   RNAS   21.2.16   CR Kent46
USBORNE,Thomas Richard Guy.MID   Sub Lt   RN   HMCMB No79A   kia   18.8.19 MR3
USHER,Sidney J   Lt   RNR   HMS Ramsey   kia   8.8.15   MR3

V

VALLINGS,Frederick Francis Orr.MID   Sub Lt   RN   HMDrifter Catspaw   31.12.19   CR Europe178A
VALLINGS,Ranulph Kingsley Joyce   Flt Sub-Lt   RN   attRNAS   kld   13.1.17 CR Greece9
VAN ALLEN,Kenneth Marsden   TFlt Sub-Lt   RNAS   4.5.16   CR Belgium388 Lt
VAN DER BYL,Charles Philip Voltelyn   Sub-Lt   RN   HM S/M G1   accdrd 9.10.16 MR1
VAN STRAUBENZEE,Percival   Lt Comdr   RN   HMS Good Hope   kia   1.11.14 MR3
VANCE,Patrick Hugo Gerald Irving   Sub-Lt   RN   HMS Shark   kia   31.5.16 MR3
VARDEN,Medwin Seymour   TFlt Sub-Lt   RNAS   drd   4.9.17   MR1
VARLEY,Frederick Victor   Lt   RNR   HMTrawler Benton Castle   kld   10.11.16   CR Lancs2
VAUGHAN,Alfred F C   Sub-Lt RNVR   HMS Cordelia   1.3.15   CR Lancs170
VEITCH,Alfred Harry   Ft Paymr   RN   HMS Good Hope   kia   1.11.14 MR3
VENABLES,Harry Adrian   TMidmn   RNVR   HMS Narbrough   drd   12.1.18   MR3
VENNING,Thomas Arnold   Eng Lt Comdr   RN   HMS Pathfinder   kia   5.9.14   MR1
VEREKER,F.G.P.   Lt   RN   HMS Venturous   drd   14.2.21   CR Europe46
VERNER,Rudolf Henry Cole   Comdr RN   HMS Inflexible   dow   18.3.15   MR1
VERNON,Henry Doone   Flt Lt   RNAS   30.9.14   MR1
VERNON,Humphrey Fane   Sub-Lt RN   HMS Hampshire   kld   5.6.16   MR3
VERNON,Theophilus C   ASqd Comdr   RNAS   15.9.17   CR France1360
VESTEY-JONES,Alan P Flt Offr   RNAS   23.3.18   CR Lincs78
VICKERY,John Robert   Art Eng   RN   HMS Flirt   kia   26.10.16   MR2
VICKERY,Samuel Henry   SurgCmdr   RN   HMS Thalia   ded   25.7.19   CR Scot926
VINCENT,Thomas Montague   Lt   RNR   HMT Cave   11.4.15   CR Scot722
VINCENT,Walter   Ch Offr   CG   CG Stn King's Lynn   18.4.16   CR Norfolk151
VINEY,Taunton Elliott.DSO.   Flt Lt   RNAS   21.5.16   CR Belgium175
VIZARD,Leonard Foley   Paymstr   RN   HMS Talbot   18.9.15   CR Europe6
VOSPER,George Francis   ChBosn   RN   HMS Powerful   16.4.15   CR Devon1

W

WACE,Stephen Charles CBE   Lt Col RMA   21.5.20   CR Middx26
WADDELL,William   Sub-Lt RNR   HMYacht Rhiannon   kld   20.7.15 MR1
WADE,Jack   TWt Tel   RNR   HMTrawler Star of Freedom   kld   19.4.17 MR2
WADE,J J   Ch Offr   RN   HM CG Withernsea Stn   30.11.19   CR Yorks96
WADE,Richard R.   Midmn RN   HMS Irresistible   13.8.15   CR Hamps117
WAGANOFF,W.G.   Lt   RN   HMS Fox   25.8.19 CR Europe179 &MR70
WAGNER,Caspar Henry Granville   TSub-Lt   RNVR   Howe Bn RNDiv   13.11.16   MR21
WAGSTAFF,John   AssPaymr   RNR   HMS Viknor   13.1.15   CR Scot57
WAINWRIGHT,Oswald Johnston   Lt Paymr   RNVR   Hawke Bn RNDiv   25.8.18   MR16

59

WAIT,Percy Arthur Wells   Midmn RN   HMS Queen Mary   kia   31.5.16MR3
WAKEFORD,Charles Asst Paymr   RNR   HMS Champagne   kia   9.10.17MR2
WAKELY,Alfred Henry   ArtEng RN   HM S/M L55 kia   9.6.19 CR Hamps5 &MR1
WALCOT,Henry C   TLt   RM   Eastney Barracks   10.10.15 CR Hamps7
WALKER,Albert T   AGnr   RN   HMS Indefatigable   kia   31.5.16MR2
WALKER,Claude Bennett.DSC.   Lt   RNR   HMS Perdita   18.5.18 CR Kent46
WALKER,Cyril Gordon.MC. Lt   RNVR Anson Bn RNDiv   kia   27.3.18CR France233
WALKER,David Henry   Lt   RMLI 2 RM Bn RNDiv   28.4.17 MR20
WALKER,F.M.   Capt   RN   HMS President   7.2.19 CR Somerset37
WALKER,Frederic Clocke   TFlt Sub-Lt   RNAS 6Sqn   17.3.17 CR France95
WALKER,Godfrey Alan   Surg   RN   RNDiv 1FA   kia   14.11.16 CR France701
WALKER,Gordon Patrick   TSurg Prob   RNVR HMS Pheasant kld   1.3.17 MR2
WALKER,Harold Stratton   Lt   RMLI HMS Good Hope   kia   1.11.14MR3
WALKER,Henry Ellis TSkipper   RNR   HMTrawler Lord Roberts   kld   26.10.16 MR1
WALKER,James Mansergh   Eng Lt Comdr RN   HMS Russell dow   28.4.16   CR Europe6
WALKER,Robert   TSurg Prob   RNVR HMS Shark   kia   31.5.16MR3
WALL,Frank Tobin   TAsst Paymr   RNR   HMS Triumph kia   25.5.15MR2
WALLACE,Hugh D.M.   FltSubLt   RNAS   7.6.17 CR France285
WALLACE,James   TCh Eng   RNR   HMS Princess Irene   kld   27.5.15MR3
WALLACE,M.A.   Sub Lt RNR   HMTug Alice   7.5.19 CR Europe6
WALLACE,William James   Ch Gnr RN   HMS Hogue   kia   22.9.14MR3
WALLACE,William Ross   PTFlt Sub-Lt RNAS   kld   21.7.16CR Hamps5
WALLEN,John William   Lt   RNVR HMPMS Ascotkia   10.11.18 MR3
WALLER,Thomas Herbert Ashley   LtCmdr   RNVR Howe Bn RNDiv   7.5.15 CR Gallipoli14
WALLICE,Thomas Henry   EngCapt   RN   HMS Pembroke   6.6.17 CR Devon158
WALLIS,Alan Bowley Lt   RNVR Drake Bn RNDiv   23.4.17 MR20
WALLIS,Alfred   Lt   RMLI 1 RM Bn RNDiv   8.10.18MR16
WALLIS,Frank Arthur George SubLt   RNR   HMCMB 33A kia   12.4.18CR France1359
WALLIS,HarryTNaval Instr   RN   HMS Indefatigable   kia   31.5.16MR2
WALLIS,Kenneth Ferguson Arnold   Lt   RN   HMS St Vincent   22.1.18 CR Scot900
WALLS,Thomas Andrew.DSC.   Carp   RN   HMS Invincible   kia   31.5.16MR3
WALLWORTH,C.R.C.   see WALWORTH,C.R.C.
WALMESLEY,Oswald Noel Flt Lt RNAS   drd   4.5.16 MR1
WALSH,James Joseph Ft Surg   RN   HMS Good Hope   kia   1.11.14MR3
WALSH,Michael Joseph   Gnr   RN   HMS Vivid   3.10.17CR Eire45
WALSINGHAM,John Henry TSub-Lt   RNR   HMS Lynn   acckld 6.5.15 MR1
WALTER,Eric Blount Jackson TFlt Sub-Lt   RNAS   24.4.17 MR20
WALTERS,Lancelot John Barrington Lt   RN   HMS Partridgekia   12.12.17 MR3
WALTON,Cyril Ambrose   TChapn   RN   HMS Chester kia   31.5.16MR1
WALTON,Ernest SA/343   Skipper   RNR   HMTrawler Pomona drd   30.9.18   CR Suffolk130
WALWORTH,Clement Robert Carmichael TFlt Sub-Lt RNAS   kia   18.2.18 CR France68 WALLWORTH
WAMBOLT,Harry Redmond FltLt   RNAS   kia   4.3.17 CR France568
WANKLYN,Herbert Graham FltLt   RNAS Dunkirk Stn kia   31.5.15CR France8
WANSBROUGH,Lionel Bernard Roy Eng Lt RN   HMS Monmouth   kia   1.11.14MR2
WARD,A.E. ChArtEng   RN   HMS Magic   12.2.19 CR Devon153
WARD,Clinton Granville Brooks   PTFlt Sub-Lt RNAS   23.1.16 CR Surrey2
WARD,Edward Copley   FtSurg RN   HMS Pembroke   7.8.17 CR Kent46
WARD,Harold Henshaw   Midmn RN   HMS Hogue kia   22.9.14MR1
WARD,Henry De Courcy   Ft Paymr   RN   HMS Cressy kia   22.9.14MR1
WARD,John Scott   Surg Lt RN   att Hawke Bn RNDiv   13.11.16 MR21
WARD,Norman Claude   Surg Prob   RNVR HMS Sarnia   kia   12.9.18MR3
WARDE,Cecil ALt   RN   HM S/M K17 drd   31.1.18 MR1
WARDER,Leonard Clifton.DSC.   ATLt   RNR   HMS Q12   kia   30.4.17MR3
WARDER,Richard Bertram Graham   Maj   RMA HMS Resolution   ded   22.1.21   CR Europe46
WARE,George Henry Warrender   WtVictOff   RN   HMS Cyclops II   8.5.18 CR Hamps9
WARING,Ruric Henry Lt   RN   HMS Hawke kia   15.10.14 MR1
WARLTERS,Raymond Alfred Price   TAsst Paymr RNR   HM Airship C17   kia   21.4.17MR2
WARMAN,Edgar Leslie   Lt   RMA How Bde   kia   8.8.18 CR France745
WARNEFORD,Reginald Alexander John VC Flt Sub-Lt RNAS   kld   17.6.15CR London4
WARNER,Frederick Archibald.DSO.   Lt Comdr   RN   HMS Torrent kld   23.12.17 MR3

WARREN,J T Skipper RNR HMS Arctic Whale 23.11.19 CR Lincs156
WARREN,William George Carp RN HMS Natal kld 30.12.15 MR1
WATCHMAN,Collingwood ALt RNR HMDrifter Gavinwood kld 20.2.16 MR1
WATERLOW,Clive Maitland WingComdr(TLtCol) RN RE att RNAS kld 20.7.17 CR Lincs86
WATERLOW,John Beauchamp.DSO. Comdr RN HMS Black Prince kia 31.5.16 MR3
WATERS,George Alexander Ft Surg RN HMS Goliath kia 13.5.15 MR1
WATERS,William Eng Lt RN HMS Formidable kia 1.1.15 MR1
WATKINS,Arthur L. SubLt RNVR HMS President 24.11.17 CR Beds23
WATKINS,George Newton TSub-Lt RNR HMS Viknor drd 13.1.15 MR3
WATKINS,John SubLt RNVR Hood Bn RNDiv 31.12.17 CR France668
WATKINSON,William Jenkinson Skipper RNR HMTrawler Zebulun ded 28.9.15 CR Yorks42
WATNEY,B.DSC. Lt RNVR HML 236 28.10.19 CR Europe26A
WATSON,Alexander Skipper RNR HMS Vivid 30.5.19 CR Scot123
WATSON,Harold Sydney TEng Lt RNR HMS Louvain kia 20.1.18 MR2
WATSON,James George Lt RNR HMS Aboukir kia 22.9.14 MR1
WATSON,James Gibb Sub-Lt RNVR Hood Bn RNDiv 14.11.16 MR21
WATSON,James Henry Digby TSurg RN HMS Hawke kia 15.10.14 MR1
WATSON,John Galloway TLt RNR HM S/M G8 kld 3.1.18 MR3
WATSON,Kenneth Falshaw Flt Lt RNAS drd 3.8.15 MR1
WATSON,Preston Albert FltSubLt RN RNAS kld 30.6.15 CR Scot386
WATSON,Sidney Frederick Lt RN HM S/M E5 kld 11.3.16 MR3
WATSON,Stuart Asst Paymr RN HMS Good Hope kia 1.11.14 MR3
WATSON-PAUL,G.V. Lt RNR HMS Egmont 19.8.19 CR Europe6
WATT,Edward G B Lt RNR HMS Bulwark kld 26.11.14 MR3
WATT,James Hamilton.RD. EngCmdr RNR HMS Moldavia 15.7.16 CR Kent46
WATTERSON,Thomas Arthur.DSC. Lt RNR HM S/M K4 drd 31.1.18 MR3
WAUCHOPE,George William Alfred TSub-Lt RNVR Anson Bn RNDiv 13.11.16 MR21
WAUTON,Hubert O Lt RN 10.14
WEAVER,Frederick C. SubLt RNVR Anson Bn RNDiv 13.11.16 CR France339
WEAVER,Horace William SubLt RNVR Howe Bn RNDiv dow 15.7.15 CR Gallipoli1
WEBB,Thomas Paul.DSO. Lt Cmdr RNR ded 19.7.19 CR Canada180
WEBBER,C.F. PaymrCmdr RN HMS President 6.2.19 CR Hamps7
WEBBER,Edward Charles Clerk RN HMS Good Hope kia 1.11.14 MR3
WEBBER,Joseph Edward Sub-Lt RNVR Hood Bn RNDiv 4.9.18 MR16
WEBBER,William Farel Chapn RN HMS Black Prince kia 31.5.16 MR3
WEBLEY,Herbert John Lt RN HMS Paragon kia 17.3.17 MR3
WEBLEY,W.T.MBE. Lt RN HMS President 15.5.19 CR Hamps9
WEBSTER,E.J.E. LtPaymr RN 22.4.19 CR Devon72
WEIGHTMAN,John TSub-Lt RNVR Armoured Cars 4.6.15 MR4
WEIL,Louis Marcus Basil FltLt RNAS attRFC kia 6.4.17 CR France1749
WEIR,Adam TEng Sub-Lt RNR HMS Ben-My-Chree 5.4.16 CR Egypt16
WEIR,Charles H TFlt Sub-Lt RNAS 8.17
WEIR,Frederick Stanley Eng Lt Cmdr RN HMS Britannia 9.11.18 CR Europe23
WEIR,John Cunning ChOff RN HM Coastguard 14.3.18 CR Scot94
WELDRICK,George Joseph Lt RNR HMS Clan McNaughton drd 3.2.15 MR1
WELLBURN,George W.RD. Lt Comdr RNR HMYacht Rhiannon kld 20.7.15 MR1
WELLESLEY,Claud Michael Ashmore Lt RN HM S/M K4 drd 31.1.18 MR3
WELMAN,Henry Bolton ALt RMLI kia 13.11.16 CR France131
WELSH,John Lt RN HMS Vernon 3.7.16 CR Hamps9
WELTON,Patrick Bosn RN 5.16
WERRY,J.S. WtShptRN HMS Redoubtable 22.1.16 CR Devon1
WESCOMB,Ernest William WOgrade2 RNAS acckld 8.7.16 CR Cornwall48
WEST,Charles Skeffington.DSO. Cmdr RNVR Howe Bn RNDiv kia 30.12.17 CR France662
WEST,George TSkipper RNR HMTrawler Flicker kld 4.3.16 MR1
WEST,James Skipper 1171 RNR HMTrawler C.A.West ded 13.11.18 CR Scot838
WESTALL,N.C. Lt RN HMS Pyramus 4.11.14 CR Aust456
WESTBROOK,T.H. Sub Lt RNVR Anson Bn RNDiv 25.8.18 CR France84
WESTBROOK,William Gnr RN HMS Bulwark kld 26.11.14 MR3
WESTBY,Thomas.MC. Lt RM 190MG Bn RNDiv 30.12.17 CR France662
WESTERBY,Jeremiah Skipper RNR 9.9.18 CR Lincs156

WESTMACOTT,Eric W.P.   Lt   RN   HMS Arethusa   28.8.14 CR Essex213
WESTON,Thomas Reginald   TPFlt Offr   RNAS   3.11.17CR Middx25
WETHERALL,George P C   Midmn RN   HMS Russell   27.4.16 CR Europe6
WEVILL,Frederick Arthur Valdimir   Midmn RNR   HMS Vanguard   kld   9.7.17 MR1
WHALE,John Patrick TLt   RNR   HMTug Char   drd   16.1.15   MR3
WHARF,George James.MC.   Capt   RMLI   1Bn   6.4.18 CR France233
WHARTON,Arnold   Art Eng   RN   HMS Irresistible   kia   18.3.15MR3
WHEATLAND,Arthur Lt   RNVR HMPMS Ascotkia   10.11.18 MR3
WHEATLEY,James Atkinson Lt   RN   HM S/M L10 kia   4.10.18MR3
WHELEN,John William   TSkipper   RNR   HMTrawler Commander Fullerton   kia   12.12.17 MR1
WHELTON,Patrick   Bosn   RN   HMS Defence kia   31.5.16MR2
WHETNALL,Arthur John   Flt Sub-Lt   RNAS   kld   18.11.16 MR40
WHIGHAM,Robert Scott   TFlt Sub-Lt   RNAS   drd   9.5.17 MR1
WHINCOP,Philip   TSkipper   RNR   HMS Silonian   12.3.16 CR Lincs123
WHITAKER,Hubert J TSub-Lt   RNVR Nelson Bn RNDiv   3.5.15 MR4
WHITAKER,Trevor   Lt   RN   HM S/M E10 kld   21.1.15MR3
WHITE,A.   Capt   SS Strombus   5.7.16 CR Egypt15
WHITE,Alfred Archie DSC   Lt   RNVR   5.2.19 CR Essex83
WHITE,Charles.MID   Lt   RM   RNDiv   28.5.15 CR Gallipoli2
WHITE,Frederick Ernest   Wt EngRNR   HMS Queen Mary   kia   31.5.16MR2
WHITE,Geoffrey Sexton.VC.   Lt Cmdr   RN   HM S/M E14 kia   28.1.18MR3
WHITE,James Percy   FltLt   RNAS   kia   4.3.17 CR France421
WHITE,John Lt Comdr   RN   HMS Genista kia   23.10.16 MR3
WHITE,Leonard H   Lt   RN   see HALE-WHITE,L.
WHITE,Thomas   SubLt   RNVR Nelson Bn RNDiv   28.12.17 CR France379
WHITE,W.C.   Eng Sub Lt   RNR   HMS Snaefell   15.6.18 CR Europe6
WHITEHOUSE,Alfred Edward   Lt Cmdr   RN   HM S/M L10 kia   4.10.18MR3
WHITEMAN,John.MID   LtCol   RN   4MiddxR attRNDiv Cmdg Hawke Bn dow   25.4.17   CR France95
WHITESIDE,Reginald Cuthbert   TSub-Lt   RNVR & RFC 18 Sqdn   20.12.16 MR20
WHITING,Arthur   Lt   RNVR HNNL No403 kld   22.8.18MR1
WHITING,Baden H.   F/O   RNAS   9.3.18 CR France1844
WHITTAKER,John Edward   SubLt RNR   RFA Thermol   26.5.21 CR Yorks3
WHITTIER,Douglas H.   FltSubLt   RNAS   20.7.16 CR Kent25
WHITTLE,Harold Worsley   ALt   RNR   HMTug Char   drd   16.1.15   MR3
WHITTON,David John   Surg Prob   RNVR HMS Cullist   kia   11.2.18MR3
WHITTON,Frederic William   LtCmdr   RNR   HMS Edinburgh Castle   accdrd   20.10.14 MR2
WHYTE,Lewis   Skipper   RNR   HMT Theresa Boyle   ded   1.6.16 CR Scot280
WHYTE,Marcus Francis Beresford   ACapt   RN   HMS President   7.1.17 CR London4
WIATT,Charles Barrington   Lt   RNR   HMS Princess Irene   kld   27.5.15MR3
WICKS,Ernest Edward   Sub-Lt RNVR Hawke Bn RNDiv   3.9.18 MR16
WILDE,Fred   Sub-Lt RNR   HMS Rhododendron   kia   5.5.18 MR1
WILDE,Percy Montague Clifton   Capt   RMA   HMS Indefatigable   kia   31.5.16MR3
WILDER,E.   SubLt RNR   HMYacht Oriana   23.4.15 CR Hamps160
WILDING,Anthony F. Capt   RM   Armoured Car Div   9.5.15 CR France632
WILDMAN,George W TLt   RNVR att RNAS   19.4.17 CR Norfolk43
WILKES,Albert   Ch Art Eng   RN   HMS Acheron accdrd   27.10.16 MR3
WILKIE,David MID   Maj   5 BlkW att RNDiv   24.4.17 MR20
WILKINS,Cecil Edward   Cmdr RN   HMS Lowestoft   ded   1.11.18CR Italy17
WILLIAMS,Archibald C R   .TMidmn   RNR   see WILLIAMS,C A R
WILLIAMS,Charles Archibald Rees   Midmn RNR   HMS K George V   ded   12.11.16 CR Scot900
WILLIAMS,Charles Lawrence Wyndham   Midmn   RN   HMS Russell kld   27.4.16MR1
WILLIAMS,Evan Hughes   TLt   RNR   HMS Hampshire   kld   5.6.16   MR3
WILLIAMS,Francis John   TSkipper   RNR   HMTrawler Fraser   kld   17.6.17MR2
WILLIAMS,Frank Thomas Penry   Flt SubLt   RNAS   kld   30.1.18CR Belgium175
WILLIAMS,Geoffrey Hugh Collman   Lt   RN   HNDrifter Catspaw   31.2.19 CR Europe178A
WILLIAMS,George Knox   FlySubLt   3Wing kldacc 10.6.16   CR France1826
WILLIAMS,Harold Richard   TCh Eng   RNR   HMS Bayano kia   11.3.15MR3
WILLIAMS,Hugh Powell Evan Tudor Capt   RN   HMS Hawke kia   15.10.14 MR1
WILLIAMS,John Francis   Lt   RN   HMS Russell kld   27.4.16MR1
WILLIAMS,John Richard   Lt   RNVR HMMS Blackmorevalekld   1.5.18 MR2

62

WILLIAMS,Mongomery.MID Capt   RMA   23.8.16 CR France296
WILLIAMS,Nicholas G.   Gnr   RN   HMS Caesar   29.2.16 CR Bermuda1
WILLIAMS,Penry G. FtSurg RN   HMS Hampshire   drd   5.6.16 CR Scot900
WILLIAMS,Percy Gerald   Clerk   RN   HMS Russell   kld   27.4.16 MR1
WILLIAMS,Richard   TSub-Lt   RNVR HM Mersey Examination Vessel No1 kld   28.12.17 MR2
WILLIAMS,Robert John Seaborn   Eng Lt RNR   HMS Tara   ded PoW 28.1.16   CR Egypt1
WILLIAMS,Robert Pennington   Lt Cmdr   RNR   HMS Pembroke   8.11.15 CR Norfolk131
WILLIAMS,Thomas Christopher Harry.MVO. Comdr RN   HMS Viking   kld   29.1.16 MR3
WILLIAMS,W.C.J.   SubLt RNVR Anson Bn RNDiv   13.11.16 CR France339
WILLIAMS,Walter Kent.MVO.   Eng Capt   RN   HMS Bulwark kld   26.11.14 MR3
WILLIAMS,Wilfred Thompson   PaymrLt   RNR   HMS PrincessMargaret   19.1.19 CR Scot252
WILLIAMS,William   WtEng RN   HMS Pembroke   21.4.20 CR Kent46
WILLIAMS,William   Ch Offr   RN/CG Caister-on-Sea,CG Stn   26.8.18 CR Norfolk85
WILLIAMS,William Arthur RD   Cmdr   RNR   HMS Presidentded   8.1.19 CR Essex88
WILLIAMS,William C J   TSub-Lt   RNVR   11.16
WILLIAMSON,Evelyn James Midmn RN   HMS Bulwark kld   26.11.14 MR3
WILLIAMSON,George Henry Walker.MID ATLt   RNR   HMS Chester kia   31.5.16 MR1
WILLIAMSON,Henry Skipper   RNR   HMTrawler T.W.Mould   drd   1.12.18 MR1
WILLIAMSON,James Alexander   TLt   RNR   HMS Lavenderkia   5.5.17 MR3
WILLIS,Howard   FltSubLt   RNAS 5Sqn   kld   15.1.18 CR France1359
WILLIS,John Edwin   TSub-Lt   RNVR 190 MG Coy RNDiv   dow   22.4.17   CR France95
WILLISON,Walter Leigh   Sub-Lt RNVR Hawke Bn RNDiv   dow   25.8.18   CR France578
WILLOUGHBY,Alfred Herbert   Lt   RN   HMS Ghurka   kld   8.2.17 MR3
WILLOUGHBY,Henry Ernest Digby Hugh Comdr   RN   HMS Indefatigable   kia   31.5.16 MR2
WILLOUGHBY,Peter Robert Heathcote Drummond Lt Cmdr RN   HMS Monmouth   kia   1.11.14 MR2
WILMOT,Wilfred Henry   Flt Sub Lt   RNAS 10Sqn   3.2.18 CR Belgium157
WILMOT-SITWELL,Stanton Degge   ALt   RM   Portsmouth Bn RNDiv   14.7.15 MR4
WILSHIN,John Barton Eng Comdr   RN   HMS Monmouth   kia   1.11.14 MR2
WILSON,A.   Sister QARNNS   5.11.18 CR Scot347
WILSON,Arthur Wellesley Alister   Midmn RN   HMS Vanguard   kld   9.7.17 CR Scot900
WILSON,Charles Hubbard   Midmn RN   HMS Bulwark kld   26.11.14 MR3
WILSON,Charles Peter.RD.   Comdr RNR   HMYacht Verona   kld   24.2.17 MR2
WILSON,Douglas Henry Vernon   Lt   RN   HMS Bulwark   26.11.14 CR Kent46
WILSON,Francis Stuart   Maj   RM   1Bde HQ   kia   24.5.15 CR Gallipoli14
WILSON,James   Sub-Lt RNVR Drake Bn RNDiv   25.3.18 MR20
WILSON,John N.   Lt   RNR   HMTrawler Longset   20.5.16 CR Durham26
WILSON,John Gnr   RN   3.10.17 CR Eire267
WILSON,John SkinnerLt Comdr   RN   HMS Indefatigable   kia   31.5.16 MR2
WILSON,Robert   Art Eng   RN   HMS Candytuft   kia   18.11.17 MR2
WILSON,T.R. LtCmdr   RNR   HMYacht Vagrant   17.10.17 CR Devon21
WILSON,William   2Lt   RNVR Hawke Bn RNDiv   2.1.18 CR France398
WILSON,William Joseph   Skipper   RNR   HMTrawler Ben Ardra ded   25.12.14 CR France1359
WIMBER,Lewis Roland   PaymrLtCmdr RN   HMS President   6.6.20 CR Kent46
WIMBUSH,Lea Ewart Barnes Flt Lt   RNAS   28.3.18 CR Middx15
WINCHESTER,John W   Mate   HMTrawler Loch Garry   13.9.16 CR Scot313
WINCHESTER,William James   TSkipper   RNR   HMTrawler Evangel   kia   25.3.17 CR Lancs14
WINGFIELD-STRATFORD,Esme John Richard Lt   RN   HM S/M D3   drd   15.3.18   MR3
WINGROVE,George Stephenson   Midmn RN   HMS Formidible   kia   1.1.15 MR1
WINN,John Hilton   Flt Sub-Lt   RNAS 1 Sqdn   20.9.17 MR20
WINPENNY,Frederick Enos   TSub-Lt   RNR   HMYacht Aries   kld   31.10.15 MR3
WINSLOW,Thomas Maitland.RD.   Lt Comdr   RNR   HMS Stephen Furness kia   13.12.17 MR3
WINTER,Rupert Randolph   Flt Cmdr   RNAS   3.2.18 CR Belgium140
WINTOUR,Charles John   Capt   RN   HMS Tipperary   kia   1.6.16 MR3
WISE,Edward S   Lt   RN   10.14
WISE,J.D.   Midmn RN   HMS Iron Duke   19.11.19 CR Asia51
WISE,Stacey Lt   RN   HMS Cressy   kia   22.9.14 MR1
WITTING,Stanley Newson   2Lt   RMLI   2 RM Bn RNDiv   22.3.18 MR20
WODEMAN,Bertram Howard FtPaymstr   RN   HMS Benbow drd   30.3.18   MR3
WOLFE MURRAY,Philip G   TLt   RNVR see MURRAY,P G W
WOLFE,Arthur Frederick   TSub-Lt   RNVR Nelson Bn RNDiv   4.2.17 MR21

WOOD,Alfred Victor TLt   RNVR HMTug Guiana   drd   29.1.18   MR1
WOOD,Charles H.P. Lt   RNVR HMS Victory   1.4.17 CR Sussex144
WOOD,Charles Sinclair   Lt   RNR   HMS Motagua kld   19.3.18MR3
WOOD,Christopher Eric   Flt Comdr   RNAS   kia   12.9.17MR37
WOOD,D.E.   WtShptRN   HMS Yarmouth   3.12.19CR Devon3
WOOD,Francis Cleveland   Midmn RN   HMS Russell kld   27.4.16MR1
WOOD,George Douglas Harry TMidmn   RNR HMS India   kia   8.8.15 MR1
WOOD,J.B.   EngLt RNR   HMS Otranto   6.10.18CR Scot713
WOOD,John TSkipper   RNR   HMDrifter Ladysmith drd   27.12.15 MR3
WOOD,John TSkipper   RNR   HMDrifter Plantin   kld   26.4.17MR3
WOOD,Melville Cornelius   TFlt Lt RNAS HMDrifter Ladysmith drd   9.10.17MR1
WOOD,Norman Edward   TSub-Lt   RNR   HMPMS Queen of the North kld   20.7.17 MR1 Norma
WOOD,William   TSkipper   RNR   HMDrifter Boy Haroldkld   3.3.16 MR3
WOOD,William Andrew   Eng Lt RN   HMS Bulwark kld   26.11.14 MR3
WOOD-ROBINSON,Thomas Mansergh   TSurg RN   HMS Black Prince   kia   31.5.16MR3
WOODALL,Aubrey Samuel   TFlt Sub-Lt   RNAS   drd   22.8.17   MR1
WOODFORD,Charles James DSM   ATLt   RNVR Drake Bn RNDiv   30.12.17 MR21
WOODGATE,Charles A.   Skipper   RNR   HMTrawler Linsdell   3.9.14 CR Suffolk93
WOODHALL,George Frederick Gerald   Cmdr RN   HMS Presidentded   13.9.16   CR Sussex17
WOODHOUSE,George William   Skipper   RNR   HMT Lucknowkia   18.5.17CR Scot288
WOODHOUSE,Mosley Grodon   FltSubLt   RNAS   9.8.17 CR France1361
WOODROW,James   Art Eng   RN   HMS Black Prince   kia   31.5.16MR2
WOODS,Henry   Staff Surg   RN   HMS Monmouth   kia   1.11.14MR2
WOODWARD,Thomas Claude   AssPaymr   RNR   HMS Pekin   ded   2.3.18 CR Suffolk138
WOOLEY,Samuel Downes   Lt   RN   HMS Victory ded   8.11.18CR Hamps9
WOOLLCOMBE-BOYCE,Harold Courtney Lt   RN   HMS Ghurka kld   8.2.17 MR3
WOOLNOUGH,Herbert James   Skipper   RNR   HMTrawler Royallien kldacc 23.9.16   CR Suffolk86
WOOLSTON,Ash Jeremiah Skipper   RNR   HMDrifter New Dawn kld   23.3.18MR1
WORTH,Silvanus Eales (2398SA)   TSkipper   RNR   HMDrifter Emulate   accdrd 21.4.17   MR2
WORTHINGTON,Arthur Gordon   Wt Elect   RN   HMS Invincible   kia   31.5.16MR3
WOUTON,Hubert Osmond Lt   RN   HMS Falcon kia   28.10.14 CR Kent5
WRAY,Reginald   Gnr   RN   HMS Princess Irene   kld   27.5.15MR3
WRIGHT,Arthur   Carp RN   HMS Highflyer   13.12.16 CR Hamps9
WRIGHT,Douglas Ross Cameron   FltSubLt   RNAS   kia   23.12.17 CR France1359
WRIGHT,James   TSkipper   RNR   HMTrawler Rose II   kld   23.4.17MR2
WRIGHT,Lawrence William TEng Lt   RN   HMS Bulwark kld   26.11.14 MR3
WRIGHT,Noel Stafford   FltSubLt   RNAS   18.9.17 CR France285
WRIGHT,William Drury   Gnr   RN   HMS Good Hope   kia   1.11.14MR3
WRIGHT,William Villiers   Gnr   RN   HMS Ghurka kld   8.2.17 MR1
WYARD,Roy TSub-Lt   RNVR Hood Bn RNDiv   dow   16.11.17 CR France145
WYATT,Arnold Baker TMidmn   RNR   HMS Partridge   12.12.17 CR Europe146
WYATT,Charles Joshua   FltLt RNAS   kld   21.8.17CR France1359
WYLDBERE-SMITH,H.F.   Capt RN   8.5.19 CR Dorset52
WYNNE,Hugh Tom Donald.DSC.   Lt   RNR   HM S/M E34   20.7.18 CR Europe96

Y

YATES,Walter Charles   Lt   RN   HMS Hyacinth   29.8.18 CR SAfrica158
YEOMAN,William Robert   TSub-Lt   RNVR Howe Bn RNDiv   24.4.17 MR20
YORSTON,T, Lt   RNVR served as STOUT,T.
YOUNG,Charles Henry   Gnr   RN   HMS Tartar kld   17.6.17MR3
YOUNG,Daniel   Skipper   RNR   HMTrawler Internos   7.3.16 CR Scot871
YOUNG,E.C.R.   EngSubLt   RNR   HMS Teutonic   19.12.18 CR Hamps5
YOUNG,Harry SubLt RNVR Anson Bn RNDiv   10.11.18 CR France1142
YOUNG,J.D. LtCmdr   RNVR   23.4.18 CR Bucks121
YOUNG,James H   Lt   RNR   HMS Malaya   31.5.16 CR Scot900
YOUNG,John Joshua Gnr   RN   HMS Queen Mary   kia   31.5.16MR3
YOUNG,Richard St J FtPaymr   RN   HMS Temeraire   8.10.17CR Scot900

YOUNG,William Henry.MID Bosn   RN   RN College Dartmouthded   11.3.21   CR Devon1

65

SECTION II

OFFICERS WHO DIED IN THE SERVICE OF THE ROYAL AIR FORCE

A

ABELL,Claude Edwin Capt   RAF   11 TDSqn   14.11.18 CR Wilts 129
ABRAHAMS,Cecil Robert George   2Lt   RAF   99 Sqdn   26.9.18 CR France 1667
ACHURCH,H G   2Lt   RAF   24.4.18 CR Hunts 124
ADAM,C P   Lt   RAF   1.4.18 CR France 149
ADAM,Henry William Lt   RAF   HMS Glorious kld   4.7.18 CR Lancs 92
ADAM,Matthew.MC. Lt   5RSFus attRAF   15 Sqdn   kia   7.8.18 CR France 805
ADAMS,Allen Percy.DFC.   Capt   RAF   47 Sqdn   kia   6.3.19 CR Asia 82
ADAMS,Harold Towns   Lt   RAF & Gen List   43 Sqdn   28.3.18 MR20
ADDERLEY,William Harris 2Lt   RAF & 9WRidR   59 Sqdn   27.10.18 CR France 398
ADKINS,Reginald   Capt   RAF   2 Sch Nav & Bomb Dropping   22.4.19 CR Hamps 98
AGAR,Egan Zinkan   Capt   Can Inf & RAF54 Sqdn   kia   13.4.18CR France 346
AGERUP,Harold   Lt   RAF & GL att222MGC   195Sqnacckld 5.6.18 CR Egypt8
AGG,William Tom   F/Cadet   RAF   48 Trng Depot   26.10.18 CR Lincs 181
AGNEW,Joseph Paul.MC.   Lt   RAF   42 Trng Sch   acc kld 14.8.18   CR Kent 160
AIRD,Arthur William 2Lt   RAF   209 Sqdn   23.5.18 MR 20
AITCHISON,Douglas James   Lt   RFA att RAF   dow   17.4.18   CR London 3
AITKEN,Alex Hunter 2Lt   RAF   57 Sqdn   27.10.18 CR France 948
AITKEN,J   2Lt   RAF   49 Sqdn   16.7.18 CR France 1410
AITKEN,J T   2Lt   RAF   218 Sqdn   28.9.18 CR Belgium 173
AIZLEWOOD,Leslie Peech.MC.AFC. Maj   RAF   2 Flying Trng Sch   29.9.18 CR Yorks 127
ALDER,Thomas Gordon Edgecombe   2Lt   RAF & ELancsR   kld   28.7.18CR Gloucs 86
ALDERSON,Reginald Liddon Maj   RAF   30.6.18 CR Leics 70
ALDERTON,T D H   2Lt   RAF   16.6.18 CR Norfolk 247
ALDRED,William Boyes   2Lt   RAF   84 Sqdn   20.9.18 CR France 146
ALDRICH,Leo Edwin 2Lt   RAF   37 TDS   kld   14.11.18 CR Somerset 25
ALEXANDER,Thomas Malcolmson   2Lt   RAF   41 Sqdn   17.8.18 CR Belgium 116
ALLAN,John Alexander Macdonald   Capt   RAF   63 Trng Sqdn   20.5.18 CR Yorks 173
ALLAN,John Roy.DSC   Capt   RAF   215 Sqdn   12.4.18 MR 20
ALLAN,Ramsay   2Lt   RAF & Gen List   2 Sqdn kld   22.4.18CR France 179
ALLANSON,Wilfred George   Lt   RAF   7 Sqdn   21.9.18 CR Belgium 18
ALLARDICE,Harry F Cadet RAF   153797   acc kld 28.7.18   CR Canada 1245
ALLBUTT,H F   2Lt   RAF   88 Sqdn   15.7.18 CR France 1359
ALLCROFT,G Cadet RAF   183749   10.11.18 CR Leics 25
ALLEN,Charles Arthur   2Lt   RAF   48 Sqdn   kld acc 12.3.19   CR Germany 1
ALLEN,Dudley George Antoine   Capt   RAF   209 Sqdn   8.10.18CR France 482
ALLEN,Francis Robert Leslie 2Lt   RAF   213 Sqdn   14.10.18 MR 20
ALLEN,Herbert   2Lt   RAF   56 Sqdn   10.8.18 MR 20
ALLEN,Raymond Francis   2Lt   1/6RWarR att RAF   kld   18.11.18 CR Ches 182
ALLEN,Victor William.MC.MM.   2Lt   RAF & 4SAI   103 Sqdn   9.6.18 CR France 360
ALLISON,Reginald   Cadet RAF   184690   8 Cadet Wing   8.11.18CR Kent 180
ALLMAN,K W   Lt   RAF   2.6.18 CR Lancs 420
ALLOWAY,C W   2Lt   RAF   27.5.18 CR Hunts 125
ALSFORD,Herbert Edward   2Lt   RAF   99 Sqdn   31.8.18 CR France 1678
ALYEA,Norman W   Cadet RAF   173941   ded   22.10.18 CR Canada 1297
AMEY,A E   2Lt   RAF   55 Sqdn   16.9.18 CR France 1675
AMOS,J   2Lt   RAF   22 Sqdn   29.8.18 CR France 646
ANDERSON,George   Lt   RAF   57 Sqdn   kia   16.9.18CR France 512
ANDERSON,John Lawrence King   Lt   RAF   55 Sqdn   kia   31.5.18CR Germany 3
ANDERSON John Reginald   Lt   RAF   60 Sqdn   kia   13.8.18CR France 649
ANDERSON,William.MC.   2Lt   RGA 114HB attRAF   7 Sqdn kld   21.9.18CR Belgium18
ANDERSON,William Alwin   Lt   RAF   32 Sqdn   18.7.18 MR 20
ANDREWS,Eric Bernard   2Lt   RAF & RFA   16.9.18 CR France 1252
ANDREWS,John Alfred Raymond   2Lt   6LincsR att RAF   kia   14.4.18CR France 31
ANDREWS,J G   2Lt   RAF   kia   14.8.18CR France 755
ANGELOFF,Claude George   Cadet RAF   ex Sgt S4/256101 ASCkld   5.11.18CR Essex 221

ANGUS,Roy William Frederick   Lt   RAF   148 Sqdn   kia   13.8.18 CR France 10
ANKERS,John 2Lt   RAF   218 Sqdn   16.7.18 MR 20
ANKETELL,Charles Edward.MM.   2Lt   RFus attRAF 206 Sqdn   kld   11.5.18 CR France134
ANKRETT,Herbert Henry   2Lt   RAF   107 Sqdn   11.7.18 CR Belgium 406
ANNIS,Wilbur Fawcett   Lt   RAF   44 Wing   ded   3.5.18 CR Canada 1688
ANSTEY,Chisholm Wilfred   Sqdn Comdr   RAF   ded   3.5.20 CR Hamps 146
ANSTEY-BENNETT,L E   Capt   RAF   7.6.21 CR Devon 138
APPLEBY,Edwin Alec 2Lt   RAF   ex RNAS   kld   24.6.18 CR London 20
APPLEY,Clarence Wasson   2Lt   RAF   8 Sqdn kia   2.9.18 CR France 427
ARBUTHNOT,R G U Lt   16 Lcrs att RAF   3.12.18 CR Herts 10
ARBUTHNOT,Lenox Stanley Capt   RAF   21 Wing   kld   1.11.18 CR Oxford 74
ARCHAMBAULT,Percy   Cadet RAF   272603   ded   13.10.18 CR Canada 174
ARCHER,S J Cadet RAF   331065   9 Cadet Wing   7.11.18 CR Hunts 83
ARCHIBALD,Max Stanfield Eaton.MC.MID Capt   RE att RAF   18 Sqdn   kia   12.5.18 CR France 95
ARCHIBALD,W A   2Lt   RAF   29 TDS   8.11.18 CR Hamps 31
ARCHIBALD,Walter Roy   Lt   RAF   80 Sqdn   27.6.18 MR 20
ARDEN,John Henry Morris.DSO.MID   LtCol   RoR,2WorcsR att RAF 3 Cadet Wing   22.7.18 CR Egypt 1
ARKLE,C W Lt   RAF   1 Acft Supply Depot Repair Pk   27.9.18 CR France 34
ARMSTRONG,D Urlan Victor   Capt   RAF   151 Sqdn   13.11.18 CR France 446
ARMSTRONG,G P   Lt   RAF   12 Group   15.7.18 CR Lincs 78
ARMSTRONG,George Wheeler   Lt   RAF   kld   2.9.18 CR Kent 180
ARMSTRONG,William Ash   F/O   RAF   208 Sqdn   kld   14.4.21 CR Egypt 8
ARMSTRONG,William Austin   2Lt   RAF   73 Sqdn   25.7.18 MR 20
ARN,Roy Mellington Cadet RAF   272834   Cadet Wing   27.11.18 CR Canada 1192
ARNOLD,Joseph V   Lt   4RWFus att RAF   3.9.18 CR Lancs 33
ARNOLD,Peter Forrester   Capt   RAF & 8LanFus   8.8.18 CR Egypt 1
ARNOT,Arthur Alison McDonald.MC.   2Lt   RAF & Gen List   3 Sqdn   12.4.18 CR France 220
ARNOTT,Harold Dwight   2Lt   RAF   104 Sqdn   29.10.18 CR France 1894
ARNOTT,Leslie   2Lt   RAF   11 Sqdn   16.9.18 CR France 1390
ARTHUR,J   Maj   RAF   5 Group HQ   6.6.18 CR France 1359
ARUNDEL,Philip Walter Rivers   Lt   RAF   43 Sqdn   8.8.18 MR 20
ASBURY,Edward Dannett   Capt   RAF   49 Sqdn   24.9.18 MR 20
ASHBY,Maurice Grassam   2Lt   RAF   42 Sqdn   4.7.18 CR France 31
ASHFIELD,L A.DFC. Lt   RAF   202 Sqdn 61 Wing   16.7.18 CR Belgium 173
ASHTON,Cecil George   Capt   RAF   ded   24.2.19   CR Middx 29
ASHTON,Frederick William Chapn RAF   18.11.18 CR Yorks 551
ASHTON,G G 2Lt   RAF   8 Sqdn   23.7.18 CR France 526
ASHWIN,Guy Arthur Jones   Lt   RAF   L Flight 1 Wing   kia   16.9.18 CR France 95
ASHWORTH,Roger William   2Lt   RAF   15 Trng Sqdn kld   26.4.18 CR London 14
ASPINALL,John Vincent   Capt   RAF & Gen List   11 Sqdn   15.5.18 CR France 62 & MR 20
ATHERTON,Francis Wright.MC.   Lt   RFA att RAF   30 Sqdn   15.5.18 MR 38
ATKINSON,Charles Henry   2Lt   RAF   54 Sqdn   4.7.18 MR 20
ATKINSON,Frank   Lt   RAF   62 Sqdn   ded   10.7.18   CR Germany 3
ATKINSON,R N G.MC.DFC & bar   Capt   RAF   90 Sqdn   7.3.19 CR Herts 31
ATTEWELL,John Charles   Lt   RAF   7 TDS   8.5.18 CR Surrey 35
ATTWATER,Keith Falconer   2Lt   RAF   97 Sqdn   28.10.18 CR France 1678
ATTWOOD,J T Leslie 2Lt   RAF   55 Sqdn   25.9.18 CR France 1678
AUDEN,Geoffrey William   Cadet RAF   ded   4.11.18 CR Derby 129
AUSTER,N C L   2Lt   3SWales Bord att RAF 27 Sqdn   16.7.18 CR France 1410
AUSTIN,Edward Valentine   2Lt   RAF   98 Sqdn   kia   11.7.18 CR France 33
AUSTIN-SPARKS,Ralph Harold   Col   RAF   kld   25.7.18 CR Warwick 89
AYLES,Francis Powell   Lt   RAF   5 Trng Sqdn   1.6.18 CR Dorset 111
AYLES,Walter Matthew William   Lt   RAF   21 Sqdn   kia   20.12.18 CR France 1029

70

BABBITT,Thomas Emerson   2Lt   RAF   43 Sqdn   15.7.18 MR20
BACH,Edward Lambert   2Lt   RAF   4 Fighting Sch kld   30.8.18 CR Lincs 6
BACKHOUSE,St J S 2Lt   RAF & CamH   3.4.18 CR Europe 20
BACKLER,A M.MID 2Lt   RAF   45 Trng Sqdn   25.5.18 CR London 23
BAILEY,Eric Henry Platt   Lt   RAF   206 Sqdn   kia   11.8.18 CR France 1032
BAILEY,Gerald W   2Lt   RAF   dedacc 1.9.18 CR Canada 1438
BAILEY,Hugh Courtenay   FCadet RAF   212 TDS   kld   30.10.18 CR France 1844
BAILLIE,F W 2Lt   RAF   42 TDS   15.9.18 CR Mddx 68
BAILLIE,William.MC.MID   Lt   RAF   49 Wing HQ   dedacc 6.4.19 CR Scot 792
BAINBRIGGE,William Arthur De Lannoy Yates Capt   RAF   Wireless Telegrphy Sch   2.4.19 CR Hamps 13
BAIRD,Daniel Dougal Lt   RAF   31.10.18 CR Scot 674
BAIRD,John Donald   Lt   RAF   acckld 8.5.18 CR Essex 1
BAIRD,Robert Oliver 2Lt   RAF   107 Sqdn   9.8.18 CR France 1472
BAIRD,William Dodds Haldane.AFC. Lt   RAF   112 Sqdn   22.11.18 CR Scot 241
BAKER,Albert Nathaniel   Lt   RAF   73 Sqdn   25.4.18 MR 20
BAKER,Arthur William   2Lt   RAF   53 Sqdn   kia   11.8.18 CR France 324
BAKER,Douglas Walter   FCadet RAF   29 TDS   kld   26.10.18 CR Hamps 31
BAKER,Thomas Matthew   2Lt   RAF   8 Sqdn kld   17.10.18 CR France 940
BALCH,Percy Frederick   Lt   RAF   26.2.19 CR Lincs 156
BALCOMBE-BROWN,R.MC.Maj   RAF   56 Sqdn   2.5.18 CR France 513
BALDIE,John Boyd   Lt   RAF   215 Sqdn   6.11.18 CR France 1678
BALDWIN,Claude Loraine   Capt   RAF   30 Sqdn   dedacc 5.11.18 CR Egypt 8
BALDWIN,W 2Lt   RAF   31 TDS   26.10.18 CR Durham 167
BALDWIN,William Everton   2Lt   ManchR att RAF   18 Sqdn   dow   25.8.18   CR France 41
BALFOUR,Bernard   Lt   RAF & 1ScotRif   65 Sqdn   16.4.18 MR 20
BALL,Frank Ephraim Lt ·   RAF   1 Sch of Aerial Fighting   kld   8.4.18 CR Scot 503
BALL,Henry James   Lt   RAF   22 Trng Sqdn kld   24.7.18 CR Egypt 1
BALLS,Frank William Lt   3SuffR attRAF   ded   1.7.18 CR Egypt 1
BANBURY,Fred Everest.DSC.   Capt   RAF   209 Sqdn   dedacc 1.4.18 CR France 200
BAND,R F G 2Lt   RAF   7 Sqdn   18.9.18 CR Belgium 18
BANKES,P A.MC.   Lt   RAF   22.2.19 CR London 19
BANKS,Frederick   2Lt   RAF & 3EssR   doi   2.6.18 CR London 12
BANNERMAN,G G   Lt   RAF   110 Sqdn   8.6.19 CR Belgium 265
BANNISTER,E G   Capt   RAF   111 Sqdn   14.2.19 CR Palestine 9
BANNISTER,Herbert Stanley Lt   10CanInf seconded RAF   21.6.18 CR France102
BANNISTER,Q W   2Lt   RAF   10.4.18 CR Canada 1688
BARBE,Adrian Espinasson   Lt   5HLI attRAF   drd   27.5.18   MR 41
BARBER,C S 2Lt   RAF   55 Sqdn   25.9.18 CR France 1678
BARBER J H FltCdt RAF   110352 5 TDS   3.12.18 CR Lancs 39
BARBER,Victor Leslie   Lt   RAF   14 Trng Sqdn   24.5.18 CR Yorks 173
BARCLAY,F Capt   RAF   7.12.18 CR Somerset 197
BARCLAY,J G   2Lt   RAF   25 Sqdn   kldacc 10.5.19   CR Belgium 241
BARING,Reginald Arthur   2Lt   RAF   73 Sqdn   9.6.18 MR 20
BARK,Norman   Lt   RAF & 6KOSB   kia   1.10.18 CR Belgium 157
BARKER,Cecil Norman   Lt   RAF   2 Aircraft supply depotdedacc 4.8.18 CR France792
BARKER,Frank Edward   Lt   RAF & W'land&C'landYeo Cent Despatch Pool   ded   13.1.19   CR Essex 40
BARKER,James   2Lt   RAF   21 TDS   4.10.18 CR Durham 106
BARKER,Joseph Claude .   2Lt   RAF   109 Sqdn   19.5.18 CR Wilts 3
BARKER,L I Capt   RAF   7 Sqdn   19.5.19 CR Germany 1
BARKER,Richard Raymond.MC.   Maj   RAF & NumbF   3 Sqdn kia   20.4.18 MR 20
BARKER,Robin E   Cdt   RAF 183681 8Cdt Wing   7.11.18 CR Yorks 175
BARKER,William Frank   F/Cadet   RAF   191 Sqdn   13.6.18 CR Norfolk 73
BARKER,William John   2Lt   RAF   dedacc 27.4.18   CR Egypt 8
BARKER,W S G   2Lt   RAF   205 TDS   21.6.18 CR France1844
BARLOW,Harold Frederick   2Lt   RAF   kld   30.8.18 CR Staffs 70
BARLOW,Leslie Charles Jackson   2Lt   RAF   82 Sqdn   kia   18.6.18 CR France 1170
BARLOW,Robin Tudor   Capt   RAF   52 Sqdn   30.7.18 CR France267
BARNATO,J H W   Capt   RAF   25.10.18 CR Mddx 40
BARNBROOKE,Arthur E   FltCdt   RAF   CentFlying Schkld   16.1.19 CR Wilts 116
BARNES,A   Lt   RAF   4.2.19 CR Warwick 10

BARNES,Alan 2Lt   RAF · 5 Sqdn kia   26.9.18 CR France 113

BARNES,Goodwin Howard Thomas.MIDx2 Capt   RAF   353 Sqdn   29.10.18 CR Hamps 214

BARNET,D G Lt   RAF   11 Sqdn   31.10.18 CR France 512

BARNETT,John Ivor Arthur RossingtonLt   RAF   kld   24.7.18CR Scot 252

BARNETT,Thomas William   2Lt   EYorks attRAF   17.1.19 CR Yorks244

BARNETT,W R   2Lt   RAF   Ex KSLI   5.9.18 CR Shrop 138

BARON,Harold Hartley   Capt   RAF   SE Area OffPool Ex 1RhodR ded   7.2.19 CR Oxford 69

BARRADELL,Harry Leslie   2Lt ·   RAF   Ex RWarR   kld   20.4.18CR Warwick 19

BARRE,Gerald Benedict   2Lt   RAF & 11RDubF   6 Sqdn   9.8.18 MR 20

BARRETT,J H P   Capt   RAF & LincsR   1.11.18CR London 12

BARRETT,Leland Kelly Willson   Lt   RAF   82 Sqdn   kia   24.4.18CR France 52

BARRON,Leslie   2Lt   RAF   kld   28.7.18CR Kent 217

BARSTOW,J E J   Capt   RAF   See JACKSON-BARSTOW,John Eric

BARTER,William George   Cdt   RGA att RAF   16.10.18 CR Dorset 73

BARTLETT,Guy George   2Lt   RAF   48 Sqdn   6.4.18 MR 20

BARTLETT,Malcolm Capt   RAF   Airship Stn   kldacc 30.8.18   CR London 8

BARTON,Harwood Woodwark   FCadet RAF   kld   2.7.18 CR Yorks 222

BARTON,Lambert Francis   Lt   RAF   74 Sqdn   kld   17.5.18CR France 180

BARWICK,Richard Lawrence Cotter 2Lt   RAF   93 Sqdn   kldacc 5.7.18 CR Sussex 5

BATCHELOR,Thomas Archibald.DFC.AFC.Maj   RAF   2Sch of Nav&Bomb Dropping acckld   22.4.19   CR Hamps98

BATE,William Franklin   2Lt   RAF   22.2.20 CR Berks 86

BATEMAN,Eric Charles   Lt   RAF   84 Sqdn   7.9.18 MR 20

BATES,Cyril Montague   . 2Lt   RAF   24.4.18 CR Lincs 78

BATHE,H M de   Lt   See De BATHE,H.M.

BATHHURST NORMAN,Alfred George   Lt   RAF   3 Aircraft Depot   acckld 20.11.18 CR France 1170

BATTEL,Andrew JohnLt   RAF   74 Sqdn   9.7.18 MR 20

BATTY,Horace Walter   2Lt   RAF   99 Sqdn   30.7.18 CR France 1632

BAUER,D C.DFC.   Capt   RAF   12 Balloon Coy   3.11.18CR France 380

BAUCHOPE,Leslie Cyril William   Lt   RAF   21.5.18 CR Lancs 256

BAWLF,David Leland 2Lt   RAF   203 Sqdn   21.4.18 CR France 31

BAYETTO,Tone Hippolyte   Capt   RAF & Gen List   28.7.18 CR Mddx 34

BAYLEY,F G.DFC.   Lt   RAF   204 Sqdn   23.10.18 CR Belgium 357

BAYNES,Evan John   Lt   RAF   42 Wing   kld   26.6.18CR Canada 1570

BEACHCROFT,W F Lt   RAF   21.7.18 CR Berks 39

BEAMAN,Edgar Robert Hulme   Capt   RAF   kld   17.12.18 CR Shrop 82

BEAN,A R   SgtCdt RAF 100446 54 TD kld   29.7.18CR Staffs 105

BEANLANDS,Bernard Paul Gascoigne.MC.Capt   RAF & HampsR   8.5.19 CR Kent 154

BEAUMONT,C C A 2Lt   RAF   52 Sqdn   22.5.18 CR France 1334

BEAUCHAMP-PROCTOR,Andrew Frederick Weatherby.VC.DSO.MC&Bar.DFC. Capt RAF   dedacc 21.6.21 CR SAfrica 130

BECK,Thomas.MC.   Lt   RAF & 2HLI   48 Sqdn   1.10.18MR 20

BEESLEY,A B2Lt   RAF   1.12.18CR London 13

BEET,G W A   Cadet RAF   8 TDS   21.7.18 CR Mddx 35

BEGBIE,Sydney Claude Hamilton   Lt   3ESurrR att RAF   kia   22.4.18CR France 1027

BEIRNE,William   2Lt   RAF   89 Sqdn   18.8.18 CR Hamps 87

BELGRAVE,James Dacres.MC&Bar Capt   2.O&BLI attRAF   60 Sqdn   kia   13.6.18CR France 105

BELL,A McC 2Lt   RAF   29.3.19 CR Scot 232

BELL,Andrew Robertson   2Lt   RAF   28 Sqdn   kia   22.9.18CR Italy 11

BELL,Benedict Godfrey Allen 2Lt   RAF   48 Sqdn   6.4.18 MR 20

BELL,C C M 2Lt   RAF   16.8.18 CR Lancs 181

BELL,C G   Capt   RAF   29.7.18 CR France 473

BELL,Douglas John.MC&Bar Capt   RAF   3 Sqdn   27.5.18 MR 20

BELL,Edwin Martin Lt   RAF   217 Sqn 61 Wing   28.9.18 CR Belgium 157

BELL,Edward Vaughan   Lt   RAF   209 Sqdn   14.5.18 MR 20

BELL,J D   Lt   RAF   see DOBREE-BELL,J

BELL,John Mercer Grimshaw.MC.   Lt   RFA att RAF   7 Sqdn dow   11.10.18 CR France 34

BELL,L   2Lt   RAF   54 TDS   29.7.18 CR Hamps 13

BELL,Leslie Harrison 2Lt   10GloucR att RAF   58 Sqdn   kld   26.9.18CR France 134

BELL,Oliver 2Lt   RAF   99 Sqdn   24.8.18 CR France 1678

BELLAMY,Harold Edward   Lt   RAF & 19MddxR   kld   28.7.18CR Ches 158   18

BELLEY,Francois Joseph   2Lt   RAF   2 FlgTrng Sch   22.7.18 CR Yorks 127

72

BELLOC,Louis   2Lt   RAF   209 Sqdn   26.8.18 MR 20
BELLORD,Charles Edward 2Lt   RAF   104 Sqdn   kia   14.9.18 CR France 1667
BELYEA,Arthur Fred 2Lt   RAF   kld   17.9.18 CR Hamps 31
BENBOW Edwin Louis.MC. Capt   RFA att RAF 85 Sqdn   kia   30.5.18 CR Belgium 20
BENDER,Carl A   Cadet RAF 153630   dedacc 10.6.18   CR Canada 1304
BENFIELD,Alfred Westbrook Lt   RAF   29.11.18 CR Norfolk 43
BENITZ,F A Lt   RAF   5.8.18 CR Lincs 136
BENNETT,Andrew Russell 2Lt   RAF   82 Sqdn   kia   14.10.18 CR Belgium 157
BENNETT,Arthur Charles   Lt   RAF   142 Sqdn   23.9.18 CR Palestine 3
BENNETT,Harry James   Lt   RAF & 21CanInf 49 Sqdn   kia   24.9.18 CR France 924
BENNETT,O H D   Lt   RAF   26.4.18 CR Heref/Worc 156
BENNETT Rex George   Lt   RAF   20 Sqdn   28.5.18 MR 20
BENNETT,Risdon Mackenzie Lt   RAF &RNAS 204 Sqdn   kld   28.9.18 MR 20
BENNETT,William Harris   Capt   MddxR att HQ RAF   ded   16.1.20   MR 53
BENSON,Donald Good   2Lt   RAF   99 Sqdn   25.6.18 CR Germany 3
BENSON,R C Lt   RAF   11.5.18 CR Mddx 85
BENTON,J W 2Lt   RAF   31.5.18 CR France 34 &1693
BERESFORD,Harry   Lt   RAF   34 TDS   15.10.18 CR Lancs 474
BERKELEY Christopher   2Lt   RAF & 2CldGds   30 TDS   kld   30.1.19 CR Mddx 30
BERRY,Charles Frank 2Lt   RAF   10 Sqdn   17.7.18 CR France 142
BERRY,E A   2Lt   RAF   Sch of Photography   6.8.18 CR Sussex 144
BERRY,Eustace Carlton   2Lt   RFA att RAF   5.7.16 CR Numb 4
BERRY,H H Lt   RAF   27.9.18 CR Essex 86
BERTRAM-SCOTT,G 2Lt   RAF See SCOTT,G.B.
BERTRAND,Phillippe(Angus)   Lt   RAF   4 Sqdn   16.6.18 CR France 193
BETTS,Conrad Coryton   Lt   RAF   G'Sqdn   17.4.18 CR Greece 10
BEVINGTON,Colin Corry   2Lt   RAF   72 Trng Sqdn kld   22.5.18 CR Surrey 160
BICKELL,William Burt   Lt   RAF   13 TDS   kldacc 12.10.18 CR Shrop 145 or BICKWELL
BIDDLE,Frank Henry Herbert 2Lt   RAF   42 Trng Sqdn kld   22.5.18 CR Mddx 39
BILLINGTON,Frank Norman Lt   RAF & AOC   30.9.18 CR France 1483
BINCKES,Reginald   Lt   RAF   214 Sqdn   21.7.18 CR France 65 or BINKES
BINGHAM,H W   2Lt   RAF   108 Sqdn   14.10.18 CR Belgium 140
BINGHAM,R G A   2Lt   RAF   209 Sqdn   8.10.18 CR France 482
BINNIE,A D   FCadet RAF   15.10.18 CR Scot 237
BINNIE,William Harold   Lt   7RScots att RAF   206 Sqdn   kia   22.7.18 CR France 134
BION,Rupert Euston   Lt   RAF & 20Huss 40 Sqdn   9.4.18 MR 20
BIRCH,Edward Cecil Lt   RAF   26.1.19 CR Surrey 153
BIRCHARD,Gordon Frank   2Lt   RAF   44 Wing(BordonCamp)   dedacc 23.5.18   CR Canada 1197
BIRD,Clarence Oscar.DFC.   F/O   RAF   kld   27.5.20 CR Egypt 10
BIRD,Frederic Valentine   Lt   RAF   12 Sqdn   kia   21.8.18 CR France 745
BIRD,Montagu Herbert   Lt   1CanInf att RAF   9.7.18 CR France 71
BIRKETT,H   2Lt   RAF   No3 Flying Sch   24.10.18 CR C'land&W'land 11
BIRRELL,Albert   2Lt   RAF   13 Sqdn   18.9.18 CR France 95
BISHOP,Alfred Glanville   Lt   RAF   239 Sqdn   lost at sea   3.9.18 MR 40
BISHOP,Noel Frederick   2Lt(Pilot)   RAF   56 Sqdn   16.9.18 MR 20
BISHOP,Willie Stanley   Cdt   RAF   180344 6 Cdt Wing   ded   11.10.18 CR Kent 180
BISSELL,Lynn Newton   Lt   RAF   201 TDS   31.10.18 CR Scot 626
BIZIOU,Henry Arthur Richard.DFC. Lt   RAF   RAE(Farnborough)Experimental Sqdn 14.7.19   CR Hamps 1
BLACK,D C Lt   RAF   5 TDS   23.4.18 CR London 12
BLACKIE,Austin Wyard   Lt   RAF   29 TDS   kld   17.9.18 CR Hamps 31
BLADWELL,Stanley Frederick   FCadet RAF   kld   19.11.18 CR France 1844
BLAIN,C W.AFC.   RAF   22.1.19 CR Suffolk 83
BLAIR,Thomas Finkall   2Lt   RAF   kld   6.4.18 CR Numb 96
BLAKE,Harry Hutton.MID   Cadet RAF 181853 8Cdt Wing   1.10.18 CR Kent 180
BLATHERWICK,Wilfred George   2Lt   RAF   56 Trng Sqdn   19.5.18 CR Herts 87
BLOUNT,J H 2Lt   RAF & O&BLI   6.7.18 CR Suffolk 55
BLUNDELL,Alfred Gresham Lt   RAF   252 Sqdn   23.8.188 CR Lancs 43
BLUNDELL,Jack Benson   2Lt   RAF   211 Sqdn   29.9.18 MR 20
BLYTH,Wilfred Ernest Hill 2Lt   RAF   88 Sqdn   22.4.18 CR Norfolk 209
BOARDMAN,Alex Gilmour 2Lt   RAF   1 Obs Sch of Aerial Gnry   kld   29.4.18 CR Essex 40

BOARDMAN,P M H Cadet RAF 182130 8Cdt Wing   ded   29.9.18 CR Kent 180
BOCKETT-PUGH,Henry Charles Edward.DFC.F/O RAF   94 Sqdn   22.9.20 MR 38
BODDAM-WHETHAM,Arthur Courtney   LtCol RAF   HQ Middle East   kld   22.6.19CR Palestine 9
BOGER,William Otway DFC Capt   RAF &LSH   56 Sqdn   kia   10.08.18 MR 20
BOLAY,A R   2Lt   RAF &Gen List   65 Sqdn   27.5.18 CR France 71
BOLES,J L   Lt   RAF 39 Sqdn   13.6.18 CR Essex 172
BOND,Reginald Harry 2Lt   RAF   kld   26.9.18CR Egypt 9
BOND,T J   2Lt   RAF 104 Sqdn   13.9.18 CR France 1678
BONNER,William   2Lt   RLancsR attRAF   19.6.18 CR France 84
BONYNGE,Edward Besserer Cadet RAF 74993   dedacc   17.4.18   CR USA 132
BOOKER,Charles Dawson.DSC.   Maj   RAF   201 Sqdn   kia   13.8.18CR France 71
BOOKER,C S Lt   RAF 35 Sqdn   3.10.18CR France194
BOOLE,J O   2Lt   RAF   9.7.18 CR Wales 107
BOOTH,Lawrence Howard   2Lt   RAF   105 Sqdn   kld   13.11.18 CR NIreland 242
BOOTH,Sydney E   2Lt   RAF 20 Sqdn   3.12.18CR Belgium 330
BOOTH,Stanley Charles   2Lt   RAF 6TDS kldacc 24.8.18   CR London 35
BOOTHMAN,C D   2Lt   RAF 210 Sqdn   26.6.18 CR France 705
BORDEN,Harold Hunter   Lt   RAF 65 Sqdn   1.7.18 CR France 526
BORROWMAN,J J   2Lt   RAF 22 Sqdn   29.8.18 CR France 646
BOSWELL,Alan Thompson Watt   2Lt   RAF 108 Sqdn   2.10.18MR 20
BOSWOOD,Leslie John   Lt   RAF 1 Obs Sch of AerialGnry   3.9.18 CR Kent 180
BOULTON,Nicholson Stuart 2Lt   RAF 20 Sqdn   29.9.18 CR France 375
BOURKE,J P SqnLdr RAF   Air Ministry   8.2.20 CR London 7
BOURKE,Thomas Leslie   2Lt   RAF 10 TDS   doi   9.9.18 CR Eire 24
BOURNE,Richard Balfour   Capt   RAF   kld   6.11.19CR Eire 14
BOURNER,Reginald Robert   2Lt   RAF   1.6.18 CR Kent 268
BOUSFIELD,Harold W   Cadet RAF 170771   dedacc   11.9.18   CR Canada 50
BOWDEN,N   2Lt   8N&DR attRAF   25.4.18 CR France 1170
BOWEN,Laurence Grant   Lt   RAF 56 Sqdn   kia   15.9.18CR France 336
BOWER,Frederick   2Lt   RAF   ded   2.3.19 CR Sussex 110
BOWER-BINNS,John Simpson   Lt   RAF 138 Sqdn   6.11.18CR Essex 40
BOWERMAN,H E   Cdt   RAF 184450 6 Sqn No1 CdtWing   30.4.20 CR Devon 246
BOWICK,William Robie   Lt   RAF   kld   11.6.18CR Suffolk 173
BOWLER,Herbert Cyril   2Lt   RAF 101 Sqdn   4.11.18CR France 528
BOWMAN,Carl Welch   Lt   RAF   ded   1.8.21 CR Canada 183
BOX,G H.DFC.   Lt   RAF &Sp List 100 Sqdn   26.8 18 CR France 1678
BOYCE,Edward Francis   2Lt   RAF 25 Sqdn   kia   3.9.18 CR France 792
BOYD,Cecil Nicholas 2Lt   RAF 19 Sqdn   dow   5.11.18CR Belgium 231
BOYD,Henry Lt   RAF 100 Sqdn   25.8.18 CR France 1678
BOYD,R H   Lt   RAF & Gen List   5 Sqdn   12.4.18 CR France 95
BOYT,Horace George Richard 2Lt   RAF 3 Fighter Sqdn kld   31.7.18CR Norfolk 67
BRACHER,Herbert Hector   2Lt   RAF 55 Sqdn   16.8.18 CR France 1675
BRABROOK,Edward John   2Lt   18LondR att RAF   8 Sqdn   20.4.18 CR France 40 or BRADBROOK
BRADBURN,Frederick James Lt   RAF 28 Wing   17.11.18 CR Lancs 14
BRADBURY,Duncan 2Lt   RAF 6 Sqdn dow   5.8.18 CR France 119
BRADLEY,Harold Bartlett   Lt   RAF 1 Sqdn   25.6.18 MR 20
BRADLEY,Walter Robinson Lt   1N&DR &RAF   ded   29.6.18   CR Greece 7
BRADSHAW,Roland Latimer Cdt   RAF 184232 8Cdt Wing   ded   28.10.18 CR Kent 180
BRAGG,Eric Lowe.MID   Lt   RAF   Ex RNAS   21.7.18 MR 37
BRAGG,E W Lt   RAF 201 TDS   31.10.18 CR Scot 626
BRAIN,William John 2Lt   RAF 110 Sqdn   21.10.18 CR Germany 3
BRAMHAM,Ernest Stewart   Capt   RAF   Aero Constr Serv   7.11.18CR Surrey 1
BRAMWELL,E H   Lt   RAF   1.1.20 CR Mddx 58
BRAMWELL,Robert 2Lt   RAF 80 Sqdn   29.9.18 MR 20
BRAND,Francis Robert   Lt   RAF 29 Sqdn   kia   27.6.18CR France 298
BRANDON,E 2Lt   RAF 9 Sqdn   11.8.18 CR France 1170
BRANDT,J A Lt   RAF 47 Sqdn   18.9.18 CR Greece 5
BRAVERY,Frederick James Lt   RAF   kld   19.8.18CR Sussex 95
BRAY,Cyril Ivor   2Lt   RAF 206 Sqdn   kld   7.7.18 CR France 255
BRAY,Charles Leslie Lt   RAF 211 Sqdn   19.5.18 CR Belgium 390

74

BRAY,Horace Edgar Kingsmill   2Lt   RAF   67 Trng Sqdn   9.7.18 CR Ches 35
BREAKLEY,Henry Leopold   2Lt   RAF   dow   15.7.18   CR Wilts 129 or BREAKEY
BRENNAN,David P   Lt   RAF   12.11.18 CR Canada 1391
BRENNAN,Thomas L Lt   RAF   ded   16.10.18 CR Canada 653
BRETT,Wesley Arthur2Lt   RAF   73 Sqdn   27.9.18 MR 20
BREWE,Cyril PltOff RAF   84 Sqdn   22.6.21 CR Iraq 6
BREWER,T E 2Lt   RAF   55 Sqdn   12.6.18 CR France 1678
BREWSTER,Joseph Lamonby 2Lt   RAF   73 Sqdn   21.5.18 MR 20
BRIDGE,Charles Henry Ardley   2Lt   RAF   23 Sqdn   31.8.18 MR 20
BRIDGE,C J   FltCdt RAF   86103   7.11.18 CR Essex 86
BRIDGETT,Claude   2Lt   RAF   99 Sqdn   kia   13.9.18 CR France 1667
BRIGGS,C   Lt   RAF   25.6.18 CR Belgium 371
BRIGHT,Ronald Ernest   Lt   RAF   74 Sqdn   8.5.18 MR 20
BRINDLEY,Victor George   2Lt   RAF   80 Sqdn   kia   30.8.18 CR France 1170
BRINKWORTH,Wilfred Henry   2Lt   RAF & RFus 215 Sqdn   4.8.18 MR 20
BRISLEY,C E Maj   RAF   13 TDS   30.7.188 CR Shrop 82
BRITTAIN,Richard Arthur Henry   2Lt   RAF   120 Trng Sqdn   15.5.18 CR Numb 4
BRITTOROUS,Oswald George   2Lt   RAF   209 Sqdn   15.5.18 MR 20
BROADHEAD,F   FCadet RAF   42 Trng Sqdn   18.8.18 CR Lincs 159
BROADLEY,Thomas Harding Lt   RAF   62 Sqdn   15.9.18 CR France 1193
BROCK,Frederick Albert.MM.   2Lt   RAF   206 Sqdn   7.8.18 MR 20
BRODIE,Eric Brownlee   Lt   RAF   43 Sqdn   11.2.19 CR Germany 1
BRODIE,Phililp Wyndham   Capt   1SfthH attRAF   ded   18.11.18 CR Italy 6
BROMLEY,John Ledger   Lt   RAF &ASC MT   11 Sqdn   kld   29.9.18 MR 20
BROOKE,Leonard Stopford   Lt   RAF   110 Sqdn   kia   25.9.18 CR Germany 5
BROOKES,Eric Guy.DFC.   Capt   RAF &WorcR 65 Sqdn   kia   8.8.18 CR France 526
BROOKES,William Leslie   Lt   RAF   209 Sqdn   8.8.18 CR France 652
BROOKS,Robert Elesmere   Lt   RAF & QuebecRegtDepot   8.4.18 CR Scot 503
BROOKS,Walter J   Lt   RAF   65 Sqdn   dow   9.10.18 CR Belgium365
BROOMHALL,O A   Lt   RAF &LpoolR 4 Sqdn   18.4.18 CR France 180
BROTHERIDGE,Frederick John   2Lt   RAF   3 Sqdn   19.5.18 MR 20
BROUNCKER,Charles Crawfurd   2Lt   RAF   211 Sqdn   4.11.18 MR 20
BROWN,Alexander Claud Gordon   2Lt   RAF   48 Sqdn   7.5.18 CR France 526
BROWN,C A Capt   RAF   15 Aicraft Acc Park   15.1.19 CR Lancs 34
BROWN,Charles Alexander   Lt   RAF   24.4.18 CR Scot 244
BROWN,Charles David   FCdt   RAF   kld   27.7.18 CR Essex 16
BROWN,C F Lt   RAF   203 Sqdn   27.7.18 CR France 525
BROWN,Charles Redmond   2Lt   RAF   218 Sqdn   28.9.18 CR Belgium 24
BROWN,E C Lt   RAF &RWKentR   18.10.18 CR France 341
BROWN,G   Lt   RAF   23.10.18 CR Belgium 349
BROWN,G C Lt   RAF   53 Sqdn   dow   10.10.18 CR Belgium 11
BROWN,Jack 2Lt   RAF   ded   30.12.19 CR Canada 1691
BROWN,John Horace Lt   RAF   ded   18.2.19   CR Canada 1322
BROWN,Jonathon Martin.DFC.   Lt   RAF   3.10.18 CR France 234
BROWN,J S Lt   RAF   20.10.18 CR Lancs 243
BROWN,Nelson W   Cadet   RAF   273002   ded   22.10.18 CR Canada 1156
BROWN,Norman Ainslie   Cdt   RAF   173798 Burwash Hall Toronto ded   21.10.18 CR Canada 1688
BROWN,P L 2Lt   RAF   40 Trng Sqdn   16.10.18 CR Surrey 6
BROWN,R R 2Lt   RAF   73 Trng Sqdn   18.6.18 CR Hamps 31
BROWN,T. 2Lt   RAF   27 Sqdn   29.9.18 CR France 1352
BROWN,William Gordon   Lt   RAF &Gen List   19 Sqdn   kia   7.5.18 CR France 95
BROWN,W J Lt   1C of LondYeo attRAF   kldacc   21.2.18   CR Egypt 9
BROWNE,George Ernest Melford   2Lt   RAF   42 Sqdn   23.9.18 MR 20
BROWNE,Hedley Goldsmith Browne 2Lt   RAF   Ex RE acckld 8.4.18 CR Glouc 67
BROWNE,Harold Johnston   Lt   RAF   15 Sqdn   kia   3.5.18 CR France 116
BROWNE,John Sandfield McDonald Lt   RAF   4 AFC Sqdn   27.6.18 MR 20
BROWNHILL,Ernest Albert.MM&Bar   2Lt   RAF   55 Sqdn   16.8.18 CR Germany 3
BROWNING,Frederick Adolphus   Lt   RAF   101 Sqdn   22.9.18 CR France 1170
BROWNRIGG,Thomas   Lt   RAF   37 TDS   drd   21.8.18   CR Hamps 57
BRUCE,J A Lt   RAF   27TDS   6.1.19 CR Scot 549

75

BRUCE,Nigel Lt   RAF   46 Sqdn   19.9.18 MR 20
BRUCE,Philip Thomson   Lt   RAF   43 Sqdn Ex 87 Sqdn   30.5.18 MR 20
BRUCE,William   Lt   RAF &SaskatchR   104 Sqdn   25.5.18 CR France 1658
BRUCE-CLARKE,W R   Capt   14LondR attRAF   1.12.18 CR Cambs 19
BRUNEL,Eugene   Cadet RAF 172297   ded   7.10.18 CR Canada 254
BRUTEY,Harold Reginald   Capt   RAF   7 Aircraft Acc Park   16.11.18 CR London 12
BRYANT,James Henry Rattenbury   Lt   RAF   28 Sqdn   kia   4.10.18 CR Italy 9
BRYARS,George Leonard   FltLt RAF   20 Sqdn   kia   16.9.18 CR France 1390
BUCHANAN,Arthur Noel   Lt   RAF   45 Wing   ded   14.10.18 CR London 4
BUCHANAN,Edward Lawrence   Capt   RFA & RAF   kia   15.8.20 CR Iraq 8
BUCHANAN,Irwin Frank   Cadet RAF 153685   42 Wing   dedacc   13.7.188 CR USA 107
BUCK,Geoffrey Sebastian.MC.DFC.   Capt   RAF   215 Sqdn   kld   3.9.18 CR France 1678
BUCKBY,R   2Lt   RAF   99 Sqdn   25.9.18 CR France 1671
BUCKERIDGE,W H   Lt   RAF   52 Sqdn   2.10.18 CR France 421
BUCKINGHAM,P E.MC.   Lt   RWKentR attRAF   7 Sqdn   8.11.18 CR Belgium 159
BUCKLAND,Cecil John   2Lt   5RFus & RAF   kld   19.8.18 CR Wilts 18
BUCKLEY,H FltCadet   RAF 85960 53 Trng Sqdn   17.7.18 CR Yorks 620
BUDDS,Percy Harold Lt   6EKentR attRAF   12 Sqdn   ded   29.10.18 CR France 40
BUGG,Eric Gordon   2Lt   RAF   11 Sqdn   6.9.18 MR 20
BULL,Marshall John   Cadet   RAF 17970   ded   19.10.18 CR Canada 440
BULLOCK,Geoffrey Ernest   Lt   5NStaffsR att148RAF   kia   16.7.18 CR France 10
BULLOCK,Reginald Henry   2Lt   RAF   Seaplane Stn(Felixstowe)   drd   21.8.18   CR Essex 186
BULLOUGH,J 2Lt   RAF   64 Sqdn   dow PoW 29.3.18   CR France 1142
BUNBURY,Thomas St Pierre Capt   RAF &RFA   64 Sqdn   kia   31.8.18 CR France 421
BURCH,Raymond Sanderson Lt   RAF   4 Sqdn   28.6.18 CR France 28
BURDEN,Sydney Edward   2Lt   RAF   32 Sqdn   kia   1.11.18 CR Belgium 229
BURDETT,William Robert   2Lt   RAF   207 TDS   kld   19.5.18 CR London 12
BURDICK,Frederick William.MC.   Capt   20LondR attRAF   4 Sqdn kia   29.8.18 CR France 352
BURFOOT,W M   2Lt   RAF   37 Sqdn   22.5.18 CR Kent 133
BURGE,Philip Scott.MC.MM.   Capt   RAF   kia   24.7.18 CR France 219
BURGESS,A Theodore   Cadet RAF 171189   ded   25.4.18   CR Canada 1379
BURNAY,Percy Samuel   Lt   RAF   57 Sqdn   6.3.19 CR Belgium 269
BURNET,Stanley   Lt   5BedsR attRAF   17 Trng Sqdn   31.5.18 CR Beds 75
BURNETT,H R.MM. 2Lt   RAF   55 Sqdn   25.9.19 CR France 1667
BURNS,James Rattray.MC.   Lt   ScotRifs AttRAF   193 Trng Sqdn   10.6.18 CR Egypyt 1
BURNS,T R R Lt   RAF   16.12.18 CR Essex41
BURREE,S A 2Lt   RAF   16 Trng Sqdn kldacc 5.7.18 CR Surrey 15
BURT,H C   Cdt   RAF   Ex 28LondR   4.7.18 CR Dorset 93
BURT,J   2Lt   RAF   70 Sqdn   8.11.18 CR Belgium 448
BURT,T   FltCdt 17314 ACycCps 61DivCycCoy attRAF Sch of Aeronautics   kld   11.9.18 CR Durham 88
BURTON,Stanley George Harold Edgar 2Lt   RAF   99 Sqn Ex 15LondR   kia   30.7.18 CR France 1678
BUSBY,Donald Arthur   2Lt   RAF   3 TDS kld   3.9.18 CR Surrey 15
BUSBY,Vernon Earle George Capt   RAF   Accident Dept kld   8.6.18 CR Warwick 7
BUSHELL,Durlin Duncan   Cadet RAF 173722   2.11.18 CR Canada 1689
BUTLER,Frederick Charles 2Lt   RAF   25.4.18 CR Wilts 184
BUTLER,J O Lt   Gen List &RAF   3 Sqdn   11.4.18 CR Belgium 241
BUTLER,Reginald Arthur   Lt   RAF   55 Sqdn   kia   20.7.18 CR Germany 3
BUTLER,William Amos Norris   2Lt   RAF   10 TDS Ex PPCLI   kld   2.8.1818 CR Norfolk 259
BUTOW,J M F/O   RAF   2.9.20 CR SAfrica 144
BUTT,Frank Wilfred Lt   RAF   102 Sqdn   kia   26.5.18 CR France 63
BUTTERWORTH,F   2Lt   1/2WYorksR attRAF   14.9.18 CR Belgium 192
BUTTERWORTH,Howard   2Lt   RAF   107 Sqdn   9.8.18 CR France 1472
BYRNE,Brennan Claude Sydney   Obs/Off   RE & RAF   47 Sqdn   3.9.20 CR Egypt 9
BYRNES,James Arthur   Cadet RAF 152840 44 Wing   dedacc 28.6.18   CR USA 147

C

CABBURN,Frank   Lt   RAF   48 Sqdn   25.6.18 CR France 692
CAIN,Richard Claude.DFC.   Capt   RAF   2 Aircraft Acc Park Ex CHA kld   18.7.19 CR Lancs 410
CAIRNES,William Jameson   Capt   RAF & 1LeinstR   74 Sqdn   kia   1.6.18 MR 20
CAIRNS,A F Lt   RAF   29.7.18 CR Yorks 276
CALDERWOOD,David Millar   2Lt   RAF   20 Sqdn Ex Pte 1CMR   20.9.18 MR 20
CALDWELL,Edward Vaughan James Lydale FCadet RAF 110938   14 TDS   6.9.18 CR Warwick 3
CALDWELL,James   Lt   RAF   2 Sqdn   28.8.18 MR 20
CALDWELL,Russell Roberts 2Lt   RAF   CentFlying Schkldacc 15.9.18   CR Wilts 116
CALLAGHAN,J C.MC.   Maj   7RMunstF att RAF   87 Sqdn   2.7.18 CR France 63
CALLAWAY,Frank Le Moignan   Maj   RAF   HQ (Malta)   2.3.19 CR Hamps 1
CALLENDER,Alwin Andrew   Capt   RAF   32 Sqdn   30.10.18 CR France 1142
CALVERLEY,Osbert Leveson 2Lt   RAF   124 Sqdn   12.7.18 CR Cambs 16
CALVERT,Ernest   2Lt   RAF   206 Sqdn   dow   14.8.18   CR France 134
CAMERON,Charles Logie   Cadet   RAF 178158 Cadet Dist Centre   ded   10.7.18   CR Surrey 1
CAMERON,James   2Lt   RAF   kldacc 21.6.18   CR Lancs 434
CAMM,Percy 2Lt   RAF   22 TDS   kld   20.10.18 CR Lancs 205
CAMPBELL,Kenneth Preston Lt   RAF   28.11.18 CR Mddx 34
CAMPBELL,Kenneth Turner 2Lt   RAF   210 Sqdn   kia   17.6.18 CR France 10
CAMPBELL,Lynn   Capt   RAF   62 Sqdn   9.10.18 CR France 1078
CAMPBELL,Norman Cecil SandersonLt   RAF   12 Grp kld   19.8.18 CR Lincs 78
CAMPBELL,R O.DCM.   2Lt   RAF   65 Sqdn   27.9.18 CR Belgium 140
CANGIAMILA,Joseph 2Lt   RAF   32 TDS   12.8.188 CR Scot 398
CANN,Percy Reginald Lt   RAF   65 Sqdn   2.4.18 CR France 145
CANNELL,Hugh Featherstone Cameron Lt   Indian Army 1 Lcrs att RAF 72 Sqdn dow   31.10.18 MR 38
CANNING,Ernest Harold.DFC.   Lt   RAF & GloucR   102 Sqdn   kia   5.10.18 CR France 404
CANNON,Frederick William 2Lt   RAF   189 NTS   2.8.18 CR Mddx 5
CANNON,S L Lt   KSLI att RAF(EEF)   ded   14.9.18   CR Egypt 1
CAPES,Cyril Wentworth   Lt   RAF   lost at sea   6.7.18 MR 40
CAPLE,Leonard Norman Akerman   Lt   RAF   22 Sqdn   kld   21.11.18 CR France 938 from954
CAPPER,Harry Kent Lt   RAF   5TDS Ex 28LondR   kld   4.6.18 CR Lincs 100
CARDWELL,Fred   P/O   RAF   HMS Vindictive   25.10.19 CR Europe 180 & MR 70
CARLETON-SMITH,Beavan 2Lt   RAF   100 Sqdn   kld   6.2.19 CR Germany 1
CARLING,John Burleigh   Lt   RAF   ded   5.5.18 CR Canada 1245
CARPENTER,Ernest Lt   RAF &WorcR 24 Sqdn   3.10.18 MR 20
CARPENTER,Eric Edwin   Lt   RAF   35 TDS   kldacc 24.8.18   CR Essex 12
CARR,A W   2Lt   ConnRgrs att RAF   22Trng Sqdn   6.7.18 CR Egypt 1
CARR,George Thompson   2Lt   RAF   82 Sqdn   14.10.18 MR 20
CARR,John Henry Talbot   F/O   RAF   kld   20.5.21 CR Suffolk 137
CARR-HALFEY,John Albert Bernard F/O   RAF   5 Sqdn   15.5.21 MR 43
CARRIGAN,Leo Patrick Sarsfield   Lt   RAF   2.11.18 CR London 1
CARROLL,Patrick Mordaunt FltLt   RAF   ded   9.3.20 CR Scot 248
CARRUTHERS,Gordon Kinraid   2Lt   RAF   98 Sqdn   25.7.18 CR France 1429
CARRUTHERS,W J 2Lt   RAF   59 Sqdn   8.10.18 CR France 277
CARSON,J A B   Capt   RAMC att RAF   9.8.18 CR Egypt 9
CARSON,Samuel Edward   2Lt   RAF   103 Sqdn   20.7.18 CR Belgium 451
CARTER,Alan 2Lt   RAF   8 Sqdn kia   25.6.18 CR France 1564
CARTER,Albert Desbriszy.DSO&Bar Maj   RAF   11 Trng Grp Ex CanInf   kld   22.5.19 CR Sussex 55
CARTER,Audsley Ralph   Maj   RGA att RAF 1 Wing dow   28.8.18   CR France 95
CARTER,Gerald MarkF/O   RWarR & RAF   17.1.21 CR Hamps 53
CARTER,J A 2Lt   RAF   10 Kite Balloon Sect   30.10.18 CR France 1266
CARTER,Robert George ·   Cadet   RAF 176468 1 Wing   20.6.18 CR Sussex 178
CARTHEW,J H   2Lt   RAF   53 Trng Sqdn   3.5.18 CR Lincs 61
CARTMEL,George Musgrove Lt   RAF   205 Sqdn   kia   6.4.18 CR France 197
CARTWRIGHT,Andrew William Clarence Capt   RAF   ded   22.11.18 CR London 12
CARTWRIGHT,Edward.MID Lt   RAF   104 Sqdn   22.8.18 CR France 1633
CARTWRIGHT,Joseph Harold   Lt   RAF   34 TDS   26.7.18 CR Staffs 33

CARTWRIGHT,John William Plush.MID 2Lt   RAF   13.5.19 CR Hamps 4
CARTWRIGHT,Pybus 2Lt   RAF   25 Sqdn   kia   4.11.18 CR France 1224
CARVER,Robin Creswell   Lt   RAF   17.7.18 CR Surrey 6
CASE,Bernard Sydney 2Lt   RAF   104 Sqdn   dow   10.11.18 CR France 1664
CASE,Charles Henry   2Lt   . RAF & 11ManchR   ded   29.9.18 CR France 376
CASE,Sidney Foley   2Lt   RAF   22.8.18 CR Heref/Worc 120
CASEY,J P N Capt   RAMC att RAF   13.12.18 CR Glouc 9
CASH,Frederick Alfred   2Lt   RAF   Sch of Aerial Gnry   24.7.18 CR Scot 639
CASSERLY,Cyril Ignatius   FCadet RAF   10 TDS   7.11.18 CR Norfolk 209
CATHLES,George Kinlock   Lt   RAF   24 Kite Balloon Sect   11.8.18 CR Egypt 7
CATON,Frederick   2Lt   RAF   215 Sqdn   dow   1.9.18 CR France 1678
CATTLE,Frank L   Lt   RAF   213 Sqdn   kldacc 29.6.18   CR Belgium 172
CAUDELL,John Harry Lt   RAF   211 TDS   kld   8.7.18 CR Hunts 83
CAVANAGH,John Charles   2Lt   RAF   218 Sqdn   kld   19.8.18 CR France 65
CAVE,A D   Lt   RAF &DLI   10.11.18 CR Sussex 111
CAVE,Clement Forte 2Lt   RAF   108 Sqdn   22.10.18 CR Belgium355
CAVE,Edward Jasper Shalcross   2Lt   RAF   8 Sqdn Ex CanInf   kia   14.8.18 CR France 526
CAVERS,James Pomeroy.MID   Lt   . RAF   150 Sqdn   kia   3.9.18 MR 37
CAWLEY,Frederick   2Lt   RAF   35 TDS   dedacc 13.10.18 CR Mon 82
CAWSTON,G 2Lt   RWSurrR att RAF   29.10.18 CR Surrey 83
CEMERY.T G 2Lt   RAF   23.8.20 CR Scot 241
CHADWICK,F W   2Lt   RAF   59 Sqdn   29.9.18 CR France 379
CHAFFEY,Harward Eastman   Lt   RAF   42 Sqdn   kia   27.10.18 CR France 1030
CHAMBERLAIN,John Boyd 2Lt   RAF   13 Trng Sqdn   23.4.18 CR Cornwall 37
CHAMBERS,John Harold   2Lt   RAF   7 TDS kld   1.2.19 CR Norfolk 261
CHAMBERS,William Geoffrey   Capt   RAF & 1/2LincsR   49 Sqdn   15.5.18 MR 20
CHAMPNEYS,J A L 2Lt   RAF   73 Sqdn   3.4.18 CR France 1233
CHANEY,Henry Edward.OBE.MIDx2   Maj   RAF   27.2.19 CR Surrey 150
CHANT,Earle Marion Lt   RAF & Brit ColmbiaR 16 Sqdn   4.4.18 CR France 403
CHAPLIN,Elliot Adams   Lt   RAF   99 Sqdn   kia   27.6.18 CR France 1667
CHAPMAN,Cecil   FCadet RAF   110297   kld   18.11.18 CR Lincs 179
CHAPMAN,C R   Lt   RAF   13.10.18 CR Sussex 144
CHAPMAN,Stephen James   Lt   RAF   1 Obs Sch of Gnry   6.6.18 CR Sussex 183
CHARLES,Basil Stuart   Lt   RAF   1 Aircraft Supply Depot   7.12.18 CR France 34
CHARLTON,Brian   Lt   TankCps att RAF   82 Sqdn   kia   27.10.18 CR Belgium 159
CHAVASSE,P 2Lt   RAF & IA RoO   59 Sqdn   8.10.18 MR 20
CHEERS,Donald Heriot Anson   2Lt   3ESurrR att RAF   kldacc 17.4.18   CR Scot 235
CHESTER,Ronald Henry Venn   Lt   RAF   1 TDS dedacc 13.7.18   CR Mddx 18
CHILD,Jack Escott   Lt   RAF   185(N) Trng Sqdn   3.11.18 CR Essex 40
CHILD,James Martin.MC.   Capt   ManchR & RAF   84 Sqdn   acckld   23.8.18   CR Essex 40
CHILD,M H   2Lt   RAF   Armament Sch(Uxbridge)   16.11.18 CR Berks 86
CHISHOLM,R J   Lt   RAF   218 Sqdn   14.5.18 CR France 13359
CHISNALL,Charles Alain   Lt   RAF   28.5.19 CR Yorks 294
CHOATE,Frederick Henry   Lt   LSH &RAF   4.6.18 CR Wilts 116
CHRISTIE,David   Lt   RAF   4 Sch of Aerial Gnry   2.4.18 CR Scot 762
CHRISTIE,Donald Murdoch   Lt   RAF   3 Sqdn   23.2.19 CR London 12
CHRISTIE,Edgar Watchorn   2Lt   RAF   60 Sqdn   2.4.18 MR 20
CHURCH,Frederick James   2Lt   RAF   74 Sqdn   13.7.18 CR France285
CHURCHER,A E C   2Lt   RAF   29 Sqdn   kld   23.9.18 CR Hamps 8
CHUCHILL,John   2Lt   RAF   kia   14.8.18 CR France 755
CILLIERS,Gabriel Pietar   2Lt   RAF   13 TDS   10.11.18 CR Shrop 145
CLARK,Algernon Basil.MC.MIDx2   Capt   3BlkW att RAF   2 Sqdn kia   3.10.18 CR France 223
CLARK,Ernest George 2Lt   RAF   27.11.18 CR Essex 193
CLARK,H T   Lt   RAF   84 Sqdn   16.6.19 CR Germany 1
CLARK,J F   2Lt   RAF   10.9.18 CR Bucks 63
CLARK,James Hyatt.MM&Bar   2Lt   RAF   119 Sqdn   4.11.18 CR Wilts 115
CLARK,Norman   FltLt   RAF   54 Sqdn   kld   18.3.18 CR France 333
CLARK,Stanley   2Lt   RAF   208 Sqdn   kia   17.9.18 CR France 10
CLARKE,Charles Edward   2Lt   WYorks att RAF   20 Sqdn   27.9.18 CR France 1061
CLARKE,Clarence Victor   2Lt   RAF   Ex 1CanInf   ded   16.2.19   CR Derby 117

78

CLARKE,E C 2Lt   RAF   104 Sqdn   13.8.18 CR France 1662
CLARKE,Fred 2Lt   RAF   105 Sqdn Ex SurrYeo dedacc 6.6.19 CR Surrey 41
CLARKE,Gerald Wilfred Francis   2Lt   RAF   42 Trng Sqdn   23.8.18 CR London 4
CLARKE,G M.AFC.   FltLt   RAF   208 Sqdn   14.4.21 CR Egypt 8
CLARKE,Hubert Wilton   Lt   RAF   2.9.18 CR France426
CLARKE,Herbert Palmer   2Lt   RAF   46 Sqdn   1.10.18 CR France 329
CLARKE,Joseph.MC. Lt(P/O)   RAF & WorcR 99 Sqdn   1.10.19MR 65
CLARKE,John 2Lt   RAF & 5SLancsR   35 Sqdn   18.9.18 MR 20
CLARKE,J K 2Lt   RAF   103 Sqdn   kia   22.7.18 CR France924
CLARKE,R A R.MC. Lt   RAF   10 Trng Sqdn   19.10.18 CR Hamps 4
CLARKSON,Thomas Cooke   2Lt   RAF   36 Trng Sqdn kldacc 2.7.18 CR Yorks 501
CLAY,Norman Andrew   FCdt   RAF 319104   ded   29.10.19 CR Durham 56
CLAYDON,A.DFC.   Capt   RAF   32 Sqdn   kia   8.7.18 CR France 924
CLAYE,Charles Geoffrey   Lt   RAF   99 Sqdn   5.7.18 CR France 1678
CLAYTON,Edward Harold   2Lt   RAF   98 Sqdn   24.8.18 CR France 1142
CLAYTON,John Alfred   2Lt   RAF   kld   21.4.18CR Shrop 48
CLEGHORN,William Fulton.DFC.   Capt   RAF   218 Sqdn   2.10.18MR 20
CLELLAND,R F/O   RAF   30.11.19 MR67
CLEMENS,Williard Ewart   Lt   RAF   Sch of Aerial Gnry   17.5.18 CR Canada 1217
CLEMENTS,Wallace Alexander Prince Cadet   RAF 182855 Cadet Dist Centre   ded   21.10.18 CR Surrey 1
CLENDENAN,Edwin Harvey Cadet RAF 272924   ded   25.10.18 CR Canada 1494
CLIFFORD,Colin Hamley   Lt   RAF   18 Wing   10.2.19 CR London 12
CLITHEROE,James Norman   Lt   RAF   53 Sqdn   22.5.18 CR Lancs 43
CLOETE,M N 2Lt   RAF   188 Night Trng Sqdn   7.8.18 CR London 8
CLUTE,Victor Maxwell   Cadet RAF 272823 Recruits Depot ded   18.10.18 CR Canada 1691
COAPE-ARNOLD,   Lt   RAF   48 Wing 200 Sqdn   26.6.18 CR Warwick 82
COBBIN,Arthur John 2Lt   RAF   57 Sqdn   14.7.18 CR France 1076
COBDEN,Frank Pargeter   Lt   MGC attRAF   104 Sqdn   kld   7.7.18 CR Germany 3
COCKBURN,Edward Colin   Lt   RAF   16.3.21 CR Yorks 361
COCKMAN,Charles Burton Blenheim   F/O   RAF   111 Sqdn   kldacc   10.12.19 CR Palestine 9
COE,David Edward   Lt   RAF   5 Sqdn kia   3.11.18CR France 1144
COFFEY,Charles Reay   Lt   RAF & Gen List   52 Sqdn   27.5.18 MR 20
COFFING,George Lee 2Lt   RAF   2 TD   kld   24.2.19CR USA 51
COGHILL,Alexander Oswin   2Lt   RAF   52 TDS   kld   11.9.18CR Eire 11
COHEN,B   2Lt   RAF   6TDS   7.5.18 CR Scot 764
COLBOURNE,J L   2Lt   RAF   16 Trng Sqdn kldacc 4.7.18 CR Sussex 93
COLE,C C   Capt   RAF   Air Ministry Ex EssR   2.11.18CR Essex 1
COLE,G   2Lt   RAF   & RNAS   21.6.18 CR Sussex 191
COLE,Montague Henry   2Lt   3SAI attRAF   30.6.18 CR France 1632
COLE,Reginald Herbert   2Lt   RAF   216 Sqdn   30.9.18 CR France 1667
COLE,William Holland   2Lt   RAF   103 Sqdn   16.9.18 MR 20
COLE,William Thomas   Lt   RAF   23.10.18 CR Dorset 60
COLEMAN,C M   2Lt   RAF   11 Sqdn   6.9.18 CR France 426
COLEMAN,Leslie   Lt   RAF   5 Sqdn   2.9.18 CR France 421
COLERIDGE,C G.MBE.   Lt   RAF   dedacc 23.7.18   CR Canada 1303
COLLIER,Douglas Charles   2Lt   RAF   56 Sqdn   24.8.18 MR 20
COLLINGE,Charles Inham   Lt   RAF   216 Sqdn Ex TankCps drd   25.7.19   CR Italy 29
COLLINGS,Lionel Lapidge   2Lt   RAF   ded   3.10.18CR Sussex 112
COLLINGWOOD,Richard Milne   Lt   RAF   204 TDS   acckld 10.7.18   CR Kent 68
COLLINS,C F Lt   RAF   24 Trng Sqdn   17.11.18 CR London 12
COLLINS,Frederick Ferdinand   2Lt   RAF   206 Sqdn   19.5.18 MR 20
COLLINS,L E 2Lt   RAF   100 Sqdn   5.4.18 CR France 1404
COLLINS,Valentine St Barbe Lt   RAF & Sp List 22 Sqdn   2.9.18 MR 20
COLLIS,T B 2Lt   RAF   22 Sqdn   27.8.18 CR France 530
COLQUHOUN,A S   2Lt   RAF & Gen List   kld   20.04.18 CR France 788
COLTSON,Charles Sydney.DSC.   Capt   RAF & RN   25.11.18 CR Essex 145
COLVILL-JONES,T Capt   RAF   48 Sqdn   dow   24.5.18   CR Germany 4
COMBER-TAYLOR,Eric Horace   Capt   RAF & Gen List   10 Sqdn   kia   16.6.18CR France 142
CONATY,D G Lt   RAF(EEF)   26.7.19 CR Egypt 1
CONLON,James T   Cadet RAF 172942   ded   10.10.18 CR Canada 1387A

CONNOR,W 2Lt RAF 11 Sqdn 4.10.18 CR France 512
CONRON,Hatton Charles Ronayne Lt RAF 205 Sqdn 18.5.18 MR 20
CONROY,Paul Servillion Cadet RAF 174014 Cadet Wing ded 11.10.18 CR Canada 254
COOCH,T A Capt WorcR & RAF 2 Comn Sqdn 17.9.19 CR France 457
COOK,Francis R Cadet RAF 153929 dedacc 7.8.18 CR Canada 35
COOK,Frederick Charles Lt BedsR att RAF dow 9.10.19 CR Beds 75
COOK,Frederick Oliver Lt RAF 99 Sqdn 26.9.18 CR France 1667
COOK,James Drue Lt RAF 107 Sqdn 11.7.18 CR Belgium 406
COOK,Murdoch 2Lt RAF 28 TDS kld 3.10.18 CR Scot 775
COOMBE,Alfred Stanley Naylor 2Lt RAF 7 Sqdn 17.4.18 MR 20
COOMBS,Herbert Milbourne.DFC. F/O RAF 216 Sqdn 8.6.21 CR Egypt 9
COONS,John Walter Lt RAF 11 Sqdn 3.10.18 CR France 84
COOPER,D G Lt RAF kld 09.5.19 CR Ches 18
COOPER,George William 2Lt RAF 67 Sqdn 30.8.18 MR 37
COOPER,Lawrence George 2Lt RAF 107 Sqdn 9.8.18 MR 20
COOPER,Maurice Lea.DFC. Capt RAF 213 Sqdn B'Flight 2.10.18 CR Belgium 157
COOPER,W J Lt RAF 101 Sqdn 4.11.18 CR France 528
CORBETT,Cyril Dudley Hely LtCol RAF &RAMC 4.12.18 CR Mddx 26
CORBETT,William Launcelot Cdt RAF 13 TDS dow 9.6.18 CR Derby 99
CORDINER,George Galloway 2Lt RAF 28 TDS 25.6.18 CR Scot 383
CORKERY,Philip Joseph 2Lt RAF kia 23.8.18 MR 37
CORMACK,Philip Frederick 2Lt RAF 204 Sqdn 27.10.18 MR 20
CORT,A B Lt RAF 62 Sqdn 12.8.18 CR France 624
COSGROVE,Albert Vail 2Lt RAF 27 Sqdn 25.9.18 CR France 1061
COTE,Joseph Arthur Robert Lt RAF 46 Sqdn ded 28.10.18 CR France 145
COTTER,Brian Charles 2Lt RAF 216 Sqdn 28.10.18 CR France 1678
COTTERELL,Basil William Lt N&DR attRAF 49 Sqdn 30.10.18 CR Belgium 241
COTTERELL,Robert James 2Lt RAF 236 Sqdn kld 18.1.19 CR Wilts 138
COTTON,Ernest 2Lt RAF 73 Sqdn 29.7.18 MR 20
COULSON.William Eugene Lt RAF kld 5.9.19 CR Surrey 91
COULTHURST,William Gordon 2Lt RAF 46 Sqdn 10.11.18 CR Belgium 234
COURT,Leslie Simpson 2Lt RAF 26 TDS 10.12.18 CR Kent 225
COURTENAY,W J 2Lt RAF 66 Sqdn kia 7.10.18 CR Italy 8
COURTENAY-DUNN,Adrian Lancelot F/O RAF 99 Sqdn 21.3.20 MR 43
COURTHORPE,W G Lt RAF & 4BedsR 21.10.18 CR France 1858
COWAN,Albert Arthur 2Lt RFA & RAF 16.7.18 CR Egypt 9
COWAN,James Basil Lt RAF 48 Sqdn 3.10.18 CR Belgium 157
COWAN,W W Lt 8RScots & RAF 6.6.19 CR Scot 239
COWPER-COLES,S W Capt RAF 7 Sqdn 14.10.18 CR Belgium 18
COX H F C Cdt RAF 183071 8 Cdt Wing 9.10.18 CR Kent 180
COX,J W 2Lt RAF 7 TDS 11.6.18 CR Glouc 6
COX,W J 2Lt RAF 29.7.18 CR Canada 1688
CRABBE,H L B 2Lt RAF & 3Hrs 15.5.18 CR France 513
CRADDOCK,H C 2Lt RAF kld 27.11.18 CR Glouc 27
CRAIB,William Brice 2Lt RAF 65 Sqdn 28.5.18 MR 20
CRAIG,Alexander Campbell 2Lt RAF 9.2.19 CR Scot 447
CRAIG,James Lt RAF 53 Sqdn kia 11.4.18 CR France 324
CRAIG,Stewart 2Lt RAF & Gen List 22.4.18 CR France 103
CRAIG,William Benson.DFC. Lt RAF 204 Sqdn kia 26.9.18 CR Belgium 371
CRAIGE,Victor Raleigh 2Lt RAF 92 Sqdn 7.4.18 CR Sussex 83
CRAM,John Mitchell 2Lt RAF 43 Wing dedacc 26.8.18 CR Canada 1245
CRANE,John Wilber Capt RAF & 1COR 19 Sqdn 30.10.18 MR 20
CRAWFORD,James Currie Lt RAF 56 Sqdn 12.11.18 CR France 441
CRAWFORD,Kelvin Capt RAF & MGC 60 Sqdn kia 11.4.18 MR 20
CREESE,A R Lt RAF 76 Wing 13.11.18 CR London 14
CRESSWELL,Ralph Neal 2Lt RAF 6 Sqdn 23.10.18 MR 20
CRISTIANI,Francis Ricado 2Lt RAF 84 Sqdn 29.9 18 CR France194
CRITCHLEY,Burton 2Lt RAF 26.6.18 CR France 10
CRITCHLEY,George Edgar FCadet RAF 42 Trng Sqdn 8.11.18 CR Lancs 164
CRITCHLEY,Roland 2Lt RAF 22 Sqdn 2.4.18 MR 20

CROCKETT,Wallace John   Lt   RAF   34 Sqdn   19.9.19 CR Italy 11
CROMBIE,W E.MC. Lt   RAF   215 Sqdn   31.8.18 CR France 1678
CRONE,Leonard   2Lt   RAF   47 Sqdn   kld   1.7.18 CR Lincs 181
CROOK,Henry Edward   2Lt   RAF   50 TDS   kld   9.11.18 CR London 12
CROSBY,Edward Eno 2Lt   RAF   99 Sqdn   13.9.18 CR France 1678
CROSBY Harold Edward   2Lt   RAF   61 Sqdn   kld   31.10.18 CR Essex 65
CROSS,Arthur Moulter   2Lt   RAF   20 Trng Sqdn kld   29.7.18 CR Lancs 43
CROSS,G J   2Lt   RAF   11.3.20 CR Mddx 80
CROSS,Russell W   Lt   RAF   kld   24.7.19 CR Canada 116
CROSSLAND,Ernest Ford   Lt   RAF   43 Wing   ded   20.10.18 CR Canada 1688
CROUCH,James Edward   2Lt   RAF   46 Sqdn   kia   14.8.18 MR 20
CROUCHER,Richard Lt   RAF   Palestine Bde HQ   23.7.19 CR Egypt 8
CROUDACE,H   Lt   RAF   36 Sqdn   13.1.19 CR London 25
CROIZIER,George C Cadet RAF 153518   dedacc 2.7.18 CR Canada 1598
CRUISE,Milton George   2Lt   RAF   213 Sqdn   20.9.18 CR France 646
CRUMMEY,Francis Cyprian Capt   RAF   27 Sqdn   20.11.18 CR France 146
CRUMP,Francis Laurent Delsaux   2Lt   RAF   21 Sqdn   dow   16.10.18 CR France 88
CRYAN,J S   2Lt   RAF   218 Sqdn   11.8.18 CR Belgium 390
CRYSLER,Carleton Aquilla Lt   RAF   23 Sqdn   20.5.18 CR France 144
CUFFE,R T   Lt   RAF   54 Sqdn   21.7.18 CR France 1429
CUMMING,Charles Linnaeus Lt   RAF   206 Sqdn   31.1.19 CR Germany 1
CUMMING,Herbert William Mackarsie Lt   RAF   204 Sqdn   5.9.18 CR France 1359
CUNNINGHAM,Harold Sherratt   Lt   47CanInf att RAF   dow   17.8.18   CR France 1170
CUNNINGHAM,James Brightwell   2Lt   RAF   205 Sqdn   22.8.18 CR France 1525
CUNNINGHAM,Michael Francis   Lt   RAF   27 Sqdn   6.6.18 MR 20
CUNNINGHAM,P J   2Lt   RAF   55 Sqdn   30.8.18 CR France 1678
CUNNINGHAM,Ronald   FCadet RAF 100453 39 Wing(Thetford)   10.8.18 CR Beds 75
CURRIE,J E   FltCdt RAF   26.10.18 CR Essex 80
CURRIE,W H 2Lt   RAF   55 Sqdn   16.7.18 CR France 1678
CURTIS,Herbert Cecil 2Lt   RAF   107 Sqdn   21.8.18 MR 20
CURTIS,Hubert James Lt   RAF & Sp List 87 Sqdn Ex 28LondR   4.11.18 MR 20
CURZON-HOWE,T S Lt   RAF   see Howe,T S C
CUTHBERT,John Bryan   Lt   RAF   13 Sqdn   28.8.18 MR 20
CUTHBERTSON,George Chapman.MC   Capt   RAF & Gen List   54 Sqdn   dow   8.4.18 CR France 145
CUTMORE,William Cecil   Lt   RAF   206 Sqdn   24.6.18 CR France 360
CUTTLE,George Robin.MC. Lt/2Lt RFA 50Bty & RAF   C'Flt 49 Sqdn kia   9.5.18 MR 20

D

d'ALBENAS,Paul Desire   2Lt   RAF   85 Sqdn   11-10-18 MR 20
DALGLEISH,Neil John   2Lt   RAF   N'Flt   30.10.18 CR London 12
DALLAS,Roderick Stanley.DSO.DSC&Bar.Maj   RAF   40 Sqdn   kia   1.6.18 CR France 10
DALLAS,William Reid   2Lt   ASC MT att RAF   215 Sqdn   kld   24.12.18 CR France 134
DALRYMPLE-WILLES,Patrick   Lt   RAF & R LancsR   ded   29.09.18
DALY,John Albert Edward Robinson DFC LtRAF   24 Sqdn   8.7.18 CR France 805
DALY,Joseph James Lt   RAF   8 TDS kld   24.5.18 CR Wilts 4
DANBY,Charles David.MC. Capt   RAF &RE   kld   18.7.18 CR Durham 182
DANIEL,Arthur Hector Ross Lt   RAF   85 Sqdn   29.8.18 CR France 1170
DANKS,E R   Lt   RAF   26.6.21 CR Glouc 94
DANN,Wilfred Stephen   Lt   3EKentR att RAF   70 Sqdn   dow   16.5.18   CR France 63
D'ARCY,Samuel Hollis Alfred.DSO. Lt   RAF   8.6.18 CR Suffolk 83
D'ARCY-LEVY,John Martin Capt   RAF   10.8.19 CR Europe 180 & MR 70
DARLEY,Cecil Hill.DSC&Bar.DFC. Maj   RAF   274 Sqdn   kld   28.9.19 CR Italy 59
DARLINGTON,Cecil Dutton Lt   RAF   204 Sqdn   kia   15.8.18 CR Belgium 63
DAUNT,Conrad O'Neill   Lt   RAF &8SLancR   29.9.18 CR France 329
DAVENPORT,D   2Lt   RAF   24.9.18 CR France 557
DAVEY,Albert Victor Patrick Lt   RAF &RFA   82 Sqdn   kld   2.6.18 CR France 1564
DAVID,Charles Frederick   Lt   RAF   97 Sqdn   kia   14.8.18 CR France 1678

DAVIDSON,Bruce Thomas   Lt   RAF   20 Sqdn   2.7.18 MR 20
DAVIDSON,Freeman A   Cadet   RAF   173757   ded   13.10.18 CR Canada 180
DAVIDSON,George Edwin   2Lt   RAF   34 TDS   kld   13.10.18 CR Lincs 181
DAVIDSON,James Thomas Gardiner Lt   RAF   2 Aircraft Supply Depot   5.7.18 CR France 40
DAVIDSON,Reuben John   2Lt   RAF   36TDS   27.7.18 CR Wilts 28
DAVIDSON,R W   2Lt   RAF   7 Sqdn   14.10.18 CR Belgium 18
DAVIDSON,Sydney   2Lt   RAF & Gen List   21.5.18 CR Belgium 24
DAVIDSON,William Dunlop 2Lt   RAF   48 Sqdn   kia   30.5.18 CR France 303
DAVIES,E G.DFC&Bar   Lt   RAF   29 Sqdn   6.2.19 CR Germany 1
DAVIES,Frederick George   2Lt   RAF   107 Sqdn   21.8.18 MR 20
DAVIES,Herbert John St Aubrey   FltCdt RAF   17.12.18 CR Essex 158
DAVIES,I G   Capt   RAF   54 TDS   2.9.18 CR Wales 335
DAVIES,J H   2Lt   RAF   98 Sqdn   19.8.18 CR France 605
DAVIES,John Cdt   RAF 175380   dedacc 8.12.18 CR Wales 241
DAVIES,Norman   2Lt   RAF   70 Sqdn   kld   5.9.18 CR Frane 134
DAVIES,Noel Parry Lt   RAF   kld   8.4.18 CR Wales 165
DAVIES,Ralph Llewelyn John 2Lt   RAF   89 Sqdn   5.5.18 CR Wales 439
DAVIES,Thomas Llewelyn.MC.   Maj   RFA att RAF   kldacc 16.9.18   CR Wales 167
DAVIS,Albert Charles 2Lt   RAF   kld   28.6.18 CR Surrey 16
DAVIS,Cecil Sealey 2Lt   RAF   kld   7.5.19 CR Scot 106
DAVIS,Charles William John FCadet RAF   acckld 13.10.18 CR Glouc 67
DAVIS,E E   Lt   RAF   21 Sqdn   dow   27.10.18 CR France 1725
DAVIS,Harry.MM.   2Lt   3RWarR att RAF   59 Sqdn   20.5.19 CR Germany 1
DAVIS,Harold Charles2Lt   9EssR att RAF 104 Sqdn   kld   26.6.18 CR France 1632
DAVIS,Harold Eborall.MC.   Lt   RAF   19.6.18 CR Essex 73
DAVIS,Leslie Sansome   2Lt   RAF   92 Sqdn   kia   30.9.18 CR France 234
DAVIS,Ronald Herbert   Lt   RAF   48 Sqdn   dedacc 19.8.18   CR France 692
DAVIS,W J   2Lt   RAF   38 Trng Sqdn   26.9.18 CR Egypt 9
DAVISON,Charles William   Lt   RAF   85 Sqdn   4.10.18 CR France 1266
DAVISON,S.DCM.   Lt   RAF   112 Sqdn   30.11.18 CR Lancs 32
DAWE,James Jeffery Lt   RAF & Gen List   24 Sqdn   7.6.18 CR France 649
DAWKINS,Frank   Lt   RAF   HQ ACS   11.10.18 CR Hamps 57
DAWSON,Samuel.DFC.   Lt   RAF   17.9.19 MR 70
DAWSON,Stephen Arthur   Lt   RAF   73 Sqdn   10.8.18 MR 20
DAWSON,William   2Lt   RAF   215 Sqdn   15.7.18 MR 20
DAWSON,William Ernest   Capt   RFA att RAF   kld   16.9.18 CR Mon 81
DAY,G S   Lt   RAF   52 Sqdn   kld   1.10.18 CR France 113
DEACON,Ernest Charles Watson   2Lt   YLI att RAF   27 Sqdn   kia   22.4.18 CR France 140
DEANE,Bernard Frederic   F/O   RAF   Sch of Art Co-op   15.4.21 CR Wilts 129
DEANE,Frederick William.DFC.   FltOff RAF   56 Sqdn   29.4.21 CR Egypt 6
DEANE,William.MC. Lt   4NorfR att RAF   20 Sqdn   20.3.20 MR 43
DEARDS,Charles   Lt   RAF   19 Balloon Sect   5.10.18 CR France 146
De BATHE,Henry Michael   Lt   RAF   56 TDS   kld   4.11.18 CR Sussex 89
DeBUSSEY,Walter   2Lt   Y&LR att RAF82Sqdn   14.10.18 CR Belgium 157
DEEGAN,George M   Cadet   RAF 174420   ded   12.10.18 CR Canada 912
De KOCK,Dink Wouter   2Lt   RAF   5 Sqdn   2.4.19 CR Egypt 9
DELANEY,Michael   Capt   RAF &YorkR 16 Grp HQ   29.3.19 CR Yorks 557
DELAY,Aladdin Richard   2Lt   RAF   1 Trng Sqdn kld   23.7.18 CR Surrey 162
DELL CLARKE,G C.MC.   Capt   RAF   60 Sqdn   16.7.18 CR France 1525
DELMAR-WILLIAMSON,George Frederick Lt   RAF &BlkW   kld   12.7.18 CR Glouc 31
DELTEIL,Edmond Louis Roger   2Lt   RAF   kld   27.10.18 CR France 1783
DENISON,John   2Lt   RAF   kia   13.4.18 CR France 10
DENNETT,Pruett Mullens   Lt   RAF   208 Sqdn   2.6.18 MR 20
DENNIS,Charles Cowley   2Lt   1/19LondR att RAF   kia   25.9.18 CR France 120
DENNIS,L V 2Lt   RAF   99 Sqdn   31.7.18 CR France 1675
DENNITTS,Kenneth John Wolfe   2Lt   RAF   98 Sqdn   3.9.18 MR 20
DENNY,Francis George   FltCdt   RAF 110251   kld   11.6.18 CR Suffolk 83
DENSHAM,Walter John   2Lt   RAF   54 Sqdn   2.10.18 CR France 147
DENTON,J E FCadet RAF 5/96503   3.9.18 CR Yorks 383
De PENCIER,John Dartnell   F/O   RAF   12 Sqdn   17.5.20 CR Germany 1

82

DEREK-LUTYONS,L F   Lt   RAF   see LUTYONS,L F D
DERRICK,Leslie James   2Lt   RAF & EKentR   15 Sqdn   kia   3.5.18 CR France 116
DERWIN,Edward Claude England   Lt   RAF   32 TDS   kld   14.10.18 CR Devon 3
DESMOND,Sidney Maurice   2Lt   RAF   206 Sqdn   kld   6.9.18 CR France 100
DESY,Joseph Rudolphe   2Lt   RAF   8 Sqdn   27.10.18 MR 20
d'ETCHEGOYEN,Louis Paul Bryant Adalbert Lt   RAF   210 Sqdn   13.5.18 CR France 100
DE VILLIERS,David John James   2Lt   RAF   6.7.18 CR Scot 252
DEVITT,Alan 2Lt   RAF   65 Sqdn   2.6.18 MR 20
DEVONSHIRE,Feray Vullramy   Lt   RAF & 7Hrs   20.7.19 MR 43
DEWAR,Walter Craig Kerr   2Lt   RAF   1.12.18 CR Scot 675
DEXTER,E I   Lt   RAF   16 Trng Sqdn   4.5.18 CR Notts 84
DICK,Archibald Logan   Cadet RAF 171042 44 Wing   dedacc 8.10.18 CR Canada 1660
DICK,Charles William Lt   RAF   ded   9.11.18 CR Scot 237
DICKIE,Cecil Barron Lt   RAF &BlkW   107 Sqdn   18.7.18 MR 20
DICKINSON,H N   Lt   RAF   22 Sqdn   10.7.18 CR France 705
DICKINSON,Thomas Malcolm DFC Capt   IA 16Cav att RAF   ded   4.1.21 CR Egypt 15
DICKSON,John Hetherington 2Lt   RAF   27 Sqdn   14.8.18 CR France 57
DIFFORD,William Membry   Lt   8ManitobaR att RAF 8 Sqdn kia   3.10.18 CR France 240
DILLON,Edward Joseph.MM. 2Lt   RAF   7 TDS kld   12.4.18 CR London 9
DILLON,W H 2Lt   RAF   70 Sqdn   24.8.18 CR France 134
DILLOWAY,Reginald Herbert 2Lt   RAF   62 Sqn Ex 16LondR   kia   15.9.18 CR France 1193
DIMMOCK,Edward Harold   Lt   RAF   Wireless Telegraphy Sch   3.2.19 CR Hamps 13
DINGWALL,John David   2Lt   RAF   25 Sqdn   21.4.18 CR France 31
DINWOODIE,George Sinclair 2Lt   RAF   38 TDS Ex Pte 7HLI dedacc 29.8.18   CR Scot 757
DIXON,Charles.MM. 2Lt   RAF (EEF)   kld   19.9.18 CR Egypt 1
DIXON,Harold George Lt   3DorsR att RAF   4.11.18 CR France 521
DIXON,Harry 2Lt   RAF   Sch of Aerial Fighting   4.4.18 CR London 9
DIXON,Michael Godfrey   Cdt   RAF 181516   ded   16.11.18 CR C'land&W'land 44
DIXON,William   2Lt   3SfthH att RAF   25 Sqdn   dow   23.6.18   CR France 40
DOBBIE,Robert William.AFC.   Capt   RAF   Aerial Obs Sch   23.12.18 CR Egypt 9
DOBELL,G L Lt   RAF   53 Sqdn   kia   11.8.18 CR France 324
DOBESON,George Edward   Lt   RAF   25 Sqdn   1.7.18 CR Belgium 384
DOBSON,Algernon Richard   Cadet RAF 172541   ded   4.10.18 CR Canada 1667
DODD,Albert Lt   RAF   11 Kite Ballon Sect   30.10.18 CR France 1266
DODD,Francis Coupe 2Lt   RAF   210 Sqdn   10.6.18 CR France 276
DODD,Hugh Reginald Lt   RAF   215 Sqdn   17.9.18 MR 20
DODDS,Sidney James Allan 2Lt   RAF   Cent Flying Sch A'Sqdn   kld   20.7.18 CR Wilts 116
DODKINS,Lionel Claud   F/O   25LondR reposted to BordR & RAF 31 Sqdn ded   13.6.21   CR Surrey 6
DODSON,Herbert Leigh Midelton   Lt   ASC att RAF 73 Sqdn Ex 46 Sqdn kia   25.8.18 CR France 421
DOGGART,Norman Alexander   Capt   RAF & ScotRif33TDS   10.10.18 CR Oxford 69
DOE,J E K   FCadet RAF 89753   25.9.18 CR Beds 23
DOIDGE,E L Lt   RAF & Manitoba Regt 99 Sqdn   31.7.18 CR France 1675
DOLAN,H E.MC.   Lt   RAF   12.5.18 CR Belgium 60
DOMEGAN,Christopher Patrick   Lt   RAF & RIrFus (on board RMS Leinster)   drd   10.10.18 CR Eire 437
DOMVILLE,William Kellock 2Lt   RAF   kld   7.7.18 CR Canada 1667
DONALD,C 2Lt   RAF   108 Sqdn   28.9.18 CR France 1359
DONALDSON,Duncan Lane   2Lt   RAF   40 TDS   8.10.18 CR Surrey 6
DONCASTER,Ellis Lynn   2Lt   RAF   107 Sqdn   8.8.18 MR 20
DONEY,C A F/Cadet   RAF   212 TDS   13.8.18 CR France 1844
DOOLITTLE,Charles Massie 2Lt   RAF   33 TDS   8.10.18 CR Oxford 97
DORE,William Henry Capt   RAF & CanSakatchR 107 Sqdn   kld   9.8.18 MR 20
DORNONVILLE de la COUR,Paul Victor Lt   RAF & SAfrInf 11 Sqdn   15.5.18 CR France 63
DOUCET,Arthur Cecil Lt   RAF   2 Flg Trng Sch kld   19.12.18 CR Yorks 127
DOUGHTY,Albert Edward.MM.   Lt   Gen List att RAF   4 Sqdn   14.4.18 CR France 31
DOUGLAS,Alexander Anderson   2Lt   RAF   98 Sqdn   30.10.18 MR 20
DOUGLAS,Arthur James   Cadet RAF 182273 8 Cdt Wing   ded   29.9.18   CR Kent 180
DOUGLAS,Brian Charles O'Driscoll Capt   ConnRgrs att RAF   21.10.18 CR Mddx 66
DOUGLAS,Frederick William Lt   RAF   41 Sqdn   12.8.18 MR 20
DOUGLAS,John McGregor   2Lt   RAF   4 Aircraft Supply Depot   18.6.18 CR France 65
DOUGLAS,Roland Keith   2Lt   RAF   19 Sqdn   26.11.18 CR Germany 3

DOWLER,George Emerson.DFC.   2Lt   RAF   46 Sqdn   10.11.18 CR Belgium 234
DOWLING,Brian Laidley   Capt   RAF   22 Sqdn   kld   2.9.18 MR 20
DOWLING,John William   2Lt   RAF   Sch of Aerial Gnry   26.6.18 CR Lincs 6
DOWSE,Henry Harvey   2Lt   RAF & ASC   139 Sqdn   ded   10.11.18 CR Italy 12
DOWSETT,Henry George   2Lt   RAF   kld   17.7.18CR Mddx 53
DRABBLE,Charles Frederick Lt   19DLI att RAF   13.8.18 CR France 1483
DRAKE,Edward Barfoot   Capt   RAF   209 Sqdn   29.9.18 MR 20
DRAKE,Ernest Francis   Lt   RAF   Ex 3ChesR   10.12.18 CR Ches 147
DREW,John   FltLt RAF   Ex 7CamH   21.9.20 CR Mddx 16
DRINKWATER,Edward Oscar   Lt   RAF   23.8.18 CR France 260
DRISCOLL,D O'N   Lt   RAF &MddxR   13.8.18 CR Surrey 152
DRIVER,Hubert Weeks   Lt   RAF   kia   19.9.18 CR France 154
DRUMMOND,John Cecil George   2Lt   RAF   59 Sqdn   8.10.18 MR 20
DRUMMOND,J R   Lt   RAF   22 Sqdn   27.9.18 CR France 404
DUBBER,Roy Edward Capt   RAF   107 Sqdn   18.7.18 MR 20
DUDLEY-SCOTT,Herries Knocker Lt   RAF   kld   22.9.18CR Suffolk 2
DUERDEN,George   2Lt   LNLancs att RAF   kia   10.4.18CR France 37
DUGGAN,G W.MC.   Lt   RAF   12.11.18 CR Wilts 115
DUKE,Wilfred Douglas   Cadet   RAF 182133 8 Cdt Wing   ded   2.10.18CR Kent 180
DULIN,W W Lt   RAF   Cent Despatch Pool   29.7.18 CR France 34
DUMVILLE,Ernest   2Lt   RAF   62 Sqdn   24.6.18 CR France 924
DUNBAR,J D 2Lt   RAF   1 Fighting Sch   25.7.18 CR Scot 520
DUNBAR,John Campbell   2Lt   1/5HLI & RAF   kld   18.9.18CR Egypt 9
DUNBAR,Talbot Clyde   Cadet   RAF 153765 Sch of Aerial Gnry   dedacc 27.7.18   CR Canada 1688
DUNCAN,Robert Ronald   2Lt   RAF   41 TDS   kld   16.7.18CR Scot 881
DUNCAN,Thomas Wilfrid   2Lt   RAF   25.9.18 CR Canada 1154
DUNCAN,William Gardiner   2Lt   RAF   206 Sqdn   24.6.18 CR France 360
DUNFEE,William Vickers   FltLt   RAF   2 Wing   1.5.18 CR Greece 9
DUNFORD,Bertram Fred   Lt   RAF   206 Sqdn   19.5.18 MR 20
DUNHAM,Morbel L   2Lt   RAF   91 Sqdn   26.6.18 CR Sussex 5
DUNLOP,Hugh Stewart Archer   2Lt   RAF   5TDS Ex 9HLI kldacc 4.4.18 CR Scot 674
DUNN,Arthur Cadet RAF   131 Sqdn   kld   26.8.18CR Lancs 34
DUNN,James Balfour 2Lt   RAF   55 Sqdn   25.9.18 CR Germany 3
DUNNETT,Lawrence Edwin   2Lt   RAF   27 Sqdn   kia   10.5.18CR France 652
DUNSTAN,John Leonard   Lt   Gen List & RAF   ded   28.10.18 CR London 14
DURANT,Wilfred Ellis   Lt   RAF   29 Sqdn   kld   2.7.18 CR France 134
DURRANT,Lombe Atthill   2Lt   RAF & Gen List   65 Sqdn   kia   6.6.18 CR France 71
DURRANT,Trevor   Capt   RAF   56 Sqdn   16.5.18 CR France 397
DUTHIE,David Ogilvie   2Lt   RAF & Gen List   2 Sqdn   23.8.18 MR 20
DUVAL,John Fergie   Cadet RAF 153256 44 Wing   dedacc 25.4.18   CR Canada 600
DYKE,E P W 2Lt   RAF & 8Y&LR   kia   30.10.18 CR Belgium 205
DYNES,Norman Oliver   Cadet   RAF 173593   Burwash Hall(Toronto)   ded   15.10.18 CR Canada 1688
DYSON,Stanley Gilbert   Lt   RAF   82 Sqdn   dow   1.6.18 CR France 71

E

EALAND,Arthur Noel 2Lt   RAF   88 Sqdn   dedacc 15.7.18   CR France 1359
EARLL,Harry.DSM.   2Lt   RAF   Eastchurch Air Stn   6.3.19 CR Kent 65
EASTON,George Cyril 2Lt   RAF   66 Sqdn   kia   5.8.18 CR Italy 9
EASTON,Philip Reginald   2Lt   RAF   4 TDS   30.7.18 CR Herts 28
EASTY,Walter Harry 2Lt   RAF   201 Sqdn   22.4.18 MR 20
EASTWOOD,Richard Gordon Cadet   RAF 110027 29 TDS   8.10.18CR Yorks 361
EATON,Edward Carter   Lt   RAF & SakatchR   65 Sqdn   kia   26.6.18CR France 516
EATON,Frederick Charles Boswell   2Lt   RAF   107 Sqdn   4.9.18 MR 20
EAVES,Clement Clough   2Lt   RAF   215 Sqdn   21.9.18 MR 20
EDDLESTON,Bert   Lt   RAF   43 Sqdn   dedacc 25.4.18   CR France 46
EDGECOMBE,Charles Hedley   2Lt   RAF   11 Sqdn   6.10.18CR Wilts 129
EDGELL,Edward Henry   2Lt   RAF   98 Sqdn   11.8.18 MR 20

84

EDRIDGE-GREEN,Henry Allan   Lt   RAF   attCapel Airship Stn Ex RWFus   5.11.18 CR Kent 7
EDWARDES,R H   Cadet   RAF   181906   8 Cdt Wing   ded   15.10.18 CR Kent 180
EDWARDS,A S   Capt   RAF   30 Sqdn   14.5.18 CR Iraq 8
EDWARDS,Brian Wallie   Lt   RAF & 4RDubF   59 Sqdn Ex RE   ded   10.11.18 CR Mddx 46
EDWARDS,Cedric George.DFC.   Lt   RAF   209 Sqdn   27.8.18 MR 20
EDWARDS,Frank Graham   2Lt   RAF   kld   3.5.18 CR Ches 72
EDWARDS,R S   2Lt   RAF   7.7.18 CR Wales 17
EDWARDS,S T   Capt   RAF   22.11.18 CR Yorks 319
EDWARDS,T J   FltCdt RAF 181262   1.12.18 CR Wales 85
EDWARDS,W D   2Lt   RAF   61 TDS   2.3.19 CR Yorks 547
ELDER,James Jarvis   Lt   RAF   13 Sqdn   3.10.18 CR France 481
ELLERCAMP,W A H   Lt   RAF   4 Sqdn   30.12.18 CR Essex 45
ELLIOTT,A E 2Lt   RAF   TDS   7.1.19 CR Egypt 9
ELLIOTT,Arthur Stanley.DSC Capt   RAF   NSea Airship NoXI   lost at sea 15.7.19   MR 40
ELLIOTT,Claude E   2Lt   RAF   4 TDS Ex Can AMC   kld   5.9.18 CR Ches 192
ELLIOTT,Duncan   Lt   RAF & BordR 4 Sqdn   15.4.18 MR 20
ELLIOTT,H J Lt   RAF   62 Wing   29.6.18 CR Gallipoli
ELLIOTT,Hugh William   Lt   RAF   accdrd 5.6.18 CR Cambs82
ELLIS,Thomas Arthur Capt   RAF   Ministry of Munitions   20.11.18 CR Chesh 28
ELLISON,Sydney Wright   Lt   RAF   28 Sqdn 14 Wing   kia   16.6.18 CR Italy 11
ELWORTHY,Sydney Richard 2Lt   RAF   1.9.18 CR Herts 44
ELY,Frank Wayman   Lt   RAF   20 Sqdn   8.10.18 MR 20
EMTAGE,John Edmund   2Lt   RAF   107 Sqdn   9.8.18 MR 20
ENGLAND,N H   Capt   RAF   92 Sqdn   7.4.18 CR Sussex 83
ENGLISH,Joseph Patrick Fitzgerald   2Lt   RAF   4TDS   21.7.18 CR Chesh 194
ENGLISH,Maurice Graham   Lt   RAF   202 Sqdn 61 Wing Ex RNAS kia   16.7.18 CR Belgium173
ENRIGHT,P A A.DFC.   Lt   RAF   222 Sqdn   2.11.18 MR 37
ERSKINE,J   Lt   RAF   19.6.18 CR Glouc 9
ESSELL,Robert Narcissus.DFC.   F/O   RAF   6 Sqdn   9.12.20 CR Iraq 8
EUNSON,John Tullock   Cadet   RAF 152900   Sch of Aerial Gnry   dedacc 2.5.18 CR Canada 1518
EVANS,Arthur Frederick   Lt   RAF   100 Sqdn   30.10.18 CR France 1678
EVANS,D R   FltCdt RAF   17.12.18 CR Wales 149
EVANS,David Rees   2Lt   RAF   123 Sqdn   kld   29.7.18 CR Yorks 154
EVANS,Donald Singleton   F/O   RAF   27.5.21 CR India 48
EVANS,Eric Henry   FltCdt RAF   53 TDS   kld   13.9.18 CR Surrey 150
EVANS,Evan Lindsey Price   Lt   RAF   7.11.18 CR Norfolk 127
EVANS,Griffith William   2Lt   RWFus attRAF   21.4.18 CR Lincs 181
EVANS,John.MM.   2Lt   RAF & EYorksR   13 Sqdn   dow   29.10.18 CR France 332
EVANS,Llewellyn Lewis Meredith.AFC.Lt   RAF   9.5.19 CR Essex 120
EVANS,P J   Cdt   RAF 182002   9.9.18 CR Warwick 106
EVANS,Percy Lewis Lt   RAF   kld   22.11.18 CR Yorks 643
EVANS,Richard Ralph   Lt   RAF   5 Sqdn   20.8.19 CR Germany 1
EVANS,Simon Davies Lt   RAF   12 Sqdn   1.11.18 CR France 398
EVANS,Victor Raymond   Cadet   RAF 153457   25.4.18 CR Canada 1125
EVANS,William David   Lt   RAF & 46CanadianInf   kld   11.6.18 CR Wales 551
EVANS,Walter George   Lt   RAF   213 Sqdn   27.6.18 MR 20
EVERETT,Frank S   FCadet RAF   8.10.18 CR London 3
EVERSDEN,Robert Ernest   Capt   RAF & 3SuffYeo   47 Sqdn   kldacc   15.8.19   CR Asia 81
EXLEY,Alfred Tennyson   2Lt   RAF   kld   22.4.18   CR Yorks 283
EYDEN,Herbert.MC.   Capt   Gen List & RAF   21 Sqdn   7.4.18 CR Belgium 18
EYRE,Arthur Noel   2Lt   RAF & 6N&DR   57 Sqdn   26.9.18 MR 20
EYRE,Hugh Clement 2Lt   RAF   110 Sqdn   dow   6.10.18 CR Germany 1
EYRES,H T   2Lt   RAF & RWSurrR   101 Sqdn   9.11.18 CR France 1754

F

FAIR,V A.MC.2Lt   KRRC att RAF 212 Sqdn   29.9.18   CR Belgium140
FAIRBAIRN,Dudley Churchill2Lt   RAF   18 Trng Sqdn   8.5.18 CR Scot 398
FAIRBURN,Frederick Archibald   2Lt   RAF   80 Sqdn   23.9.18 MR 20
FARMER,A O 2Lt   RAF   69 Trng Sqdn   30.5.18 CR Norfolk 247
FARNHAM,J H   2Lt   RAF   17 Trng Sqdn   25.4.18 CR Wilts 28
FARQUHAR,J Lt   RAF   204 Sqdn   1.8.18 CR Belgium 125
FARQUHAR,Robert Wallace Lt   RAF   32 Sqdn   dow   30.10.18 CR France 1196
FARRALL,James Garney Marshall   2Lt   RAF   lost at sea 18.7.18   MR 40
FATTORINI,Thomas Lt   RAF   205 Sqdn   kia   13.8.18 CR France 360
FAULKS,H C 2Lt   RAF   8 Sqdn kia   8.8.18 CR France 1172
FAWCETT,F 2Lt   RAF   64 Sqdn   12.11.18 CR France 40
FAWDRY,Harry   Lt   RAF   218 Sqdn   kia   11.8.18 CR Belgium 390
FEARNSIDES,E G   Maj   RAF   26.6.19 CR Wales 480
FEATHERSTONE,G A   Lt   RAF   108 Sqdn   1.10.18 CR Belgium 140
FELHAUER,Carl Varl 2Lt   RAF   44 Sqdn   kld   9.7.18 CR Lincs 181
FELTON,H A 2Lt   RAF   22 Sqdn   16.9.18 CR France611
FENNELL,Frederick Vibond Lt   RAF   8 Sqdn kld   30.6.18 CR France 1564
FENTON,Cedric Edgar   2Lt   RAF   44 Sqdn   ded   24.10.18 CR Yorks 253
FENTON,James Andrew   Lt   RAF   209 Sqdn   28.9.18 CR France 273
FENWICK,Cecil James   F/O   RAF   X'Engine Repair Depot   dedacc 18.10.19 CR Egypt 9
FENWICK,Frederick Lt   RAF   kldacc 24.3.19   CR Numb 7
FENWICK,Horace Edgar   F/O   RAF   24 Sqdn   kld   4.11.20 CR herts 87
FERGUSON,Frank Willard   2Lt   RAF   87 Sqdn   3.9.18 CR France 1059
FERGUSON,John Alvin Arthur   Lt   RAF   ded   27.10.20 CR Canada 1688
FERGUSON,John Ferrier   Lt   RAF   43 Wing   ded   16.10.18 CR Canada 487
FERGUSON,John Shannon   2Lt   RAF   215 Sqdn   21.9.18 MR 20
FERGUSON,William Bruce.MC.   Lt   9CanRlyTrps & RAF   7.7.18 CR Essex 45
FERNALD,Van Dyke Lt   3RWSurrR att RAF   139 Sqdn   kia   23.7.18 CR Italy 9
FERREIRA,Julien Percy   2Lt   RAF   57 Sqdn   kld   16.9.18 MR 20
FESSER,Charles Frederic   F/Cadet   RAF   44 Sqdn   29.7.18 CR Lincs 181
FEURER,Sydney Moss   2Lt   RBerksR att RAF   27 Sqdn   kia   22.7.18 CR France 1107
FFRENCH,Evelyn Wilson   Capt   RAF &RFA   kld   23.12.18 CR Mddx 26
FFRENCH,George Edward   2Lt   RAF   27 Sqdn   kia   23.5.18 CR France 10
FIELD,T R   Cdt   RAF 178852   26.6.18 CR London 8
FINBOW,William George   2Lt   RAF   201 Trng Sqdn   27.10.18 CR Suffolk 83
FINCH,R E   Lt   RAF   30.11.18 CR London 5
FINDLAY,F 2Lt   RAF   21 TDS   27.2.19 CR Surrey 1
FINE,S Lt   RAF   15 Sqdn   kia   18.5.18 CR France 59
FINLAY,Kenneth Neil 2Lt   RAF   26 Trng Sqdn kld   3.6.18 CR Essex 96
FINNEY,George   TR/8/25444 FCdt   3HampsR att RAF   kld   1.8.18 CR Berks 6
FINNIGAN,Joseph   2Lt   RAF   205 Sqdn   18.5.18 MR 20
FINZI,Edgar Cecil.MID   Lt   RAF   221 Sqdn   kia   5.9.18 CR Greece 9
FIRTH,James William Lt   RAF & NorfR 108 Sqdn   1.10.18 MR 20
FIRTH,P R   2Lt   RAF   kld   17.10.18 CR Yorks 361
FISH,William Raymond.MC&Bar   Capt   RAF   54 Sqdn   2.6.18 CR France 180
FISHER,Bertram   2Lt   RAF   54 Sqdn   21.7.18 MR 20
FISHER,Hubert Frank.OBE.   Maj   RAF   Home Establishment(from CanRAF)   22.3.19   CR Glouc 88
FISHER,Oscar   240260 FCdt   4SfthH & RAF   30.7.18 CR Lincs 156
FISHER,Sidney John Lt   BRCD att RAF   kldacc 30.9.18   CR France 1844
FITTON,James Clifford   2Lt   RAF   48 Sqdn   15.5.18 MR 20
FITTON,William.MM.   2Lt   RAF & 1/2LancF   6 Sqdn acckld 19.8.18   CR Fraqnce 1525
FITZGERALD,Roy James.MC.MID   Lt   GloucR att RAF   35 Sqdn   kia   1.7.18 CR France 71
FITZGERALD-EAGER,N   F/O   RAF   14 Sqdn   14.6.20 CR Egypt 20
FLAVELL,Alfred Victor   2Lt   RAF   8 Trng Sqdn   dedacc 4.5.18 CR Warwick 10
FLEET,Eric Thomas   48106   Cadet(Sgt)   4RSFus att RAF   22.10.18 CR Mddx 66
FLEET,John George 2Lt   RAF   3 Sqdn   6.8.18 CR France 84

FLEISCHER,Derric Cecil   2Lt   RAF   55 Sqdn   kia   3.11.18 CR France 1678
FLEMING,Alfred   2Lt   RAF   4 Sqdn   29.4.18 CR France 100
FLETCHER,C A.MM. 2Lt   RAF   1 Fighting Sch   20.10.18 CR Shrop 120
FLETCHER,Charles   2Lt   RAF   7 Sqdn dow   29.9.18   CR Belgium 38
FLETCHER,Edward Corston 2Lt   RAF   214 Sqdn   drd   22.8.18 CR Europe 90
FLOWER,C K Lt   RAF   218 Sqdn   15.5.18 CR France 1359
FLOWERS,Humphrey French Capt   RFA & RAF   82 Sqdn   14.10.18 CR Belgium157
FLOYD,John Marcon 2Lt   RAF   ded   22.2.19   CR Suffolk 240
FLYNN,Jerry Hope Laurice Wilfrid   Capt   RAF   32 Sqdn   3.9.18 CR France 1307
FOGGIN,Cyril Edgar Maj   RAF   40 Sqdn   kldacc   30.7.18   CR France 1564
FOGGIN,G W 2Lt   NCycBn att RAF   48 Sqdn   14.7.18 CR France 71
FOLEY,F Y   Capt&QM   ASC att RAF   12.5.18 CR Hamps 64
FOLKARD,W L   2Lt   RAF   15.11.18 CR Suffolk 138
FORBES,Ian Grant   Cadet RAF 174147   ded   30.10.18 CR Canada 1689
FORBES,N J 2Lt   RAF   10 Sqdn   17.7.18 CR France 142
FOORD,Edward Alec Lt   78 CanadianInf att RAF   kia   27.6.18 CR France 1170
FORD,Clarence James 2Lt   RAF   Cent Flying Sch   kldacc 3.5.18 CR Yorks 267
FORD,N   2Lt   RAF   100 Sqdn   5.4.18 CR France 1404
FORD,Norman Stanley.MC.   2Lt   RAF & RWSurrR   19.7.18 CR Wilts 116
FORDER,E   Lt   RAF   25.2.19 CR Dorset 18
FORREST,Arthur Cecil   2Lt   RAF   201 Sqdn   kia   29.7.18 CR France 10
FORREST,L J Lt   RAF   102 Sqdn   5.10.18 CR France 404
FORREST-DUNLOP,John James   FCdt   RAF 181870 8 Cdt Wing   29 9.18 CR Kent 180
FORSTER,Douglas   2Lt   RAF   11 TDS   7.10.18 CR Durham 121
FORSTER,Robert Cyril   2Lt   RAF   75 Trng Sqdn kld   9.5.18 CR Durham 9
FORSYTH,William Allan   Capt   RAF & 56RFA   27.6.18 CR Belgium 31
FOSS,F K   F/Cadet   RAF   43 TDS   24.10.18 CR Hamps 90
FOSTER,W A Lt   ManchR att RAF   20.2.19 CR Dorset 50
FOTHERGILL,Wilfrid Thompson   Lt   RAF   5 Sqdn kia   20.8.18 CR France 1170
FONTAIN,Cecil Charles   Lt   RAF   210 Sqdn   kia   14.10.18 CR Belgium 157
FOURNIER,Ludger L Cadet RAF 154484   ded   7.4.19 CR Canada 1687
FOWLER,Alfred Charles Garrett   2Lt   RAF   215 Sqdn   21.9.18 MR 20
FOWLER,Cecil James Lt   RAF   30 TDS   kld   25.7.18 CR Mddx 53
FOWLER,D A 2Lt   RAF   6 Bde HQ   26.6.19 CR Beds 23
FOX,Benson Charles   Lt   RAF   34 TDS   kld   23.7.18 CR Lincs 181
FOX,Hiram Claude   2Lt   RAF   46 TDS   26.10.18 CR Lincs 181
FOX,John Francis   FCdt   RAF   17.12.18 CR Somerset 30
FOX,John Robert   2Lt   RAF   55 Sqdn   16.8.18 CR France 1630
FOX,Walter Robert Seymour 2Lt   RAF   15 Sqdn 12 Wing   kia   22.8.18 CR France 84
FOX RUSSELL,Harry Thornbury.MC.   Capt   RAF   kld   18.11.18 CR Wales 461
FRANK,Hugh Robert 2Lt   RAF   209 Sqdn   4.7.18 MR 20
FRANKLIN,Leslie Nansen   Lt   RAF   56 Sqdn   kld   14.7.18 CR France 1489
FRASER,Alistair Hay Lt   RAF   41 Sqdn   11.8.18 CR France 1525
FRASER,Donald   Cadet RAF 272308 Cdt Wing   ded   12.10.18 CR Canada 1178
FRASER,M   2Lt   RAF   ded   22.7.18   CR Scot 874
FRASER,Robert Alexander   2Lt   RAF   15 Sqdn   18.5.18 CR France 59
FREDERICK,Leonard Martin 2Lt   RAF   6 Trng Sqdn kld   8.7.18 CR Scot 398
FREEMAN,Harold Augustus 2Lt   RAF   Cent Flying Sch C'Sqdn   kld   9.9.18 CR Wilts 116
FREEMAN,Joseph Arthur   2Lt   RAF   9 TDS   29.7.18 CR Beds 75
FREEMAN,Russell Herbert.MC.   Maj   RAF &WorcR 73 Sqdn   kia   21.7.18 CR France 524
FREER,Walter 2Lt   RAF   108 Sqdn Ex 4CamH   6.10.18 MR 20
FRENCH,Edwin Valentine   FltCdt RAF   acckld 16.10.18 CR Essex 80
FRIZZELL,Norman S Cadet RAF 152752   dedacc   22.8.18   CR Canada 1688
FRONEMAN,Everil Edwin.MC.   Capt   RAF   44 TDS   21.7.18 CR Berks 39
FROOM,Allman Minor   Cadet RAF 154228 Sch of Aerial Fighting dedacc   23.9.188 CR Canada 487
FROST,Douglas Greenhalgh 2Lt   RAF   5 Fighting Sch dedacc   29.1.19   CR Egypt 9
FROST,Frederick Donald   Cadet RAF 184094 Cdts Dist Depot   ded   18.10.18 CR Mon 67
FRY,A A.MBE.   Capt   RAF   12 Wing   27.6.19 CR Surrey 94
FUHR,Hugh Robert   Lt   RAF   67 Trng Sqdn kldacc   16.6.18   CR Ches 35
FULLERTON,Charles Alan Clarke   2Lt   RAF   72 Trng Sqdn kld   29.5.18 CR Yorks 537

FULLERTON,Roe Robertson Lt   RAF   16.2 19CR Canada 1688
FURLEY,J D 2Lt   RAF   5 Fighting Sch 20.10.18 CR Egypt 9
FUTCHER,H E   Lt   RAF   3 Aircraft Depot   21.10.18 CR France 1787
FYFE,R J   Lt   RAF   84 Sqdn   18.6.18CR France 1170
FYFIELD,A J F/O   RAF   29.4.20CR Suffolk 55

G

GABELL,D R C   Capt   RAF   12.7.18 CR Glouc 34
GADPAILLE,Louis Granville Surridge Lt   RAF   88 Sqdn   18.5.18 MR 20
GALBRAITH,John Gershia   2Lt   RAF   13 Sqdn   28.7.18 CR France 95
GALLANT,Francis Joseph   Lt   RAF   drd   13.3.19   CR France 1211
GALVAYNE,Vernon Frederick Attride FltLt RAF   4.6.18 CR Ches 8
GAMMELL,B E   Lt   · RAF   107 Sqdn   7.9.18 CR France 1252
GANGE,Percival Hookway   2Lt   RAF   1 TDS   10.6.18 CR Glouc 5
GANNAWAY,Charles Henry 2Lt   RAF   27 Sqdn   16.6.18 CR France 425
GANT,Robert Wilfred Lt   RAF   Malta Garrison   3.8.18 CR Europe 1
GANTER,F S Lt   RAF   72 Sqdn   27.6.18 CR France 924
GARDEN,Clarence Scott   2Lt   RAF   ·4 TDS kld   2.6.18 CR Ches 192
GARDEN,Duncan   FCdt   RAF 110331   kldacc 24.7.188 CR Scot 876
GARDEN,James Scott Cdt   RAF 173497   ded   16.10.18 CR Canada 1689
GARDEN,Kenneth Clinton William   2Lt   RAF   1 Obs Sch of Aerial Gnry   kld   3.9.18 CR London 4
GARDENNER,John Vernon   2Lt   RAF   6 Sqdn   9.10.18CR France 725
GARDNER,H W   F/O   RAF   10.3.21 CR Surrey 15
GARDINER,H Cdt   RAF 132566 5 Cdt Wing   12.11.18 CR Kent 180
GARDINER,Ivan Jephson   Lt   5NorfR att RAF   drd   27.5.18   MR 41
GARDNER,C V.DFC. Capt   RAF   19 Sqdn   dow   30.9.18   CR France 512
GARDNER,F A   FCdt   RAF 119621 1 TDS   10.8.18 CR Sussex 64
GARDNER,John Harrison   2Lt   RAF   100 Sqdn   kia   9.1.19 CR Germany 1
GARLICK,Tom   2Lt   RAF   4 Sqdn   28.6.18 CR France 28
GARNER,Ernest James.AFC. Obs/Off   RAF   HMS Pegasus   18.10.20 CR Asia 51
GARNER,Frank Leslie   2Lt   RAF   5 Sqdn kld   20.12.16 CR Ches 146
GARNONS-WILLIAMS,Aylmer Curtis.MC   Capt   RAF &SWB   14.5.18 CR Sussex 27
GARROD,Basil Rahere   Lt   1LNLancsR att RAF   149 Sqdn   ded   4.2.19 CR Germany 1
GARSIDE,Jack   2Lt   RAF   kld   18.11.18 CR Warwick 50
GASSON,Fitzroy Arthur Bell. Lt   RAF   kia   26.9.18CR Belgium 390
GASTER,Percy Stuart 2Lt   Gen List & RAF   18 Trng Sqdn kld   21.4.18CR London 3
GATECLIFF,James Noel   Lt   RAF   53 Sqdn   kia   29.6.18CR France 24
GATTENS,Charles   Lt   RAF   63 Sqdn   15.6.19 CR Iraq 8
GAUKROGER,Herbert   Lt   RAF   7.5.19 CR Yorks 701
GAUKROGER,J Kenneth   Lt   RAF   107 Sqdn   kld   8.8.18 MR 20
GEARY,Brian Charles 2Lt   RAF   98 Sqdn   11.8.18 MR 20
GEEKIE,Archibald   2Lt   RAF (EEF)   24.5.19 CR Egypt 1
GEIDT,Charles Uppleby   Lt   CamH att RAF   kldacc 10.4.18   CR Egypt 1
GEORGE,John Frederick.DSM.   2Lt   RAF   226 Sqdn   kia   26.8.18CR Italy 8
GEORGE,L   Lt   RAF &ASC   ded   12.5.18
GERHARDI,Harold James   2Lt   RAF   47 Sqdn   kia   18.9.18CR Greece 5
GIBBONS,J E 2Lt   RAF   9.10.18CR France 482
GIBBS,David FCdt   RAF 242005 38 Sqdn   8.8.18 CR Warwick 97
GIBSON,D P 2Lt   RAF   6.7.18 CR Canada 1688
GIBBS,Stanley Lt   RAF   206 Sqdn   14.5.19 CR Germany 1
GIBSON,Vernon Francis   FCdt   RAF   51 TDS   9.11.18CR Ches 35
GILBERT,Anson Elliott   Lt   CanFA att RAF   ded   5.11.18CR Canada 1667
GILBERT,Charles Oliver   Cadet RAF 172217   ded   8.10.18CR Canada 1612
GILBERT,Kenneth Nigel Wilson MC Capt   RAF & 32 RFA   ded   15.10.18 CR Norfolk 138
GILBERT,S C Lt   RAF   99 Sqdn   26.9.18 CR France 1674
GILBERTSON,Dennis Henry Stacey Lt   RAF   70 Sqdn   4.9.18 CR France 1201
GILCHRIST,ArchibaldLt   RAF & 1/4RB   kia   3.10.18CR France 234

GILFILLAN,A W   Lt   RAF   7.11.18 CR Glouc 9
GILL,Kenneth Carlyle.MC.MID   Capt   RAF & 1CambR   22 Sqdn   dow   23.10.18 CR France 1512
GILLESPIE,A E.MM. 2Lt   RAF   191 Trng Depot   9.5.18 CR Scot 385
GILLESPIE,Douglas Victor.MID   2Lt   RAF   70 Sqdn   kia   6.4.18 CR France 1170
GILLESPIE,R H   2Lt   RAF   15 Sqdn   7.8.18 CR France 805
GILLETT,Howard Raymond   2Ltt   RAF   RNAS Stn Manston   6.4.18 CR Lond 12
GILLIES,J W Lt   RAF   25.5.18 CR Mddx 80
GILLMAN,Bernard Tuite   2Lt   RAF   49 Sqdn   24.9.18 MR 20
GILMAN,Walter   Lt   RAF   211 Sqdn   13.7.18 MR 20
GILPIN,Robert Rooke 2Lt   RAF   kldacc   22.12.18 CR France 1868
GIRDLESTONE,H W Lt   RGA att RAF   4 Sqdn kld   30.4.18   CR France 134
GITSHAM,J Lt   RAF   35 Sqdn   29.6.18 CR France 71
GLANVILLE,H F.MID   Capt   RAF   2 TDS   24.5.18 CR Scot 627
GLASSE,E S Lt   RAF   48 Sqdn   19.8.18 CR France 586
GLEN,James   Capt   RAF & 5ScotRif   70 Sqdn   16.9.18 MR 20
GLENDINNING,Stanley Hill Lt   RAF   I.A.G.Sqdn   dedacc   17.7.18   CR Canada 1575
GLENTWORTH,Edmond William Claude Gerrard deVere.Viscount Capt RAF   32 Sqdn   kia   18.5.18 CR France 421
GLEW,W   2Lt   RAF   99 Sqdn   7.11.18 CR France 1675
GLIDDON,Reginald Arthur   Lt   RAF &MddxR   kld   9.5.18 CR London 33
GLOVER,Clifford L   Lt   RAF &ChesR   48 Sqdn   15.5.18 MR 20
GODDARD,Frank Edward   2Lt   RAF   Ex RE kld   10.6.18 CR Hamps 139
GODET,Lennock De Graaff   Lt   RAF   55 Sqdn   1.6.18   CR France 1677
GODFREY,Charles Henry Albert   2Lt   RAF   1 Fighting Sch kld   11.12.18 CR Surrey 6
GODFREY,Chester H 2Lt   RAF   ded   14.3.20   CR Canada 1268
GOLLER,John Morrisey   Lt   RAF   62 Sqdn   kia   16.6.18 CR France 987
GONDRE,Jean 2Lt   RAF   48 Sqdn   20.7.19 CR Europe 180 & MR 70
GONNE,Michael Edward.MC.   Capt   RAF &RFus   54 Sqdn   kia   8.8.18 CR France 526
GOOD,Herbert Barrett Lt   RAF   92 Sqdn   5.9.18 MR 20
GOODALE,Walter Henry   Lt   46CanInf att RAF   104 Sqdn   1.8.18 CR France 1667
GOODBURN,R   2Lt   RAF   7.8.18 CR Lancs 475
GOODCHILD,Victor George   Lt   RAF   2 Aircraft Supply Depot   ded   31.10.18 CR France 52
GOODE,Frank Valentine   Lt   RAF   18.12.19 CR Warwick 84
GOODEARLE,F R   Lt   RAF   20 Sqdn   23.10.18 CR France 332
GOODHUGH,P H   2Lt   RAF   46 Sqn Ex CMGC   dow   29.9.18   CR France 658
GOODMAN,Gilbert Anthony Lt   1LNLancsR att RAF   66 Sqdn   kia   28.10.18 CR Italy 9
GOODWILL,Eric Ainsworth   Lt   RAF   42 Sqdn   kia   3.11.18 CR France 1030
GOODYEAR,Charles Frederick Richards 2Lt   RAF   55 Sqdn   25.6.18 CR France 34
GOOSEY,H   2Lt   RAF   8.8.18 CR Nhants 143
GORDON,Erskine W   Lt   RAF &PPCLI   98 Sqdn   31.7.18 CR France 1429
GORDON,J A Lt   RAF & BCR   12.8.18 CR France 1472
GORDON,H A Lt   RAF   60 Sqdn   7.7.18 CR France 526
GORDON,Robert Bissett.DFC.   ObsOff RAF   20 Sqdn   20.3.20 MR 43
GORDON,Ralph Vivian   2Lt   RAF   55 Sqdn   25.9.18 CR France 1678
GORDON-BELL,C   Capt   RAF   see BELL,C G
GORMAN,R E 2Lt   RAF   36 TDS   27.7.18 CR Wilts 28
GOTCH,G W 2Lt   RAF   22.10.18 CR Bucks 51
GOULD,Herbert Rusca.MC.   Capt   RAF   18 Sqdn   14.8.18 MR 20
GOURLAY,William Miller   2Lt   RAF   91 Sqdn   1.10.18 CR Surrey 9
GOW,John Eckford   2Lt   CanFA att RAF   204 Sqdn   dow   10.8.18   CR Belgium 140
GOWSELL,Leonard   Lt   Gen List & RAF   4 Sqdn dow   20.4.18   CR France 134
GOY,E G   Lt   RAF   1 Sch of Navgn & Bombg(RNAS)   25.4.18   CR Ches 8
GRADY,James Fraser 2Lt   RAF   Gnry Sch(Eastchurch)   19.7.18 CR Kent 79
GRAHAM,David Liddell   Lt   RAF   47 Sqdn   kia   24.6.18 CR Greece 6
GRAHAM,Edward William   Lt   RAF   56 Sqn Ex CASC   3.1.19 CR France 658
GRAHAM,G W   See HOFFMAN,G W real name
GRAHAM,George Wilson   Lt   RAF   204 Sqdn   13.7.18 CR Europe 90
GRAHAM,Vernon William   FltCdt RAF   41 TDS(Denham)   16.7.18 CR Herts 87
GRAHAM,W J K   2Lt   RAF   6 Trng Sqdn   17.5.18 CR Scot 398
GRANT,Charles Frederick   2Lt   RAF   5 Sqdn kia   10.8.18 MR 20
GRANT,H C R 2Lt   RAF   80 Sqdn   4.11.18 CR France 521

89

GRANT,P T   2Lt   RAF   65 Sqdn   21.1.19 CR Belgium 393
GRANT,Richard Craven   Capt   RAF & 3ScoRif   209 Sqdn   kia   2.9.18 MR 20
GRAY,Allan Cyril   2Lt   RAF   29.12.18 CR Canada 1608
GRAY,Victor Samuel Lt   RAF &4SuffR 48 Sqdn   8.8.18 MR 20
GREY,William McNeil   2Lt   RAF   ded   22.1.19   CR Canada 1688
GREASLEY,John Richard   2Lt   RAF   65 Sqdn   1.4.18 MR 20
GREATWOOD,F S   2Lt   RAF & RSussR   drd   12.4.18   CR Kent 7
GREAVES,N 2Lt   RAF   70 Sqdn   28.10.18 CR Belgium 406
GREEN,Merle Livingstone   Lt   RAF   65 Sqdn   6.8.18 CR France 71
GREEN,Smith 2Lt   RAF   ·70 Sqdn   18.2.19 CR Germany 1
GREENE,John Edmund.DFC. Capt   RAF   213 Sqdn   kia   14.10.18 CR Belgium 24
GREENWELL,J E   Lt   RAF   16.7.18 CR Durham 162
GREENWOOD,Leonard Aspinall   Lt   RAF   43 Sqdn   13.4 18 CR France 226
GREGORY,Miles Sells   Lt   RAF   19 Sqdn   11.8.18 MR 20
GREIG,Charles William   FltLt   RAF(RNAS)   12.9.18 CR Europe 17
GRESWELL,Eric Walter   Lt   8ChesR att RAF   111 Sqdn   kia   9.6.18 CR Palestine 9
GRIFFIN,Edward William   Lt   6GloucR att RAF   kia   16.9.18 CR France 792
GRIFFIN,Stephen   2Lt   RAF   88 Sqdn   18.5.18 MR 20
GRIFFITH,Donovan Baldwin 2Lt   RAF   209 Sqdn   19.7.18 CR France 1170
GRIFFITHS,Reginald Hopkin Hill.MC. 2Lt   RAF &9WelshR   kld   17.10.18 CR Belgium 140
GRIGG,Dennis Hugh 2Lt   RAF   98 Sqdn   kld   11.10.18 CR France 788
GRIGSON,Claude Vivian   Cdt   RAF 183204 1 Cdt Wing   ded   15.10.18 CR Kent 180
GRIMSHAW,A V S   Lt   RAF   20.5.20 CR C'land&W'land 78
GRIMSHAW,George Henry   2Lt   RAF   kld   8.7.18 CR Ches 72
GRIMSELL,George Eldon   Cadet RAF 272237   13.10.18 CR Canada 1143
GRIMWADE,Sidney Arthur   2Lt   RAF   54 TDS   4.8.18 CR Staffs 156
GROVES,Robert Marsland.CB.DSO.AFC.   AirCdre   RAF   Cmdg Mid East Area dedacc 27.5.20   CR Egypt 10
GUNDILL,Robert Percy   2Lt   RAF &YLI   108 Sqdn   2.10.18 MR 20
GUNTHER,Harry Hall 2Lt   RAF   63 Trng Sqdn kld   18.7.18 CR Kent 125
GUTHRIE,Arthur Calderwood 2Lt   RE att RAF   42 Sqdn   9.8.18 CR France 31
GUTHRIE,J B Lt   RAF   34 Sqdn   10.5.18 CR Italy 9
HACKER,James M   Cadet · RAF 74813   dedacc 23.8.18 CR Canada 911
HACKLETT,Leslie Arnold   Lt(Pilot) RAF   1 Comms Sqn 2 Sch of Navgn & Bombg kldacc 26.2.19   CR Mddx 66
HACKMAN,Clifford 2Lt   RAF   92 Sqdn   7.4.18 CR Glouc 217
HACON,William Charles   Capt   RAF   ded   19.2.19   CR Essex 48
HADDON,W Lt   RAF   12.5.20 CR Staffs 6
HADLOW,A L 2Lt   RAF   70 Sqdn   6.10.18 CR Belgium 38
HAIGH,John Scot   2Lt   RAF   24 Sqdn   15.8.18 CR France 71
HAGAN,J W 2Lt   RAF   18
HAGAN,William Becker   Cadet RAF 171565 Cdt Wing   ded   11.5.18   CR USA 79
HAGGERSTON,T   Maj   RAF   Air Ministry   20.2.19 CR Surrey 160
HAINES,Alfred John.DFC.   Lt   RAF   45 Sqdn   10.8.18 CR Italy 11
HAINSWORTH,George   2Lt   RAF   ded   4.12.18 CR Yorks 256
HALCOMBE,Norman Marshall.MIDx3   Maj   RE att RAF   ded   13.2.19   CR Egypt 7
HALE,P R   2Lt   RAF   att HMS Tiger kld   16.10.18 CR London 24
HALES,John Playford Capt   RAF   203 Sqdn   23.8.18 CR France 370
HALEY,A   2Lt   RAF &EssR   55 Sqdn   1.6.18 CR France 1667
HALFORD,William Henry Loffill   2Lt   RAF   202 Sqdn   28.9.18 MR 20
HALFPENNY,William Henry Lt   LancF att RAF 49 TDS   dedacc 24.11.18 CR Lancs 2
HALL,Clifford Lt   RAF   214 Sqdn   9.7.19 CR France 1571
HALL,Frederick Vincent   Lt   RAF   210 Sqdn   kia   15.5.18 CR France 180
HALL,G W   2Lt   RAF & Gen List   3 Sqdn   20.11.17 CR France 336
HALL,Geoffrey Lawrence Dobney   Lt   RAF   3 Sqn 13 Wing   2.5.18 CR France 63
HALL,Henry Glaze   Lt   RAF   17 Sqdn   17.7.18 MR 37
HALL,John Francis Ashley   2Lt   RAF & 1EYorksR   21 Sqdn   kia   14.8.18 CR France 88
HALL,James Grantley Lt   RAF   60 Sqdn   kia   8.8.18 CR France 1467
HALL,James Hervey   Lt   RAF &LancF   25.8.18 CR Lancs 263
HALL,Russell McKay Lt   RAF & QuebecR   98 Sqdn   28.5.18 CR Belgium 385
HALL,S   2Lt   RAF   4 Sqdn   18.10.18 CR France 1029
HALL-SMITH,Philip Lt   RAF   kld   1.8.19 CR Scot 131

HALLEY,David Bowie   2Lt   RAF   22 Sqdn   kia   30.8.18 CR France 10
HALLIDAY,J G W   2Lt   RAF   98 Sqdn   3.9.18 CR France 526
HALSTEAD,G W.MM.   Lt   RAF   31.1.19 CR Hamps 83
HALSTED,Francis Neville.DSC.DFC.FltLt   RAF   drd   3.10.20 MR 40
HAMAR,Richard Clarence   Cadet   RAF 152564 Sch of Aerial Gnry   dedacc 4.6.18 CR Canada 1518
HAMES,Clifford Robinson   2Lt   RAF   25.4.18 CR Kent 7
HAMILTON,Alexander   Lt   RAF   3 Sqdn   8.8.18 MR 20
HAMILTON,David Shaw   Lt   RAF   62 Sqdn   kia   1.9.18 CR France 1196
HAMILTON,H J.MC. Capt   RAF   13.6.18 CR Mddx 15
HAMILTON,William Whitfield   FltCdt RAF 36936   kld   4.10.18 CR Durham 173
HAMMOND,H C   2Lt   RAF   70 Sqdn   11.2.19 CR Germany 1
HAMMOND,Henry Lloyd   Lt   RAF   215 Sqdn   4.8.18 MR 20
HAMMOND,Joseph Joel   Capt   RAF   acckld   22.9.18   CR USA 52
HAMMOND,Vernon John   Capt   RAF   2 Trng Wing ded   23.2.19   CR Essex 1
HAMPTON,F A F   Lt   RAF &NFus   23.8.18 CR Mddx 17
HAMPTON,John Henry   2Lt   RAF   3 Sqdn   29.10.18 MR 20
HANCOCK,John Mervyn   Lt   RAF   kld   1.3.19 CR Mddx 34
HAND,P A   Lt   RAF   107 Sqdn   9.7.18 CR France 134
HANDEL,Kenneth Douglas   2Lt   RAF   53 att 4 Sqdn kia   25.6.18 CR France 31
HANNA,Harold Leander   Lt   RAF   3 Trng Depot   23.4.18 CR Wilts 115
HANNA,William Neil Lt   RAF   36 Sqdn   dedacc 20.11.18 CR Italy 11
HARBORD,Lionel Anthony   Lt   RAF   21.8.19 MR 67
HARBORD,Sidney Bertram   FltCdt RAF   40 TDS   19.12.18 CR Norfolk 131
HARDING,Cyril George   2Lt   RAF   103 Sqdn   9.11.188 CR Glouc 189
HARDY,J   2Lt   RAF   8 Aircraft Park   21.10.18 CR France 1359
HARGRAVE,William George 2Lt   RAF   28 Sqdn   kia   17.4.18 CR Italy 10
HARGREAVES,William Henry   Lt   15MddxR att RAF   8.5.18 CR Palestine
HARINGTON,J R   Lt   RAF   206 Sqdn   7.7.18 CR France 255
HARKER,E K 2Lt   RAF &RGA   dow   18.4.18   CR Belgium 38
HARKER,Howard Redmayne.MC.   Capt   RAF   2 Sch of Navgn & Bombg   ded   27.2.19   CR Lancs 34
HARMAN,Leslie Woodward.MID   Lt   RAF   40 Trng Sqdn ded   4.11.18 CR London 12
HARMON,Burdette William.MC.DCM.   Lt   RAF & ManitobaR   56 Sqdn   10.5.18   CR France 1170
HARPER,George Victor   2Lt   RAF   104 Sqdn   26.9.18 CR France 1667
HARPER,N S Lt   RAF   99 Sqdn   25.6.18 CR Germany 3
HARRAN,F St P   Lt   RAF   20.6.18 CR Devon 1
HARRIES,A G FltCdt RAF 100322 10 Sch of Aerial Gnry kld   6.6.18 CR Ches 182
HARRIS,Howard Vernon   Cadet   RAF 273065   ded   23.10.18 CR Canada 1689
HARRIS,Ralph Joseph Lt   RAF   9.11.18 CR London 12
HARRIS,S E   Lt   RAF   9 Sqdn   4.7.18 CR France 1170
HARRIS,T W S   Capt   RAF   4.10.18 CR Essex 48
HARRIS,W J Cdt   RAF 144219 2 Wing   8.6.18 CR Sussex 178
HARRISON,Alexander   FltCdt RAF 100046 1 Sch of Navgn &Bombg   5.7.18 CR Lancs 30
HARRISON,C 2Lt   RAF   186 Sqdn   3.5.19 CR Hamps 4
HARRISON,Edward   Lt   RAF & RE   24 Sqdn   17.5.18 MR 20
HARRISON,E A   2Lt   RAF   5 Sqdn   1.10.18 CR France 597
HARRISON,Henry Leslie   Lt   4YorksR att RAF   28.10.18 CR London 14
HARRISON,Herbert Rowland FltCdt RAF   kld   7.9.18 CR Lancs 7
HARRISON,J 2Lt   RAF   53 Sqdn   29.6.18 CR France 24
HARRISON,James Ingleby   Maj   RAF   214 Sqn Ex LtCmdr RN   16.5.18 CR Belgium 132
HARRISON,Norman Victor   Capt   RAF   kld   22.4.18 CR Surrey 2
HARRISON,R Lt   RAF &RE   ded   17.5.18
HARRISON,Walter Wingrave 2Lt   RAF   205 Sqdn   21.9.18 MR 20
HARROW,R W T   2Lt   RAF   3 TDS   16.6.18 CR Kent 272
HARSTON,Sidney   Lt   RAF   204 Sqdn   29.6.18 MR 20
HART,Eric Stanley   2Lt   RAF   96 Sqdn   kld   5.6.18 CR USA 143
HART,F W   2Lt   RAF   20 Trng Wing   22.7.18 CR Egypt 1
HART,William Cecil Frederick Nicol Lt   RAF & 11 RLancsR   57 Sqdn   kia   1.4.18 MR 20
HARTLEY,Walter Noel   2Lt   RAF   49 Sqdn   8.8.18 MR 20
HARVEY,Charles Almond   2Lt   RAF   7 Sqdn   29.6.18 CR Belgium 152
HARVEY,Edwin Sinclair   2Lt   RAF   20 Sqdn   29.9.18 CR France 660

HARVEY,Gerald Myles   Cadet   RAF 272592 Recruits Depot ded   12.10.18 CR Canada 180
HARVEY,R W2Lt   RFus att RAF   22.10.18 CR London 22
HARVEY,Thomas Francis   Lt   RAF &SfthH   49 Sqdn   7.6.18 MR 20
HARWOOD,Gerald.AFC.   Lt   3SuffR att RAF   acckld 1.5.19 CR Kent 103
HASKEW,Clement Charles   FltCdt RAF 1958   Ex 80549 3DLI   kld   25.7.18CR Staffs 84
HASTIE,Harry Nelson Lt   RAF 95 Sqdn   12.4.18 CR Ches 35
HATCH,Arthur Vernon   Cadet RAF 153352   ded   25.5.18   CR Canada 1028
HATCHER,H B   2Lt   RAF   30.7.18 CR Somerset 157
HATHAWAY,I W   2Lt   RAF 12 TDS   11.8.18 CR Wilts 4
HAVELOCK-SUTTON,G H.MC.   F/O   RAF   Depot(HaltonCamp) Ex Lt KEdwHorse   30.7.20   CR Bucks 20
HAWKEN,G W   2Lt   RAF & Gen List   18.5.18 CR Hamps 192
HAWKINS,Reginald Lt   RAF 74 Sqdn   29.7,18 CR France 134
HAWKINS,Trevor Emlyn Ockwell 2Lt   RAF 103 Sqdn   20.7.18 CR Belgium 451
HAWKSWELL,Louis Bertram Lt   RAF   18.9.18 CR Yorks 469
HAWLEY,Arthur Charles Richard   Lt   RAF 54 Sqdn   9.8.18 MR 20
HAYE,Ronald George 2Lt   RAF 204 TDS   kld   25.6.18CR London 10
HAYNE,Edwin Tufnell.DSC.DFC.   Capt   RAF   kld   28.4.19CR Warwick 65
HAYNES,Charles Graham.MC&Bar   Capt   RAF &KRRC   23.10.18 CR Belgium 349
HAYNES,E B 2Lt   RAF   1 Aircraft Repair Depot   14.11.18 CR Mon 89
HAYNES,G W N R   Capt   6RMunstF att RAF   30.5.19 CR Germany 1
HAYNES,P A 2Lt   RAF 108 Sqdn   28.9.18 CR France 1359
HAYNES,William Harold.DSO.   Capt   RAF 151 Sqdn   26.9.18 CR France 52
HAYWARD,F R   2Lt   RAF 36 TDS   23.8.18 CR Lancs 23
HAZELL,Dudley Howard   Lt   2 RLancsR att RAF   kld   27.9.18CR France 924
HAZEN,Thomas Douglas   Lt   RAF 56 Sqdn   19.8.18 MR 20
HEADLAM,John   Lt   RAF 60 Sqdn   kia   30.5.18 CR France 226
HEARD,Murray   2Lt   RAF 209 Sqdn   11.10.18 CR France 113
HEATER,Roy Esworth2Lt   RAF 44 Sqdn   7.6.18 CR Lincs 181
HEATH,Grahame   Lt   RAF   20.8.18 CR Warwick 3
HEATHERS,P C   2Lt   RAF   2.2.19 CR London 8
HEBLEY,J B C   302817   FltCdt RAF & 5LondR   ded   14.2.19   CR Herts 87
HEEBNER,Carl Hastings   Lt   RAF   103 Sqdn   24.9.18 CR France 557
HEFFERNAN,Michael James 2Lt   RAF   28 TDS   kld   30.1.19CR Lancs 1
HEIGHAM-PLUMTRE,L G 2Lt   RAF &BedR   4.6.18 CR France 1564
HEINZMAN,Thomas Herman 2Lt   RAF 42 Wing   kld   29.5.18CR Canada 1688
HELM,Henry Paul Dundas.MID   Capt   RAF &BordR   ded   6.11.18CR C'land &W'land 17
HELMER,Elton Williams   Lt   RAF 23 Sqdn   kld   8.8.18 CR France 652
HELMORE,Stanley Thomas John   2Lt   23RFus att RAF   18 Sqdn   kia   14.5.18CR France 21
HEMINGWAY,Arnold2Lt   RAF 104 Sqdn   6.11.18CR France 1675
HEMSWORTH,Gore William Lt   RAF 1 Sqdn drd   15.8.19   CR France 34
HENDERSON,Ernest Brian · Lt   3CanInf att RAF   3.11.18CR Canada 1121
HENDERSON,Frederick William   Cadet RAF 171360   ded   2.6.18 CR USA 97
HENDERSON,George Andrew Falconer   Lt   RAF &GordH Ex 2GordH   4.7.18 CR Scot 339
HENDERSON,Ian Henry David.MC Capt   A&SH att RAF   21.6.18 CR Scot 520
HENDERSON,Kenneth Selby Capt   RAF & Sp List 1 Sqdn   2.6.18 MR 20
HENDERSON,L H   2Lt   RAF   29.10.18 CR Numb 7
HENDERSON,Tom Ormand   Lt   RAF 4 Sqdn   14.9.18 CR Belgium 192
HENDERSON,William Douglas   F/Cadet   RAF 32 TDS   28.11.18 CR Glouc 86
HENDRY,J C S.AM 2Lt   RAF   Isle of Scilly   6.7.18 CR France 1808
HENNESSY,Harold Stephen Lt   RAF 1 Sqdn   5.6.18 MR 20
HENRY,John Aloysius Gerard2Lt   RAF 7 Sqdn kia   28.9.18CR Belgium 13
HEPBURN,Andrew Anderson FltCdt RAF 1 Flying Sch kldacc 23.8.18   CR Scot 111
HEPBURN,Reginald Victor 2Lt   RAF & Gen List   kia   16.9.18CR France 365
HEPWORTH,Arthur Montague.MC. Lt   RWSurrR & RAF   kia   4.5.18 CR Palestine 9
HERBERT,Robert Stannard 2Lt   RAF 108 Sqdn   8.10.18CR France 1359
HERITAGE,Edward Wilmot Cadet RAF 204 TDS   kld   15.9.18CR Lancs 34
HERITAGE,Herbert Alec   2Lt   RAF 125 Sqn Ex 14LondR doi   28.6.18CR London 14
HERLIY,P J Lt   RAF   5.12.18CR Eire 132 & 14
HERON,Francis Turretin   2Lt   RAF 206 Sqdn   25.7.18 MR 20
HERON,William Frederick 2Lt   RAF 5 Fighting Sch   3.3.19 CR Egypt 9

92

HERRING,Albert Henry   Lt   RAF   25 Sqdn   20.5.18 CR France 941
HERRON,K C Lt   RAF   82 Sqdn   24.4.18 CR France 71
HESLOP,A V 2Lt   RAF   4 Sqdn   9.11.18CR France 276
HEWAT,Richard Alexander   Lt   RAF   87 Sqdn   14.8.18   MR 20
HEWENS,F A Lt   RAF   16.7.18 CR Mddx 64
HEWETT,H D Lt   RAF   13 Sqdn   27.10.18 CR France 332
HEWETT,Leonard Stanley   Lt   RAF   100 Sqdn   kldacc 6.2.19 CR Germany 1
HEWSON,Arlof DavidCadet RAF 154244   42 Wing   dedacc 5.5.18 CR Canada 1119
HEYES,A E   2Lt   RAF & Gen List   21 Sqdn   14.4.18 CR Belgium 38
HEYWOOD,Alan Charles Albert   Lt   RAF   Artly Obs Sch   20.6.18 CR Egypt 9
HEYWOOD,Francis Kirkman Lt   RAF   98 Sqdn   kld   1.10.18CR France 512
HICKES,Robert Ian Alexander2Lt   RAF   5 Sqdn   30.8.18 CR France 1660
HICKEY,Charles Robert Reeves.DFC&Bar.Capt   RAF   204 Sqn 61 Wing   kldacc 3.10.18CR Belgium 24
HICKEY,Leonard Charles   Lt   RAF   46 Sqdn   2.5.18   MR 20
HICKS,Wilfred Noel   2Lt   RAF   16 Sqn Ex Gnr HAC   dow   27.10.18 CR France 1285
HIELD,William Cecil 2Lt   RAF   7 TDS   12.4.18 CR Yorks 357
HIGGINS,H   2Lt   RAF   91 Can Trng Sqdn   13.7.18 CR Lincs 78
HIGGINSON,George Havelock   Cadet RAF 154655   Recruits Depot ded   12.5.18   CR Canada 112
HIGGS,Lloyd Alfred 2Lt   RAF   35 Sqdn   7.10.18CR France 194
HILBORN,William Carnall.DFC.   Capt   RAF   45 Sqdn   26.8.18 CR Italy 11
HILL,Aubrey Charels Finch   Capt   RAF   Aerodrome Serv Unit ded   24.10.18 CR France 1512
HILL,Arthur Hadden   Lt   RAF   27 Sqdn   kia   10.5.18CR France 652
HILL,Angus Joseph   Cadet RAF 272983   ded   27.10.18 CR Canada 1688
HILL,Alan Purdie Dunlop   Maj   RGA & RAF   59 Sqdn   8.2.19 CR Belgium 330
HILL,Arnold Whittier 2Lt   RAF   dedacc 13.7.18   CR USA 92
HILL,H   FltCdt RAF   204 Fog Wing Depot Stn   28.8.18 CR Ches 153
HILL,H B   Lt   RAF   6.9.18 CR Warwick 40
HILL,Hepworth Ambrose Vyvian   F/O   RAF   100 Sqdn   25.2.21 CR NIreland 33
HILL,Richard Alexander Gathorne   Lt   RAF & SomLI 204 Sqdn   kld   12.8.18MR 20
HILL,Robert Brinton Lt   RAF   29.4.18 CR Wilts 3
HILL,R F   Lt   RAF   17.9.18 CR Sussex 219
HILL,S J   2Lt   RAF   65 Sqdn   4.10.18   CR Belgium140
HILL,Stafford Norman Lt   RAF   101 Sqdn   2.3.19 CR Eire 14
HILLIS,Bruce Sinclair Lt   RAF   48 Sqdn   kia   5.7.18 CR France 425
HILLOCK,Charles Alexander 2Lt   RAF 154732? 1 Fighting Sch kld   8.1.19 CR Scot 520
HILLS,William Henry F/O   RAF   Instr Depot   17.10.20 CR London 29
HILTON,Robert   2Lt   RAF &5ManchR   13 Sqdn   6.4.18   MR 20
HIND,Ivan Frank   Capt   RAF   40 Sqdn   kia   12.8.18CR France 511
HINDER,Arthur   2Lt   RAF   97 Sqdn   16.9.18 CR France 1788
HINDLEY,Aaron   Lt   RAF   45 Sqdn   19.5.18 CR Ches 160
HINSLEY,W Lt   RAF   HQ (Mudros) ded   6.12.18CR Greece 9
HINTON,A W 2Lt   RAF   4.5.18 CR Oxford 94
HINTON,Francis Athol   2Lt   RAF   51 TDS   kldacc 9.11.18CR Ches 35
HIRST,Sidney 2Lt   RAF   103 Sqdn   16.6.18   MR 20
HISCOX,A H Lt   RAF   208 Sqdn   28.9.18 CR France 646
HITCH,George Stewart   Lt   5LpoolR att RAF   ded   9.11.18CR Ches 182
HITCHCOCK,Albert Edward 2Lt   RAF   28 Sqdn   kia   29.1.19CR Italy 11
HITCHCOCK,S R   Cdt   RAF   4.10.18CR Mddx 53
HITCHIN-KEMP,R P 2Lt   RAF   see KEMP,R P H
HITCHMOUGH,J E   Cdt   RAF   1 Sch of Aeronautics(Reading)   15.7.18 CR Warwick 16
HOBBS,Thomas Goodwin.DFC.   2Lt   RAF   59 Sqdn   dow   23.8.18   CR France 84
HOCKING,Edward Cuthbert Lt   RAF &RFA   151 Sqdn   28.10.18 CR France 646
HODGKINSON,William   Lt   RAF   62 Sqdn   9.10.18CR France 1078
HODGSON,Francis Herbert Capt   RAF   O'Flight   kld   19.11.18 CR France 441
HODGSON,Richard Eveleigh Lt   RAF &LpoolR 204 Sqn Ex 4LpoolR   kia   15.9.18CR Belgium 24
HOFFMAN,George William.MM.   2Lt   RAF   Served as GRAHAM,G.W. 64 Sqdn   1.11.18CR France 1142
HOFMEISTER,A W   2Lt   RAF   53 TDS   29.8.18 CR Kent 7
HODGE,W   2Lt   RAF   99 Sqdn   24.4.18 CR NIreland 222
HODSKIN,Archibald Francis Lt   RAF   6.9.18 MR 37
HODSON,George Frederick   Lt   RAF   lost at sea   5.8.18   MR 40

HOGAN,J W 2Lt RAF 149 Sqdn 15.9.18 CR France 134
HOGG,William Bease Lt RAF 18 Sqdn 4.9.18 MR 20
HOJEL,Jonathan George 2Lt RAF 210 Sqdn kia 21.8.18 CR France 1359
HOLDER,Evelyn Lt RAF 1 Aerial Grp ded 17.2.19 CR France 40
HOLIDAY,Richard Alan.MM. Lt RAF 98 Sqdn 3.5.18 MR 20
HOLLAND,Algernon Capt RAF 21.9.18 CR Scot 385
HOLLAND,Horace Lloyd F/O RAF B'Flt 141 Sqdn drd 21.2.20 MR 40
HOLLAND,J H 2Lt 22RFus att RAF 16.6.18 CR France 1233
HOLLICK,John Lt RAF 210 Sqdn 18.5.18 MR 20
HOLLIDAY,Walter Cadet RAF 174418 ded 16.10.18 CR Canada 1689
HOLLINGS,Hubert 2Lt RAF 202 Sqdn 28.9.18 CR Belgium 132
HOLLINGWORTH,A Lt QuebecR att RAF 8 Sqdn 25.6.18 CR France 1564
HOLLOWAY,Claude Abrey MarseilleCapt RAF & RWKentR 19.2.19 CR Kent 289
HOLMAN,Eric Lt RAF ded 13.7.21 CR Wales 671
HOLMES,Douglas William Lt RAF 98 Sqdn 30.10.18 CR Belgium 203
HOLMES,Herbert 2Lt RAF 97 Sqdn 28.10.18 CR France 1678
HOLMES,James Cuthbert Lt RAF Aircraft Park kia 1.9.18 CR Egypt 2
HOLMES,John Charles Holland Lt RAF 15 Sqdn kia 9.11.18 CR France 1223
HOLT,C T Lt See SLACK,George William real name
HOLTHOUSE,Arthur Reginald 2Lt RAF 42 Sqdn 10.4.18 MR 20
HOMAN,Henry Biorn 2Lt RAF 66 Sqdn kia 4.4.18 CR Italy 11
HOMERSHAM,Ronald 2Lt 4EYorksR att RAF 4 Sqdn kia 30.4.18 CR France 134
HOMEWOOD,C 2Lt RAF 8.7.18 CR Kent 184
HOOD,John Lt 8A&SH & RAF 57 Sqdn kia 18.8.17 CR Belgium 140
HOOK,Geoffrey Lt RAF Sch of Aerial Gnry 4.10.18 CR Canada 152
HOOPER,Ernest Andrew 2Lt RAF 27 Sqdn 30.10.18 CR France 646
HOPCRAFT,Peter Lt RAF 97 Sqdn 28.10.18 CR France 1678
HOPGOOD,Edward William Frank Lt 87CanInf att RAF 188 Light Trng Sqdn 14.10.18 CR Kent 216
HOPKINS,F Lt RAF 108 Sqdn 1.10.18 CR Belgium 140
HOPKINS,H L Lt RAF 185 Sqdn 11.5.18 CR Essex 45
HOPKINSON,Bertram.CMG. Col RAF 26.8.18 CR Cambs 3
HOPPERTON,Harry Robert Capt RAF Coastal Airship XXV drd 1.8.18 MR 40
HOPTON,Herbert William 2Lt RAF 205 Sqdn 12.8.18 CR France 806
HORRIDGE,John Leslie Capt RAF 91 Sqdn 21.11.18 CR Lancs 322
HORSLEY,O.MC. Capt GordH att RAF 19.8.18 CR Hamps 179
HORTON,G D Capt RAF 98 Sqdn 31.5.18 CR Belgium 167
HORTON,Robert Edmund Lt(Obs) RAF att RNAS (Cherbourg) kldacc 13.8.18 CR France 1848
HOSKING,Fernly John Capt RAF Corp Repair Depot 3.12.18 CR Greece 10
HOSTETTER,T R Lt RAF 3 Sqdn 27.9.18 CR France 1467
HOUGHTON,Frank Magens Caulfeild Lt RAF 6.5.18 CR Shrop 11
HOUSTON,C T 2Lt RAF 103 Sqdn 22.7.18 CR France 924
HOUSTON,W D 2Lt RAF 16 Sqdn 27.8.18 CR France 95
HOWARD,Andrew Capt RAF Ex RNVR AssPaymrLt HMS Carribean 28.10.19 CR Lancs 8
HOWARD,George Edwy Caldwell Lt RAF 204 Sqdn 26.9.18 CR Belgium 371
HOWARD,George Stanley 2Lt RAF 21.5.18 CR Yorks 354
HOWARD,Guy Robert.DSO. Maj RAF &EssR 18 Sqdn 23.10.18 CR France 113
HOWARD,James William 2Lt RAF 99 Sqdn 26.9.18 CR France 1678
HOWARD,Murray Leo Lt RAF 64 Sqdn& CanLocalForce 25.7.18 CR France 10
HOWARTH,Norman Capt RAF & 3RLancsR 23 Sqdn 6.9.18 MR 20
HOWDEN,William Albert 2Lt RAF 29 Sqdn kld 9.11.18 CR Belgium 348
HOWE,Thomas Sydney Curzon.MC. 2Lt RAF &ConnR 54 Sqdn 17.4.18 MR 20
HOWELL,Evan Idres Lt NhantsR att RAF 72 Trng Sqdn 21.4.18 CR Wales 135
HOWELL-JONES,Athol Cuthbert 2Lt(Obs) RAF 206 Sqdn 19.5.18 MR 20
HOWELLS,Evan Llewellyn 2Lt RAF 23 Sqdn 23.10.18 CR France 1477
HOWETT,W F 2Lt RAF 4 Fighting Sch 17.12.18 CR Notts 81
HOWSON,Charles James Lt RAF 95 Sqdn 5.7.18 CR Lancs 2
HOYLAND,L B 2Lt RAF 25.11.18 CR Yorks 543
HUBY,O M 2Lt 5RWarR att RAF kld 23.10.18 CR Yorks 1
HUBBARD,Hugh Belmont 2Lt RAF 67 Wing 30.8.18 MR 37
HUCKS,Bentfield Charles Capt RAF Aircraft Manf Coy 7.11.18 CR London 14

94

HUDSON,F D 2Lt   RAF   ded PoW   6.4.18
HUDSON,Frederick Derek   Lt   RAF   43 Sqdn   dow   27.4.18   CR Germany 3
HUDSON,Frederick James David   2Lt   RAF   88 Sqdn   21.5.18 MR 20
HUDSON,Harold Edgar   2Lt   RAF   80 Sqdn   8.8.18 CR France 526
HUGHES,Harold   Lt   RAF & Gen List   7 Sqdn   11.4.18 CR Belgium 18
HUGHES,John FltCdt RAF   1 Sqdn kld   25.11.18 CR Wales 454
HUGHES,John Meirion   Lt   RAF & 4LancsR   103 Sqdn   16.6.18 MR 20
HUGHES,W Lt   RAF   Artly Obs Sch   19.11.18 CR Egypt 9
HUGHES,William Barton   Lt   RAF   5 Grp (Dunkirk)   dedacc   17.5.18   CR Kent 7
HULL,E P J   2Lt   RAF   2.7.18 CR London 10
HUMBERSTONE,J   2Lt   RAF   Aerial Fighting Sch   18.6.18 CR Egypt 9
HUMBLE-CROFTS,A M   Capt   RAF   5 Grp HQ   19.11.18 CR Sussex 225
HUMMERSTONE,L G   Lt   5LondR att RAF   12 Sqdn   21.8.18 CR France 103
HUMPHREY,J A   2Lt   RAF   28 TDS   16.1.19 CR Oxford 23
HUMPHREY,Thomas Albert 2Lt(Obs)   RAF &8RWSurrR   205 Sqdn   3.5.18 CR France 425
HUMPHREYS,Cecil James Gaston   2Lt   RAF   42 Wing   dedacc   15.7.18   CR Canada 1303
HUNT,Charles Basil Lt   RAF   4 Sqdn kia   25.4.18 CR France 28
HUNT,Cyril Frank   Lt   RAF   97 Sqn(India)   kld   23.4.19 CR Surrey 152
HUNT,David Reginald Lt   RAF   1 Repair Park   kia   18.8.18 CR France 65
HUNT,George Ede   2Lt   YLI att RAF   kld   21.7.18 CR Yorks 172
HUNT,H H   2Lt   RAF   1 Sqdn   26.10.18 CR France 446
HUNT,William Victor Lt   MGC att RAF   82 Sqdn   dow   17.10.18 CR Belgium 20
HUNTER,Alfred James   Lt   17MddxR att RAF   101 Sqdn   kia   7.8.18 CR France 29
HUNTER,Douglas Young·   Lt   RAF   209 Sqdn   7.7.18 MR 20
HUNTER,G T F   Lt   RAF   23.2.21 CR Yorks 428
HUNTER,Henry Thomas   Lt   RAF   3 Aircraft Depot   19.10.18 CR France 1787
HUNTER,William Alexander 2Lt   RAF   TDS   3.7.18 CR Scot 811
HURLEY,Stanley George   Lt   RAF   1.3.19 CR Surrey 152
HURNDALL,Charles Douglas 2Lt   RAF   kld   30.12.18 CR Essex 86
HUSSELBY,Thomas Law   Cdt   RAF   30.10.18 CR Warwick 50
HUTCHESON,Charles Edward   Lt   RAF   27 Sqdn   30.10.18 CR France 646
HUTCHESON,Gordon James Lt   RAF   53 Sqdn   dow   27.5.18 CR FRance 102
HUTCHINSON,Harold   F/O   RAF   6 Sqdn   2.8.20 CR Iraq 8
HUTCHINSON,H   2Lt   RAF   149 Sqdn   27.3.19 CR Germany 1
HUTTON,William Douglas Campbell Lt   RAF   110 Sqdn   dedacc   27.3.19   CR Germany 1
HUYCKE,Frederick Arthur   2Lt   RAF   Ex CanArtly   drd   3.9.18 MR 40
HYDE,Alfred Neal   2Lt   RAF   205 Sqdn   21.9.18 MR 20
HYDE-THOMSON,Douglas Hyde   LtCol   RAF   Directorate of Air Organisation   21.5.18   CR Kent 7

I

IBISON,Karl George   2Lt   RAF   213 Sqdn   kia   4.10.18 CR Belgium 148
IDDON,S R   FltCdt RAF   9 Trng Depot   6.9.18 CR Lancs 143
ILIFF,George   2Lt   RAF   213 Sqdn   25.9.18 MR 20
ILLINGWORTH,Frederick William.MIDx2.Lt   RAF   23 Sqn Ex ScotRif   ded   6.2.19 CR Scot 247
ILLINGWORTH,M O Capt   RAF   15.7.20 CR Lancs 96
INCHES,Robert Kirk.DFC.   Lt   RAF   100 Sqdn Ex RE   25.8.18 CR France 1678
INGRAM,Raymond Thompson   2Lt   RAF   98 Sqdn   3.9.18 MR 20
IPSWICH,William Henry Alfred Fitzroy Lt   RAF & 5CldGds   23.4.18 CR Suffolk 173
IRA-SMITH,Herbert William Edwin   Capt   1/5BedsR & RAF   ded   7.12.20 CR Asia 82
IRELAND,Edward   2Lt   RAF   Airship Trng Wing   kld   31.7.19 CR Lancs 14
IRVINE,Von Reusseler Van Tassel   Lt   RAF   43 Sqdn   19.7.18 MR 20
IRVING,George Budd.DFC.   Capt   RAF   19 Sqdn   11.8.18 MR 20
IRWIN,R V   Lt   RAF   2.10.18 CR Germany 1
ISHERWOOD,H   2Lt   RAF & LNLancsR   23.10.18 CR Lancs 257
ISAAC,Wallace Alexander   2Lt   RAF   4 Sqdn   7.8.18 CR France 134

J

JACKMAN,John Robinson   Lt   RAF & 6WRidR   17.6.18   CR France 518
JACKMAN,William J Cadet   RAF   174205   ded   31.10.18 CR Canada 1607
JACKS,Robert Le Roy 2Lt   RAF   dedacc   11.9.18   CR USA 12
JACKSON,C F S   2Lt   RAF   207 TDS   30.4.18 CR Essex 84
JACKSON,Cyril Robert Howard   Lt   RAF   139 Sqdn   kia   16.6.18CR Italy 8 & 72
JACKSON,Cecil Thomas   Lt   1/12LNLancsR att RAF   kia   31.8.18CR Egypt 1
JACKSON,Frederick John   2Lt   RAF &1/3LondR   14.10.18 CR Belgium157
JACKSON,Francis Xavier   Lt   RAF   108 Sqdn   kld   21.9.18CR Belgium 140
JACKSON,Hugh Arthur Bruce2Lt   RAF   104 Sqdn   25.6.18 CR France 1678
JACKSON,W E   2Lt   RAF   104 Sqdn   15.9.18 CR France 1678
JACKSON,Walter   Cdt   RAF 142829 11 Aircraft Park   19.12.18 CR France 1359
JACKSON,William Vernon   2Lt   RAF   206 Sqdn   30.10.18 CR Fraqnce 276
JACKSON-BARSTOW,John Eric   Capt   RAF & NSomYeo   27.1.19 CR Somerset 197
JACOB,C G   Lt   RAF   Sch of Navgn & Bombg   1.4.18   CR Hamps 90
JACOB,John Victor Reed   Lt   RAF   16.3.19 CR France 34
JACOBI,Edward William Sydney   Lt   RAF   1 Marine Obs Sch   kld   24.5.19CR Suffolk 1
JAMES,Bert   Capt   RAF   3 Sqdn dedacc 7.5.18 CR Norfolk 96
JAMES L E   Cdt   RAF   27.11.18 CR Warwick 134
JAMES,Reginald Arthur   Capt   RAF &5MddxR   54 Sqdn   16.6.18 MR 20
JAMES,Wallace Henry   Cadet RAF   171261   ded   22.9.20   CR Canada 1667
JAMES,William Leslie   FltCdt RAF   205 TDS   dedacc   29.10.18 CR Numb 75
JAMESON,James Bruce   Lt   RAF   48 Sqdn   24.8.18 CR France 1170
JAMESON,Wilfred Chalmers Capt   RAF   ded PoW 15.9.18   MR 38
JANES,Charles William   2Lt   RAF   2 AG &HG   11.4.18 CR London 10
JAQUES,Harry Moffat 2Lt   RAF   43 Sqdn   kld   30.7.18CR France 1429
JAQUES,John Barclay.MC.AFC.   F/O   DLI att RAF   216 Sqdn   kld   1.4.20 CR EAfrica 116
JAQUES,T H 2Lt   RAF   12 Sqdn   30.9.18 CR France 1483
JARDINE,Douglas Graeme Burness.MC. Capt   RAF &1/2HLI   kia   5.8.18   CR Europe 74
JARVIS,E McD   Lt   RAF   32 Sqdn   6.6.18 CR France 1233
JASSBY,Harry Walter 2Lt   RAF   6.11.18CR Essex 46
JEFCOATE,Frank.MBE.MID Capt   RAF   111 Sqdn   kld   14.2.19CR Palestine 9
JEFFERSON,Elgie Blyth Barwise   Capt   1LpoolR att RAF   15.5.19 CR France 1359
JEFFERY,Harold Greensmith Lt   RAF & Gen List   58 Sqdn   kld   4.7.18 CR France 223
JEMMESON,George Edwin   2Lt   RAF   221 Sqdn   kldacc   15.5.19   CR Asia 81
JENKIN,W W L   2Lt   RAF   99 Sqdn   25.6.18 CR France 1678
JENKINS,A E 2Lt   RAF   7 Sqdn   28.9.18 CR Belgium 18
JENKINS,Basil Oliver.CBE.   LtCol RAF   7.2.19 CR Germany 1
JENKINS,Beavon Pendleton   2Lt   RAF   103 Sqdn   20.10.18 CR Germany 1
JENKINS,John Alexander   FltCdt RAF   114 Sqdn   kld   22.9.18CR Scot 229
JENKINS,Leoline.DSO.MC&Bar.   LtCol RAF   SE HQ ded   20.11.18 CR Mddx 44
JENNER,P H 2Lt   RAF   66 Sqdn   14.12.18 CR Italy 11
JENNINGS,Clarence John   Cadet RAF 152677 43 Wing9 (Texas,USA)   dedacc 4.4.18 CR Canada 1668
JENNINGS,Eric Kingsley Young   FltCdt RAF   48 TDS   18.8.18 CR Lincs 181
JENNINGS,Frederick Robert Lt   RAF   67 Wing   2.9.18 CR Italy 6
JENNINGS,R FltCdt RAF   24.7.18 CR Yorks 156
JEPPE,Ferdinand Alexander Lt   RAF   Armnt Sch   22.10.18 CR Mddx 83
JEWELL,H J Lt   RAF   MO Pilots Sch   17.7.21 CR Kent 27
JEWELL,J B Lt   RAF & Gen List   6.4.18 CR Mddx 34
JINMAN,Ewart William Fred Lt   RAF   18 Sqdn   14.8.18 MR 20
JOFFE,William.DSO. 2Lt   RAF   1 Sqn Ex 5YLI   1.10.18CR France 1760
JOHN,F E   Capt   RAF   204 Sqdn   26.2.19 CR London 12
JOHN,Wilbur Arnold Lt   SussYeo att RAF   1.8.18 CR Belgium 112
JOHNS,Reginald Leach   Lt   RAF   208 Sqdn   kia   11.6.18CR France 31
JOHNSON,Arthur Edward   F/Cadet   RAF   Ex Can AMC   drd   28.10.18 MR 40
JOHNSON,Benjamin 2Lt   RAF   104 Sqdn   29.10.18 CR France 1894

JOHNSON,Clarence Everard 2Lt RAF dedacc 22.5.18 CR Notts 81
JOHNSON,Cecil Marland 2Lt RAF &GenList2 Sqdn 6.6.18 CR France 12
JOHNSON,C S Lt RAF 206 Sqdn 13.8.18 CR France 285
JOHNSON,E H.DFC. Lt RAF 205 Sqdn 9.11.18CR Belgium 221
JOHNSON,John Hercules Lt RAF 43 Sqdn kia 9.6.18 CR France 1065
JOHNSON,R W 2Lt RAF 7 DS 2.11.18 CR London 10
JOHNSON,Roland Walker 2Lt RAF 210 Sqdn 1.10.18 MR 20
JOHNSON,T A Lt RAF 13 Sqdn 28.8.18 CR France 1489
JOHNSON,William John 2Lt RAF 211 Sqdn 13.10.18 CR Germany 3
JOHNSTON,James Mills 2Lt RAF kld 18.5.18CR Lincs 78
JOHNSTON,Noble J Cadet RAF 152681 dedacc 12.5.18 CR Canada 1206
JOHNSTON,Robin Louis Lt RAF 2 Sqdn kia 9.5.18 CR France 279
JOHNSTON,Samuel Beatty Cadet RAF 272708 18.10.18 CR Canada 1175
JOHNSTONE,John Ritchie Lt RAF 244 Sqdn lost at sea 14.8.18 MR 40
JONES A N C Cdt RAF 8 Cdt Wing 8.10.18CR Warwick 19
JONES A P 2Lt RAF 22.9.18 CR Wales 506
JONES,Arthur Saunders 2Lt RAF 108 Sqdn 27.9.18 CR Belgium 453
JONES,B H M Lt RAF 14.4.18 CR Suffolk 113
JONES,Basil R 2Lt RAF 4 Sqdn kia 28.9.18CR France 25
JONES,David Bracegirdle.DCM. 2Lt RAF 84 Sqdn dow 3.7.18 CR France 29
JONES,E B F/O RAF 208 Sqdn 14.4.21 CR Egypt 8
JONES,Eric Berkeley 2Lt RAF 5 TDS kld 11.11.18 CR Lincs 100
JONES,Ernest David Lt RAF 52 Sqdn 3.4.18 MR 20
JONES,Evon Davies Lt RAF 2 att 10 Sqdn kia 2.4.18 CR Belgium 11
JONES,Francis Joseph Lt RAF 45 Sqdn kia 1.6.18 CR Italy 11
JONES,George William RevCapt RAF 4.11.18CR Scot 240
JONES,Herbert Linley 2Lt RAF ded 23.10.18 CR London 18
JONES J J.MM. 2Lt RAF 46 Trng Sqdn 31.5.18 CR Lancs 1
JONES,Joseph Wesson 2Lt RAF 107 Sqdn 9.8.18 MR 20
JONES,Ludlow Norman Lt RAF 48 Sqdn 3.10.18CR Belgium 140 & MR 20
JONES,Leslie Seymour Ross 2Lt RAF &3DevR 65 Sqdn kia 6.10.18CR Belgium 371
JONES,Max Greville.MC. Lt 1NumbF att RAF 55 Sqdn 12.6.18 CR France 1678
JONES,Percy Griffith 2Lt RAF &RE 20 Sqdn kld 2.7.18 CR France 134
JONES,R Colville 2Lt RAF & 13RB kld 4.11.18
JONES,Thomas Alfred2Lt RAF 55 Sqdn 30.8.18 CR France 1660
JONES,Tom Bright Capt RAF &GenList kia 11.4.18CR France 95
JONES,Thomas Pargeter.MBE. 2Lt RAF 101 Sqdn 31.10.18 CR France 528
JONES,William Rice FltCdt RAF 6509 Ex L/Cpl HAC 13.9.18 CR Wales 240
JONSSON,Hallgrimur.MC. Lt RAF & BCR 12 Sqdn 3.9.18 MR 20
JORDAN,Charles Henry Lt RAF 39 Sqdn 31.7.18 CR Essex 172
JOWETT,T 2Lt RAF 29.5.18 CR Yorks 707
JOYCE,Cyril Gordon 2Lt RAF 78 Sqdn acckld 22.5.18 CR Essex 45
JOYCE,James Alfred Lt RAF Boys Sch of Tech Trng 20.12.20 CR Kent 46
JOYCE,Norman Roy Lt RAF &GenList23 Sqdn 1.4.18 MR 20
JUKES,Sydney Lt RAF TDS kld 27.11.18 CR Wilts 102
JUPP,Lawrence Borrie 2Lt RAF 34 Sqdn 26.7.18 CR Italy 11
JUNOR,Kenneth William MC Capt RAF & 11CanMGC 56 Sqdn 23.4.18 MR 20

K

KANE,Augustine George 2Lt 3SWBord att RAF kia 24.6.18CR Greece 6
KANN,Raymond Victor Lt RScotsF & RAF Cent Flying Sch 21.8.19 CR London 12
KAPLAN,Harry W Cadet RAF 153703 44 Wing dedacc 4.7.18 CR Canada 114
KAVANAGH,Charles Francis 2Lt RAF Air Ministry 28.2.19 CR London 12
KAYE,Arthur Edward Cadet BedsR att RAF kldacc 17.10.18 CR Oxford 69
KEARNEY,E M S 2Lt RAF 35 Sqdn kia 27.10.18 CR France 441
KEARNEY,Norman Charles Lt RAF 27.4.18 CR London 25

KEATING,T J Capt   RFA att RAF   63 Sqdn   14.6.18 CR Iraq 8
KEEN,Arthur William.MC.   Maj   RAF   40 Sqdn   2.9.18 CR France 34
KEEN,Stephen Whitworth.MC.   Lt   RAF   60 Sqdn   kia   21.8.18CR France 226
KEEPIN,W F 2Lt   RAF   139 Sqdn   kia   16.8.18CR Italy 8 & 72
KEEVIL,Cecil Horace Case   Capt   18WYorksR xffed to RFC or RAF   kld   13.6.17CR London 12
KELLER,Roderick Leopold.MC.   Capt   RWarR att RAF   15.8.18 CR Herts 10
KELLOUGH,William Roy   2Lt   RAF   88 Sqdn   kld   3.3.19 CR Belgium 330
KELLOW,W 2Lt   RAF   kia   17.9.18CR France 611
KELLY,Charles Leonard   Lt   RAF &LNLancsR   204 Sqdn   20.9.18 CR Belgium 452 & MR20
KELLY,Ernest Tilton SumpterLt   RAF   1 Sqdn   19.6.18 CR France 924
KELLY,John 2Lt   RAF   52 Sqdn   30.7.18 CR France 41
KELLY,M S Lt   RAF & ManitobaR   15.5.18 CR France 180
KELLY,Roy Hamilton 2Lt   RAF   4.1.20 CR Canada 506
KELLY,Thomas Paul Cdt   RAF 183505 Cdt Dist Depot   28.10.18 CR Surrey 1
KELLY,Thomas William   2Lt   RAF   211 Sqdn   29.9.18 CR France 1359
KELLY,William Joseph   Lt   RAF   26.9.18 CR Nhants 60
KELSEY,William James   2Lt   RAF   5 TDS kld   30.5.18CR Wales 135
KELTY,George William Albert   2Lt   RAF   11 Sqdn   kia   3.10.18CR France 84
KEMP,Frederick Henry   Lt   RAF   5 Grp HQ   12.11.18 CR London 7
KEMP,George Hubert 2Lt   DCLI att RAF 20 Sqdn   kia   1.6.18 CR France 134
KEMP,R P H 2Lt   RAF   25.9.18 CR Mddx 30
KEMP,S A   Lt   RAF   3 Sqn att1 Aerial Range   21.2.19 CR France 40
KENDALL,Frederick Denys 2Lt   RAF   67 Wing   30.8.188 CR Greece 7
KENDALL,George   2Lt   WYorksR att RAF   ded   15.10.18 CR Ches 56
KENNEDY,James Gilbert   Lt   RAF   65 Sqdn   4.4.18 MR 20
KENNEDY,William 2Lt   RAF   48 Sqdn   kldacc 12.3.19   CR Germany 1
KERR,D McC Capt   RAF   see McCONNELL KERR,D
KERR,R W   Lt   RAF   2 Flying Trng Sch   12.8.18 CR Yorks 127
KERRUISH,Evan Francis   2Lt   RAF   1 Torpedo Sqdn   13.7.18 CR Yorks 178
KESTERTON,Thomas Frederick   2Lt   RAF   204 TDS   kld   6.8.18 CR Kent 68
KETTLEWOOD,Arthur John FltCdt RAF   kld   20.11.18 CR Yorks 79
KEYMER,Basil Graham Homfray.DFC&Bar.Capt   RAF   kia   24.10.19 CR Asia 81
KIBBY,Herbert Cecil 2Lt(Pilot)   RAF   kld   27.10.18 CR Mddx 69
KIDD,E J C   2Lt   RAF &WYorksR   10.4.18 CR Yorks 474
KIDD,James Alexander   2Lt   RAF   Air Stn(Polegate) Ex RNAS   ded   31.10.18 CR Essex 1
KIDD,James Forrest Lt   12KRRC & RAF   20 Sqdn   kld   1.11.18CR France 937
KIDD,Vernon Monroe 2Lt   RAF   29 TDS   kld   30.8.18CR Hamps 31
KIDDLE,C H E   Cdt   RAF   20.11.18 CR Dorset 67
KIERAN,John F J   Lt   RAF   ded   18.12.20 CR Canada 254
KIME,Gilbert Henry Ernest.MM   2Lt   RAF   10 Sqdn   12.5.19 CR Essex 7
KING,Alexander John Gavin Lt   RAF   149 Sqdn   15.9.18 CR France 134
KING,Charles Capt   RAF   Constr Stn (Kingsnorth)   30.8.18 CR Kent 46
KING,Cecil Frederick.MC.DFC.   Capt   RAF   43 Sqdn   kldacc 24.1.19   CR Norfolk 58
KING,John Stephen   2Lt   RAF   13 Sqdn   kia   1.10.18CR France 240
KING,Kenneth Vivian Lt   RAF   52 Sqdn   kia   30.7.18CR France 41
KING,Lionel Richard Thacker.MID 2Lt   RAF   Ex RNAS   kld   3.5.18 CR Ches 62
KING,Stewart 2Lt   RAF   kld   26.9.18CR Belgium 178
KING,Vernon Lt   RM att RAF   kia   11.4.18CR France 95
KING,Wilfrid John   Lt   RAF   214 Sqdn   16.5.18 CR Belgium132
KING,William Hugh   Lt   RAF &EssR   7 Sqdn kld   11.4.18CR Belgium18
KINGHORN,W   2Lt   RAF   57 Sqdn   kia   5.11.18CR France 521
KINNEAR,John Lawson.DSO.MC.   Maj   RAF   1 Trng Sqdn   28.4.18 CR Hamps 31
KIRBY,Cecil Francis 2Lt   RAF   83 Sqdn   kld   6.9.18 CR France 1564
KIRB,E J C   Lt   RAF   8.8.19 CR Scot 131
KIRBY,J R   2Lt   RAF   acckld 16.12.18 CR Hamps 211
KIRKLAND,James TweeddaleLt   RAF   57 Sqdn   kia   20.7.18CR France 245
KIRTON,Ralph Imray.AFC.   2Lt   RAF &KOSB   kld   22.11.18 CR London 3
KIRWAN,L   2Lt   RAF &1SLancsR   30 Sqdn   20.8.18 CR Iraq 8
KIRWAN,Milo William   Cadet   RAF 152392   dedacc 8.4.18 CR USA 228
KISSEL,Gustav Hermann   Lt   US AviationSect attRAF 43 Sqdn   kia   12.4.18CR France 705

KITCHEN,J F R	Lt	RAF	& RNAS		21.6.18 CR Sussex 191

KITCHEN,J F R   Lt   RAF   & RNAS   21.6.18 CR Sussex 191
KITE,A W   2Lt   RAF   61 TDS   12.5.18 CR Hamps 176
KNIGHT,C R W   Lt   RAF   21.6.19 CR Europe 179 & MR 70
KNIGHT,George Bertram   Lt   RAF   54 Sqdn   dow   7.4.18 CR France 145
KNIGHT,Gerald Fetherston   Lt   RAF &DevR   ded   30.10.19
KNIGHT,James Burghleigh Caxton   2Lt   RAF &GenList   15.4.18 CR Egypt 9
KNIGHT,William Harry Duncan   2Lt   RAF   65 Sqdn   2.5.18 CR France 526
KNOLL,Wilhelm Jacobus   2Lt   RAF   Sch of Fighting   20.5.18 CR Yorks 183
KNOTT,E M.AFC.   Capt   RAF   1 Comm Sqdn   3.5.19 CR Warwick 135
KNOWLES,A R   2Lt   RAF   2.4.18 CR France 630
KNOWLES,Harry   Lt   RAF   48 Sqdn   dow   11.8.18   CR France 71
KNOWLES,W 2Lt   RAF   9 Sqdn   4.7.18 CR France 1170
KNOX,William   2Lt   RAF   30 TDS   31.10.18 CR Durham 19
KNYASTON,John Valentine Lt   RAF   14 TDS   15.7.19 CR Wilts 3
KORSLUND,Milo Franklin   Lt   RAF   73 Sqdn   12.4.18 MR 20
KRETMAR,William Forrest King   Lt   RAF   141 Sqdn   kld   7.5.19 CR Eire 14

L

LACEY,William George   Lt   RAF &RASC 27 Sqdn   4.11.18 CR France 1154
LACKEY,Herbert David   FltLt   RAF   70 Sqn Ex RNAS   7.10.18CR Belgium 140
LAING,Thomas Henry 2Lt   RAF   55 Sqdn   kia   30.8.18CR France 1644
LAIRD,Archibald Burns   Cadet RAF 153073   24.6.18 CR Canada 1113
LAKE,Harold Caldecott   2Lt   RAF   209 TDS   kld   5.4.18 CR London 25
LAMB,Edward Woollard Penistone   2Lt   RAF &GenList11 Sqdn   kia   24.4.18CR France 62
LAMB,Harold Alfred Lt   1ResCavR att RAF   98 Sqdn   kia   7.4.18 CR France 31
LAMB,Herbert Joseph 2Lt   RAF   9.10.18CR Oxford 23
LAMBURN,Gerald Arthur   Lt   RAF   1 Fighting Sch kld   30.9.18CR Scot 520
LANCE,William George   Lt   RAF   19 Sqdn   13.8.18 CR France 71
LANE,A G H Lt   RAF   218 Sqdn   15.5.18 CR France 1359
LANE,Reginald William   2Lt   1/2HampsR & RAF   kia   9.11.18CR France 276
LANGDON,John Henry.MC. Lt   2GloucR att RAF   kld   5.6.18 CR Egypt 8
LANGLEY,John Basil Robert Lt   RAF   15.5.18 CR Hamps 4
LANGSDON,Walter Thomas   FltCdt RAF 60158   46 TDS   11.3.19 CR Kent 296
LANIGAN,William Leonard   2Lt   RAF   202 TDS   12.7.18 CR Lincs 78
LANKIN,C G Lt   RAF   20 Sqdn   25.4.18 CR France 134
LARDNER,R 2Lt   RAF   211 Sqn 65 Wing   26.5.18 CR France 1359
LARKIN,J P.DSO.DCM.   Maj   7KOSB & RAF   4.11.19CR Durham 28
LASHFORD,Vincent Clarke   2Lt   RAF   kld   30.5.18CR Wales 17
LASKER,Robert Sydney   2Lt   RAF   25 Sqdn   20.5.18 CR France 941
LATHAM,J H V   2Lt   RAF   kld   20.4.18CR Lancs 108
LATIMER,Alfred.MM.   Lt   RAF & RFA   4.10.18CR Italy 2
LATTO,Edward Campbell   Lt   RAF   11.8.18 CR Scot 14
LAUGHTON,Henry Philip Walter   Lt   RAF   kld   27.5.18CR Warwick 55
LAVARACK,Philip James Vaughan.MC&Bar.   Maj   RAF   120 Sqdn   14.5.18 CR Numb 4
LAVINGTON,L J   Lt   RAF   12 Sqdn   22.8.18 CR France 745
LAW,John   Lt   RAF   39 Trng Sqdn   11.6.18 CR Lancs 217
LAWRENCE,Percy   2Lt   RAF   8 Sqdn   9.8.18 CR France 526
LAWRENCE,P W B   Capt   RAF   149 Sqdn   27.2.19 CR Germany 1
LAWRIE,Ian Gray   Cadet RAF 154579   ded   7.4.18 CR Canada 1695
LAWSON,Harold.MBE.   Capt   RAF   HQ NW Area ded   15.2.19   CR Lincs 181
LAZENBY,James Arthur Leonard   FltCdt RAF   18.10.18 CR Yorks 410
LEACH,F   Lt   RAF &1/8ManchR   16.6.18 MR 65
LEAF,William Henry Lt   RAF   92 Sqdn   30.10.18 CR France 441
LEAKE,Eric Gilbert.MC.   Capt   7ManchR att RAF   59 Sqdn   31.7.18 CR France 84
LEARN,Gerald Alfred Lt   RAF   210 Sqdn   kld   24.6.18MR 20
Le BLANC,Edgar P   Cadet RAF 153342   dedacc 29.4.18   CR Canada 1055
LECKENBY,J G   2Lt   RAF   4 Sqdn   9.11.18CR Belgium 367

LECKIE,George Arthur   Lt   RAF   49 Sqdn   9.5.18 MR 20
LEE,Charles Percy   2Lt   RAF & 3LondR   107 Sqdn   kld   22.10.18 CR France 788
LEE,Edward Arthur Richard   2Lt   RAF   98 Sqdn   30.10.18 MR 20
LEE,Fred   FltCdt RAF 53058   30.11.18 CR Yorks 408
LEE,J A   2Lt   RAF   55 Sqdn   25.8.18 CR France 1678
LEE,John Owen   Cdt   RAF 181191   2 Sch of Mil Aeros   ded   1.11.18 CR Oxford 69
LEE,John Varley   2Lt   RAF   27 Sqdn   14.8.18 CR France 57
LEE,William   Lt   RAF &5RIrFus   kldacc 19.8.18   CR Egypt 15
LEEB,Mercer Eric   Capt   LNLancsR & RAF   10.7.19 CR Sussex 144
LEED,David   2Lt   RAF &1/2HampsR   209 Sqdn Ex 10SfthH kld   12.8.18 MR 20
LEEMING,Louis   2Lt   RAF   73 Wing   kld   5.12.18 CR Lancs 226
LEFEBVRE,René Hector   2Lt   RAF   66 Sqdn   13.4.18 CR Italy 11
Le FEUVRE,William Ernest   Lt   RAF   27 Trng Sqdn   9.5.18 CR Herts 87
LEFFLER,Leonard John Wilfred   Cadet RAF 182290 8Cdt Wing Ex SAInf   ded   25.9.18   CR Sussex 111
LEGGE,William   Lt   RAF   55 Sqdn   kld   13.6.18 CR Germany 1
LEIGH,Reginald Lea   Lt   RAF   3 Sqdn   18.6.18 MR 20
LEIGHTON,George Roy   Lt   RAF   66 Sqdn   mbk   7.10.18 CR Italy 8
LEITH,Sydney Angus   Lt   RAF   38 Sqdn   kld   19.4.18 CR Warwick 50
LE LIEVRE,Frank Lyndon   2Lt   RAF   85 Sqdn   4.10.18 MR 20
LE LIEVRE,Roger Horace   Lt   RAF   kld   31.8.18 CR Mddx 66
Le MESURIER,Thomas Frederick.DSO&2Bars.   Capt   RAF   211 Sqn 65 Wing   kia   26.5.18 CR France 1359
Le MOINE,Claude Melvin   2Lt   RAF   20.8.19 CR Europe 179 & MR70
LENIHEN,John Harold   2Lt   RAF   14 TDS   14.11.18 CR London 9
LEONARD,Thomas Laurence Washington 2Lt   RAF   101 Sqdn   kia   30.10.18 CR France 332
LESLIE,George Buchanan   Lt   RAF   12 Sqdn   28.10.18 CR France 40
LETHBRIDGE,Thomas James 2Lt   RAF   34 Sqdn   dedacc 25.9.18   CR Italy 11
LETTS,John Herbert Towne.MC.   Capt   RAF &LincsR 64 Sqdn   kldacc 11.10.18 CR France 103
LEVICK,Cyril 2Lt   RAF   4 Sqdn   16.6.18 MR 20
LEVINE,Myer Joseph 2Lt   RAF   53 Trng Sqdn kld   8.5.18 CR Norfolk 209
LEVY,A G   2Lt   RAF   42 Trng Sqdn   25.4.18 CR Mddx 40
LEVY,J M D A   See D'ARCY-LEVY
LEWIN,P   2Lt   RAF   66 Sqdn   9.9.19 CR Dorset 93
LEWIS,Alan Vivian   Lt   RAF   9.9.18 CR Heref/Worc 112
LEWIS,J H E Cdt   RAF 183163 8Cdt Wing   1.10.18 CR Glouc 86
LEWIS,Jack Arthur   2Lt   RAF   210 Sqdn   kld   16.9.18 MR 20
LEWIS,John Aicken Carleton 2Lt   RAF   kld   4.6.18 CR Kent 83
LEWIS,Meredith B   Lt   RAF   54 Sqdn   kia   15.7.18 CR France 1753
LEWIS,Richard Francis   Lt   RAF   73 Sqdn   25.7.18 MR 20
LIDDELL,John Gillespie   2Lt   RAF   20.4.18 CR Scot 212
LIDDELL,Matthew Henry Goldie   2Lt   RAF &7ScotRif   54 Sqdn   kld   17.4.18 MR 20
LIGHTBODY.John Douglas   2Lt   RAF   204 Sqdn   4.11.18 CR Belgium 364
LIMERICK,Victor   Lt   RFA & RAF   5 Sqdn kld   20.8.19 CR Germany 1
LIND,J V   2Lt   RAF   62 Sqdn   kld   18.9.18 CR France 788
LINDLEY,Bryant Lutellus.MC.   Lt   RAF   25 Sqdn   kld   29.6.18 CR Belgium 132
LINDNER,Philip Edward   Lt   RAF   66 Wing   21.7.18 CR Greece 7 & MR 37,LINDER
LINDSAY,R   FltCdt RAF 316027   3 TRDS   6.1.19 CR Hamps 90
LINDSAY,Robert Edmond   Lt   RAF   6.12.18 CR Scot 118
LING,William Frederick Edward   FltCdt RAF 54051   kld   14.6.18 CR Herts 84
LINK,Frederick Leslie Cuff   Lt   RAF   74 Sqdn   7.6.18 CR France 180
LINKLETTER,Silas Montague   2Lt   RAF   2 Sqdn   27.8.19 CR Lancs 383
LIPSETT,George Arthur   Lt   RAF   91 Sqdn   kld   27.7.18 CR Sussex 5
LISTER,Ronald   2Lt   RAF   8 Sqdn   27.10.18 MR 20
LITCHFIELD,Richard William   Cadet RAF 152897 Sch of Aerial Gnry   dedacc 2.5.18 CR Canada 183
LITTLE,D L   2Lt   RAF   21.6.18 CR Warwick 97
LITTLE,I C   FltLt RAF   Airship Base Hampden R38   kldacc 24.8.21   CR Yorks 2
LITTLE,Robert Alexander.DSO&Bar.DSC&Bar.FltCmdr RAF   203 Sqdn Ex RNAS   kia   27.5.18 CR France 1525
LITTLE,R K   2Lt   RAF   Marine Obs Sch   18.11.18 CR Kent 68
LLOYD,A E   Lt   RAF   14.12.18 CR Devon 128
LLOYD,Colin Corden   Lt   RAF   54 Sqdn   kld   17.4.18 MR 20
LLOYD,E   FltCdt RAF   2 Sqdn drd   28.10.18 MR 40

100

LLOYD,F   2Lt   RAF   1.2.19 CR Staffs 60
LLOYD,Lionel Bertie Eld   Lt   RAF & CMR   12.10.18 CR Dorset 109
LLOYD,Robert Aubrey Hastings   2Lt   RAF   85 Sqdn   14.10.18 CR France 512
LOCHEED,Ralph William   2Lt   RAF   12 Sqdn   28.5.18 CR France 103
LOCKE,E P   2Lt   RAF   48 Sqdn   19.8.18 CR France 586
LOCKWOOD,Frederick G   Cadet   RAF 172260   ded   29.10.18 CR Canada 115
LODER-SYMONDS,William Crawshay   Capt   RAF &WiltsR   kld   30.5.18CR Berks 56
LOFTS,Wilfred   2Lt   RAF   42 Sqdn   doi   9.8.18 CR France 31
LOGAN,Thomas Edgar   Lt   RAF   dedacc 22.11.18 CR Canada 818
LOMAX,Leslie John 2Lt   RAF   113 Sqdn   accdrd 24.6.18   CR Palestine 9
LORD,Ernest Owen   Lt   RAF   7 Sqdn   18.9.18 CR Belgium 18
LORD,Lawrence McLenn   2Lt   RAF   Cent Flying Sch   kld   15.9.18CR Wilts 116
LOTT,C W   Lt   RAF   20.7.18 CR Europe 1
LOUPINSKY,JLt   RAF   38 Trng Sqdn   26.7.19 CR Yorks 500
LOVE,F B   2Lt   RAF   39 Trng Sqdn   8.6.18 CR Essex 27
LOVELL,Cyril Thomas   2Lt   MGC & RAF   kia   15.6.18CR France 27
LOWCOCK,Reginald John.DSO.MC..Maj   RAF &N&DR Artly Co-op Sqdn   acckld   22.7.18   CR Wilts 4
LOWE,H A   2Lt   RAF   10 TDS   4.11.18CR Norfolk 259
LOWENSTEIN,Jack Charles Lt   RAF   1 Aircraft Supply Depot   dedacc 9.5.18 CR France 102
LOWRIE,Victor William Valette   Lt   RAF   27.4.18 CR Wales 17
LOXLEY,Reginald Victor Byron   Capt   RAF   ded   18.10.18 CR France 455
LUCAS,Humphrey William Herbert.MC. Lt   RAF   61 Sqdn   kld   2.10.18 CR Surrey 6
LUCAS,J   Cdt   RAF 180864 8 Cdt Wing   1.10.18CR Kent 180
LUCAS,T H   Lt   RAF & HampsR   15.5.18 CR Egypt 9
LUGARD,Edward March   Capt   RLancR att RAF   kld   30.7.18CR London 8
LUKER,Frank Percy 2Lt   1WorcR & RAF   1.11.18CR Bucks 39
LUPTON,Charles Roger.DSC. Capt   RAF   205 Sqdn   kld   9.5.18 CR France 71
LUSH,Eric Raven   PltOff   RAF   2 Fly Trng Sch kld   19.8.21CR Mddx 16
LUTYENS,L F D   Lt   RAF   RAE (Farnborough)   8.5.18 CR Surrey 143
LYGO,F A   Lt   RAF   50 Trng Sqdn   25.8.18 CR Yorks 542
LYNE,E.MBE.Lt   RAF   97 Sqdn   26.8.18 CR France 1678
LYON,Lloyd Diets St A.MM. 2Lt   RAF   54 Sqdn   drd   28.2.19   MR 40
LYSTER-SMYTHE,Richard Litton.MID   Capt   RAF   Ex 3GordH   drd   19.6.19   CR Palestine 9

M

MACALLISTER,George Wesley   2Lt   RAF   2 TDS   12.8.18 CR Scot 235
MACARTNEY,David Allen   Lt   RAF   98 Sqdn   17.6.18 CR France 518
MACASKILL,G H   2Lt   RAF   Sch of Aeronautics   4.7.18 CR Hamps 202
MACBETH,Robert Edward Andrew   Lt   RAF   kld   19.8.18CR Warwick 70
MACCARTNEY-FILGATE,Desmond Maurice 2Lt   RAF   42 Trng Sqdn acckld   31.5.18   CR Kent 197
MacDONALD,A W   2Lt   RAF   1 TDS   11.11.18 CR Lincs 100
MACDONALD,Charles Davie 2Lt   RAF   211 Sqdn   4.11.18 MR 20
MacDONALD,Donald J   Cadet   RAF 272600   ded   10.10.18 CR Canada 469
MacDONALD,Guyon KennethCapt   RAF & 3N&DR   ded   21.11.19
MACDONALD,George Oxley 2Lt   RAF   1 Sch of Aeronautics Ex 63 CanInf   1.5.18 CR Berks 86
MacDONALD,J A   2Lt   RAF   13.3.19 CR Canada 1091A
MacDONALD James Burgess 2Lt   RAF   6 Sqdn   30.8.18 CR France 427
MacDONALD,Kenneth   Lt   RAF &5NFus 21 Sqdn   16.8.18 MR 20
MACDONALD,R O C Capt   RAF   53 TDS(Dover)   10.8.18 CR kent 7
MacDONELL,Edward C   Lt   RAF   ded   31.7.21   CR Canada 254
MacDOUGALL,Baldwin Childerboss 2Lt   RAF   141 Sqdn   22.9.18 CR Kent 96
MacDOUGALL,Dugald.DFC. Capt   RAF   25.8.19 CR Europe 179 & MR 70
MACFARLAND,Foster Murray   Lt   RAF & Sp List 18 Sqdn   3.9.18 MR 20
MACFARLANE,Peter Lt   RAF   32 Sqdn   10.8.18 MR 20
MacFARLANE,William Smith.MC.   Lt   5RScots att RAF   kld   20.6.18CR Scot 237
MACHIN,J F 2Lt   RAF   123 Sqdn   29.5.18 CR Staffs 82
MACILROY,T S   FltCdt RAF   10.7.18 CR Scot 752

MACKAY,D D A   Lt   RAF   70 Sqdn   14.10.18 CR Belgium 16
MACKAY,Duncan Ronald Gordon.DFC.MID.Capt   RAF   55 Sqdn   dow PoW 11.11.18 CR France 1649
MacKAY,John Wood   FltCdt· RAF 110338 39 Sqdn   kld   13.6.18 CR Scot 239
MACKAY,M W H   Lt   RAF   24.11.18 CR Scot 790
MACKENZIE,A D   2Lt   RAF   104 Sqdn   15.9.18 CR France 1667
MacKENZIE,Donald Alvin MM   Lt   CanFA att RAF   10 Sqdn   kia   28.10.18 CR Belgium 159
MACKENZIE,D E   2Lt   RAF   4.8.18 CR Bucks 64
MacKENZIE,Ewen Cameron Lt   RAF   9.11.18 CR Scot 752
MACKENZIE,George Osborne   Lt   RAF   56 Sqdn   27.9.18 MR 20
MACKIE,James Matthew DCM   Lt   RAF & 27CanadianInf 25 Sqdn   16.7.18 MR 20
MACKLIN,Charles Pursell   Lt   RAF   3 Sqdn   30.5.18 MR 20
MacLAREN,John Augustine   Cdt   RAF 183101 1 Sch of Aeros ded   29.10.18 CR Suffolk 176
MACLEAN,Alexander Murchison   Capt   RAF &ScotH 10 Sqdn   12.4.18 MR 20
MacLEAN,A P Lt   RAF &4RScots   17.9.18 CR Egypt 15
MacLEAN,Roderick Sutherland Gunn Lt   RAF   29 Sqdn   27.10.18 CR Belgium 435
MacLEOD,Malcolm MacKay   Capt   RAF   1 TDS   24.7.18 CR Lincs 100
MacNAIR,Ian   Lt   RAF   54 Sqdn   12.4.18 MR 20
MACNAMARA,Arthur William.DFC.Lt   RAF   12 Sqdn   kia   3.9.18 CR France 438
MacNAUGHTON,A P F   Cadet   RAF 272728   ded   16.10.18 CR Canada 256
MacPHERSON,C S   Lt   RCanR att RAF   18.9.18 CR Cambs 16
MACQUEEN,A J   F/O   RAF   12 Sqdn   5.7.20 CR Germany 1
MacRAE,John Nigel   Capt   RAF &GenList 83 Sqdn   kld   11.4.17 CR France 88
MacTAVISH,I A B   2Lt   RAF   218 Sqdn   15.5.18 CR France 1359
MacVICKER,John Everard Churchill Lt   RAF & Gen List   22.7.18 CR France 429
MADEN,Frederick   Capt   RAF   13 Trng Sqdn kld   9.7.18 CR Warwick 3
MADGE,William Thomas   2Lt   RAF   55 Sqdn   kia   16.8.18 CR Germany 3
MAGOR,Gerald Atkinson   Capt   RAF   201 Sqdn   22.4.18 MR 20
MAGOR,Norman Ansley.DSC.   Capt   RAF   kld   25.4.18 MR 40
MAHONEY,Brian Gerald   2Lt   RMunstF att RAF   189(N) Trng Sqdn   3.9.18 CR London 4
MAISEY,Harold Charels   2Lt   RAF   3 Sqdn   29.10.18 MR 20
MAITLAND,Edward Maitland.CMG.DSO.AFC.AirComdre   RAF   Airship base R 38   kldacc   24.8.21   CR Yorks 2
MAKEPEACE,Reginald Milburn.MC.Lt   RAF   1 Sch of Aerial Fighting   kld   28.5.18 CR Lancs 2
MAKER,William Ferley   2Lt   RAF   kld   16.8.18 CR Cornwall 17
MALCOLM,Alan Alexander   Lt   RAF &17Lancers   98 Sqdn   17.5.18 MR 20
MALCOLM,Allan Gilbert   2Lt   RAF   52 Sqdn   kld   2.10.18 CR France 421
MALCOLM,O L   Lt   RAF   104 Sqdn   26.9.18 CR France 1667
MALLETT,Ray   2Lt   RAF   3 TDS acckld 16.7.18   CR Hamps 192
MALLEY-MARTIN,James.MC.   Lt   RAF &1/2BordR   30.10.18 CR France 332
MALTBY,Alfred Henry   Lt   RAF &GenList 4 Sqdn   4.6.18 MR 20
MALTBY,Alfred John 2Lt   RAF   6 Trng Sqdn   20.6.18 CR Kent 179
MANDERS,A 2Lt   RAF   15 Sqdn   16.11.18 CR France 658
MANDERS,Stanley George   Capt   RAF   3 Ballon Wing   9.12.18 CR France 289
MANLEY,Francis Cyril Churchill   Lt   RAF   188(N) Trng Sqn Ex RFA   kldacc   11.8.18   CR Yorks 45
MANNOCK,Edward.VC.DSO&2Bars.MC.   Maj   RAF &RE 85 Sqdn   26.7.18 MR 20
MANUEL,E G Lt   RAF   2 A/C Acc Park   8.6. 18 CR London 23
MANUEL,John Gerald.DSC. Capt   RAF   210 Sqdn   10.6.18 CR France 276
MANZETTI,Charles Albert   Lt   RAF   kld   21.8.18 CR Sussex 144
MARCHANT,Clarence Henry Lt   RAF   5 Fighting Sch   3.3.19 CR Egypt 9
MARCHANT,Frederick Newland   Lt   RAF   66 Sqdn   6.6.18 CR Italy 11
MARCHBANK,O J   Lt   Can Engrs att RAF   2.6.18 CR Wilts 3
MARKQUICK,Edward Burleigh   2Lt   RAF   210 Sqdn   16.9.18 MR 20
MARCUS,Stephen Percival   F/O   RAF   6 Flying Trng Sch   kld   15.8.21 CR Surrey 2
MARKS,C   2Lt   RAF   6.1.19 CR Wilts 141
MARKS,L T   Lt   RAF   1 Aeroplane Supply Depot Recepn Park 29.10.18 CR France 34
MARRIOTT,Geoffrey 2Lt   RAF   32 Trng Sqdn dedacc 19.7.18   CR Berks 111
MARRIOTT,K M H   Lt   RAF & 1/2WRidR   kia   28.9.18
MARSH,Cuthbert Alban   2Lt   SLancsR att RAF   42 Sqdn   doi   24.6.18 CR France 31
MARSH,Philip Everard Graham.MC. Capt   RAF &ASC 7 TDS   20.12.18 CR Essex 110
MARSHALL,William Edward Ilsley Lt   RAF   acckld 26.6.18   CR Lancs 2
MARTIN,Bruce   Lt   RAF   105 Sqdn   ded   1.3.19 CR Sussex 85

MARTIN,Frederick William Herbert Lt   RAF   41 Sqdn   9.8.18 MR 20
MARTIN,Harold Leslie   2Lt   RAF   39 TDS   kld   30.9.18 CR Derby 99
MARTIN,Thomas Cranston   Lt   RAF   85 Sqdn   12.8.18 MR 20
MASON,Cecil John   Lt   RAF   54 Sqdn   21.4.18 MR 20
MASON,Nelson   Lt   RAF   210 Sqdn   11.6.18 CR France 180
MASTERS,Albert Charles   2Lt   RAF   1.5.18 CR Nhants 107
MASTERS,Ernest Harold   Lt   RAF   45 Sqdn   24.12.18 CR France 113
MATHER,A W   Lt   RAF & BlkW   29.10.18 CR Lincs 61
MATHER,Edward   Lt   RAF   43 Sqdn   kia   6.4.18 CR France 1266
MATHEWS,J W   Capt   RAF   206 Sqdn   1.8.18 CR Belgium 112
MATHEWSON,Thomas Frederick.AFC.   F/O 270912 RAF   Airship base R 38   kldacc   24.8.21   CR Yorks 2
MATHIE,Tom FltCdt RAF   kld   6.6.18 CR Scot 754
MATTHEWS,Ernest Alan   Lt   RAF &11SomLI   2.4.18 CR France 630
MATTHEWS,Harry Cecil TR10/90398   FltCdt Trng Res Bn att RAF   kld   12.11.18 CR Essex 234
MATTHEY,Schomberg Edward   2Lt   RAF   204 Sqdn   kia   3.10.18 CR Belgium 24
MATURIN,William Henry   Lt   RAF   4.7.19 CR Hamps 9
MAWER,John Bailey   Lt   RAF   57 Sqdn   28.11.18 CR Lincs 236
MAXTED,William Henry   Lt   RAF   3 Sqdn   17.12.18 CR France 40
MAY,Thomas Radcliffe Agnew   2Lt   RAF   4 Aircraft Supply Depot   9.8.18 CR France 65
MAYO,Alexander John   Capt   RAF   107 Sqdn   9.8.18 CR France 526
McADAM,George R   F/Cadet   RAF Served as WALLACE,G.R.   26.7.18 CR Surrey 10
McALLISTER,Allan James   2Lt   RAF   20 Sqdn   kia   4.7.18 CR France 134
McALPIN,Donald Davis   2Lt   RAF   2 Sqdn drd   28.10.18 MR 40
McARTHUR,Hector MacDonald   Cdt   RAF 176693   Off Tech Trng Wing   30.6.18 CR Scot 66
McBAIN,G B S.DSC. Capt   RAF   27 Sqdn   10.5.18 CR France 1472
McBRIDE,John Gordon   2Lt   RAF &3GloucR   20 Sqdn   8.10.18 MR 20
McCAIG,Peter Lt   ScotHorse att RAF   54 Sqdn   27.9.18 CR France 147
McCAIG,William George   2Lt   RAF   13 Sqdn   1.10.18 CR France 256
McCALLUM,Arthur Richard Lt   RAF   3 TDS kld   29.8.18 CR Hamps 90
McCALLUM,John Mervin   Lt   RAF   Cent Despatch Pool   kld   8.8.18 CR France 792
McCALLUM,John Ross Robert Gordon   Lt   RAF   8 Sqdn kld   23.8.18 CR France 927
McCALLUM,R P F   FltCdt RAF 110648   8.10.18 CR Scot 253
McCARTER,Duncan 2Lt   RAF   kld   1.5.18 CR Scot 245
McCARTHY,T   2Lt   RAF   82 Sqdn   24.8.18 CR Belgium 451
McCHLERY,James Morrison 2Lt   RAF   6 Sqdn   8.10.18 CR France 699
McCLURE,T A   2Lt   RAF &ConnR   28.5.18 CR Eire 512
McCONNELL KERR,David   Capt   RAF   4.10.18 CR SAfrica 136
McCONNELL,D E   2Lt   RAF   7.12.18 CR Hamps 179
McCONNELL,Harold Jeffrey Lt   5RIrRif att RAF   98 Sqdn   31.5.18 CR Belgium 132
McCREARY,Harry Charles   Lt   RAF   20 Sqdn Ex RNAS   kia   2.7.18 CR Belgium 140
McCUDDEN,James Thomas Byford.VC.DSO&Bar.MC&Bar.MM. Maj RAF   60 Sqdn   dow   9.7.18 CR France 1525
McCULLOCH,R C S   Capt   ASC att RAF   1.3.19 CR Scot 228
McCUTCHEON,Bernard John 2Lt   RAF   48 Sqdn   8.8.18 MR 20
McDONALD,Hugh   2Lt   RAF   42 Sqdn   24.6.18 CR France 31
McDONALD,Ian Donald Ray.MC.DFC.   F/O   RAF   84 Sqdn   22.9.20 MR 38
McDONALD,John Garwood   2Lt   RAF   52 Trng Sqdn kld   1.5.18 CR Scot 687
McDONALD,J J   Lt   RAF   29.3.19 CR Canada 657
McDONALD,Roderick Capt   RAF   208 Sqdn   8.5.18 MR 20
McDOWALL,H S   2Lt   RAF   62 Trng Sqdn   28.6.18 CR Yorks 46
McEACHRAN,Neil   Lt   3HLI att RAF 59 Sqdn   kld   20.5.19 CR Germany 1
McELHINNEY,Arthur Mark 2Lt   RAF   Flying Sch   21.11.18 CR France 1844
McELROY,G E H.MC&2Bars Capt   RAF   kia   31.7.18 CR France 1887
McELROY,Victor Henry DFC   Lt   RAF &CanadianEng   3 Sqdn   2.9.18 CR France 687
McEVOY,Edward   2Lt   RAF   36 TDS   4.8.18 CR Yorks 406
McEWAN,George Clapperton Lt   RAF   7.6.18 CR France 1063
McFARLAN,Archibald   2Lt   RAF   1 Fighting Sch   23.8.18 CR Scot 520
McFARLAND,Foster Murray Lt   RAF &SpList   kld   3.9.18 MR 20
McFARLANE,Donald McIntyre   Lt   RAF &9ScotRif   18.4.18 CR Egypt 9
McFAUL,Leonard Lawrence Lt   RAF   80 Sqdn   kia   10.7.18 CR France 1040
McGEE,E J   2Lt   RAF   12.2.19 CR Beds 22

McGEE,Wilfred Raworth   Lt   RAF   103 Sqdn   11.6.18 MR 20
McGIBBON,D H   2Lt   RAF   42 Trng Sqdn   15.9.18 CR Kent 197
McGIBBON,John   2Lt   RAF   16.8.18 CR Scot 810
McGILL,James Andrew   2Lt   RAF   80 Sqdn   6.9.18 MR 20
McGILLIVRAY,A G   2Lt   RAF   131 Sqdn   16.6.18 CR Ches 86
McGREGOR,D M   Lt   RAF   45 TDS   16.7.18 CR Scot 239
McGUIRE,T F 2Lt   RAF   208 Sqdn   21.12.18 CR Belgium 330
McHARDY,Alexander William   2Lt   RAF   20 Sqdn   10.11.18 CR Belgium 226 & 406
McHARG,L H Lt   RAF   54 Sqdn   31.7.18 CR France 1429
McHATTIE,James William   Lt   Y&LR att RAF 20 Sqdn   kia   25.4.18 CR France '134
McILHARGEY,Cyril Aloysius Cadet RAF 152933   22.5.18 CR Canada 1181
McINTOSH,Victor Brown   Lt   RAF   3 Sqdn   10.8.18 MR 20
McINTYRE,David Percival   2Lt   RAF   10 Sqdn   25.4.18 CR Scot 395
McINTYRE,James Bennett   'Lt   RAF   55 Sqdn   16.8.18 CR France 1675
McINTYRE,Lorne Howson   Lt   RAF   3 Sqdn   21.8.18 MR 20
McKAY,John Thomas Lt   RAF   23 Sqdn   3.7.18 MR 20
McKEEVER,Andrew Edward Maj   RAF   1 Sqdn kldacc 26.12.19 CR Canada 1200
McKEEVER,J C   Lt   RAF   16.3.21 CR Canada 1200
McKENZIE,A 2Lt   RAF   55 Sqdn   13.6.18 CR Germany 1
McKERRELL,William Archibald Struthers Lt 8RScots att RAF   4 Sqdn dow   10.4.18   CR France 98
McKIEL,Rolfe E   2Lt   RAF   2Trng Depot   6.9.18 CR Scot 235
McLAURIN,John Henry   FltCdt RAF 117030 1 TDS   29.9.18 CR Eire 34
McLEAN,Alexander FltCdt RAF 110038 1 Sch of Instrn   5.9.18 CR Scot 752
McLEAN,Chesley   2Lt   RAF   4 Sqdn drd   16.8.18   MR 40
McLEISH,Gordon   2Lt   RAF   31.7.18 CR Scot 387
McLELLAN,Harry Linton   Lt   RAF   108 Sqdn   kld   21.9.18 CR Belgium 140
McLELLAN,Jarvis O Lt   RAF   kld   10.7.18 CR Canada 1028
McLENNAN,John Lawrence.MC.   Capt   RASC att RAF   kia   28.8.19 CR Asia 81
McLEOD,Alan.VC.   Lt   RAF   ded   6.11.18 CR Canada 112
McLEOD,George Earl Lt   RAF   204 TDS   acckld 11.2.19   CR Kent 68
McLEOD,G Donald   Lt   RAF   ded   22.1.19   CR Canada 256
McLEOD,S E S   Lt   RAF   4 Sqdn   11.8.19 CR Suffolk 55
McMAHAN,William John   Lt   RAF   8.12.20 CR Canada 1166
McMASTER,F H   Capt   RAF   31.5.18 CR Surrey 57
McMILLAN,Charles McWhirter   Lt   RAF   70 Sqdn   27.6.18 MR 20
McMURDO,G B M   Lt   ·RAF   27.9.18 CR Scot 808
McMURTRY,L B   2Lt   RAF   213 Sqdn   13.10.18 CR Belgium 381
McNAUGHTON,Archibald Alex   Cadet RAF 174197 Cdt Wing   15.10.18 CR Canada 256
McNAY,Frank Hutchinson   2Lt   RAF   20.11.18 CR Yorks 110
McNEALE,Terence Charles   2Lt   RAF   9.10.18 CR France 341
McNEANEY,John Henry.DFC.   Capt   RAF   1.3.19 CR London 5
McNEIL,A Gordon   Lt   RAF   87 Sqdn   kia   6.9.18 CR France 145
McNISH,Hugh 2Lt   RAF   22.10.18 CR Belgium 355
McQUEEN,H J   2Lt   RAF   46 Sqdn   4.9.18 CR France 1170
McSWEENEY,G B   2Lt   RAF   1 Sch of Navgn & Bombg   25.7.18 CR Wilts 3
McTAVISH,I A B   2Lt   RAF &GenList   kld   15.5.18
MEADWAY,Brian Wilton   Lt   7NhantsR att RAF   56 Trng Sqdn kld   4.6.18 CR Herts 87
MEARS,Henry Frank Lt   RAF   HMS Furious kld   29.4.18 CR London 4
MEDCALF,James Harry   Capt   RAF   45 Trng Sqdn   25.5.18 CR Lincs 181
MEDLICOTT,H W   2Lt   RAF   21.5.17 CR Germany 3
MEDDINGS,Wilfred Walter   2Lt   RAF   201 TDS   dedacc 8.7.19 CR Warwick 10
MEEK,John Freele 2Lt   RAF   4 Fighting Sch kldacc 14.8.18   CR Lincs 6
MEES,Ian Rudolph Lt   RAF   48 Sqdn   14.11.18 CR Wilts 129
MEFF,William.MID 2Lt   RAF   54 TDS   25.7.18 CR Scot 280
MEIKLE,A J B   2Lt   RAF   4 TDS   acckld 5.8.18 CR Glouc 210
MELANSON,Albert Joseph   Lt   RAF & CanFC 2 Sqdn   9.5.18 MR 20
MELBOURNE,Arthur Robert 2Lt   RAF   80 Sqdn   14.6.18 MR 20
MELLING,Harold   Lt   .RAF   10 TDS   dedacc 7.11.18 CR Norfolk 259
MELLINGS,Harold Thomas.DSC&Bar.DFC Capt   RAF   210 Sqdn   22.7.18 CR Belgium 173
MELLOR,Douglas John Thompson   Lt   RAF   205 Sqdn   7.9.18 MR 20

104

MELLOR,Norman   Lt   RAF   drd   10.10.18 CR Yorks 619
MELVILLE,Harry Taylor   Lt   RAF   99 Sqdn   31.7.18 CR France 1675
MELVILLE,Jack Turner   FltCdt RAF 52563   55 Wing   kldacc 30.1.18   CR Scot 766
MELVIN,Will Simpson   2Lt   1/4RB att RAF   23.8.18 CR France 223
MERCIER,Herbert Blennerhassett   2Lt   RAF   55 Sqn Ex RIrRif   kia   3.11.18CR France 1678
MEREDITH,E M   2Lt   RAF &GenList21 Sqdn   13.4.18 CR Belgium 38
MEREDITH,Robert Ellaby   Lt   1CanBCR & RAF   25.7.18 CR France 1107
MERRILL,Volney Norris   2Lt   RAF   3 TDS   8.11.18CR Hamps 90
MESHAM,James Herbert   Lt   RAF   204 Sqn 61 Wing   kld   13.7.18CR Europe 90
MESSENGER,Leonard William   2Lt   RAF   3 TDS Ex RFA   4.7.18 CR Hamps 13
METCALFE,Neville   2Lt   RAF   7.8.18 CR Essex 45
MIDDLECOTE,Edwin William Alfred George Lt   16 KRRC att RAF   kia   3.10.18CR France 915
MIDDLETON,Alfred Saunders   Lt   RAF   56 Sqdn   kld   26.10.18 CR France 398
MIDGLEY,Gordon George   Lt   RAF   13.1.19 CR Eire 14
MILDMAY,B W St.J 2Lt   RAF &GenList See St.JOHN MILDMAY.   kld   16.4.18
MILES,W N   2Lt   RAF   1 Sch of Aeros   24.7.18 CR Norfolk 210
MILL,J 2Lt   RAF   201 Sqdn   20.9.18 CR France 332
MILLAR,Arthur Frederick   2Lt   RAF   27 Sqdn   14.8.18 CR France 57
MILLAR,G H   Capt   RAF   HMS Furious   29.4.18 CR Scot 112
MILLAR,Keith Ogilvie   Lt   RAF   88 Sqdn   21.5.18 MR 20
MILLARD,S H FltCdt RAF   3 TDS   16.10.18 CR Hamps 90
MILLER,A   Cdt   RAF 117467 5 Sch of Aviation   7.7.18 CR Bucks 56
MILLER,B M C   2Lt   RAF &RGA SR   kld   29.5.18CR Belgium 36
MILLER,Donald   Lt   RAF   70 Sqdn   30.6.18 CR France 1525
MILLER,John Jewett   2Lt   RAF   95 Sqdn   25.4.18 CR Ches 35
MILLER,Hector S   Cadet   RAF 153240   dedacc 2.6.18 CR Canada 1688
MILLER,William Joseph   2Lt   RAF   24 Sqdn   17.9.18 MR 20
MILLHOUSE,Archie Percival FltCdt RAF   kld   29.11.18 CR Lancs 475
MILLIKEN,James   2Lt   12RIrRif att RAF   kld   31.12.18 CR NIreland 42
MILLINGTON,Cyril Bertram 2Lt   RAF   200 Trng Sqdn kld   1.10.18CR Scot 86
MILLS,John McFarlane Denholm.DFC.MID. Lt   RAF   5 Wing   22.6.19 CR Palestine p
MILLS,Kenneth Charles   Capt   RAF   1 Sqdn   8.8.18 MR 20
MILLS,William John 2Lt   20 NFus att RAF   20 Sqdn   dow   4.9.18 CR France 142
MILLS-ADAMS,A H 2Lt   RAF   57 Sqdn   1.10.18CR France 658
MILNE,R   Lt   RAF   206 Sqdn   11.8.18 CR France 1032
MILNER,Eric Lt   RAF   5 Sqdn   3.11.18CR France 1144
MILLWARD,J Cdt   RAF   35 Sqdn   6.8.18 CR Staffs 87
MINORS,Ronald Towers   Capt   RAF &WorcR   kld   27.3.19CR Belgium 265
MISENER,Milburn Smith   Lt   RAF   201 Sqdn   9.8.18 MR 20
MISENHIMER,William Kay   2Lt   RAF   Cent Flying Sch 6 Sqdn   kld   6.9.18 CR Wilts 116
MITCHELL,E P H   2Lt   BordR & RAF   7.5.18 CR Egypt 9
MITCHELL,John   Lt   7ScotRif att RAF   25 Sqdn   dow   3.4.18 CR France 52
MITCHELL,James Kinnaird   2Lt   RAF   57 Sqdn   10.8.18 CR France 1525
MITCHELL,James Norman   2Lt   RAF   62 Sqdn   kia   12.8.18CR France 624
MITCHELL,J T   Lt   RAF   112 Sqdn   24.1.19 CR Kent 216
MITCHELL,Leslie Edwin   2Lt   RAF   62 Sqdn   kia   29.9.18CR France 1727
MITCHELL,N R   Lt   RAF   1 Sch of Aerial Gnry   6.6.18 CR Scot 239
MITCHELL,William   2Lt   RAF   41 Sqdn   10.10.18 CR Belgium 409
MOCATTA,F E   Capt   RFA & RAF   26.8.19 CR Mddx 27
MOGRIDGE,Lewis Lt   8LpoolR att RAF   5 Sqdn kia   12.4.18CR France 95
MOIR,A E.MM.   Lt   RAF   65 Sqdn   26.10.18 CR Belgium 413
MOIR,Clifford James Lt   RAF   217 Sqdn   kia   30.6.18MR 20
MOIR,G A   2Lt   RAF   Cent Flying Sch   18.10.18 CR Scot 280
MOLLET,Frederick Norman   Lt   RAF &9HampsR   107 Sqdn   kia   18.7.18CR France 1107
MOLLISON,John(Jack)   Lt   RAF   208 Sqdn   kia   27.8.18 CR France 309
MOLYNEAUX,G   2Lt   RAF   11.5.18 CR NIreland 33
MOND,Francis Leopold   Capt   RFA att RAF   kia   15.05.18
MONK,Harry Ivor Montague 2Lt   RAF   1.10.18CR Mddx 26
MONTAGU,Rupert Samuel.DSC.   FltLt   RAF & NavOffLt RN   Airship base R 38   kldacc   24.8.21   CR Yorks 2
MONTGOMERY,Glyde Gregory   Cadet   RAF &CFA   19

MONTGOMERY,James Richardson Lt   RAF   3 Sqdn   16.9.18 CR France 1727
MOODIE,H M 2Lt   RAF &9SfthH   16.9.18 CR France 1359
MOON,Edwin Rowland.DSO&Bar.   SqnLdr RAF   29.4.20 CR Hamps 57
MOORE,Andrew Walter   Cadet RAF 272805   Recruits Depot ded   19.10.18 CR Canada 1689
MOORE,Frank Simpson   Cadet RAF 272868   26.10.18 CR Canada 1094
MOORE,G B.MC.   Capt   RAF &GenList   7.4.18 MR 20
MOORE,Jack Greville Lt   RAF   81 Sqdn   2.4.18 CR Lincs 181
MOORE,James George.MM.MIDx2   Lt   2RB att RAF   5.7.18 CR Durham 27
MOORE,James Gordon   Lt   RAF   2 Repatn Camp   13.8.19 CR London 12
MOORE,M V Lt   RAF   5.3.19 CR Kent 180
MOORE,Raymond   Lt   RAF   46 Sqdn   12.8.18 MR 20
MOORE,W H 2Lt   RAF   17.2.19 CR Surrey 160
MOORHEAD,Edmund George   Cadet RAF 272468   14.10.18 CR Canada 1175
MOORHOUSE,William   2Lt   RAF   104 Sqdn   kld   22.8.18 CR Frqance 1678
MORANGE,Leonard S   Lt   RAF   55 Trng Sqdn kld   11.8.18 CR Ches 35
MORBEY,John Samuel   2Lt   RAF   kld   1.8.18 CR Essex 1
MORCK,L S 2Lt   RAF   Sch of Navgn &Bombg   26.6.18 CR Durham 26
MORETON,Norman Houghton   Lt   RAF   34 Sqdn   kia   16.5.18 CR Italy 11
MORGAN,B.DCM.   Lt   RAF & ScoRif 59 Wing   kld   16.10.18 CR Scot 674
MORGAN,E P Lt   RAF   206 Sqdn   22.5.18 CR France 134
MORGAN,E S Lt   RAF   211 Sqdn   7.9.18 CR France 1359
MORGAN,Frederick James   Lt   7RFus att RAF 18 Sqdn   dow   16.5.18   CR France 31
MORGAN,Frank Robert   2Lt   RAF   5 TDS   19.10.18 CR Mddx 16
MORGAN,John Towlson   Capt   1RWFus att RAF   70 Sqdn   kia   29.10.18 CR France 283
MORGAN,Lewis Laugharne.MC.   Lt   RAF   kld   28.4.18 CR Kent 175
MORLEY,Edward Lionel   2Lt   RAF   42 Wing(Deseronto)   26.7.18 CR Canada 1178
MORLEY,Hubert Arthur   Cdt   RAF 180148   7 Sqn 7 Obs Sch of Aeros   ded   27.10.18 CR Somerset 25
MORRIS,Corbett Wiley   2Lt   RAF   120 Sqdn   acckld   30.11.18 CR Kent 68
MORRIS,J F.MC&BarCapt   RAF   14.8.18 CR Scot 222
MORRIS,John Clarke Lt   3WRidR att RAF   19 Sqdn   13.1.19 CR France 1252
MORRIS,Norman Preston   Capt   RAF   17.9.18 CR Surrey 41
MORRIS,W A Lt   RAF   41 Sqdn   2.10.18 CR Belgium 11
MORRISON,Cyril Osiris   2Lt   RAF   209 TDS   kld   12.8.18 CR Hamps 5
MORRISON,Ernest Alexander Augustus   Lt   KRRC att RAF   13.11.18 CR Yorks 172
MORRISON,Eric Simpson   2Lt   RAF   27 Sqdn   7.7.18 CR France 792
MORRISON,John Lindsay   2Lt   RAF   29 TDS   31.7.18 CR Hamps 31
MORTIMER,Ernest George Smith   2Lt   RAF &GenList   3.4.18 CR France 169
MORTON,Edward Basil Gowan   Capt   RAF   98 Sqdn   16.7.18 MR 20
MORTON,G M J   2Lt   RAF   40 Sqdn   27.9.18 CR France 273
MORTON,Matthew Charles.DCM.   2Lt   RAF   Artly Co-op Sch   5.4.18 CR Yorks 294
MORTON,Ruby Harold.MM. 2Lt   RAF   66 Trng Sqdn kld   3.7.18 CR Herts 30
MOSES,James David Lt   RAF &CanadianInf   57 Sqdn   1.4.18 MR 20
MOSSMAN,Charles Frederick   2Lt   RAF   Sch of Aerial Gnry & Fighting   14.5.18   CR Essex 40
MOSSOP,Charles Stanley.DSC.   Lt   RAF   243 Sqdn   dedacc 13.8.18   CR France 1848
MOSSOP,Ralph   FltCdt RAF   kld   30.10.18 CR C'land&W'land 60
MOUSLEY,Oscar Oliver   2Lt   RAF   4 TDS   25.6.18 CR Ches 192
MOXEY,Sydney   Lt   RAF   4 Sqdn   14.7.18 CR France 134
MOYNIHAN,P C   Lt   RAF   22.5.18 CR Warwick 65
MUCKLOW,Edward Gerald   2Lt   RAF   37 Sqdn Served as MILBURN,E.G.   22.4.18   CR Essex 222
MUIR,George Victor 2Lt   RAF   B'Sqdn   18.10.18 CR Scot 239
MUIRDEN,Norman Hadley   Lt   RAF   48 Sqdn   8.8.18 CR France 441
MULLEN,Arnold George Leighton   Lt   5DLI att RAF 104 Sqdn   kia   22.8.18 CR France 1633
MULROY,Herbert James   Lt   RAF   56 Sqdn   18.6.18 MR 20
MUMFORD,L R   2Lt   23LondR att RAF   ded   21.10.18 CR Mddx 17
MUNDAY,Edward Richard   Lt   RAF   5.8.18 MR 40
MUNDY,Clarence Reginald . Lt   RAF & 16CanadianInf   kld   23.11.18 CR Scot 106
MUNRO,John William   Lt   RAF   44 Wing (BordenCamp)   kldacc 10.8.18   CR Canada 1231
MUNT,R R   2Lt   Gen List & RAF(EEF)   1.5.18 CR Egypt 1
MURCHISON,Roderick John F/O   RAF   25.2.20 CR Egypt 9
MURPHY,Harry Eustace   Lt   RAF &1/4RFus   kld   22.4.18 CR Eire 78

106

MURRAY,Gordon Lautre   2Lt   RAF   80 Sqdn   12.4.18 MR 20
MURRAY,Huson Grand   Lt   RAF   204 Sqdn   kia   27.10.18 CR Belgium 359
MURRAY,Kenneth William   Lt   RAF &Can BCR   13 Sqdn   1.7.18 CR France 924
MURRAY,Ronald Stewart   2Lt   RAF   49 TDS   kld   14.8.18 CR Yorks 178
MURRAY,Robert William Skinner   Capt   RAMC att RAF   5 Fighting Sch   6.5.19 CR Egypt 9
MURRAY,W L   2Lt   RAF   2 Flying Trng Sch   26.10.18 CR Yorks 127
MURRAY,Walter Scott   2Lt   RAF   4 TDS   27.5.18 CR Ches 192
MUSGROVE,Harold Stone   2Lt   RAF &CanadianCycCps   57 Sqdn   9.8.18 MR 20
MYERS,Philip Bryce 2Lt   RAF   40 Sqdn   27.9.18 MR 20
MYRING,Thomas Frank Leslie   2Lt   RAF   55 Sqdn   kia   30.8.18 CR France 1644

N

NAISH,Jasper Paull   Lt   RAF   209 Sqdn   kia   25.7.18 CR France 134
NAPIER,Charles George Douglas.MC.DCM.Capt   RAF   48 Sqdn   15.5.18 MR 20
NAPIER,James   2Lt   RAF &GenList52 Sqdn   7.4.18 MR 20
NASH,Gordon 2Lt   RAF & Gen List   63 Sqdn   kld   7.5.18 CR Kent 156
NASH,H A   2Lt   RAF   55 Sqdn   14.5.18 CR France 1678
NASH,Percival Swaby Lt   RAF   27.6.19 CR Canada 440
NASH,Thomas Stuart Lt   RAF   80 Sqdn   9.8.18 CR France 71
NASH,Thomas Walter.DFC&Bar.   Capt   RAF   204 Sqdn   23.10.18 CR Belgium 357
NAYLOR,Leyland Ashwell   Lt   RAF   drd   7.7.19 CR Canada 116
NAYLOR,Wilson   2Lt   RAF   4 Sqdn   15.4.18 MR 20
NEIL,James Wilson   2Lt   RAF   108 Sqdn   6.10.18 MR 20
NEILL,Geoffrey William.MC. Lt   6LeistR att RAF   kldacc 8.6.18 CR Egypt 8
NEILSON,Allan Alfred   2Lt   RAF   12 Sqdn   dow   23.8.18   CR France 103
NEILSON,P Lt   RAF   84 Sqdn   18.6.18 CR France 526
NELSON,Harold Ludlow   Lt   RAF   210 Sqdn & RNAS 10 Sqdn   29.4.18 MR 20
NELSON,James Noel Lt   RAF   213 Sqdn   dow   14.6.18   CR Belgium375
NELSON,Kenneth Alonzo   2Lt   RAF   4 TDS   23.5.18 CR Ches 28
NESBITT,William Joseph   2Lt   RAF   19 Sqdn   27.10.18 CR France 1142
NEVIN,Frederick Desmond   2Lt   RAF   49 Sqdn   19.5.18 CR France 526
NEWBY,William   Lt   RAF   1 SAfr Sqdn   kia   29.10.18 CR France 1272
NEWSON,Douglas Arthur   2Lt   RAF   42 Sqdn   23.9.18 MR 20
NEWTH,William Bernard   2Lt   RAF   60 Sqdn   25.2.19 CR Glouc 164
NEWTON,Fleming   2Lt   RAF   201 Sqdn   9.5.18 CR France 239
NEWTON,Robert Francis   2Lt   RAF   52 Sqdn   3.4.18 MR 20
NICHOL,Edward Frank.MC.   Capt   3LNLancs & RAF   24.9.19 CR Kent 27
NICHOLAS,J L   Cdt   RAF 177637   17.12.8 CR Mon 11
NICHOLLS,Edward Cecil Henry Robert   Lt   RAF &RWSurrR   41 Sqdn   kld   20.9.18 CR Essex 222
NICHOLLS,J J Lt   RAF   103 Sqdn   30.10.18 CR France 1027
NICHOLLS,Oscar Lancelot   2Lt   RAF   Cent Flying Sch   kld   6.9.18 CR Wilts 116
NICHOLLS-PRATT,Edward George   2Lt   RAF   13 TDS   kld   2.7.18 CR Mddx 84
NICHOLS,D M   2Lt   RAF   7.9.18 CR Surrey 16
NICHOLS,Edgar   Lt   RAF   35 TDS   kld   24.1.19 CR Cambs 16
NICHOLSON,Owen Harrow   Lt   RAF   3 Sqdn   18.6.18 MR 20
NICKELS,Christopher Charles Gordon   Lt   RAF   (Great Yarmouth)   9.6.18 CR Essex 1
NICOLSON,James   Lt   RAF   20 Sqdn   23.9.18 MR 20
NIEGHORN,Karl   2Lt   RAF   34 Trng Sqdn   19.6.18 CR Hamps 90
NIELSEN,Peter   Lt   RAF   84 Sqdn   18.6.18 MR 20
NIGHTINGALE,Alfred John Lt   RAF   F'Sqn(Mudros)   dedacc 3.6.18 CR Greece 10
NIGHTINGALE,Eric Lt   RAF &EKentR   kia   25.6.18 CR France 526
NIGHTINGALE,S   Cadet   RAF 153324   dedacc 24.9.18   CR Canada 1687
NIXON,L M   FltLt   RAF   74 Sqdn   17.5.18 CR France 346
NIXON,Stanley   Lt   16PPCLI att RAF   55 Sqdn   1.1.19 CR France 1512
NOAD,T   Lt   RAF   27 Sqdn   10.6.18 CR France 1230
NOEL,Hugh Clobery   Lt   RAF   103 Sqdn   24.9.18 MR 20
NOEL,Tom Cecil.MC&Bar   Lt   RAF   20 Sqdn   kia   22.8.18 CR Belgium 115

NOLAN,Philip John Noel.DFC.   Lt   RAF &RFA   7.4.18 CR France 988
NORD,Harry Alexander   F/Cadet   RAF 128210 59 Wing   9.7.18 CR Lincs 78
NORMAN,Geoffrey Hamilton.MIDx3 SqnLdr RAF   RAE   18.8.21 CR London 16
NORMAN,Harry   2Lt   RAF   204 TDS   2.6.18 CR Yorks 119
NORRIS,R W 2Lt   RAF   20.10.18 CR Eire 446
NORTON,George   Lt   RAF   1 Obs Sch of Aerial Gnry   dedacc 10.5.19   CR Europe 28
NUGENT,Anthony   2Lt   RAF   52 Sqdn   1.6.18 CR France 1693
NUNAN,Noel Daniel 2Lt · RAF   dow 24.2.19   CR Europe 180 & MR 70
NUNN,Frederick Arthur William   Lt   RAF &1LondR 65 Sqdn   2.4.18 MR 20
NUTCOMBE,Thomas Arthur 2Lt   ELancsR att RAF   101 Sqdn   dedacc 2.8.18 CR France 29
NUTKINS,Vernon William   Lt   1RScots att RAF   21 Sqdn   19.2.18 CR Egypt 8
NUTTALL,Frank.MC.DFC.AFC.   FltLt   RAF   30 Sqdn   18.9.20 CR Asia 82
NUTTER,Leonard Henry   Cdt   RAF   7 Sch of Aviation   ded   7.11.18 CR C'land&W'land 89

O

OAKLEY,Maurice Ford   Lt   RAF   66 Wing   3.7.18 CR Italy 37
O'BRIEN,Humphrey Donatus Stafford MC &Bar,MID Capt RAF & 1 NHantsR   63 Sqdn   kld   14.9.18 CR Iraq 8
OCCOMORE,Frank Samuel.DFC   2Lt   RAF   52 Sqdn   1.10.18 CR France 113
O'CONNELL,C W.MC.   Lt   1stSurrRifs att RAF   kld   18.6.18 CR Essex 9
O'CONNELL,Patrick Maurice Lt   RAF   15.10.18 CR Eire 109
O'CONNOR,R V   2Lt   RAF   17 Sqdn   29.10.18 CR Greece 3
O'CONNOR,T.DSC. Capt RAF   2.9.18 CR Hamps 64
O'CONNOR-GLYNN,E P   Lt   RAF   66 Sqdn   15.8.18 CR Italy 11
O'DONOGHUE,James   2Lt   RAF   46 Sqdn   4.11.18 CR France 936
OERTLING,Lewis John Francis   Lt   BedR att RAF 5 Sqdn dow   8.8.18 CR France 71
O'FLYNN,G B   2Lt   RAF   3.9.18 CR Wales 17
OGILVY,David Pearson   .2Lt   RAF   52 Sqdn   kia   30.7.18 CR France 41
OGILVY-RAMSAY,Max   Lt   RAF   139 Sqdn   dedacc 4.8.18 CR Italy 11
O'GRADY,James Henry   Lt   RAF   215 Sqdn   24.12.18 CR France 134
O'HARA,H E Lt   RAF   74 Sqn 11 Wing   25.5.18 CR France 180
O'HARA WOOD,Arthur Holroyd   Maj   RAF   46 Sqn 22 Wing   4.10.18 CR France 329
OLDFIELD,Henry Hammersley   2Lt   RAF   20.2.19 CR Lancs 380
O'LEARY,Hugh Barker   Cadet   RAF 152558   dedacc 6.5.18 CR Canada 1687
OLIVER,Thomas Kenneth Graham   Lt   RAF   73 Sqdn   kia   5.9.18 CR France 273
OLMSTEAD,George Tait   Lt   RAF   64 Sqdn   1.8.18 CR France 95
O'NEIL,Thomas Michael   2Lt   RAF & RDubF 43 Sqdn   8.5.18 MR 20
ORAM,William   2Lt   RAF   56 Sqdn   8.7.18 CR France 40
ORANGE,Harold Starling   2Lt   RAF   55 Sqdn   25.9.18 CR Germany 3
ORDE,M A J FltLt   RAF   5.8.20 CR Hamps 36
O'REILLY,N Lt   RAF   Cent Pay Off   12.4.19 CR London 19
O'REILLY,Richard Hamilton Lt   RAF &CanadianEng1TunCoy 62 Sqdn   kia   29.9.18 CR France 1727
ORMEROD,Walter   2Lt   RAF   43 Sqdn   29.8.18 CR France 481
ORR,John Richard   Lt   177CanInf att RAF   80 Sqdn   kia   9.8.18 CR France 247
ORR,Osborne John.DFC.   Lt   RAF   204 Sqdn   23.10.18 MR 20
ORR,Robert Seton Scott   Lt   RAF   201 Sqdn   8.8.18 CR France 526
OSBORN,J E 2Lt   RAF   22.12.18 CR Essex 1
OSBORNE,Donald Springer   2Lt   RAF   Cent Flying Sch   kld   5.10.18 CR Wilts 116
OSBORNE,Geoffrey William 2Lt   RAF   7 Sqdn   29.6.18 CR France 134
OSBORNE,T L   Lt   RAF &5DevR   30.9.18 CR France 1483
O'SHEA,Harry Arthur Lt   RAF &SpList 92 Sqdn   14.8.18 MR 20
OSTLER,Alan.MC.   Lt   RAF &17RFA 13 Sqdn   16.9.18 CR France 481
OSTIGNY,J G Rene   Cadet   RAF 172998   ded   8.10.18 CR Canada 254
OSTLER,John Eric   F/O   RAF   17.4.20 CR Mddx 16
OSWIN,W A Cdt   RAF 183223   28.9.18 CR Leics 15
OTTEWELL,John Miller   Lt   RAF   Wireless Telegraphy Sch   kld   2.4.19 CR Hamps 13
OUBRIDGE,Dinsdale John Arthur   Cdt   RAF 183482   8.2.19 CR Notts 84
OUGHTIBRIDGE,Robert   FltCdt RAF   51 TDS   kld   11.8.18 CR Yorks 361

OWEN,Frank.DCM.   2Lt   RAF   108 Sqdn   kld   1.10.18 CR Belgium 140
OWEN,N   2Lt   RAF   63 Trng Sqdn   3.6.18   CR Wales 536
OWEN,R E   2Lt   RAF   103 Sqdn   18.9.18   CR France 525
OWEN,Sidney Smith   Lt   BCR Depot att RAF   42 Sqdn   11.12.18 CR France 1142
OWEN,T J   Lt   RAF   13.11.18 CR Glouc 8
OWEN,William Thomas   Lt   RAF   213 Sqdn   14.10.18 MR 20
OWEN-HOLDSWORTH,James Philip.MC   2Lt   RAF & Gen List   101 Sqdn   12.4.18 CR France 300

P

PACE,W J.DFC.   Capt   RAF   3 Commn Sqdn   27.4.19 CR Mddx 66
PACEY,Frederick Carman   2Lt   RAF   32 Sqdn   3.9.18   MR 20
PACKER,Joseph   2Lt   RAF   20.8.18 CR Wilts 141
PACKHAM,Conroy Thomas 2Lt   RAF   17 TDS   17.10.18 CR Egypt 8
PADMORE,Alan Reynolds   Lt   RAF   217 Sqdn   kia   28.9.18 CR France 1359
PAGDIN,Jabez Gilbert Lt   RAF   ded   30.10.18 CR Wales 637
PAGE,A B   Cdt   RAF 176156 206 Sqdn   14.5.19 CR Germany 1
PAGE,D F V   Lt   7SuffR att RAF   21.9.18 CR France 256
PAGE,Lance St Allard March.MIDx2   Capt   RAF &10EKent   kia   20.8.18 CR Iraq 8
PAGET,Augustus.DFC.   2Lt   RAF   66 Sqdn   mbk   30.10.18 CR Italy 8 & 81
PAGET,Frederick James   2Lt   RAF   206 Sqdn   dow   6.8.18   CR France 134
PAICE,Stanley Cecil   2Lt   RAF   kld   4.6.1818 CR Wilts 116
PAINE,Roy Dickson   Cadet RAF 174370   ded   10.10.18 CR Canada 32
PALARDY,Guy   Lt   RAF &GenList 62 Sqdn   dow   7.5.18   CR France 792
PALFREYMAN,Audubon Eric   Capt   RAF   27 Sqdn   23.5.18 CR Belgium 384
PALLEN,Henry G   Cadet RAF 173465   ded   12.10.18 CR Canada 180
PALLISER,L H   2Lt   RAF   5.6.19 CR Mddx 74
PALK,William Eustace.MC.DFC.   Lt   RAF   dedacc 27.8.21   CR Wales 174
PALMER,Arthur Bailey Bentick   Lt   RAF   35 TDS Ex 17MddxR kld   23.8.18 CR Mddx 53
PALMER,B B Lt   RAF   HMS Pegasus   17.4.18 CR Herts 27
PALMER,J W 2Lt   RAF   2 Sqdn   25.12.18 CR France 1042
PALMER,R D C.DFC. F/O   RAF   6 Sqdn   2.8.20 CR Iraq 8
PARKER,Allen Foggett   Lt   1WYorksR att RAF   31.5.18 CR Yorks 294
PARKER,F H Lt   RAF   ded   26.10.18 CR Canada 487
PARKER,Herbert   2Lt   RAF   43 Sqdn   dedacc 6.9.18 CR France 805
PARKES,Samuel James   2Lt   RAF   205 Sqdn   13.8.18 MR 20
PARKINSON,George Robert John   Lt   RAF   drd   13.4.18   MR 40
PARKS,Albert Ernest 2Lt   RAF   191(night)Trng Sch   kld   7.9.18   CR Hunts 90
PARKS,Herbert Clifford   Lt   RAF   29 Sqdn   19.12.18 CR Belgium 330
PARLEE,George William Hugh   Lt   RAF   5 Sqdn   20.8.18 CR France 1170
PARNELL,Edgar Alan 2Lt   RAF   64 Sqdn   29.8.18 MR 20
PARR,D A   FltCdt RAF   13.8.18 CR Scot 235
PARRY,S   2Lt   RAF &RE   62 Sqdn   kld   3.5.18   CR France 792
PARSONS,E   Lt   RAF   17.7.18 CR Glouc 9
PARTINGTON,Cyril Walter   Lt   1WarR att RAF   22 Sqdn   kld   30.8.18 CR France 788
PARTRIDGE,Frederick George   FltCdt RAF 176975   ded   22.11.18 CR Nhants 79
PARTRIDGE,H E   2Lt   RAF   61 Trng Sqdn kld   25.5.18 CR Lincs 181
PARTRIDGE,Henry Treneman   Lt   1/4RSussR att RAF   Aerial Flight Sch   kld   14.7.18 CR Egypt 9
PASCOE,Christopher Willoughby   Lt   RAF   226 Sqn 67 Wing kia   1.7.18 CR Italy 6
PASHBY,Frank Edwin   2Lt   RBerksR att RAF   53 Sqdn   dow   13.4.18   CR Belgium 11
PATERSON,G I   Capt   RAF &152CanInf   82 Sqdn   kia   2.4.18 CR France 425
PATERSON,James   Cdt   RAF 176805 1 OTTW   3.6.18   CR Scot 764
PATERSON,John Herbert   Lt   RAF & 19Lancers IA 21 Sqdn   21.6.18 CR Egypt 9
PATEY,Herbert Andrew.DFC.Capt   RAF   210 Sqdn   ded   18.2.19   CR London 12
PATRICK,J   Capt   RAF   HQ Malta Sqdn   19.12.18 CR London 12
PATRICK,Thomas V Cadet RAF 153643   dedacc 18.5.18   CR Canada 10
PATTISON,C E   Capt   RAF   2.4.18 CR Scot 242
PATTISON,John Herbert   Lt   IARO att RAF   acckld 21.6.18

109

PATTON,Idris Knox   Lt   RAF   Wireless Telegraphy Sch   25.11.18 CR Durham 9
PATTULLO,Ronald Campbell 2Lt   RAF   204 Sqdn   15.9.18 MR 20
PAUL,Arthur Reginald 2Lt   RAF   20 Sqdn   kia   22.1.18 CR Belgium 140
PAUL,Herbert Fielding   Cadet RAF 153008   42 Wing   dedacc 4.5.18 CR Canada 699
PAULINE,Victor REginald   .2Lt   RAF &GenList 23 Sqdn   8.5.18 CR France 134
PAULL,Charles William Trevelyn   Lt   RAF   31 Balloon Sect   ded   18.11.18 CR France 34
PAULL,J A.AFC.   Lt   RAF   HQ 13 Grp   12.6.19 CR Heref&Worc 208
PAUSCH,Arthur Walter   Lt   RAF & Gen List   16.7.18 CR France 792
PAWSON,George St Vincent.MC.   Lt   RAF   6.11.18 CR Kent 201
PAWSON,Walter Stead   2Lt   RAF   70 Trng Sqdn kld   6.5.18 CR Hamps 31
PAXTON,Gerald Arthur   Lt   RSussR att RAF   17 Sqdn   18.8.18 CR Greece 1
PAYNE,A A Lt   RAF   4.4.18 CR Derby 61
PAYNE,Leonard Allan.MC.   Capt   RAF   48 Sqdn   18.2.19 CR Germany 1
PAYNE,Stanley James.MIDx3 Maj   RAF   5 A/C Acc Park   ded   3.3.19 CR Somerset 197
PAYNE,Sydney Thomas   Lt   RAF &GenList 13 Sqdn   6.4.18 MR 20
PAYNTER,J De C.DSC.   Capt   RAF   215 Sqdn   6.6.18 CR France 1359
PAYTON,Clement Wattson.DFC.   Lt   RAF   210 Sqdn   2.10.18 CR Belgium 140
PAYTON,John Leslie Lt   RAF &RFA   84 Sqdn   16.8.18 MR 20
PEACOCK,Ernest   2Lt   RAF   8 TDS   kld   26.5.18 CR Numb 5
PEACOCK,John Thomas   Lt   RAF &DCLI   49 Sqdn   16.7.18 CR France 1440
PEACOCK,Thomas.MM   2Lt   RAF   11 Sqdn   kia   3.10.18 CR France 84
PEARCE,Sydney Martin   Maj   RAF &4LeicsR   ded   6.12.18 CR Sussex 199
PEARSON,W R G   Capt   RAF   4 TDS   20.6.18 CR Ches 192
PEDDIE,Henry Scott Crawford   Cadet RAF 173934   ded   1.11.18 CR USA 230
PEDDIE,J   FltCdt RAF 316091   Cdt Dist Depot   5.12.18 CR Wales 17
PEEL,W S.MC.   Lt   1LincsR att RAF   59 Sqdn   27.9.18 CR France 512
PEGRAM,Jack Arthur Horton 2Lt   RAF   kia   18.7.18 MR 40
PEIRCE,George F   Lt   RAF   4 Sqdn   26.5.18 CR France 180
PELCHAT,Louis J A   Cadet RAF 172893   ded   23.10.18 CR Canada 254
PELL,Willard Augustus   Lt   RAF   80 Sqdn   12.4.18 MR 20
PELLETIER,Charles Adolphe Lt   RAF &CETD   1 Sqdn   11.5.18 MR 20
PELLOW,Richard Carter   2Lt   RAF   kld   9.7.18 CR Cornwall 111
PELTON,Roy Edgar   Cadet RAF 152779   ded   15.4.18   CR Canada 180
PEMBLE,Frederick Philip   Lt   RAF   213 Sqdn   29.6.18 CR Belgium 172
PENNAL,Howard Laurence   2Lt   RAF   20 Sqdn   kia   23.10.18 CR France 963
PENROSE,Keith   2Lt   RAF   20 Sqdn   3.9.18 CR France 245
PENROSE-WELSTED,Samuel Richard.DFC Capt   RAF &RIrRif   17 Sqdn   17.7.18 MR 37
PEPPER,Edward Herbert   2Lt   RAF   2 Sqdn kld   23.8.18 CR France 223
PERCIVAL,Ernest Russel   2Lt   RAF   13.3.19 CR Kent 180
PERCIVAL,Harold Kingsley FltCdt RAF 137709   kld   23.9.18 CR Scot 398
PERCIVAL,John Frederick Spencer.MID FltLt   RAF   206 Sqdn   1.3.19 CR Mddx 17
PERCY-SMITH,V   Maj   RAF & Gen List   29.9.20 MR 65
PERRIN,E C.OBE.   FltLt   RAF   2 Wing Ex Capt 4ChesR   5.7.21 MR65
PERRIN,Maurice NaSmith   Maj   RAMC att RAF   kld   28.4.19 CR Surrey 157
PERRING,Charles Richard   Lt   RAF   A/C Acc Park(Hendon)   doi   9.8.18 CR London 12
PERRIS,Noel Felix   Lt   RAF   143 Sqdn   kld   20.7.18 CR Kent 221
PERRY,Alfred Frederick   2Lt   RAF   N'Flight   28.10.18 MR 20
PERRY,Lawrence Percy   2Lt   RAF   48 Sqdn   2.9.18 MR 20
PERRYMAN,Arthur Charles 2Lt   MddxR att RAF   7.1.18 CR Mddx 17
PERSHOUSE,G B   F/O   RAF   12 Sqdn   4.5.21 CR Germany 1
PERTUS,Rennie Alphonse   Lt   CFC seconded RAF   kia   29.8.18 CR France 1170
PETERS,Albert Henry Lt   RAF   54 Sqdn   doi   15.5.18 CR France 65
PETERSEN,Aaron   2Lt   RAF &3EYorksR   18 Sqdn   3.9.18 MR 20
PETIPAS,Herbert Edward   2Lt   RAF   ded   24.3.20   CR Canada 637
PETTITT,M S Lt   RAF   11.8.18 CR Kent 99
PHAIR,Terence H C   Cadet RAF 173567   ded   14.6.18   CR Canada 1440
PHILIP,L A   Lt   RAF   204 TDS   15.9.18 CR Kent 68
PHILLIPS,Donald Robert   2Lt   RAF   11 Sqdn   4.10.18 CR France 512
PHILLIPS,James Ewing   Capt   RAF   16.9.18 CR France 365
PHILLIPS,John Edgar 2Lt   RAF   Cent Flying Sch   20.5.18 CR Essex 40

110

PHILLIPS,T   Capt   RLancsR & RAF   19.8.18 CR Lancs 76
PHILLIPS,Thomas   2Lt   RAF   52 Sqdn   kia   13.10.18 CR France 1196
PHILLIPS,Thomas Martin   2Lt   RAF   103 Sqdn   18.9.18 CR France 525
PHIPSON,H G S   Lt   RAF   27 Sqdn   16.7.18 CR France 1410
PICK,A J   Lt   3DLI att RAF   kld   2.12.18 CR Numb 26
PICKARD,Cecil Gerald Verity2Lt   RAF   104 Sqdn   kia   22.8.18 CR Germany 3
PICKEN,Ronald Baynton   Lt   RAF   6.9.18 MR 37
PIERCE,John Basil   Lt   RAF   53 Sqdn   2.10.18MR 20
PIERCE,Percy John Emerson   Lt   RAF   19 Sqdn   dedacc   13.8.18   CR France 71
PIERCE,Robert Graham   Lt   RAF   29 Sqdn   kia   2.7.18 CR France 134
PIKE,Henry George   2Lt   RAF   65 Sqdn   30.8.18 MR 20
PILLING,J E   2Lt   RAF &LpoolR   25 Sqdn   1.7.18 CR Belgium 384
PIM,Thomas   Lt   RAF &RFA   13 Sqdn   28.8.18 MR 20
PINEO,Harold MacDonald   Lt   RAF   ded   18.12.18 CR Canada 11
PINK,Alan Luis   Lt   RAF &1/4RB   41 Sqdn   kia   30.10.18 CR Belgium 441
PIPE,James   F/O   RAF   31 Sqdn   1.1.20 MR 67
PIPER,Edward Hoernle   Lt   RAF   57 Sqdn   15.5.18 CR France 513
PITHER,C E   Capt   RAF   12 Sqdn   22.8.18 CR France 745
PITHER,Sidney Edward   Capt   RAF &1KOSB   dedacc   11.6.18   CR Egypt 15
PITHEY,Croye Rother.DFC&Bar   F/O   RAF   2 Sqdn drd   21.2.20   MR 40
PITOT,A L A M   2Lt   RE & RAF   103 Sqdn   8.10.18 CR France 512
PITTS-PITTS,Walter John   Lt   RAF   57 Sqdn   9.8.18 CR France 307
PLANT,Charles Robert   2Lt   RAF   5 TDS   8.8.18 CR Mddx 13
PLATT,A   Lt   RAF   57 Sqdn   5.9.18 CR France 1307
PLAYER,Frank   2Lt   RAF   4.9.18 CR France 1252
PLENTY,Edward Pellew   Maj   RAF   96 Sqdn   ded   22.11.18 CR Berks 72
PLUMMER,Frederick Lt   RAF   12.9.18 CR London 26
POE,James Morris   2Lt   RAF   70 Sqdn   9.10.18 CR Belgium 140
POLLARD,Wilfred Walter   2Lt   RAF   206 Sqdn   5.7.18 CR Warwick 7
POLLINS,Jay   2Lt   RAF   21 Sqdn   28.9.18 CR France 10
POLLOCK,J F 2Lt   RAF   55 Sqdn   20.7.18 CR France 1678
PONTING,W   Lt   RAF   25.10.18 CR Glouc 123
POOLE,B G   2Lt   RAF   53 Sqdn   22.3.18 CR France 1061
POOLE,Harry Rowland   Lt   RAF   ded   15.11.18 CR London 12
POOLE,H W A   Cdt   RAF 175287   1 Cdt Wing   1.8.18 CR Sussex 178
POOLE,Leslie Stanley Richard   Lt   RAF   1 Ballon Wing   3.12.18CR France 1277
POOLE,Roland Barrett   2Lt   RAF   62 Wing   kld   18.12.18 CR Greece 10
PORTER,E M   Lt   RAF   Suda Bay Seaplane Base   6.8.18 CR Greece 16
PORTER,William   2Lt   RAF   83 Sqdn   28.2.19 CR France 1571
POTTER,Sydney Hugh.MID   F/O   RAF   47 Sqdn   kldacc   14.8.21   CR Egypt 9
POTTS,George Joseph Leslie 2Lt   RAF   218 Sqdn   kia   8.10.18 CR France 1359
POUCHOT,Jack Auguste.DCM.   Lt   RAF   56 Sqdn   5.10.18CR France 911
PRAGNELL,Sidney Ralph   2Lt   RAF   4 Sqdn kld   10.8.18 CR Dorset 87
PRANCE,John Edward.DCM. 2Lt   RAF   Sch of Aeros(Reading) ded   24.6.18   CR Devon 38
PREECE,B G   FltCdt RAF   16.11.18 CR Scot 596
PREECE,Charles Evered   Lt   RAF   2 Sqdn Ex WorcYeo   18.2.19 CR Heref&Worc 199
PREECE,Ellis   2Lt   RAF   57 Sqdn   2.10.18CR France 911
PRENTICE,A J   2Lt   RAF   16.10.18 CR Scot 811
PRESCOTT,Lewis William   2Lt   RAF   23 Sqdn   22.4.18 MR 20
PRESS,H W   2Lt   RAF   29 Sqdn   23.9.18 CR Mddx 29
PRESTON,Harry Dennis   2Lt   RAF   14.5.18 CR Wilts 129
PRESTON,Maxwell Edden   2Lt   RAF   32 TDS   23.9.18 CR Scot 398
PRICE,C L   Lt   RAF   11.5.18 CR Kent 28
PRICE,John Warren   Lt   RAF   ded   9.10.18CR Canada 1054
PRICE,Oliver   2Lt   RAF   56 Sqdn   4.11.18CR France 1142
PRICE,Thomas John   Lt   RAF   27.5.18 MR 34
PRIDEAUX,Edwin Ravenhill 2Lt   RAF   203 Sqdn   17.5.18 MR 20
PRIME,H L   2Lt   RAF   206 Sqdn   6.10.18CR Belgium 140
PRINCE,Frederick George   2Lt   RAF   58 Sqdn   kld   17.5.19CR Italy 59
PRINCE,W F J2Lt   9LondR att RAF   1 Obs Sch of Aerial Gnry   ded   30.5.18   CR Essex 40

111

PRIOR,Harry Leonard 2Lt 30ResBnRFus att RAF 117 Sqdn acckld 3.7.18 CR Kent 71
PRITCHARD,Cyril John 2Lt RAF 98 Sqdn 30.10.18 CR Belgium 203
PRITCHARD,J E M.OBE.AFC. FltLt RAF kldacc 24.8.21 CR Yorks 2
PRITCHARD,Joshua Leonard 2Lt RAF 218 Sqdn 29.9.18 MR 20
PRITCHARD,R O 2Lt RAF 1 Sch of Aeros ded 6.11.18 CR Wales 550
PROCTER,Charles Austin 2Lt RAF & Gen List 82 Sqdn dedacc 24.4.18 CR France 52
PROCTER,H N J Lt RAF 60 Sqdn 16.5.18 CR France 381
PROCTER,Leslie Horner Lt RAF &ASC 10 Sqdn 17.11.18 CR Belgium 393
PROFFITT,John Thomas Read 2Lt RAF 66 Wing 224 Sqdn 20.10.18 MR 37
PROSSER,D H 2Lt RAF 27 Sqdn 10.5.18 CR France 652
PROSSER,John Edward 2Lt RAF 98 Sqdn 30.10.18 CR Belgium 203
PROTHERO,O I Lt RAF C'Flt 4 Sqdn 23.3.20 CR Bucks 14
PROUDFOOT,Cyril Dallas 2Lt SNottsHrs att RAF 22.4.18 CR France 103
PROUT,Harold Oliver.AFC. F/O RAF 24 Sqdn kldacc 4.11.20 CR Surrey 15
PROVAN,Alexander 2Lt RAF 110 Sqdn kia 25.9.18 CR Germany 5
PUGH,John Edwin Lt RAF 210 Sqdn dow 13.11.18 CR Belgium 332
PUGHE,Robert F/O RAF 5 Sqdn kld 16.4.20 MR 43
PULLAR,John 2Lt RAF 25 Sqdn kia 24.9.18 CR France 792
PULLEN,William Stanley 2Lt RAF 206 TDS 12.6.18 CR Bucks 96

Q

QUERRIE,Harry Walker Lt RAF kld 31.8.18 CR Canada 1688
QUIGLEY,Frank G Capt RAF 20.10.18 CR Canada 1688
QUIN,J E 2Lt RAF 2 Fighting Sch kld 15.10.18 CR Durham 12
QUINAN,Barrington Chadwick Capt RAF &5CanadianInf ded 20.7.18 CR Scot 674
QUINTON,J G 2Lt RAF 55 Sqdn 30.8.18 CR France 1678

R

RABY,Laurence Frederick 2Lt RAF 53 Sqdn kia 9.10.18 CR Belgium 11
RADHILL,P J Lt 5ChesR att RAF ded 2.6.18
RADLOFF,Heinrich Lt RAF & 1/11LondR dedacc 14.9.18 CR Palestine 3
RADNOR,Allan Cuthbert Cdt RAF 204 TDS kld 7.12.18 CR Kent 68
RAHILL,Peter Joseph Lt 5ChesR att RAF kld 2.6.18 CR Ches 28
RALPH,Francis James.DFC. 2Lt RAF 20 Sqdn 3.9.18 CR France 1170
RAMSAY,George Strachan Lt RAF 49 Sqdn 8.8.18 MR 20
RAMSAY,James W M Lt RAF 57 Sqdn 2.10.18 CR France 270
RAMSAY,M O Lt RAF See OGILVY-RAMSAY,Max
RAMSDEN,Samuel Lt RAF 4 Sqdn 12.4.18 CR France 134
RANNEY,Kenneth Alexander Lt RAF 53 Sqdn kia 31.7.18 CR France 20
RATH,H C.DFC. Lt RAF 29 Sqdn 26.10.18 CR Belgium 406
RATTLE,Louis Chaloner 2Lt RAF 100 Sqdn kia 10/11.10.18 CR France 1678
RAVEN,C H R E Capt RAF 2.6.19 CR Mddx 56
RAVINE,C C G Lt RAF 1st L'Flt Wing 16.9.18 CR France 95
RAW,W A 2Lt RAF ded 16.3.19 CR Essex 45
RAWLEY,R W 2Lt RAF 18 Sqdn 13.8.18 CR France 1483
RAWLINGS,Benjamin.MM. 2Lt RAF 107 Sqdn 18.7.18 CR France 1107
RAWLINGS,Percy Townley.DSC. Capt RAF Est Dept A/C Protn kld 26.5.19 CR London 14
RAWLINSON,Percy Ivan Lt RAF ded 30.11.18 CR Lincs 152
RAYNER,Albert Stanley Lt 1/2NhantsR att RAF 2 Issue Sect 2 Air Supply Depot dow 15.7.18 CR France 792
RAYNER,Eric Bottomley FltCdt RAF 5/97201 204 TDS kld 17.10.18 CR Yorks 717
READ,Stanley Charles 2Lt RAF 27 Sqdn 25.9.18 CR France 1061
REDDIE,Frederick Graham 2Lt RAF 206 Sqdn 19.5.18 MR 20
REDLER,H B.MC. Lt RAF 21.6.18 CR Somerset 176
REDMOND,H F 2Lt RAF 53 Sqdn 10.7.18 CR France 134

REECE,F B   Capt   RE att RAF   4 Sqdn   20.4.18 CR France 134
REED,Alan Thomas   Lt   RAF   94 Sqn Ex 16LondR &2/4EKentR kld 1.11.18CR Surrey 34
REED,Frederick Horace   2Lt(Obs)   RAF   6 Sqdn dow   23/27.10.18 CR France 734
REEMAN,A C 2Lt   RAF   202 Sqdn   10.8.18 CR France 1359
REES,D C   2Lt   RAF   30.9.18 CR France 716
REES,Francis Edward 2Lt   RAF   215 Sqdn   22.8.18 CR France 1675
REID,Cecil Dugald   Cadet   RAF 93546   327 D'Sqdn   kld   5.9.18 CR Scot 752
REID,Cecil Glenford   F/Cadet   RAF   6 Sqn Ex 74CanInf   kld   10.1.19CR Lincs 181
REID,David Simpson 2Lt   RAF   16 Sqdn   27.8.18 CR France 95
REID,Frank Rice   2Lt   RAF   29 TDS   kld   30.9.18CR Hamps 31
REID,James   Lt   RAF   65 Sqdn   kia   4.11.18CR Belgium 354
REID,John C M   Lt   RAF   213 Sqdn   12.5.18 MR 20
REID,J D M   Lt   RAF   9.5.18 CR Warwick 89
REID,W R   Lt   RAF   21 TDS   28.2.19 CR Yorks 43
REID,W S   Cdt   RAF   9.6.19 CR Scot 718
REILLY,Frederick Holmes   Lt   RAF   98 Sqdn   kia   28.5.18CR Belgium 385
RENNIE,Arthur Muir   FltCdt RAF   19.10.18 CR Scot 65
RENNIE,Edward Clement   Lt   RGA att RAF   dow   16.6.18   CR Greece 4
RENTON,Eric George 2Lt   RAF   8 Sqdn   14.8.18 CR France 526
RENWICK,Hugh Archibald   Capt   SWBord att RAF   19.8.18 CR Hamps 145
REPTON,C T   Lt   RAF &NottsYeo   kia   25.4.18CR Palestine 3
REVELLE,Roy Cyril   2Lt   RAF & 8 O&BLI   kia   16.9.18 CR Palestine 9
REYNOLDS,Charles Edward   Lt   RAF   55 Sqdn   23.10.18 CR France 1678
REYNOLDS,E F   2Lt   RAF   10.12.18 CR Yorks 319
REYNOLDS,Edward Guthrie 2Lt   RAF   73 Sqdn   8.7.18 CR France 924
REYNOLDS,Francis William Ponnsett 2Lt(Pilot)   RAF   36 Sqdn   kld   13.8.18CR London 4
REYNOLDS,Gerald Ellis   Lt   RAF & PPCLI 102 Sqdn   kld   27.6.188 CR France 806
REYNOLDS,J E   2Lt   RAF   55 Sqdn   18.5.18 CR France 1678
REYNOLDS,Victor Oliver   F/O   RAF   24 Sqn Ex HampsR   kldacc 12.7.20   CR Surrey 6
RHODES,Thomas George   Lt   3WRidR att RAF   57 Sqdn   11.6.18 CR France 792
RICE,Edmund Gabriel Lt   RAF   2 Sch of Instr   kld   3.5.18 CR Warwick 50
RICE,E J   FltCdt RAF   316204   14.12.18 CR Devon 71
RICHARDS,Henry Stokes   2Lt   RAF &12EssR   kld   1.8.18 CR Kent 180
RICHARDSON,Arthur Cadet   RAF   171458   42 Wing   drd   4.10.18CR USA 121
RICHARDSON,Edward Earle.MM.   2Lt   1/2ESurrR att RAF   15 Sqdn   kia   9.11.18 CR France 1223
RICHARDSON,Ernest James 2Lt   RAF   35 Sqdn   dow   27.10.18 CR France 441
RICHARDSON,Gurth Alwyn   FltLt   RAF   drd   10.10.20 MR 40
RICHARDSON,Ian Dacre   Lt   RAF   Repatn Camp   5.3.19 CR Surrey 1
RICHARDSON,J   2Lt   RAF   155 Sqdn   kld   3.12.18CR Yorks 98
RICHARDSON,Stuart Herbert 2Lt   RAF   3 Sqdn   23.9.18 CR France 714
RIDGWAY,Philip Ambrose Favard   Lt   RAF   21.4.18 CR Yorks 2
RIDLEY,Cyril Burfield.DSC.   FltLt   RAF   12 Sqdn   kld   17.5.20CR Germany 1
RIDOUT,Allan Gibbs 2Lt   RAF   Cent Flying Sch B'Sqdn   kld   28.7.18CR Wilts 116
RIEKIE.Harry Heatly   Lt   RAF   9 Sqdn   4.7.18 MR 20
RIGBY,Charles   Lt   RAF &RFus 62 Sqdn   4.11.18 MR 20
RIGBY,F B   Maj   RAF   25.9.18 CR Lancs 464
RIGBY,J   Lt   RAF   16 Trng Grp   20.11.18 CR Lancs 104
RIGDEN,C O   F/O   RAF   216 Sqdn   29.11.20 CR Egypt 9
RIGHTON,Wilfrid   Lt   RAF   Air Stn (Kingsnorth)   kld   30.8.18CR Kent 179
RILEY,Benjamin   2Lt   RAF   49 Sqdn   kia   24.11.18 CR France 403
RINGROSE,Ronald   Lt   RAF   202 Sqdn   28.9.18 CR Belgium 132
RIPLEY,R C P Lt   RAF & BrWIndiesR 110 Sqdn   5.10.18CR Germany 3
RITCHIE,George Thornhill   Lt   RAF   13.12.18 CR Wilts 129
RITCHIE,Stanley Edward   Capt   RAF   HMS Argus   16.4.19 CR Surrey 75
ROACH,D J   2Lt   RAF   6 Trng Sqdn   kld   23.5.18CR Scot 398
ROBERTS,C H   Lt   RAF   98 Sqdn   19.8.18 CR France 605
ROBERTS,Donald Arthur   Lt   RAF   HMS Iron Duke   30.1.19 CR London 22
ROBERTS,John Herbert   Lt   RAF &RFA   8 Sqdn   24.9.18 MR 20
ROBERTS,S T C   Lt   RAF   52 Sqdn   30.7.18 CR France 41
ROBERTS,W A   Lt   RAF   31.7.19 CR Derby 47

ROBERTSON,Andrew Gilchrist   2Lt   RAF   205 Sqn 22 Wing   16.9.18 CR France 526
ROBERTSON,David Brown 2Lt   RAF   25 Sqdn   kia   27.9.18 CR France 924
ROBERTSON,Elliot Gairn   2Lt   RAF   85 Sqdn   27.9.18 MR 20
ROBERTSON,John Shirley   Lt   43CanInf attRFC   kld   16.11.17 CR Lincs 181
ROBERTSON,Peter   Lt   RAF &3CamH   ded   16.1.19   CR Ches 8
ROBERTSON,Tom   Cdt   RAF   8 Cdt Wing   28.11.18 CR Scot 484
ROBERTSON,W S   Lt   RAF   85 Sqdn   13.7.18 CR France 922
ROBINSON,A D   Lt   RAF   12.8.18 CR France 652
ROBINSON,A J   2Lt   RAF   55 Sqdn   25.9.18 CR France 1667
ROBINSON,Cyril Charles Edward   Lt   RAF   27 or 59 Sqdn kia 28.4or24.07.18 CR France 63 & 1429
ROBINSON,Cyril Evan   2Lt   RAF   27 Sqdn   24.7.18 MR 20
ROBINSON,Ernest Charles   Lt   RAF   10 Sqdn   20.1.19 CR France 1027
ROBINSON,Frederick Colyer 2Lt   RAF   34 Trng Sqdn   17.8.18 CR Hamps 90
ROBINSON,G.MC.   Capt   CanCav att RAF   19.5.18 CR Kent 197
ROBINSON,Gathorne Clegg   2Lt   YLI att RAF   kld   6.6.18 CR Yorks 570
ROBINSON,George Lancaster F/Cadet   RAF &PPCLI 13 TDS   ded   1.11.18 CR Shrop 145
ROBINSON,H E   Lt   RAF   72 TDS   21.4.18 CR Mddx 80
ROBINSON,Henry   Lt   RAF   1 A/C Depot   3.3.19 CR France 134
ROBINSON,Hugh Huntley MC & bar   Maj   RAF &RAMC   kld   3.5.19 CR Belgium 241
ROBINSON,Harry Percival   2Lt   RAF   6 TDS kld   25.6.18 CR Yorks 2
ROBINSON,Ralph   Lt   RAF   206 Sqdn   12.4.18 CR France 134
ROBINSON,R W   Lt   RAF   Dunkirk   11.8.18 CR Europe 86A
ROBINSON,Thomas Vivian   2Lt   RAF   20 Sqdn   4.7.18 CR France 134
ROBINSON,William Frederick Rokeby Lt   RAF   8 Sqdn   24.9.18 MR 20
ROBINSON,William Hartley   Lt   RAF   66 Sqdn   2.5.18 CR Italy 11
ROBINSON,William Leefe.VC.   Capt   WorcR att RAF   31.12.18 CR Mddx 23
ROBSON,John Cadet   RAF 154486   3.7.18 CR Canada 1303
ROCHFORT,A D'O   Lt   RGA att RAF 58 Trng Sqdn   13.10.18 CR Egypt 15
RODGER,William Alexander   Lt   RAF &ManitobaR   10.11.18 CR Belgium 226 & 406
ROE,Henry Alfred Havilland Lt   RAF   214 Sqdn   19.5.18 CR Belgium 390
ROEBUCK,Leonard   2Lt   RAF   38 Sqdn   4.4.18 CR Yorks 642
ROGERS,Arthur Forbes   2Lt   RAF   16.7.18 CR Kent 180
ROGERS,David Halsted   Cdt   RAF 152024 43 Wing   dedacc 15.6.18   CR USA 169
ROGERS,Thomas Harold   2Lt   RAF   56 Sqdn   27.10.18 MR 20
ROGERSON,G C   2Lt   RAF   50 Sqdn   16.9.18 CR Herts 20
ROPER,George   2Lt   RAF   131 Sqdn   kld   25.5.18 CR Shrop 130
ROSCOE,James Franck   2Lt   RAF   13 Grp kld   6.8.18 CR Ches 192
ROSE,Alexander   2Lt   HLI att RAF   6.9.18 CR Scot 752
ROSE,Algernon Winter.MC.   Capt   EssYeo att RAF   29.10.18 CR Essex 256
ROSE,S   2Lt   RAF   12.9.18 CR Bucks 6
ROSENTHAL,Samuel Cadet   RAF 154067 42 Wing   kld   29.5.18 CR Canada 257
ROSEVEAR,Stanley Wallace.DSC&Bar   Capt   RAF   201 Sqdn   kia   25.4.18 CR France 226
ROSS,Allan James Ferguson 2Lt   RAF   204 Sqdn   27.10.18 CR Belgium 406
ROSS,Douglas Nicol.MM.   Lt   BrColumbiaR & RAF 24 Sqdn   17.2.18 MR 20
ROSS,G A B Lt   6LpoolR att RAF   1.6.18 CR France 1693
ROSS,J   Lt   RAF   49 Sqdn   8.8.18 CR France 987
ROSS,James Stewart 2Lt   RAF   2 Sch of Aeros   29.7.18 CR Scot 287
RISSINGTON-BARNETT,J A Lt   RAF   see BARNETT,J I A R
ROSS-JENKINS,M   2Lt   RAF   62 Sqdn   16.6.18 CR France 987
ROURKE,Bernard Stanley   2Lt   RAF   26 TDS   3.9.18 CR Scot 280
ROWDEN,Cuthbert Roger.MC.   Maj   RAF & 5WorcR   78 Sqdn   20.4.18 CR Sussex 114
ROWDON,Alfred William   Lt   RAF   80 Sqdn   10.5.18 MR 20
ROWE,Marcus E   2Lt   RAF   62 TDS   kld   19.8.18 CR Wilts 28
ROWE,Robert Ronald Lt   RAF   73 Sqdn   3.5.18 MR 20
ROWELL,W C Capt   RAF   22.5.19 CR Devon 130
ROWELL,T.MC.   2Lt   RAF &RBerksR   20.5.18 CR Nhants 79
ROY,David Charles 2Lt   RAF   49 Sqdn   25.8.18 MR 20
ROY,Indrulal.DFC. FltLt   RAF   22.7.18 CR France 1737
ROYDS,Thomas Alington   2Lt   RAF &GenList 59 Sqdn   20.4.18 CR France 76
ROYLE,Leopold Victor Arnold.MC.   Capt   RAF   111 Sqdn   kld   17.8.18 CR Palestine 9

ROYLE,Raynes Lord Charles 2Lt RAF 7 Sqdn 8.11.18 CR Belgium 159
ROYSTON,N Lt RAF 5.11.18 CR Scot 722
RUCKER,Robin Sinclair Lt RAF 43 Sqdn kld 12.10.18 CR France 1170
RUDD,Thomas Herbert Lt RAF ded 19.2.21 CR Europe 51
RUDGE,A E Lt RAF 203 Sqdn 22.7.18 CR France 1312
RUFFRIDGE,George Albert 2Lt RAF 44 Wing dedacc 6.5.18 CR USA 137
RUMSBY,Richard William MC Lt 9SussR att RAF kia 9.5.18 CR France 792
RUMSEY,Reginald English Capt RAF 9.12.18 CR Shrop 19
RUSH,Edward Arthur P/O RAF 2 Flying Trng Sch 19.8.21 CR Mddx 16
RUSHTON,Cecil George Capt RAF 214 Sqdn kia 16.5.18 CR Belgium 132
RUSHTON,Wallace 2Lt RAF 57 Sqdn 4.11.18 CR France 521
RUSSELL,C G 2Lt RAF 99 Sqdn 30.8.18 CR France 1678
RUSSELL,Cyril Ernest Shaftesbury Capt RAF 149 Sqdn 5.3.19 CR Germany 1
RUSSELL,Henry Thornbury Fox MC Capt RAF &6RWFus kld 18.11.18
RUSSELL,James Gordon Lt RAF 28 Sqdn kia 15.6.18 CR Italy 11
RUSSELL,Robert Francis. 2Lt RAF 70 Sqdn kia 28.10.18 CR Belgium 406
RUSSELL,William Lt RAF ex RE 3.4.18 CR France 792
RUSSELL,William Havery 2Lt RAF 1 Sch of Navgn & Bombg acckld 6.10.18 CR Durham 19
RUTLEDGE,William Thomas 2Lt RAF 38 Sqdn 2.11.18 CR France 34
RUXTON,Wilfred Hay Lt RAF 22 TDS doi 29.8.18 CR Eire 14
RYAN,H H W FltCdt RAF 100539 5 TDS (Huntingdon) kld 28.8.18 CR Hunts 83
RYAN,P S F/Cadet RAF 13.7.18 CR Wilts 3
RYLANDS,Peter Wolfertstan Lt RAF 9.8.18 CR Dorset 103

S

SABEY,Albert Robert Lt RAF 104 Sqdn dow 11.9.18 CR France 1675
SADLER,Roland Albert James 2Lt RAF &RWarR kldacc 23.9.18 CR Norfolk 24
SALES,Norman Lt RAF &2YLI 87 Sqdn 30.6.18 CR France 1525
SALMON,Frederick Charles 2Lt RAF 97 Sqdn kld 1.5.19 CR Kent 83
SALMON-BACKHOUSE,S J Lt RAF see BACKHOUSE,St J S
SALMONS,W J.MM. 2Lt RAF 65 Sqdn 23.4.18 CR Warwick 50
SALTER,Geoffrey Charles Taylor.MC. Lt RAF & EYorksR 28.5.18 MR 20
SALTON,William Fletcher Lt RAF 66 Wing 9.6.18 CR Italy 37
SALTON,W K 2Lt RAF 10 Sqdn 17.11.18 CR Belgium 393
SAMPSON,Amyas Terrell Lt RAF 3 Sqdn 8.8.18 MR 20
SAMPSON,Wilfred John Lt RAF 81 Sqdn 2.12.18 CR Oxford 69
SAMS,Mervyn Alfred Lt RAF 13.12.18 CR France 1844
SAMUELSON,Frank Albert 2Lt RAF 51 TDS 29.10.18 CR Ches 35
SANDERS,Frederic Joseph Lt RAF 7 Sqdn kld 3.5.18 CR France 180
SANDERS,H Cdt RAF 138312 8 Cdt Wing 8.3.19 CR Devon 41
SANDERS,Harry Creighton Cadet RAF 153688 17.9.18 CR Canada 1224
SANDERS,R F 2Lt RAF 61 Sqdn 27.9.18 CR Warwick 7
SANDERS,R H 2Lt RAF 50 TDS 5.9.18 CR London 12
SANDERSON,Albert Montague Lt RAF 74 Sqdn 1.10.18 MR 20
SANDERSON,Charles Buswell 2Lt RAF 27 Sqdn dow 17.10.18 CR France 934 & MR 20,25.9.18
SANGSTER,Albert Burnett 2Lt RAF 206 Sqdn 13.8.18 CR Belgium 453 & MR 20
SANKEY,C M.MC. 2Lt EKentR att RAF 15.5.18 CR Mddx 53
SANSOM,Roland Charles Lt RAF & Gen List 55 Sqdn 16.5.18 CR Germany 3
SATTERTHWAITE,George Edward Lt RAF 20 Trng Wing kld 11.6.18 CR Egypt 1
SATTERTHWAITE,J Lt RAF 12.6.18 CR Lancs 263
SAUNDERS,Herbert Clement.MM. Lt BCR Depot att RAF 46 Sqdn kia 18.9.18 CR France 1495
SAUNDERS,James Foster Cdt RAF 153720 44 Wing dedacc 17.6.18 CR Canada 1484
SAUNDERS,James Oscar Reginald Stuart 2Lt RAF 100 Sqdn kia 21.10.18 CR Germany 3
SAUNDERS,Lorn Lamont 2Lt RAF 46 Sqdn 4.10.18 CR France 329
SAUNDERSON,S T Capt RAF 131 Sqdn 22.4.18 CR Shrop 130
SAVAGE,H L Lt RAF 47 TDS kldacc 11.9.18 CR Yorks 500
SAVAGE,Henry William Lt RAF 21 Sqdn kia 14.8.18 CR France 88

115

SAVILLE,Albert Edward   Lt   RAF   drd   14.8.18   MR 40
SAWYER,C H 2Lt   RAF   46 Sqdn   8.10.18CR France 446
SAWYER,R H Lt   RAF   3.8.18 CR Mddx 48
SAYERS,Leslie Frederick Cecil   2Lt   RAF   98 Sqdn   kia   31.7.18 CR France 1429
SAYERS,Percy Langley   Lt   RAF   26.11.18 CR Lincs 156
SCHINGH,Joseph Emery   Lt   RAF   15 TDS   kld   7.2.19 CR Notts 60
SCALES,Herbert James.MC. Capt   RAF   150 Sqdn   dedacc 12.6.18   CR Greece 1
SCARAMANGA,James John Lt   RAF   22 Sqdn   dow   10.7.18   CR France 31
SCARBOROUGH,Edward Owen   2Lt   RAF   119 Sqdn   25.5.18 CR Cambs 16
SCARR,Ggeoffrey Campbell Lt   RAF   1 Obs Sch of Aerial Gnry   18.11.18 CR Kent 180
SCARRATT,John Arthur   FltCdt RAF 128917   28.12.18 CR Scot 106
SCHMOLLE,James Gustave Lt   RAF   189 Night Fighting Sch   ded   22.10.18 CR Essex 45
SCHOLES,A V.MM. 2Lt   RAF   WT Flight 21 Wing   1.11.18CR Yorks 643
SCHOLTE,O J F.MC. Capt   RAF & BedsR 60 Sqdn   30.7.18 CR France 1564
SCOBIE,Caldwell Graves   Lt   RAF &SpList 88 Sqdn   21.5.18 MR 20
SCOBIE,Keith MacDonald   Lt   RAF   43 TDS   acckld 27.10.18 CR Hamps 90
SCOTCHER,William Goodliff.MC.MID   Capt   RAF   50 Sqdn   kld   15.9.18CR Essex 48
SCOTT,Blaney Edmund MC,DFC   Lt   RAF & CanFA 20TMB   ded   9.10.19CR Canada 183
SCOTT,Clive Keeling Lt   RAF   kld   1.6.18 CR Mddx 80
SCOTT,E S   2Lt   RAF   28 TDS   7.11.18CR Oxford 23
SCOTT,Francis Charles Dudley   Lt   RAF &DLI   52 Sqdn   4.11.18MR 20
SCOTT,G B   2Lt   RAF   28 TDS   17.8.18 CR Oxford 69
SCOTT,G M Lt   RAF   11.6.18 CR Greece 10
SCOTT,Herbert   2Lt   RAF   8 Sqdn   23.8.18 CR France 593
SCOTT,Harold George2Lt   RAF &O&BLI 52 Sqdn   30.7.18 MR 20
SCOTT,Norman MM Lt   RAF &PPCLI   kld   20.6.18CR Lancs 78
SCOTT,Raymond.MM.   Lt   RAF   205 Sqdn   3.5.18 CR France 425
SCOTT,R J   2Lt   RAF   111Sqn   8.5.18 CR Palestine 9
SCOTT,Snowden Appleton   Cadet RAF TR5/13234   57 Sqdn   19.8.18 CR Durham 17
SCOTT,Stuart Harvey Lt   RAF   6 Sqdn   29.9.18 CR France 212
SCOTT,Tom Farrar.MM.   2Lt   RAF   75 Sqn Ex Can AMC kld   21.5.18CR Norfolk 259
SCOVIL,Earle Markee.MM.   Lt   RAF   Res Depot   dedacc 21.7.18   CR Canada 961
SCRACE,John Lt   5EKentR att RAF   21 TDS   kld   24.8.18CR Kent 44
SCROGGIE,Leonard Charles Lt   RAF   213 Sqdn   25.9.18 MR 20
SCRIBBINS,William Howard 2Lt   RAF   22.8.18 CR Berks 43
SCRIVEN,S A 2Lt   RAF   14.3.20 CR Glouc 25
SCUDAMORE,W S K Lt   RAF   208 Sqdn   18.7.18 CR France 255
SEDDON,Alfred   FltCdt RAF   41 TDS   kld   24.10.18 CR Lancs 327
SEDGWICK,Francis Belfour Capt   RAF   18.10.18 CR Surrey 160
SEAGRAVE,P 2Lt   RAF &7LpoolR   1.11.18CR France 937
SEED,William Ernest Lt   RAF   12.12.18 CR Lancs 101
SELLAR,William Ritchie   2Lt   RAF   98 Sqdn   kia   29.8.18CR France 392
SELLARS,Herbert Whitely.MC.   Lt   RAF   11 Sqdn   15.5.18 MR 20
SELLS,C P.MC.   Capt   RAMC att RAF   4.7.19 CR Dorset 93
SEMPLE,F M Cdt   RAF   Trng Sch of Aeros   30.10.18 CR Berks 85
SEPHTON,Stanley   2Lt   RAF   55 Sqdn   14.5.18 CR France 1678
SESSIONS,Donald Humphrey.MC.   Lt   RAF   2 Sch of Aerial Gnry   20.6.18 CR Glouc 97
SESSIONS,F H N   Lt   RAF & RDFus   5.6.18 CR Eire 24
SEXTON,Edgar Zephania   2Lt   RAF   21.11.18 CR Canada 1183
SEYMOUR,Charles Benjamin2Lt   RAF   11 Sqdn   6.9.18 MR 20
SEYRES,J A Lt   RAF   6.5.21 CR Surrey 38
SHACKELL,Cecil John   Lt   RAF   210 Sqdn   dedacc 18.6.18   CR France 180
SHANKS,Daniel Albert   2Lt   RAF   108 Sqdn   21.9.18 MR 20
SHARMAN,C L   2Lt   RAF   22.2.19 CR Susses 111
SHARP,Christopher Harold   2Lt   NorfR att RAF 99 Sqdn   26.9.18 CR France 1667
SHAW,Erwin David   1stLt   USarmy AviationSect att RAF 48 Sqdn   kia   9.7.18 CR France 314
SHAW,Frank Aubrey.MC.   Lt   RAF &LancF 98 Sqdn   16.7.18 MR 20
SHAW,George Edward   FltCdt RAF 137459 Harrowby Disperal Centre   ded   21.4.19   CR Cambs 1
SHEAD,S G Lt   RAF   29.11.18 CR London 5
SHEARD,Henry Wigglesworth   2Lt   RAF   10 Sqdn   11.8.18 CR France 142

SHEARER,Frederick James   Lt   RAF   kia   25.7.18 CR Belgium 157
SHEEHAN,M J   2Lt   RAF   13 Sqdn   1.10.18 CR France 256
SHEIL,Charles 2Lt   2MunstF att RAF   2 Sqdn   22.4.18 CR France 179
SHELDON,Charles Stanley   Lt   RAF   70 Sqdn   27.6.18 MR 20
SHELDRAKE,Archibald Turner   Lt   RAF &7HLI   64 Sqdn   28.9.18 MR 20
SHEPARD,F H G.AFC.   F/O   RAF   1 Commn Sqdn   2.10.19 CR Mddx 80
SHEPERD,J A 2Lt   RAF   53 Trng Sqdn   28.7.18 CR Yorks 547
SHEPPARD,Edmund Culver   Capt   RAF &196CanadianInf   21
SHEREK,Paul Lt   RAF &NStaffsR   57 Sqdn   1.10.18 CR France 658
SHERIDAN,Charles James Cameron   2Lt   RAF   54 Sqdn   kldacc 29.8.18   CR France 46
SHERIDAN,John Wilton   Lt   CamH & RAF   54 Sqdn   dedacc 27.9.18   CR Essex 73
SHERLOCK,Clarence Edward 2Lt   RAF   57 TDS   kld   19.8.18 CR Bucks 54
SHERWOOD,C L A   Lt   RAF   23 Sqdn   1.7.18 CR France 1170
SHERWOOD,Francis Colin   Lt   RAF   248 Sqdn   30.10.18 CR London 4
SHIELD,F L   2Lt   RAF   63 Trng Sqdn   2.6.18 CR Warwick 7
SHIELDS,C C S   2Lt   RAF   80 Sqdn   10.5.18 CR France 699
SHIER,M R   2Lt   RAF   drd   6.9.18 MR 40
SHILLINGFORD,Stanley Charles   Lt   RAF &2Fus   16.6.18 CR France 324
SHIRLEY,Frank Lawrence James.MC.   FltLt   RAF   ded   30.11.20 CR Warwick 97
SHOOTER,John Harold.MC.   2Lt   Y&LR att RAF   10.4.18 CR France 303
SHORROCK,Walter   2Lt   RAF   4 TDS   3.11.18 CR Lancs 193
SHORTLEY,Francis W   Cadet   RAF 272548   ded   11.10.18 CR Canada 256
SHUM,Brian Godfrey   2Lt   RAF   22 Sqdn   27.9.18 MR 20
SHUTTLEWORTH,R W   2Lt   RAF &9LancF   ded   16.8.18   CR Yorks 487
SIBLEY,Desmond Wilkie   P/O   RAF   216 Sqdn   1.4.20 CR EAfrica 116
SIBLEY,Robert Dymond Gladman   Maj   RAF   210 Sqdn   1.10.18 MR 20
SIDDALL,Joseph Henry   Lt   RAF   209 Sqdn   25.7.18 MR 20
SIDEBOTTOM,William.DFC. F/O   RAF   30 Sqdn   8.12.20 MR 61
SIEVEKING,Valentine Edgar.DSC&Bar   Capt   RAF   214 Sqdn   kld   18.5.18 CR Belgium 390
SIM,James Copland   FltCdt   RAF   209 TDS   19.11.18 CR Hamps 5
SIMMONDS,Leslie Bernard   2Lt   RAF   57 Sqdn   16.9.18 MR 20
SIMMONS,A D   Lt   RAF   189(N) Sqdn   26.2.19 CR Yorks 275
SIMMONS,G E   2Lt   RAF   254 Tech Stores   9.2.19 CR London 7
SIMMS,A L.DSC.   Capt   RAF   14.7.18 CR Heref&Worc 186
SIMMS,J B P   2Lt   RAF &3NFus   4 Sqdn   4.6.18 MR 20
SIMPSON,A L FltLt   RAF   7.4.18 CR Canada 1691
SIMPSON,D   Cdt   RAF 183870   20.11.18 CR Scot 442
SIMPSON,Joseph   FltCdt   RAF G/28822   kld   20.7.18 CR Wilts 4
SIMPSON,Robert   2Lt   RAF   211 Sqdn   7.9.18 CR France 1359
SIMPSON,Thomas Barton   Lt   RAF   54 TDS   kld   19.12.18 CR Essex 76
SIMPSON,Thomas Edmund   2Lt   RAF   65 Sqdn   1.6.18 CR France 71
SINCLAIR,R   2Lt   RAF   70 Sqdn   24.1.19 CR Germany 1
SINCLAIR,Robert Black   2Lt   RAF   14 TDS   22.3.19 CR London 12
SISSING,Arthur Edgar 2Lt   RAF   66 Sqdn   1.11.18 CR Italy 80
SKEDDEN,Charles Edwin Lloyd   Lt   RAF &1CentOntarioR 74 Sqdn   8.5.18 CR France 180
SKINNER,Robert Leonard Grahame   2Lt   RAF & 1/2BlkW   46 Sqdn   3.5.18 MR 20
SLACK,George William   Lt   RAF   49 Trng Sqn Served as HOLT,C.T.   28.6.18   CR Yorks 500
SLADE,Robert Bishop Lt   RAF   23.7.18 CR Berks 89
SLATER,Ian Cecil   FlgOff   RAF   208 Sqdn   15.8.21 CR Egypt 8
SLAVIK,John Frederick   Lt   RAF   34 Trng Sqdn   26.5.18 CR Hamps 90
SLINGER,Albert   2Lt   RAF   206 Sqdn   3.5.18 MR 20
SLOCOMBE,David William   Lt   RAF   44 TDS   ded   24.10.18 CR Somerset 99
SLOSS,James Duncan 2Lt   RAF   108 Sqdn   dow   23.11.18 CR France 34
SMAILES,Eric Bramall   2Lt   RAF   104 Sqdn   13.9.18 CR Germany 3
SMALL,Gordon Folger   Cadet   RAF 152753   ded   12.5.18   CR USA 155
SMALL,James Bruce   Lt   RB att RAF   101 Sqdn   kia   2.8.18 CR France 29
SMEE,Arthur Joseph   Lt   3WiltsR att RAF   kldacc 28.10.18 CR Surrey 15
SMITH,Albert Edward 2Lt   RAF   218 Sqdn   29.9.18 MR 20
SMITH,Algernon Sydney   2Lt   RAF   57 Sqdn   20.3.19 CR Belgium 268
SMITH,C G V Lt   RAF   66 Trng Sqdn   21.5.18 CR Wilts 28

SMITH,D E	Lt	RAF	20 Sqdn		14.8.18 CR Belgium 125		
SMITH,Donald Graham	2Lt	RAF &4MddxR	42 Sqdn Ex RAMC		10.4.18 MR 20		
SMITH,Donald McQuiston	Lt	RAF	Cent Despatch Pool	kld	20.8.18CR Lincs 181		
SMITH,E	2Lt	RAF &GenList		28.4.18 CR France 184			
SMITH,Eric Avery	2Lt	RAF	57 Sqdn	dow	27.9.18	CR France 84	
SMITH,Francis Beacroft.MC.	Lt	RNVR RN Div att RAF			28.5.18 CR Essex 1		
SMITH,Frank James.MC.MM.		ObsOff RAF	208 Sqdn		14.4.21 CR Egypt 8		
SMITH,Frederick Charles.DSC.		Lt	RAF	62 Wing	22.7.18 CR Gallipoli 1		
SMITH,Fred Forster	2Lt	RAF	Seaplane Stn(Cattewater)	drd	1.9.18 CR Durham 164		
SMITH,Frederick Lawrence Percy	2Lt	RAF	108 Sqdn		9.11.18CR Belgium 159		
SMITH,George	2Lt	RAF	80 Sqdn		15.8.18 CR France 71		
SMITH,George William Kenneth	Lt	RAF	70 Sqdn	dow	22.10.18 CR France 34		
SMITH,Hugh Cassillis	2Lt	RAF	78 Sqdn	kld	15.5.19CR Essex 45		
SMITH,Harold Spencer	2Lt	3LondR att RAF	att 53 Sqdn		31.7.18 CR France 20		
SMITH,Harry Stuart	2Lt	RAF	60 Sqdn		15.9.18 CR France 1496		
SMITH,Joseph Edward	Lt	RAF	60 Sqdn		17.9.18 CR France 427		
SMITH,John Henry	2Lt	10MddxR att RAF	103 Sqdn	kia	9.7.18 CR France 31		
SMITH,James Hamilton Reid	2Lt	RAF	24 Sqdn	kia	10.11.18 CR Belgium 275		
SMITH,John Charles Samuel	Cdt	RAF 110051		ded	26.4.18	CR Essex 14	
SMITH,Joseph Lawrence	F/Cadet	RAF 531665	192Nthn Trng Sqdn	kld	17.7.18CR Cambs 74		
SMITH,Leslie George	2Lt	RAF	20 Sqdn	kia	26.9.18CR France 415		
SMITH,Ralph Eustace	Capt	RAF &NumbYeo		kia	18.4.18CR France 303		
SMITH,S	Lt	RAF	203 Sqdn		11.4.18 CR France 193		
SMITH,Sydney Arnold	2Lt	RAF	65 Sqdn	kia	6.8.18 CR France 71		
SMITH,Sydney Philip	Capt	RAF	46 Sqdn		6.4.18 MR 20		
SMITH,T E	2Lt	RAF &WorcR		11.6.18 CR Warwick 60			
SMITH,Theodore Thomas	2Lt	RAF	11 Sqdn		29.9.18 MR 20		
SMITH,Wansey	2Lt	11ELansR attRAF	10 Sqdn	kia	2.4.18 CR Belgium 11		
SMITH,William	Lt	RAF	HMS Valiant		29.1.19 CR Ches 8		
SMITH,William Percival	2Lt	RAF	38 Trng Wing		7.9.18 CR Egypt 9		
SMITH-GRANT,John Gordon Smith Cheetham	Capt	9RScots att RAF	70 Sqdn	kld	30.5.18CR France 84		
SMUTS,C L	2Lt	RAF	TDS		23.4.18 CR Lincs 100		
SMYTH,G H	2Lt	RAF	2 Fighting Sch		5.9.18 CR Cambs 39		
SNEATH,Wilfred Harry	Lt	RAF	208 Sqdn		6.4.18 MR 20		
SNOWDEN,H J	Lt	SLancsR att RFC			11.8.17 CR London 12		
SNYMAN,Gabriel Daniel Nel	2Lt	RAF		8.10.18CR France 341			
SOLOMON,Harry Mayer	2Lt	RAF	4 A/C Supply Depot		5.12.18CR Hamps 67		
SOLOMON,L B	Lt	2RFus att RAF		12.4.18 CR France 193			
SOMERVILLE,C W	2Lt	RAF	82 Sqdn		24.8.18 CR Belgium 451		
SOMERVILLE,P T	2Lt	RAF	101 Sig Coy		16.8.18 CR France 74		
SONNENBERG,Charles Melville	Lt	RAF	35 Sqdn	dow	19.9.18	CR France 194	
SORLEY,James Campbell	Lt	RAF	213 Sqdn		25.9.18 CR Belgium 132		
SOTHERON-ESTCOURT,Arthur Charles.MC.	Lt	RAF	5 Sqn Ex 8GloucR	kia	8.8.18 CR France 652		
SOUCHOTTE,Charles Campbell	2Lt	RAF	57 Sqdn	kia	23.4.18CR France 792		
SOULBY,Herbert Westgarth	Lt	RAF	51 TDS		19.10.18 CR Ches 35		
SOUTER,T H	2Lt	RAF	103 Sqdn		4.7.18 CR France 924		
SOUTHALL,William Percival	Lt	RAF	64 Sqdn		28.5.18 MR 20		
SOUTHWELL,Charles Reginald	2Lt	RAF	66 Trng Sqdn	kld	6.5.18 CR Durham 26		
SPAIN,David Victor	Cdt	RAF 182119	8Cdt Wing		28.9.18 CR Kent 180		
SPARGO,Percy Gardiner.DCM.	2Lt	RAF	17 Sqdn		18.9.18 CR Greece 1		
SPARKS,Seba Walter	Lt	RAF	17 Sqdn		14.6.18 CR Greece 4		
SPEAKE,Thomas Gordon	2Lt	RAF	82 Sqdn		20.11.18 CR Belgium 393		
SPEER,John Richard	Cadet	RAF 152957		dedacc	24.10 18 CR Canada 110		
SPEIR,G	2Lt	RAF	5 TDS		1.4.18 CR Scot 503		
SPENCE James Hamilton	Lt	RGA & RAF	54 Sqdn		16.7.18 MR 20		
SPENCE,Lyell Campbell.MC.	Lt	RAF	& CanFldArt	kia	25.5.18CR France 10		
SPENCER,Evan David	Lt	5CRT att RAF		kld	11.6.18CR France 792		
SPENCER,Herbert	Lt	RAF	22 Trng Sqdn	ded	29.11.18 CR Egypt 1		
SPENCER,T K	2Lt	RAF	2 A/C Engine Depot		24.8.18 CR France 34		
SPENCER,William	Lt	RAF	27 Sqdn		10.5.18 CR France 1472		

SPENSLEY,Frank Oswald   Capt   RAMC att RAF   ded   23.10.18 CR Dorset 110
SPICER,Edward Arthur   Lt   RAF   53 Trng Sqdn   2.11.18 CR London 2
SPILHAUS,John Arnold   Lt   RAF   70 Sqdn   4.9.18 CR France 1277
SPINKS,Cyril Edwin 2Lt   RAF   11 Sqdn   4.10.18 CR France 512
SPINNEY,William Leslie Gordon   F/O   RAF   24.2.21 CR Mddx 38
SPONG,R W   Lt   RAF   30.10.18 CR Kent 180
SPOONER,Arthur Bruce   Cadet   RAF 153175 42 Wing   dedacc 28.8.18   CR Canada 474
SPRATT,Sidney   2Lt   RAF   58 Sqdn   kld   17.5.19 CR Italy 59
SPROSON,William Wilson   Lt   LancFus att RAF   101 Sqdn   kia   7.8.18 CR France 29
SPURGIN,F R G   Lt   RAF   27 Sqdn   16.6.18 CR France 987
SPURRELL,Herbert George Flaxman   Capt   RAMC att RAF(EEF)   ded   8.11.18 CR Egypt 1
SQUIRE,Leonard Percy   Cadet   RAF   34 TDS   23.8.18 CR Lincs 181
STACE,Arthur Howard Bartlett   2Lt   RAF   3.5.19 CR Belgium 241
STACEY,John Randolph   Lt   RAF   Ex 1CanInf   kld   8.4.18 CR Mddx 66
STACK,James Charles Lt   LabCps att RAF   4 Sqdn kld   30.4.18 CR France 134
STAFFORD,John Foster   2Lt   RAF   210 Sqdn   29.9.18 CR Belgium 126
STAGG,Leslie William Gilbert   2Lt   RAF   99 Sqdn   kia   31.7.18 CR France 1675
STAHL,Alfred Magnus   2Lt   RAF   4.9.18 CR France 1277
STANDRING,Wilfrid Montague   2Lt   RAF   65 Sqdn   kia   8.7.18 CR France 71
STANLEY,Charles Gordon   2Lt   RWarR att RAF   34 Sqdn   kia   19.9.18 CR Italy 11
STANSELL,Lionel Brough.MM.   2Lt   RAF &10RWKentR   ded   26.10.18 CR Kent 232
STANSFIELD,W   Cdt   RAF 182941   8 Cdt Wing   4.10.18 CR Yorks 417
STANTON.P C H   Cdt   RAF   1 Sch of Aeros(Reading)   28.10.18 CR Yorks 195
STATA,Bernard Hill Lt   RAF   218 Sqdn   28.9.18 CR Belgium 24
STEDMAN,Arthur Roy   Lt   RAF   88 Sqdn   14.8.18 MR 20
STECKLEY,H B   2Lt   RAF   27 Sqdn   22.7.18 CR France 1107
STEEL,Arthur Edward Lt   RAF &21MddxR   206 Sqdn   3.5.18 MR 20
STEEL,Leonard George   Lt   RAF   62 Wing   22.7.18 CR Gallipoli 1
STEELE,T L.MC.   2Lt   RAF   10.4.18 MR 34
STEGGALL,Frank Lavis   2Lt   RAF   58 TRng Sqdn dow   9.6.18 CR Egypt 15
STELL,Jack   2Lt   RAF &3RScots   19.6.18 CR Lancs 206
STENNETT,W R   Lt   RAF   202 Sqn 61 Wing   kld   4.5.18 CR France 1359
STENT,Harold Rodolph   2Lt   2/4WRidR att RAF   kia   20.7.18 CR France 622
STEPHEN,James Davidson   2Lt   RAF   42 Wing   ded   21.10.18 CR Canada 1688
STEPHENS,Alexander Thomas   FltCdt RAF 318351   20.9.19 CR Mddx 77
STEPHENS,Donald Ernest   2Lt   RAF   57 Sqdn   19.9.18 CR Germany 3
STEPHENS,Henry Hill   2Lt   RAF   42 Sqdn   dow   28.6.18   CR France 31
STEPHENSON-PEACH,William George   FltLt RAF   ded   23.4.21   MR 43
STEPTOE,Martin   10958   Cdt   2.O&BLI att RAF   2 Cdt Wing   ded   18.11.18 CR Kent 103
STERLING,William Charles   Lt   RAF   24 Sqdn   3.10.18 MR 20
STERN,Leopold Grahame   Lt   RAF   99 Sqdn   26.9.18 CR France 1667
STEVENS,Alfred James   2Lt   1WarR att RAF   142 Sqdn   kia   21.9.18 CR Palestine 9
STEVENS,Alexander MacKay Lt   RAF   202 Sqdn   28.9.18 MR 20
STEVENS,Howard Knight   2Lt   RAF   13 TDS   30.8.18 CR Shrop 82
STEVENS,Richard Henry Burkwood Lt   RAF   49 Sqdn   kld   30.5.18 CR France 1564
STEVENSON,Alan McDonald   Lt   RAF & Gen List   5.4.18 CR Egypt 9
STEWART,A R   Lt   RAF   54 Sqdn   3.5.18 CR France 65
STEWART,E R.DFC. 2Lt   RAF   55 Sqdn   12.8.18 CR France 1678
STEWART,George S 2Lt   Gen List & RAF   18.6.19 CR USA 184
STEWART,Harold Malcolm   2Lt   RAF   27 Sqdn   kia   16.6.18 CR France 1233
STEWART,John Malcolm   Cadet   RAF 154535   44 Wing   ded   24.4.18   CR Canada 180
STEWART,Roy Theodore   2Lt   RAF   13.9.18 CR Sussex 191
STILL,George 2Lt   RAF &CamH   3.4.18 CR Europe 20
ST JOHN MILDMAY,Bouverie Walter   2Lt   Gen List & RAF   70 Sqdn   kld   16.4.18 CR France 169
STOCK,Albert Ernest 2Lt   RAF   18 Sqdn   4.9.18 CR France 273
STOCK-REES,P G   Lt   RAF   205 TDS   18.6.18 CR France 1844
STOCKENSTROM,Andries Lars   Lt   RAF   70 Sqdn   23.5.18 MR 20
STOCKHAUSEN,Ivan Lancelot   Lt   BrWIndiesR att RAF   17 Sqdn   kia   3.10.17 CR Greece 3
STOCKINS,William James   2Lt   22LondR & RAF   6.6.18 MR 20
STOCKLEY,Harold Brodie   2Lt   RAF & 2LondR   kld   22.7.18

119

STODDART,George Benjamin Johnstone 2Lt RAF &GenList 65 Sqdn   kia   10.4.18 CR France 37

STOKES,Claud Harry.DFC.   Capt   RAF   57 Sqdn   dow   7.11.18 CR Belgium 199

STOKES,H J E   Lt   RAF   9.5.19   CR Kent 27

STOKES,William Allen   LtCol   RE att RAF   28.8.20   CR Egypt 6

STONE,Richard   Lt   RAF   201 Sqdn   9.8.18   CR France 526

STONE,William Holloway   Lt   RAF   49 Sqdn   kld   5.9.18   CR France 227

STONEHOUSE,Ronald   .Lt   RAF   kld   1.4.18   CR France 62

STORRS,H L   Lt   RAF   10 Sqdn   dow   20.6.18   CR France 134

STORY,Leslie Campbell   2Lt   RAF   209 Sqdn   1.7.18   MR 20

STOTT,J   2Lt   RAF   215 Sqdn   23.8.18   CR France 1675

STOVIN,Frederick Cecil   Lt   RAF   209 Sqdn   24.4.18   MR 20

STOYLE,Arthur Percy Lt   RAF   2 Tent Depot   ded   27.2.19   CR France 40

STRACHAN,Andrew Robert   2Lt   RAF   20 Sqdn   20.9.18   MR 20

STRANGE,Gilbert John   Capt   RAF &DorsR   40 Sqdn   24.9.18   MR 20

STRANGE,Hector Stanley   2Lt   RAF &2/4DorsR   7.10.18 CR Egypt 15

STRANSOM,Norman Garner   Lt   RAF   48 Sqdn   kia   10.5.18 CR France 526

STRAW,Lionel Liffard Kay   Lt ·   RAF   25 Sqdn   4.11.18   CR Belgium 262

STREET,Brooks Henry   Lt   2/7WelshR att RAF   34 Sqdn   kia   6.8.18   CR Italy 11

STRINGFELLOW,James Herbert   2Lt   RAF   2 Air Supply Depot   22.7.18   CR France 792

STRONG,Robert Abraham   2Lt   RAF   273 Sqdn   1.12.18 CR Essex 28

STROUD,Eric Hubert Noel   Lt   RAF &LeicR   53 Sqdn   kia   21.4.18 CR Belgium 453

STRUBEN,Henry Marinus   F/O   RAF   25 Sqdn   kld   24.6.21 CR Kent 200

STRUGNELL,Leonard William MM 2Lt   RAF & 1/4MddxR   98 Sqdn   kia   16.6.18 CR France 792

STUART,Peter Dudley Capt   RAF   5 TDS   acckld 1.6.18   CR Lancs 2

STUART,T C   2Lt   RAF   12.12.18   CR Eire 528

STUART-SMITH,Philip James   Lt   RAF & CanCpsCavR   74 Sqdn   8.5.18   MR 20

STUBBS,William Henry   Lt   RAF   54 Sqdn   kia   25.6.18 CR Belgium 88

STUBLEY,L M   Lt   RAF   12 Sqdn   21.8.18   CR France 745

STURGESS,George Minshall   Lt   EssR att RAF   kld   5.4.18   CR Egypt 8

SULLIVAN,Frank Harrington 2Lt   RAF   216 Sqdn   kldacc   29.3.19   CR France 34

SUMNER,E Ralph   Cadet   RAF   272949   ded   7.11.18 CR Canada 256

SUMNER,Francis Cyril   Lt   RAF   214 Sqdn   kld   9.7.19   CR France 1571

SUMNER,G   2Lt   RAF   11.5.18   CR Lancs 170

SUMSION,Francis   Lt   RAF &WelshR 62 Sqdn   4.11.18 CR Belgium 218

SUTCLIFFE,Geoffrey 2Lt   RAF   204 Sqdn   23.10.18   CR Belgium 357

SUTHERLAND,Alexander Macbeth   2Lt   RAF   2.7.18   CR France 652

SUTHERLAND,Hugh Capt   RAF   58 TDS   4.11.18 CR Lincs 78

SUTHERLAND,Hugh Angus 2Lt   RAF   HMS Furious   5.9.18   CR Scot 112

SUTHERLAND,James Lawrence Cathcart.MC.Lt   RWKentR att RAF   104 Sqdn   19.8.18   CR France 1667

SUTHERLAND,J H R.OBE.AFC.   Lt   RAF   ded   11.2.20   CR Canada 112

SUTHERLAND,Thomas   Capt   RAF & 2/6LpoolR   dow   14.6.20   CR Lancs 2

SUTTLE,William Parker   Capt   RAF   215 Sqdn   ded   2.2.19   CR France 134

SUTTON,Arthur Eldred Barker   Lt   RAF   4.7.18   CR Ches 3

SUTTON,H L 2Lt   RAF   50 Trng Sqdn   22.4.18   CR Lancs 383

SUTTON,Oliver Manners.MC.   FltLt   RAF   Aero Exptl Est kldacc   16.8.21   CR Sussex 163

SUTTON-JONES,Cecil Gwyn FltCdt   RAF   kld   11.9.18 CR Numb 56

SWAIN,Clifford Maxwell   2Lt   RAF   52 Sqdn   kia   4.4.18   CR France 37

SWAINE,Sydney W   Lt   RFA attRAF   52 Sqdn   4.4.18   CR France 37

SWANNELL,C E.MM.   Lt   RAF   19.7.18   CR Sussex 178

SWANSON,George William   Capt   4HampsR att RAF   drd   10.10.18   MR 40

SWANSTON,J R.DFC.   F/O   RAF   60 Sqdn   28.6.20   MR 67

SWAYZE,William K   Lt   ·RAF   ded   26.2.20   CR Canada 1498

SWEENEY,Leo John.MC.   Lt   RAF &BrColumbiaR   4 Sqdn   30.4.18   CR France 134

SWEETING,Alan Ernest   Lt   RAF   kld   2.8.19   CR Staffs 71

SWORDER,Norman   Lt   BrColumbiaR att RAF   17.4.18   CR France 268

SYDES,W J A Lt   RAF   Arm Sch Ealing   24.2.19   CR London 12

SYKES,J A   Lt   RAF   48 Sqdn   kia   3.10.18 CR Belgium 157

SYKES,John Acton   Lt   RAF   65 Sqdn   16.6.18   CR France 526

SYMONDSON,Vernon Francis   Lt   RAF   210 Sqdn   13.11.18   CR France 658

SYMONS,James Godfrey   2Lt   RAF   27 Sqdn   4.11.18 CR France 1154

SYMONS,Keith William Allardyce   Lt   RAF   73 Sqdn   30.7.18 MR 20
SYMONS,T S Capt   RAF & 3RSussR   kld   29.9.18CR France 379

T

TAIT,Wilfred Burt   2Lt   RAF   43 Wing   dedacc 16.7.18 CR Canada 1688
TALBOT,A   Lt   RAF   1 Trng Sqdn   acckld 3.6.18 CR Hamps 31
TALBOT,Ralph Frederick   2Lt   RAF   8 Sqdn   2.9.18 MR 20
TALBOT,William Caithness   Lt   RAF   20.7.18 CR Wilts 116
TANNER,F C 2Lt   RAF   34 Trng Sqdn   28.6.18 CR Hamps 90
TANNER,John Champion   Capt   RAF   56 TDS   kld   1.8.18 CR Hamps 150
TAPP,F E   Cdt   RAF 184575 8 Cdt Wing   24.11.18 CR Devon 100
TARBUTT,Fraser Coventry   Lt   RAF   56 Sqdn   16.6.18 MR 20
TART,Edmund Graham   Lt   RAF   6 TDS   31.5.18 CR Ches 3
TATE,Alan Charles RichmondLt   RAF &GenList79 Sqdn   kld   2.5.18 CR France 788
TATTON,Eric Hudson.MID   CaptFltCmdr   RAF   84 Sqdn   kia   20.4.18CR France 37
TAVINER,E   2Lt   RAF   drd   28.10.18 MR 40
TAYLER,John Allingham Churchill   Lt   RAF   213 Sqn 61 Wing   7.8.18 CR France 1359
TAYLERSON,N A   Lt   RAF   211 Sqdn   19.5.18 CR Belgium 390
TAYLOR,Ashley Dudley   Capt   RAF   99 Sqdn   24.8.18 CR France 1678
TAYLOR,Edgar   Lt   RAF   79 Sqdn   25.8.18 MR 20
TAYLOR,Frederick Charles   2Lt   RAF   206 Sqdn   22.5.18 CR France 134
TAYLOR,Hugh John   Cadet   RAF 272376   ded   6.10.18CR Canada 115
TAYLOR,James   2Lt   RAF   34 Sqdn   kia   26.7.18CR Italy 11
TAYLOR,John Hector 2Lt   RAF   O'Flight   kldacc 19.11.18 CR France 441
TAYLOR,Joseph Hugh   FltSubLt   RAF   G'Sqdn   17.4.18 CR Greece 10
TAYLOR,Mervill Samuel   Lt   RAF   209 Sqdn   7.7.18 MR 20
TAYLOR,Norman Samuel   Lt   RAF   66 Sqn 14 Wing   kld   13.8.19MR 70
TAYLOR,Ronald John William   2Lt   RAF   Cranwell Stn   kld   9.5.18 CR Devon 69
TAYLOR,William Edward   Lt   RAF   70 Sqdn   31.5.18 CR France 247
TEDBURY,Ralph Newman   2Lt   RAF   3 Sqdn dow   4.9.18 CR France 103
TEETZEL,Harry Duncan   2Lt   RAF   60 Trng Sqdn   10.7.18 CR Yorks 12
TELFER,William Houston   2Lt   RAF   27 Sqdn   24.7.18 CR France 1429
TERRY,Eric Charles   2Lt   RAF   16 Trng Sqdn   kld   12.4.18CR Wilts 28
TERRY,H   Lt   RAF   28.11.18 CR Warwick 4
TEUNON,M   Lt   RGA att RAF   4.1.19 CR Scot 378
THACKER-KING,L R Lt   RAF   see KING,L R T
THERON,W V Lt   RAF   205 Sqdn   20.9.18 CR France 526
THEOBALD,C S   Cadet   RAF   38 TDS   26.10.18 CR Yorks 319
THOMAS,B S B.MC. Lt   RAF   11 Sqdn   4.10.18CR France 512
THOMAS,Desmond   2Lt   4SLancsR att RAF   14 N'Wing   kia   28.6.18CR Italy 9
THOMAS,D U 2Lt   RAF   57 Sqdn   27.10.18 CR France 948
THOMAS,G M.DFC. Flt Lt   RAF   kldacc 24.8.21   CR Yorks 2
THOMAS,Hugh Spencer   2Lt   RAF   27 Sqdn   29.9.18 CR France 1352
THOMAS,O V FltCmdr   RAF   29.7.18 CR Essex 175
THOMPSON,Adam Howie   2Lt   4GordH att RAF   191 (night) Trng Sqdn   7.9.18 CR Hunts 90
THOMPSON,Alfred Hamilton Lt   RAF &5ResBnCanadianInf   ded   26.9.18   CR France 134
THOMPSON,A R   Lt   RAF   6 Sqdn   10.8.18 CR France 1170
THOMPSON,Cecil Frederick Johnstone Lt   RAF   45 TDS   kld   6.9.18 CR Surrey 150
THOMPSON,Clifford FltCdt RAF   kldacc 3.1.19 CR Lancs 317
THOMPSON,C R J   Capt   RAF   63 Trng Sqdn   17.7.18 CR Kent 125
THOMPSON,Douglas Blaxland   Lt   RFA att RAF   47 Sqdn   24.10.19 CR Asia 81
THOMPSON,Henry   2Lt   RAF   103 Sqdn   11.6.18 MR 20
THOMPSON,Leonard 2Lt   RAF   209 Sqdn   kia   8.8.18 CR France 526
THOMPSON,Leroy Herbert   Cadet   RAF 173637 Cdt Wing   ded   30.10.18 CR USA 149
THOMPSON,Robert Ellerton 2Lt   RAF   80 Sqdn   1.10.18 MR 20
THOMPSON,Robert Henry   2Lt   RAF   203 Sqdn   9.12.18CR France 550
THOMPSON,Sidney   Lt   RAF   27 Sqdn   26.1.19 CR Durham 8

THOMPSON,Samuel Frederick Henry.MC.DFC.　　Capt　RAF　22 Sqdn　　　　27.9.18　MR 20
THOMPSON,S P　　FltCdt　RAF　205 TDS　　　12.7.18　CR France 1844
THOMPSON,W M　Lt　　RAF　107 Sqdn　　　20.10.18　CR Belgium 241
THOMSON,G E.DSO.MC.　Capt　RAF　7 TDS　　　23.5.18　CR Oxford 74
THOMSON,John　Lt　　RAF &CanEngrs　　N'Flt　　27.10.18　MR 20
THOMSON,J　Lt　　RAF &RE　　　　25.2.19　CR Scot 115
THOMSON,John Eric　Cadet　RAF　182223　8 Cdt Wing　ded　5.10.18CR Kent 180
THOMSON,J H　　2Lt　　RAF & 5A&SH　　107 Sqdn　　　9.10.18　CR Belgium 205
THOMSON,Roy Reid　Lt　　RAF　70 Sqdn　　　3.11.18CR Belgium 143
THOMSON,Samuel Andrew　2Lt　RAF　60 Sqdn　　　5.9.18　MR 20
THORN,Harold Jarvis Cave　2Lt　RAF　84 Sqdn　dow　31.10.18　CR France 441
THORNE,Arthur Burrell　Lt　　RAF　　　8.5.18　CR Norfolk 60
THORNHILL,Archibald George　　Lt　　RAF　kld　13.5.19CR Glouc 69
THORNTON,F O.DFC.　　Lt　　RAF　57 Sqdn　kld　6.3.19　CR Belgium 269
THORNTON,Harold Victor　Lt　　RAF　34 Sqdn　kia　10.5.18CR Italy 9
THORNTON,Percy　2Lt　RAF　59 Sqdn　doi　28.4.18CR France 63
THORP,Charles Evans2Lt　RAF　55 Sqdn　kld　30.8.18CR France 1678
THROWER,Leonard Albert　2Lt　RAF　Seaplane Stn　lost at sea　18.7.18　　MR 40
THURSTON,D R.AFC.　　Capt　RAF　Airship Trng Wing Ex RN　ded　24.2.19　　CR Lincs 181
THWAITE,Mendel Francis　2Lt　RAF　58 TDS　kld　28.10.18　CR Lincs 78
TIDMARSH,John Moriarty　Lt　　RAF &12WRidR　　kld　3.9.18　CR Eire 167
TILL,E 2Lt　RAF　57 Sqdn　　　6.11.18CR France 788
TIMSON,Percy Walter Johnson　　Lt　　RAF　57 Sqdn　　　26.9.18　MR 20
TISDALL,Michael Henry　　Lt　　RAF　48 Sqdn　　23.12.19　MR 43
TITCHENER,Frank　Lt　　RAF　202 Sqdn　　14.5.18　MR 20
TODD,John　2Lt　RAF　9 Trng Sqdn　kld　29.7.18CR Lancs 383
TODD,Leslie Graham 2Lt　RAF　99 Sqdn　ded　26.2.19　　CR France 1142
TODMAN,Charles Vincent　Lt　　10LondR att RAF　16 Sqdn　kia　3.8.18　CR France 95
TOES,Arthur　2Lt　RAF　18 Sqdn　kia　27.10.18　CR France 725
TOFT,H　2Lt　RAF　　　12.10.18　CR Lincs 491
TOLLER,R A　Lt　　2WelshReg att RAF　　　27.2.19　CR London 4
TOLLEY,Charles Robert　Lt　　RAF　　　21.4.19　CR Hamps 1
TOLMAN,Clifford John　2Lt　RAF　22 Sqdn　　　27.9.18　MR 20
TOLSON,Douglas Irvine　Cdt　RAF　177552　　　1.11.18CR Yorks 631
TOMKINSON,H C　2Lt　RAF　　　5.11.18CR Ches 51
TOMLIN,Alfred Hare　2Lt　RAF　　dow　16.9.18　　CR Herts 30
TOMPSON,Eric Barton　　Capt　RAF　　　8.4.18　CR Greece 10
TONG,Arthur Frederick　Lt　　RAF　217 Sqdn　kld　28.9.18CR France 1358
TONKS,Adrian James Boswell　　Capt　RAF　217 Sqn(EEF)　kld　14.7.19CR Egypt 1
TOPLEY,E P A　　2Lt　RAF　29 TDS　　30.10.18　CR Hamps 31
TOPPING,J　2Lt　2BlkW att RAF　　　16.9.18　MR 34
TOUCHARD,Gustave　Lt　　RAF　44 Wing　ded　5.9.18　CR Canada 1688
TOUCHE,Eric Percy Johnstone　　2Lt　　RAF　kld　17.5.18CR Hamps 192
TOULMIN,Harold.MC.　　Lt　　RAF &6LNLancsR　46 Sqdn　　17.9.18　MR 20
TOWER,W C C　Capt　10EKentR att RAF　　　30.11.18　CR Sussex 144
TOWLER,Cyril John　2Lt　RAF　41 TDS　　4.9.18　CR Sussex 200
TOWLER,F S 2Lt　RAF　110 Sqdn　　　5.10.18CR Germany 3
TOWNSEND,William Henry　Lt　　RAF　57 Sqdn　　　23.4.18　CR France 792
TOWNSHEND,Roy Cowell　2Lt　RAF　7 TDS kld　29.5.18CR Berks 66
TOWNSLEY,H A　　2Lt　RAF　7 Sqdn　　14.10.18　CR Belgium 157
TOWNSON,Herbert Johnston 2Lt　15WYorksR att RAF　　kldacc　21.4.18　　CR France 52
TOY,Edmund Charles 2Lt　RAF　213 Sqdn　　25.8.18　MR 20
TRACEY,Ernest Osborn　　FltCdt　RAF　100438　13 Sqdn(Yatesbury)　kld　31.5.18CR Devon 67
TRAFFORD,Arthur Ernest　FltCdt　RAF　　　31.10.18　CR Essex 45
TRAPP,Donovan Joseph　Lt　　RAF　85 Sqdn　　　19.7.18　CR France 255
TRAUNWEISER,G N Lt　　RAF　　　16.4.18　CR France 1094
TRELEASE,R A　Maj　RAF　HQ Indt AF　　27.11.18　CR London 26
TREMBLAY,Albert Jaques　Lt　　RAF &2PnrBn CE(WOntarioR)　　acckld　31.8.18　　CR Hamps 202
TRENDELL,Mervyn Henry WollastonLt　　RAF　HMS Galatea　kld　19.5.18CR Norfolk 109
TRIGG,H F E 2Lt　Gen List att RAF　　　8.5.18　CR Hamps 15

TRIMBLE,Alan Vincent 2Lt RAF 41 Sqdn 25.8.18 MR 20
TROLLIP,Douglas Price Lt RAF 57 Sqdn 1.4.18 MR 20
TROTH,George Norman 2Lt RAF 101 Sqdn 21.9.188 CR France 1170
TROTTER,Claude Hendley Lt RAF &10CanadianInf (AlbertaR) 44 Sqdn kld 13.10.18 CR Essex 164
TRUBRIDGE,R W Lt RAF 6.5.18 CR France 29
TUCKER,H G Lt RAF 5 TDS 4.4.18 CR Kent 125
TUCKWELL,Humphrey Ansell Henry Lt RAF 65 Sqdn kia 4.7.18 CR France 526
TUGWOOD,James Cdt RAF 181919 2 Sch of Obsvrs 8.11.18 CR NHants 6
TUNBRIDGE,Richard Geoffrey Lt RAF 4 Aux Sch of Gnry kld 1.5.18 CR Norfolk 133
TUNSTALL,G S Lt ManitobaRegDepot seconded RAF 18.5.18 CR Lincs 181
TUPMAN,Arthur Lyon 2Lt 2N&DR att RAF 80 Sqdn kia 22.8.18CR France 329
TIRKINGTON,Ivan Lt RAF 79 Sqdn dedacc 23.6.19 CR Germany 1
TURNBULL,Herbert Philip Lt RAF 42 Sqdn kia 27.10.18 CR France 1030
TURNBULL,John Seymour Lt RAF & WorcR 41 Sqdn 17.6.18 MR 20
TURNBULL,Owen McIlwraith 2Lt RAF 57 Sqdn 21.9.18 MR 20
TURNBULL,Thomas Henry Lt RAF 40 Sqdn 26.10.18 CR France 1085
TURNER,A L Cdt RAF 180516 Trng Wing 5.8.18 CR Sussex 178
TURNER,Bertram Eric Nelson Lt RAF 221 Sqdn ded 15.5.19 CR Asia 81
TURNER,Frederick Eley 2Lt RAF &WYorksR 27.9.18 CR France 1061
TURNER,G J Lt ManitobaR seconded RAF 10.4.18 CR Palestine 9
TURNER,Henry Capt RAF 103 Sqdn 5.6.18 CR France 1235
TURNER,R Capt RAF 212 TDS 31.7.18 CR France 1844
TWILTON,Reginald John Lt RAF 88 Sqdn kld 25.4.19CR Belgium 336
TWOHEY,William Francis PFO RAF 205 TDS 3.7.18 CR Lincs 78
TYRRELL,John Marcus Capt 3ResBnRIrFus att RAF 20.6.18 CR France 102
TYRRELL,Walter Alexander.MC. Capt RAF 32 Sqdn kia 9.6.18 CR France 1232
TYSON,T M 2Lt RAF 2 Sch of Aeros 12.6.18 CR Norfolk 247

U

UHRICH,Charles Philip Lt RAF 28 Sqn 14 Wing dedacc 24.6.18 CR Italy 11
ULLYOTT,Herbert Norman 2Lt RAF 8 Sqdn dedacc 15.8.18 CR France 71
UNDERHILL,R J Lt RAF 22.2.19 CR Kent 180
UNDERWOOD,Ewart Nutman Lt RAF 11 Sqdn kia 6.9.18 CR France 426
UNDERWOOD,Frederick Nelson 2Lt RAF HMS Furious kld 2.7.19 CR Scot 235
UNDERWOOD,Roy Garon Lt RAF acckld 25.9.18 CR Essex 86
UNWIN,Francis John Lt RAF Ex KSLI HMS Vindictive drd 17.9.19 CR Europe 180 & MR 70
UPFILL,Thomas Henry.MC. Lt RFA att RAF 59 Sqdn 18.10.18 CR France 658
UPTON,William George Lt RAF 213 Sqdn 4.10.18 CR Belgium 157
URINOWSKI,Alexander 2Lt RAF 48 Sqdn kia 24.8.18CR France 1170
URWIN,Wilfred Lt RAF ded 19.11.19 CR Numb 96

V

VANDENBERG,Frederick Alfred 2Lt RAF 22 Trng Sqdn kld 20.5.18 CR Egypt 1
van de SPUY,J S V R 2Lt RAF 3 TDS acckld 25.11.18 CR Hamps 90
VANDE WATER,Malcolm Gifford 2Lt RAF 29 TDS 26.10.18 CR Hamps 31
VAN RYNEVELD,J P Lt RAF 63 Trng Sqdn 2.6.18 CR Kent 125
VAN STADEN,L J 2Lt RAF 26.4.18 CR Lincs 136
VAN VELDEN,C J H 2Lt RAF Repatn Camp Ex SARif 24.2.19 CR London 8
VAUCOUR,Awdry Morris.MC&Bar.DFC. Maj RAF &RA kia 16.7.18CR Italy 11
VERNON,R G 2Lt RAF 110 Sqdn 21.10.18 CR Germany 3
VICKERS,Alfred 2Lt RAF 56 Sqdn 3.9.18 MR 20
VICKERS,S W.MC.DFC. Capt RAF 18.2.19 CR Ches 59
VINCENT,Frederick Charles FltCdt RAF 176712 1 TDS (Stamford) kld 3.1.19 CR Devon 1
VIVEASH,A J Lt RAF 13 Sqdn 28.8.18 CR France 1489

VON POELLNITZ,Herman Walter   CaptMaj   RAF & 2LincsR   72 Sqdn   kld   11.5.18CR Iraq 8
VORSTER,William Lennox   Lt   RAF   139 Sqdn   23.7.18 CR Italy 71

W

WADDINGTON,George Walter   2Lt   RAF   49 Sqdn   25.11.18 CR France 403
WADDINGTON,J H   2Lt   RAF   80 Sqdn   22.10.18 CR France 528
WADDY,Sidney Norman   2Lt   RAF   48 Sqdn   24.7.18 CR France 402
WADSWORTH,Leonard   2Lt   RAF   25 Sqdn   dow   29.6.18   CR France 71
WAINWRIGHT,Clifford Ernest   2Lt   KRRC att RAF11 Sqdn   dow   14.10.18 CR France 375
WAITE,Lawrence Phelps   2Lt   RAF   4 TDS kld   16.7.18CR Ches 192
WAKEFORD,F R S   2Lt   RAF   25.12.18 CR Wales 108
WAKEMAN,Malcolm Winser 2Lt   RAF   53 Sqdn   dow   18.10.18 CR France 65
WALD,Alexander.MC.   Lt   RAF   36 Sqdn   11.6.18 CR Numb 4
WALFORD,William Geoffrey Capt   RAF &RE Mon   62 Sqdn   kia   4.11.18CR Belgium 218
WALKER,Frank Frederick   2Lt   RAF   84 Sqn 22 Wing   dow   14.4.18   CR France 145
WALKER,George Bruce   Lt   17HLI attRAF   1.3.19 CR Scot 674
WALKER,Henry Hunt 2Lt   RAF   13.7.18 CR Canada 1444
WALKER,Howard Napier OBE,MC LtCol   1WelshR att RAF   ded   3.6.19 CR Devon 2
WALKER,Hubert William   Lt   RAF   8 Sqn Ex Sgt RAMC kia   23.7.18CR France 526
WALKER,John Cyril 2Lt   RAF   10.8.18 CR France 658
WALKER,J E 2Lt   RAF   209 Sqdn   17.9.18 CR France 1280
WALKER,John Gill   2Lt   RAF   22 Sqdn   30.8.18 CR France 10
WALKER,J P Lt   RAF   3.8.18 CR Essex 50
WALKER,Kenneth MacKenzie   2Lt   RAF &3WiltsR   209 Sqdn   12.8.18 MR 20
WALKER,L H 2Lt   RAF   80 Sqdn   26.9.18 CR France 725
WALKER,Stephen   2Lt   CambR att RAF   kld   14.5.18CR Essex 246
WALKER,William.DFC.   Capt   RAF &GenList6 Sqdn   8.10.18MR 20
WALLACE,G R   F/Cadet   RAF   See McADAM,George R
WALLACE,John Ewing   2Lt   RAF   107 Sqdn   kia   9.8.18 MR 20
WALLACE,Kenneth Houston 2Lt   RAF   70 Sqdn   4.9.18 MR 20
WALLER,Hardress De Warrenne   P/O   RAF   lost at sea   21.2.20   MR 40
WALLER,Richard Percy   2Lt   RAF   kld   22.5.18CR Scot 64
WALLIS,Frank   2Lt   RAF   18 Sqdn   ded   13.2.19   CR Belgium 241
WALSH,Laurence William   Lt   RAF   85 Wing   28.10.18 CR France 1678
WALTERS,Herbert Aidan   2Lt   RAF &GenList21 Sqdn   kld   7.4.18 CR Belgium 18
WALTON,John Willie Capt   RAF   3.12.18CR Surrey 2
WARD,Frank Marshall   2Lt   RAF   22 Sqdn   kia   22.4.18CR France 31
WARD,Harry Bronard 2Lt   RAF   12 TDS   23.10.18 CR Wilts 167
WARD,John Gordon   2Lt   RAF   63 Trng Sqdn   7.5.18 CR Lancs 256
WARD,L J B 2Lt   RAF   55 Sqdn   2.1.19 CR France 1675
WARE,Denys Charles Capt   RAF   209 Sqdn   kia   20.9.18CR France 1727
WAREING,Guy Wilbraham.DFC.   Capt   RAF   29 Sqdn   27.10.18 CR Belgium 432
WARMAN,Clive Wilson.DSO.MC.MID   Capt   RAF   81 Sqdn   dedacc 12.5.19   CR Surrey 1
WARMAN,William Alfred   2Lt   RAF   Ex 1/4EssR   13.10.18 CR Egypt 9
WARNEFORD,Walter Kemeys Francis   Capt   RAF   N'sea Airship XI   lost at sea   15.7.19   MR 40
WARNER,Henry Ernest   2Lt   RAF   3 TDS   23.6.18 CR Hamps 192
WARNER,John Weston.DFC. Lt   RAF   85 Sqdn   4.10.18CR France 1061
WARNER,William Henry   2Lt   RAF   218 Sqdn   kia   27.6.18CR Germany 2
WARREN,Edward Dunley   2Lt   RAF   73 Wing   kld   5.12.18CR Norfolk 85
WARREN,F   Designer   RAF   kldacc 28.8.21   CR Yorks 2
WARRILOW,Reginald Arthur Bakewell 2Lt RAF   29 TDS   kld   13.1.19CR Wilts 30
WARWICK,John Lacy 2Lt   RAF   63 Sqdn   14.6.18 CR Iraq 8
WASE,John Edgelow Lt   RAF   218 Sqdn   19.8.18 CR France 65
WASHINGTON,William Frederick   2Lt   RAF   20 Sqdn   kld   3.9.18 CR France 245
WATCHORN,Claude Edmund2Lt   RAF   kldacc 17.6.18   CR Ches 86
WATERER,M A   2Lt   RAF &RE Mon   6 Sqdn dow   11.10.18 CR France 446
WATERHOUSE,Joseph   Lt   RAF   37 TDS   18.2.19 CR London 25

WATERLOW,E.MC. Capt RAF 25 Sqdn 16.7.18 CR Belgium 84
WATERS,Andrew John 2Lt RAF 206 Sqdn 31.1.19 CR Germany 1
WATKINS,Jack Eric.MID Lt RAF 67 Wing kia 30.8.18 CR Greece 7
WATKINS,Loudon Pierce.MC. Capt RAF 148 Sqdn 1.7.18 CR France 14
WATKINS,William 2Lt 3WelshReg att RAF 139Sqnkia 23.7.18 CR Italy 9
WATSON,George Lt RAF 40 Sqdn 20.5.18 MR 20
WATSON,Howard 2Lt RAF 53 Trng Sqdn 8.5.18 CR Scot 170
WATSON,Percy Frederick FltCdt RAF kld 12.8.18 CR Warwick 97
WATSON,W E 2Lt RAF 61 Wing 6.6.18 CR France 1359
WATTS,Wilfred John Capt RAF &4CanadianInf 44 Wing ded 21.10.18 CR Canada 1688
WAYMAN,Robert Frederick 2Lt RAF 38 Trng Wing 23.9.18 CR Egypt 9
WEALE,Frederick Hubert Archibald 2Lt RAF 57 Sqdn 2.10.18 CR France 911
WEAVER,E J FltCdt RAF 5.7.18 CR France 1844
WEAVER,Herbert John Lt RAF 8 Sqdn dedacc 6.5.19 CR France 34
WEAVER-ADAMS,Philip Clive 2Lt RAF kld 28.10.18 CR Bucks 95
WEBB,Derek Errol Lt RAF 107 Sqdn dow 9.10.18 CR Belgium219
WEBB,G 2Lt 1/2SStaffsR att RAF 5.6.18 CR France 1235
WEBB,Paul Frederick Hobson Lt RAF 27 Sqdn 7.7.18 CR France 792
WEBBER,William Harold 2Lt RAF 5 Sqdn 10.8.18 MR 20
WEBER,Victor Joseph Lt RAF 15.12.18 CR France 1056
WEBSTER,Alexander Lt RAF 70 Sqdn 24.1.19 CR Germany 1
WEBSTER,Arthur Nugent Lt RAF 203 Sqdn kia 5.6.18 CR France 260
WEHR,Charles R Cadet RAF 272195 ded 22.10.18 CR Canada 300
WEIGHT,James Lt RAF 42 Sqdn kia 4.7.18 CR France 31
WEIR,C G 2Lt RAF 4 Sqdn 7.8.18 CR France 134
WEIR,G M Cdt RAF 183670 8 Cdr Wing ded 28.10.18 CR Kent 180
WEIR,H Roy Cadet RAF 153510 dedacc 25.6.18 CR Canada 151
WEIR,Noble Alexander 2Lt RAF 19 Sqdn 27.11.18 CR France 1196
WELCH,Hubert John Lt RAF 80 Sqdn kld 29.9.18 CR France 375
WELCH,S B Lt RAF 49 Sqdn 25.8.18 CR France 421
WELCHMAN,Patrick Eliot.MC.DFC. Capt 2KOSB att RAF 99 Sqdn dow 29.11.18 CR France 1678
WELFORD,L C Lt RAF 80 Sqdn 7.6.18 CR France 1421
WELINKAR,Shri Krishna Chauda Lt RAF 23 Sqdn dow 30.6.18 CR France 425
WELLS,A H Cadet RAF 182104 8Cdt Wing 5.10.18 CR Kent 180
WELLS,Charles Douglas.MC.MID Lt RAF 62 Sqdn kia 16.5.18 CR France 23
WELLS,Sydney 2Lt RAF 48 Sqdn 26.3.19 CR Germany 1
WELLS,William Lewis.MC&Bar Capt 8MddxR att RAF 48 Sqdn dow 6.5.18 CR France 145
WEMYSS-GORMAN,Dundas FltCdt RAF 205TDS 9.7.18 CR France 1844
WEST,E A Cdt RAF 13774 18.12.18 CR EAfrica 47
WEST,John Sprout Lt RAF 88 Sqdn 28.6.18 CR Belgium 132
WEST,Percy Charles Lt RAF 16 Sqdn 3.8.18 CR France 95
WEST,Sidney John 2Lt RAF 9 Sqdn dow 11.8.18 CR France 119
WESTALL,Arthur 2Lt RAF 216 Sqdn kia 30.3.19 CR France 34
WESTCOTT,William Ernest 2Lt RAF 8 Trng Sqdn ded 28.4.18 CR Kent 83
WESTHOFEN,Philip Charles 2Lt RAF 4 Sqdn 12.4.18 MR 20
WESTMORELAND,Edwin Herbert Lt RAF 44 TDS kld 20.8.18 CR Oxford 74
WESTON,John Everard 2Lt RAF 4 Sqdn 14.7.18 CR France 134
WHALLEY,Gilbert Walter Lt RAF 129 Sqdn 27.4.18 CR Suffolk 173
WHALLEY,Reginald Livesey Capt 4ELancsR & RAF 16.9.18 CR France 403
WHATELY,George Alfred 2Lt RAF 80 Sqdn 10.5.18 MR 20
WHELAN,Cyril Lt RAF 42 Trng Sqdn 25.4.18 CR London 9
WHEELER,Alexander James Paterson2Lt RAF 1A/C Supply Depot Repair Park 9.5.18 CR France 102
WHEELER,George Ray 2Lt RAF 19 TDS kld 26.11.18 CR Egypt 8
WHITCOMBE,Hugh Donald Gore Cdt RAF ded 23.7.20 CR Greece 9
WHITCUT,H M Lt RAF &5SStaffsR kld 28.4.18 CR Wilts 115
WHITE,Alan Geoffrey Lt RAF 211 Sqdn kia 29.9.18 CR Belgium 157
WHITE,Cecil Godfrey.MC Capt RAF &RFA 53 Sqdn 21.4.18 CR Belgium 453
WHITE,Edward Alfred 103684 Cadet RE att RAF 26.7.18 CR Mddx 83
WHITE,Evelyn Neville Lewis Maj RAF Air Ministry Ex LtCmdr RN 29.7.19 CR Cornwall 29
WHITE,G J Cadet RAF 153535 dedacc 13.7.18 CR Canada 1558

125

WHITE,T H.MC.   2Lt   RAF   46 TDS   24.1.19 CR London 10
WHITEHEAD,E J   2Lt   RAF   3.5.18 CR Surrey 57
WHITEHEAD,George William Edendale Lt RAF &RFA   53 Sqdn   kld   17.10.18 CR Belgium 140
WHITEHEAD,Joseph Lt   RAF   drd   1.9.18 MR 40
WHITEHEAD,Lewis Ewart   Capt   RAF & Gen List   65 Sqdn   20.5.18 MR 20
WHITEHOUSE,Frank 2Lt   RAF   52 Sqdn   27.5.18 CR France 1334
WHITELAW,Frederick John   2Lt   RAF   148 Sqdn   ded   28.2.19   CR Sussex 178
WHITELOCK,Charles Railton Lt   RAF   55 Sqdn   16.7.18 CR France 1678
WHITESIDE,Arthur Barlow.MC&Bar Lt   RAF   2 Sch of Navgn & Bombg   22.4.19 CR Hamps 98
WHITESIDE,M B D   Lt   HLI att RAF   13.6.18 CR Wales 31
WHITFIELD,Edgar   2Lt   RAF   57 Sqdn   1.4.18 MR 20
WHITFELD,N B   Lt   RAF   62 Sqdn   7.7.18 CR Sussex 159
WHITFORD-HAWKEY,Antony H   Lt   RAF   43 Sqdn   9.5.18 MR 20
WHITHAM,J H   Lt   RAF   26.11.18 CR Yorks 612
WHITLEY,Thomas Turner   FltCdt RAF 321403   drd   24.7.18   CR Yorks 396
WHITMAN,Thomas   2Lt   RAF   80 Sqdn   4.10.18 MR 20
WHITMILL,George Harris   Lt   RAF   202 Sqn 61 Wing   21.4.18 CR France 1359
WHITTALL,Garth   2Lt   RAF   23 Sqdn   12.11.18 CR France 658
WHITTAKER,Fred Poulton   2Lt   RAF   54 TDS Ex 8ManchR kld   25.10.18 CR Lancs 43
WHITWELL,Patrick Henry   2Lt   RAF &YorksR 4 Sqdn kia   25.4.18 CR France 28
WHYTE,Cecil Bertram   2Lt   RAF &RScots 98 Sqdn   3.5.18 MR 20
WICKETT,Royston Clement   2Lt   RAF   6 Sqdn   9.8.18 MR 20
WICKS,Victor Houghton   F/O   RAF   Airship Base (Howden) in R38 kld   24.8.21 CR Berks 86
WICKS,William Dixon   2Lt   RAF   42 Sqdn   11.12.18 CR France 1142
WIENER,Louis de Villier   Lt   RAF   57 Sqdn   4.11.18 MR 20
WIGGINS,Harold Claud   2Lt   RAF   23 Trng Sqdn kld   1.4.18 CR Egypt 1
WIGGINS,T   2Lt   17LancF att RAF   99 Sqdn   27.6.18 CR France 1667
WIGRAM,Aarthur Dunbar   Capt   RAF   30.4.19 CR Berks 125
WILBERFORCE,W R S   2Lt   RAF &KRRC   2.6.18 CR Hamps 130
WILCOCK,John   FltCdt RAF 175355 1 Sch of Navgn & Bombg   kld   22.9.18 CR Ches 142
WILD,Harold Lt   RAF   27 Sqdn   kia   16.6.18 CR France 360
WILDIG,N H   2Lt   RAF   104 Sqdn   kia   7.7.18 CR France 1672
WILDISH,James Edmund   2Lt   RAF   8 Sqdn ded   27.10.18 CR France 146
WILKIN,C S   Lt   RAF   2 Aux Sch of Aerial Gnry   11.9.18 CR Suffolk 83
WILKINSON,C   Lt   RAF   42 Sqdn   21.11.18 CR Essex 124
WILKINSON,Ernest Fletcher 2Lt   RAF   18 Sqdn   22.11.18 CR France 1512
WILKINSON,L   2Lt   RAF   18.6.18 CR Yorks 613
WILLES,Patrick Dalrymple   Lt   RAF   3 A/C Acctnce Park Ex 3RLancsR   29.9.18   CR Norfolk 209
WILLEY,Reginald   2Lt   RAF   57 Sqdn   kia   20.5.18 CR France 792
WILLIAMS,Alfred Edmund   2Lt   RAF   35 Sqdn   25.4.18 CR France 1170
WILLIAMS,Arthur Henry   2Lt   RAF   204 Sqdn   31.10.18 CR Belgium 159
WILLIAMS,Charles Henry   Lt   RAF   63 Trng Sqdn acckld 2.8.18 CR Kent 125
WILLIAMS,Edward Albert   2Lt   Gen List & EgyptLabCps att RAF   31.12.18 CR Egypt 8
WILLIAMS,Frederick Lt   RAF & 7RWFus   62 Sqdn   kia   24.6.18 CR France 924
WILLIAMS,Fred   Lt   RAF   22 Sqdn   2.4.18 MR 20
WILLIAMS,Frank Emlyn.MC.Capt   1/5 WelshR att RAF   57 Sqdn   dow   7.4.18 CR Egypt 8
WILLIAMS,Frank Stanley   Lt   RAF   34 Sqdn   kia   28.6.18 CR Italy 9
WILLIAMS,Gwilym Francis   2Lt   RAF   7 TDS   26.5.18 CR Mddx 39
WILLIAMS,Harvey Tennant   Lt   RAF   lost at sea   5.9,18 MR 40
WILLIAMS,H W W   FltCdt RAF 110760 2 Flying Sch   17.8.18 CR Lancs 149
WILLIAMS,Philip Edward   Lt   RAF   43 Wing   ded   22.10.18 CR Canada 1688
WILLIAMS,Trevor Lewis   Lt   RAF   72 Sqdn   kldacc 1.1.19 CR Iraq 8
WILLIAMS,W H   Capt   RAF &6LancF   kld   3.5.18 CR Palestine 9
WILLIAMSON,G F D See DELMAX-WILLIAMSON,George Frederick
WILLIAMSON,James Lt   RAF   70 Sqdn   15.5.18 MR 20
WILLIAMSON,R B   2Lt   RAF   107 Sqdn   29.10.18 CR France 446
WILLIS,Arthur Ernest Lt   RAF   Cent Flying Sch C'Sqdn   27.8.18 CR Wilts 116
WILLIS,Ernest Maj   RAF   Kite Balloon Sect   1.7.18 CR Europe 1
WILLIS,Francis John Harrhy   2Lt   RAF   kld   20.9.18 CR Devon 267
WILLIS,George White 2Lt   RAF   1 A/C Supply Depot Recep Park   4.1.19 CR France 34

126

WILLIS,Philip.MM   2Lt   RAF & 31CanInf   107 Sqdn   9.8.18 MR 20
WILLISCROFT,Walter Balmer   2Lt   RAF   73 Trng Sqdn   26.9.18 CR Oxford 69
WILLOUGHBY,William V   2Lt   RAF   ded   4.12.19CR Canada 146
WILLS,O B W.MC.   Lt   RAF   10.11.18 CR Suffolk 113
WILSON,Brodie Wyatt   Lt   19LondR att RAF   205 Sqdn   23.9.18 CR France 1061
WILSON,Cecil Kidd   2Lt   RAF   1.4.18 CR Kent 180
WILSON,Claud Melnot.DFC. Lt   RAF   29 Sqdn   kia   14.10.18 CR Belgium 157
WILSON,David   2Lt   SLancsR att RAF   143 Sqdn   12.7.18 CR Scot 774
WILSON,Geoffrey   Lt   RAF &ASC 19DivTrn 209 Sqdn   15.5.18 MR 20
WILSON,Harold   Lt   RAF   32 Sqdn   kia   1.11.18CR Belgium 229
WILSON,Harry Beckford   Lt   RAF   36 TDS   kld   15.8.18CR Warwick 177
WILSON,H B B   Lt   RAF   18.7.18 CR Germany 2
WILSON,Horace Levick   2Lt   RAF   13 Sqdn   1.7.18 CR France 924
WILSON,Jack Morris Lt   RAF   204 Sqdn   30.6.18 CR Germany 2
WILSON,J M 2Lt   RAF   13.11.18 CR Scot 761
WILSON,J S   Lt   RAF   70 Sqdn   29.9.18 CR Belgium 38
WILSON,N   2Lt   RAF   43 Sqdn   18.10.18 CR Germany 1
WILSON,Robert B   Cadet   RAF 70583   dedacc 6.11.18CR Canada 1667
WILSON,V Bruce   Lt   RAF   ded   1.11.18CR Canada 1430
WILSON,Wesley Holford   2Lt   RAF   3 TDS kld   23.9.18CR Hamps 192
WILSON,William Nichol   Lt   RAF   110 Sqdn   dedacc 8.6.19 CR Belgium 265
WILTON,Ernest Parkin   Lt   RAF & ASC   ded   5.11.18CR Yorks 643
WILTSHIRE,C E   Cadet   RAF   58 TDS   19.8.18 CR Notts 37
WIMBUSH,Ewart Austin Bourchier.DFC.Lt RAF   C Sqdnkld   23.5.18CR Asia 81
WINCHESTER,Philip George Dulton FltCdt RAF 45514   63 TRng Sqdn kld   29.8.18CR Sussex 144
WINDOW,Kenneth Percival   2Lt   RAF   43 TDS   kld   28.8.18CR Wales 107
WINDRIDGE,Edwin Arthur   Lt   RAF   103 Sqdn   kia   9.6.18 CR France 360
WINKLEY,Stanley H Lt   RAF   84 Sqdn   1.4.18 MR 20
WINKS,James Grant 2Lt   RAF   51 Sqdn   9.7.18 CR Scot 755
WINNETT.Wilfred Henry   Cadet   RAF 154452   27.5.18 CR Canada 1175
WINSTANLEY,ArthurFltCdt RAF   9.9.18 CR Lancs 2
WINTER,R R C   2Lt   RAF &DLI   54 Sqdn   9.8.18 CR France 526
WINTHROP-ANDREWS,John   Lt   RAF   80 Sqdn   4.10.18MR 20
WINTON,Harold Barkley   Lt   RAF &GenList 1 Sqdn dedacc 21.4.18   CR France 134
WODEHOUSE,C E   Lt   RAF   Marine Obs Sch   18.11.18 CR Kent 68
WOGAN-BROWNE,C P   2Lt   RAF   99 Sqdn   13.9.18 CR France 1678
WOLLASTON,John Dudley   2Lt   RAF   Trng Depot(Beverley) kld   3.4.18 CR Ches 147
WOLSTENHOLME,J B W   Lt   RAF   20.8.18 CR Mddx 42
WOOD,A H O'H   Maj   RAF   see O'HARA WOOD,A H
WOOD,Charles Campbell.MID   Lt   RAF   1 Tech Wireless Sch   10.1.20 CR Mddx 16
WOOD,Charles L   Lt   RAF   201 Sqdn   17.8.18 CR Belgium 406
WOOD,Harvey Cecil Cdt   RAF   2 Offrs Tech Trng Wing   ded   16.7.18   CR Sussex 178
WOOD,Herbert Frederick   Maj   9Lancers att RAF   11.12.18 CR Canada 24
WOOD,John   116826   FltCdt 6ResBn RFA att RAF   kld   19.10.18 CR Lancs 257
WOOD,J   2Lt   RAF   100 Sqdn   9.1.19 CR Germany 1
WOOD,Patrick Bryan Sandford   Lt   RAF   67 Wing   kldacc 24.5.18   CR Italy 6
WOOD,R   2Lt   RAF   65 Sqdn   18.10.18 CR France 1359
WOODCOCK,Frederick.MC. Capt   RGA & RAF   101 Sqdn   31.10.18 CR France 528 & MR 20
WOODEND,Charles William 2Lt   RAF   48 Sqdn   kia   19.8.18CR France 692
WOODHEAD,Harry Tordoff Capt   RAF   14.1.20 CR Yorks 425
WOODHOUSE,Lionel Mostyn.MC.DFC.   Capt   RAF   59 Sqdn   27.9.18 CR France 512
WOODLAND,G H   2Lt   RAF   52 TDS   kldacc 5.11.18CR Somerset 141
WOOLHOUSE,Leslie George 2Lt   RAF   2 Fighting Sch kld   18.1.19CR London 5
WOOLLARD,George Frederick   Lt   RAF   3.9.18 CR Yorks 439
WOOLLEY,Frederick William   2Lt   RAF   99 or 108 Sqdn   14.10.18 CR Belgium 393 & France 1675,31.7.18
WOOLLETT,J C   Capt   RAF   16.11.18 CR Kent 230
WORDEN,Elmer   Cadet   RAF 154631   42 Wing   dedacc 16.9.18   CR USA 238
WORKMAN,Guy   2Lt   RAF   6.5.20 CR Glouc 166
WORMALD,William Montague   2Lt   RAF   209 Sqdn   2.9.18 MR 20
WRAIGHT,L C   2Lt   RAF   17.6.18 CR Kent 217

127

WREATHALL,Robert Scott   2Lt   RAF   82 Sqdn   15.11.18 CR France 1029
WRIGHT,B W Lt   RAF   4 Sqdn   4.5.18 CR France 193
WRIGHT,C V C   Lt   RAF   1 Marine Obs Sch   24.5.19 CR Suffolk 1
WRIGHT,Francis Beattie   Lt   RAF & RFA   10 Sqdn   12.4.18 MR 20
WRIGHT,H C FltCdt RAF   29.9.18 CR Yorks 104
WRIGHT,J T Capt RNAS/RAF   17.7.19 CR Lancs 40
WRIGHT,Leonard Reginald   Lt   RAF   1 (T)Wireless Sch 26 Wing ded   23.10.18 CR Hamps 1
WRIGHT,S H 2Lt   RAF   33 Sqdn   kld   17.12.18 CR Notts 84
WRIGHT,Stephen Sydney   Lt   RAF   7 Sqdn   17.4.17 MR 20
WRIGHT,T   2Lt   RAF   143 Sqdn   20.7.18 CR Lancs 46
WRIGHT,William   Lt   RAF &31CanadianInf   ded   20.11.18 CR Scot 592
WRIGHT,William Milne   2Lt   RAF   2 TDS   1.10.18CR Scot 82
WYATT,William   Lt   RAF   1 Marine Obs Sch   26.5.19 CR Suffolk 1
WYKES,C E Lt   RAF   13.8.18 CR Herts 44
WYLIE,J R   2Lt   RAF   23.4.18 CR Lancs 487
WYMAN,A   Lt   RAF   91 Sqdn   27.5.18 CR Sussex 5
WYNN,Harold William   2Lt   RAF   13 Sqdn   12.10.18 CR France 240

Y

YEOMAN,B F L   2Lt   1/4LondR att RAF   11.5.18 CR Oxford 97
YEULETT,W A.DFC. Lt   RAF   19.7.18 CR Europe 72
YOKUM,C F 2Lt   RAF   59 Sqdn   10.2.19 CR Belgium 330
YORKE,Frederick   Lt   ChesR att RAF   13.1.19 CR Durham 26
YOUNG,Charles Leslie.DFC. Capt   RAF   kia   30.5.18MR 40
YOUNG,Christopher Lt   RAF   55 Sqdn   kia   20.7.18CR Germany 3
YOUNG,Clarence EarlPFO   RAF   Cent Flying Sch   kld   10.11.18 CR Wilts 116
YOUNG,Fred John   2Lt   RAF   24 Trng Sqdn kld   1.5.18 CR Essex 118
YOUNG,Frederick Royston   2Lt   RAF   72 Trng Sqdn   31.8.18 CR Yorks 12
YOUNG,Gavin Ferguson   Lt   RAF   3 Sqdn   2.9.18 CR France 1484
YOUNG,H N.DFC&Bar.MID F/O   RAF   12 Sqdn   13.7.21 CR Shrop 129
YOUNG,Leslie   Lt   RAF   25 Sqdn   kia   4.10.18CR France 403
YOUNG,William Barrie.MID Capt   RAF   62 Trng Sqdn   8.8.18 CR Scot 556
YUILLE,William Beresford   2Lt   RAF   46 Sqdn   kia   30.5.18CR France 303

Z

ZEALLEY,Eric Ralph Lt   RLanR att RAF   30.8.18 CR France 788

APPENDIX 1

A list of the memorials and cemeteries mentioned in the list of officers.

MEMORIALS.

MR1   Naval Memorial,Chatham.
MR2   Naval Memorial,Plymouth.
MR3   Naval Memorial,Portsmouth.
MR4   Helles Memorial,Gallipoli.
MR15 La Ferte-Sous-Jouarre Memorial,France.
MR16 Vis-En-Artois Memorial,France.
MR17 Cambrai Memorial,France.
MR18 Soissons Memorial,France.
MR19 Loos Memorial,France.
MR20 Arras Memorial,France.
MR21 Theipval Memorial,France.
MR22 Le Touret Memorial,France.
MR27 Pozieres Memorial,France.
MR28 Neuve-Chapelle Indian Memorial,France.
MR29 Ypres (Menin Gate) Memorial,Belgium.
MR30 Tyne Cot Memorial,Belgium.
MR31 Nieuport Memorial,Belgium.
MR32 Ploegsteert Memorial,Belgium.
MR34 Jerusalem Memorial,Israel.
MR35 Mikra Memorial,Salonica,Greece.
MR37 Dorian Memorial,Greece.
MR38 Basra Memorial,Iraq.
MR40 Hollybrook Memorial,Southampton,England.
MR41 Chatby Memorial,Egypt.
MR43 Delhi Memorial,India.
MR46 Mombasa British Memorial,East Africa.
MR47 Tanga British Memorial Cemetery,East Africa.
MR50 Nairobi British and Indian Memorial,East Africa.
MR52 Dar Es Salaam British and Indian Memorial,East Africa.
MR53 Aden Memorial,Arabia.
MR59 Bardera Fort Memorial,Somaliland.
MR61 Tehran Memorial,Iran.
MR64 Bombay (St Thomas) Cathedral Memorial,India.
MR65 Kirkee Memorial,India.
MR66 Madras Memorial,India.
MR67 Karachi Memorial,Pakistan.
MR68 Taukkyan Memorial,Burma.
MR69 Delhi 1914-1918 War Memorial,India.
MR70 Brookwood (Russia) Memorial,England.

CEMETERIES.

EAST AFRICA.
2   Handeni Cemetery.
6   Korogwe Churchyard.
7   Korogwe Military Cemetery.
8   Lindi Cemetery.
9   Mhonda Mission Cemetery.
10   Mingoyo Cemetery.
11   Mtama Cemetery.
12   Mwanza Cemetery.
13   New Moshi British Cemetery.
15   Songea European Cemetery.
19   Tanga Main Cemetery.
22   Bweho Chini Military Graves.
23   Chogowali Military Grave.
24   Dakawa (Mgeta River and Wami River) Military Graves.
28   Longido Cemetery.
29   Luchomo Military Grave.
30   Mahiwa Military Graves.
32   Mikese Military Grave.
33   Mkwera Military Graves.
35   Dar Es Salaam (Sea View) Cemetery.
36   Dar Es Salaam (Upanga Street) Cemetery.
38   Kilwa Kivinje Cemetery.
39   Morogoro Cemetery.
40   Iringa Cemetery.
42   Kajiado Cemetery.
43   Kisii Boma Military Grave.
44   Kisumu Cemetery.
46   Molo Military Grave.
47   Mombasa Protestant Cemetery.
49   Mumias European Cemetery.
50   Mwele Ndogo Military Grave.
51   Nairobi Forest Cemetery.
52   Nairobi South Cemetery.
53   Naivasha Cemetery.
54   Nakuru Cemetery.
56   Taveta Military Cemetery.
58   Voi Cemetery.
59   Wajir Cemetery.
60   Hargeisa War Cemetery.
61   Mogadishu African War Cemetery.
66   Port Louis Western Cemetery.
67   Port Louis (Roche-Bois) Eastern Cemetery.
77   Mangochi Town Cemetery.
78   Karonga Church of Central Africa Presbyterian Cemetery.
80   Karonga New War Cemetery.
86   Zomba Town Cemetery.
87   Beira Christian Cemetery.
89   Maputo Cemetery.
90   Lumbo British Cemetery.
92   Pemba Cemetery.
101 Harare (Pioneer)Cemetery.
116 Khartoum War Cemetery.
124 Entebbe European Cemetery.
125 Jinja Roman Catholic Churchyard.
126 Kabarole Mission Cemetery.
127 Kampala (Jinja Road) European Cemetery.
128 Mbarara (St James) Churchyard.

SOUTH AFRICA.
18   Trekkopjes Cemetery.
26   Durban (Ordnance Road) Military Cemetery.
30   Durban (Stellawood) Cemetery.
42   Benoni Cemetery.
52   Johannesburg (Braamfontein) Cemetery.
53   Johannesburg (Brixton New) Cemetery.
63   Potchefstroom European Cemetery.
69   Roberts Heights Military Cemetery,Pretoria.
72   Tzaneen Estate Cemetery,Selati Valley.
81   Rooidam Military Cemetery,Tempe.

130   Mafeking Cemetery.
136   Muizenberg Cemetery,Cape Town.
144   Plumstead Cemetery,Cape Town.
158   Simonstown (Dido Valley) Cemetery.
171   Woltemade Cemetery,Cape Town.
172   Wynberg (Church Street) Cemetery,Cape Town.

WEST AFRICA.

1   Christiansborg Civil Cemetery.
2   Gambaga European Cemetery.
3   Kumasi European Cemetery.
4   Sekondi (Shama Road) European Cemetery
      now Takoradi European Cemetery,Ghana.
5   Chra Village Cemetery now Whala Cemetery.
6   Kumasi Memorial.
8   Elisabethville Cemetery.
12   Bougie Communal Cemetery,Algeria.
17   Relizane Communal Cemetery.
23   Bathurst Memorial.
24   Funchal British Cemetery,Maderia.
28   Freetown Memorial.
30   Freetown (King Tom) Cemetery.
33   Bakundi Military Grave.
35   Bauchi European Cemetery.
39   Enugu Military Grave.
40   Ibadan Mission Church Cemetery.
41   Lkoyi New Cemetery,Lagos.
42   Kaduna Cemetery.
45   Lokoja Town Cemetery.
46   Mamfe European Cemetery.
47   Maio Kalei Military Grave.
48   Nsanakang Cemetery Enclosure.
49   Nsanakang European Cemetery.
50   Udi Military Grave.
52   Yola Station Cemetery.
53   Zaria European Cemetery.
54   Zungeru Cemetery.
55   Calabar Memorial.
56   Ibadan Memorial.
57   Lokoja Memorial.
58   Zaria Memorial.
61   Duala Cemetery.

ASIA.

9   Colombo (Kanatte) General Cemetery,Sri Lanka.
20   Sai Wan Bay Memorial (UMA & UMB),Hong Kong.
33   Hong Kong Cemetery,Hong Kong.
40   Yokohama War Cemetery,Japan.
45   Kranji War Cemetery,Singapore.
51   Haidar Pasha Cemetery,Istanbul.
52   Chanak Consular Cemetery,Asiatic side of the Dardanelles.
53   Famagusta Military Cemetery,Cyprus.
60   Maala Cemetery,Aden.
61   Perim Cemetery,Aden.
62   Sheikh Othman Cemetery,Aden.
64   Horth Point Christian Cemetery,Kamaran Island.
66   Muscat Old Cemetery,Oman.
81   Haidar Pasha Memorial.
82   Tehran War Cemetery,Iran.

AUSTRALIA.

112   Sydney (Waverley) General Cemetery.
307   Brighton General Cemetery.

BELGIUM.

1   Ferme-Olivier Cemetery,Elverdinghe.
2   Hop Store Cemetery,Vlamertinghe.
3   Nine Elms British Cemetery,Poperinghe.
4   Vlamertinghe Military Cemetery.
5   Poperinghe New Military Cemetery.
6   Brandhoek Military Cemetery,Vlamertinghe.
7   Brandhoek New Military Cemetery,Vlamertinghe.
8   Brandhoek New Military Cemetery No.3,Vlamertinghe.
9   Hospital Farm Cemetery,Elverdinghe.
10   Vlamertinghe New Military Cemetery.
11   Lijssenthoek Military Cemetery.
12   Canada Farm Cemetery,Elverdinghe.
13   Bleuet Farm Cemetery,Elverdinghe.
15   Reninghelst New Military Cemetery.
16   Dozinghem Military Cemetery,Westvleteren.
17   Kemmel Chateau Military Cemetery.
18   Mendinghem Military Cemetery,Proven.
19   Huts Cemetery,Dickebusch.
20   Duhallow A.D.S. Cemetery,Ypres.
21   La Clytte Military Cemetery,Reninghelst.
22   Oxford Road Cemetery,Ieper.
23   Bard Cottage Cemetery,Boezinge.
24   Coxyde Military Cemetery.
25   Solferino Farm Cemetery,Brielen.
26   Divisional Collecting Post Cemetery,Boesinghe.
27   Track "X" Cemetery,St Jean-Les-Ypres.
28   Dickebusch New Military Cemetery.
29   Dickebusch New Military Cemetery Extension.
30   Gunners Farm Cemetery,Ploegsteert.
31   Motor Car Corner Cemetery,Ploegsteert.
32   Le Touquet Railway Crossing Cemetery,Ploegsteert.
33   Calvaire (Essex) Military Cemetery,Ploegsteert.
34   Belgian Battery Corner Cemetery,Ypres.
35   Divisional Cemetery,Dickebusch Road,Vlamertinghe.
36   Gwalia Cemetery,Poperinghe.
37   Ridge Wood Military Cemetery,Voormezeele.
38   Haringhe (Bandaghem) Military Cemetery.
40   Abeele Aerodrome Military Cemetery,Watou.
41   Watou Churchyard.
42   Kandahar Farm Cemetery,Neuve-Eglise.
43   St Quentin Cabaret Military Cemetery,Ploegsteert.
44   Potijze Burial Ground.
45   Potijze Chateau Grounds Cemetery.
46   Potijze Chateau Lawn Cemetery.
47   Potijze Chateau Wood Cemetery.
48   La Plus Douve Farm Cemetery,Ploegsteert.
49   Ration Farm (La Plus Douve) Annexe,Ploegsteert.
50   Underhill Farm Cemetery,Ploegsteert.
52   Prowse Point Military Cemetery,Warneton.
53   Hyde Park Corner (Royal Berks) Cemetery,Ploegsteert.
54   Berks Cemetery Extension,Ploegsteert.
56   Chester Farm Cemetery,Zillebeke.
57   Ypres Town Cemetery,Menin Gate.
58   Ypres Town Cemetery Extension,Menin Gate.

59 Ramparts Cemetery,Lille Gate,Ypres.
60 La Laiterie Military Cemetery,Kemmel.
61 Spanbroekmolen British Cemetery,Wytschaete.
62 Lone Tree Cemetery,Spanbroekmolen,Wytschaete.
63 St Julien Dressing Station Cemetery,Langemarck.
64 Minty Farm Cemetery,St Jan.
65 No Man's Cot Cemetery,Boezinge.
66 Welsh Cemetery (Caesar's Nose),Boezinge.
67 Colne Valley Cemetery,Boezinge.
68 Lancashire Cottage Cemetery,Ploegsteert
69 Ploegsteert Churchyard.
70 Ploegsteert Wood Military Cemetery,Warneton.
71 Rifle House Cemetery,Warneton.
72 Menin Road South Military Cemetery,Ypres.
73 Essex Farm Cemetery,Boesinghe.
74 Wytschaete Military Cemetery.
75 Derry House Cemetery No.2,Wytschaete.
76 Torreken Farm Cemetery No.1,Wytschaete.
77 Somer Farm Cemetery,Wytschaete.
78 Cabin Hill Cemetery,Wytschaete.
79 Lindenhoek Chalet Military Cemetery,Kemmel.
80 Dickebusch Old Military Cemetery.
81 Reninghelst Churchyard.
82 Reninghelst Churchyard Extension.
83 Clement House Cemetery,Langemarck.
84 Ypres Reservoir Cemetery.
85 Talana Farm Cemetery,Boesinghe.
86 Dragoon Camp Cemetery,Boesinghe.
87 Ruisseau Farm Cemetery,Langemarck.
88 Aeroplane Cemetery,Ypres.
89 Wulverghem-Lindenhoek Road Military Cemetery.
90 Westhof Farm Cemetery,Neuve-Eglise.
91 La Brique Military Cemetery No.1,St Jean-Les-Ypres.
92 La Brique Military Cemetery No.2,St Jean-Les-Ypres.
93 Wieltje Farm Cemetery,St Jean-Les-Ypres.
94 Buffs Road Cemetery,St Jean-Les-Ypres.
96 New Irish Farm Cemetery,St Jean-Les-Ypres.
97 Dranoutre Military Cemetery.
98 Dranoutre Churchyard.
99 Packhorse Farm Shrine Cemetery,Wulverghem.
100 Pond Farm Cemetery,Wulverghem.
101 White House Cemetery,St Jean-Les-Ypres.
102 Klein-Vierstraat British Cemetery,Kemmel.
103 Suffolk Cemetery,Vierstraat,Kemmel.
104 Godezonne Farm Cemetery,Kemmel.
105 Elzenwalle Brasserie Cemetery,Voormezeele.
106 Artillery Wood Cemetery,Boesinghe.
107 R.E. Farm Cemetery,Wytschaete.
111 Voormezeele Enclosure No.3.
112 Hooge Crater Cemetery,Zillebeke.
113 Birr Cross Roads Cemetery,Zillebeke.
114 R.E. Grave,Railway Wood,Zillebeke.
115 Perth Cemetery (China Wall),Zillebeke.
116 Zantvoorde British Cemetery.
117 Zantvoorde Churchyard.
118 Oak Dump Cemetery,Voormezeele.
120 Woods Cemetery,Zillebeke.
121 1/D.C.L.I. Cemetery,The Bluff,Zillebeke.
122 Hedge Row Trench Cemetery,Zillebeke.
123 Passchendaele New British Cemetery.

124 Voormezeele Enclosures No.1 & No.2.
125 Tyne Cot Cemetery,Passchendaele.
126 Poelcapelle British Cemetery.
127 Railway Dugouts Burial Ground (Transport Farm),Zillebeke.
128 Dochy Farm New British Cemetery,Langemarck.
129 Seaforth Cemetery,Cheddar Villa,Langemarck.
130 Bridge House Cemetery,Langemarck.
131 Spoilbank Cemetery,Zillebeke.
132 Larch Wood (Railway Cutting) Cemetery,Zillebeke.
133 Tuileries British Cemetery,Zillebeke.
134 Zillebeke Churchyard.
135 Railway Chateau Cemetery,Vlamertinghe.
136 London Rifle Brigade Cemetery,Ploegsteert.
137 Tancrez Farm Cemetery,Ploegsteert.
138 Maple Leaf Cemetery,Romarin,Neuve-Eglise.
140 Harlebeke New British Cemetery.
141 Staceghem Communal Cemetery,Harlebeke.
143 Vichte Military Cemetery.
147 Hulste Communal Cemetery.
149 Wielsbeke Churchyard.
150 Poperinghe Communal Cemetery.
151 Poperinghe Old Military Cemetery.
152 Oosttaverne Wood Cemetery,Wyschaete.
153 Croonaert Chapel Cemetery,Wyschaete.
154 Bus House Cemetery,Voormezeele.
155 Irish House Cemetery,Kemmel.
156 Dadizeele Communal Cemetery.
157 Dadizeele New British Cemetery.
158 Moorseele Military Cemetery.
159 Kezelberg Military Cemetery,Moorseele.
160 Ledeghem Churchyard.
161 Ledeghem Military Cemetery.
162 Moorslede Communal Cemetery.
163 Slypskappelle Churchyard,Moorslede.
165 Bedford House Cemetery,Enclosure No.2,Zillebeke.
166 Bedford House Cemetery Enclosure No.3,Zillebeke.
167 Bedford House Cemetery Enclosure No.4,Zillebeke.
167a Bedford House Cemetery Enclosure No.6,Zillebeke.
168 Messines Ridge British Cemetery.
169 Wulverghem Churchyard.
170 Neuve-Eglise Churchyard.
171 Adinkerke Churchyard Extension.
172 Adinkerke Military Cemetery,Furnes.
173 Ramscappelle Road Military Cemetery,St Georges.
174 Nieuport Communal Cemetery.
175 Ostende New Communal Cemetery.
176 Steenkerke Belgian Military Cemetery.
178 Breedene Churchyard.
182 Locre Churchyard.
183 Locre Hospice Cemetery.
184 Locre No.10 Cemetery.
185 Grootebeek British Cemetery,Reninghelst.
186 Kemmel Churchyard.
187 Dickebusch Churchyard.
188 Hagle Dump Cemetery,Elverdinghe.
191 Westoutre Churchyard Extension.
192 Westoutre British Cemetery.
193 Boesinghe Churchyard.
195 Angreau Communal Cemetery.

197 Audregnies Churchyard.
198 Elouges Communal Cemetery.
199 Erquelinnes Communal Cemetery.
201 Hautrage Military Cemetery.
202 Frameries Communal Cemetery.
203 Quievrain Communal Cemetery.
204 Roisin Communal Cemetery.
205 Thulin New Communal Cemetery.
206 Flenu Communal Cemetery.
214 Jemappes Communal Cemetery.
216 Wiheries Communal Cemetery.
218 Blaugies Communal Cemetery.
219 Boussu Communal Cemetery.
221 Boussu-lez-Walcourt Communal Cemetery.
226 Froidchapelle Communal Cemetery.
229 Harchies Communal Cemetery.
231 Jurbise Churchyard.
234 Monbliart Communal Cemetery,Beaumont.
236 Quevy-Le-Petit Communal Cemetery.
241 Mons Communal Cemetery.
242 St Symphorien Military Cemetery.
243 La Louviere Communal Cemetery.
244 Maisieres Communal Cemetery.
246 Asquillies Churchyard.
256 Harveng Churchyard.
261 Nouvelles Communal Cemetery.
262 Rouveroy Communal Cemetery.
265 Belgrade Cemetery,Namur.
266 Liege (Robermont) Cemetery.
267 Huy (La Sarte) Communal Cemetery.
268 Houyet Churchyard.
269 Theux Communal Cemetery.
275 Gougnies Communal Cemetery.
302 Malonne Communal Cemetery.
307 Polygon Wood Cemetery,Zonnebeke.
308 Buttes New British Cemetery,Polygon Wood,Zonnebeke.
310 Divisional Collecting Post Cemetery Extension,Boesinghe.
316 Halle Communal Cemetery.
320 Louvain Communal Cemetery.
321 Nivelles (Nijvel) Communal Cemetery.
330 Charleroi Communal Cemetery.
332 Gosselies Comunal Cemetery.
336 Marcinelle New Communal Cemetery.
337 Soumoy Communal Cemetery.
339 Berks Cemetery Extension (Rosenberg Chateau Plots),Ploegsteert.
342 Schoonselhof Cemetery,Antwerp.
344 Audenarde Communal Cemetery.
348 Bottelaere Churchyard,East Flanders.
349 Bouchaute Churchyard.
353 Ghent City Cemetery.
354 Gysenzelle Churchyard,East Flanders.
355 Landeghem Churchyard,East Flanders.
357 Meerendre Churchyard,East Flanders.
358 Mooregem Churchyard.
359 Nazareth Churchyard,East Flanders.
364 Scheldewindeke Churchyard,East Flanders.
365 Termonde Communal Cemetery Extension,East Flanders.
367 Escanaffles Communal Cemetery,Hainault.
370 Beveren-Sur-Yser Churchyard.

371 Blankenberghe Communal Cemetery.
375 Hoogstaede Belgian Military Cemetery.
376 Houttabe Churchyard,West Flanders.
378 Knocke Churchyard,West Flanders.
379 Oostcamp Churchyard.
380 Oostnieuwkerke Churchyard.
381 Oostrosbeke Communal Cemetery.
383 Roulers Communal Cemetery.
384 Ruddervoorde Communal Cemetery.
385 Stalhille Churchyard,West Flanders.
388 Wenduyne Churchyard,West Flanders.
390 Zeeburugge Churchyard,Bruges.
391 Zeeburugge Memorial,West Flanders.
392 Courtrai (La Madeleine) Cemetery.
393 Courtrai (St Jean) Cemetery.
396 Ath Communal Cemetery.
400 Lessines Communal Cemetery.
402 Bisseghem Communal Cemetery.
405 Winkel-St Eloi Churchyard.
406 Tournai Communal Cemetery Allied Extension.
408 Heestert Military Cemetery.
409 Leuze Communal Cemetery.
410 Menin Communal Cemetery.
413 Anbaing Churchyard.
414 Bleharies Communal Cemetery.
417 Esplechin Churchyard.
420 Froidmont Communal Cemetery.
423 La Glanerie Churchyard.
428 Orcq Communal Cemetery.
432 Rumillies Churchyard.
435 Taintegnies Communal Cemetery.
438 Warcoing Churchyard.
441 Coyghem Churchyard.
442 Dottignies Communal Cemetery.
443 Espierres Churchyard.
448 Rolleghen Churchyard.
449 St Genois Churchyard.
450 Wevelghem Communal Cemetery.
451 Strand Military Cemetery,Ploegsteert.
452 Kemmel Cemetery.
453 Sanctuary Wood Cemetery, Zillebeke.
454 Voormezele Churchyard.

BERMUDA.
1   Bermuda Royal Naval Cemetery,Ireland Island.

BURMA.
122a Rangoon War Cemetery.
129a Taukkyan War Cemetery.

CANADA.
10   Souris (Glenwood) Cemetery.
11   Virden Cemetery.
32   Basswood Cemetery,Marquette.
35   Clanwilliam Presbyterian Cemetery,Marquette.
50   MacGregor Cemetery,Neepawa.
99   Deloraine Cemetery,Souris,Manitoba.
110   Springfield (Sunnyside) Cemetery,Springfield.
112   Kildonan Cemetery,Winnipeg.
114   West Kildonan Jewish Cemetery,Winnipeg.

115 Winnipeg (Brookside) Cemetery,Winnipeg.
116 Winnipeg (Elmwood) Cemetery.
151 Trail (Mountain View) Cemetery,Kootenay.
152 Cobble Hill (St John the Baptist) Anglican Church Cemetery,Nanaimo.
154 Esquimalt Veterans' Cemetery,Nanaimo.
55 Gabriola Island Graveyard,Nanaimo,British Columbia.
174 New Westminster (Fraser) Cemetery,St Peter's Romam Catholic Sect.
180 Vancouver (Mountain View) Cemetery,Vancouver.
183 Victoria (Ross Bay) Cemetery,Victoria.
254 Montreal (Notre Dame des Neiges) Cemetery,Hochelaga.
256 Montreal (Mount Royal) Cemetery,Hochelaga,Quebec.
257 Montreal (Shaar Hashomayin) Cemetery,Hochelaga.
261 Aylmer (St Paul's) Roman Catholic Cemetery,Hull,Quebec.
300 Notre Dame de Stanbridge Roman Catholic Cemetery,Missiquoi.
323A Quebec City (Mount Hermon) Cemetery,Quebec.
423 Preeceville Cemetery,Mackenzie,Saskatchewan.
440 Moose Jaw Cemetery,Moose Jaw.
449 North Battleford Cemetery,North Battleford.
469 Grenfell Cemetery,Qu'Appelle.
487 Moosomin South Cemetery,Regina.
506 Saskatoon (Woodlawn) Cemetery,Saskatoon.
547 Edmonton Cemetery,East Edmonton,Alberta.
609 Annapolis Royal (St Alban's) Anglican Cemetery.
637 Tracadie Roman Catholic Cemetery.
653 North Sydney (St Joseph's) Roman Catholic Cemetery.
657A Sydney (Calvary)Roman Catholic Cemetery.
658 Sydney (HardwoodHill) Cemetery.
699 Springhill (Hillside) Cemetery.
740 Halifax (Camp Hill) Cemetery,Nova Scotia.
745A Halifax (St John's) Cemetery.
818 New Glasgow (Riverside) Cemetery.
911 Summerside People's Cemetery.
912 Summerside (St Paul's) Cemetery.
961 St Stephen Rural Cemetery.
1028 St John (Fernhill) Cemetery,New Brunswick.
1054 Moncton (Elmwood) Cemetery.
1055 Moncton (Shediac Road) Roman Catholic Cemetery.
1060 Sackville Rural Cemetery.
1087 Kincardine Cemetery,Bruce,Ontario.
1091 Port Elgin (Sanctuary Park) Cemetery,Bruce.
1094 Teeswater Cemetery,Bruce.
1113 Cottam (Trinity) Anglican Churchyard.
1114 Kingsville (Greenhill) Cemetery,Essex,Ontario.
1119 Sandwich (St John's) Anglican Churchyard.
1121 Walkerville (St Mary's) Anglican Cemetery Essex.
1125 Bayfield Cemetery,Huron.
1143 Chatham (Maple Leaf) Cemetery,Kent,Ontario.
1245 Ottawa (Beechwood) Cemetery,Carleton,Ontario.
1154A Forest (Beechwood) Cemetery,Lambton.
1156 Sarnia (Lake View) Cemetery,Lambton.
1166 Wyoming Cemetery,Lambton.
1175 London (Mount Pleasant) Cemetery,Middlesex.
1178 London (Woodland) Cemetery,Middlesex.
1181 Lucan (St Patrick's) Roman Catholic Cemetery,Middlesex.
1183 Strathroy Cemetery,Middlesex.
1192 Norwich Cemetery,Oxford.
1197 Woodstock (Hillview) United Cemetery,Oxford.

1200 Listowel (Fairview) Cemetery,Perth.
1206 St Mary's Cemetery,Perth.
1217 Kitchener (Mount Hope) Roman Catholic Cemetery,Waterloo.
1224 Erin Cemetery,Wellington.
1231 Morristown (Crown) Cemetery,Wellington.
1246 Ottawa (Notre Dame) Roman Catholic Cemetery,Carleton.
1268 Godfrey (Piccadilly) Cemetery,Frontenae.
1297 Albury Cemetery,Hastings.
1300 Belleville Cemetery,Hastings.
1303 Deseronto Cemetery,Hastings.
1304/1305 Deseronto (St Vincent de Paul) Cemetery,Hastings.
1322 Beckwith (St Fillan's) Cemetery,Lanark.
1379 Norwood Protestant Cemetery,Peterborough.
1380 Peterborough (Little Lake) Cemetery,Peterborough,Ontario.
1387A Vanleek Hill Roman Catholic Cemetery,Prescott.
1391 Picton (Mount Olivet) Cemetery,Prince Edward.
1430 Lindsay (Riverside) Cemetery,Victoria,Ontario.
1438 Kenora (Lake of the Woods) Cemetery,Kenora.
1440 Fort Frances Cemetery,Rainy River.
1444 Fort William (Mountain View) Cemetery,Thunder Bay.
1464 Brantford (Greenwood) Cemetery,Brant,Ontario.
1484 Durham Cemetery,Grey.
1494 Thornbury Cemetery,Grey.
1498 Dunnville (Riverside) Cemetery,Haldimand.
1518 Beansville (Mount Osborne) Cemetery,Lincoln.
1522 Grimsby (St Andrew's) Anglican Cemetery,Lincoln.
1531 St Catharines (Victoria Lawn) Cemetery,Lincoln,Ontario.
1558 Delhi Cemetery,Norfolk.
1570 Oshawa union Cemetery,Ontario.
1575 Sunderland Cemetery,Ontario.
1598 Mono Mills (Mitchell's) Cemetery,Peel.
1600 Alliston Union Cemetery,Simcoe.
1607 Collingwood (St Mary's) Roman Catholic Cemetery,Simcoe.
1608 Collingwood United Cemetery,Simcoe.
1612 Elmvale Presbyterian Cemetery,Simcoe.
1660 Welland (Woodlawn) Cemetery,Welland.
1667 Hamilton Cemetery,Wentworth,Ontario.
1687 Toronto (Mount Hope) Cemetery,York.
1688 Toronto (Mount Pleasant) Cemetery,York,Ontario.
1689 Toronto Necropolis,York.
1691 Toronto (Prospect) Cemetery,York,Ontario.
1694 Toronto (St James's) Cemetery,York,Ontario.
1695 Toronto St John's,Norway)Cemetery,York.

CENTRAL AMERICA.
6 Quirigua Hospital Cemetery,Guatemala.

EGYPT.
1 Alexandria (Hadra) War Memorial Cemetery.
2 Kantara War Memorial Cemetery
3 Chatby Military Cemetery.
6 Chatby War Memorial Cemetery.
7 Port Said War Memorial Cemetery.
8 Ismailia War Memorial Cemetery.
9 Cairo War Memorial Cemetery.
10 Cairo New British Protestant Cemetery.
13 Cairo Civil International Cemetery.

15   Suez War Memorial Cemetery.
19   Mersa Matruh Military Cemetery.

EUROPE.
1   Pieta Military Cemetery,Malta.
3   Ta Braxia Cemetery,Malta.
4   Addolorata Cemetery,Malta.
5   Rinella Military Cemetery,Malta.
6   Malta Naval Cemetery.
7   Pembroke Military Cemetery,Malta.
9   Marsa Jewish Cemetery,Malta.
17   Plovdiv Central Cemetery,Bulgaria.
20   Sofia War Cemetery,Bulgaria.
23   Gibraltar (North Front) Cemetery,Gibraltar.
26A   Rakoskeresztur Hungarian National Cemetery,Hungary.
28   Lisbon (St George) British Churchyard,Portugal.
30   Bucharest War Cemetery,Romania.
34   Bilbao British Cemetery,Lujua,Spain.
42   Madrid British Cemetery,Spain.
46   Villagarcia British Naval Cemetery,Spain.
51   Vevey (St Martin's) Cemetery,Switzerland.
56   Belgrade New Cemetery,Yugoslavia.
57   Chela Kula Military Cemetery,Nish,Yugoslavia.
58   Skoplje (Uskub) British Cemetery,Yugoslavia.
58a   Kuzala Cemetery,Rijeka,Yugoslavia.
64   Skagen Cemetery,Denmark.
66   Copenhagen Western Cemetery,Denmark.
67   Borsmose Churchyard,Aal,Denmark.
72   Haurvig Churchyard,Denmark.
74   Vederso Churchyard,Denmark.
86A   Bergen-Op-Zoom War Cemetery,Holland.
90   Flushing Vlissingen Northern Cemetery,Holland.
96   Noordwijk General Cemetery,Holland.
97   Orthen Protestant Cemetery,Hertogenbosch,Holland.
99   Rotterdam (Crooswijk) General Cemetery,Holland.
100   'S Hertogenbosch General Cemetery,Holland.
110   Kragero Cemetery,Norway.
131   Narvik Cemetery,Norway.
135   Faberg Churchyard,Norway.
136   Lillehammer Churchyard,Norway.
146   Fredrikstad Military Cemetery,Norway.
148   Tonsberg Old Cemetery,Norway.
149   Poznan Old Garrison Cemetery,Poland.
150a Malbork Commonwealth War Cemetery,Poland.
178A Kviberg Cemetery,Sweden.
179   Archangel Allied Cemetery,Russia.
180   Archangel Memorial,Russia.
193   Churkin Russian Naval Cemetery,Vladivostok,Siberia.
195   Vladivostok Memorial,Siberia.

FRANCE.
1   Le Treport Military Cemetery.
2   Forceville Communal Cemetery Extension.
3   Louvencourt Military Cemetery.
4   Acheux British Cemetery.
5   Bertrancourt Military Cemetery.
8   Calais Southern Cemetery.
10   Pernes British Cemetery.
12   Barlin Communal Cemetery Extension.
13   Mont Huon Military Cemetery,Le Treport.

14   Ligny-St Flochel British Cemetery,Averdoingt.
15   Maroeuil British Cemetery.
16   BoisGuillaume Communal Cemetery.
18   Morbecque British Cemetery.
19   Le Grand Hasard Military Cemetery,Morbecque.
20   Thiennes British Cemetery.
21   Tannay British Cemetery,Thiennes.
22   Corbie Communal Cemetery.
23   Corbie Communal Cemetery Extension.
24   Cinq Rues British Cemetery,Hazebrouck.
25   La Kreule Military Cemetery,Hazebrouck.
26   Le Peuplier Military Cemetery,Caestre.
27   Caestre Military Cemetery.
28   Borre British Cemetery.
29   Crouy British Cemetery,Crouy-Sur-Somme.
30   Crouy Communal Cemetery,Crouy-Sur-Somme.
31   Aire Communal Cemetery.
32   Bruay Communal Cemetery Extension.
33   Sandpits British Cemetery,Labeuvriere.
34   Terlincthun British Cemetery,Wimille.
35   Auchonvillers Military Cemetery.
37   Picquigny British Cemetery.
39   Longpre-Les-Corps Saints British Cemetery.
40   Etaples Military Cemetery.
41   Varennes Military Cemetery.
43   Warloy-Baillon Communal Cemetery.
44   Warloy-Baillon Communal Cemetery Extension.
46   Avesnes-Le-Comte Communal Cemetery Extension.
49   Izel-Les-Hameau Communal Cemetery.
51   Abbeville Communal Cemetery.
52   Abbeville Communal Cemetery Extension.
53   Haute-Avesnes British Cemetery.
54   Dainville British Cemetery.
55   Dainville Communal Cemetery.
57   Wanquetin Communal Cemetery Extension.
58   La Chaudiere Military Cemetery,Vimy.
59   Contay British Cemetery.
60   Harponville Communal Cemetery.
61   Harponville Communal Cemetery Extension.
62   Doullens Communal Cemetery Extension No.1.
63   Doullens Communal Cemetery Extension No.2.
64   Wimereux Communal Cemetery.
65   Les Baraques Military Cemetery,Sangatte.
66   La Neuville British Cemetery,Corbie.
67   La Neuville Communal Cemetery,Corbie.
68   Ecoivres Military Cemetery,Mont-St Eloy.
69   Pernois British Cemetery,Halloy-Les-Pernois.
71   Vignacourt British Cemetery.
74   Puchevillers British Cemetery.
76   Toutencourt Communal Cemetery.
77   Herissart Communal Cemetery.
79   Molliens-Au-Bois Communal Cemetery.
80   Bethune Town Cemetery.
81   Villers Station Cemetery,Villers-Au-Bois.
82   Ration Farm Military Cemetery,La Chapelle-D'Armentieres.
83   Brewery Orchard Cemetery,Bois-Grenier.
84   Bagneux British Cemetery,Gezaincourt.
85   Ste Marie Cemetery,Le Havre.
87   Sanvic Communal Cemetery.

88	Lapugnoy Military Cemetery.
94	Marles-Les-Mines Communal Cemetery.
95	Aubigny Communal Cemetery Extension.
96	Ste Catherine British Cemetery.
97	St Nicholas British Cemetery.
98	Chocques Military Cemetery.
100	Arneke British Cemetery.
102	Boulogne Eastern Cemetery.
103	Bac-Du-Sud British Cemetery,Bailleulval.
104	Gouy-En-Artois Communal Cemetery Extension.
105	Grove Town Cemetery,Meaulte.
106	Houchin British Cemetery.
107	Houchin Communal Cemetery.
108	Fouquieres Churchyard.
109	Fouquieres Churchyard Extension.
112	Gosnay Communal Cemetery.
113	Duisans British Cemetery,Etrun.
114	Cambrin Churchyard Extension.
115	Philosophe British Cemetery,Mazingarbe.
116	Querrieu British Cemetery.
119	Daours Communal Cemetery Extension.
120	Warlincourt Halte British Cemetery,Saulty.
121	Etretat Churchyard.
122	Etretat Churchyard Extension.
123	Tourgeville Military Cemetery.
131	Mailly Wood Cemetery.
133	Courcelles-Au-Bois Communal Cemetery Extension.
134	Longuenesse (St Omer) Souvenir Cemetery.
139	Godewaersvelde British Cemetery.
140	Godewaersvelde Churchyard.
141	Dive Copse British Cemetery,Sailly-Le-Sec.
142	Esquelbecq Military Cemetery.
144	Adelaide Cemetery,Villers-Bretonneux.
145	St Sever Cemetery,Rouen.
146	St Sever Cemetery Extension,Rouen.
147	Haynecourt British Cemetery.
149	Maroc British Cemetery,Grenay.
150	Bapaume Post Military Cemetery,Albert.
151	Peake Wood Cemetery,Fricourt.
152	Munich Trench British Cemetery,Beaumont-Hamel.
153	Waggon Road Cemetery,Beaumont-Hamel.
154	Monchy British Cemetery,Monchy-Le-Preux.
155	Windmill British Cemetery,Monchy-Le_Preux.
156	Euston Road Cemetery,Colincamps.
157	Louez Military Cemetery,Duisans.
158	Habarcq Communal Cemetery Extension.
160	Bully-Grenay Communal Cemetery French Extension.
161	Bully-Grenay Communal Cemetery British Extension.
162	Wancourt British Cemetery.
163	Cambrin Military Cemetery.
164	Bray Military Cemetery.
166	Bray-Sur-Somme Communal Cemetery.
167	Beauval Communal Cemetery.
169	Gezaincourt Communal Cemetery Extension.
172	Beauquesne Communal Cemetery.
174	Wailly Orchard Cemetery.
175	Fermont Military Cemetery,Riviere.
176	Dernancourt Communal Cemetery.
177	Dernancourt Communal Cemetery Extension.
178	Noeux-Les-Mines Communal Cemetery.
179	Noeux-Les-Mines Communal Cemetery Extension.
180	Ebblinghem Military Cemetery.
184	Roclincourt Military Cemetery.
185	Namps-Au-Val British Cemetery.
188	Dartmoor Cemetery,Becordel-Becourt.
189	Norfolk Cemetery,Becordel-Becourt.
190	Highland Cemetery,Le Cateau.
192	Neuvilly Communal Cemetery Extension.
193	Oursteene Communal Cemetery Extension,Bailleul.
194	Doingt Communal Cemetery Extension.
196	Ribemont Communal Cemetery Extension.
197	Millencourt Communal Cemetery Extension.
198	Buire-Sur-L'Ancre Communal Cemetery.
200	Hazebrouck Communal Cemetery.
201	Lillers Communal Cemetery.
202	Lillers Communal Cemetery Extension.
203	Couin British Cemetery.
204	Couin New British Cemetery.
206	Romeries Communal Cemetery Extension.
207	Mericourt-L'Abbe Communal Cemetery Extension.
208	Franvillers Communal Cemetery.
209	Franvillers Communal Cemetery Extension.
210	Bonnay Communal Cemetery Extension.
212	Unicorn Cemetery,Vend'Huile.
214	Bucquoy Road Cemetery,Ficheux.
215	Connaught Cemetery,Thiepval.
216	Sailly-Saillisel British Cemetery.
217	Morval British Cemetery.
218	Rancourt Military Cemetery.
219	Dud Corner Cemetery,Loos.
220	Knightsbridge Cemetery,Mesnil-Martinsart.
221	Beaumont-Hamel British Cemetery.
222	Mazingarbe Communal Cemetery.
223	Mazingarbe Communal Cemetery Extension.
224	Hersin Communal Cemetery Extension.
225	St Hilaire Cemetery,Frevent.
226	St Hilaire Cemetery Extension,Frevent.
228	Montay Communal Cemetery.
229	Montay British Cemetery.
230	Montay-Neuvilly Road Cemetery,Montay.
231	Pommereuil British Cemetery.
232	Martinsart British Cemetery.
233	Mesnil Communal Cemetery Extension.
234	Prospect Hill Cemetery,Gouy.
235	Ramicourt British Cemetery.
236	Joncourt British Cemetery.
237	Joncourt East British Cemetery.
238	Joncourt Communal Cemetery.
239	Adanac Military Cemetery,Miraumont and Pys.
241	Ramillies British Cemetery.
242	Proville British Cemetery.
244	Neuville-St Remy Churchyard.
245	Lebucquiere Communal Cemetery Extension.
246	Blighty Valley Cemetery,Authuile Wood,Authuile and Aveluy.
247	Beacon Cemetery,Sailly-Laurette.
248	St Venant-Robecq Road British Cemetery,Robecq.
249	Gonnehem Churchyard.
250	Gonnehem British Cemetery.
251	Aveluy Communal Cemetery Extension.

252 Aveluy Wood Cemetery (Lancashire Dump),Mesnil-Martinsart.
253 Sailly-Sur-La-Lys Churchyard.
254 Sailly-Sur-La-Lys Canadian Cemetery.
255 Anzac Cemetery,Sailly-Sur-La-Lys.
256 Anneux British Cemetery.
257 Sailly-Labourse Communal Cemetery.
258 Sailly-Labourse Communal Cemetery Extension.
259 Labourse Communal Cemetery.
260 Brown's Road Military Cemetery,Festubert.
261 Post Office Rifles Cemetery,Festubert.
262 Pont-D'Achelles Military Cemetery,Nieppe.
263 Pont-De-Nieppe Communal Cemetery.
264 Nieppe Communal Cemetery.
265 Roclincourt Valley Cemetery.
266 Anzin-St Aubin British Cemetery.
267 Gordon Dump Cemetery,Ovillers-La Boisselle.
268 La Targette British Cemetery (Aux-Rietz),Neuville-St Vaast.
269 Petit-Vimy British Cemetery,Vimy.
270 St Aubert British Cemetery.
271 Avesnes-Le-Sec Communal Cemetery Extension.
272 Quarry Cemetery,Marquion.
273 Chapel Corner Cemetery,Sauchy-Lestree.
274 Sains-Les-Marquion British Cemetery.
275 Erquinghem-Lys Churchyard Extension.
276 "Y" Farm Military Cemetery,Bois-Grenier.
277 Bulls Road Cemetery,Flers.
278 Thilloy Road Cemetery,Beaulencourt.
279 Guards Cemetery,Windy Corner,Cuinchy.
280 Courcelette British Cemetery.
281 Foncquevillers Military Cemetery.
283 Hannescamps New Military Cemetery.
284 Bailleul Communal Cemetery.
285 Bailleul Communal Cemetery Extension.
286 Briastre Communal Cemetery.
287 Belle Vue British Cemetery,Briastre.
288 Solesmes Communal Cemetery.
289 Solesmes British Cemetery.
290 Crucifix Cemetery,Vendegies-Sur-Ecaillon.
292 Vertain Communal Cemetery Extension.
293 Lonsdale Cemetery,Aveluy and Authuile.
294 Guillemont Road Cemetery,Guillemont.
295 Bouzincourt Communal Cemetery.
296 Bouzincourt Communal Cemetery Extension.
297 Trois-Arbres Cemetery,Steenwerck.
298 Le Grand Beaumart British Cemetery,Steenwerck.
299 St Acheul French National Cemetery,Amiens.
300 St Pierre Cemetery,Amiens.
303 Longueau British Cemetery.
304 Camon Communal Cemetery.
306 Bancourt Communal Cemetery.
307 Bancourt British Cemetery.
308 Manchester Cemetery,Riencourt-Les-Bapaume.
309 Sun Quarry Cemetery,Cherisy.
311 Orange Trench Cemetery,Monchy-Le-Preux.
312 Happy Valley British Cemetery,Fampoux.
314 Regina Trench Cemetery,Grandcourt.
315 Haspres Coppice Cemetery,Haspres.
316 York Cemetery,Haspres.

319 Quievy Communal Cemetery Extension.
320 St Hilaire-Les Cambrai British Cemetery.
321 Canonne Farm British Cemetery,Sommaing.
323 Montrecourt Churchyard.
324 Meteren Military Cemetery.
327 Brie British Cemetery.
328 Ennemain Communal Cemetery Extension.
329 Bronfay Farm Military Cemetery,Bray-Sur-Somme.
330 Devonshire Cemetery,Mametz.
331 Gordon Cemetery,Mametz.
332 Awoingt British Cemetery.
333 Awoingt Churchyard.
336 Estourmel Churchyard.
337 Carnieres Communal Cemetery Extension.
338 Forenville Military Cemetery.
339 Ancre British Cemetery,Beaumont-Hamel.
340 Busigny Communal Cemetery.
341 Busigny Communal Cemetery Extension.
342 Sailly-Au-Bois Military Cemetery.
343 Hedauville Communal Cemetery Extension.
344 Mailly-Maillet Communal Cemetery Extension.
345 Merville Communal Cemetery.
346 Merville Communal Cemetery Extension.
347 Rue-David Military Cemetery,Fleurbaix.
348 Rue-Du-Bois Military Cemetery,Fleurbaix.
349 White City Cemetery,Bois-Grenier.
350 Vieux-Berquin Communal Cemetery.
352 Aval Wood Military Cemetery,Vieux-Berquin.
353 Nieppe-Bois (Rue-Du-Bois) British Cemetery,Vieux-Berquin.
354 La Gorgue Communal Cemetery.
355 Lestrem Communal Cemetery.
356 Calonne-Sur-La-Lys Communal Cemetery.
357 Lowrie Cemetery,Havrincourt.
358 Grand Ravine British Cemetery,Havrincourt.
359 Ribecourt Railway Cemetery.
360 Bouchoir New British Cemetery.
363 Villers-Faucon Communal Cemetery.
364 Villeers-Faucon Communal Cemetery Extension.
365 Ste Emilie Valley Cemetery,Villers-Faucon.
366 Jeancourt Communal Cemetery Extension.
368 Epehy Communal Cemetery.
369 Epehy Wood Farm Cemetery,Epehy.
370 Meaulte Military Cemetery.
372 Fricourt British Cemetery (Bray Road).
373 Fricourt New Military Cemetery.
374 Guards' Cemetery,Lesboeufs.
375 Bellicourt British Cemetery.
376 Uplands Cemetery,Magny-La-Fosse.
377 Janval Cemetery,Dieppe.
379 Fifteen Ravine British Cemetery,Villers-Plouich.
380 Delsaux Farm Cemetery,Beugny.
381 Red Cross Corner Cemetery,Beugny.
382 Haplincourt Communal Cemetery.
383 Mill Road Cemetery,Thiepval.
384 Grandcourt Road Cemetery,Grandcourt.
385 Warlencourt British Cemetery.
386 Bazentin-Le-Petit Communal Cemetery.
387 Bazentin-Le-Petit Communal Cemetery Extension.
388 Bazentin-Le-Petit Military Cemetery.

389	Thistle Dump Cemetery,High Wood,Longueval.
390	London Cemetery and Extension,High Wood,Longueval.
392	Martinpuich British Cemetery.
393	Ovillers Military Cemetery.
394	Citadel New Military Cemetery,Fricourt.
395	Bray Hill British Cemetery,Bray-Sur-Somme.
396	Bray Vale British Cemetery,Bray-Sur-Somme.
397	Dantzig Alley British Cemetery,Mametz.
398	Rocquigny-Equancourt Road British Cemetery,Manancourt.
399	Quarry Cemetery,Montauban.
400	Bernafay Wood British Cemetery,Montauban.
401	Longueval Road Cemetery.
402	Delville Wood Cemetery,Longueval.
403	Cambrai East Military Cemetery.
404	Drummond Cemetery,Raillencourt.
406	Sucrerie Cemetery,Epinoy.
407	Villers Hill British Cemetery,Villers-Guislain.
410	Hinges Military Cemetery.
411	Le Vertannoy British Cemetery,Hinges.
412	Mont-Bernenchon British Cemetery,Gonnehem.
413	Mont-Bernenchon Churchyard.
414	Annezin Communal Cemetery.
415	Gouzeaucourt New British Cemetery.
417	Heudicourt Communal Cemetery Extension.
418	Beaurains Road Cemetery,Beaurains.
419	Achicourt Road Cemetery,Achicourt.
420	Agny Military Cemetery.
421	Vis-En-Artois British Cemetery,Haucourt.
423	Vermelles British Cemetery.
424	Crucifix Corner Cemetery,Villers-Bretonneux.
425	Hangard Communal Cemetery Extension.
426	Dury Mill British Cemetery.
427	Dury Crucifix Cemetery.
429	Sauchy-Cauchy Communal Cemetery Extension.
430	Albert Communal Cemetery Extension.
432	Caterpillar Valley Cemetery,Longueval.
433	Ecoust-St Mein British Cemetery.
434	Heninel-Croisilles Road Cemetery.
435	Lagnicourt Hedge Cemetery.
437	Morchies Australian Cemetery.
438	Morchies Military Cemetery.
439	Fins New British Cemetery,Sorel-Le-Grand.
441	Premont British Cemetery.
443	Montbrehain British Cemetery.
444	Calvaire Cemetery,Montbrehain.
445	High Tree Cemetery,Montbrehain.
446	Tincourt New British Cemetery.
448	Aizecourt-Le-Bas Churchyard.
451	Athies Communal Cemetery Extension.
452	Point-Du-Jour Military Cemetery,Athies.
453	Flatiron Copse Cemetery,Mametz.
457	City of Paris Cemetery,Pantin.
461	Levallois-Perret Communal Cemetery.
462	Neuilly-Sur-Seine New Communal Cemetery.
473	Les Gonards Cemetery,Versailles.
477	St Germain-En-Laye Old Communal Cemetery.
480	Aix-Noulette Communal Cemetery Extension.
481	Ontario Cemetery,Sains-Les-Marquion.
482	Triangle Cemetery,Inchy-En-Artois.
484	Moeuvres British Cemetery.
485	Hourges Orchard Cemetery,Domart-Sur-La-Luce.
487	Demuin British Cemetery.
489	Hangard Wood British Cemetery.
490	Gentelles Communal Cemetery.
495	St Venant Communal Cemetery.
496	St Venant Communal Cemetery Extension.
498	Berguette Churchyard.
500	Busnes Communal Cemetery.
501	Berles-Au-Bois Churchyard Extension.
502	Berles New Military Cemetery.
503	Berles Position Military Cemetery.
504	Bellacourt Military Cemetery,Riviere.
505	De Cuisine Ravine British Cemetery,Basseux.
506	Beaumetz-Les-Loges Communal Cemetery.
511	Peronne Communal Cemetery Extension,Ste Radegonde.
512	Grevillers British Cemetery.
513	Carnoy Military Cemetery.
514	Queens Cemetery,Bucquoy.
515	Becourt Military Cemetery,Becordel-Becourt.
516	Bouzincourt Ridge Cemetery,Albert.
517	Achiet-Le-Grand Communal Cemetery.
518	Achiet-Le-Grand Communal Cemetery Extension.
521	Cross Roads Cemetery,Fontaine-Au-Bois.
522	Thelus Military Cemetery.
523	Nine Elms Military Cemetery,Thelus.
524	Raperie British Cemetery,Villemontoire.
525	Rue-Petillon Military Cemetery.
526	Heath Cemetery,Harbonnieres.
527	Roisel Communal Cemetery.
528	Roisel Communal Cemetery Extension.
529	Hermies British Cemetery.
530	Hermies Hill British Cemetery.
531	Feuchy Chapel British Cemetery,Wancourt.
532	Tigris Lane Cemetery,Wancourt.
533	Frankfurt Trench British Cemetery,Beaumont-Hamel.
534	New Munich Trench British Cemetery,Beaumont-Hamel.
535	Stump Road Cemetery,Grandcourt.
536	Guemappe British Cemetery,Wancourt.
537	Tank Cemetery,Guemappe.
538	Heninel Communal Cemetery Extension.
539	Bootham Cemetery,Heninel.
540	Cherisy Road East Cemetery,Heninel.
541	Rookery British Cemetery,Heninel.
543	Vis-En-Artois Communal Cemetery.
544	Fampoux British Cemetery.
545	Level Crossing Cemetery,Fampoux.
546	Crump Trench British Cemetery,Fampoux.
547	Sucrerie Cemetery,Ablain-St Nazaire.
548	Givenchy-En-Gohelle Canadian Cemetery,Souchez.
549	Zouave Valley Cemetery,Souchez.
550	Loos British Cemetery.
551	St Patrick's Cemetery,Loos.
552	Bois-Carre Military Cemetery,Haisnes.
553	Ninth Avenue Cemetery,Haisnes.
554	Fosse 7 Military Cemetery (Quality Street),Mazingarbe.
557	Lievin Communal Cemetery Extension.
558	Bois-De-Noulette British Cemetery,Aix-Noulette.
559	Tranchee De Mecknes Cemetery,Aix-Noulette.
560	Beaulencourt British Cemetery,Ligny-Thilloy.
561	Beugnatre Communal Cemetery.

721 Woburn Abbey Cemetery,Cuinchy.
725 Vadencourt British Cemetery,Maissemy.
727 Le Touret Military Cemetery,Richebourg-L'Avoue.
728 Highland Cemetery,Roclincourt.
729 Mindel Trench British Cemetery,St Laurent-Blangy.
730 Hervin Farm British Cemetery,St Laurent-Blangy.
731 Bunyans Cemetery,Tilloy-Les-Mofflaines.
733 Ghissignies British Cemetery.
734 Englefontaine Churchyard.
735 Englefontaine British Cemetery.
737 Poix-Du-Nord Communal Cemetery Extension.
738 Preux-Au-Bois Communal Cemetery.
739 Bermerain Communal Cemetery.
742 Serre Road Cemetery No.1,Beaumont-Hamel,Hebuterne
and Puisieux.
743 Serre Road Cemetery No.3,Puisieux.
744 A.I.F. Burial Ground,Grass Lane,Flers.
745 Bienvillers Military Cemetery.
747 Humbercamps Communal Cemetery Extension.
748 Bailleulmont Communal Cemetery.
749 Barly French Military Cemetery.
755 Ruyaulcourt Military Cemetery.
756 Beaumetz Cross Roads Cemetery,Beaumetz-Les-Cambrai.
757 Beaumetz-Les-Cambrai Military Cemetery No.1
758 Bertincourt Chateau British Cemetery.
759 Louverval Military Cemetery,Doignies.
760 Iwuy Communal Cemetery.
761 Niagara Cemetery,Iwuy.
765 Gorre British Cemetery,Beuvry.
768 Estaires Communal Cemetery.
769 Estaires Communal Cemetery Extension.
770 Blargies Communal Cemetery Extension.
772 Forges-Les-Eaux Communal Cemetery.
777 Orchard Dump Cemetery,Arleux-En-Gohelle.
779 Lens Communal Cemetery,Sallaumines.
782 Billy-Montigny Communal Cemetery.
783 Izel-Les-Equerchin Communal Cemetery.
785 Combles Communal Cemetery Extension.
786 Guards' Cemetery,Combles.
787 St Pol Communal Cemetery Extension.
788 St Pol British Cemetery,St Pol-Sur-Ternoise.
790 Hesdin Communal Cemetery.
792 Huby-St Leu British Cemetery.
795 St Georges Churchyard.
798 Gommecourt British Cemetery No.2,Hebuterne.
800 Rossignol Wood Cemetery,Hebuterne.
801 Luke Copse British Cemetery,Puisieux.
802 Queens Cemetery,Puisieux.
803 Ten Tree Alley Cemetery,Puisieux.
804 Quesnoy Farm Military Cemetery,Bucquoy.
805 Fienvillers British Cemetery.
806 Pont-Remy British Cemetery.
808 St Ouen Communal Cemetery.
813 Bonneville Communal Cemetery.
816 Conde-Folie Communal Cemetery.
817 Coulonvillers Communal Cemetery.
818 Cramont Communal Cemetery.
832 Pozieres British Cemetery,Ovillers-La Boisselle.
833 Heilly Station Cemetery,Mericourt-L'Abbe.
834 Caulaincourt Communal Cemetery.

835 Trefcon British Cemetery,Caulaincourt.
836 Hancourt British Cemetery.
837 Beaumetz Communal Cemetery.
839 Mons-En-Chaussee Communal Cemetery.
840 Tertry Communal Cemetery.
841 Vraignes Communal Cemetery.
844 Beaurevoir British Cemetery.
845 Guizancourt Farm Cemetery,Gouy.
846 Serain Communal Cemetery Extension.
847 Fresnoy-Le-Grand Communal Cemetery Extension.
848 Brancourt-Le-Grand Communal Cemetery.
849 Brancourt-Le-Grand Military Cemetery.
855 Bertenacre Military Cemetery,Fletre.
856 Mont-Noir Military Cemetery,St Jans-Cappel.
857 Borre Churchyard.
858 Caestre Communal Cemetery.
860 Hondeghem Churchyard.
861 La Creche Communal Cemetery,Bailleul.
864 Vauxbuin French National Cemetery.
865 Buzancy Military Cemetery.
866 Oulchy-Le-Chateau Churchyard Extension.
867 Crouy-Vauxrot French National Cemetery,Crouy.
870 Chacrise Communal Cemetery.
874 Ste Marguerite Churchyard.
878 Villemontoire Communal Cemetery.
879 Boves East Communal Cemetery.
880 Boves West Communal Cemetery.
881 Boves West Communal Cemetery Extension.
882 Allonville Communal Cemetery.
885 Frechencourt Communal Cemetery.
886 Bavelincourt Communal Cemetery.
887 Montigny Communal Cemetery (Somme).
888 Montigny Communal Cemetery Extension (Somme).
889 Blangy-Tronville Communal Cemetery.
891 Bertangles Communal Cemetery.
904 Neuville-Bourjonval Communal Cemetery.
905 Neuville-Bourjonval British Cemetery.
906 Five Points Cemetery,Lechelle.
907 Ytres Communal Cemetery.
908 Manancourt Communal Cemetery.
910 Marcoing Communal Cemetery.
911 Marcoing British Cemetery.
912 Masnieres British Cemetery,Marcoing.
913 Noyelles-Sur-L'Escaut Communal Cemetery.
914 Noyelles-Sur-L'Escaut Communal Cemetery Extension.
915 Rumilly Communal Cemetery Extension.
916 Cagnoncles Communal Cemetery.
920 Niergnies Communal Cemetery.
921 Le Bizet Cemetery,Armentieres.
922 Cite Bonjean Military Cemetery,Armentieres.
924 Cabaret-Rouge British Cemetery.Souchez.
925 Ayette British Cemetery.
927 Douchy-Les-Ayette British Cemetery.
928 Avesnes-Sur-Helpe Communal Cemetery.
929 Fontaine-Au-Bois Communal Cemetery.
930 Dourlers Communal Cemetery Extension.
931 Maubeuge (Sous-Le-Bois) Cemetery.
932 Landrecies Communal Cemetery.
933 Landrecies British Cemetery.
934 Hautmont Communal Cemetery.

935 Berlaimont Communal Cemetery.
936 Berlaimont Communal Cemetery Extension.
937 Pont-Sur-Sambre Communal Cemetery.
938 Sebourg British Cemetery.
939 Sebourg Communal Cemetery.
940 Ors British Cemetery.
941 Aulnoye Communal Cemetery.
943 Grand-Fyat Communal Cemetery.
944 Maroilles Communal Cemetery.
948 Bermeries Communal Cemetery.
949 Brttrechies Communal Cemetery.
952 Ecuelin Churchyard.
953 Eth Communal Cemetery.
954 Feignies Communal Cemetery.
955 Gommegnies Communal Cemetery.
957 Hargnies Communal Cemetery.
963 Leval Communal Cemetery.
965 Malplaquet Communal Cemetery,Taisnieres-Sur-Hon.
968 Monceau-St Waast Communal Cemetery.
978 St Remy-Chaussee Communal Cemetery.
979 St Waast-La-Vallee Communal Cemetery.
981 Semousies Churchyard.
982 Taisnieres-En-Thierache Communal Cemetery.
984 Wargnies-Le-Grand Churchyard.
985 Wargnies-Le-Petit Communal Cemetery.
987 Roye New British Cemetery.
988 Moreuil Communal Cemetery Allied Extension.
1003 Hailles Communal Cemetery.
1008 Rouvrel Communal Cemetery.
1012 Englebelmer Communal Cemetery.
1013 Englebelmer Communal Cemetery Extension.
1014 St Amand British Cemetery.
1016 Henu Churchyard.
1017 Mondicourt Communal Cemetery.
1022 Ignaucourt Churchyard.
1027 Lille Southern Cemetery.
1028 St Andre Communal Cemetery.
1029 Tourcoing (Pont-Neuville) Communal Cemetery.
1030 Ascq Communal Cemetery.
1031 Halluin Communal Cemetery.
1032 Linselles Communal Cemetery.
1033 Fretin Communal Cemetery.
1034 Cretinier Cemetery,Wattrelos.
1039 Bousbecques Communal Cemetery.
1040 Camphin-en-Pevele Communal Cemetery.
1041 Criox Communal Cemetery.
1042 Genech Communal Cemetery.
1044 hem Communal Cemetery.
1049 Mouvaux New Comunal Cemetery.
1050 Neuville-En-Ferrain Communal Cemetery.
1054 Sailly-Les-Lannoy Churchyard.
1056 Templeuve Communal Cemetery.
1058 Willems Communal Cemetery.
1059 Arras Road Cemetery,Roclincourt.
1061 Grand-Seraucourt British Cemetery.
1063 Noyon New British Cemetery.
1065 Thiescourt French National Cemetery.
1066 Montescourt-Lizerolles Communal Cemetery.
1071 Blerancourt Communal Cemetery.
1074 Jussy Communal Cemetery.

1076 Le Quesnoy Communal Cemetery.
1078 Preseau Communal Cemetery.
1079 Preseau Communal Cemetery Extension.
1080 Villers-Pol Communal Cemetery Extension.
1081 Ruesnes Communal Cemetery.
1082 Capelle-Beaudignies Road Cemetery,Capelle.
1084 Artres Communal Cemetery.
1085 Curgies Communal Cemetery.
1087 Maresches Communal Cemetery.
1091 Steenwerck Communal Cemetery.
1092 Croix-Du-Bac British Cemetery,Steenwerck.
1094 Haverskerque British Cemetery.
1095 Laventie Communal Cemetery.
1100 Steenbecque Churchyard.
1106 Vieille-Chapelle New Military Cemetery,Lacouture.
1107 Vailly British Cemetery.
1108 Guards' Grave,Villers-Cotterets Forest.
1110 Braine Communal Cemetery.
1111 Soupir Churchyard.
1112 Soupir Communal Cemetery.
1113 Montreuil-Aux-Lions British Cemetery.
1117 Bezu-Le-Guery Communal Cemetery.
1128 Gandelu Communal Cemetery.
1129 Haramont Communal Cemetery.
1134 Priez Communal Cemetery.
1139 Vieil-Arcy Communal Cemetery.
1140 Houplines Communal Cemetery Extension.
1141 Ferme Buterne Military Cemetery,Houplines.
1142 Valenciennes (St Roch) Communal Cemetery.
1144 Raismes Communal Cemetery.
1147 Bruille-St Amand Churchyard.
1154 Thivencelle Churchyard.
1157 Rue-Du-Bacquerot No.1 Military Cemetery,Laventie.
1158 Fauquissart Military Cemetery,Laventie.
1159 Quesnoy-Sur-Deule Communal Cemetery.
1160 Quesnoy-Sur-Deule Communal Cemetery,German Extension.
1161 Isbergues Communal Cemetery.
1169 St Hilaire-Cottes Churchyard.
1170 Villers-Bretonneux Military Cemetery,Fouilloy.
1172 Fouilloy Communal Cemetery.
1173 Aubigny British Cemetery (Somme).
1180 Neufchatel Churchyard.
1182 Faubourg-D'Amiens Cemetery,Arras.
1183 Boisleux-Au-Mont Communal Cemetery.
1184 Sunken Road Cemetery,Boisleux St Marc.
1185 London Cemetery,Neuville-Vitasse.
1186 Henin Communal Cemetery Extension.
1187 Summit Trench Cemetery,Croisilles.
1188 Feuchy British Cemetery.
1190 Sunken Road Cemetery,Fampoux.
1191 Albuera Cemetery,Bailleul-Sire-Berthoult.
1192 Naval Trench Cemetery,Gavrelle.
1193 Chili Trench Cemetery,Gavrelle.
1194 Roeux British Cemetery.
1196 Auberchicourt British Cemetery.
1198 Masny Churchyard.
1201 Villers-au-Tertre Communal Cemetery.
1202 Ham Communal Cemetery.
1203 Ham British Cematery,Muille-Villette.

1204 Foreste Communal Cemetery.
1205 Douilly Communal Cemetery.
1206 Eppeville Churchyard.
1211 Maubeuge-Centre Cemetery.
1216 Sains-Du-Nord Communal Cemetery.
1219 Floursies Churchyard.
1223 Solre-Le-Chateau Communal Cemetery.
1225 Senlis French National Cemetery.
1227 Compiegne South Communal Cemetery.
1228 Royallieu French National Cemetery,Compiegne.
1230 Verberie French National Cemetery.
1231 Nery Communal Cemetery.
1232 Beauvais Communal Cemetery.
1233 Marissel French National Cemetery.
1234 Dompierre French National Cemetery.
1235 Vignemont French National Cemetery.
1236 Annel Communal Cemetery,Longueil-Annel.
1242 Hardivillers Communal Cemetery.
1252 Denain Communal Cemetery.
1254 Famars Communal Cemetery Extension.
1256 Maing Communal Cemetery extension.
1257 Querenaing Communal Cemetery.
1258 Thiant Communal Cemetery.
1259 Vendegies Cross Roads British Cemetery,Bermerain.
1260 Verchain British Cemetery,Verchain-Maugre.
1266 St Souplet British Cemetery.
1268 Vaux-Andigny British Cemetery.
1269 La Vallee-Mulatre Communal Cemetery.
1270 La Vallee-Mulatre Communal Cemetery Extension.
1271 Wassigny Communal Cemetery.
1272 Le Rejet-De-Beaulieu Communal Cemetery.
1274 St Benin Communal Cemetery (Nord).
1276 Douai Communal Cemetery.
1277 Douai British Cemetery,Cuincy.
1278 Brebieres British Cemetery.
1279 Annoeullin Communal Cemetery German Extension.
1280 Abscon Communal Cemetery.
1281 Arleux-Du-Nord Communal Cemetery.
1284 Auby Communal Cemetery.
1285 Auchy Churchyard.
1287 Brillon Communal Cemetery.
1290 Flers-en-Escrebieux Communal Cemetery.
1293 Hem-Lenglet Communal Cemetery.
1295 Lallaing Communal Cemetery.
1296 Lecelles Churchyard.
1301 Paillencourt Churchyard.
1307 Sin-le-Noble Communal Cemetery.
1308 Somain Communal Cemetery.
1310 Beaumont Communal Cemetery.
1311 Corbehem Communal Cemetery.
1312 Courrieres Communal Cemetery.
1314 Noyelles-Godault Communal Cemetery.
1316 Quiery-La-Motte Communal Cemetery.
1321 Bois-Carre British Cemetery,Thelus.
1325 Vimy Communal Cemetery,Farbus.
1326 Hebuterne Communal Cemetery.
1327 Hebuterne Military Cemetery.
1328 Vendresse Churchyard.
1329 Vendresse British Cemetery.
1331 hermonville Military Cemetery.

1332 Jonchery-Sur-Vesle British Cemetery.
1333 Beaurepaire French National Cemetery,Pontavert.
1334 Berry-au-Bac French National Cemetery.
1337 Longueval Communal Cemetery.
1339 Bourg-Et-Comin Communal Cemetery.
1340 Moulins Churchyard.
1341 Moulins New Communal Cemetery.
1342 Paissy Churchyard.
1345 Bois-Des-Angles British Cemetery,Crevecoeur-Sur-L'Escaut.
1346 Moulin-De-Pierre British Cemetery,Villeers-Outreau.
1347 Esnes Communal Cemetery.
1348 Fontaine-Au-Pire Communal Cemetery.
1349 Ligny-En-Cambresis Communal Cemetery.
1350 Haucourt Communal Cemetery.
1351 Becquigny Communal Cemetery.
1352 Escaufort Communal Cemetery.
1354 Selvigny Communal Cemetery.
1355 Wambaix Communal Cemetery.
1357 Bleue-Maison Military Cemetery,Eperlecques.
1358 Croix-Rouge Military Cemetery,Quaedypre.
1359 Dunkerque Town Cemetery.
1360 Malo-Les-Bains Communal Cemetery.
1361 Zuydcoote Military Cemetery.
1364 Buysscheure Churchyard.
1366 Houtkerque Churchyard.
1367 Ledeerzeele Churchyard.
1369 Steenvorde Communal Cemetery.
1372 Wormhoudt Communal Cemetery.
1374 Audruicq Churchyard.
1386 Quietiste Military Cemetery,Le Cateau.
1387 Beauvois-En-Cambresis Communal Cemetery.
1388 Bethencourt Communal Cemetery.
1390 Bevillers Communal Cemetery.
1391 Bertry Communal Cemetery.
1392 Maurois Communal Cemetery.
1393 Montigny Communal Cemetery (Nord).
1394 Reumont Churchyard.
1395 Troisvilles Communal Cemetery.
1396 Viesly Communal Cemetery.
1402 Nesles-La-Gilberde Communal Cemetery.
1404 Mailly-Le-Camp French Cemetery.
1410 Dormans French National Cemetery.
1415 Sezanne Communal Cemetery.
1416 Soulieres Churchyard.
1420 Baron Communal Cemetery.
1421 Catenoy French National Cemetery.
1422 Creil Communal Cemetery.
1425 Bassevelle Churchyard.
1426 Bellot Communal Cemetery.
1429 Coulommieers Communal Cemetery.
1432 Fretoy Communal Cemetery.
1436 La Haute-Maison,Ferme Des Arceries.
1438 Meaux Communal Cemetery.
1439 Melun North Cemetery.
1440 Montereau Communal Cemetery.
1441 Nangis Communal Cemetery.
1443 Orly-Sur-Morin Communal Cemetery.
1445 Perreuse Chateau French National Cemetery,Signy-Signets.

1451 Sablonnieres New Communal Cemetery.
1461 Hargicourt British Cemetery.
1462 Hargicourt Communal Cemetery Extension.
1463 Ronssoy Communal Cemetery.
1464 Villeret Churchyard.
1465 Hesbecourt Communal Cemetery.
1467 Somme American Cemetery,Bony.
1468 La Chapelette British Cemetery,Peronne.
1472 Assevillers New British Cemetery.
1473 Foucaucourt Communal Cemetery.
1475 Vendegies-Au-Bois British Cemetery.
1476 Amerval Communal Cemetery Extension,Solesmes.
1477 Ovillers New Communal Cemetery,Solesmes.
1478 Forest Communal Cemetery (Nord).
1479 Ors Communal Cemetery.
1480 Beaurain British Cemetery.
1482 Bousies Communal Cemetery.
1483 Flesquieres Hill British Cemetery.
1484 Vaulx Hill Cemetery,Vaulx-Vraucourt.
1485 Vaux Australian Field Ambulance Cemetery,Vaulx-Vraucourt.
1486 Vraucourt Copse Cemetery,Vaulx-Vraucourt.
1487 L'Homme Mort British Cemetery,Ecoust-St Mein.
1488 Noreuil Australian Cemetery.
1489 Croisilles British Cemetery.
1490 "Y" Ravine Cemetery,Beaumont-Hamel.
1491 Redan Ridge Cemetery No.1,Beaumont-Hamel.
1492 Redan Ridge Cemetery No.2,Beaumont-Hamel.
1494 Templeux-Le-Guerard Communal Cemetery Extension.
1495 Templeux-Le-Guerard British Cemetery.
1496 Moeuvres Communal Cemetery Extension.
1497 Sanders Keep Military Cemetery,Graincourt-Les-Havrincourt.
1498 Orival Wood Cemetery,Flesquieres.
1499 Demicourt Communal Cemetery,Boursies.
1500 Hawthorn Ridge Cemetery No.1,Auchon-Villers.
1501 Hawthorn Ridge Cemetery No.2,Auchon-Villers.
1502 Hunter's Cemetery,Beaumont-Hamel.
1504 Miraumont Communal Cemetery.
1512 Fillievres British Cemetery.
1525 Wavans British Cemetery.
1545 Doudelainville Communal Cemetery.
1553 Le Crotoy Communal Cemetery.
1564 Quend Communal Cemetery.
1568 Vaux-En-Amienois Communal Cemetery.
1571 Mazargues Cemetery Extension.
1586 Fruges Communal Cemetery.
1597 Rimboval Churchyard.
1615 Rethel French National Cemetery.
1630 Ingwiller Communal Cemetery.
1632 Plaine French National Cemetery.
1633 Roppenheim Communal Cemetery.
1643 Neuf-Brisach Communal Cemetery.
1644 Arnaville Churchyard.
1649 Joeuf Communal Cemetery.
1658 Commercy French National Cemetery.
1660 Latour-en-Woevre Communal Cemetery.
1662 Antilly Churchyard.
1664 Ars-sur-Moselle Churchyard.
1667 Chambieres French National (Mixed) Cemetery,Metz.
1671 Moulin-les-Metz Communal Cemetery.
1672 Rechicourt-le-Chateau Communal Cemetery.
1674 Ste Ruffine Communal Cemetery.
1675 Sarralbe Military Cemetery.
1678 Charmes Military Cemetery,Essegny.
1689 Chambrecy British Cemetery.
1690 Courmas British Cemetery.
1693 Epernay French National Cemetery.
1695 La Neuville-Aux-Larris Military Cemetery.
1697 St Imoge Churchyard.
1699 Vandieres Churchyard.
1700 Berthaucouer Communal Cemetery,Pontru.
1701 Chapelle British Cemetery,Holnon.
1703 Guise (La Desolation) French National Cemetery,Flavigny-Le-Petit.
1704 La Baraque British Cemetery,Bellenglise.
1706 Levergies Communal Cemetery.
1707 Ribemont Communal Cemetery.
1710 Sequehart British Cemetery No.1
1712 Brissay-Choigny Churchyard.
1715 Moy-De-L'Aisne Communal Cemetery.
1717 Sery-Les-Mezieres Communal Cemetery.
1723 St Mary's A.D.S. Cemetery,Haisnes.
1724 Carvin Communal Cemetery.
1725 Don Communal Cemetery.Annoeullin.
1726 Phalempin Communal Cemetery.
1727 Rumaucourt Communal Cemetery.
1730 Wicres Churchyard.
1732 Santes Churchyard.
1737 Estevelles Communal Cemetery.
1744 Monchy-Breton Churchyard.
1745 Nedonchel Churchyard.
1749 Sauchy-Lestree Communal Cemetery.
1751 Etreux British Cemetery.
1752 Etreux Communal Cemetery.
1753 La Ville-Aux-Bois British Cemetery.
1754 St Erme Communal Cemetery Extension.
1755 Sissonne British Cemetery.
1760 Esqueheries Communal Cemetery.
1766 Etroeungt Communal Cemetery.
1775 Nice (Caucade) British Civil Cemetery.
1776 Nice (Caucade) Communal Cemetery.
1778 Troyes Town Cemetery.
1779 Gruissan Communal Cemetery.
1783 Senas Communal Cemetery.
1787 Courban RAF Cemetery.
1788 Dijon (Les Pejoces) Cemetery.
1798 Conches-En-Ouche Communal Cemetery.
1799 Evreux Communal Cemetery.
1805 Maintenon Communal Cemetery.
1808 Guilvinec Communal Cemetery.
1822 Talence Communal Cemetery.
1826 Luxeuil Communal Cemetery.
1830 Champagnole Communal Cemetery.
1839 St Nazaire (Toutes-Aides) Cemetery.
1841 Orleans Main Cemetery.
1844 Vendome Town Cemetery.
1845 Angers West Cemetery.
1848 Tourlaville Communal Cemetery.
1849 Tourlaville Communal Cemetery Extension.

1856 Lyon (La Guillotiere) Old Communal Cemetery.
1858 St Germain-Au-Mont-D'Or Communal Cemetery Extension.
1862 Le Mans West Cemetery.
1866 Asnieres-Sur-Oise Communal Cemetery.
1868 Louvres Communal Cemetery.
1886 Monaco Principality Cemetery,La Condamine.
1887 Laventie Military Cemetery.
1888 Haubourdin Communal Cemetery.
1890 Serre Road Cemetery No.2,Beaumont-Hamel and Hebuterne.
1891 Thiepval Anglo-French Cemetery,Authuile.
1893 Chauny Communal Cemetery British Extension.
1894 Montcornet Military Cemetery.
1896 Canadian Cemetery No.2,Neuville-St Vaast.

GALLIPOLI.
1 Lancashire Landing Cemetery,Helles.
2 Redoubt Cemetery,Helles.
3 Pink Farm Cemetery,Helles.
4 Azmak Cemetery,Sulva.
5 Green Hill Cemetery,Sulva.
6 Twelve Tree Copse Cemetery,Helles.
7 Lone Pine Cemetery,Anzac.
13 The Farm Cemetery,Anzac.
14 Skew Bridge Cemetery,Helles.
15 "V" Beach Cemetery,Helles.
17 7th Field Ambulance Cemetery,Anzac.
18 Embarkation Pier Cemetery,Anzac.
19 No.2 Outpost Cemetery,Anzac.
20 New Zealand No.2 Outpost Cemetery,Anzac.
26 Lala Baba Cemetery,Sulva.
27 Hill 10 Cemetery,Sulva.
29 Ari Burnu Cemetery,Anzac.
30 Beach Cemetery,Anzac.
31 Shrapnel Valley Cemetery,Anzac.

GERMANY.
1 Cologne Southern Cemetery.
2 Hamburg Cemetery,Ohlsdorf.
3 Niederzwehren Cemetery,Cassel.
4 Berlin South-Western Cemetery,Stahnsdorf.
5 Aachen Military Cemetery.
9 Coblenz Jewish Cemetery.

GREECE.
1 Sarigol Military Cemetery.
2 Kirechkoi-Hortakoi Military Cemetery.
3 Struma Military Cemetery.
4 Lahana Military Cemetery.
5 Doiran Military Cemetery.
6 Karasouli Military Cemetery.
7 Salonika Anglo-French Military Cemetery,Lembet Road.
8 Salonika Protestant Cemetery.
9 Mikra British Cemetery,Salonika.
10 East Mudros Military Cemetery,Lemnos.
11 Portianos Military Cemetery,West Mudros,Lemnos.
14 Syra New British Cemetery.

16 Suda Bay War Cemetery,Crete.
17 Corfu British Cemetery.
18 Bralo British Cemetery.
19 Dedeagatch British Cemetery.
21 Athens New Protestant Cemetery.
23 Volo Municipal Cemetery.

INDIA.
48 Delhi War Cemetery.
97a Calcutta (Bhowanipore) Cemetery.
164 Madras (St Mary's) Cemetery.

IRAQ.
1 Kut War Cemetery.
5 Amara War Cemetery.
6 Basra War Cemetery.
8 Baghdad (North Gate) War Cemetery.
9 Baghdad East Jewish Cemetery.

ITALY.
1 Barenthal Military Cemetery.
2 Boscon British Cemetery.
3 Magnaboschi British Cemetery.
4 Granezza British Cemetery.
5 Cavalletto British Cemetery.
6 Taranto Town Cemetery Extension.
7 Giavera British Cemetery.
8 Memorial to the Missing,Giavera British Cemetery.
9 Tezze British Cemetery,Vazzola.
10 Dueville Communal Cemetery Extension.
11 Montecchio Precalcino Communal Cemetery Extension.
12 Staglieno Cemetery,Genoa.
13 Savona Town Cemetery.
14 Savona Memorial.
15 Arquata Scrivia Communal Cemetery Extension.
16 Bordighera British Cemetery.
17 Bari War Cemetery.
19 Faenza Communal Cemetery.
24 Carloforte Communal Cemetery.
29 Foggia Communal Cemetery.
35 Porto Empedocle Communal Cemetery.
37 Otranto Town Cemetery.
42 Messine Town Cemetery.
45 Carmignano Di Brenta Communal Cemetery.
48 Padua Main Cemetery.
56 Oneglia Town Cemetery.
57 San Remo Town Cemetery.
59 Testaccio Protestant Cemetery,Rome.
61 Syracuse Communal Cemetery.
65 Turin Town Cemetery.
71 Mattarello Communal Cemetery.
72 Romagnano Communal Cemetery.
74 Altivole Communal Cemetery.
75 Conegliano (San Giuseppe) Communal Cemetery.
76 Falze Communal Cemetery,Trevignano.
80 Corva Cemetery.
81 Fontanafredda Communal Cemetery.
83 Venice (San Michele) Cemetery.

LEBANON.
1   Beirut British War Cemetery.

NEW ZEALAND.
134   Epsom (St Andrew) Churchyard.
194   Purewa Cemetery.
243   Featherston Soldiers' Cemetery.
320   Suva Cemetery,Fiji.

NEWFOUNDLAND.
59   St John's Church of England Cemetery.

PAKISTAN.
50a   Rawalpindi War Cemetery.

PALESTINE or ISRAEL.
1   Beersheba War Cemetery.
2   Deir El Belah War Cemetery.
3   Jerusalem War Cemetery.
5   Jerusalem Protestant Cemetery,Mount Zion.
8   Gaza War Cemetery.
9   Ramleh War Cemetery.
11   Haifa War Cemetery.
14   Richon-Le-Zion Jewish Cemetery.

SOUTH AMERICA.
6   The Timehri Memorial (U.M.A.),Guyana.
12   Guayacan Protestant Cemetery,Chile.

SYRIA.
2   Damascus Commonwealth War Cemetery.

TANZANIA.
1   Dar Es Salaam War Cemetery,Bagamoyo Road.

U.S.A.
11   San Diego (Greenwoood) Cemetery,California.
12   San Diego Masonic Cemetery,California.
13   San Francisco (Cypress Lawn) Cemetery,California.
51   Covington (Mount Hope) Cemetery,Indiana.
52   Indianapolis (Crown Hill) Cemetery,Indiana.
77   Avon (St Michael's) Cemetery (Norfolk),Massachusetts.
79   Brookline (Holy Hood) Cemetery,Massachusetts.
92   Mount Auburn Cemetery,Cambridge &
Watertown,Massachusetts.
97   Weston (Linwood) Cemetery,Massachusetts.
107   Detroit (Mount Olivet) Cemetery,Michigan.
121   St Louis (Bellefontaine) Public Cemetery,Missouri.
132   Asbury First Presbyterian Church Cemetery,New Jersey.
137   Rosedale Cemetery,Montclair & Orange,New Jersey.
143   Amityville Cemetery,New York.
147   Bronx (St Raymond's) Cemetery,New York.
149   Brooklyn (Greenwood) Cemetery,New York.
155   Cape Vincent (Riverside) Cemetery,New York.
169   New York (Woodlawn) Cemetery,New York.
184   Akron (Glendale) Cemetery (Summit),Ohio.
187   Chillicothe (Grandview) Cemetery (Ross),Ohio.
228   Fort Worth (Greenwood) Cemetery (Tarrant),Texas.
230   Memphis (Fairview) Cemetery,Texas.
234   Arlington National Cemetery (Arlington),Virginia.

234a   Newport News (Green Lawn) Cemetery
(Warwick),Virginia.
238   Colville (Highland) Cemetery,Washington.
246   Nuuanu Cemetery,Honolulu,Hawaii.

WEST INDIES.
29   Port of Spain Memorial (U.M.A.),Trinadad & Tobago.
36   Kingstown (St George) Cathedral Close,St Vincent.

ENGLISH,IRISH SCOTTISH and WELSH COUNTIES.

BEDFORD & HUNTINGDON.
8   Higham Gobion (St Mary) Churchyard,Beds.
22   Ampthill (St Andrew) Churchyard,Beds.
23   Bedford Cemetery,Beds.
34   Pavenham (St Peter) Churchyard,Beds.
48   Campton and Shefford Cemetery,Beds.
65   Biggleswade Cemetery,Beds.
66   Dunstable Cemetery,Beds.
70   Eaton Socon Churchyard,Beds.
74   Luton Church Burial Ground,Beds.
75   Luton General Cemetery,Beds.
78   Houghton Regis (All Saints) Churchyard,Beds.
83   Huntingdon Cemetery,Hunts.
90   Upwood Cemetery,Hunts.
102   Ramsey (St Thomas a Becket) Churchyard,Hunts.
104 · St Ives Public Cemetery,Hunts.
111   Somersham (St John the Baptist) Churchyard,Hunts.
113   Wyton (All Saints) Churchyard,Hunts.
124   St Neots Cemetery,Hunts.
125   Molesworth (St Peter) Churchyard,Hunts.

BERKSHIRE.
1   Abingdon Cemetery.
2   Abingdon (SS Mary & Edmund) Roman Catholic
Churchyard,St Helen Without.
6   Kennington Cemetery,Radley.
15   Wootton (St Peter) Churchyard.
19   Bradfield (St Andrew) Churchyard.
23   Stratfield Mortimer (St Mary) Churchyard.
27   Yattendon (SS Peter & Paul) Churchyard.
28   Bisham (All Saints) Churchyard.
29   Boyne Hill (All Saints) Chhurchyard,Bray.
31   Cookham Cemetery.
33   Hurley (St Mary) Churchyard.
37   Stubbings (St James the Less) Churchyard,Bisham.
39   Ascot (All Saints) Churchyard Extension,Winkfield.
42   Cranbourne (St Peter) Churchyard,Winkfield.
43   Crowthorne (St John the Baptist) Churchyard.
45   Sandhurst Royal Military College Cemetery.
47   Warfield (St Michael) Churchyard Extension.
56   Hinton Waldrist (St Margaret) Churchyard.
66   Hungerford Church Cemetery.
71   Maidenhead Cemetery.
72   Newbury Old Cemetery.
73   Chieveley (St Mary) Churchyard.
83   Clewer (St Andrew)Churchyard.
84   Windsor Cemetery.
85   Reading (Caversham) Cemetery.
86   Reading Cemetery.

93   Long Wittenham (St Mary) Churchyard.
94   Sotwell (St James) Churchyard.
112 Wokingham (All Saints) Churchyard.
113 Wokingham (St Paul) Churchyard.
116 Bearwood (St Catherine) Churchyard,Hurst St Nicholas.
117 Earley (St Peter) Churchyard.
119 Hurst (St Nicholas) Churchyard Extension.
121 Sonning (St Andrew) Churchyard.
124 Wargrave (St Mary) Churchyard.
125 Wokingham (St Sebastian) Churchyard,Wokingham
Without.

BUCKINGHAMSHIRE.
12   Penn Street (Holy Trinity) Churchyard,Penn.
32   Weston Turville (St Mary) Churchyard.
36   Beaconsfield Cemetery.
37   Bletchley (St Mary) Churchyard.
39   Buckingham Cemetery.
50   Twyford (The Assumption) Churchyard.
51   High Wycombe Cemetery.
54   Cliveden War Cemetery,Taplow.
55   Datchet Cemetery.
57   Dorney Burial Ground.
69   Wyrardisbury (St Andrew) Churchyard.
76   Long Crendon (St Mary) Churchyard.
80   Marlow Cemetery.
82   Marlow (St Peter) Roman Catholic Churchyard.
86   Moulsoe (St Mary) Churchyard.
91   Wavendon (St Mary) Churchyard.
96   Upton-Cum-Chalvey (St Mary) Churchyard.
116 Great Hampden (St Mary Magdalene) Churchyard,Great &
Little Hampden.
120 Monks Risborough (St Dunstan) Churchyard.
è123 Tylers Green (St Margaret) Churchyard,Chepping
Wycombe Rural.

CAMBRIDGESHIRE.
1   Cambridge General Cemetery.
2   Cambridge (Mill Road) Cemetery.
3   Cambridge (SS Gile's & Peter's) Cemetery.
16   Cambridge Borough Cemetery,Fen Ditton.
19   Cottenham (All Saints) Churchyard.
21   Dry Drayton (SS Peter & Paul) Churchyard.
25   Great Shelford (St Mary) Churchyard.
31   Horningsea (St Peter) Churchyard.
37   Stapleford (St Andrew) Churchyard.
39   Trumpington (SS Mary & Michael) New Churchyard.
51   Weston Colville (St Mary) Churchyard.
74   Newmarket Cemetery,Wood Ditton
82   Boxworth (St Peter) Churchyard.
84   Chatteris General Cemertery.
91   Wilburton (St Peter) Church.
97   Doddington (St Mary) Churchyard.
103 Wisbech Borough Cemetery.

CHESHIRE.
1   Alsager (Christ Church) Churchyard.
2   Ashton-Upon-Mersey (St Martin) Churchyard.
3   Bebington Cemetery.
4   Bebington (St Andrew) Churchyard.

6   Higher Bebington (Christ Church) Churchyard.
8   Birkenhead (Flaybrick Hill) Cemetery.
11   Bowdon (St Mary) Churchyard.
18   Northenden (St Wilfrid) Churchyard.
19   Over Peover (St Lawrence) Churchyard,Peover Superior.
22   Rostherne (St Mary) Churchyard.
26   Cheadle and Gatley Cemetery.
28   Chester General Cemetery.
30   Christleton (St James) Churchyard.
31   Eccleston (St Mary) Churchyard.
32   Great Saughall (All Saints) Churchyard.
35   Shotwick(St Michael) Churchyard.
44   Church Lawton (All Saints) Churchyard.
51   Crewe Cemetery.
53   Ashton-Under-Lyne and Dunkinfield Joint Cemetery.
56   Altrincham Cemetery.
59   Norbury (St Thomas) Churchyard.
61   Hoylake (Holy Trinity) Churchyard.
62   West Kirby (St Bridget) Churchyard.
72   Macclesfield Cemetery.
74   Alderley Edge Cemetery.
84   Prestbury (St Peter) Churchyard.
86   Siddington (All Saints) Churchyard.
97   Middlewich Cemetery.
98   Mottram-In-Longdendale Cemetery.
111 Wybunbury (St Chad) Churchyard.
113 Nantwich (All Saints) Church Cemetery.
114 Nantwich General Cemetery.
117 Neston-Cum-Parkgate Cemetery.
119 Davenham (St Wilfred) Churchyard.
123 Lostock Gralam (St John) Churchyard.
127 Northwich Cemetery.
128 Northwich (St Helen) Churchyard.
131 Appleton Thorn (St Cross) Churchyard,Appleton.
133 Daresbury (All Saints) Churchyard.
137 Halton Cemetery.
142 Stockton Heath (St Thomas) Churchyard.
143 Stretton (St Matthew) Churchyard.
146 Runcorn Cemetery.
147 Sale Cemetery.
153 Stalybridge (St Paul) Churchyard.
154 Heaton Mersey Congregational Churchyard.
158 Stockport Borough Cemetery.
160 Stockport (Willow Grove) Cemetery.
175 Waverton (St Peter) Churchyard.
178 Egremont (St John) Churchyard.
181 Woodchurch (Holy Cross) Churchyard.
182 Wallasey (Rake Lane) Cemetery.
183 Lindow (St John) Churchyard.
184 Wilmslow Cemetery.
186 Over (St Chad) Churchyard.
190 Bidston (St Oswald) Churchyard.
192 Eastham (St Mary) Churchyard.
193 Heswall (St Peter) Churchyard.
194 hooton (St Mary of the Angels) Roman Catholic Cemetery.
197 Thurstaton (St Bartholomew) Churchyard.
198 Willaston (Christ Church) Churchyard.

CORNWALL.
1   Bodmin Cemetery.

4   Egloshayle Church Cemetery.
13   St Mabyn Churchyard.
17   Callington Cemetery.
20   Calstock Cemetery.
23   Camborne (St Martin) Churchyard.
29   Forrabury (St Symphorian) Churchyard,Forrabury and Minster.
36   Mawnan (SS Mawnan and Stephen) Churchyard.
37   Mylor (St Mylor) Churchyard.
40   Falmouth Cemetery.
48   Grade (St Grade and Holy Cross) Churchyard.
49   Gunwalloe (St Winwalloe) Churchyard.
55   Porthleven Cemetery,Sithney.
56   Ruan Minor (St Ruan) Churchyard.
61   St Martin's Churchyard.
64   Launceston Cemetery.
68   North Hill (St Torney) Churchyard.
79   Morval Church Cemetery.
96   Penzance Cemetery.
106   St Day (Holy Trinity) Churchyard.
109   Redruth Cemetery.
111   Biscovey (St Mary) Churchyard,St Blazey.
123   St Austell Cemetery.
128   St Columb Major Cemetery.
132   Antony Cemetery.
135   Maker (SS Macra,Mary and Julia) Churchyard.
136   Millbrook Church Cemetery.
138   Rame (St Germanus) Churchyard.
140   St Stephens-By-Saltash (St Stephen) Churchyard.
142   St Ives Cemetery.
148   Launcells (St Swithin) Churchyard.
161   Feock Church Cemetery.
163   Kenwyn (St Kenwyn) Churchyard,Kenwyn Rural.
172   Gulval (St Gulval) Churchyard.
175   Perranuthnoe (SS Piran and Nicholas) Churchyard.
177   St Erth (St Ercus) Churchyard,St Erth Rural.

CUMBERLAND AND WESTMORLAND.

6   Aspatria (St Kentigern) Churchyard,Cumberland.
11   Muncaster (St Michael) Churchyard,Cumberland.
13   Brampton (St Martin) Old Churchyard,Cumberland.
17   Carlisle (Dalston Road) Cemetery,Cumberland.
18   Carlisle (Upperby) Cemetery,Cumberland.
25   Wetheral Cemetery,Cumberland.
40   Cockermouth Cemetery,Cumberland.
44   Silloth (St Paul) Churchyard,Cumberland.
45   Crosthwaite (St Kentigern) Churchyard,Cumberland.
46   Keswick (St John) Churchyard,Cumberland.
50   Maryport Cemetery,Cumberland.
54   Great Salkeld (St Cuthbert) Churchyard,Cumberland.
59   Penrith Cemetery,Cumberland.
60   Whitehaven Cemetery,Cumberland.
68   Allonby (Christ Church) Churchyard,Cumberland.
74   Wigton Cemetery,Cumberland.
78   Kirkby Stephen Cemetery,Westmoreland.
82   Kendal (Parkside) Cemetery,Westmorland.
83   Kirkby Lonsdale (St Mary) Churchyard,Westmorland.
85   Arnside Cemetery,Westmorland.
86   Barbon (St Bartholomew) Churchyard,Westmorland.
89   Burton (St James) Churchyard,Westmoreland.

91   Heversham (St Mary) Churchyard,Westmorland.
98   Selside (St Thomas) Churchyard,Whitwell and Selside,Westmorland.
100   Troutbeck (Jesus) Churchyard,Westmorland.
107   Bowness-On-Windermere Cemetery,Westmorland.
108   Windermere (St Mary's) Cemetery,Westmorland.

DERBYSHIRE.

2   Alfreton (Lea Brooks) Cemetery.
3   Alfreton (St Martin) Churchyard.
26   Tideswell (St John the Baptist) Churchyard.
29   Bakewell Cemetery.
30   Baslow (St Anne) Churchyard.
32   Crich (St Mary) Churchyard.
34   Denby (St Mary) Churchyard.
39   Mackworth (All Saints) Churchyard.
42   South Wingfield (Park) Burial Ground.
47   Shirebrook Cemetery.
51   Bolsover (St Mary) Old Churchyard.
57   Buxton Cemetery.
58   Fairfield (St Peter) Churchyard.
61   Castleton (St Edmund) Churchyard.
66   Edale (Holy Trinity) Churchyard.
76   Whittington (St Bartholomew) Churchyard.
97   Derby (Normanton) Cemetery.
98   Derby (Nottingham Road) Cemetery.
99   Derby (Uttoxeter Road) Cemetery.
117   Heanor Cemetery.
120   Long Eaton Cemetery.
122   Cromford (St Mary) Churchyard.
127   Dore (Christ Church) Churchyard.
129   Church Broughton (St Michael) Churchyard.
135   Newton Solney (St Mary) Churchyard.
145   Ockbrook (All Saints) Churchyard.
146   Risley (All Saints) Churchyard.

DEVONSHIRE.

1   Plymouth Old Cemetery.
2   Efford Cemetery,Plymouth.
3   Weston Mill Cemetery,Plymouth.
6   Beer Church Cemetery.
10   Hawkchurch (St John the Baptist) Churchyard.
11   Kilmington (St Giles) Churchyard.
12   Musbury (St Michael) Churchyard.
15   Axminster Cemetery.
17   Barnstaple Cemetery.
21   Braunton (St Brannock) Churchyard.
29   Horwood Churchyard.
33   Morte Hoe Cemetery.
36   Westleigh (St Peter) Churchyard.
37   Bideford Church Cemetery.
38   Bideford Public Cemetery.
39   Abbotsham Churchyard.
40   Alwington (St Andrew) Churchyard.
41   Bucks Mills Church Cemetery,Woolfardisworthy.
46   Brixham Noncomformist Cemetery.
47   Brixham (St Mary) Churchyard.
50   Budleigh Salterton Cemetery.
67   Townstall (St Clement) Churchyard.
68   Dawlish Cemetery.

69   Exeter Higher Cemetery.
70   Exeter (Exwick) Cemetery.
71   Heavitree (St Michael) Churchyard Extension.
72   Littleham (SS Margaret and Andrew) Churchyard.
73   Withycombe Raleigh (St John in the Wilderness) Churchyard.
74   Great Torrington Cemetery.
76   Bradworthy (St John the Baptist) Churchyard.
86   Feniton (St Andrew) Churchyard.
87   Gittisham (St Michael) Churchyard.
91   Ilfracombe (Holy Trinity) Churchyard.
92   Ilfracombe (St Brannock's Road) Cemetery.
96   Chivelstone (St Silvester) Churchyard.
100   Loddiswell (St Michael) Churchyard.
102   Modbury (St George) Churchyard.
107   Thurlestone (All Saints) Churchyard.
128   Highweek (All Saints) Churchyard Extension.
130   Wolborough (St Mary) Churchyard.
132   Northam (St Margaret) Churchyard.
138   Hatherleigh (St John the Baptist) Churchyard.
152   Collaton (St Mary) Churchyard.
153   Paignton Cemetery.
158   Plympton St Maurice Churchyard.
172   Pennycross (St Pancras) Churchyard,Weston Peverell.
185   Exminster (St Martin) Churchyard.
200   Topsham Cemetery.
206   Seaton (St Gregory) Churchyard.
207   Sidmouth Cemetery.
230   Marystow (St Mary) Churchyard.
233   Sheepstor Churchyard.
236   Whitchurch (St Andrew) Churchyard.
237   Tavistock New Cemetery.
238   Shaldon (St Nicholas) Churchyard.
239   Teignmouth Cemetery.
243   Bradfield (All Saints) Churchyard.
246   Cullompton Cemetery.
247   Halberton (St Andrew) Churchyard.
248   Huntsham (All Saints) Churchyard.
258   Torquay Extramural Cemetery.
266   Bridgetown and Berry Pomeroy Cemetery.
267   Totnes Cemetery.
274   Kingswear Cemetery.
276   Marldon (St John the Baptist) Churchyard.

DORSET AND CHANNEL ISLANDS.

6   Parnham Private Cemetery,Beaminster,Dorset.
9   Blandford Cemetery.
18   Winterborne Stickland (St Mary) Churchyard.
20   Bridport Cemetery,Dorset.
22   Burton Bradstock Cemetery,Dorset.
27   Whitchurch Canonicorum (St Candida and Holy Cross) Churchyard.
28   Cattistock (SS Peter and Paul) Churchyard,Dorset.
33   Dorchester Cemetery,Dorset.
42   Stratton (St Mary) Churchyard,Dorset.
46   Branksome Park (All Saints) Churchyard,Dorset.
48   Longfleet (St Mary) Churchyard,Dorset.
49   Poole (Branksome) Cemetery,Dorset.
50   Poole Cemetery,Dorset.
51   Poole (Parkstone) Cemetery,Dorset.

52   Broadstone Cemetery,Canford Magna,Dorset.
53   Kinson (St Andrew) Churchyard,Dorset.
57   Portland Royal Naval Cemetery,Dorset.
58   Portland (St George) Churchyard,Dorset.
60   Shaftesbury (Holy Trinity) Churchyard.
67   Gillingham New Cemetery,Dorset.
70   Milton-on-Stour (SS Simon and Jude) Churchyard,Gillingham,Dorset.
73   Sutton Waldron (St Bartholomew) Churchyard.
85   Yetminster (St Andrew) Churchyard,Dorset.
87   Sherborne Cemetery,Dorset.
93   Swanage Old Cemetery,Dorset.
94   Wareham Cemetery,Dorset.
95   Affpuddle (St Laurence) Churchyard,Dorset.
102   Kimmeridge Churchyard,Dorset.
103   Langton Matravers Church Cemetery.
109   Wool (Holy Rood) Churchyard,Dorset.
110   Melcombe Regis Cemetery,Dorset.
111   Weymouth Cemetery,Dorset.
115   Owermoigne (St Michael) Churchyard,Dorset.
133   Witchampton (All Saints) Churchyard,Dorset.
135   Wimborne Minster Cemetery,Dorset.
139   Fort George Military Cemetery,St Peter Port,Guernsey.
141   St Martins New Cemetery,Guernsey.
144   St Peter Port (St John) Churchyard,Guernsey.
149   St Brelade Churchyard,Jersey.
151   St Helier (Almorah) Cemetery,Jersey.
152   St Helier (Mont-A-L'Abbe) New Cemetery,Jersey.
156   St Lawrence Churchyard,Jersey.
160   St Peter Churchyard,Jersey.
162   St Saviour Churchyard,Jersey.

DURHAM.

1   Blaydon (St Cuthbert,Stella) Cemetery.
8   Gateshead East Cemetery.
9   Gateshead (Saltwell) Cemetery.
12   Hebburn Cemetery.
13   Jarrow Cemetery.
15   Ryton Cemetery.
17   Seaham Harbour Cemetery.
18   Harton (St Peter) Churchyard.
19   South Shields (Harton) Cemetery.
23   Boldon Cemetery.
25   Whitburn (St Mary) Churchyard.
26   Sunderland (Bishopwearmouth) Cemetery.
27   Sunderland (Mere Knolls) Cemetery.
28   Sunderland (Ryhope Road) Cemetery.
39   Annfield Plain (Harelaw) Cemetery.
42   Auckland St Andrew Old Churchyard.
55   New Shildon (All Saints) Churchyard,Middridge Grange.
56   West Auckland Cemetery.
59   Gainford (St Mary) Churchyard.
62   Barnard Castle Roman Catholic Cemetery.
64   Benfieldside Cemetery.
81   West Pelton (St Paul) Churchyard,Urpeth.
88   Darlington West Cemetery.
97   Durham (St Oswald's) Burial Ground.
102   Pittington Burial Ground.
106   Shincliffe (St Mary) Churchyard.
108   Castle Eden (St James) Churchyard.

109 Dalton-Le-Dale (Holy Trinity) Churchyard.
115 Monk Hesleden Cemetery.
121 Wingate (Holy Trinity) Churchyard.
124 Hartlepool (Hart Road) New Cemetery.
140 Lanchester (All Saints) Churchyard.
162 Stanley New Cemetery.
164 Egglescliffe (St Mary) Churchyard.
165 Norton (St Mary) Churchyard.
167 Stockton-on-Tees (Durham Road) Cemetery.
173 Edmondbyers (St Edmund) Churchyard.
180 Seaton Carew (Holy Trinity) Churchyard.
181 West Hartlepool North Cemetery.
182 West Hartlepool (Stranton) Cemetery.

EIRE or IRELAND.
2 Chapelizod (St Lawrence) Church of Ireland Churchyard,Dublin City.
3 Clondalkin (St John) Church of Ireland Churchyard.
5 Dean's Grange Cemetery,Monkstown.
11 Dublin Friends' Burial Ground,Blackrock.
12 Glasnevin Cemetery,Dublin City.
14 Grangegorman Military Cemetery,Dublin City.
17 Kilgobbin Old Church Cemetery.
24 Mont Jerome Cemetery,Harold's Cross,Dublin City.
27 Royal Hospital Cemetery,Kilmainham,Dublin City.
30 Ballynacally (Kilchreest) Cemetery,County Clare.
34 Ennis (Drumcliff) Cemetery.
45 Scattery Island Graveyard.
48 Ardnagashel Private Burial Ground,County Cork.
49 Ballincollig Military Cemetery,County Cork.
57 Ballynakilla Churchyard,Bere Island,County Cork.
58 Baltimore (Tullagh) Graveyard,County Cork.
63 Blackrock (St Michael) Church of Ireland Churchyard,County Cork.
70 Castlehyde Church of Ireland Churchyard,County Cork.
71 Castlelyons Churchyard,County Cork.
75 Cloyne (St Coleman) Cathedral Churchyard,County Cork.
76 Cobh Old Church Cemetery,County Cork.
77 Cork Military Cemetery,County Cork.
78 Cork (St Finbarr's) Cemetery,County Cork.
81 Corkbeg Church of Ireland Churchyard,County Cork.
84 Currykippane Jewish Cemetery,County Cork.
86 Donoughmore Catholic Churchyard,County Cork.
88 Douglas (St Luke) Church of Ireland churchyard,County Cork.
90 Drinagh Old Graveyard.
94 Fermoy Military Cemetery,County Cork.
95 Fort Carlisle Military Cemetery,County Cork.
109 Kilnamartyra Catholic Churchyard.
114 Kinsale (St Multose) Church of Ireland Churchyard,County Cork.
122 Millstreet Churchyard,County Cork.
132 Skibbereen (Chapel) Graveyard.
138 Timoleague Church of Ireland Churchyard,County Cork.
143 Youghal (St Mary's) Collegiate Churchyard,County Cork.
148 Dromod Church fo Ireland Churchyard,Waterville,County Kerry.
159 Tralee New Cemetery,County Kerry.
160 Tralee (Ratass) Cemetery,County Kerry.
161 Ardcanny Churchyard,Mellon,County Limerick.

163 Bruree Church of Ireland Churchyard,County Limerick.
166 Limerick (King's Island) Military Cemetery,County Limerick.
167 Limerick (St Lawrence's) Catholic Cemetery,County Limerick.
168 Limerick (St Mary) Cathedral Churchyard,County Limerick.
185 Clonmel Friends' Burial Ground,County Tipperary.
186 Clonmel (St Patrick's) Cemetery,County Tipperary.
194 Lorrha Old Graveyard,County Tipperary.
205 Terryglass (St Columba) Catholic Churchyard,County Tipperary.
215 Ballynakill House Private Burial Ground,County Waterford.
216 Ballynaneashagh (St Otteran's) Catholic Cemetery.
234 Stradbally Church of Ireland Churchyard,County Waterford.
237 Tramore (Holy Cross) Catholic Churchyard,County Waterford.
238 Waterford Protestant Cemetery,County Waterford.
251 Ballymachugh (St Paul) Church of Ireland Churchyard,County Cavan.
260 Kilmore Church of Ireland Cemetery,County Cavan.
267 Clonmany Catholic Churchyard,County Donegal.
270 Cockhill Catholic Cemetery,County Donegal.
286 Lower Fahan (Christ Church) Churchyard,County Donegal.
292 Rathmullan (Old Abbey) Graveyard,County Donegal.
295 Upper Fahan Church of Ireland Churchyard,County Donegal.
301 Galway (Bohermore) New Cemetery,County Galway.
309 Omey (Christ Church) Church of Ireland Churchyard,Clifden,County Galway.
313 Athy (St John's) Old Cemetery,County Kildare.
319 Clane (St Michael) Church of Ireland Churchyard,County Kildare.
322 Curragh Military Cemetery,County Kildare.
336 Nass (Maudlings 0r St Magdalen's) Protestant Cemetery,County Kildare.
350 Foulkstown Catholic Churchyard,County Kilkenny.
355 Kilkenny (St Canice) Church of Ireland Cathedral Cemetery,County Kilkenny.
356 Kilkenny (St John) Church of Ireland Churchyard,County Kilkenny.
362 Knocktopher (St David) Church of Ireland Churchyard,County Kilkenny.
381 Durrow Catholic Churchyard,County Leix.
394 Ballymacormick Church of Ireland Churchyard,County Longford.
398 Longford (Ballymacormick) Cemetery,County Longford.
401 Newtown Forbes (St Ann) Church of Ireland Churchyard,County Longford.
406 Drogheda (St Mary) Church of Ireland Churchyard,County Louth.
408 Dromin Old Graveyard,County Louth.
411 Dundalk (St Patrick's) Cemetery,County Louth.
422 Ballina Catholic Cathedral Churchyard,County Mayo.
432 Kilmaine (Holy Trinity) Church of Ireland Churchyard,County Mayo.
434 Newport Presbyterian Churchyard,County Mayo.
437 Ardcath Graveyard,County Meath.
440 Bective (St Mary) Church of Ireland Churchyard,County

Meath.
446 Julianstown (St Mary) Church of Ireland Churchyard,County Meath.
451 Loughcrew Church of Ireland Churchyard,County Meath.
459 Slane (St Patrick) Church of Ireland Churchyard,County Meath.
468 Currin Church of Ireland Churchyard,County Monaghan.
475 Ballyburley Church of Ireland Churchyard,Offaly.
476 Ballycumber (Liss) Churchyard,Offaly.
480 Bir Old Graveyard,Offaly.
487 Killoughy Church of Ireland Churchyard,Offaly.
492 Ardcarn (St Beaidh) Church of Ireland Churchyard,County Roscommon.
499 Killaraght Church of Ireland Churchyard,County Sligo.
505 Ballyglass Cemetery,Mullingar,County Westmeath.
506 Cornamagh Cemetery,Athlone,County Westmeath.
510 Rathconnell Church of Ireland Churchyard,County Westmeath.
512 Toberclare Catholic Churchyard,County Westmeath.
522 Kilscoran Church of Ireland Churchyard,County Wexford.
528 Arklow Cemetery,County Wicklow.
531 Delgany (Christ Church) Church of Ireland Churchyard,County Wicklow.
532 Dunlavin (St Nicholas) Churchyard,County Wicklow.
533 Glenealy Church of Ireland Churchyard,County Wicklow.
534 Greystones (Redford) Cemetery,County Wicklow.
537 Kilcommon Church of Ireland Churchyard,County Wicklow.
539 Killiskey Church of Ireland Churchyard,County Wicklow.
541 Powerscourt (St Patrick) Church Of Ireland Churchyard,County Wicklow.

ESSEX.
1 The City of London Cemetery,Manor Park.
5 Manor Park Cemetery.
7 Woodgrange Park Cemetery.
9 Leytonstone (St Patrick's) Roman Catholic Cemetery.
10 Walthamstow (Queen's Road) Cemetery.
11 Walthamstow (St Mary) Churchyard.
12 Walthamstow (St Peter-on-the-Forest) Churchyard.
13 East London Cemetery,Plaistow.
14 West Ham Cemetery.
16 Barking (Rippleside) Cemetery.
29 Shenfield (St Mary) Churchyard.
36 Thorndon Hall (Our Lady & St Lawrence) Chapel.
37 Buckhurst Hill (St John the Baptist) Churchyard.
40 Chingford Mount Cemetery.
43 Grays New Cemetery.
45 Hornchurch (St Andrew) Churchyard.
48 Ilford Cemetery.
50 Loughton Burial Ground.
56 North Ockenden (St Mary Magdalene) Churchyard.
69 Hockley (St Peter) Churchyard.
73 Rochford (St Andrew) Churchyard.
75 Great Warley (Christchurch) Cemetery.
80 Romford Cemetery.
81 Shoeburyness (St Andrew) Churchyard.
83 Southend on Sea (Leigh on Sea) Cemetery.
84 Southend on Sea (North Road) Cemetery.
86 Southend on Sea (Sutton Road) Cemetery.

88 Wanstead (St Mary) Churchyard.
95 Great Henny (St Mary) Churchyard.
96 Liston Churchyard.
102 Fairsted (SS Mary and Peter) Churchyard.
105 Coggeshall Burial Ground.
106 Hatfield Peverel (St Andrew) Churchyard.
107 Kelvedon (St Mary) Churchyard Extension.
110 Wethersfield (St Mary Magdalene) Churchyard.
112 Brightlingsea (All Saints) Churchyard.
118 Chelmsford (Rectory Lane) Cemetery.
119 Chelmsford (Writtle Road) Cemetery.
120 Springfield (Holy Trinity) Churchyard.
122 Broomfield (St Mary) Churchyard.
123 Danbury (St John the Baptist) Churchyard.
124 East Hanningfield (All Saints) Churchyard.
128 Great Waltham (SS Mary and Lawrence) Churchyard.
130 Ingatestone and Fryerning Cemetery.
132 Little Waltham (St Martin) Churchyard.
137 Sandon (St Andrew) Churchyard.
141 Widford (St mary) Churchyard.
145 Berechurch (St Michael) Churchyard.
146 Colchester Cemetery.
149 Lexden (St Leonard) Churchyard.
158 Little Dunmow (St Mary) Churchyard.
164 Chigwell Row (All Saints) Churchyard,Chigwell.
167 Harlow (St Mary) Churchyard.
172 North Weald Bassett (St Andrew) Churchyard.
175 Coopersale (St Alban) Churchyard.
176 Frinton-on-Sea (St Mary) Churchyard.
185 Dovercourt (All Saints) Churchyard.
186 Harwich Cemetery.
193 East Donyland (St lawrence) Churchyard.
196 Great Horkesley (All Saints) Churchyard.
208 Maldon Cemetery.
209 Maldon (St Mary) Churchyard.
210 Bradwell-near-the-Sea (St Thomas the Apostle) Church Cemetery.
211 Goldhanger (St Peter) Churchyard.
212 Great Braxted (All Saints) Churchyard.
213 Heybridge Cemetery.
221 Southminster (St Leonard) Churchyard.
222 Stow Maries (SS Mary and Margaret) Churchyard.
231 Woodham Walter (St Michael) Churchyard.
234 Chipping Ongar Cemetery,Ongar.
242 Stapleford Abbots (St Mary) Churchyard.
246 Saffron Walden Friends' Burial Ground.
254 Littlebury (Holy Trinity) Churchyard.
255 Newport (Sr Mary) Churchyard.
256 Quendon Churchyard,Quendon and Rickling.
258 Rickling (All Saints) Churchyard,Quendon and Rickling.
261 Birchanger (St Mary) Churchyard.
267 Alresford (St Peter) Churchyard.
268 Ardleigh Cemetery.
270 Bradfield (St Lawrence) Churchyard.
274 Kirby-Le-Soken (St Michael) Churchyard.
275 Little Bentley (St Mary) Churchyard.
285 Witham (All Saints) Churchyard.
287 Wivenhoe (Bellevue Road) Cemetery.

GLOUCESTERSHIRE.

5   Bristol (Arno's Vale) Cemetery.
6   Bristol (Holy Souls) Roman Catholic Cemetery.
9   Bristol (Canford) Cemetery.
10   Bristol Cathedral Burial Ground.
11   Bristol (Greenbank) Cemetery.
15   Bristol (Shirehampton) Cemetery.
19   Westbury-on-Trym (Holy Trinity) Churchyard.
24   Charlton Kings Cemetery.
27   Cheltenham Cemetery,Prestbury.
30   Great Witcombe (St Mary) Churchyard.
31   Leckhampton (St Peter) Churchyard.
32   Prestbury (St Mary) Churchyard,Dowdeswell.
38   Frenchay (St John the Baptist) Churchyard,Winterbourne.
40   Little Badminton Churchyard,Hawkesbury.
51   Brimpsfield (St Michael) Churchyard.
61   Quenington Cemetery.
67   Cirencester Cemetery.
69   Lower Cam (St Bartholomew) Churchyard,Cam.
72   Slimbridge (St John) Churchyard.
86   Gloucester Cemetery.
88   Barnwood (St Lawrence) Churchyard.
92   Hempsted (St Swithun) Churchyard.
102   Wotton Congregational Church Cemetery,Wotton St Mary With-Out.
109   Lydney (St Mary) Churchyard.
124   Newnham (St Peter) Churchyard.
126   Chedworth (St Andrew) Churchyard.
133   Whittington Cemetery.
138   Great Barrington Cemetery.
143   Amberley Church Cemetery,Minchinhampton.
159   Rodborough (St Mary Magdalene) Churchyard.
164   Stonehouse (St Cyr) Churchyard Extension.
168   Stroud Cemetery.
176   Ashchurch (St Nicholas) Churchyard.
178   Kemerton (St Nicholas) Churchyard.
182   Berkeley Cemetery.
190   Thornbury Cemetery.
203   Eastington (St Michael) Churchyard.
214   Stanton (St Michael) Churchyard.

HAMPSHIRE.

1   Aldershot Military Cemetery.
4   Gosport (Ann's Hill) Cemetery.
5   Haslar Royal Naval Cemetery.
6   Alverstoke (Sr Mark) Churchyard.
7   Eastney Cemetery,Portsmouth.
8   Milton Cemetery,Portsmouth.
9   Portsea Cemetery,Portsmouth.
10   Portsdown (Christ Church) Cemetery,Portsmouth.
11   Portsdown (Christ Church) Military Cemetery,Portsmouth.
12   Wymering (SS Peter and Paul) Churchyard,Portsmouth.
13   Bournemouth East Cemetery.
15   Bournemouth (Wimborne Road) Cemetery.
17   Christchurch Cemetery.
19   Highcliffe (St Mark) Churchyard.
22   Throop Congregational Churchyard,Holdenhurst.
23   Fordingbridge Cemetery.
28   Lymington Cemetery.
30   Brockenhurst (St Nicholas) Cemetery.
31   East Boldre (St Paul) Churchyard.
34   Milton (St Mary Magdalene) Churchyard.
36   Beaulieu Cemetery.
41   Eling (St Mary) Churchyard Extension.
43   Exbury (St Catherine) Church.
53   North Stoneham (St Nicholas) Churchyard.
56   Southampton (Hollybrook) Cemetery.
57   Southampton Old Cemetery.
58   Southampton (St Mary Extra) Cemetery.
60   Botley (All Saints) Churchyard.
62   Hound (St Mary) Churchyard Extension.
64   Netley Military Cemetery,Hound.
65   West End (St James's) Cemetery.
67   Aldershot Jewish Cemetery.
70   Cheriton (St Michael) Churchyard.
76   Bentley (St Mary) Churchyard.
83   Grayshott (St Luke) Churchyard.
85   Headley (All Saints) Churchyard Extension.
87   Kingsley (St Nicholas) Old Churchyard.
90   Andover Cemetery.
98   Penton Mewsey (Holy Trinity) Churchyard.
106   Basingstoke (South View) Cemetery.
115   Newnham (St Nicholas) Churchyard.
117   Preston Candover (St Mary) Old Churchyard.
119   Sherfield-Upon-Loddon (St Leonard) churchyard.
122   Upton Grey (St Mary) Churchyard.
130   Shedfield (St John the Baptist) Churchyard.
132   Swanmore (St Barnabas) Churchyard.
136   Crofton (Holy Rood) Old Churchyard.
138   Porchester (St Mary) Churchyard.
139   Sarisbury (St Paul's) Burial Ground.
144   Farnborough Abbey Roman Catholic Churchyard.
145   Farnborough Burial Ground.
146   Fleet (All Saints) Churchyard.
150   Eversley (St Mary) Churchyard Extension.
151   Ewshott (St Mary) Churchyard,Crookham.
153   Hartley Wintney (St Mary) Old Churchyard.
157   Odiham Cemetery.
159   Yateley (St Peter) Churchyard.
160   Bedhampton (St Thomas) Churchyard.
161   North Hayling (St Peter) Churchyard.
173   Highclere Cemetery.
176   Buriton (St Mary) Churchyard.
179   Steep (All Saints) Churchyard.
180   Petersfield Cemetery.
182   Braishfield (All Saints) Churchyard,Michelmersh.
186   Rownhams (St John) Churchyard.
191   Nether Wallop (St Andrew) Churchyard.
192   Stockbridge Cemetery.
202   Winchester (West Hill) Old Cemetery.
205   Compton (All Saints) Churchyard.
214   Ryde Borough Cemetery,Isle of Wight.
216   East Cowes Cemetery,Isle of Wight.
217   Oakfield (St John's) Cemetery,Isle of Wight.
218   St Helens Churchyard,Isle of Wight.
219   Sandown (Christ Church) Churchyard,Isle of Wight.
220   Shanklin Cemetery,Isle of Wight.
221   Ventnor Cemetery,Isle of Wight.
232   Carisbrooke Cemetery,Isle of Wight.
234   Freshwater (All Saints) Churchyard,Isle Of Wight.

240 Parkhurst Military Cemetery,Carisbrooke,Isle of Wight.
241 Shalfleet Churchyard,Isle of Wight.
242 Shorwell (St Peter) New Churchyard,Isle of Wight.
245 Wippingham (St Mildred) Churchyard,Isle of Wight.
246 Whitwell New Burial Ground,Isle of Wight.

HEREFORD AND WORCESTER.
9   Whitbourne (St John the Baptist) Churchyard
Extension,Hereford.
18   Hereford Cemetery,Hereford.
51   Bosbury (Holy Trinity(Churchyard,Hereford.
54   Colwall (St James the Great) Churchyard,Hereford.
56   Much Marcle (St Bartholomew) Churchyard,Hereford.
59   Ledbury Cemetery,Hereford.
96   Mansell Gamage (St Giles) Churchyard,Hereford.
110 Bromsgrove Cemetery,Worcester.
116 Martin Hussingtree (St Michael) Churchyard,Worcester.
129 Broadway (St Eadburgh) Churchyard,Worcester.
144 Kidderminster (St John the Baptist) Churchyard,Worcester.
154 Great Malvern Cemetery,Worcester.
162 Harpley (St Bartholomew) Churchyard,Lower
Sapey,Worcester.
166 Martley (St Peter) Churchyard,Worcester.
182 Blockley Church Cemetery,Worcester.
186 Stourbridge Cemetery,Worcester.
189 Lower Mitton (St Michael) Churchyard,Worcester.
191 Tenbury (St Mary) Churchyard,Worcester.
201 Kempsey (St Mary) Churchyard,Worcester.
208 Worcester (Astwood) Cemetery,Worcester.

HERTFORD.
10   Shenley (St Botolph) Churchyard.
12   Chipping Barnet Church Burial Ground.
24   Layston Churchyard.
29   Chorley Wood (Christ Church) Churchyard.
30   Great Northern London Cemetery.
31   Great Birkhamsted (St Peter) Churchyard.
37   Harpenden (St Nicholas) Churchyard.
38   Bishop's Hatfield (St Etheldreda) Church Cemetery.
60   Tewin (St Peter) Churchyard.
72   Knebworth (St Mary) Churchyard.
81   Hitchin Cemetery.
84   Rickmansworth Cemetery.
87   St Albans Cemetery.
91   Redbourn (St Mary) Churchyard.
108 Wareside (Holy Trinity) Churchyard,Ware Rural.
110 Watford Cemetery.
115 Radlett (Christ Church) Churchyard,Aldenham.
116 Welwyn Cemetery.

HUNTINGDON.   see BEDFORDSHIRE & HUNTINGDON

KENT.
2   Deal Cemetery.
5   Charlton Cemetery.
7   Dover (St Jame's) Cemetery.
8   Dover (St Mary's) New Cemetery.
14   River (St Peter) Churchyard.
15   St Margaret's-at-Cliffe (St Margaret) Churchyard.
24   Birchington (All Saints) Churchyard.

25   Minster Cemetery.
27   Margate Cemetery.
28   Ramsgate Cemetery.
29   Ramsgate (St Augustine) Roman Catholic Churchyard.
30   St Lawrence Cemetery.
34   Walmer (St Mary) Old Churchyard.
37   Hackington (St Stephen) Churchyard.
38   Herne Bay Cemetery,Herne.
42   Chatham Cemetery.
44   Luton (Christ Church) Churchyard.
46   Gillingham New Cemetery.
47   Rainham (St Margaret) Churchyard.
61   Fort Pitt Military Cemetery.
62   Frindsbury (All Saints) Churchyard.
63   Rochester (St Margaret's) Cemetery.
64   Rochester (St Nicholas) Cemetery.
65   Eastchurch (All Saints) Churchyard.
67   Isle of Sheppey General Cemetery,Minster-in-Sheppey.
68   Leysdown (St Clemeny) Churchyard.
71   Sittingbourne Cemetery.
82   Beckenham (St George) Churchyard.
83   Crystal Palace District Cemetery.
85   Bexley Heath Cemetery.
86   East Wickham (St Michael) Churchyard.
89   Bromley Hill Cemetery.
90   Bromley (London Road) Cemetery.
91   Plaistow (St Mary's) Cemetery.
95   Hayes Churchyard.
96   Keston Churchyard.
97   Knockholt (St Katharine) Churchyard.
99   Orpington (All Saints) Churchyard.
100 St Paul's Cray (St Paulinus) Churchyard.
102 Chislehurst Cemetery.
103 Chislehurst (St Nicholas) Churchyard.
105 Crayford (St Paulinus) Churchyard.
109 Darenth (St Margaret) Churchyard.
122 Wilmington (St Michael) Churchyard.
124 Dartford (East Hill) Cemetery.
125 Dartford (Watling Street) Cemetery.
127 Erith (Brook Street) Cemetery.
129 Gravesend Cemetery.
130 Northfleet Cemetery.
141 Fordcombe (St Peter) Churchyard,Penshurst.
147 Riverhead (St Mary) Churchyard.
153 Sevenoaks (Greatness Park) Cemetery.
154 Sevenoaks (St Nicholas) Churchyard.
156 Foots Cray Baptist Chapelyard.
157 Sidcup Cemetery.
160 Ashford Cemetery.
164 Bridge (St Peter) Churchyard.
175 Canterbury Cemetery.
177 Canterbury (St Martin) Churchyard.
179 Cheriton (St Martin) Churchyard.
180 Shorncliffe Military Cemetery.
182 Cranbrook Cemetery.
191 Chilham (St Mary) Churchyard.
197 Wye (SS Gregory and Martin) Churchyard.
200 Hawkinge (St Michael) Churchyard.
201 Lyminge (SS Mary & Eadburg) Churchyard.
203 Saltwood (SS Peter and Paul) Churchyard.

205 Faversham Cemetery.
212 Ospringe (SS Peter and Paul) Churchyard.
216 Throwley (St Michael) Churchyard.
217 Folkestone Old Cemetery.
221 Detling (St Martin) Churchyard.
224 Harrietsham (St John the Baptist) Churchyard.
225 Hollingbourne (All Saints) Churchyard.
230 Hythe Cemetery.
231 Lydd (All Saints) Churchyard Extension.
232 Maidstone Cemetery.
234 Bearstead (Holy Cross) Churchyard Extension.
235 Boughton Monchelsea (St Peter) Churchyard.
239 Linton (St Nicholas) Churchyard.
243 Staplehurst (All Saints) Churchyard.
252 East Peckham (St Michael) Churchyard.
259 West Malling (St Mary) Churchyard.
261 New Romney (St Nicholas) Churchyard.
267 Rusthall (St Paul) Churchyard.
268 Tunbridge Wells Cemetery.
269 Southborough Cemetery.
272 Tenterden (St Mildred's) Cemetery.
279 Brenchley (All Saints) Churchyard.
280 Groombridge (St John) Churchyard,Speldhurst.
281 Hildenborough (St John the Devine) Churchyard.
282 Horsmonden (St Margaret) Churchyard.
284 Matfield (St Luke) Churchyard,Brenchley.
285 Paddock Wood (St Andrew) Churchyard,Brenchley.
287 Speldhurst (St Mary) Churchyard.
289 Tonbridge Cemetery.
296 Kingsnorth Churchyard.
298 Westwell Burial Ground.
301 Wrotham (St George) Churchyard Extension.

LANCASHIRE.
1 Allerton Cemetery,Liverpool.
2 Anfield Cemetery,Liverpool.
4 Everton Cemetery,Liverpool.
7 Kirkdale Cemetery,Liverpool.
8 Knotty Ash (St John the Evangelist) Churchyard.
9 Lingfield Road (Broad Green) Jewish Cemetery,Liverpool.
10 Much Woolton (St Mary's) Roman Catholic Cemetery,Liverpool.
12 St Jame's Cemetery,Liverpool.
14 Toxteth Park Cemetery,Liverpool.
18 Wavertree (Holy Trinity) Churchyard,Liverpool.
19 Birch-in-Rusholme (St James) Churchyard,Manchester.
23 Cheetham Hill (St Luke) Churchyard.
24 Cheetham Hill Wesleyan Cemetery,Manchester.
30 Manchester Crematorium.
32 Manchester (Gorton) Cemetery.
33 Manchester (Philips Park) Cemetery.
34 Manchester Southern Cemetery.
35 Moston (St Joseph's) Roman Catholic Cemetery,Manchester.
37 Newton Heath (All Saints) Churchyard,Manchester.
39 Withington (St Paul) Churchyard.
40 Barrow-in-Furness Cemetery.
42 Bispham (All Hallows) Churchyard.
43 Blackpool Cemetery.
46 Fleetwood Protestant Dissenters' Cemetery.

48 Fleetwood (St Peter) Churchyard Extension.
52 Lund (St John) Churchyard,Clifton-with-Salwick.
71 Grange-Over-Sands Cemetery.
76 Lancaster Cemetery.
77 Lancaster (Scotforth) Cemetery.
80 Bolton-le-Sands (Holy Trinity) Churchyard.
86 Warton (St Oswald) Churchyard,Warton-with-Lundeth.
92 Lytham (St Cuthbert) Churchyard.
95 St Anne's-on-Sea Churchyard.
96 Heysham (St Peter) Churchyard.
98 Morecombe (Torrisholme) Cemetery.
101 Ashton-on-Ribble (St Andrew) Churchyard.
102 Preston (New Hall Lane) Cemetery.
103 Broughton (St John the Baptist) Churchyard.
104 Cottam (St Andrew) Churchyard,Lea Ashton,Ingol and Cottam.
108 Grimsargh (St Michael) Churchyard,Grimsargh-with-Brockholes.
111 Longton (St Andrew) Churchyard.
112 Longton (St Oswald) Roman Catholic Churchyard.
114 Penwortham (St Mary) Churchyard.
143 Walton-Le-Dale (St Leonard) Churchyard.
146 Bootle Cemetery.
149 Great Crosby (St Luke) Churchyard.
150 Great Crosby (SS Peter and Paul) Roman Catholic Churchyard.
152 Huyton (St Agnes) Roman Catholic Churchyard.
154 Roby (St Bartholomew) Churchyard.
155 Liverpool (West Derby) Cemetery.
156 Liverpool (Yew Tree) Roman Catholic Cemetery.
157 Newton-in-Makerfield Cemetery.
160 Prescot (St Mary) Churchyard.
164 St Helens Cemetery.
168 Ince Blundell Roman Catholic Cemetery.
169 Liverpool (Ford) Roman Catholic Cemetery.
170 Sefton (St Helen) Churchyard.
171 Warrington Cemetery.
176 Hollinfare Cemetery,Rixton-with-Glazebrook.
179 Eccleston (Christ Church) Churchyard.
181 Halewood (St Nicholas) Churchyard.
186 Farnworth (St Luke) Churchyard.
189 Accrington Cemetery.
193 Blackburn Cemetery.
198 Mellor (St Mary) Churchyard.
199 Mellor Wesleyan Methodist Chapelyard.
205 Burnley Cemetery.
206 Habergham (All Saints) Churchyard.
209 Briercliffe (St James) Churchyard.
210 Foulridge (St Michael) Churchyard.
211 Haggate Baptist Chapelyard,Briercliffe.
216 Newchurch-in-Pendle (St Mary) Churchyard,Goldshaw Booth.
217 Read (St John) Churchyard.
219 Wheatley Lane Inghamite Chapelyard,Wheatley Carr Booth.
222 Church and Clayton-le-Moors Joint Cemetery.
226 Clitheroe (St Mary's) Burial Ground.
233 Whalley (Queen Mary's Hospital) Military Cemetery.
235 Colne Cemetery.
237 Great Harwood Cemetery.

243 Nelson Cemetery.
246 Padiham Cemetery.
255 Bolton (Astley Bridge) Cemetery.
256 Bolton (Heaton) Cemetery.
257 Bolton (Tonge) Cemetery.
261 Halliwell (St Peter) Churchyard.
263 Bury Cemetery.
266 Bury (St Paul) Churchyard.
267 Elton (All Saints) Churchyard.
277 Darwen Cemetery.
278 Hoddlesden (St Paul) Churchyard.
283 Haslingden Holden Hall) Cemetery.
284 Haslingden (St James the Great) Churchyard.
313 Rawtenstall (Longholme) Wesleyan Chapelyard.
317 Rochdale Cemetery.
321 Tottington (St Anne) Churchyard.
322 Tottington (St John) Free Church of England Churchyard.
327 Harwood (Christ Church) Churchyard.
336 Whitworth Cemetery.
342 Ashton-in-Makerfield (St Thomas) Churchyard.
343 Ashton-in-Makerfield (St Thomas) Churchyard,Heath Lane Extension.
346 Chorley Cemetery.
366 Formby (St Peter) Churchyard.
368 Wigan Cemetery.
380 Southport (Birkdale) Cemetery.
381 Southport (Duke Street) Cemetery.
383 Southport (St Cuthbert) Churchyard.
386 Aughton (Christ Church) Churchyard.
387 Aughton (St Michael) Churchyard.
391 Maghull (St Andrew) Churchyard.
401 Douglas Cemetery,Isle of Man.
403 Kirk Braddan (St Brendan) New Churchyard,Isle of Man.
405 Kirk Christ Lezayre (Holy Trinity) Churchyard,Isle of Man.
410 Kirk Malew (St Malew) Churchyard,Isle of Man.
413 Kirk Maughold (St Machut) Churchyard,Isle of Man.
416 Ashton-under-Lyne (Hurst) Cemetery.
420 Audenshaw Cemetery.
421 Audenshaw (St Stephen) Churchyard.
427 Oldham (Chadderton) Cemetery.
434 Eccles (Peel Green) Cemetery.
436 Monton Unitarian Churchyard.
438 Hindley (All Saints) Churchyard.
441 Hey (St John the Baptist) Churchyard Extension.
443 Leigh Cemetery.
450 Middleton New Cemetery.
463 Prestwich (St Margaret) Churchyard.
464 Prestwich (St Mary) Churchyard.
471 Higher Broughton (St John) Churchyard.
472 Kersal (St Paul) Churchyard.
474 Salford (Weaste) Cemetery.
475 Stretford Cemetery.
478 Pendlebury (St Augustine of Canterbury) Churchyard.
481 Swinton Cemetery.
483 Tyldesley Cemetery.
487 Urmston Cemetery.
489 Whitefield British Jews' Cemetery.
491 Worsley (St Mark) Churchyard.

LEICESTERSHIRE.
13 Barrow-upon-Soar Cemetery.
15 Leicester (Gilroes) Cemetery,Gilroes.
24 Woodhouse Eaves (St Paul) Churchyard Extension,Woodhouse.
25 Bottesford (St Mary) Churchyard.
55 Burbage (St Catherine) Churchyard.
63 Leicester (Welford Road) Cemetery.
64 Loughborough (Leicester Road) Cemetery.
70 Lutterworth (St Mary) Churchyard.
87 Shenton (St John) Churchyard.
97 Market Harborough (Northampton Road) Cemetery.
117 Sysonby Churchyard.
119 Quorn (St Bartholomew) Churchyard.
120 Shepshed Cemetery.

LINCOLNSHIRE.
1 Boston Cemetery.
6 Freiston (St James) Churchyard.
10 Skirbeck Quarter (St Thomas) Churchyard.
14 Fleet (St Mary Magdalene) Churchyard.
25 Gosberton Cemetery.
29 Spalding Cemetery.
34 Folkingham (St Andrew) Churchyard.
38 Market Deeping Cemetery.
44 Bourne Cemetery.
53 Waddington (St Michael) Churchyard.
57 Fulbeck (St Nicholas) Churchyard.
60 Stubton (St Martin) Churchyard.
61 Grantham Cemetery.
67 Harlaxton (SS Mary and Peter) Churchyard.
69 Londonthorpe (St John the Baptist) Churchyard.
76 Billinghay Cemetery.
78 Cranwell (St Andrew) Churchyard.
86 Leasingham (St Andrew) Churchyard.
98 Quarrington (St Botolph) Churchyard.
100 Stamford Cemetery.
115 Middle Rasen (St Peter) Churchyard.
123 Cleethorpes Cemetery.
136 Gainsborough General Cemetery.
142 Broughton Cemetery.
152 Scawby (St Hibald) Churchyard.
156 Grimsby (Scartho Road) Cemetery.
158 Scartho (St Giles) Churchyard.
159 Great Coates (St Nicholas) Churchyard.
160 Immingham (St Andrew) Churchyard.
162 Stallingborough (SS Peter and Paul) Churchyard.
179 Lincoln (Canwick Road) Cemetery.
181 Lincoln (Newport) Cemetery.
183 Louth Cemetery.
202 Mablethorpe (St Mary) Churchyard.
220 Hogsthorpe (St Mary) Churchyard.
225 Spilsby Cemetery.
236 Goltho (St George) Churchyard.
239 Nettleham (All Saints) New Churchyard.

LONDON.
1 Wandsworth Cemetery.
2 Nunhead (All Saints) Cemetery.
3 Camberwell (Forest Hill Road) Cemetery.

4   Brompton Cemetery,Kensington.
5   Fulham Old Cemetery.
6   Fulham (St Thomas of Canterbury) Roman Catholic Cemetery.
7   Hammersmith Cemetery.
8   Kensal Green (All Souls) Cemetery,Kensington and Hammersmith.
9   Kensal Green (St Mary's) Roman Catholic Cemetery,Hammersmith.
10   Abney Park Cemetery,Stoke Newington.
11   City of London and Tower Hamlets Cemetery,Stepney.
12   Hampstead Cemetery.
13   Hampstead (St John) Additional Burial Ground.
14   Highgate Cemetery,St Pancras.
15   St Paul's Cathedral.
16   Savoy Chapel.
18   Battersea (St Mary's,Battersea Rise) Cemetery.
19   Deptford Cemetery,Brockley.
20   Lambeth Cemetery,Tooting.
22   Lewisham (Ladywell) Cemetery.
23   Norwood Cemetery.
24   Putney Cemetery.
25   Putney Vale Cemetery.
26   Streatham Cemetery (Garratt lane).
27   Tooting (St Nicholas) Churchyard.
28   Charlton Cemetery,Greenwich.
29   Greenwich Cemetery.
30   Greenwich Royal Naval Cemetery.
32   Eltham (St John the Baptist) Churchyard,Woolwich.
33   Plumstead Cemetery,Woolwich.
35   Woolwich Cemetery.

MIDDLESEX.
1   Edmonton Cemetery.
5   Enfield Chase Cemetery.
6   Enfield Highway Cemetery.
7   Enfield Highway (St James) Churchyard.
9   Southgate Cemetery.
12   South Mimms (St Giles) Churchyard.
13   Tottenham and Wood Green Cemetery.
15   Islington Cemetery.
16   St Marylebone Cemetery.
17   St Pancras Cemetery.
18   Harrow on the Hill (St Mary) Lower Churchyard.
19   Harrow on the Hill Cemetery.
21   Edgware (St Margaret) Churchyard.
23   Harrow Waeld (All Saints) Churchyard Extension.
25   Pinner Cemetery.
26   Golders Green Crematorium.
27   Golders Green Jewish Cemetery.
28   Hampstead Garden Suburb (St Jude) Church.
29   Hendon Park Cemetery.
30   Hendon (St Mary) Churchyard.
34   Ruislip (St Martin) Churchyard Extension.
35   Wealdstone Cemetery.
37   Wembley Old Burial Ground.
38   Wembley (St John the Evangelist) Churchyard.
39   Paddington Cemetery.
40   Willesden Jewish Cemetery.
41   Willesden Liberal Jewish Cemetery.

42   Willesden New Cemetery.
43   Willesden Old Cemetery.
44   Acton Cemetery.
46   Chiswick Cemetery.
47   New Brentford (St Lawrence) Churchyard.
48   Ealing and Old Brentford Cemetery.
49   Greenford (Holy Cross) Churchyard.
51   Kensington (Hanwell) Cemetery.
52   Perivale Cemetery.
53   Westminster City Cemetery.
56   Feltham Cemetery.
58   Hampton Burial Ground.
62   Harlington (SS Peter and Paul) Churchyard.
64   Hayes (St Mary) Churchyard.
66   Heston (St Leonard) Churchyard.
68   New Brentford Cemetery.
69   Southall Cemetery.
70   Ashford Cemetery.
74   Littleton (St Mary Magdalene) Churchyard.
76   Sunbury New Cemetery.
77   Teddington Cemetery.
78   Hounslow Cemetery.
80   Twickenham Parochial Cemetery.
83   Hillingdon Cemetery.
84   Uxbridge Cemetery.
85   Harmondsworth (St Mary) Churchyard.

MONMOUTHSHIRE.
4   Abergavenny New Cemetery,Llanfoist.
9   Llanfoist (St Faith) Churchyard.
11   Llanover (St Bartholomew) Churchyard.
19   Trevethin (St Cadoc) Churchyard.
34   Caldicot (St Mary) Churchyard.
52   Newport (Christchurch) Cemetery,Christchurch.
67   Newport (St Woollos) Cemetery.
69   Panteg Cemetery.
76   Graig Congregational Chapelyard.
81   Malpas (St Mary) Churchyard.
82   Marshfield (St Mary) Churchyard.
83   Rogerstone (Bethesda) Baptist Chapelyard.
89   Usk (St Mary Magdalene) Churchyard.

NORFOLK.
11   Heydon (SS Peter and Paul) Churchyard.
15   Stratton Strawless (St Margaret) Churchyard.
21   Cantley (St Margaret) Churchyard.
24   Redenhall (The Assumption) Churchyard,Redwnhall-with-Harleston.
26   Thorpe-Next-Norwich (St Andrew) Church Cemetery.
30   Cromer No.2 Burial Ground.
43   Pulham St Mary the Virgin Churchyard.
58   Docking (St Mary) Churchyard.
60   Heacham (St Mary) Churchyard.
61   Hunstanton (St Mary) Churchyard.
67   Stanhoe (All Saints) Churchyard.
73   Marham (Holy Trinity) Churchyard.
74   Runcton Holme (St James) Churchyard,South Runcton.
77   Stradsett (St Mary) Churchyard.
85   Great Yarmouth (Caister) Cemetery,East Caister.
88   Ormesby St Margaret Churchyard,Ormsby.

94   Aldborough (St Mary) Churchyard.
96   Beeston Regis (All Saints) Churchyard.
101 Mundesley (All Saints) Churchyard.
103 Overstrand (St Martin) Churchyard.
109 Upper Sheringham (All Saints) Churchyard.
110 West Runton (Holy Trinity) Churchyard,Runton.
111 Weybourne (All Saints) Churchyard.
118 Kimberley (St Peter) Churchyard.
127 Hillington (St Mary) Churchyard.
128 Little Massingham (St Andrew) Churchyard.
131 Great Yarmouth (Gorleston) Cemetery.
132 Great Yarmouth New Cemetery.
133 Great Yarmouth Old Cemetery.
137 Colney (St Andrew) Churchyard.
138 Cringleford (St Peter) Churchyard.
139 East Carleton (St Mary) Churchyard.
151 King's Lynn Cemetery.
162 Hedenham (St Peter) Churchyard.
172 Woodton (All Saints) Churchyard.
179 Upwell (St Peter) Churchyard.
184 East Bilney (St Mary) Churchyard,Beetley.
195 Mileham (St John the Baptist) Churchyard.
207 Eaton (St Andrew) New Churchyard,Norwich.
209 Norwich Cemetery.
210 Norwich (The Rosary) Cemetery.
231 Hoveton St John Churchyard,Hoveton.
235 Sloley (St Bartholomew) Churchyard.
247 Narborough (All Saints) Churchyard.
254 Swaffham (SS Peter and Paul) Churchyard.
255 Thetford Cemetery.
256 Blo'Norton (St Andrew) Churchyard.
259 East Harling Cemetery,Harling.
261 Feltwell (St Nicholas) Churchyard.
285 Attleborough Cemetery.
288 Breckles (St Margaret) Churchyard,Stow Bedon.
301 Watton Nonconformist Burial Ground.

NORTHAMPTON.
1   Brackley (St Peter) Churchyard.
6   Helmdon (St Mary Magdalene) Churchyard.
13   Church Brampton (St Botolph) Churchyard.
27   Barby (St Mary) Churchyard.
31   Yelvertoft (All Saints) Churchyard.
32   Daventry (Holy Cross) Churchyard.
38   Newnham (St Michael) Churchyard.
55   Castle Ashby (St Mary Magdalene) Churchyard.
60   Northampton (Towcester Road) Cemetery,Hardingstone.
67   Cottingham (St Mary Magdalene) Churchyard.
74   Kettering Cemetery.
76   Middleton Cheney (All Saints) Churchyard.
78   Abington (SS Peter and Paul) Churchyard.
79   Northampton General Cemetery.
80   Dallington Cemetery.
82   Great Billing (St Andrew) Churchyard Roman Catholic Extension.
107 Raunds Wesleyan Methodist Chapelyard.
143 Wellingborough (Doddington Road) Cemetery.
144 Wellingborough (London Road) Cemetery.
146 Barnack Cemetery,Soke of Peterborough.
151 Peterborough Old Cemetery,Soke of Peterborough.

161 Hambleton (St Andrew) Churchyard,Rutland.
164 Oakham Cemetery,Rutland.

NORTHERN IRELAND.
14   Layde Church of Ireland Churchyard,Cushendall,County Antrim.
33   Belfast City Cemetery,County Antrim.
37   Carnmoney Cemetery,County Antrim.
40   Carrickfergus (Victoria) Cemetery,County Antrim.
42   Ballylinney Presbyterian Cemetery,County Antrim.
45   Glenarm New Cemetery,County Antrim.
52   Larne New Cemetery,County Antrim.
56   Drumbeg (St Patrick) Church of Ireland Churchyard,County Antrim.
57   Dundrod Presbyterian Churchyard,County Antrim.
68   Kilmore (St Aidnan) Church of Ireland Churchyard,County Armagh.
71   Armagh (St Mark) Church of Ireland Churchyard,County Armagh.
74   Derrytrasna Roman Catholic Churchyard,County Armagh.
79   Seagoe Cemetery,County Armagh.
80   Lurgan (Dougher) Roman Catholic Cemetery,County Armagh.
85   Bessbrook (Christ Church) Church of Ireland Churchyard Extension,County Armagh.
102 Tullylish (All Saints) Church of Ireland Churchyard,County Down.
105 Banbridge Roman Catholic Cemetery,County Down.
106 Banbridge Town Cemetery,County Down.
107 Bangor New Cemetery,County Down.
110 Belfast (Dundonald) Cemetery,County Down.
124 Down Cathedral New Cemetery,County Down.
136 Hillsborough (St Malachi) Church of Ireland Churchyard,County Down.
137 Knockbreda Church of Ireland Churchyard,Newtownbreda,County Down.
138 Holywood Cemetery,County Down.
145 Newcastle (St John's) Cemetery,County Down.
146 Colonallan Church of Ireland Churchyard,County Down.
è165 kinawley Church of Ireland Churchyard,Derrylin,County Fermanagh.
168 Enniskillen New Cemetery,County Fermanagh.
181 Coleraine Cemetery,County Londonderry.
183 Killowen (St John) Church of Ireland Churchyard,County Londonderry.
188 Kilrea (St Patrick) Church of Ireland Churchyard,County Londonderry.
196 Londonderry City Cemetery,County Londonderry.
201 Glendermot Church of Ireland Churchyard,County Londonderry.
222 Killeeshil (St Paul) Church of Ireland Churchyard,County Tyrone.
229 Dungannon Borough Cemetery,County Tyrone.
231 Cappagh (St Eugenius) Church of Ireland Churchyard,East Mountjoy,County Tyrone.
239 Kilskeery Church of Ireland Churchyard,County Tyrone.
242 Omagh New Cemetery,County Tyrone.
248 Strabane Cemetery,County Tyrone.

NORTHUMBERLAND.
1   Newcastle-upon-Tyne (All Saints) Cemetery.
2   Newcastle-upon-Tyne (Byker and Heaton) Cemetery.
3   Newcastle-upon-Tyne (Old Jesmond) General Cemetery.
4   Newcastle-upon-Tyne (St Andrew's and Jesmond) Cemetery.
5   Newcastle-upon-Tyne (St John's,Westgate and Elswick) Cemetery.
7   Newcastle-upon-Tyne (St Nicholas) Cemetery.
11 Alnwick Cemetery.
11a Bolton Churchyard.
19 South Charlton (St James) Churchyard.
20 Warkworth (St laurence) Church Burial Ground.
26 Bedlington (St Cuthbert) Churchyard.
34 Berwick-upon-Tweed Cemetery.
36 Blyth Cemetery.
39 Horton (St Mary) Churchyard,Blyth.
43 North Gosforth Joint Burial Ground.
49 Earsdon (St Alban) Churchyard,Seaton Valley.
56 Old Bewick (Holy Trinity) Churchyard.
58 Wooler (St Mary) Church Burial Ground.
60 Gosforth (St Nicholas) Churchyard.
74 Longbenton (Benton) Cemetery.
75 Morpeth (SS Mary and James) Churchyard.
78 Cresswell (St Bartholomew) Churchyard.
83 Newburn (Lemington) Cemetery.
86 Ancroft (St Anne) Churchyard.
87 Norham (St Cuthbert) Churchyard.
96 Tynemouth (Preston) Cemetery.
97 Wallsend (Church Bank) Cemetery.
99 Whitley Bay (Hartley South) Cemetery.

NOTTINGHAMSHIRE.
2   Annesley and Felley Cemetery,Annesley.
32   Plumtree (St Mary) Churchyard.
39   East Retford Cemetery.
60   Hucknall Cemetery.
66   East Leake (St Mary the Virgin) Churchyard.
68   Mansfield (Nottingham Road) Cemetery.
70   Forest Town (St Alban) Churchyard.
84   Nottingham Church Cemetery.
85   Nottingham General Cemetery.
96   Halam (St Michael) Churchyard.
106 Southwell Minster (St Mary) Churchyard.
112 Sutton-in-Ashfield Cemetery.
121 Worksop (Retford Road) Cemetery.

OXFORDSHIRE.
1   Banbury Cemetery.
3   Alkerton (St Michael) churchyard.
24 Bicester Cemetery.
32 Spelsbury (All Saints) Churchyard.
36 Dorchester Cemetery.
44 Goring (St Thomas of Canterbury) Churchyard.
45 Mapledurham (St Margaret) Churchyard.
51 Henley-on-Thames Cemetery.
69 Oxford (Botley) Cemetery.
71 Oxford (Holy Cross) Cemetery.
73 Oxford (Rose Hill) Cemetery.
74 Oxford (Wolvercote) Cemetery.
85 Brize Norton (St Brice) Churchyard Extension.

97 Witney Burial Ground.

SCOTLAND.
1   Applin Old Churchyard,Lismore and Applin,Argyll.
2   Applin (St Cross) Episcopalian Churchyard,Lismore and Applin,Argyll.
4   Ardmarnoch House Burial Ground,Filfinan,Argyll.
9   Campbeltown (Kilkerrean) Cemetery,Argyll.
14   Dunoon Cemetery,Dunoon and Kilmun,Argyll.
15   Dunoon (Holy Trinity) Episcopalian Churchyard,Dunoon and Kilmun,Argyll.
22   Kiells Old Churchyard,Jara,Argyll.
26   Kilbride Parish Churchyard,Kilfinan,Argyll.
31   Kilchoman New Cemetery,Argyll.
41   Kilmhoiri Old Churchyard,Craignish,Argyll.
44   Kilmory Castle Burial Ground,Glassary,Argyll.
45   Kilmun Cemetery,Dunoon and Kilmun,Argyll.
50   Kilvickeon Old Churchyard,Kilfinichen and Kilvickeon,Argyll.
52   Lochgoilhead Parish Churchyard,Lochgoilhead and Kilmorich,Argyll.
54   Oban (Pennyfuir) Cemetery,Kilmore and kilbride,Argyll.
60   Tarbert Burial Ground,Kilcalmonell,Argyll.
64   Alloa (Sunnyside) Cemetery,Clackmannan.
69   Tillicoultry Cemetery,Clackmannan.
76   Boturich Castle Private Cemetery,Kilmaronock,Dumbarton.
77   Cardross Parish Churchyard,Dumbarton.
80   Dumbarton Cemetery,Dumbarton.
81   Faslane Cemetery,Row,Dumbarton.
82   Helensburgh Cemetery,Row,Dumbarton.
84   Kirkintilloch (Auld Aisle) Cemetery,Dumbarton.
86   New Patrick Cemetery,Dumbarton.
87   New Kilpatrick Parish Churchyard,Dumbarton.
92   Abercrombie Old Chapelyard,Fife.
97   Ballingry Cemetery,Fife.
105 Cowdenbeath Cemetery,Beath,Fife.
109 Cupar New Cemetery,Fife.
112 Dunfermline Cemetery,Fife.
115 East Wemyss Cemetery,Wemyss,Fife.
118 Forgan (Vicarsford) Cemetery,Fife.
119 Inverkeithing Cemetery,Fife.
122 Kilconquhar Parish Churchyard,Fife.
127 Kirkcaldy Cemetery,Kirkcaldy and Dysart,Fife.
136 Newburgh Cemetery,Fife.
141 St Andrews Eastern Cemetery,Fife.
142 St Andrews Western Cemetery,Fife.
151 Kinross East Burying Ground,Kinross.
153 Orwell Parish Churchyard,Kinross.
167 Callander Cemetery,Perth.
169 Comrie Cemetery,Perth.
171 Crieff Cemetery,Perth.
180 Innerwick-in-Glenlyon Parish Churchyard,Fortingall,Perth.
187 Kinfauns Parish Churchyard,Perth.
199 Perth (Wellshill) Cemetery,Perth.
200 Pitlochry New Cemetery,Moulin,Perth.
203 St Madoes Parish Churchyard,Perth.
204 Scone Cemetery,Perth.
208 Trossachs Parish Churchyard,Callander,Perth.
211 Denny Cemetery,Stirling.
212 Falkirk Cemetery,Stirling.

214 Grangemouth Burial Ground,Stirling.
226 Stirling (Ballengeich) Cemetery,Stirling.
228 Stirling (Mar Place) Cemetery,Stirling.
229 Stirling (Valley) Cemetery,Stirling.
231 Colinton Parish Churchyard,Edinburgh.
232 Corstorphine Parish Churchyard,Edinburgh.
235 Edinburgh (Comely Bank) Cemetery.
236 Edinburgh (Dalry) Cemetery.
237 Edinburgh (Dean,Western) Cemetery.
238 Edinburgh Eastern Cemetery.
239 Edinburgh (Grange) Cemetery.
240 Edinburgh (Liberton) Cemetery.
241 Edinburgh (Morningside) Cemetery.
242 Edinburgh (New Calton) Burial Ground.
244 Edinburgh (Newington) Cemetery.
245 Edinburgh (North Merchiston) Cemetery.
246 Edinburgh (Piershill) Cemetery.
247 Edinburgh (Portobello) Cemetery.
248 Edinburgh Roman Catholic Cemetery.
249 Edinburgh (Rosebank) Cemetery.
252 Edinburgh (Seafield) Cemetery.
253 Edinburgh (Warriston) Cemetery.
258 Cockpen Old Churchyard,Edinburgh.
259 Cranston Parish Churchyard,Midlothian.
262 Dalkeith (Eskbank) Cemetery,Midlothian.
263 Dalmahoy (Sr Mary) Episcopalian
Churchyard,Ratho,Midlothian.
267 Inveresk Parish Churchyard,Midlothian.
269 Lasswade Old Churchyard,Midlothian.
270 Loanhead Cemetery,Lasswade,Midlothian.
274 Penicuik Cemetery,Midlothian.
275 Penicuik Parish Churchyard,Midlothian.
277 Roslin Cemetery,Lasswade,Midlothian.
279 West Calder Cemetry,Midlothian.
280 Aberdeen (Allenvale) Cemetery.
281 Aberdeen (Grove) Cemetery.
283 Aberdeen (Nellfield) Cemetery.
286 Aberdeen (St Peter's) Cemetery.
287 Aberdeen (Springbank) Cemetery.
288 Aberdeen (Trinity) Cemetery.
294 Belhelvie Old Cemetery,Aberdeen.
308 Ellon Cemetery,Aberdeen.
310 Folla-Rule (Sr George) Episcopalian
Churchyard,Fyvie,Aberdeen.
313 Fraserburgh (Kirkton) Cemetery,Aberdeen.
319 Huntly Cemetery,Aberdeen.
329 Kincardine O'Neil (Christ Church) Episcopalian
Churchyard,Aberdeen.
330 Kincardine O'Neil Old Churchyard,Aberdeen.
333 Kintore Parish Churchyard,Aberdeen.
339 Longside New Parish Churchyard,Aberdeen.
341 Lonmay Parish Churchyard,Aberdeen.
353 New Pitsligo Parish Churchyard,Tyrie,Aberdeen.
357 Old Machar Cathedral Churchyard,Aberdeen.
358 Peterculter Parish Churchyard,Aberdeen.
359 Peterculter New Burial Ground,Aberdeen.
360 Peterhead New Cemetery,Aberdeen.
378 Turriff Cemetery,Aberdeen.
380 Arbroath Eastern Cemetery,Arbroath and St
Vigeans,Angus.

381 Arbroath western Cemetery,Arbroath and St
Vigeans,Angus.
383 Brechin Cemetery,Angus.
385 Dundee Eastern Necropolis,Angus.
386 Dundee Western Cemetery,Angus.
387 Dundee Western Necropolis,Angus.
395 Monifieth Cemetery,Angus.
396 Montrose (Rosehill) Cemetery,Angus.
398 Montrose (Sleepyhillock) Cemetery,Angus.
422 Cuier Churchyard,Barra,Inverness.
424 Daviot Parish Churchyard,Daviot and Dunlichity,Inverness.
430 Fort William (St Andrew) Episcopalian
Churchyard,Kilmallie,Inverness.
435 Heisker Island Graves,North Uist,Inverness.
438 Insh (St Eunan) Churchyard,Kingussie,Inverness.
442 Inverness (Tomnahurich) Cemetery.
447 Kilmallie Old Churchyard,Inverness.
455 Kilmuir Old Churchyard,Duirinish,Inverness.
458 Kingussie Parish Churchyard,Kingussie and Insh,Inverness.
484 Banchory Ternan Parish Churchyard,Kincardine.
495 Laurencekirk Cemetery,Kincardine.
497 Nigg New Parish Churchyard,Kincardine.
500 St Cyrus Upper (Parish) Churchyard,Kincardine.
501 Ardrossan Cemetery,Ayr.
503 Ayr Cemetery.
508 Colmonell Parish Churchyard,Ayr.
510 Cumnock New Cemetery,Old Cumnock,Ayr.
514 Darvel Cemetery,Ayr.
517 Dundonald (Troon) Cemetery,Ayr.
520 Girvan (Doune) Cemetery,Ayr.
522 Irvine Cemetery,Ayr.
523 Irvine Parish Churchyard,Ayr.
525 Kilmarnock Cemetery,Ayr.
528 Kirkmichael Parish Churchyard,Ayr.
530 Largs Cemetery,Ayr.
531 Mauchline Cemetery,Ayr.
533 Monkton and Prestwick Cemetery,Ayr.
546 Symington Parish Churchyard,Ayr.
547 Tarbolton Parish Churchyard,Ayr.
549 West Kilbride Cemetery,Ayr.
556 Earlston Parish Churchyard,Berwick.
558 Eyemouth Cemetery,Berwick.
561 Greenlaw Parish Churchyard,Berwick.
563 Hutton Parish Churchyard,Berwick.
566 Lennel Old Churchyard,Berwick.
567 Longformacus New Burial Ground,Berwick.
569 Mordington Burial Ground,Berwick.
579 Rothesay Cemetery,Bute.
581 Annan Cemetery,Dumfries.
582 Applrgarth Parish Churchyard,Dumfries.
591 Dryfesdale Cemetery,Dunfries.
596 Dunfries (St Michael's) New Cemetery,Dumfries.
608 Kirkpartick-Juxta Parish Churchyard,Dumfries.
612 Moffat Cemetery,Kirkpatrick-Juxta,Dumfries.
613 Morton New Cemetery,Dumfries.
617 St Mungo Old Parish Churchyard,Dumfries.
621 Troqueer New Burial Ground,Dumfries.
625 Aberlady Parish Churchyard,East Lothian.
626 Athelstaneford Parish Churchyard,East Lothian.
627 Dirleton Parish Churchyard,East Lothian.

632 Haddington Cemetery,East Lothian.
639 Prestonkirk Parish Churchyard,East Lothian.
640 Prestonpans New Cemetery,East Lothian.
644 Tynninghame Burial Ground,East Lothian.
660 Kirkbean Parish Churchyard,Kirkcudbright.
669 Innerleithen Cemetery,Peebles.
671 Peebles Cemetery.
674 Cathcart Cemetery,Renfrew.
675 Eastwood Cemetery,Renfrew.
677 Greenock Cemetery,Renfrew.
679 Kilbarchan Cemetery,Renfrew.
680 Kilmacolm Cemetery,Renfrew.
682 Neilston Cemetery,Renfrew.
683 Paisley Abbey Cemetery,Renfrew.
684 Paisley (Hawkhead) Cemetery,Renfrew.
685 Piasley (Woodside) Cemetery,Renfrew.
686 Port Glasgow Cemetery,Renfrew.
687 Renfrew (Arkleston) Cemetery,Renfrew.
696 Kelso Cemetery,Roxburgh.
711 Ashkirk Parish Church,Selkirk.
713 Galashiels (Eastlands) Cemetery,Selkirk.
717 Selkirk Parish Churchyard.
718 Selkirk (shawfield) Cemetery,Selkirk.
721 Bo'ness Cemetery,Bo'ness and Carriden,West Lothian.
722 Dalmeny Cemetery,West Lothian.
723 Ecclesmachan Cemetery,West Lothian.
725 Kirkliston Burial Ground,West Lothian.
726 Linlithgow Cemetery,West Lothian.
728 Polkemmet Private Burying Ground,Whitburn,West Lothian.
729 Uphall Cemetery,West Lothian.
730 Whitburn Cemetery,West Lothian.
742 Portpatrick Cemetery,Wigtown.
746 Stoneykirk Parish Churchyard,Wigtown.
752 Glasgow (Craigton) Cemetery.
754 Glasgow Eastern Necropolis.
755 Glasgow (Lambhill) Cemetery.
756 Glasgow Necropolis.
757 Glasgow (Riddrie Park) Cemetery.
758 Glasgow (St Kentigern's) Roman Catholic Cemetery.
760 Glasgow (Sandymount) Cemetery.
761 Glasgow (Sighthill) Cemetery.
762 Glasgow Southern Necropolis (Central Division).
764 Glasgow Western Necropolis.
766 Tollcross (Central) United Free Churchyard,Glasgow.
774 Cadder Cemetery,Lanark.
775 Cambuslang (Westburn) Cemetery,Lanark.
776 Cambusnethan Cemetery,Lanark.
780 Carluke (Wilton) Cemetery,Lanark.
783 Carnwath New Cemetery,Lanark.
789 Culter Parish Churchyard,Lanark.
790 Dalziel (Airbles) Cemetery,Lanark.
792 Dalziel (Old Manse Road) Burial Ground,Lanark.
795 East Kilbride Cemetery,Lanark.
798 Hamilton (Bent) Cemetery,Lanark.
799 Hamilton Parish Cemetery,Lanark.
803 Lanark (St Leonard's) Cemetery.
805 Lanark (St Nicholas) Cemetery.
807 Lesmahagow Cemetery,Lanark.
808 New Monkland Cemetery,Lanark.

810 Old Monkland Cemetery,Lanark.
811 Pettinain Parish Churchyard,Lanark.
812 Rutherglen Cemetery,Lanark.
816 Strathaven New Cemetery,Avondale,Lanark.
820 Banff Cemetery,Banff.
827 Cullen Cemetery,Banff.
832 Gamrie Old Churchyard,Banff.
835 Keith (Broomhill) Cemetery,Banff.
838 Macduff Parish Churchyard,Banff.
840 Martlach Parish Churchyard,Banff.
843 Rathven (Hillhead) Cemetery,Banff.
854 Halkirk Parish Churchyard,Caithness.
858 Olrig New Cemetery,Caithness.
862 Thurso Cemetery,Caithness.
871 Duffus Cemetery,Moray.
874 Elgin New Cemetery,Moray.
876 Forres (Cluny Hill) Cemetery,Moray.
877 Grantown-on-Spey New Burial Ground,Cromdale,Moray.
879 Kinloss Abbey Churchyard,Moray.
881 Knockando Parish Churchyard,Moray.
886 Nairn Cemetery,Nairn.
893 Evie Cemetery,Evie and Rendall,Orkney.
899 Kirkwall (St Olaf's) Cemetery,Kirkwall and St Olaf,Orkney.
900 Lyness Naval Cemetery,Hoy and Graemsay,Orkney.
902 Osmondwall Cemetery,Walls and Flotta,Orkney.
909 Stenness Parish Churchyard,Orkney.
926 Cromarty Parish Cemetery,Ross and Cromarty.
935 Fodderty Old Churchyard,Ross and Cromarty.
936 Foich Burial Ground,Lochbroom,Ross and Cromarty.
956 Londubh Old Churchyard,Gairloch,Ross and Cromarty.
963 Rosskeen Parish Churchyard Extension,Ross and Cromarty.
965 Sandwick Cemetery,Stornoway,Ross and Cromarty.
966 Suddie Old Churchyard,Knockbain,Ross and Cromarty.
967 Tain (St Duthus) Cemetery,Ross and Cromarty.
968 Tarbat Parish Churchyard,Ross and Cromarty.
975 Brora Cemetery,Clyne,Sutherland.
990 Melness Cemetery,Tongue,Sutherland.
1014 Lerwick New Cemetery,Zetland.
1030 Voe Old Churchyard,Delting,Zetland.

SHROPSHIRE.
11 Dorrington (St Edward the Confessor) Churchyard,Condover.
19 Shrewsbury General Cemetery,Meole Brace.
37 Church Stretton (St Lawrence) Churchyard Extension.
48 Dawley Magna (Holy Trinity) Churchyard.
52 Stoke-upon-Tern (St Peter) Churchyard Extension.
60 Little Ness (St Martin) Churchyard.
63 Petton Churchyard.
67 Ludlow New Cemetery.
70 Ashford Bowdler (St Andrew) Churchyard.
74 Caynham (St Mary) Churchyard.
81 Little Drayton (Christ Church) Churchyard.
82 Market Drayton Cemetery.
89 Newport Cemetery.
93 Oswestry General Cemetery.
95 Haughton (St Chad) Churchyard,West Felton.
97 Knockin (St Mary) Churchyard.
100 Moreton (SS Philip and James) Churchyard,Llanyblodwel.

101 Nantmawr Congregational Chapelyard,Oswestry Rural.
104 St Martin's Churchyard.
111 Donington (St Cuthbert) Churchyard.
114 Shifnal (St Andrew) Churchyard.
120 Hadley General Cemetery.
125 Clive (All Saints) Churchyard.
129 Prees (St Chad) Churchyard.
130 Shawbury (St Mary) Churchyard.
138 Broseley Cemetery.
143 Willey (St John the Devine) Churchyard.
145 Tilstock (Christ Church) Churchyard,Whitchurch Rural.
147 Whitchurch Cemetery.

SOMERSET.
10 Burrington (Holy Trinity) Churchyard.
17 Uphill (St Nicholas) Churchyard.
19 Wedmore (St Mary Magdalene) Churchyard.
25 Bath (Locksbrook) Cemetery.
26 Bath (St James's) Cemetery.
30 Bathwick Church Cemetery.
31 Bathampton (St Nicholas) Churchyard.
33 Bathford (St Swithun) Churchyard.
35 Charlcombe (St Mary) Churchyard.
37 Lansdown Cemetery,Charlcombe.
40 Wellow Cemetery.
42 Bridgwater (Wembdon Road) Cemetery (Chapel Portion).
43 Bridgwater (Wembdon Road) Cemetery (Church Portion).
49 Middlezoy (Holy Cross) Churchyard.
67 Hinton St George (St George) Churchyard.
71 Clevedon (St Andrew) Churchyard.
96 Frome (St John the Baptist) Churchyard.
99 Highbridge Cemetery.
101 Corston (All Saints) Church.
103 Keynsham Cemetery.
118 Kingweston (All Saints) Churchyard.
126 Easton-in-Gordano (St George) Churchyard.
139 Minehead Cemetery.
141 Radstock (St Nicholas) Churchyard.
153 Shepton Mallet Burial Ground.
157 Taunton (St Mary's) Cemetery.
161 Churchstanton (St Paul) Churchyard.
172 Staple Fitzpaine (St Peter) Churchyard.
173 Staplegrove (St John) Churchyard.
176 West Monkton (St Augustine) Churchyard.
183 Sampford Arundel (Holy Cross) Churchyard.
185 Wells Cathedral Cemetery.
186 Wells Cemetery.
196 Wookey (St Matthew) Churchyard Extension.
197 Weston-Super-Mare Cemetery.
198 Carhampton (St John the Baptist) Churchyard.
199 Crowcombe (Holy Ghost) Churchyard.
210 Holford (St Mary) Churchyard.
219 Redlynch (St Peter) Church,Bruton.
222 South Cadbury (St Thomas A Becket) Churchyard.

STAFFORDSHIRE.
4 Brierley Hill (South Street) Baptist Churchyard.
6 Ogley Hay (St James) Churchyard.
21 Coseley (Christ Church) Churchyard.
33 Cradley Heath (St Luke) Churchyard.

35 Rowley Regis (St Giles) Churchyard.
41 Codsall (St Nicholas) Churchyard Extensions.
45 Pattingham (St Chad) Churchyard.
47 Pennfields (St Philip) Churchyard,Trysull and Seisdon.
49 Wombourn (St Benedict) churchyard.
52 Smethwick (Uplands) Cemetery.
57 Tetenhall Regis (St Michael) Churchyard.
60 Walsall (Bloxwich) Cemetery.
61 Walsall (Ryecroft) Cemetery.
65 Pelsall (St Michael) Churchyard.
67 Rushall (St Michael) Churchyard.
70 Wednesbury Cemetery.
71 Wednesfield (St Thomas) Churchyard Extension.
73 West Bromwich Cemetery.
78 Wolverhampton General Cemetery.
82 Biddulph (St Lawrence) Churchyard.
84 Burton-upon-Trent Cemetery.
85 Horninglow (St John) Churchyard.
87 Alton (St John) Roman Catholic Churchyard.
91 Cheddleton (St Edward the Confessor) Churchyard.
93 Kingsley (St Werburgh) Churchyard.
94 Upper Tean (Christ Church) Churchyard,Checkley.
105 Norton-in-the-Moors (St Bartholomew) Churchyard.
108 Lichfield (St Chad) Churchyard.
109 Lichfield (St Michael) Churchyard.
114 Cannock Chase Military Burial Ground,Brereton.
125 Whittington (St Giles) Churchyard.
134 Castle Church (St Mary) Chuhrchyard.
135 Stafford Cemetery.
140 Great Haywood (St Stephen) Churchyard,Colwick.
143 Ingestre (St Mary) Churchyard.
152 Normacot (Holy Evangelists) Churchyard.
153 Stoke-on-Trent (Burslem) Cemetery.
156 Stoke-on-Trent (Hartshill) Cemetery.
170 Rangemore (All Saints) Churchyard,Tatenhill.
176 Blithfield (St Leonard) Churchyard.
177 Denstone (All Saints) Churchyard.
180 Newborough (All Saints) Churchyard.
183 Uttoxeter Cemetery.

SUFFOLK.
1 Aldeburgh (SS Peter and Paul) Churchyard.
2 Beccles Cemetery.
3 Aldringham (St Andrew) Churchyard.
9 Dunwich (St James) Churchyard.
23 Wenhaston (St Peter) Churchyard.
45 Bungay Cemetery.
54 Felixstowe New Cemetery.
55 Felixstowe (SS Peter and Paul) Churchyard.
64 Redgrave (St Botolph) Churchyard.
69 Badingham (St John the Baptist) Churchyard.
83 Ipswich Cemetery.
85 Lowestoft (Beccles Road) Cemetery.
86 Lowestoft (Kirkley) Cemetery.
91 Burgh Castle (St Peter) Churchyard.
92 Carlton Colville Additional Churchyard.
93 Carlton Colville (St Peter) Churchyard.
98 Oulton (St Michael) Churchyard.
106 Earl Soham Cemetery.
113 Orford (St Bartholomew) Churchyard.

121   Brantham (St Michael) Churchyard.
126   East Bergholt Cemetery.
128   Holbrook (All Saints) Churchyard.
130   Shotley (St Mary) Churchyard.
133   Stutton (St Peter) Churchyard.
137   Southwold (St Edmund) Churchyard.
138   Stowmarket Cemetery.
173   Euston (St Genevieve) Churchyard.
176   Bury St Edmunds Cemetery.
207   Nayland Cemetery,Nayland-with-Wissington.
215   Icklingham (St James) Churchyard.
224   Exning Cemetery.
225   Sudbury Cemetery.
240   Flempton (St Catherine) Churchyard.
242   Great Livermere (St Peter) Churchyard.

SURREY.

1   Brookwood Military Cemetery.
2   Barnes (East Sheen) Cemetery.
3   Barnes Old Cemetery.
4   Mortlake Burial Ground.
6   Bandon Hill Cemetery,Beddington.
8   Carshalton (All Saints) Churchyard.
9   Caterham Burial Ground.
10   Warlingham (All Saints) Churchyard.
11   Whyteleafe (St Luke) Churchyard.
13   Sanderstead (All Saints) Churchyard.
15   Croydon (Mitcham Road) Cemetery.
16   Croydon (Queen's Road) Cemetery.
18   Shirley (St John) Churchyard.
21   Chelsham (St Leonard) Churchyard.
27   Godstone (St Nicholas) Churchyard.
29   Limpsfield (St Peter) Churchyard.
32   Tandridge (St Peter) Churchyard.
34   Battersea Cemetery,Morden.
35   Merton (St Mary) Churchyard.
36   Morden (St Laurence) Churchyard.
37   Mitcham Burial Ground.
38   Streatham Park Cemetery.
41   Reigate Cemetery.
42   Betchworth (St Michael) Churchyard.
43   Buckland (St Mary) Churchyard.
45   Chipstaed (St Margaret) Churchyard.
47   Kingswood (St Andrew) Churchyard.
52   Walton-on-the-Hill (St Peter) Churchyard.
55   Sutton Cemetery.
57   Wimbledon (Gap Road) Cemetery.
58   Wimbledon (St Mary-on-the-Hill) Churchyard.
60   Byfleet (St Mary) Churchyard.
62   Valley End (St Saviour) Churchyard,Chobham.
64   Addlestone Burial Ground.
70   Holmwood (St Mary Magdalene) Churchyard,Capel.
72   Ockley Cemetery.
75   Dorking Cemetery.
76   East Molesey Cemetery.
78   Egham (St Jude's) Cemetery.
80   Ashtead (St Giles) Churchyard.
83   Cobham Cemetery.
84   Ewell (St Mary) Churchyard.
86   Hatchford (St Matthew) Churchyard,Cobham.

88   Little Bookahm Churchyard.
91   Epsom Cemetery.
93   Claygate (Holy Trinity) Churchyard.
94   Esher (Christ Church) Churchyard.
95   Long Ditton (St Mary) Churchyard.
96   Thames Ditton (St Nicholas) Churchyard.
97   Ash Cemetery;Ash and Normandy.
99   Frensham (St Mary) Churchyard.
102   Shottermill (St Stephen) Churchyard.
103   Tilford (All Saints) Churchyard,Farnham Rural.
104   Wyke (St Mark) Churchyard,Ash and Normandy.
106   Farnham Civil Cemetery.
110   Wrecclesham (St Peter) Churchyard Extension.
112   Frimley (St Peter) Churchyard.
113   York Town (St Michael) Churchyard.
114   Busbridge (St John the Baptist) Churchyard.
115   Godalming New Cemetery.
118   Guildford (Stoke) Cemetery.
126   Send (St Mary) Churchyard,Send and Ripley.
128   Shere (St James) Churchyard.
131   Worplesdon (St Mary) Churchyard.
132   Ham (St Andrew) Churchyard.
134   Bramley Cemetery.
135   Chiddingfold (St Mary) Churchyard.
136   Cranleigh Cemetery.
138   Grayswood (All Saints) Churchyard,Witley.
142   Shamley Green (Christ Church) Churchyard,Wonersh.
143   Thursley (St Michael) Churchyard.
148   Kingston-on-Thames Cemetery.
150   Fulham New Cemetery,North Sheen.
151   Petersham (St Peter) Churchyard.
152   Richmond Cemetery.
153   Surbiton Cemetery.
154   Malden (St John the Baptist) Churchyard.
156   Walton-on-Thames Cemetery.
157   Weybridge Cemetery.
158   Windlesham Additional Burial Ground.
159   Windlesham (Bagshot) Burial Ground.
160   Brookwood Cemetery (The London Necropolis).
161   Horsell (St Mary) churchyard.
162   Woking Crematorium.

SUSSEX.

2   Arundel Roman Catholic Cemetery.
4   Bognor Regis Cemetery.
5   Chichester Cemetery.
9   Lyminster (St Mary Magdalene) Churchyard.
13   Coolhurst Churchyard,Lower Beeding.
15   Crawley Monastery Burial Ground.
17   Ifield (St Margaret) Churchyard.
19   Nuthurst (St Andrew) Churchyard.
23   Slinfold (St Peter) Churchyard.
24   Warnham (St Margaret) Churchyard.
27   Horsham (Hills) Cemetery.
30   Easebourne (St Mary) Churchyard.
52   Stopham (St Mary) Churchyard.
55   Old Shoreham Cemetery.
57   Southwick (St Michael) Churchyard.
58   Henfield Cemetery.
64   Pulborough (St Mary) Churchyard.

72   West Dean Cemetery.
83   Oving (St Andrew) Churchyard Extension.
85   Selsey Cemetery.
88   Westhampnett (St Peter) Churchyard.
89   West Stoke (St Andrew) Churchyard.
93   Heene (St Botolph) Churchyard Extension.
95   Worthing (Broadwater) Cemetery.
102   Sedlescombe (St John the Baptist) Churchyard.
107   Bexhill Cemetery.
109   Little Common (St Mark) Churchyard.
110   Brighton and Preston Cemetery.
111   Brighton Borough Cemetery.
112   Brighton Extramural Cemetery.
114   Rottingdean (St Margaret) Churchyard.
124   Glynde Churchyard.
125   Hamsey (St Peter) Churchyard.
128   Ringmer (St Mary) Churchyard.
134   Hurstpierpoint (Holy Trinity) Churchyard.
135   Hurstpierpoint New Cemetery.
136   Hurstpierpoint Old Cemetery.
138   Lindfield (Walstead) Cemetery.
139   Newtimber (St John) Churchyard.
143   Cuckfield Cemetery.
144   Eastbourne (Ocklynge) Cemetery.
151   Pevensey (St Nicholas) Churchyard.
156   Coleman's Hatch (Holy Trinity) Churchyard,Hartfield.
159   Forest Row Cemetery.
163   Withyham (St Michael) Churchyard.
164   Worth (St Nicholas) Churchyard.
165   East Grinstead (Mount Noddy) Cemetery.
176   Fairlight (St Andrew) Churchyard.
177   Guestling (St Lawrence) Churchyard.
178   Hastings Cemetery,Ore.
182   Aldrington (St Leonard) Churchyard.
183   Hove Cemetery.
184   Hove (St Andrew) Churchayrd.
185   Lewes Cemetery.
187   Lewes (St John the Baptist-Subcastro) Churchyard.
189   Southover (St John the Baptist) Churchyard.
190   Kingston-near-Lewes (St Pancras) Churchyard.
191   Newhaven Cemetery.
197   Rye Cemetery,Rye Foreign.
199   Winchelsea (St Thomas) Churchyard.
200   Seaford Cemetery.
201   Burwash (St Bartholomew) Churchyard.
203   Eridge Green (Holy Trinity) Churchyard,Frant.
204   Frant (St Alban) Churchyard.
216   Framfield (St Thomas Becket) Churchyard.
219   High Hurstwood (Holy Trinity) Churchyard,Buxted.
220   Isfield (St Margaret) Churchyard.
225   Waldron (All Saints) Churchyard.
226   Uckfield Cemetery.

WALES.
1   Aberdare Cemetery,Glamorgan.
3   Barry (Merthyr Dyfan) Cemetery,Glamorgan.
4   Bridgend Cemetery,Glamorgan.
7   Nolton (St Mary) Churchyard,Glamorgan.
9   Caerphilly (St Martin) Churchyard.
12   Llanfabon (St Mabon) Churchyard,Glamorgan.

13   Llanfaban (St Mabon) Churchyard Extension,Glamorgan.
16   Ystrad Mynach (Holy Trinity) Churchyard,Glamorgan.
17   Cardiff Cemetery,Glamorgan.
19   Cardiff (Llandaff) Cemetery,Glamorgan.
20   Llanishen (St Isan) Churchyard,Glamorgan.
26   Radyr (St John the Baptist) Old Churchyard,Glamorgan.
29   St Fagans (St Fagan) Churchyard,Glamorgan.
30   St George-super-Ely (St George) Churchyard,Glamorgan.
31   St Nicholas Churchyard,Glamorgan.
35   Whitchurch (St Mary) Churchyard,Glamorgan.
37   Llanblethian (St John the Baptist) Churchyard,Glamorgan.
54   Reynoldston (St George) Churchyard,Glamorgan.
77   Merthyr Tydfil (Ffrwd) Cemetery,Glamorgan.
78   Merthyr Tydfil (Pant) Cemetery,Glamorgan.
83   Mountain Ash (Maesyrarian) Cemetery,Glamorgan.
85   Neath (Ynysmaerdy) Cemetery,Glamorgan.
86   Aberpergwm (St Cattwg) Churchyard Private Extension,Neath Higher,Glamorgan.
95   Pontrhydyfen (Jerusalem) Calvinistic Methodist Chapelyard,Michaelston Higher,Glamorgan.
107   Penarth Cemetery,Glamorgan.
108   Penarth (St Augustine of Canterbury) Churchyard.
118   Pyle (St James) Churchyard,Glamorgan.
119   St Bride's Major (St Bridget) churchyard,Glamorgan.
135   Pontypridd (Glyntaff) Cemetery,Glamorgan.
137   Newton Nottage (St John the Baptist) Churchyard,Glamorgan.
149   Rhondda (Treorchy) Cemetery,Glamorgan.
152   Cockett (St Peter) Churchyard,Glamorgan.
163   Morriston (Horeb) Congregational Chapelyard,Glamorgan.
165   Sketty (Bethel) Welsh Congregational Chapelyard,Glamorgan.
166   Sketty (St Paul) Churchyard,Glamorgan.
167   Swansea (Cwmgelly) Cemetery,Glamorgan.
168   Swansea (Danygraig) Cemetery,Glamorgan.
171   Swansea (Oystermouth) Cemetery.Glamorgan.
174   Brecon (St David) Churchyard,Brecknock.
177   Cwmswyg Congregational Chapelyard,Traianglas,Brecknock.
178   Devynnock (St Cynog) Churchyard,Maescar,Brecknock.
195   Penderyn (St Cynog) Churchyard,Brecknock.
199   Ystradgynlais (St Cynog) Churchyard,Ystradgynlais Lower,Brecknock.
201   Llanfihangel Ystrad (St Michael) Churchyard,Cardigan.
203   Aberystwyth Cemetery,Cardigan.
212   Cardigan Cemetery.
214   Llandygwydd (St Tygwydd) Churchyard,Cardigan.
219   lampeter (St Peter) Churchyard,Cardigan.
231   Llangranog (St David) Churchyard,Cardigan.
238   Llangeitho (St Ceitho) Churchyard,Cardigan.
240   Tregaron (Bwlchgwynt) Calvinistic Methodist Chapelyard,Caron Township,Cardigan
241   Tredaron (Sr Caron) Churchyard Extension,Caron Township,Cardigan.
245   Carmarthen Cemetery.
251   Llanllwch (St Luke) Churchyard,Carmarthen.
278   Llanegwad (St Egwad) Churchyard,Carmarthen.
289   Llanelly Church Cemetery,Carmarthen.
306   Llanfihangel Ar Arth (St Michael) Churchyard,Carmarthen.
335   Cemmaes Calvinistic Methodist Chapelyard,Montgomery.

358 Welshpool (Christ Church) Churchyard,Montgomery.

361 Fishguard Church Cemetery,Pembroke.

367 Haverfordwest St Mary Church Cemetery,Pembroke.

368 Haverfordwest (St Thomas of Canterbury) Churchyard,Pembroke.

372 Herbrandston (St Mary) Churchyard,Pembroke.

383 Treffgarne (St Michael) Churchyard,Pembroke.

389 Milford Haven Cemetery,Pembroke.

393 Llawhaden (St Aidan) Churchyard,Pembroke.

402 Pembroke Dock (Llanion) Cemetery,Pembroke.

404 Pembroke (St Daniel) Churchyard,Pembroke.

416 Stackpole Elidor (SS Elidyr and James) Churchyard,Pembroke.

429 Llandrindod Wells Cemetery,Radnor.

439 Llansantffraid Cwmdeuddhr (St Winifred) Churchyard,Radnor.

440 Llanyre (St LLyr) Churchyard,Radnor.

447 Llanedwen (St Edwen) Churchyard,Anglesey.

454 Amlwch Cemetery,Anglesey.

460 Holyhead (St Mary) Roman Catholic Churchyard,Anglesey.

461 Holyhead (St Seiriol) Churchyard,Anglesey.

462 Llangefni Cemetery,Anglesey.

463 Llandysilio (St Tyssilio) Churchyard,Anglesey.

480 Four Mile Bridge Wesleyan Chapelyard,Rhoscolyn,Anglesey.

491 Bangor (Glanadda) Cemetery,Caernarvon.

497 Llanbeblig (St Peblig) Churchayrd,Caernarvon.

498 Conway (St Agnes) Churchyard,Caernarvon.

506 Llysfaen (St Cynfran) Churchyard,Caernarvon.

518 Clynnog Fawr (St Beuno) Churchyard,Clynnog,Caernarvon.

531 Llanwnda (St Gwyndaf) Churchyard,Caernarvon.

535 Llandudno (Great Orme's Head) Cemetery,Caernarvon.

536 Llandudno (St Tudno) Churchyard,Caernarvon.

537 Llanrhos (SS Eleri and Mary) Churchyard,Caernarvon.

546 Llanbedrog Cemetery,Caernarvon.

550 Llangybi (Capel Helyg) Independent Chapelyard,Caernarvon.

564 Penmaenmawr (Dwygyfylchi) Cemetery,Caernarvon.

568 Abergele Cemetery,Denbigh.

571 Colwyn Bay (Bronynant) Cemetery,Denbigh.

597 Llanbedr Dyffryn Clwyd (St Peter) Churchyard,Denbigh.

603 Rhewl Calvinistic Methodist Chapelyard,Llanynys Rural,Denbigh.

609 St George (St George) Churchyard,Denbigh.

613 Wrexham Cemetery,Denbigh.

619 Gresford (All Saints) Churchyard,Denbigh.

629 Ruabon Cemetery,Denbigh.

637 Hawarden (St Deiniol) Churchyard,Flint.

646 Caerfallwch (St Paul) Churchyard,Northop,Flint.

648 Gwernafield (Holy Trinity) Churchyard,Mold Rural,Flint.

651 Holywell (Zion) Congregational Chapelyard,Holywell Rural,Flint.

658 Pontblyddyn (Christ Church) Churchyard,Mold Rural,Flint.

659 Whitford (SS Beuno and Mary) Churchyard,Flint.

664 Bangor Monachorum (St Dunawd) Churchyard,Flint.

671 Rhyl Church Cemetery,Flint.

672 Rhyl Town Cemetery,Flint.

673 Bodelwyddan (St Margaret) Churchyard,Flint.

677 St Asaph Cathedral Churchyard,Flint.

681 Harlech (St Tanwg) Churchyard,Merioneth.

684 Llanfair (St Mary) Churchyard,Marioneth.

690 Trawsfynydd (Penycefn) Cemetery,Merioneth.

692 Brithdir (St Mark) Churchyard,Brithdir and Islaw'roreth,Merioneth.

693 Llanaber (St Mary) Churchyard,Merioneth.

706 Corwen (SS Mael and Sulien) Churchyard,Merioneth.

713 Festiniog (Llan) Cemetery,Merioneth.

714 Festiniog (Newborough) Burial Ground,Merioneth.

725 Aberdovey Cemetery,Merioneth.

WARWICKSHIRE.

1 Acock's Green (St Mary) Churchyard.

3 Birmingham (Brandwood End) Cemetery.

4 Birmingham Crematorium.

5 Birmingham General Cemetery.

6 Birmingham (Handsworth) Cemetery.

è7 Birmingham (Lodge Hill) Cemetery.

9 Birmingham (Witton) Cemetery.

10 Birmingham (Yardley) Cemetery.

12 Edgbaston (St Bartholomew) Churchyard.

14 Erdington (St Barnabas) Churchyard.

16 Handsworth (St Mary) Churchyard.

19 King's Norton (St Nicholas) Churchyard.

22 Northfield (St Laurence) Churchyard Extension.

23 Perry Barr (St John) Churchyard.

30 Coughton Church Cemetery.

32 Studley (St Mary) Churchyard.

37 Atherstone Cemetery.

40 Polesworth (St Editha) Churchyard.

47 Long Compton (SS Peter and Paul) Churchyard.

50 Coventry (London Road) Cemetery.

55 Radford (St Nicholas) Churchyard.

57 Farnborough (St Botolph) Churchyard.

60 Wyken (St Mary Magdalene) Churchyard.

63 Kenilworth (St Nicholas) Churchyard.

65 Castle Bromwich (SS Mary and Margaret) Churchyard.

66 Coleshill Cemetery.

67 Curdworth (St Peter) Churchyard.

69 Hampton-in-Arden (SS Mary and Bartholomew) Churchyard.

70 Maxstoke (St Michael) Churchyard.

74 Monks Kirby (St Edith) Churchyard.

75 Chilvers Coton (All Saints) Churchyard.

81 Astley (St Mary) Churchyard.

82 Wolvey Cemetery.

83 Leamington (Milverton) Cemetery.

84 Leamington (Whitnash Road) Cemetery.

88 Brinklow Cemetery.

89 Clifton-on-Dunsmore (St Mary) Additional Churchyard.

96 Wolston Cemetery.

97 Rugby (Clifton Road) Cemetery.

98 Rugby (St Marie) Roman Catholic Churchyard.

100 Knowle (SS John the Baptist and Ann) Churchyard.

101 Olton Franciscan Cemetery,Solihull.

102 Salter Street (St Patrick) Churchyard,Tanworth.

106 Temple Balsall (St Mary) Churchyard,Balsall.

112 Napton-on-the-Hill Cemetery.

115 Southam (St James) Churchyard.

117 Stratford-on-Avon Cemetery.

129 Wellesbourne (St Peter) Churchyard,Wellesbourne

Hastings.

134 Hill (St James the Great) Churchyard.
135 Sutton Coldfield Cemetery.
143 Budbrooke (St Michael) Churchyard.
151 Warwick Cemetery,Budbrooke.
152 Wasperton (St John the Baptist) Churchyard.

WILTSHIRE.

1   Amesbury Cemetery.
2   Bulford Church Cemetery.
3   Durrington Cemetery.
4   Figheldean (St Michael) Churchyard.
12   Wilsford (St Michael) Churchyard.
14   Winterbourne Gunner (St Mary) Churchyard.
16   Atworth (St Michael) Churchyard.
18   Holt Cemetery.
25   East Tytherton Moravian Burial Ground,Bremhill.
28   Yatesbury (All Saints) Churchyard.
29   Chippenham Cemetery.
56   Devizes Cemetery,Roundway.
64   Chiseldon Cemetery.
86   Sopworth (St Mary) Churchyard.
100 Melksham Cemetery.
115 Tidworth Military Cemetery,North Tidworth.
116 Upavon Cemetery.
121 Chilton Foliat (St Mary) Churchyard.
128 East Harnham (All Saints) Churchyard.
129 Salisbury (London Road) Cemetery.
142 Swindon (Radnor Street) Cemetery.
145 Chicklade (All Saints) Churchyard.
153 Swallowcliffe (St Peter) Churchyard.
157 Bishopstrow (St Aldhelm) Churchyard.
167 Sutton Veny (St John) Churchyard.
176 Keevil (St Leonard) Churchyard.
179 Wilton Cemetery.
180 Barford St Martin Cemetery.
186 Burcombe (St John the Baptist) Churchyard,Burcombe
Without.
194 Salisbury (Devizes Road) Cemetery,Bemerton.

YORKSHIRE.

1   Hull (Hedon Road) Cemetery.
2   Hull Western Cemetery.
3   Hull Northern Cemetery.
5   Hull General Cemetery.
6   Hull (Holy Trinity,Hessle Road) Cemetery.
11   Beverley (St Martin's) Cemetery.
12   Beverley (St Mary's) Cemetery.
22   Bridlington Cemetery.
35   Sledmere (St Mary) Churchyard.
38   Fulford Water Burial Ground.
42   Filey (St Oswald) Churchyard.
43   Great Driffield Cemetery.
45   Hessle Cemetery.
46   Hornsea Cemetery.
62   Burstwick (All Saints) Churchyard.
63   Easington Cemetery.
79   Wilberfoss (St John the Baptist) Churchyard.
81   Barlby (All Saints) Churchyard.
83   Kirk Ella Church Cemetery.

93   Sigglesthorne (St Laurence) Churchyard.
96   Withernsea Cemetery.
97   Withernsea (St Nicholas) Churchyard.
98   York Cemetery.
100 Aysgarth (St Andrew) Churchyard,Gould.
104 Fencote (St Andrew) Churchyard,Kirkby Fleetham.
106 Thornton Watlass (St Mary) Churchyard.
110 Eryholme (St Mary) Churchyard.
114 Coxwold (St Michael) Churchyard.
119 Eston Cemetery.
123 Huntington (All Saints) Churchyard.
126 Guisborough Cemetery.
127 Marske-in-Cleveland (St Germain) Churchyard.
138 Finghall (St Andrew) Churchyard.
154 Middlesbrough (Linthorpe) Cemetery.
156 North ormesby (St Joseph's) Roman Catholic Cemetery.
159 Northallerton Cemetery.
171 Thornton Dale (All Saints) Churchyard.
172 Coatham (Christ Church) Churchyard.
173 Redcar Cemetery.
175 Grinton (St Andrew) Churchyard.
176 Richmond Cemetery.
178 Catterick Cemetery.
181 Hipswell (St John) Churchyard.
183 Saltburn-by-the-Sea Cemetery.
185 Scarborough Cemetery.
186 Brompton (All Saints) Churchyard.
192 Seamer (St Martin) Churchyard.
194 Boosbeck (St Aidan) Churchyard.
195 Brotton Church Cemetery.
208 Kirk Leavington (St Martin) Churchyard.
222 Whitby Cemetery.
228 Lythe (St Oswald) Churchyard.
230 Bishopthorpe (St Andrew) Churchyard.
244 Goole Cemetery.
245 Acomb (St Stephen) Churchyard.
249 Little Ouseburn (Holy Trinity) Churchyard.
250 Moor Monkton (All Saints) Churchyard.
253 Guiseley Primitive Methodist Chapelyard.
256 Harrowgate (Grove Road) Cemetery.
264 Skelbrooke (St Michael) Churchyard.
267 Horsforth Cemetery.
274 Knaresborough Cemetery.
275 Knottingley Cemetery.
276 Normanton Cemetery.
283 Pontefract Cemetery.
292 Rawdon (St Peter) Churchyard.
294 Ripon Cemetery.
303 Selby Cemetery.
305 Acaster Selby (St John) Churchyard.
308 Healaugh (St John the Baptist) Churchyard.
311 Kirkby Wharfe (St John the Baptist) Churchyard
Extension,Kirkby Wharfe and North Milford.
319 Tadcaster Cemetery,Tadcaster West.
321 Sandal Magna (St Helen) Churchyard.
323 Wakefield Cemetery.
328 Wath-upon-Dearne Cemetery.
335 Spofforth (All Saints) Churchyard,Spofforth-with-Stockeld.
338 Wetherby Cemetery.
344 Calverley (St Wilfred) Churchyard.

Appendix 2

This is a list of abreviations used in the list of officers. The majority not mentioned as they are self evident. Others are a combination of the abreviations listed below.

ACapt,ALt,etc	Acting Captain,Acting Lieutenant,etc
A/A Bde	Anti Aircraft Brigade
acc	Accidentally
Att	Attached
Bde	Brigade
Bn	Battalion
Can	Canadian
Cmdg	Commanding
Cps	Corps
CR	Cemetery Register
Ded	Died
Dow	Died of Wounds
Drd	Drowned
Eng	Engineer
Ex	Formerly
Ft Paymr	Fleet Paymaster
HQ	Headquarters
HMCMB	His Majesty's Coastal Motor Boat
HMHS	His Majesty's Hospital Ship
HMML	His Majesty's Motor Launch
kia	Killed in action
kld	Killed
MID	Mentioned in Despatches
MR	Memorial Register
Paymr	Paymaster
RAF	Royal Air Force
Res	Reserve
RN Div	Royal Naval Division
RoO	Reserve of Officers
S/M	Submarine
Sqdn or Sqn	Squadron
TCapt,TLt,etc	Temporary Captain,Temporary Lieutenant,Etc